# COLORADO CAMPING

# COLORADO CAMPING

SECOND EDITION

Robyn Brewer

**FOGHORN ✌ OUTDOORS**

COLORADO CAMPING
SECOND EDITION

Printing History
1st edition—1998
2nd edition—June 2000

5 4 3 2 1 0

© Text and photographs copyright
Robyn Brewer, 2000. All rights reserved.

© Illustrations and maps copyright
Avalon Travel Publishing, Inc., 2000.
All rights reserved.

Some photos and illustrations are used by
permission and are the property of the
original copyright owners.

All photos by Julie Johnson unless
otherwise noted.

All illustrations by Bob Race unless
otherwise noted.

*Front cover photo:* John P. Kelly/The Image Bank © 2000

*Editors:* Jean-Vi Lenthe, Carolyn Perkins
*Design and Production:* Jon Knolle, David Hurst
*Cartography:* Chris Alvarez, Mike Morgenfeld
*Index:* Sondra Nation

*ISBN:* 1-57354-085-4
*ISSN:* 1098-8262

*Published by*
Avalon Travel Publishing, Inc.
5855 Beaudry St.
Emeryville, CA 94608, USA

Printed in the USA

Please send all comments, corrections,
additions, amendments, and critiques to:

COLORADO CAMPING
Second Edition
FOGHORN OUTDOORS
AVALON TRAVEL PUBLISHING, INC.
5855 BEAUDRY ST.
EMERYVILLE, CA 94608, USA
e-mail: info@travelmatters.com
www.travelmatters.com

Distributed in the United States and
Canada by Publishers Group West

*This book is dedicated with love*

*to my mom.*

① Sugar loafin p 212
Mon 8th Leadville.

② TUES 9th St Luis. @ GREAT
SAND DUNES P388 No 125

③ Wed 10t Thurs 11t
p. 323 no 94 Durango

④ FRIDAY

⑤ SATURDAY P360 no 62 (+ option
Gunnison. KoA. for SUNDAY)

⑥ SUNDAY P362 no 65 (Nos over
Howard. Pleasant Valley 14 tons)

# TABLE OF CONTENTS

Introduction . . . . . . . . . . . . . . . . . . . . . . . . . . . . . . . . . . . . . . . . . 12

CAMPING TIPS . . . . . . . . . . . . . . . . . . . . . . . . . . . . . . . . . . . . . . . 16

Food and Cooking Gear . . . . . . . . . . . . . . . . . . . . . . . . . . . . . . . . 16
Camping Stoves; Fuels for Camping Stoves; Building Fires;
Cooking Gear; Food and Cooking Tricks; Keeping the Price
Down

Clothing and Weather Protection . . . . . . . . . . . . . . . . . . . . . . 27
The Art of Layering; About Hats; Vests and Parkas;
Rain Gear; Other Gear . . . and a Few Tips

Hiking and Foot Care . . . . . . . . . . . . . . . . . . . . . . . . . . . . . . . . . 33
Selecting the Right Boots; Socks; A Few More Tips

Sleeping Gear . . . . . . . . . . . . . . . . . . . . . . . . . . . . . . . . . . . . . . . 39
Sleeping Bags; Insulation Pads; A Few Tricks; Tents and
Weather Protection; Family Tents; Bivouac Bags;
Pickup Truck Campers; RVs

First Aid and Insect Protection . . . . . . . . . . . . . . . . . . . . . . . 47
Mosquitoes, No-See-Ums, Gnats, and Horseflies; DEET
Versus "Natural" Repellents; Ticks; Poison Oak; Sunburn;
A Word about Giardia and Cryptosporidium; Hypothermia;
Getting Unlost

Catching Fish, Avoiding Bears, and Having Fun . . . . . . . . . . . 63
Trout and Bass; Fishing Tips; Of Bears and Food; The
Grizzly; Fun and Games; Old Tricks Don't Always Work;
Getting Revenge

Camp Ethics and Politics. . . . . . . . . . . . . . . . . . . . . . . . . . . . . . 79
Getting Along with Fellow Campers

Outdoors with Kids . . . . . . . . . . . . . . . . . . . . . . . . . . . . . . . . . . 83

Predicting Weather . . . . . . . . . . . . . . . . . . . . . . . . . . . . . . 85

Beating the Time Trap . . . . . . . . . . . . . . . . . . . . . . . . . . . . 88

Resource Guide . . . . . . . . . . . . . . . . . . . . . . . . . . . . . . . . . . 89

Camping Gear Checklist . . . . . . . . . . . . . . . . . . . . . . . . . . 90

## Special Topics

*Keep It Wild 16; Campfires 22; How to Make Beef Jerky in Your Own Kitchen 27; Travel Lightly 37; Camp with Care 46; Sanitation 53; Bear Territory 74; Keep the Wilderness Wild 78; Respect Other Users 80; Plan Ahead and Prepare 86*

**CHAPTER A1** . . . . . . . . . . . . . . . . . . . . . . . . . . . . . . . . . . . 94

**CHAPTER A2** . . . . . . . . . . . . . . . . . . . . . . . . . . . . . . . . . . 130

**CHAPTER A3** . . . . . . . . . . . . . . . . . . . . . . . . . . . . . . . . . . 228

**CHAPTER A4** . . . . . . . . . . . . . . . . . . . . . . . . . . . . . . . . . . 270

**CHAPTER B1** . . . . . . . . . . . . . . . . . . . . . . . . . . . . . . . . . . 280

**CHAPTER B2** . . . . . . . . . . . . . . . . . . . . . . . . . . . . . . . . . . 332

**CHAPTER B3** . . . . . . . . . . . . . . . . . . . . . . . . . . . . . . . . . , 414

**CHAPTER B4** . . . . . . . . . . . . . . . . . . . . . . . . . . . . . . . . . . 448

**APPENDIX** . . . . . . . . . . . . . . . . . . . . . . . . . . . . . . . . . . . . 454
Colorado's Best Campgrounds

**INDEX** . . . . . . . . . . . . . . . . . . . . . . . . . . . . . . . . . . . . . . . 457

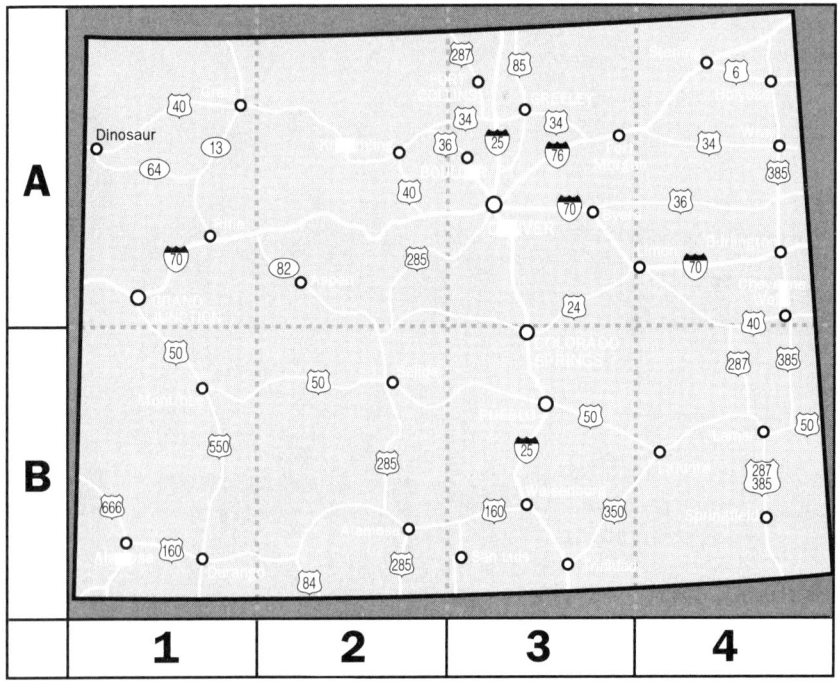

## MAPS

A1 ............................................. 94

A2 ............................................. 130

A3 ............................................. 228

A4 ............................................. 270

B1 ............................................. 280

B2 ............................................. 332

B3 ............................................. 414

B4 ............................................. 448

# How to Use This Book

## Finding a Campground
You can search for your ideal campground in two ways:

1. If you know the name of the campground you'd like to visit or the nearest town or geographical feature (national or state forest, national or state park or recreation area, wildlife area, lake, river, mountain), look it up in the index beginning on page 457.

2. If you'd like to stay in a particular part of Colorado and want to find out what campgrounds are available there, turn to the state map on the facing pages or in the back of this book. Find the zone where you want to camp, such as A2 for Rocky Mountain National Park, and turn to the corresponding chapter. Each chapter opens with a map that clearly numbers every campground in that zone. Locate individual camping destinations on the map and then turn to those numbered sites in the chapter for detailed descriptions.

## About the Maps
The maps in this book are designed to show the general location of each campground. Readers are advised to purchase a detailed state map before heading out to any campground, particularly when venturing into remote areas.

## What the Ratings Mean
Every campground in this book has been rated on a scale of 1-10. The ratings are based on the scenic beauty of the area only and do not reflect quality control issues such as the cleanliness of the campground or the temperament of the management.

## What the Symbols Mean
Listings in this book feature activity symbols that represent the recreational offerings at or very near the campground. Other symbols identify whether there are sites for RVs or tents, or any wheelchair-accessible facilities. Wheelchair accessibility has been indicated when it is mentioned by campground managers, and concerned persons should call the contact number to ensure that their specific needs will be met.

## Our Commitment

We are committed to making *Colorado Camping* the most accurate, thorough, and enjoyable camping guide to the state. With this second edition you can rest assured that every camping spot in this book has been carefully reviewed and is accompanied by the most up-to-date information. However, with the change of seasons you can bet that some of the fees listed herein have gone up and that camping destinations may have opened, closed, or changed hands. If you have a specific need or concern, it's a good idea to call the campground ahead of time.

If you would like to comment on the book, whether it's to suggest a tent or RV spot we overlooked or to let us know about any noteworthy experience—good or bad—that occurred while using *Colorado Camping* as your guide, we would appreciate hearing from you. Please address correspondence to:

Colorado Camping
Second Edition
Avalon Travel Publishing
5855 Beaudry Street
Emeryville, CA 94608
U.S.A.
e-mail: info@travelmatters.com

## ACTIVITY SYMBOLS

| | | | |
|---|---|---|---|
| = biking | | = rock climbing |
| = boating | | = sea kayaking |
| = fishing | | = snowmobiling |
| =golf | | = snowshoeing |
| = hiking | | = snow skiing |
| = historical site | | = swimming |
| = hunting | | = tennis |
| = horseback riding | | = waterskiing |
| = hot springs | | = wheelchair access |
| = PWC riding | | = RV sites |
| = motorboating | | = tent sites |
| = rafting/canoing | | = Five Percent Club |

# Introduction

Last year I had two major objectives: 1) Get married. 2) Write the second edition of this book.

Lucky for me, I was able to combine the two. After the happy pandemonium of our wedding in July, my new husband and I breathed a sigh of relief and set out for a peaceful camping honeymoon in southern Colorado. Much to his chagrin, I simply could not resist the chance to do some field research. While my romantically inclined husband gazed out the window and daydreamed about future homesites and children, I held a pen in one hand and a notebook in the other, taking copious notes on the towns and campgrounds we visited. After a few gentle reminders that this was our *honeymoon,* I put work away and joined him in a reverie about how wonderful it would be someday to take our own kids on such a great trip.

Although I felt I'd gotten to know many of Colorado's secrets when I wrote the first edition of this book, when we took this trip I was once again struck with great awe and reverence for the state's beauty. The sprawling farmland between Lake City and Creede looks like a setting for a fairy tale, and the craggy mountains near Ouray and Silverton rival the splendor of the huge ranges in Switzerland and Austria. And if you have an RV or car, all of this is absolutely accessible.

In fact, camping still is the best bargain around, with most sites ranging from a few bucks up to $30 a night, and some costing nothing at all. When my mother, sister, and I took my young nephew to Disneyland, we witnessed harried families fighting crowds and spending too much money on silly plastic toys and food devoid of nutrition. In a campground you get natural beauty, peace and quiet, and the chance to spend some quality time in nature with your loved ones. No contest, as far as I'm concerned. Of course, being a bit of an e-mail junkie, I do understand the pain of being disconnected from a computer, but in the past couple of years many campgrounds have added technological amenities such as modem hookups and computer workstations, so you can keep up with your e-mail or research recreation options on the Internet. State and federal agencies have stepped into the 21st century as well, some offering extensive websites and even on-line reservations.

Besides information on the technological advances of various campgrounds, you'll find more than 35 new campgrounds in this new edition. In order to update information on the remaining camps, I did extensive research, phoning each private campground, park, and U.S. Forest Service office personally to get the most current and correct information possible. Moreover, I listened to suggestions from my readers —comments on specific campgrounds, remarks on scenic beauty of certain areas—and incorporated them throughout the book. The result, I think, is the most comprehensive, accurate guide you'll find to camping in Colorado.

Perhaps it will even inspire you to go camping on your own honeymoon—or second honeymoon. Just remember to leave your work at home.

# CAMPING TIPS

by Tom Stienstra

## Food and Cooking Gear

It was a warm, crystal clear day, the kind of day when if you had ever wanted to go skydiving, you would go skydiving. That was exactly the case for my old pal Foonsky, who had never before tried the sport. But a funny thing happened after he jumped out of the plane and pulled on the rip cord: His parachute didn't open.

In total free fall, Foonsky watched the earth below getting closer and closer. Not one to panic, he calmly pulled the rip cord on the emergency parachute. Again nothing happened. No parachute, no nothing.

The ground was getting ever closer, and as he tried to search for a soft place to land, Foonsky detected a small object shooting up toward him, growing larger as it approached. It looked like a camper.

Figuring this was his last chance, Foonsky shouted as they passed in midair, "Hey, do you know anything about parachutes?"

The other fellow just yelled back as he headed off into space, "Do you know anything about lighting camping stoves?"

Well, Foonsky got lucky and his parachute opened. As for the other guy, well, he's probably in orbit like a NASA weather satellite. If you've ever had a mishap while lighting a camping stove, you know exactly what I'm talking about.

When it comes to camping, all gear is not created equal. Nothing is more important than lighting your stove easily and having it reach full heat without feeling as if you're playing with a short fuse to a miniature bomb. If your stove does not work right, your trip can turn into a disaster, regardless of how well you have planned the other elements. In addition, a bad stove will add an underlying sense of foreboding to your day. You will constantly have the inner suspicion that your darn stove is going to foul up again.

---

### Keep It Wild

"Enjoy America's country and leave no trace." That's the motto of the Leave No Trace program, and we strongly support it. Promoting responsible outdoor recreation through education, research, and partnerships is its mission. Look for the **Keep It Wild Tips**, developed from the policies of Leave No Trace, sprinkled throughout the introduction. For a free pocket-sized, weatherproof card printed with these policies, as well as information that details how to minimize human impact on wild areas, contact Leave No Trace at P.O. Box 997, Boulder CO, 80306; tel. (800) 332-4100; website: www.int.org.

---

If you are buying a camping stove, remember this one critical rule: **CAMPING STOVES**
Do not leave the store with a new stove unless you have
been shown exactly how to use it.

Know what you are getting. Many stores that specialize in
outdoor recreation equipment now provide experienced
campers/employees who will demonstrate the use of every
stove they sell and while they're at it, describe their respective strengths and weaknesses.

An innovation by Peak 1 is a two-burner backpacking
stove, allowing you to boil water and heat a pot of
food simultaneously. While that has long been standard for car campers using Coleman's legendary
camp stove, it was previously unheard of for
wilderness campers in high-elevation areas. Another recent invention is the flameless stove (no
kidding), which allows campers to cook in a tent
safely for the first time.

A stove that has developed a cultlike following is
the little Sierra, which burns small twigs and pinecones,
then uses a tiny battery-driven fan to develop increased heat and cooking ability. It's an excellent alternative for long-distance backpacking trips, as it
solves the problem of carrying a fuel bottle, especially on expeditions for which large quantities of fuel would otherwise be
needed. Some tinkering with the flame (a very hot one) is required, and they are legal and functional only in the
alpine zone where dry wood is available. Also note
that in years with high fire danger, the U.S. Forest
Service will enact rules prohibiting open flames, and
fires are also often prohibited above an elevation of
10,000 feet.

*Stoves are available in many styles and burn a variety of
fuels. These are three typical examples. Top:* **White gas** *stoves
are the most popular because they are inexpensive and
easy to find; they do require priming and can be
explosive. Middle:* **Gas canister** *stoves burn
propane, butane, isobutane, and mixtures of
the three. These are the easiest to use but
have two disadvantages: 1) Because the
fuel is bottled, determining how much fuel
is left can be difficult. 2) The fuel is limited
to above-freezing conditions. Bottom:* **Liquid fuel**
*stoves burn Coleman Fuel, denatured alcohol, kerosene, and
even gasoline; these fuels are economical and have a high heat
output, but most must be primed.*

I prefer a small, lightweight stove that uses white gas so I can closely gauge fuel consumption. My pal Foonsky uses one with a butane bottle because it lights so easily. We have contests to see who can boil a pot of water faster, and the difference is usually negligible. Thus, other factors are important when choosing a stove.

Of these, ease of cleaning the burner is the most important. If you camp often, especially with a smaller stove, the burner holes will eventually become clogged. Some stoves have a built-in cleaning needle; a quick twist of the knob and you're in business. Others require disassembly and a protracted session using special cleaning tools. If a stove is difficult to clean, you will tend to put off doing it, and your stove will sputter and pant while you feel humiliated watching the cold pot of water sitting there.

Before making a purchase, have the salesperson show you how to clean the burner head. Except in the case of large, multiburner family camping stoves, which rarely require cleaning, this test can do more to determine the long-term value of a stove than any other factor.

**FUELS FOR CAMPING STOVES** White gas and butane have long been the most popular camp fuels, but a newly developed fuel could dramatically change that.

LPG (liquid petroleum gas) comes in cartridges for easy attachment to a stove or lantern. At room temperature, LPG is delivered in a combustible gaseous form. When you shake the cartridge, the contents sound liquid; that is because the gas liquefies under pressure, which is why it is so easy to use. Large amounts of fuel are compressed into small canisters.

While convenience has always been the calling card for LPG, recent innovations have allowed it to become a suitable choice for winter and high-altitude mountaineering expeditions, coming close to matching white gas performance specs. For several years now, MSR, Epi (Coleman), Coleman, Primus, Camping Gaz, Markill, and other makers have been mixing propane, butane, and isobutane to improve performance capabilities.

Two important hurdles that stood in the way of LPG's popularity were recently leaped. Coleman, working in cooperation with the U.S. Postal Service, has developed a program in which three-packs of 170-gram Coleman Max fuel cartridges can be shipped by mail to any address or post office in the 50 states and Puerto Rico. Also, each Coleman Max fuel cartridge is now made of aluminum and comes with a special device that allows the consumer to puncture the cartridge safely once the fuel is gone and then toss it into any aluminum recycling container.

The following details the benefits and drawbacks of other available fuels:

*White gas:* White gas is the most popular camp fuel because it can be purchased at most outdoor recreation stores and many supermarkets and is inexpensive and effective. It burns hot, has virtually no smell, and evaporates quickly when spilled. If you are caught in wet, miserable weather and can't get a fire going, you can use white gas as an emergency fire starter; however, if you do so, use it sparingly and never on an open flame.

White gas is a popular fuel both for car campers who use the large, two-burner stoves equipped with a fuel tank and a pump and for hikers who carry a lightweight backpacking stove. On the latter, lighting can require priming with a gel called priming paste, which some people dislike. Another problem with white gas is that it can be extremely explosive.

As an example, I once almost burned my beard completely off in a mini-explosion while lighting one of the larger stoves designed for car camping. I was in the middle of cooking dinner when the flame suddenly shut down. Sure enough, the fuel tank was empty, and after refilling it, I pumped the tank 50 or 60 times to regain pressure. When I lit a match, the sucker ignited from three feet away. The resulting explosion was like a stick of dynamite going off, and immediately the smell of burning beard was in the air. In a flash, my once thick, dark beard had been reduced to a mass of little yellow burned curlicues.

My error? After filling the tank, I forgot to shut the fuel cock off while pumping up the pressure in the tank. As a result, the stove burners were slowly producing the gas/air mixture as I pumped the tank, filling the air above the stove. Then strike a match from even a few feet away and ka-boom!

*Butane:* The explosive problem can be solved by using stoves that burn bottled butane fuel. Butane requires no pouring, pumping, or priming, and butane stoves are the easiest to light. Just turn a knob and light—that's it. On the minus side, because it comes in bottles, you never know precisely how much fuel you have left. And when a bottle is empty, you have a potential piece of litter. (Never litter. Ever.)

The other problem with butane is that it just plain does not work well in cold weather or when there is little fuel left in the cartridge. Since you cannot predict mountain weather in spring or fall, you can wind up using more fuel than originally projected. That can be frustrating, particularly if your stove starts wheezing when there are still several days left to go. In addition, with most butane cartridges, if there is any chance of the temperature falling below freezing, you often have to sleep with the cartridge to keep it warm or forget about using it come morning.

*Coleman Max Performance Fuel:* This new fuel offers a unique approach to solving the consistent burn challenge facing all pressurized gas cartridges: operating at temperatures at or below 0 degrees Fahrenheit. Using a standard propane/butane blend for high-octane performance, Coleman gets around the drop-off in performance other cartridges experience by utilizing a version of fuel injection. A hose inside the cartridge pulls liquid fuel into the stove, where it vaporizes—a switch from the standard approach of pulling only a gaseous form of the fuel into a stove. By drawing liquid out of the cartridge, Coleman gets

During high fire danger the U.S. Forest Service will enact rules prohibiting open flames. Fires are also often prohibited above an elevation of 10,000 feet.

around the tendency of propane to burn off first and allows each cartridge to deliver a consistent mix of propane and butane to the stove's burners throughout the cartridge's life.

*Butane/Propane:* This blend offers higher octane performance than butane alone, solving the cold temperature doldrums somewhat. However, propane burns off before butane, so there will be a performance drop as the fuel level in the cartridge lowers.

*Propane:* Now available for single-burner stoves using larger, heavier cartridges to accommodate higher pressures, propane offers the very best performance of any of the pressurized gas canister fuels.

*Primus Tri-Blend:* This blend is made up of 20% propane, 70% butane, and 10% isobutane and is designed to burn with more consistent heat and efficiency than standard propane/butane mixes.

*Denatured alcohol:* Though this fuel burns cleanly and quietly and is virtually explosion proof, it generates much less heat than pressurized or liquid gas fuels.

*Kerosene:* Never buy a stove that uses kerosene for fuel. Kerosene is smelly and messy, generates low heat, needs priming, and is virtually obsolete as a camp fuel in the United States. As a test I once tried using a kerosene stove. I could scarcely boil a pot of water. In addition, some kerosene leaked out when the stove was packed, ruining everything it touched. The smell of kerosene never did go away. Kerosene remains popular in Europe only because most campers there haven't yet heard much about white gas. When they do, they will demand it.

**BUILDING FIRES**  One summer expedition took me to the Canadian wilderness in British Columbia for a 75-mile canoe trip on the Bowron Lake Circuit, a chain of 13 lakes, six rivers, and seven portages. It is one of the truly great canoe trips in the world, a loop that ends just a few hundred feet from its starting point. But at the first camp at Kibbee Lake, my stove developed a fuel leak at the base of the burner, and the nuclear-like blast that followed just about turned Canada into a giant crater.

As a result, the final 70 miles of the trip had to be completed without a stove, cooking on open fires each night. The problem was compounded by the weather. It rained eight of the 10 days. Rain? In Canada, raindrops the size of silver dollars fall so hard they actually bounce on the lake surface. We had to stop paddling a few times in order to empty the rainwater out of the canoe. At the end of the day we'd make camp and then face the test: either make a fire or go to bed cold and hungry.

With an ax, at least we had a chance for success. As soaked as all the downed wood was, I was able to make my own fire-starting tinder from the chips of split logs; no matter how hard it rains, the inside of a log is always dry.

In miserable weather, matches don't stay lit long enough to get the tinder started. Instead we used either a candle or the little waxlike fire-starter cubes that remain lit for several minutes. From those we could get the tinder going. Then we added small, slender strips of wood that had been axed from the interior of the logs. When the flame reached a foot high, we added the logs, their dry interior facing in. By the time the inside of the logs had caught fire, the outside would be drying from the heat. It wasn't long before a royal blaze was brightening the rainy night.

That's a worst-case scenario, and hopefully you will never face anything like it. Nevertheless, being able to build a good fire and cook on it can be one of the more satisfying elements of a camping trip. At times just looking into the flames can provide a special satisfaction at the end of a good day.

However, never expect to build a fire for every meal or in some cases even to build one at all. Many state and federal campgrounds have been picked clean of downed wood, or forest fire danger forces rangers to prohibit fires altogether during the fire season. In either case you must use your camp stove or go hungry.

But when you can build a fire and the resources for doing so are available, it will enhance the quality of your camping experience. Of the campgrounds listed in this book, those where you are permitted to build fires will usually have fire rings. In primitive areas where you can make your own fire, you should dig a ring eight inches deep, line the edges with rock, and clear all the needles and twigs in a five-foot radius. The next day, when the fire is dead, you can discard the rocks, fill over the black charcoal with dirt, and then scatter pine needles and twigs over it. Nobody will even know you camped there. That's the best way I know to keep a secret spot a real secret.

When you start to build a campfire, the first thing you will notice is that no matter how good your intentions, your fellow campers will not be able to resist moving the wood around. Watch. You'll be getting ready to add a key piece of wood at just the right spot, and your companion will stick his mitts in, confidently believing he has a better idea. He'll shift the fire around and undermine your best-thought-out plans

So I enforce a rule on camping trips: One person makes the fire while everybody else stands clear or is involved with other camp tasks such as gathering wood, getting water, putting up tents, or planning dinner. Once the fire is going strong, then it's fair game; anyone adds logs at his or her discretion. But in the early, delicate stages of the campfire, it's best to leave the work to one person.

Before a match is ever struck, you should gather a complete pile of firewood. Then start small, with the tiniest twigs you can find, and slowly add larger twigs as you go, crisscrossing them like a miniature tepee. Eventually you will get to the big chunks that will produce high heat. The key is to get one piece of wood burning into another, which then burns into another, setting off what I call the chain of flame. Conversely, single pieces of wood set apart from each other will not burn.

On a dry summer evening at a campsite where plenty of wood is available, about the only way you can blow the deal is to get impatient and try to add the big pieces too quickly. Do that and you'll get smoke,

## Keep It Wild Tip 1: Campfires

1. Fire use can scar the backcountry. If a fire ring is not available, use a lightweight stove for cooking.

2. Where fires are permitted, use existing fire rings away from large rocks or overhangs.

3. Don't char rocks by building new rings.

4. Gather sticks from the ground that are no larger than the diameter of your wrist.

5. Don't snap branches of live, dead, or downed trees, which can cause personal injury and also scar the natural setting.

6. Put the fire "dead out" and make sure it's cold before departing. Remove all trash from the fire ring and sprinkle dirt over the site.

7. Remember that some forest fires can be started by a campfire that appears to be out. Hot embers burning deep in the pit can cause tree roots to catch fire and burn underground. If you ever see smoke rising from the ground, seemingly from nowhere, dig down and put the fire out.

not flames, and it won't be long before every one of your fellow campers is poking at your fire. It will drive you crazy, but they just won't be able to help it.

**COOKING GEAR** I like traveling light, and I've found that all I need for cooking is a pot, small frying pan, metal pot grabber, fork, knife, cup, and matches. If you want to keep the price of food low and also cook customized dinners each night, a small pressure cooker can be just the ticket. (See "Keeping the Price Down" on page 24.) I store all my gear in one small bag that fits into my pack. If I'm camping out of my four-wheel-drive rig, the little bag of cooking gear is easy to keep track of. Going simple, not complicated, is the key to keeping a camping trip on the right track.

You can get more elaborate by purchasing complete kits with plates, a coffeepot, large pots, and other cookware, but what really counts is having a single pot that makes you happy. It needs to be just the right size, not too big or small, and stable enough so it won't tip over, even if it is at a slight angle on a fire, full of water at a full boil. Mine is just six inches wide and four-and-a-half inches deep. It holds better than a quart of water and has served me well for several hundred camp dinners.

The rest of your cook kit is easy to complete. The frying pan should be small, light-gauge aluminum, Teflon-coated, with a fold-in handle so it's no hassle to store. A pot grabber is a great addition. It's a little aluminum gadget that clamps to the edge of pots and allows you to lift them and pour water with total control without burning your fingers. For cleanup take a plastic scrubber and a small bottle filled with dish cleaner, and you're in business.

A Sierra Cup, a wide aluminum cup with a wire handle, is an ideal item to carry because you can eat out of it as well as use it for drinking. This means no plates to scrub after dinner, so cleanup is quick and easy. In addition, if you go for a hike, you can clip it to your belt with its handle.

If you want a more formal setup complete with plates, glasses, silverware, and the like, you can end up spending more time preparing and cleaning up from meals than you do enjoying the country you are exploring. In addition, the more equipment you bring, the more loose ends you will have to deal with, and loose ends can cause plenty of frustration. If you have a choice, go simple.

And remember what Thoreau said: "A man is rich in proportion to what he can do without."

**FOOD AND COOKING TRICKS**

On a trip to the Bob Marshall Wilderness in western Montana, I woke up one morning, yawned, and said, "What've we got for breakfast?"

The silence was ominous. "Well," finally came the response, "we don't have any food left."

"What!?"

"Well, I figured we'd catch trout for meals every other night."

On the return trip, we ended up eating wild berries, buds, and, yes, even roots (not too tasty). When we finally landed the next day at a suburban pizza parlor, we nearly ate the wooden tables.

Running out of food on a camping trip can do more to turn reasonable people into violent grumps than any other event. There's no excuse for it, not when a system for figuring meals can be outlined with precision and little effort. You should not go out and buy a bunch of food, throw it in your rig, and head off for yonder. That leaves too much to chance. And if you've ever been in the woods and real hungry, you'll know it's worth taking a little effort to make sure a day or two of starvation will not occur. Here's a three-step solution:

1. Draw up a general meal-by-meal plan and make sure your companions like what's on it.

2. Tell your companions to buy any specialty items (like a special brand of coffee) on their own and not to expect you to take care of everything.

3. Put all the food on your living room floor and literally plan out every day of your trip, meal by meal, putting the food in plastic bags as you go. That way you will know exact food quotas and will not go hungry.

Fish for your dinner? There's one guarantee as far as that goes: If you expect to catch fish for meals, you will most certainly get skunked. If you don't expect to catch fish for meals, you will probably catch so many they'll be coming out of your ears. I've seen it a hundred times.

"There must be some mistake," I said with a laugh. "Whoever paid $750 for camp food?"

But the amount was as clear as the digital numbers on the cash register: $753.27.

"How is this possible?" I asked the clerk.

"Just add it up," she responded, irritated.

Then I started figuring. The freeze-dried backpack dinners cost $6 apiece. A small pack of beef jerky went for $2, the beef sticks for 75 cents, granola bars for 50 cents. Multiply it all by four hungry men, including Foonsky, for 21 days. This food was to sustain us on a major expedition—four guys hiking 250 miles over three weeks from Mount Whitney to Yosemite Valley.

The dinners alone cost close to $500. Add in the usual goodies— jerky, granola bars, soup, dried fruit, oatmeal, Tang, candy, and coffee —and I felt as if an earthquake had struck when I saw the tab.

A lot of campers have received similar shocks. In preparation for their trips, campers shop with enthusiasm. Then they pay the bill in horror.

Well, there are solutions, lots of them. You can eat gourmet style in the outback without having your wallet cleaned out. But it requires do-it-yourself cooking, more planning, and careful shopping. It also means transcending the push-button I-want-it-now attitude that so many people can't leave behind when they go to the mountains.

The secret is to bring along a small pressure cooker. A reader, Mike Bettinger of San Francisco, passed this tip on to me. Little pressure cookers weigh about two pounds, which may sound like a lot to backpackers and backcountry campers. But when three or four people are on a trip, it actually saves weight.

The key is that it allows campers to bring items that are difficult to cook at high altitudes, such as brown and white rice; red, black, pinto, and lima beans; and lentils. You pick one or more for a basic staple and then add a variety of freeze-dried ingredients to make a complete dish. Available are packets of meat, vegetables, onions, shallots, and garlic. Sun-dried tomatoes, for instance, reconstitute wonderfully in a pressure cooker. Add herbs, spices, and maybe a few rainbow trout and you will be eating better out of a backpack than most people do at home.

"In the morning, I have used the pressure cooker to turn dried apricots into apricot sauce to put on the pancakes we made with sourdough starter," Bettinger said. "The pressure cooker is also big enough for washing out cups and utensils. The days when backpacking meant eating terrible freeze-dried food are over. It doesn't take a gourmet cook to prepare these meals, only some thought beforehand."

Now when Foonsky, Mr. Furnai, Rambob, and I sit down to eat such a meal, we don't call it "eating." We call it "hodgepacking" or "time to pack your hodge." After a particularly long day on the trail, you can do some serious hodgepacking.

If your trip is a shorter one, say for a weekend, you can bring more fresh food to add some sizzle to the hodge. You can design a hot soup/stew mix that is good enough to eat at home. Start by bringing a pot of water to a full boil, then adding pasta, ramen noodles, or macaroni. While it simmers, cut in a potato, carrot, onion, and garlic clove, and cook for about 10 minutes. When the vegetables have softened, add in a soup mix or two, maybe some cheese, and you are just about in business. But you can still ruin it and turn your hodge into slodge. Make sure you read the directions on the soup mix to determine cooking time. It can vary widely. In addition, make sure you stir the whole thing up; otherwise you will get these hidden dry clumps of soup mix that can taste like garlic sawdust.

How do I know? Well, it was up near Kearsage Pass in the Sierra Nevada, where, feeling half-starved, I dug into our nightly hodge. I will never forget that first bite—I damn near gagged to death. Foonsky laughed at me, until he took his first bite (a nice big one), then turned green.

Another way to trim food costs is to make your own beef jerky, the trademark staple of campers for more than 200 years. A tiny packet of beef jerky costs $2, and for that 250-mile expedition, I spent $150 on jerky alone. Never again. Now we make our own and get big strips of jerky that taste better than anything you can buy.

If all this still doesn't sound like your idea of a gourmet but low-cost camping meal, well, you are forgetting the main course: rainbow trout. Remember: If you don't plan on catching them for dinner, you'll probably snag more than you can finish in one night's hodgepacking.

Some campers go to great difficulties to cook their trout, bringing along frying pans, butter, grills, tinfoil, and more, but all you need is some seasoned salt and a campfire.

Rinse the gutted trout, and while it's still wet, sprinkle on a good dose of seasoned salt, both inside and out. Clear any burning logs to the side of the campfire, then lay the trout right on the coals, turning it once so both sides are cooked. Sound ridiculous? Sound like you are throwing the fish away? Sound like the fish will burn up? Sound like you will have to eat the campfire ash? Wrong on all counts. The fish cooks perfectly, the ash doesn't stick, and after cooking trout this way, you may never fry trout again.

But if you can't convince your buddies, who may insist the trout should be fried, then make sure you have butter to fry them in, not oil. Also make sure you cook them all the way through, so the meat strips off the backbone in two nice, clean fillets. The fish should end up looking like one that Sylvester the Cat just drew out of his mouth—only the head, tail, and a perfect skeleton.

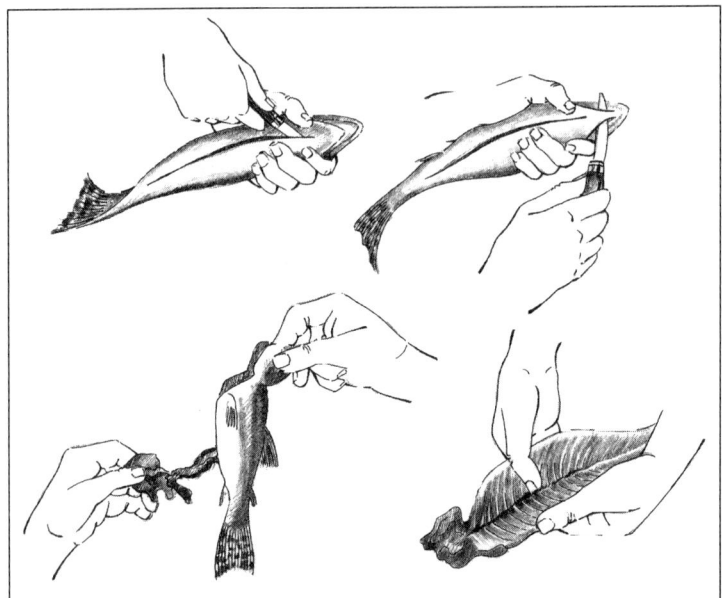

*Basic steps to cleaning a fish: First, slit belly from anal vent to gills. Then sever lower junctions of gills. Next, pull out innards and gills. And last but not least, run thumbnail along cavity to clean out dark matter.*

You can supplement your eats with sweets, nuts, freeze-dried fruits, and drink mixes. In any case, make sure you keep the dinner menu varied. If you and your buddies look into your dinner cups and groan, "Ugh, not this again," you will soon start dreaming of cheeseburgers and french fries instead of hiking, fishing, and finding beautiful campsites.

If you are car camping and have a big ice chest, you can bring virtually anything to eat and drink. If you are on the trail and don't mind paying the price, the newest premade, freeze-dried dinners provide another option.

Some of the biggest advances in the outdoors industry have come in the freeze-dried dinners now available to campers. Some of them are almost good enough to serve in restaurants. Sweet-and-sour pork over rice, tostadas, Burgundy chicken—it sure beats the poopy goop we used to eat, like the old soupy chili-mac dinners that tasted bad and looked so unlike food that consumption was near impossible, even for my dog, Rebel. Foonsky usually managed to get it down, however, but just barely.

To provide an idea of how to plan a menu, consider what my companions and I ate while hiking 250 miles on California's John Muir Trail:

### How to Make Beef Jerky in Your Own Kitchen

Start with a couple pieces of meat: lean top round, sirloin, or tri-tip. Cut it into 3/16-inch strips across the grain, trimming out the membrane, gristle, and fat. Marinate the strips for 24 hours in a glass dish. The fun begins in picking a marinade. Try two-thirds teriyaki sauce, one-third Worcestershire. You can customize the recipe by adding pepper, ground mustard, bay leaf, red wine vinegar, garlic, and, for the brave, Tabasco sauce.

After a day or so, squeeze out each strip of meat with a rolling pin, lay them in rows on a cooling rack over a cookie sheet, and dry them in the oven at 125 degrees for 12 hours. Thicker pieces can take as long as 18 to 24 hours.

That's it. The hardest part is cleaning the cookie sheet when you're done. The easiest part is eating your own homemade jerky while sitting at a lookout on a mountain ridge. The do-it-yourself method for jerky may take a day or so, but it is cheaper and can taste better than any store-bought jerky.

- Breakfast: instant soup, oatmeal (never get plain), one beef or jerky stick, coffee or hot chocolate.

- Lunch: one beef stick, two jerky sticks, one granola bar, dried fruit, half cup of pistachio nuts, Tang, one small bag of M&Ms.

- Dinner: instant soup, one freeze-dried dinner, one milk bar, rainbow trout.

What was that last item? Rainbow trout? Right! Unless you plan on it, you can catch them every night.

## Clothing and Weather Protection

What started as an innocent pursuit of a perfect campground evolved into one heck of a predicament for Foonsky and me.

We had parked at the end of a logging road and then bushwhacked our way down a canyon to a pristine trout stream. On my first cast—a little flip into the plunge pool of a waterfall—I caught a 16-inch rainbow trout, a real beauty that jumped three times. Magic stuff.

Then just across the stream, we saw it: The Perfect Camping Spot. On a sandbar on the edge of the forest, there lay a flat spot, high and dry above the river. Nearby was plenty of downed wood collected by past winter storms that we could use for firewood. And, of course, this beautiful trout stream was bubbling along just 40 yards from the site.

But nothing is perfect, right? To reach it, we had to wade across the river, although it didn't appear to be too difficult. The cold water tingled a bit, and the river came up surprisingly high, just above the belt. But it would be worth it to camp at The Perfect Spot.

Once across the river, we put on some dry clothes, set up camp, explored the woods, and fished the stream, catching several nice trout for dinner. But late that afternoon, it started raining. What? Rain in the summertime? Nature makes its own rules. By the next morning, it was still raining, pouring like a Yosemite waterfall from a solid gray sky.

That's when we noticed The Perfect Spot wasn't so perfect. The rain had raised the river level too high for us to wade back across. We were marooned, wet, and hungry.

"Now we're in a heck of a predicament," said Foonsky, the water streaming off him.

Getting cold and wet on a camping trip with no way to warm up is not only unnecessary and uncomfortable, it can be a fast ticket to hypothermia, the number one killer of campers in the woods. By definition, hypothermia is a condition in which body temperature is lowered to the point that it causes illness. It is particularly dangerous because the afflicted are usually unaware it is setting in. The first sign is a sense of apathy, then a state of confusion, which can lead eventually to collapse (or what appears to be sleep), then death.

You must always have a way to get warm and dry in short order, regardless of any conditions you may face. If you have no way of getting dry, then you must take emergency steps to prevent hypothermia. Those steps are detailed in the first-aid section on page 47.

But you should never reach that point. For starters, always have spare sets of clothing tucked away so no matter how cold and wet you might get, you have something dry to put on. On hiking trips I always carry a second set of clothes, sealed to stay dry, in a plastic garbage bag. I keep a third set waiting back at the truck.

If you are car camping, your vehicle can cause an illusory sense of security. But with an extra set of dry clothes stashed safely away, there is no illusion. The security is real. And remember, no matter how hot the weather is when you start your trip, always be prepared for the worst. Foonsky and I learned the hard way.

So both of us were soaking wet on that sandbar, and with no other choice we tried holing up in the tent for the night. A sleeping bag with Quallofil or another polyester fiberfill can retain warmth even when wet, because the fill is hollow and retains its loft. So as miserable as it was, we made it through the night.

The rain stopped the next day and the river dropped a bit, but it was still rolling big and angry. Using a stick as a wading staff, Foonsky crossed about 80% of the stream before he was dumped, but he made a jump for it and managed to scramble to the riverbank. He waved for me to follow. "No problem," I thought.

It took me 20 minutes to reach nearly the same spot where Foonsky had been dumped. The heavy river current was above my belt and pushing hard. Then in the flash of an instant, my wading staff slipped on a rock. I teetered in the river current and was knocked over like a bowling pin. I became completely submerged. I went tumbling down the river, heading right toward the waterfall. While underwater I looked up at the surface, and I can remember how close it seemed yet how out of control I was. Right then this giant hand appeared, and I grabbed it. It was Foonsky. If it weren't for that hand, I would have sailed right over the waterfall.

My momentum drew Foonsky right into the river, and we scrambled in the current, but I suddenly sensed the river bottom under my knees. On all fours, the two of us clambered ashore. We were safe.

"Thanks ol' buddy," I said.

"Man, we're wet," he responded. "Let's get to the rig and get some dry clothes on."

The most important element in enjoying the outdoor experience in any **THE ART OF** condition is to stay dry and warm. There is no substitute. You must **LAYERING** stay dry and you must stay warm.

Thus comes the theory behind layering, which suggests that as your body temperature fluctuates or the weather shifts, you simply peel off or add available layers as needed—and have a waterproof shell available in case of rain.

The introduction of a new era of outdoor clothing has made it possible for campers to turn choosing clothes into an art form. Like art, it comes much more expensive than throwing on a pair of blue jeans, a T-shirt, and some flannel, but for many it is worth the price.

In putting together your ideal layering system, there are some general considerations. What you need to do is create a system that effectively combines elements of breathability, wicking, rapid drying, insulation, durability, wind resistance, and water repellence while still being lightweight and offering the necessary freedom of movement, all with just a few garments.

The basic intent of a base layer is to manage moisture. Your base layer will be the first article of clothing you put on and the last to come off. Since your own skin will be churning out the perspiration, the goal of this second skin is to manage the moisture and move it away from you without trapping your body's heat. The only time that cotton should become a part of your base layer is if you wish to keep cool, not warm, such as in a hot desert climate where evaporative cooling becomes your friend, not your enemy.

That is why the best base layer available is from bicomponent knits, that is, blends of polyester and cotton, which work to provide wicking and insulating properties in one layer. The way it works is that the side facing your skin is water hating, while the side away from your skin is water loving; thus it pulls or "wicks" moisture through. You'll stay dry and happy, even with only one layer on, something not possible with old single-function weaves. The best include Thermax, Capilene, Driclime, Lifa, and Polartec 100.

Stretch fleece and microdenier pile also provide a good base layer, though they can be used as a second layer as well. Microdenier pile can be worn alone or layered under or over other pieces, and it has excellent wicking capability as well as more windproof potential.

The next layer should be a light cotton shirt or a long-sleeved cotton/wool shirt, or both, depending on the coolness of the day. For pants, many just wear blue jeans when camping, but blue jeans can be hot and tight, and once wet, they tend to stay that way. Putting on wet blue jeans on a cold morning is a torturous way to start the day. (I tell you this from experience, since I have suffered that fate a number of times.) A better choice is pants made from a cotton/canvas mix, which are available at outdoors stores. They are light, have a lot of give, and dry quickly. If the weather is quite warm, shorts that have some room to them can be the best choice.

Finally, you'll top the entire ensemble off with a thin windproof, water-resistant layer. You want this layer to breathe like crazy, yet not be so porous that rain runs through it like floodwaters through a leaking dike. Patagonia's Velocity shell is one of the best. Its outer fabric is DWR (durable water-repellent) treated, and the coating is by Gore. Patagonia calls it Pneumatic (Gore now calls it Activent, while Marmot, Moonstone, and North Face all offer their own versions). Though condensation will still build up inside, it manages to get rid of enough moisture.

It is critical to know the difference between "water-resistant" and "waterproof." This is covered later in the chapter under the "Rain Gear" section.

But hey, why does anybody need all this fancy stuff just to go camping? Fair question. Like the introduction of Gore-Tex years ago, all this fabric and fiber mumbo jumbo has its skeptics, including me. You don't have to opt for this aerobic-function fashion statement; it is unnecessary on many camping trips. But the fact is you must be ready for anything when you venture into the outdoors. And the truth is that the new era of outdoor clothing works, and it works better than anything that has come before.

Regardless of what you choose, weather should never be a nuisance or cause discomfort, regardless of what you experience. Instead it should provide a welcome change of pace.

**ABOUT HATS**  One final word of advice: Always pack along a warm hat for those times when you need to seal in warmth. You lose a large percentage of heat through your head. I almost always wear a wide-brimmed hat, something like the legendary outlaws wore 150 years ago. There's actually logic behind it: My hat is made out of kangaroo skin (waterproof), is rigged with a lariat (it can be cinched down when it's windy), and has a wide brim that keeps the tops of my ears from being sunburned (years ago they once were burned to a red crisp on a trip where I was wearing a baseball hat). But to be honest, I like how it looks, kind of like my pal Waylon Jennings.

In cold weather you should take the layer system one step further **VESTS AND** with a warm vest and a parka jacket. Vests are especially useful because **PARKAS** they provide warmth without the bulkiness of a parka. The warmest vests and parkas are either filled with down or Quallofil, or are made with a cotton/wool mix. Each has its respective merits and problems. Down fill provides the most warmth for the amount of weight, but becomes useless when wet, closely resembling a wet dishrag. Quallofil keeps much of its heat-retaining quality even when wet, but is expensive. Vests made of cotton/wool mixes are the most attractive and also are quite warm, but they can be as heavy as a ship's anchor when wet.

Sometimes the answer is combining the two. One of my best camping companions wears a good-looking cotton/wool vest and a parka filled with Quallofil. The vest never gets wet, so weight is not a factor.

One of the most miserable nights I ever spent in my life was on a **RAIN** camping trip where I didn't bring my rain gear or a tent. Hey, it was **GEAR** early August, the temperature had been in the 90s for weeks, and if anybody had said it was going to rain, I would have told him to consult a brain doctor. But rain it did. And as I got wetter and wetter, I kept saying to myself, "Hey, it's summer, it's not supposed to rain." Then I remembered one of the ten commandments of camping: Forget your rain gear and you can guarantee it will rain.

To stay dry, you need some form of water-repellent shell. It can be as simple as a $5 poncho made out of plastic or as elaborate as a Gore-Tex rain jacket-and-pants set that costs $300. What counts is not how much you spend, but how dry you stay.

The most important thing to realize is that waterproof and water-resistant are completely different things. In addition, there is no such thing as rain gear that is both waterproof and breathable. The more waterproof a jacket is, the less it breathes. Conversely, the more breathable a jacket is, the less waterproof it becomes.

If you wear water-resistant rain gear in a downpour, you'll get soaked. Water-resistant rain gear is appealing because it breathes and will keep you dry in the light stuff, such as mist, fog, even a little splash from a canoe paddle. But in rain? Forget it.

So what is the solution?

I've decided that the best approach is a set of fairly light but 100%-waterproof rain gear. I recently bought a hooded jacket and pants from Coleman, and my assessment is that it is the most cost-efficient rain gear I've ever had. All I can say is, hey, it works: I stay dry, it doesn't weigh much, and it didn't cost a fortune.

You can also stay dry with any of the waterproof plastics and even heavy-duty rubber-coated outfits made for commercial fishermen.

But these are uncomfortable during anything but a heavy rain. Because they are heavy and don't breathe, you'll likely get soaked anyway (that is, from your own sweat), even if it isn't raining hard.

On backpacking trips, I still stash a super lightweight water-repellent slicker for day hikes, and a poncho, which I throw over my pack at night to keep it dry. But otherwise I never go anywhere—*anywhere*—without my rain gear.

Some do just fine with a cheap poncho, and note that ponchos can serve other uses in addition to a raincoat. Ponchos can be used as a ground tarp, as a rain cover for supplies or a backpack, or can be roped up to trees in a pinch to provide a quick storm ceiling if you don't have a tent. The problem with ponchos is that in a hard rain, you just don't stay dry. First your legs get wet, then they get soaked. Then your arms follow the same pattern. If you're wearing cotton, you'll find that once part of the garment gets wet, the water will spread until, alas, you are dripping wet, poncho and all. Before long you start to feel like a walking refrigerator.

**Waterproof:** impervious to water. Though rain won't penetrate waterproof material, if you're at all mobile you'll soon find yourself wet from perspiration that can't evaporate. **Water-resistant:** resistant but not impervious to water. You'll stay dry using water-resistant material only if it isn't pouring.

One high-cost option is buying a Gore-Tex rain jacket and pants. Gore-Tex is actually not a fabric as is commonly believed, but a laminated film that coats a breathable fabric. The result is lightweight, water-repellent, breathable jackets and pants. They are perfect for campers, but they cost a fortune.

Some hiking buddies of mine have complained that the older Gore-Tex rain gear loses its water-repellent quality over time. However, manufacturers insist that this is the result of water seeping through seams, not leaks in the jacket. At each seam, tiny needles have pierced the fabric, and as tiny as the holes are, water will find a way through. An application of Seam Lock, especially at major seams around the shoulders of a jacket, can usually fix the problem.

If you don't want to spend the big bucks for Gore-Tex rain gear but want more rain protection than a poncho affords, a coated nylon jacket is the compromise that many choose. They are inexpensive, have the highest water-repellency of any rain gear, and are warm, providing a good outer shell for your layers of clothing. But they are not without fault. These jackets don't breathe at all, and if you zip them up tight, you can sweat a river.

My brother Rambob gave me a nylon jacket prior to a mountain climbing expedition. I wore that $20 special all the way to the top with no complaints; it's warm and 100% waterproof. The one problem with nylon is when temperatures drop below freezing. It gets so stiff that it feels as if you are wearing a straitjacket. But at $20, it seems like a treasure, especially compared to a $180 Gore-Tex jacket.

There's one more jacket-construction term to know: DWR, or durable water-repellent finish. All of the top-quality jackets these days are DWR treated. The DWR causes water to bead up on the shell. When the DWR wears off, even a once-waterproof jacket will feel like a wet dishrag.

Also note that ventilation is the key to coolness. The only ventilation on most shells is often the zipper. But waterproof jackets need additional openings. Look for mesh-backed pockets and underarm zippers, as well as cuffs, waists, and hems that can be adjusted to open wide. Storm flaps (the baffle over the zipper) that close with hook-and-loop material or snaps let you leave the zipper open for airflow into the jacket.

What are the three items most commonly forgotten on a camping trip? A hat, sunglasses, and lip balm.

OTHER GEAR ... AND A FEW TIPS

A hat is crucial, especially when you are visiting high elevations. Without one you are constantly exposed to everything nature can give you. The sun will dehydrate you, sap your energy, sunburn your head, and in worst cases, cause sunstroke. Start with a comfortable hat. Then finish with sunglasses, lip balm, and sunscreen for additional protection. They will help protect you from extreme heat.

To guard against extreme cold, it's a good idea to keep a pair of thin ski gloves stashed away with your emergency clothes, along with a wool ski cap. The gloves should be thick enough to keep your fingers from stiffening up, but pliable enough to allow full movement so you don't have to take them off to complete simple tasks, like lighting a stove. An alternative to gloves are glovelets, which look like gloves with no fingers. In any case, just because the weather turns cold doesn't mean that your hands have to.

And if you fall into a river as Foonsky and I did—well, I hope you have a set of dry clothes waiting back at your rig. Oh, and a hand reaching out to you.

## Hiking and Foot Care

We had set up a nice little camp in the woods, and my buddy, Foonsky, was strapping on his hiking boots, sitting against a big Douglas fir.

"New boots," he said with a grin. "But they seem pretty stiff."

We decided to hoof it down the trail for a few hours, exploring the mountain wildlands that are said to hide Bigfoot and other strange creatures. After just a short while on the trail, a sense of peace and calm seemed to settle in. The forest provides the chance to be purified with clean air and the smell of trees, freeing you from all troubles.

But it wasn't long before a look of trouble was on Foonsky's face. And no, it wasn't from seeing Bigfoot.

"Got a hot spot on a toe," he said.

Immediately we stopped. He pulled off his right boot, then his socks, and inspected the left side of his big toe. Sure enough, a blister had bubbled up, filled with fluid, but hadn't popped. From his medical kit, Foonsky cut a small piece of moleskin to fit over the blister and taped it to hold it in place. In a few minutes we were back on the trail.

A half hour later, there was still no sign of Bigfoot. But Foonsky stopped again and pulled off his other boot. "Another hot spot." On the little toe of his left foot was another small blister, over which he taped a Band-Aid to keep it from further chafing against the inside of his new boot.

In just a few days, ol' Foonsky, a strong, 6-foot-5, 200-plus-pound guy, was walking around like a sore-hoofed horse that had been loaded with a month's worth of supplies and ridden over sharp rocks. Well, it wasn't the distance that had done Foonsky in; it was those blisters. He had them on eight of his 10 toes and was going through Band-Aids, moleskin, and tape like a walking emergency ward. If he used any more tape, he would've looked like a mummy from an Egyptian tomb.

If you've ever been in a similar predicament, you know the frustration of wanting to have a good time, wanting to hike and explore the area where you have set up a secluded camp, only to be turned gimp-legged by several blisters. No one is immune—all are created equal before the blister god. You can be forced to bow to it unless you get your act together.

That means wearing the right style boots for what you have in mind and then protecting your feet with carefully selected socks. If you are still so unfortunate as to get a blister or two, it means knowing how to treat them fast so they don't turn your walk into a sore-footed endurance test.

What causes blisters? In almost all cases, it is the simple rubbing of a foot against the rugged interior of a boot. That can be worsened by several factors:

1. A very stiff boot or one in which your foot moves inside as you walk, instead of the boot flexing as if it were another layer of skin.

2. Thin, ragged, or dirty socks. This is the fastest route to blisters. Thin socks will allow your feet to move inside of your boots, ragged socks will allow your skin to chafe directly against the boot's interior, and dirty socks will wrinkle and fold, also rubbing against your feet instead of cushioning them.

3. Soft feet. By themselves, soft feet will not cause blisters, but in combination with a stiff boot or thin socks, they can cause terrible problems. The best way to toughen up your feet is to go barefoot. In fact, some of the biggest, toughest-looking guys you'll ever see, from Hell's Angels to pro football players, have feet that are as soft as a baby's butt. Why? Because they never go barefoot and don't hike much.

**SELECTING THE RIGHT BOOTS**     One summer I hiked 400 miles, including 250 miles in three weeks, along the crest of California's Sierra Nevada, and another 150 miles over several months in an earlier general training program. In that span I got just one blister, suffered on the fourth day of the 250-miler. I treated it immediately and suffered no more. One key is wearing the right boot, and for me, that means a boot that acts as a thick layer of skin that is flexible and pliable to my foot. I want my feet to fit snugly in them, with no interior movement.

There are three kinds of boots: mountaineering boots, hiking (or backpacking) boots, and canvas walking shoes. Select the right one for you or pay the consequences.

## Mountaineering Boots

The stiffest of the lot is the mountaineering boot. These boots are often identified by mid-range tops, laces that extend almost as far as the toe area, and ankle areas that are as stiff as a board. The lack of "give" is what endears them to mountaineers. Their stiffness is preferred when rock climbing, walking off-trail on craggy surfaces, or hiking down the edge of streambeds where walking across small rocks can cause you to turn your ankle. Because these boots don't give on rugged, craggy terrain, they reduce ankle injuries and provide better traction.

The drawback to stiff boots is that if you don't have the proper socks and your foot starts slipping around in the boot, you will get a set of blisters that would raise even Foonsky's eyebrows. But if you just want to go for a walk or a good tromp with a backpack, then hiking shoes or backpacking boots will serve you better.

## Canvas Walking shoes

Canvas walking shoes are the lightest of all boots, designed for day walks or short backpacking trips. Some of the newer models are like rugged tennis shoes, designed with a canvas top for lightness and a lug sole for traction. These are perfect for people who like to walk but rarely carry a backpack. Because they are flexible, they are easy to break in, and with fresh socks they rarely cause blister problems. Because they are light, general hiking fatigue is greatly reduced.

On the negative side, because canvas shoes have shallow lug soles, traction can be far from good on slippery surfaces. In addition, they provide less than ideal ankle support, which can be a problem in rocky areas, such as along a stream where you might want to go trout fishing. Turn your ankle and your trip can be ruined.

## Backpacking Boots

My preference is for a premium backpacking boot, the perfect medium between the stiff mountaineering boot and the soft canvas walking shoe. The deep lug bottom provides traction, the high ankle coverage provides support, yet the soft, waterproof leather body gives each foot a snug fit. Add it up and that means no blisters. On the negative side, they can be quite hot, weigh a ton, and if they get wet, take days to dry.

There are a zillion styles, brands, and price ranges to choose from. If you wander about, comparing all their many features, you will get as confused as a kid in a toy store. Instead, go into the store with your mind clear about what you want, find it, and buy it. If you want the best, expect to spend $85-110 for canvas walking shoes, from $130-180 and sometimes more for hiking or mountaineering boots. I have spent as much as $250 for hiking boots that I have worn for close to 2,000 miles. Yet another time I spent $185, thinking I was getting stellar quality, but they turned out to be miserable blister makers, and even after a year of trying to get my money's worth, they never worked right on the trail and now occupy a dark place deep in my closet.

This is one area where you don't want to scrimp, so try not to yelp about the high cost. Instead, walk out of the store believing you deserve the best, and that's exactly what you just paid for. Another trick I have learned is to bring several pairs of different style hiking boots on adventures, then change them constantly according to the terrain. Use heavy boots for steep trails with loose footing, lightweight models for flat routes with a hard surface. This works wonders to avoid blisters and muscle soreness because you are constantly changing what I call "the point of attack."

If you plan on using the advice of a shoe salesperson, first look at what kind of boots he or she is wearing. If he or she isn't even wearing boots, then any advice the salesperson might tender may not be worth a plugged nickel. Most people I know who own quality boots, including salespeople, will wear them almost daily if their job allows, since boots are the best footwear available. However, even these well-meaning folks can offer sketchy advice. Every hiker I've ever met will tell you he wears the world's greatest boot.

Instead, enter the store with a precise use and style in mind. Rather than fish for suggestions, tell the salesperson exactly what you want, try two or three brands of the same style, and always try on both boots in a pair simultaneously so you know exactly how they'll feel. If possible, walk up and down stairs with them. Are they too stiff? Are your feet snug yet comfortable, or do they slip? Do they have that "right" kind of feel when you walk?

If you get the right answers to those questions, then you're on your way to blister-free, pleasure-filled days of walking.

**SOCKS** The poor gent was scratching his feet as if ants were crawling over them. I looked closer. Huge yellow calluses covered the bottoms of his feet, and at the ball and heel, the calluses were about a quarter inch thick, cracking and sore.

"I don't understand it," he said. "I'm on my feet a lot, so I bought a real good pair of hiking boots. But look what they've done to my feet. My feet itch so much I'm going crazy."

People can spend so much energy selecting the right kind of boot that they virtually overlook wearing the right kind of socks. One goes with the other.

Your socks should be thick enough to cushion your feet as well as fit snugly. Without good socks you might try to get the bootlaces too tight—and that's like putting a tourniquet on your feet. You should have plenty of clean socks on hand, or plan on washing what you have on your trip. As socks are worn, they become compressed, dirty, and damp. Any one of those factors can cause problems.

My camping companions believe I go overboard when it comes to socks, that I bring too many and wear too many. But it works, so that's where the complaints stop. So how many do I wear? Well, it varies. On day hikes, I have found a sock called a SmartWool that makes my size 13s feel like I'm walking on pillows. But on long expeditions, the 200-milers, I sometimes wear three socks on each foot, believe it or not. It may sound like overkill, but each has its purpose, and like I said, it works.

The interior sock is thin, lightweight, and made of polypropylene or silk synthetic materials designed to transport moisture away from your skin. With a poly interior sock, your foot stays dry when it sweats. Without a poly sock, your foot can get damp and mix with dirt, which can cause a hot spot to start on your foot. Eventually you get blisters, lots of them.

The second sock is for comfort and can be cotton, but a thin wool-based composite is ideal. Some made of the latter can wick moisture away from the skin, much like polypropylene does. If wool itches your feet, a thick cotton sock can be suitable, though cotton collects moisture and compacts more quickly than other socks. If you're on a short hike though, cotton will do just fine.

The exterior sock should be made of high-quality, thick wool—at least 80% wool. It will cushion your feet, provide that just right snug fit in your boot, and give you some additional warmth and insulation in cold weather. It is critical to keep the wool sock clean. If you wear a dirty wool sock over and over again, it will compact and lose its cushion and start wrinkling while you hike, then your feet will catch on fire from the blisters that start popping up. Of course, when wearing multiple socks, especially a wool composite, you will likely need to go up a boot size so they fit comfortably.

**A FEW MORE TIPS** If you are like most folks—that is, the bottoms of your feet are rarely exposed and quite soft—you can take additional steps in their care. The best tip is keeping a fresh foot pad made of sponge rubber in your boot. Another cure for soft feet is to get out and walk or jog on a regular basis prior to your camping trip.

If you plan to use a foot pad and wear three socks, you will need to use these items when sizing boots. It is an unforgiving error to wear thin cotton socks when buying boots and later try to squeeze all this stuff, plus your feet, into them. There just won't be enough room.

The key to treating blisters is fast work at the first sign of a hot spot. But before you remove your socks, check to see if the sock has a wrinkle in it, a likely cause of the problem. If so, either change socks or pull them tight, removing the tiny folds, after taking care of the blister. Cut a piece of moleskin to cover the offending toe, securing the moleskin with white medical tape. If moleskin is not available, small Band-Aids can do the job, but these have to be replaced daily, and sometimes with even more frequency. At night, clean your feet and sleep without socks.

Two other items that can help your walking is an Ace bandage and a pair of gaiters.

For sprained ankles and twisted knees, an Ace bandage can be like an insurance policy to get you back on the trail and out of trouble. Over the years I have had serious ankle problems and have relied on a good wrap with a four-inch bandage to get me home. The newer bandages come with the clips permanently attached, so you don't have to worry about losing them.

Gaiters are leggings made of plastic, nylon, or Gore-Tex that fit from just below your knees, over your calves, and attach under your boots. They are of particular help when walking in damp areas or in places where rain is common. As your legs brush against ferns or low-lying plants, gaiters will deflect the moisture. Without them, your pants will be soaking wet in short order.

Should your boots become wet, a good tip is never to try to force dry them. Some well-meaning folks will try to dry them quickly at the edge of a campfire or actually put the boots in an oven. While this may dry the boots, it can also loosen the glue that holds them together, ultimately weakening them until one day they fall apart in a heap.

A better bet is to treat the leather so the boots become water repellent. Silicone-based liquids are the easiest to use and least greasy of the treatments available.

A final tip is to have another pair of lightweight shoes or moccasins that you can wear around camp and in the process give your feet the rest they deserve.

## Sleeping Gear

One mountain night in the pines on an eve long ago, my dad, brother, and I had rolled out our sleeping bags and were bedded down for the night. After the pre-trip excitement, a long drive, an evening of trout fishing, and a barbecue, we were like three tired doggies who had played too much.

But as I looked up at the stars, I was suddenly wide awake. This kid was still wired. A half hour later? No change—wide awake.

And as little kids can do, I had to wake up ol' dad to tell him about it. "Hey, Dad, I can't sleep."

"This is what you do," he said. "Watch the sky for a shooting star and tell yourself that you cannot go to sleep until you see at least one. As you wait and watch, you will start getting tired, and it will be difficult to keep your eyes open. But tell yourself you must keep watching. Then you'll start to really feel tired. When you finally see a shooting star, you'll go to sleep so fast you won't know what hit you."

Well, I tried it that night and I don't even remember seeing a shooting star, I went to sleep so fast.

It's a good trick, and along with having a good sleeping bag, ground insulation, maybe a tent, or a few tricks for bedding down in a pickup truck or motor home, you can get a good night's sleep on every camping trip.

More than 20 years after that camping episode with my dad and brother, we made a trip to the planetarium at the Academy of Sciences in San Francisco to see a show on Halley's Comet. The lights dimmed, and the ceiling turned into a night sky, filled with stars and a setting moon. A scientist began explaining phenomena of the heavens.

After a few minutes, I began to feel drowsy. Just then, a shooting star zipped across the planetarium ceiling. I went into a deep sleep so fast it was like I was in a coma. I didn't wake up until the show was over, the lights were turned back on, and the people were leaving.

Feeling drowsy, I turned to see if ol' Dad had liked the show. Oh yeah? Not only had he gone to sleep too, but he apparently had no intention of waking up, no matter what. Just like a camping trip.

SLEEPING BAGS Question: What could be worse than trying to sleep in a cold, wet sleeping bag on a rainy night without a tent in the mountains?

Answer: Trying to sleep in a cold, wet sleeping bag on a rainy night without a tent in the mountains when your sleeping bag is filled with down.

Water will turn a down-filled sleeping bag into a mushy heap. Many campers do not like a high-tech approach, but the state-of-the-art polyfiber sleeping bags can keep you warm even when wet. That factor, along with temperature rating and weight, is key when selecting a sleeping bag.

A sleeping bag is a shell filled with heat-retaining insulation. By itself it is not warm. Your body provides the heat, and the sleeping bag's ability to retain that heat is what makes it warm or cold.

The old-style canvas bags are heavy, bulky, cold, and when wet, useless. With other options available, their use is limited. Anybody who sleeps outdoors or backpacks should choose otherwise. Buy and use a sleeping bag filled with down or one of the quality poly-fills. Down is light, warm, and aesthetically pleasing to those who don't think camping and technology mix. If you choose a down bag, be sure to keep it double wrapped in plastic garbage bags on your trip in order to keep it dry. Once wet, you'll spend your nights howling at the moon.

The polyfiber-filled bags are not necessarily better than those filled with down, but they can be. Their one key advantage is that even when wet, some poly-fills can retain up to 85% of your body heat. This allows you to sleep and get valuable rest even in miserable conditions. And my camping experience is that no matter how lucky you may be, there comes a time when you will get caught in an unexpected, violent storm and everything you've got will get wet, including your sleeping bag. That's when a poly-fill bag becomes priceless. You either have one and can sleep, or you don't have one and suffer. It is that simple. Of the synthetic fills, Quallofil made by Dupont is the industry leader.

But just because a sleeping bag uses a high-tech poly-fill doesn't necessarily make it a better bag. There are other factors.

The most important are a bag's temperature rating and weight. The temperature rating of a sleeping bag refers to how cold it can get before you start actually feeling cold. Many campers make the mistake of thinking, "I only camp in the summer, so a bag rated at 30 or 40 degrees should be fine." Later they find out it isn't so fine, and all it takes is one cold night to convince them of that. When selecting the right temperature rating, visualize the coldest weather you might ever confront, and then get a bag rated for even colder weather.

*Even with the warmest sleeping bag in the world, if you just lay it down on the ground and try to sleep, you will likely get as cold as a winter cucumber. That is because the cold ground will suck the warmth right out of your body. The solution? A sleeping pad.*

For instance, if you are a summer camper, you may rarely experience a night in the low 30s or high 20s. A sleeping bag rated at 20 degrees would be appropriate, keeping you snug, warm, and asleep. For most campers, I advise bags rated at zero or 10 degrees.

If you buy a poly-filled sleeping bag, never leave it squished in your stuff sack between camping trips. Instead, keep it on a hanger in a closet or use it as a blanket. One thing that can reduce a poly-filled bag's heat-retaining qualities is if you lose the loft out of the tiny hollow fibers that make up the fill. You can avoid this with proper storage.

The weight of a sleeping bag can also be a key factor, especially for backpackers. When you have to carry your gear on your back, every ounce becomes important. Sleeping bags that weigh just three pounds are available, although they are expensive. But if you hike much, it's worth the price to keep your weight to a minimum,. For an overnighter, you can get away with a four- or four-and-a-half-pound bag without much stress. However, bags weighing five pounds and up should be left back at the car.

I have two sleeping bags: a seven-pounder that feels like I'm in a giant sponge, and a little three-pounder. The heavy-duty model is for pickup truck camping in cold weather and doubles as a blanket at home. The lightweight bag is for hikes. Between the two, I'm set.

## INSULATION PADS

Even with the warmest sleeping bag in the world, if you just lay it down on the ground and try to sleep, you will likely get as cold as a winter cucumber. That is because the cold ground will suck the warmth right out of your body. The solution is to have a layer of insulation between you and the ground. For this you can use a thin Insulite pad, a lightweight Therm-a-Rest inflatable pad, a foam pad or mattress, air bed, or a cot. Here is a capsule summary of all three:

- **Insulite pads:** They are light, inexpensive, roll up quick for transport, and can double as a seat pad at your camp. The negative side is that in one night, they will compress, making you feel that you are sleeping on granite.

- **Therm-a-Rest pads:** These are a real luxury because they do everything an Insulite pad does, but also provide a cushion. The negative side is that they are expensive by comparison, and if they get a hole in them, they become worthless without a patch kit.

- **Air beds, foam mattresses, and cots:** These are excellent for car campers. The new line of air beds available are outstanding, especially the thicker ones, and inflate quickly with an electric motor inflator that plugs into a power plug or cigarette lighter in your vehicle. Foam mattresses are also excellent, in fact, the most comfortable of all, but their size precludes many from considering them. I've found that cots work great, too. I finally wore out an old wood one just before this book went to press; replaced it immediately with one of the new high-tech and light metal ones. For camping in the back of a pick-up truck with a camper shell, the cots with three-inch legs are best, of course.

**A Few Tricks**  When surveying a camp area, the most important consideration should be to select a good spot to sleep. Everything else is secondary. Ideally, you want a flat spot that is wind sheltered and on ground soft enough to drive stakes into. Yeah, and I want to win the lottery, too.

Sometimes that ground will have a slight slope to it. In that case, always sleep with your head on the uphill side. If you sleep parallel to the slope, every time you roll over, you'll find yourself rolling down the hill. If you sleep with your head on the downhill side, you'll get a headache that feels as if an ax is embedded in your brain.

When you've found a good spot, clear it of all branches, twigs, and rocks, of course. A good tip is to dig a slight indentation in the ground where your hip will fit. Since your body is not flat, but has curves and edges, it will not feel comfortable on flat ground. Some people even get severely bruised on the sides of their hips when sleeping on flat, hard ground. For that reason alone they learn to hate camping. What a shame, especially when solved so easily with a Therm-a-Rest pad, foam insulation, air bed or a cot.

After the ground is prepared, throw a ground cloth over the spot, which will keep much of the morning dew off you. In some areas, particularly where fog is a problem, morning dew can be heavy and get the outside of your sleeping bag quite wet. In that case, you need overhead protection, such as a tent or some kind of roof, like a poncho or tarp with its ends tied to trees.

**Tents and Weather Protection**  All it takes is to get caught in the rain once without a tent and you will never go anywhere without one again. A tent provides protection from rain, wind, and mosquito attacks. In exchange, you can lose a starry night's view, though some tents now even provide moon roofs.

A tent can be as complex as a four-season, tubular-jointed dome with a rain fly or as simple as two ponchos snapped together and roped up to a tree. They can be as cheap as a $10 tube tent, which is nothing more than a hollow piece of plastic, or as expensive as a $500 five-person deluxe expedition dome model. They vary greatly in size, price, and put-up time. If you plan on getting a good one, plan on doing plenty of shopping and asking lots of questions. With a little bit of homework, you can get the right answers to these questions:

## Will It Keep Me Dry?

On many one-person and two-person tents, the rain fly does not extend far enough to keep water off the bottom sidewalls of the tent. In a driving rain, water can also drip from the rain fly and to the bottom sidewalls of the tent. Eventually the water can leak through to the inside, particularly through the seams where the tent has been sewn together.

You must be able to stake out your rain fly so it completely covers all of the tent. If you are tent shopping and this does not appear possible, then don't buy the tent. To prevent potential leaks, use a seam waterproofer such as Seam Lock, a gluelike substance, to close potential leak areas on tent seams. For large umbrella tents, keep a patch kit handy.

Another way to keep water out of your tent is to store all wet garments outside the tent, under a poncho. Moisture from wet clothes stashed in the tent will condense on the interior tent walls. If you bring enough wet clothes into the tent, by the next morning you can feel as if you're camping in a duck blind.

## How Hard Is It to Put Up?

If a tent is difficult to erect in full sunlight, you can just about forget it at night. Some tents can go up in just a few minutes, without requiring help from another camper. This might be the kind of tent you want.

The way to compare put-up time of tents when shopping is to count the number of connecting points from the tent poles to the tent and the number of stakes required. The fewer, the better. Think simple. My tent has seven connecting points and, minus the rain fly, requires no stakes. It goes up in a few minutes. If you need a lot of stakes, it is a sure tip-off to a long put-up time. Try it at night or in the rain, and you'll be ready to cash your chips and go for broke.

Another factor is the tent poles themselves. Some small tents have poles that are broken into small sections that are connected by bungee cords. It takes only an instant to convert them to a complete pole.

Some outdoor shops have tents on display on their showroom floor. Before buying the tent, have the salesperson take the tent down and put it back up. If it takes him more than five minutes, or he says he doesn't have time, then keep looking.

*A-frame style tents have gone the way of the dinosaur. With the world going high-tech, tents of today vary greatly in complexity, size, price, and put-up time. And they wouldn't be fit for the new millennium without offering options such as moon roofs, rain flies, and tent wings. Be sure to purchase the one that's right for your needs.*

### Is It Roomy Enough?

Don't judge the size of a tent on floor space alone. Some tents small on floor space can give the illusion of roominess with a high ceiling. You can be quite comfortable in them and snug.

But remember that a one-person or two-person tent is just that. A two-person tent has room for two people plus gear. That's it. Don't buy a tent expecting it to hold more than it is intended to.

**How Much Does It Weigh?**

If you're a hiker, this becomes the preeminent question. If it's much more than six or seven pounds, forget it. A 12-pound tent is bad enough, but get it wet and it's like carrying a piano on your back. On the other hand, weight is scarcely a factor if you camp only where you can take your car. My dad, for instance, used to have this giant canvas umbrella tent that folded down to a neat little pack that weighed about 500 pounds.

**FAMILY TENTS** It is always worth spending the time and money to purchase a tent you and your family will be happy with.

Though many good family tents are available for $125-175, particularly from Coleman, Cabela's, and Remington, here is a synopsis of two of the best tents available anywhere, without regard to cost, generally ranging from $350-600:

**Sierra Designs Mondo 5CD**
tel. (800) 736-8551
10.14 pounds
82 square feet / 20-square-foot vestibule / Inside peak height: five feet, five inches
If you've got a family that likes to head for distant camps, then this is your tent. It's light enough to pack along, yet big enough to accommodate a family of four. Using speed clips, this tent is by far the easiest and quickest to set up of any family tent I've used. A generous rain fly and covered entry area (new adjustment features allow various awning configurations) mean more than adequate protection from the elements, no matter how hard they are pelting down.

**Kelty Domolite 6**
tel. (800) 423-2320
16.4 pounds
81.5 square feet / Inside peak height: five feet, seven inches
Using three 18-foot-long fiberglass poles, the Domolite boasts a sleek, low profile that slips the wind very nicely. Each pole slides easily through continuous pole sleeves, thanks to rubber-tipped ends, making set-up a snap. Kelty has an optional covered entry area, since without it, the tent is barely adequate shelter should you have to weather a deluge in cramped quarters. Floor seams are taped for added waterproofness. A great package.

**BIVOUAC BAGS** If you like going solo and choose not to own a tent at all, a bivy bag, short for bivouac bag, can provide the weather protection you require. A bivy bag is a water-repellent shell in which your sleeping bag fits. It is light and tough, and for some is the perfect alternative to a heavy tent. My own bivy weighs 31 ounces and cost me $240, made by OR (Outdoor Research), and I just plain love the thing on expeditions. On the downside, however, it can be a bit difficult getting settled just right in it, and some say they feel claustrophobic at the close quarters. My biggest fear was the idea of riding out a storm. You can hear the rain hitting you, and sometimes even feel the pounding of the drops through the bivy bag. For some, it can be unsettling to try and sleep under such circumstances. On the other hand, I've always looked forward to it. In cold weather, it also helps to keep you warm.

**PICKUP TRUCK CAMPERS** If you own a pickup truck with a camper shell, you can turn it into a self-contained campground with a little work. This can be an ideal way to go: it's fast, portable, and you are guaranteed a dry environment.

But that does not necessarily mean it is a warm environment. In fact, without insulation from the metal truck bed, it can be like trying to sleep on an iceberg. That is because the metal truck bed will get as cold as the air temperature, which is often much colder than the ground temperature. Without insulation, it can be much colder in your camper shell than it would be on the open ground.

When I camp in my rig, I use a large piece of foam for a mattress and insulation. The foam measures four inches thick, 48 inches wide, and 76 inches long. It makes for a bed as comfortable as anything one might ask for. In fact, during the winter, if I don't go camping for a few weeks because of writing obligations, I sometimes will throw the foam on the floor, lie down the old sleeping bag, light a fire, and camp right in my living room. It's in my blood, I tell you. Air beds and cots are also extremely comfortable and I've used both many times. Whatever you choose, just make sure you have a comfortable sleeping unit. Good sleep makes for great camping trips.

**RVs** The problems RVers encounter come from two primary sources: lack of privacy and light intrusion.

The lack of privacy stems from the natural restrictions of where a land yacht can go. Without careful use of the guide portion of this book, motor home owners can find themselves in parking lot settings, jammed in with plenty of neighbors. Because RVs often have large picture windows, you lose your privacy, causing some late nights; then, come daybreak, light intrusion forces an early wake up. The result is you get shorted on your sleep.

The answer is to carry inserts to fit over the inside of your windows. This closes off the outside and retains your privacy. And if you don't want to wake up with the sun at daybreak, you don't have to. It will still be dark.

## First Aid and Insect Protection

The mountain night could not have been more perfect, I thought as I lay in my sleeping bag.

The sky looked like a mass of jewels and the air tasted sweet and smelled of pines. A shooting star fireballed across the sky, and I remember thinking, "It just doesn't get any better."

Just then, as I was drifting into sleep, a mysterious buzz appeared from nowhere and deposited itself inside my left ear. Suddenly awake, I whacked my ear with the palm of my hand, hard enough to cause a minor concussion. The buzz disappeared. I pulled out my flashlight and shined it on my palm, and there, lit in the blackness of night, lay the squished intruder: a mosquito, dead amid a stain of blood.

Satisfied, I turned off the light, closed my eyes, and thought of the fishing trip planned for the next day. Then I heard them. It was a squadron of mosquitoes flying landing patterns around my head. I tried to grab them with an open hand, but they dodged the assault and flew off. Just 30 seconds later another landed in my left ear. I promptly dispatched the invader with a rip of the palm.

Now I was completely awake, so I got out of my sleeping bag to retrieve some mosquito repellent. But en route, several of the buggers swarmed and nailed me in the back and arms. After I applied the repellent and settled snugly again in my sleeping bag, the mosquitoes would buzz a few inches from my ear. After getting a whiff of the poison, they would fly off. It was like sleeping in a sawmill.

The next day, drowsy from little sleep, I set out to fish. I'd walked but 15 minutes when I brushed against a bush and felt this stinging sensation on the inside of my arm, just above the wrist. I looked down: A tick had his clamps in me. I ripped it out before he could embed his head into my skin.

After catching a few fish, I sat down against a tree to eat lunch and just watch the water go by. My dog, Rebel, sat down next to me and stared at the beef jerky I was munching as if it were a T-bone steak. I finished eating, gave him a small piece, patted him on the head, and said, "Good dog." Right then, I noticed an itch on my arm where a mosquito had drilled me. I unconsciously scratched it. Two days later, in that exact spot, some nasty red splotches started popping up. Poison oak. By petting my dog and then scratching my arm, I had transferred the oil residue of the poison oak leaves from Rebel's fur to my arm.

When I returned home, Foonsky asked me about the trip.

"Great," I said. "Mosquitoes, ticks, poison oak. Can hardly wait to go back."

"Sorry I missed out," he answered.

## MOSQUITOES, NO-SEE-UMS, GNATS, AND HORSEFLIES

On a trip to Canada, Foonsky and I were fishing a small lake from the shore when suddenly a black horde of mosquitoes could be seen moving across the lake toward us. It was like when the French army looked across the Rhine and saw the Wehrmacht coming. There was a buzz in the air. We fought them off for a few minutes, then made a fast retreat to the truck and jumped in, content the buggers had been fooled. But somehow still unknown to us, the mosquitoes gained entry to the truck. In 10 minutes, we squished 15 of them as they attempted to plant their oil derricks into our skin. Just outside the truck, the black horde waited for us to make a tactical error like rolling down a window. It finally took a miraculous hailstorm to foil the attack.

When it comes to mosquitoes, no-see-ums, gnats, and horseflies, there are times when there is nothing you can do. However, in most situations you can muster a defense to repel the attack.

The first key with mosquitoes is to wear clothing too heavy for them to drill through. Expose a minimum of skin, wear a hat, and tie a bandanna around your neck, preferably one that has been sprayed with repellent. If you try to get by with just a cotton T-shirt, you will be declared a federal mosquito sanctuary.

So first your skin must be well covered, exposing only your hands and face. Second, you should have your companion spray your clothes with repellent. Third, you should dab liquid repellent directly on your skin.

At night, the easiest way to get a good sleep without mosquitoes buzzing in your ear is to sleep in a bug-proof tent. If the nights are warm and you want to see the stars, new tent models are available that have a skylight covered with mosquito netting. If you don't like tents on summer evenings, mosquito netting rigged with an air space at your head can solve the problem. Otherwise prepare to get bitten, even with the use of mosquito repellent.

If your problems are with no-see-ums or biting horseflies, then you need a slightly different approach.

No-see-ums are tiny black insects that look like nothing more than a sliver of dirt on your skin. Then you notice something stinging, and when you rub the area, you scratch up a little no-see-um. The results are similar to mosquito bites, making your skin itch, splotch, and when you get them bad, swell. In addition to using the techniques described to repel mosquitoes, you should go one step further.

The problem is that no-see-ums are tricky little devils. Somehow they can actually get under your socks and around your ankles where they will bite to their hearts' content all night long while you sleep, itch, sleep, and itch some more. The best solution is to apply a liquid repellent to your ankles, then wear clean socks.

Horseflies are another story. They are rarely a problem, but when they get their dander up, they can cause trouble you'll never forget.

One such episode occurred when Foonsky and I were paddling a canoe along the shoreline of a large lake. This giant horsefly, about the size of a fingertip, started dive-bombing the canoe. After 20 minutes, it landed on Foonsky's thigh. He immediately slammed it with an open hand, then let out a blood-curdling "Yeeeee-ow!" that practically sent ripples across the lake. When Foonsky whacked it, the horsefly had somehow turned around and bit him in the hand, leaving a huge red welt.

In the next 10 minutes, that big fly strafed the canoe on more dive-bomb runs. I finally got my canoe paddle, swung it as if it were a baseball bat, and nailed that horsefly as if I'd hit a home run. It landed about 15 feet from the boat, still alive and buzzing in the water. While I was trying to figure what it would take to kill this bugger, a large rainbow trout surfaced and snatched it out of the water, finally avenging the assault.

If you have horsefly or yellow jacket problems, you'd best just leave the area. One, two, or a few can be dealt with. More than that and your fun camping trip will be about as fun as being roped to a tree and stung by an electric shock rod.

On most trips, you will spend time doing everything possible to keep from getting bitten by mosquitoes or no-see-ums. When that fails, you must know what to do next, and fast, if you are among those ill-fated campers who get big red lumps from a bite inflicted from even a microscopic mosquito.

A fluid called After Bite or a dab of ammonia should be applied immediately to the bite. To start the healing process, apply a first-aid gel (not a liquid), such as the one made by Campho-Phenique.

**Mosquito Repellent:** Taking vitamin B1 and eating garlic are reputed to act as natural insect repellents, but I've met a lot of mosquitoes that are not convinced. A better bet is to examine the label of the repellent in question for non-diethyl-metatoluamide, commonly known as DEET. That is the poison, and the percentage of it in the container must be listed and will indicate that brand's effectiveness. Inert ingredients are mainly fluids used to fill the bottles.

## DEET VERSUS "NATURAL" REPELLENTS

What is DEET? You're not likely to find the word DEET on any repellent label. That's because DEET stands for N,N diethyl-m-tolu-amide. If the label contains this scientific name, the repellent contains DEET. Despite fears of DEET-associated health risks and the increased attention given natural alternatives, DEET-based repellents are still acknowledged as by far the best option when serious insect protection is required.

What are the health risks associated with using DEET? A number of deaths and a number of medical problems have been attributed in the press to DEET in recent years—events that those in the DEET community vehemently deny as being specifically DEET related, pointing to reams of scientific documentation as evidence. It does seem logical to assume that if DEET can peel paint, melt nylon, destroy plastic, wreck wood finishes, and damage fishing line, then it must be hell on the skin—perhaps worse.

On one trip, I had a small bottle of mosquito repellent in the same pocket as a Swiss army knife. Guess what happened? The mosquito repellent leaked a bit and literally melted the insignia right off the knife. DEET will also melt synthetic clothes. That is why in bad mosquito country, I'll expose a minimum of skin, just hands and face (with full beard), and apply the repellent only to the back of my hands and my cheeks, perhaps wear a bandanna sprinkled with a few drops as well. That does the trick, with a minimum of exposure to the repellent.

Although nothing definitive has been published, there is a belief among a growing number in the scientific community that repeated applications of products containing low percentages of DEET can be potentially dangerous. It is theorized that this actually puts consumers at a greater risk for absorbing high levels of DEET into the body than if they had just used one application of a 30 to 50% DEET product with an efficacy of four to six hours. Also being studied is the possibility that low levels of DEET, which might not otherwise be of toxicological concern, may become hazardous if they are formulated with solvents or dilutents (considered inert ingredients) that may enhance the absorption rate.

Are natural alternatives a safer choice? To imply that essential oils are completely safe because they are a natural product is not altogether accurate. Essential oils, while derived from plants that grow naturally, are chemicals too. Some are potentially hazardous if ingested, and most are downright painful if they find their way into the eyes or onto mucus membranes. For example, pennyroyal is perhaps the most toxic of the essential oils used to repel insects and can be deadly if taken internally. Other oils used include citronella (perhaps the most common, it's extracted from an aromatic grass indigenous to Southern Asia), eucalyptus, cedarwood, and peppermint.

Three citronella-based products, Buzz Away (manufactured by Quantum), Avon's Skin-So-Soft, and Natrapel (manufactured by Tender), have received EPA registration and approval for sale as repellents for use in controlling mosquitoes, flies, gnats, and midges.

How effective are natural repellents? While there are numerous studies cited by those on the DEET and citronella sides of the fence, the average effective repelling time of a citronella product appears to range from 1.5 to two hours. Tests conducted at Cambridge University, England, comparing Natrapel to DEET-based Skintastic (a low-percentage DEET product) found citronella to be just as effective in repelling mosquitoes. The key here is effectiveness and the amount of time until reapplication.

Citronella products work for up to two hours and then require reapplication (the same holds true for other natural formulations). Products using a low-percentage level of DEET also require reapplication every two hours to remain effective. So if you're going outside for only a short period in an environment where insect bites are more an irritant than a hazard, you would do just as well to go natural.

What other chemical alternatives are there? Another line of defense against insects is the chemical permethrin, used on clothing, not on skin. Permethrin-based products are designed to repel and kill arthropods or crawling insects, making them a preferred repellent for ticks. The currently available products will remain effective, repelling and killing mosquitoes, ticks, and chiggers, for two weeks and through two launderings.

## TICKS

Ticks are nasty little vermin that will wait in ambush, jump on unsuspecting prey, and then crawl to a prime location before filling their bodies with their victim's blood.

I call them Dracula bugs, but by any name they can be a terrible camp pest. Ticks rest on grass and low plants and attach themselves to those who brush against the vegetation (dogs are particularly vulnerable). Typically they are no more than 18 inches above ground, and if you stay on the trails, you can usually avoid them.

There are two common species of ticks. The common coastal tick is larger, brownish in color, and prefers to crawl around prior to putting its clamps on you. The latter habit can be creepy, but when you feel it crawling, you can just pick it off and dispatch it. The coastal tick's preferred destination is usually the back of your neck, just where the hairline starts. The other species, the wood tick, is small and black, and when he puts his clamps in, it's immediately painful. When a wood tick gets into a dog for a few days, it can cause a large red welt. In either case, ticks should be removed as soon as possible.

If you have hiked in areas infested with ticks, it is advisable to shower as soon as possible, washing your clothes immediately. If you just leave your clothes in a heap, a tick can crawl out and invade your home. They like warmth, and one way or another, they can end up in your bed. Waking up in the middle of the night with a tick crawling across your chest can really give you the creeps.

Once a tick has its clampers on you, you must decide how long it has been there. If it has been a short time, the most painless and effective method for removal is to take a pair of sharp tweezers and grasp the little devil, making certain to isolate the mouth area, then pull him out. Reader Johvin Perry sent in the suggestion to coat the tick with Vaseline, which will cut off its oxygen supply, after which it may voluntarily give up the hunt.

If the tick has been in longer, you may wish to have a doctor extract it. Some people will burn a tick with a cigarette, or poison it with lighter fluid, but this is not advisable. No matter how you do it, you must take care to remove all of it, especially its clawlike mouth.

The wound, however small, should then be cleansed and dressed. This is done by applying liquid peroxide, which cleans and sterilizes, and then applying a dressing coated with a first-aid gel such as First-Aid Cream, Campho-Phenique, or Neosporin.

Lyme disease, which can be transmitted by the bite of the deer tick, is rare but common enough to warrant some attention. To prevent tick bites, some people tuck their pant legs into their hiking socks and spray tick repellent, called Permamone, on their pants.

The first symptom of Lyme disease is that the bite area will develop a bright red, splotchy rash. Other possible early symptoms include headache, nausea, fever, and/or a stiff neck. If this happens, or if you have any doubts, you should see your doctor immediately. If you do get Lyme disease, don't panic. Doctors say it is easily treated in the early stages with simple antibiotics. If you are nervous about getting Lyme disease, carry a small plastic bag with you when you hike. If a tick manages to get his clampers into you, put it in the plastic bag after you pull it out. Then give it to your doctor for analysis to see if the tick is a carrier of the disease.

During the course of my hiking and camping career, I have removed ticks from my skin hundreds of times without any problems. However, if you are worried about ticks, you can purchase a tick removal kit from any outdoors store. These kits allow you to remove ticks in such a way that their toxins are guaranteed not to enter your bloodstream.

If you are particularly wary of ticks or perhaps even have nightmares of them, wear long pants that are tucked into the socks, as well as a long-sleeved shirt tucked securely into the pants and held with a belt. Clothing should be light in color, making it easier to see ticks, and tightly woven so ticks have trouble hanging on. On one hike with my mom, Eleanor, I brushed more than 100 ticks off my blue jeans in less than an hour, while she did not pick up a single one on her polyester pants.

Perform tick checks regularly, especially on the back of the neck. The combination of DEET insect repellents applied to the skin and permethrin repellents applied directly to clothing is considered to be the most effective line of defense against ticks.

POISON OAK   After a nice afternoon hike, about a five-miler, I was concerned about possible exposure to poison oak, so I immediately showered and put on clean clothes. Then I settled into a chair with my favorite foamy elixir to watch the end of a baseball game. The game went 18 innings; meanwhile, my dog, tired from the hike, went to sleep on my bare ankles.

## Keep It Wild Tip 4: Sanitation

If no refuse facility is available:

1. Deposit human waste in "cat holes" dug six to eight inches deep. Cover and disguise the cat hole when finished.

2. Deposit human waste at least 75 paces (200 feet) from any water source or camp.

3. Use toilet paper sparingly. When finished, carefully burn it in the cat hole, then bury it.

4. If no appropriate burial locations are available, such as in popular wilderness camps above tree line in granite settings, then all human refuse should be double-bagged and packed out.

5. At boat-in campsites, chemical toilets are required. Chemical toilets can also solve the problem of larger groups camping for long stays at one location where no facilities are available.

6. To wash dishes or your body, carry water away from the source and use small amounts of biodegradable soap. Scatter dishwater after all food particles have been removed.

7. Scour your campsites for even the tiniest piece of trash and any other evidence of your stay. Pack out all the trash you can, even if it's not yours. Finding cigarette butts, for instance, provides special irritation for most campers. Pick them up and discard them properly.

8. Never litter. Never. Or you become the enemy of all others.

A few days later I had a case of poison oak. My feet looked as though they had been on fire and put out with an ice pick. The lesson? Don't always trust your dog, give him a bath as well, and beware of extra-inning ball games.

You can get poison oak only from direct contact with the oil residue from the leaves. It can be passed in a variety of ways, as direct as skin-to-leaf contact or as indirect as leaf to dog, dog to sofa, sofa to skin. Once you have it, there is little you can do but itch yourself to death. Applying Caladryl lotion or its equivalent can help because it contains antihistamines, which attack and dry the itch.

A tip that may sound crazy but seems to work is advised by my pal Furniss. You should expose the afflicted area to the hottest water you can stand, then suddenly immerse it in cold water. The hot water opens the skin pores and gets the "itch" out, and the cold water then quickly seals the pores.

In any case, you're a lot better off if you don't get poison oak to begin with. Remember that poison oak can disguise itself. In the spring, it is green; then it gradually turns reddish in the summer. By fall, it becomes a bloody, ugly-looking red. In the winter, it loses its leaves altogether and appears to be nothing more than barren, brown sticks of a small plant. However, at any time and in any form, its contact with skin can quickly lead to infection.

Some people are more easily afflicted than others, but if you are one of the lucky few who aren't, don't cheer too loudly. While some people can be exposed to the oil residue of poison oak with little or no effect, the body's resistance can gradually be worn down with repeated exposure. At one time I could practically play in the stuff and the only symptom would be a few little bumps on the inside of my wrist. Now, over 15 years later, my resistance has broken down. If I merely rub against poison oak now, in a few days the exposed area can look as if it were used for a track meet.

So regardless of whether you consider yourself vulnerable or not, you should take heed to reduce your exposure. That can be done by staying on trails when you hike and making sure your dog does the same. Remember, the worst stands of poison oak are usually brush-infested areas just off the trail. Protect yourself also by dressing so your skin is completely covered, wearing long-sleeved shirts, long pants, and boots. If you suspect you've been exposed, immediately wash your clothes and then wash yourself with aloe vera, rinsing with a cool shower.

*Avoiding Poison Oak Remember the old Boy Scout saying: "Leaves of three, let them be."*

And don't forget to give your dog a bath as well.

**SUNBURN**  The most common injury suffered on camping trips is sunburn, yet some people wear it as a badge of honor, believing that it somehow enhances their virility. Well, it doesn't. Neither do suntans. And too much sun can lead to serious burns or sunstroke.

It is easy enough to avoid. Use a high-level sunscreen on your skin, apply lip balm with sunscreen, and wear sunglasses and a hat. If any area gets burned, apply first-aid cream, which will soothe and provide moisture for your parched, burned skin.

The best advice is not to get even a suntan. Those who do are involved in a practice that can be eventually ruinous to their skin and possibly lead to cancer.

**A WORD ABOUT GIARDIA AND CRYPTO-SPORIDIUM**  You have just hiked in to your backwoods spot, you're thirsty and a bit tired, but you smile as you consider the prospects. Everything seems perfect—there's not a stranger in sight, and you have nothing to do but relax with your pals.

You toss down your gear, grab your cup, dip it into the stream, and take a long drink of that ice-cold mountain water. It seems crystal pure and sweeter than anything you've ever tasted. It's not till later that you find out it can be just like drinking a cup of poison.

Whether you camp in the wilderness or not, if you hike, you're going to get thirsty. And if your canteen runs dry, you'll start eyeing any water source. Stop! Do not pass Go. Do not drink.

By drinking what appears to be pure mountain water without first treating it, you can ingest a microscopic protozoan called *Giardia lamblia*. The pain of the ensuing abdominal cramps can make you feel that your stomach and intestinal tract are in a knot, ready to explode. With that comes long-term diarrhea that is worse than even a bear could imagine.

Doctors call the disease *giardiasis*, or giardia for short, but it is difficult to diagnose. One friend of mine who contracted giardia was told he might have stomach cancer before the proper diagnosis was made.

Drinking directly from a stream or lake does not mean you will get giardia, but you are taking a giant chance. There is no reason to assume such a risk, potentially ruining your trip and enduring weeks of misery.

A lot of people are taking that risk. I made a personal survey of campers in the Yosemite National Park wilderness, and found that roughly only one in 20 were equipped with some kind of water-purification system. The result, according to the Public Health Service, is that an average of 4% of all backpackers and campers suffer giardiasis. According to the Parasitic Diseases Division of the Center for Infectious Diseases, the rates range from 1% to 20% across the country.

But if you get giardia, you are not going to care about the statistics. "When I got giardia, I just about wanted to die," said Henry McCarthy, a California camper. "For about 10 days, it was the most terrible thing I have ever experienced. And through the whole thing, I kept thinking, 'I shouldn't have drunk that water, but it seemed all right at the time.'"

That is the mistake most campers make. The stream might be running free, gurgling over boulders in the high country, tumbling into deep, oxygenated pools. It looks pure. Then in a few days, the problems suddenly start. Drinking untreated water from mountain streams is a lot like playing Russian roulette. Sooner or later the gun goes off.

**Treating Your Water Means Avoiding Diarrhea:** The only sure way to beat giardia and other water-borne diseases is to filter or boil your water before drinking, eating, or brushing your teeth. And the best way to prevent the spread of giardia is to bury your waste products at least eight inches deep and 200 feet away from natural waters.

### Filters

There's really no excuse for going without a water filter: Handheld filters are getting more compact, lighter, easier to use, and often less expensive. Having to boil water or endure chemicals that leave a bad taste in the mouth has been all but eliminated.

With a filter, you just pump and drink. Filtering strains out microscopic contaminants, rendering the water clear and somewhat pure. How pure? That depends on the size of the filter's pores—what manufacturers call pore-size efficiency. A filter with a pore-size efficiency of one micron or smaller will remove protozoa like *Giardia lamblia,* and cryptosporidium, as well as parasitic eggs and larva, but it takes a

*Water filters are a wise investment since all wilderness water should be considered contaminated. Make sure the filter can be easily cleaned or has a replaceable cartridge. The filter pores must be .04 microns or less to remove bacteria.*

pore-size efficiency of less than 0.4 microns to remove bacteria. All but one of the filters recommended here do that.

A good backcountry water filter weighs less than 20 ounces, is easy to grasp, simple to use, and a snap to clean and maintain. At the very least, buy one that will remove protozoa and bacteria. (A number of cheap, pocket-size filters remove only *Giardia lamblia,* and cryptosporidium. That, in my book, is risking your health to save money.) Consider the flow rate, too: A liter per minute is good.

All filters will eventually clog—it's a sign that they've been doing their job. If you force water through a filter that's becoming difficult to pump, you risk injecting a load of microbial nasties into your bottle. Some models can be backwashed, brushed, or, as with ceramic elements, scrubbed to extend their useful lives. And if the filter has a prefilter to screen out the big stuff, use it: It will give your filter a boost in mileage, which can then top out at about 100 gallons per disposable element. Any of the filters reviewed here will serve well on an outing into the wilds, providing you always play by the manufacturer's rules. They cost from a low of about $35-75 and over $200, depending on the volume of water they are constructed to filter.

### First Need Deluxe:

The 15-ounce First Need Deluxe from General Ecology does something no other handheld filter will do: It removes protozoa, bacteria, and viruses without using chemicals. Such effectiveness is the result of a fancy three-stage matrix system. Unfortunately, if you drop the filter and unknowingly crack the cartridge, all the little nasties can get through. General Ecology's solution is to include a bottle of blue dye that indicates breaks. The issue hasn't scared off too many folks, though: the First Need has been around since 1982. Additional cartridges cost $30. A final note: The filter pumps smoothly and puts out more than a liter per minute. A favorite of mine.

### PentaPure Oasis:

The PentaPure Oasis Water Purification System from WTC/Ecomaster offers drinkable water with a twist: You squeeze and sip instead of pumping. Weighing 6.5 ounces, the system packages a three-stage filter inside a 21-ounce-capacity sport bottle with an angled and sealing drinking nozzle, ideal for mountain bikers. The filter removes and/or kills protozoa, bacteria, and viruses, so it's also suitable for world travel. It's certainly convenient: just fill the bottle with untreated water, screw on the cap, give it a firm squeeze (don't expect the easy flow of a normal sport bottle; there's more work being done), and sip. The Oasis only runs into trouble if the water source is shallow; you'll need a cup for scooping.

## Basic Designs Ceramic:

The Basic Designs Ceramic Filter Pump weighs eight ounces and is as stripped-down a filter as you'll find. The pump is simple, easy to use, and quite reliable. The ceramic filter effectively removes protozoa and bacteria, making it ideal and cost effective for backpacking—but it won't protect against viruses. Also, the filter element is too bulbous to work directly from a shallow water source; like the PentaPure, you'll have to decontaminate a pot, cup, or bottle to transfer your unfiltered water. It's a great buy, though, for anyone worried only about Giardia lamblia, and cryptosporidium.

## SweetWater WalkAbout:

The WalkAbout is perfect for the day hiker or backpacker who obsesses on lightening the load. The filter weighs just 8.5 ounces, is easily cleaned in the field, and removes both protozoa and bacteria: a genuine bargain. There are some trade-offs, however, for its diminutiveness. Water delivery is a tad slow at just under a liter per minute, but redesigned filter cartridges ($12.50) are now good for up to 100 gallons.

## MSR MiniWorks:

Like the WalkAbout, the bargain-priced MiniWorks has a bigger and more expensive water-filtering brother. But in this case the differences are harder to discern: The new 14.3-ounce MiniWorks looks similar to the $140 WaterWorks II, and like the WaterWorks is fully field-maintainable, while guarding against protozoa, bacteria, and chemicals. But the Mini is the best-executed, easiest-to-use ceramic filter on the market, and it attaches directly to a standard one-quart Nalgene water bottle. Too bad it takes 90 seconds to filter that quart.

## PUR Explorer:

The Explorer offers protection from all the bad guys—viruses as well as protozoa and bacteria—by incorporating an iodine matrix into the filtration process. An optional carbon cartridge ($20) neutralizes the iodine's noxious taste. The Explorer is also considered a trusty veteran among water filters because of its smooth pumping action and nifty back-washing feature: With a quick twist, the device switches from filtering mode to self-cleaning mode. It may be on the heavy side (20 ounces) and somewhat pricey, but the Explorer works very well on iffy water anywhere.

## Katadyn U.S.A. Mini Filter:

The Mini Filter is a much more compact version of Katadyn's venerable Pocket Filter. This one weighs just eight ounces, ideal for the minimalist backcountry traveler, and it effectively removes protozoa and bacteria. A palm-of-the-hand-size filter, however, makes it challenging to put any kind of power behind the pump's tiny handle, and the filtered water comes through at a paltry half-liter per minute. It also requires more cleaning than most filters—though the good news is that the element is made of long-lasting ceramic. Ironically, one option lets you purchase the Mini Filter with a carbon element instead of the ceramic. The pumping is easier, the flow rate is better, and the price is way down ($99), but I'd only go that route if you'll be pumping from clear mountain streams.

## MSR WaterWorks II Ceramic:

At 17.4 ounces the WaterWorks II isn't light, but for the same price as the Katadyn you get a better flow rate (90 seconds per liter), an easy pumping action, and—like the original Mini Filter—a long-lasting ceramic cartridge. This filter is a good match for the person who encounters a lot of dirty water—its three-stage filter weeds out protozoa, bacteria, and chemicals—and is mechanically inclined: The MSR can be completely disassembled afield for troubleshooting and cleaning. (If you're not so endowed, take the filter apart at home only, as the potential for confusion is somewhat high.) By the way, the company has corrected the clogging problem that plagued a previous version of the WaterWorks.

The big drawback with filters is that if you pump water from a mucky lake, the filter can clog in a few days. Therein lies the weakness. Once plugged up, it is useless, and you have to replace it or take your chances.

One trick to extend the filter life is to fill your cook pot with water, let the sediment settle, then pump from there. As an insurance policy, always have a spare filter canister on hand.

### Boiling water

Except for water filtration, this is the only treatment that you can use with complete confidence. According to the federal Parasitic Diseases Division, it takes a few minutes at a rolling boil to be certain you've killed *Giardia lamblia*. At high elevations, boil for three to five minutes. A side benefit is that you'll also kill other dangerous bacteria that live undetected in natural waters.

But to be honest, boiling water is a thorn for most people on backcountry trips. For one thing, if you boil water on an open fire, what should taste like crystal-pure mountain water tastes instead like a mouthful of warm ashes. If you don't have a campfire, it wastes stove fuel. And if you are thirsty *now*, forget it. The water takes hours to cool.

The only time boiling always makes sense, however, is when you are preparing dinner. The ash taste will disappear in whatever freeze-dried dinner, soup, or hot drink you make.

## Water-Purification Pills

Pills are the preference for most backcountry campers, and this can get them in trouble. At just $3-8 per bottle, which can figure up to just a few cents per canteen, they do come cheap. In addition, they kill most of the bacteria, regardless of whether you use iodine crystals or potable aqua iodine tablets.

The problem is they just don't always kill *Giardia lamblia,* and that is the one critter worth worrying about on your trip. That makes water-treatment pills unreliable and dangerous.

Another key element is the time factor. Depending on the water's temperature, organic content, and pH level, these pills can take a long time to do the job. A minimum wait of 20 minutes is advised. Most people don't like waiting that long, especially when they're hot and thirsty after a hike and thinking, "What the heck, the water looks fine."

And then there is the taste. On one trip, my water filter clogged and we had to use the iodine pills instead. It doesn't take long to get tired of the iodine-tinged taste of the water. Mountain water should be one of the greatest tasting beverages of the world, but the iodine kills that.

## No Treatment

This is your last resort and, using extreme care, can be executed with success. One of my best hiking buddies, Michael Furniss, is a nationally renowned hydrologist, and on wilderness trips he has showed me the difference between safe and dangerous water sources.

Long ago, people believed that just finding water running over a rock was a guarantee of its purity. Imagine that. What we've learned is that the safe water sources are almost always small springs located in high, craggy mountain areas. The key is making sure no one has been upstream from where you drink.

Furniss mentioned that another potential problem in bypassing water treatment is that even in settings free of *Giardia lamblia,* you can still ingest other bacteria that cause stomach problems.

No matter how well planned your trip might be, a sudden change in weather can turn it into a puzzle for which there are few answers. **HYPOTHERMIA**
Bad weather or an accident can set in motion a dangerous chain of events.

Such a chain of episodes occurred for my brother Rambob and me on a fishing trip one fall day just below the snow line. The weather had suddenly turned very cold, and ice was forming along the shore of the lake. Suddenly, the canoe became terribly imbalanced, and just that quick it flipped. The little life vest seat cushions were useless, and using the canoe as a paddleboard, we tried to kick our way back to shore where my dad was going crazy at the thought of his two sons drowning before his eyes.

It took 17 minutes in that 38-degree water, but we finally made it to shore. When they pulled me out of the water, my legs were dead, not strong enough even to hold up my weight. In fact, I didn't feel so much cold as tired, and I just wanted to lie down and go to sleep.

I closed my eyes, and my brother-in-law, Lloyd Angal, slapped me in the face several times, then got me on my feet and pushed and pulled me about.

In the celebration over our making it to shore, only Lloyd had realized that hypothermia was setting in. Hypothermia is the condition in which the temperature of the body is lowered to the point that it causes poor reasoning, apathy, and collapse. It can look like the afflicted person is just tired and needs to sleep, but that sleep can be the first step toward a coma.

Ultimately my brother and I shared what little dry clothing remained. Then we began hiking around to get muscle movement, creating internal warmth. We ate whatever munchies were available because the body produces heat by digestion. But most important, we got our heads as dry as possible. More body heat is lost through wet hair than any other single factor.

A few hours later, we were in a pizza parlor replaying the incident, talking about how only a life vest can do the job of a life vest. We decided never again to rely on those little flotation seat cushions that disappear when the boat flips.

Almost by instinct we had done everything right to prevent hypothermia: Don't go to sleep, start a physical activity, induce shivering, put dry clothes on, dry your head, and eat something. That's how you fight hypothermia. In a dangerous situation, whether you fall in a lake or a stream or get caught unprepared in a storm, that's how you can stay alive.

After being in that ice-bordered lake for almost 20 minutes and then finally pulling ourselves to the shoreline, we discovered a strange thing. My canoe was flipped right-side up and almost all of its contents were lost: tackle box, flotation cushions, and cooler. But remaining was one paddle and one fishing rod, the trout rod my grandfather had given me for my 12th birthday.

Lloyd gave me a smile. "This means that you are meant to paddle and fish again," he said with a laugh.

**GETTING UNLOST** You could not have been more lost. But there I was, a guy who is supposed to know about these things, transfixed by confusion, snow, and hoofprints from a big deer.

I discovered it is actually quite easy to get lost. If you don't get your bearings, getting found is the difficult part. This occurred on a wilderness trip where I'd hiked in to a remote lake and then set up a base camp for a deer hunt.

"There are some giant bucks up on that rim," confided Mr. Furnai, who lives near the area. "But it takes a mountain man to even get close to them."

That was a challenge I answered. After four-wheeling it to the trailhead, I tromped off with pack and rifle, gut-thumped it up 100 switchbacks over the rim, then followed a creek drainage up to a small but beautiful lake. The area was stark and nearly treeless, with bald granite broken only by large boulders. To keep from getting lost, I marked my route with piles of small rocks to act as directional signs for the return trip.

But at daybreak the next day, I stuck my head out of my tent and found eight inches of snow on the ground. I looked up into a gray sky filled by huge, cascading snowflakes. Visibility was about 50 yards, with fog on the mountain rim. "I better get out of here and get back to my truck," I said to myself. "If my truck gets buried at the trailhead, I'll never get out."

After packing quickly, I started down the mountain. But after 20 minutes, I began to get disoriented. You see, all the little piles of rocks I'd stacked to mark the way were now buried in snow, and I had only a smooth white blanket of snow to guide me. Everything looked the same, and it was snowing even harder now.

Five minutes later I started chewing on some jerky to keep warm, then suddenly stopped. Where was I? Where was the creek drainage? Isn't this where I was supposed to cross over a creek and start the switchbacks down the mountain?

Right then I looked down and saw the tracks of a huge deer, the kind Mr. Furnai had talked about. What a predicament: I was lost and snowed in and seeing big hoofprints in the snow. Part of me wanted to abandon all safety and go after that deer, but a little voice in the back of my head won out. "Treat this as an emergency," it said.

The first step in any predicament is to secure your present situation, that is, to make sure it does not get any worse. I unloaded my rifle (too easy to slip, fall, and have a misfire), took stock of my food (three days' worth), camp fuel (plenty), and clothes (rain gear keeping me dry). Then I wondered, "Where the hell am I?"

I took out my map, compass, and altimeter, then opened the map and laid it on the snow. It immediately began collecting snowflakes. I set the compass atop the map and oriented it to north. Because of the fog, there was no way to spot landmarks, such as prominent mountain-tops, to verify my position. Then I checked the altimeter, which read 4,900 feet. Well, the elevation at my lake was 5,320 feet. That was critical information.

I scanned the elevation lines on the map and was able to trace the approximate area of my position, somewhere downstream from the lake, yet close to a 4,900-foot elevation. "Right here," I said, pointing to a spot on the map with a finger. "I should pick up the switchback trail down the mountain somewhere off to the left, maybe just 40 or 50 yards away."

Slowly and deliberately, I pushed through the light, powdered snow. In five minutes, I suddenly stopped. To the left, across a 10-foot depression in the snow, appeared a flat spot that veered off to the right. "That's it! That's the crossing."

In minutes, I was working down the switchbacks, on my way, no longer lost. I thought of the hoofprints I had seen, and now that I knew my position, I wanted to head back and spend the day hunting. Then I looked up at the sky, saw it filled with falling snowflakes, and envisioned my truck buried deep in snow. Alas, this time logic won out over dreams.

In a few hours, now trudging through more than a foot of snow, I was at my truck at a spot called Doe Flat, and next to it was a giant, all-terrain U.S. Forest Service vehicle and two rangers.

"Need any help?" I asked them.

They just laughed. "We're here to help you," one answered. "It's a good thing you filed a trip plan with our district office in Gasquet. We wouldn't have known you were out here."

"Winter has arrived," said the other. "If we don't get your truck out now, it will be stuck here until next spring. If we hadn't found you, you might have been here until the end of time."

They connected a chain from the rear axle of their giant rig to the front axle of my truck and started towing me out, back to civilization. On the way to pavement, I figured I had gotten some of the more important lessons of my life. Always file a trip plan and have plenty of food, fuel, and a camp stove you can rely on. Make sure your clothes, weather gear, sleeping bag, and tent will keep you dry and warm. Always carry a compass, altimeter, and map with elevation lines, and know how to use them, practicing in good weather to get the feel of it.

And if you get lost and see the hoofprints of a giant deer, well, there are times when it is best to pass them by.

*To keep from getting lost (above tree line or in sparse vegetation), mark your route with **trail ducks**, small piles of rocks, which act as directional signs for the return trip.*

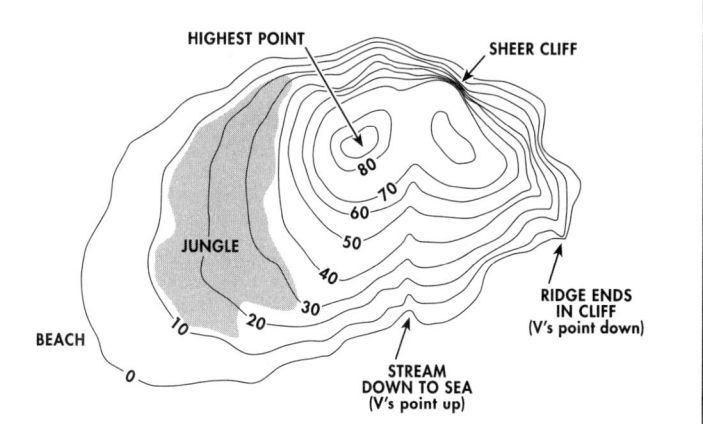

HIGHEST POINT

SHEER CLIFF

80
70
60
50
40
30
20
10
0

JUNGLE

BEACH

RIDGE ENDS
IN CLIFF
(V's point down)

STREAM
DOWN TO SEA
(V's point up)

*The topographical map is easier to read than you think. Lines close together mean steep gradients; lines farther apart mean gentle gradients; V-shaped sets of lines pointing to higher elevations mean gulleys or streambeds; V-shaped sets of lines pointing to lower elevations mean ridges.*

## Catching Fish, Avoiding Bears, and Having Fun

Feet tired and hot, stomachs hungry, we stopped our hike for lunch beside a beautiful little river pool that was catching the flows from a long but gentle waterfall. My brother Rambob passed me a piece of jerky. I took my boots off, then slowly dunked my feet into the cool, foaming water.

I was gazing at a towering peak across a canyon when suddenly, Wham! There was a quick jolt at the heel of my right foot. I pulled my foot out of the water to find that, incredibly, a trout had bitten it.

My brother looked at me as if I had antlers growing out of my head. "Wow!" he exclaimed. "That trout almost caught himself an outdoors writer!"

It's true that in remote areas trout sometimes bite on almost anything, even feet. On one high-country trip I caught limits of trout using nothing but a bare hook. The only problem is that the fish will often hit the splitshot sinker instead of the hook. Of course, fishing isn't usually that easy. But it gives you an idea of what is possible.

America's wildlands are home to a remarkable abundance of fish and wildlife. Deer browse with little fear of man, bears keep an eye out for your food, and little critters like squirrels and chipmunks are daily companions. Add in the fishing, and you've got yourself a camping trip.

Your camping adventures will evolve into premium outdoor experiences if you can work in a few good fishing trips, avoid bear problems, and occasionally add a little offbeat fun with some camp games.

**TROUT AND BASS** He creeps up on the stream as quiet as an Indian scout, keeping his shadow off the water. With his little spinning rod he'll zip his lure within an inch or two of its desired mark, probing along rocks, the edges of riffles, pocket water, or wherever he can find a change in river habitat. Rambob is trout fishing, and he's a master at it.

In most cases he'll catch a trout on his first or second cast. After that it's time to move up the river, giving no spot much more than five minutes' due. Stick and move, stick and move, stalking the stream like a bobcat zeroing in on an unsuspecting rabbit. He might keep a few trout for dinner, but mostly he releases what he catches. Rambob doesn't necessarily fish for food. It's the feeling that comes with it.

You don't need a million dollars' worth of fancy gear to catch fish. What you need is the right outlook, and that can be learned. That goes regardless of whether you are fishing for trout or bass, the two most popular fisheries in the United States. Your fishing tackle selection should be as simple and clutter free as possible.

At home I've got every piece of fishing tackle you might imagine, more than 30 rods and many tackle boxes, racks and cabinets filled with all kinds of stuff. I've got one lure that looks like a chipmunk and another that resembles a miniature can of beer with hooks. If I hear of something new, I want to try it and usually do. It's a result of my lifelong fascination with the sport.

But if you just want to catch fish, there's an easier way to go. And when I go fishing, I take that path. I don't try to bring everything. It would be impossible. Instead I bring a relatively small amount of gear. At home I will scan my tackle boxes for equipment and lures, make my selections, and bring just the essentials. Rod, reel, and tackle will fit into a side pocket of my backpack or a small carrying bag.

So what kind of rod should be used on an outdoor trip? For most camper/anglers, I suggest the use of a light, multipiece spinning rod that will break down to a small size. The lowest-priced, quality six-piece rod on the market is the Daiwa 6.5-foot pack rod, No. 6752, which is made of a graphite/glass composite that gives it the quality of a much more expensive model. And it comes in a hard plastic carrying tube for protection. Other major rod manufacturers, such as Fenwick, offer similar premium rods. It's tough to miss with any of them.

The use of graphite/glass composites in fishing rods has made them lighter and more sensitive, yet stronger. The only downside to graphite as a rod material is that it can be brittle. If you rap your rod against something, it can crack or cause a weak spot. That weak spot can eventually snap under even light pressure, like setting a hook or casting. Of course, a bit of care will prevent that from ever occurring. If you haven't bought a fishing reel in some time, you will be surprised at the quality and price of micro spinning reels on the market. The reels come tiny and strong, with rear-control drag systems. Sigma, Shimano, Cardinal, Abu, and others all make premium reels. They're worth it. With your purchase, you've just bought a reel that will last for years and years.

The one downside to spinning reels is that after long-term use, the bail spring will weaken. The result is that after casting and beginning to reel, the bail will sometimes not flip over and allow the reel to retrieve the line. Then you have to do it by hand. This can be incredibly frustrating, particularly when stream fishing, where instant line pickup is essential. The solution is to have a new bail spring installed every few years. This is a cheap, quick operation for a tackle expert.

You might own a giant tackle box filled with lures, but on your fishing trip you are better off to fit just the essentials into a small container. One of the best ways to do that is to use the Plano Micro-Magnum 3414, a tiny two-sided tackle box for trout anglers that fits into a shirt pocket. In mine, I can fit 20 lures in one side of the box and 20 flies, splitshot, and snap swivels in the other. For bass lures, which are bigger, you need a slightly larger box, but the same principle applies.

There are more fishing lures on the market than you can imagine, but a few special ones can do the job. I make sure these are in my box on every trip. For trout, I carry a small black Panther Martin spinner with yellow spots, a small gold Kastmaster, a yellow Roostertail, a gold Z-Ray with red spots, a Super Duper, and a Mepps Lightning spinner.

You can take it a step further using insider's wisdom. My old pal Ed "the Dunk" showed me his trick of taking a tiny Dardevle spoon, then spray painting it flat black and dabbing five tiny red dots on it. It's a real killer, particularly in tiny streams where the trout are spooky.

The best trout catcher I've ever used on rivers is a small metal lure called a Met-L Fly. On days when nothing else works, it can be like going to a shooting gallery. The problem is that the lure is nearly impossible to find. Rambob and I consider the few we have remaining so valuable that if the lure is snagged on a rock, a cold swim is deemed mandatory for its retrieval. These lures are as hard to find in tackle shops as trout can be to catch without one.

For bass, you can also fit all you need into a small plastic tackle box. I have fished with many bass pros, and all of them actually use just a few lures: a white spinner bait, a small jig called a Gits-It, a surface plug called a Zara Spook, and plastic worms. At times, as when the bass move into shoreline areas during the spring, shad minnow imitations like those made by Rebel or Rapala can be dynamite. My favorite is the one-inch, blue-silver Rapala. Every spring as the lakes begin to warm

**Why We Fish:** Fishing can give you a sense of exhilaration, like taking a hot shower after being coated with dust. On your walk back to camp, the steps come easy. You suddenly understand what John Muir meant when he talked of developing a oneness with nature, because you have it. That's what fishing can provide.

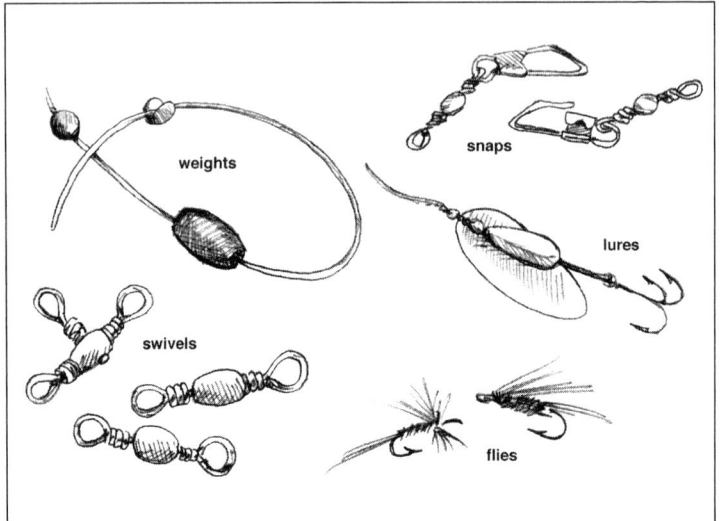

*While camping, the only fishing tackle you should bring is the essentials: several varying weights, about 20 lures, and around 20 flies, splitshot, and snap swivels. These should all fit into a container just bigger than a deck of cards.*

and the fish snap out of their winter doldrums, I like to float and paddle around in my small raft. I'll cast that little Rapala along the shoreline and catch and release hundreds of bass, bluegill, and sunfish. The fish are usually sitting close to the shoreline, awaiting my offering.

**FISHING TIPS** There's an old angler's joke about how you need to think like a fish. But if you're the one getting zilched, you may not think it's so funny.

The irony is that it is your mental approach, what you see and what you miss, that often determines your fishing luck. Some people will spend a lot of money on tackle, lures, and fishing clothes, and that done, just saunter up to a stream or lake, cast out, and wonder why they are not catching fish. The answer is their mental outlook. They are not attuning themselves to their surroundings.

You must live on nature's level, not your own. Try this and you will become aware of things you never believed even existed. Soon you will see things that will allow you to catch fish. You can get a head start by reading about fishing, but to get your degree in fishing, you must attend the University of Nature.

On every fishing trip, regardless what you fish for, try to follow three hard-and-fast rules:

1. Always approach the fishing spot so you will be undetected.

2. Present your lure, fly, or bait in a manner so it appears completely natural, as if no line was attached.

3. Stick and move, hitting one spot, working it the best you can, then move to the next.

## Approach

No one can just walk up to a stream or lake, cast out, and start catching fish as if someone had waved a magic wand. Instead, give the fish credit for being smart. After all, they live there.

Your approach must be completely undetected by the fish. Fish can sense your presence through sight and sound, though this is misinterpreted by most people. By sight, this rarely means the fish actually see you; more likely they will see your shadow on the water or the movement of your arm or rod while casting. By sound, it doesn't mean they hear you talking, but that they will detect the vibrations of your footsteps along the shore, kicking a rock, or the unnatural plunking sound of a heavy cast hitting the water. Any of these elements can spook them off the bite. In order to fish undetected, you must walk softly, keep your shadow off the water, and keep your casting motion low. All of these keys become easier at sunrise or sunset, when shadows are on the water. At midday a high sun causes a high level of light penetration in the water, which can make the fish skittish to any foreign presence.

Like hunting, you must stalk the spots. When my brother Rambob sneaks up on a fishing spot, he is like a burglar sneaking through an unlocked window.

## Presentation

Your lure, fly, or bait must appear in the water as if no line were attached, so it looks as natural as possible. My pal Mo Furniss has skin-dived in rivers to watch what the fish see when somebody is fishing.

"You wouldn't believe it," he said. "When the lure hits the water, every trout within 40 feet, like 15, 20 trout, will do a little zigzag. They all see the lure and are aware something is going on. Meanwhile, on-shore the guy casting doesn't get a bite and thinks there aren't any fish in the river."

If your offering is aimed at fooling a fish into striking, it must appear as part of its natural habitat, as if it is an insect just hatched or a small fish looking for a spot to hide. That's where you come in.

After you have sneaked up on a fishing spot, you should zip your cast upstream and start your retrieval as soon as it hits the water. If you let the lure sink to the bottom and then start the retrieval, you have no chance. A minnow, for instance, does not sink to the bottom, then start swimming. On rivers, the retrieval should be more of a drift, as if the "minnow" is in trouble and the current is sweeping it downstream.

When fishing on trout streams, always hike and cast upriver and retrieve as the offering drifts downstream in the current. This is effective because trout will sit almost motionless, pointed upstream, finning against the current. This way they can see anything coming their direction, and if a potential food morsel arrives, all they need to do is move over a few inches, open their mouths, and they've got an easy lunch. Thus you must cast upstream.

Conversely, if you cast downstream, your retrieval will bring the lure from behind the fish, where he cannot see it approaching. And I've never seen a trout that had eyes in its tail. In addition, when retrieving a downstream lure, the river current will tend to sweep your lure inshore to the rocks.

### Finding Spots

A lot of anglers don't catch fish, and a lot of hikers never see any wildlife. The key is where they are looking.

The rule of the wild is that fish and wildlife will congregate wherever there is a distinct change in the habitat. This is where you should begin your search. To find deer, for instance, forget probing a thick forest, but look for where it breaks into a meadow or a clear-cut has splayed a stand of trees. That's where the deer will be.

In a river, it can be where a riffle pours into a small pool, a rapid that plunges into a deep hole and flattens, a big boulder in the middle of a long riffle, a shoreline point, a rock pile, a submerged tree. Look for the changes. Conversely, long, straight stretches of shoreline will not hold fish—the habitat is lousy.

On rivers, the most productive areas are often where short riffles tumble into small oxygenated pools. After sneaking up from the downstream side and staying low, you should zip your cast so the lure plops gently into the white water just above the pool. Starting your retrieval instantly, the lure will drift downstream and plunk into the pool. Bang! That's where the trout will hit. Take a few more casts, then head upstream to the next spot.

With a careful approach and lure presentation and by fishing in the right spots, you have the ticket to many exciting days on the water.

**OF BEARS AND FOOD** The first time you come nose-to-nose with a bear can make your skin quiver.

Even the sight of mild-mannered black bears, the most common bear in America, can send shock waves through your body. They range from 250 to 400 pounds and have large claws and teeth that are made to scare campers. When they bound, the muscles on their shoulders roll like ocean breakers.

Bears in camping areas are accustomed to sharing the mountains with hikers and campers. They have become specialists in the food-raiding business. As a result, you must be able to make a bear-proof food hang or be able to scare the fellow off. Many campgrounds provide bear- and raccoon-proof food lockers. You can also stash your food in your vehicle, but that limits the range of your trip.

The rule of the wild is that wildlife will congregate wherever there is a distinct change in habitat. To find **where fish are hiding**, look where a riffle pours into a small pond, where a rapid plunges into a deep hole and flattens, and around submerged trees, rock piles, and boulders in the middle of a long riffle.

If you are staying at one of the easy backpack sites listed in this book, there will be no food lockers available. Your car will not be there, either. The solution is to make a bear-proof food hang, suspending all of your food wrapped in a plastic garbage bag from a rope in midair, 10 feet from the trunk of a tree and 20 feet off the ground. (Counterbalancing two bags with a rope thrown over a tree limb is very effective, but finding an appropriate limb can be difficult.)

This is accomplished by tying a rock to a rope, then throwing it over a high but sturdy tree limb. Next, tie your food bag to the rope and hoist it in the air. When you are satisfied with the position of the food bag, tie off the end of the rope to another tree. In an area frequented by bears, a good food bag is a necessity—nothing else will do.

I've been there. On one trip my pal Foonsky and my brother Rambob had left to fish, and I was stoking up an evening campfire when I felt the eyes of an intruder on my back. I turned around and saw a big bear heading straight for our camp. In the next half hour I scared the bear off twice, but then he got a whiff of something sweet in my brother's pack.

The bear rolled into camp like a truck, grabbed the pack, ripped it open, and plucked out the Tang and the Swiss Miss. The 350-pounder then sat astride a nearby log and lapped at the goodies like a thirsty dog drinking water.

Once a bear gets his mitts on your gear, he considers it his. I took two steps toward the pack, and that bear jumped off the log and galloped across the camp right at me. Scientists say a man can't outrun a bear, but they've never seen how fast I can go up a granite block with a bear on my tail.

Shortly thereafter, Foonsky returned to find me perched on top of the rock and demanded to know how I could let a bear get our Tang. It took all three of us, Foonsky, Rambob, and me, charging at once and shouting like madmen, to clear the bear out of camp and send him off over the ridge. We learned never to let food sit unattended.

**THE GRIZZLY**  When it comes to grizzlies, well, my friends, you need what we call an attitude adjustment. Or that big ol' bear may just decide to adjust your attitude for you, making your stay at the park a short one.

Grizzlies are nothing like black bears. They are bigger, stronger, have little fear, and take what they want. Some people believe there are many different species of this critter, like Alaskan brown, silvertip, cinnamon, and Kodiak, but the truth is they are all grizzlies. Any difference in appearance has to do with diet, habitat, and life habits, not speciation. By any name, they all come big.

The first thing you must do is determine if there are grizzlies in the area where you are camping. That can usually be done by asking local rangers. If you are heading into Yellowstone or Glacier National Park, or the Bob Marshall Wilderness of Montana, well, you don't

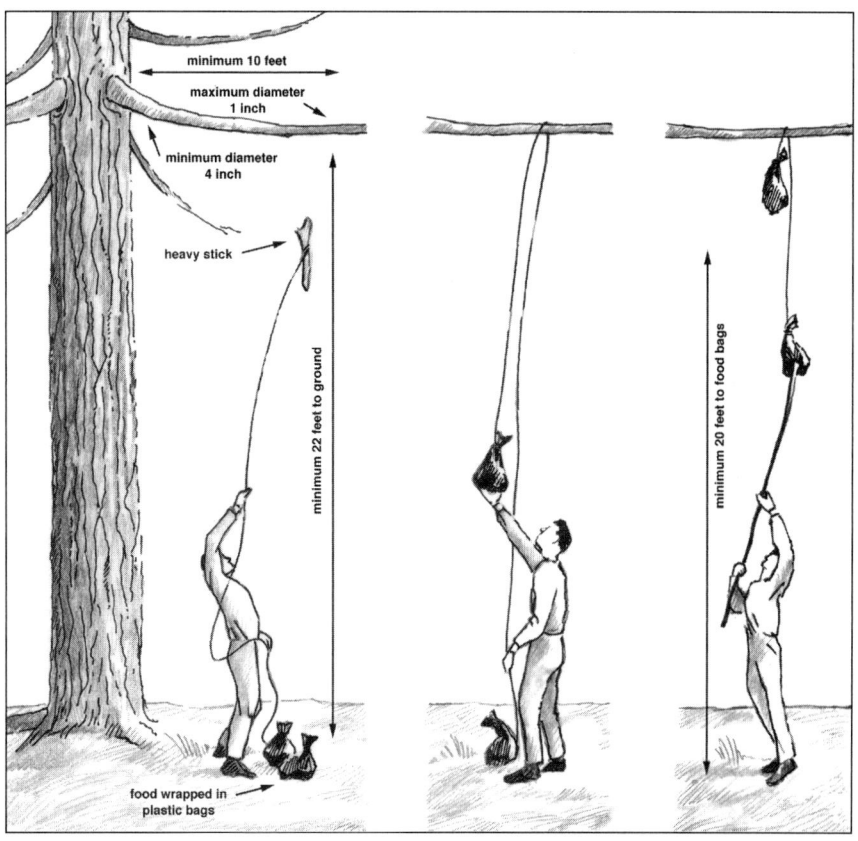

*In an area frequented by bears, a good bear-proof food hang is a must. Food should be stored in a plastic bag 10 feet from the trunk of the tree and at least 20 feet from the ground.*

have to ask. They're out there, and they're the biggest and potentially most dangerous critters you could run into.

One general way to figure the size of a bear is from his footprint. Take the width of the footprint in inches, add one to it, and you'll have an estimated length of the bear in feet. For instance, a nine-inch footprint equals a 10-foot bear. Any bear that big is a grizzly, my friends. In fact, most grizzly footprints average about nine to 10 inches across, and black bears (though they may be brown in color) tend to have footprints only four and a half to six inches across.

Most encounters with grizzlies occur when hikers fall into a silent march in the wilderness with the wind in their faces, and they walk around a corner and right into a big, unsuspecting grizzly. If you do this and see a big hump just behind its neck, well, don't think twice. It's a grizzly.

And then what should you do? Get up a tree, that's what. Grizzlies are so big that their claws cannot support their immense weight, and thus they cannot climb trees. And although their young can climb, they rarely want to get their mitts on you.

If you do get grabbed, every instinct in your body will tell you to fight back. Don't believe it. Play dead. Go limp. Let the bear throw you around a little, because after awhile you become unexciting play material and the bear will get bored. My grandmother was grabbed by a grizzly in Glacier National Park and after a few tosses and hugs, was finally left alone to escape.

Some say it's a good idea to tuck your head under his chin, since that way the bear will be unable to bite your head. I'll take a pass on that one. If you are taking action, any action, it's a signal that you are a force to be reckoned with, and he'll likely respond with more aggression. And bears don't lose many wrestling matches.

What grizzlies really like to do, believe it or not, is to pile a lot of sticks and leaves on you. Just let them, and keep perfectly still. Don't fight them; don't run. And when you have a 100% chance (not 98 or 99) to dash up a nearby tree, that's when you let fly. Once safely in a tree, you can hurl down insults and let your aggression out.

In a wilderness camp there are special precautions you should take. Always hang your food at least 100 yards downwind of camp and get it high, 30 feet is reasonable. In addition, circle your camp with rope and hang the bells from your pack on it. Thus, if a bear walks into your camp, he'll run into the rope, the bells will ring, and everybody will have a chance to get a tree before ol' griz figures out what's going on. Often the unexpected ringing of bells is enough to send him off in search of a quieter environment.

You see, more often than not, grizzlies tend to clear the way for campers and hikers. So, be smart, don't act like bear bait, and always have a plan if you are confronted by one.

My pal Foonsky had such a plan during a wilderness expedition in Montana's northern Rockies. On our second day of hiking, we started seeing scratch marks on the trees 13 to 14 feet off the ground.

"Mr. Griz made those," Foonsky said. "With spring here, the grizzlies are coming out of hibernation and using the trees like a cat uses a scratch board to stretch the muscles."

The next day, I noticed Foonsky had a pair of track shoes tied to the back of his pack. I just laughed.

"You're not going to outrun a griz," I said. "In fact, there's hardly any animal out here in the wilderness that man can outrun."

Foonsky just smiled.

"I don't have to outrun a griz," he said. "I just have to outrun you!"

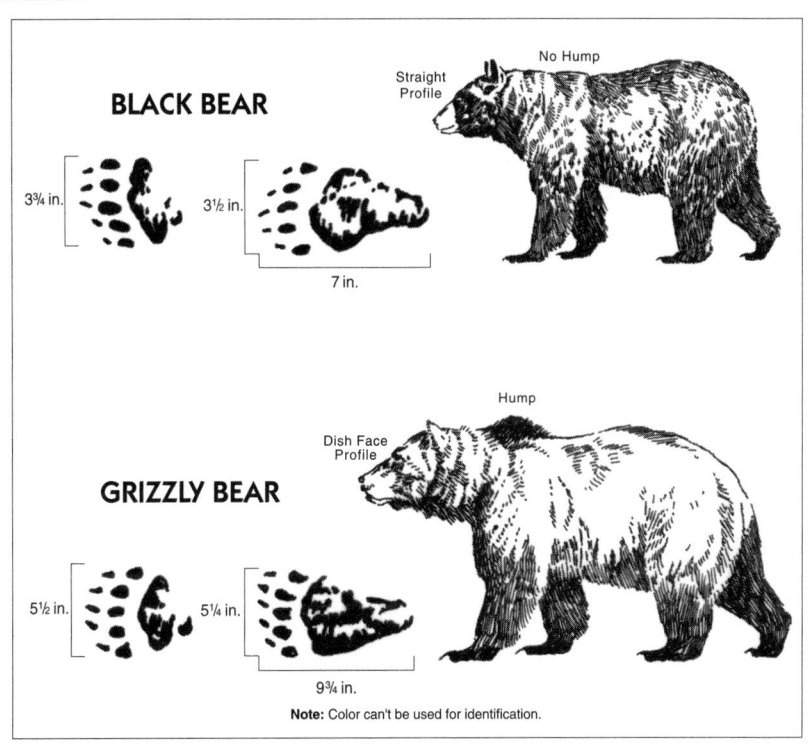

**BLACK BEAR**

Straight Profile

No Hump

3¾ in.

3½ in.

7 in.

**GRIZZLY BEAR**

Dish Face Profile

Hump

5½ in.

5¼ in.

9¾ in.

**Note:** Color can't be used for identification.

*Grizzly bears are distinguished from black bears by a pronounced shoulder hump and a concave facial profile. Grizzlies are generally brown and average 10 to 11 feet in length, while black bears (which can also be brown) maintain lengths of five to seven feet.*

**FUN AND GAMES**

"Now what are we supposed to do?" the young boy asked his dad. "Yeah, Dad, think of something," said another son.

Well, Dad thought hard. This was one of the first camping trips he'd taken with his sons and one of the first lessons he received was that kids don't appreciate the philosophic release of mountain quiet. They want action and lots of it. With a glint in his eye, Dad searched around the camp and picked up 15 twigs, breaking them so each was four inches long. He laid them in three separate rows, three twigs in one row, five twigs in another, and seven in the other.

"OK, this game is called 3-5-7," said Dad. "You each take turns picking up sticks. You are allowed to remove all or as few as one twig from a row, but here's the catch: You can pick only from one row per turn. Whoever picks up the last stick left is the loser."

## Bear Territory

If you are hiking in a wilderness area that may have grizzlies, it becomes a necessity to wear bells on your pack. That way the bear will hear you coming and likely get out of your way. Keep talking, singing, or maybe even debating the country's foreign policy, but do not fall into a silent hiking vigil. And if a breeze is blowing in your face, you must make even more noise (a good excuse to rant and rave about the government's domestic affairs). Noise is important, because your smell will not be carried in the direction you are hiking. As a result the bear will not smell you coming.

If a bear can hear you and smell you, it will tend to get out of the way and let you pass without your knowing it was even close by. The exceptions are if you are carrying fish or lots of sweets in your pack or if you are wearing heavy, sweet deodorants or makeup. All of these are bear attractants.

I remember this episode well because those two little boys were my brother Bobby, as in Rambobby, and me. And to this day, we still play 3-5-7 on campouts, with the winner getting to watch the loser clean the dishes. What I have learned in the span of time since that original episode is that it does not matter what your age is: campers need options for camp fun.

Some evenings, after a long hike or ride, you are likely to feel too worn-out to take on a serious romp downstream to fish, or a climb up to a ridge for a view. That is especially true if you have been in the outback for a week or more. At that point a lot of campers will spend their time resting and gazing at a map of the area, dreaming of the next day's adventure, or just take a seat against a rock, watching the colors of the sky and mountain panorama change minute by minute. But kids in the push-button video era, and a lot of adults too, want more. After all, "I'm on vacation; I want some fun."

There are several options, like the 3-5-7 twig game, and they should be just as much a part of your trip planning as arranging your gear.

For kids, plan on games, the more physically challenging the competition, the better. One of the best games is to throw a chunk of wood into a lake and challenge the kids to hit it by throwing rocks. It wreaks havoc on the fishing, but it can keep kids totally absorbed for some time. Target practice with a wrist-rocket slingshot is also all consuming for kids, firing rocks away at small targets like pinecones set on a log.

You can also set kids off on little missions near camp, such as looking for the footprints of wildlife, searching out good places to have a "snipe hunt," picking up twigs to get the evening fire started, or having them take the water purifier to a stream to pump some drinking water into a canteen. The latter is an easy, fun, yet important task that will allow kids to feel a sense of equality they often don't get at home. For adults, the appeal should be more to the intellect. A good example is star and planet identification, and while you are staring into space, you're bound to spot a few asteroids or shooting stars. A star chart can make it easy to locate and identify many distinctive stars and constellations, such as Pleiades (the Seven Sisters), Orion, and others from the zodiac, depending on the time of year. With a little research, this can add a unique perspective to your trip. You could point to Polaris, one of the most easily identified of all stars, and note that navigators in the 1400s used it to find their way. Polaris, of course, is the North Star and is at the end of the handle of the Little Dipper. Pinpointing Polaris is quite easy. First find the Big Dipper, then locate the outside stars of the ladle of the Big Dipper. They are called the "Pointer Stars" because they point right at Polaris.

A tree identification book can teach you a few things about your surroundings. It is also a good idea for one member of the party to research the history of the area you have chosen and another to research the geology. With shared knowledge, you end up with a deeper love of wild places.

Another way to add some recreation into your trip is to bring a board game, a number of which have been miniaturized for campers. The most popular are chess, checkers, and cribbage. The latter comes with an equally miniature set of playing cards. And if you bring those little cards, that opens a vast set of other possibilities. With kids along, for instance, just take three queens out of the deck and you can play Old Maid.

But there are more serious card games and they come with high stakes. Such occurred on one high country trip where Foonsky, Rambob, and I sat down for a late afternoon game of poker. In a game of seven-card stud, I caught a straight on the sixth card and felt like a dog licking on a T-bone. Already I had bet several Skittles and peanut M&Ms on this promising hand.

Then I examined the cards Foonsky had face up. He was showing three sevens, and acting as happy as a grizzly with a pork chop—or a full house. He matched my bet of two peanut M&Ms, then raised me three SweetTarts, one Starburst, and one sour apple Jolly Rancher. Rambob folded, but I matched Foonsky's bet and hoped for the best as the seventh and final card was dealt.

Just after Foonsky glanced at that last card, I saw him sneak a look at my grape stick and beef jerky stash.

"I raise you a grape stick," he said.

Rambob and I both gasped. It was the highest bet ever made, equivalent to a million dollars laid down in Las Vegas. Cannons were going off in my chest. I looked hard at my cards. They looked good, but were they good enough?

Catching Fish, Avoiding Bears, and Having Fun 75

Even with a great hand like I had, a grape stick was too much to gamble, my last one with 10 days of trail ahead of us. I shook my head and folded my cards. Foonsky smiled at his victory.

But I still had my grape stick.

## OLD TRICKS DON'T ALWAYS WORK

Most people are born honest, but after a few camping trips, they usually get over it.

I remember some advice I got from Rambob, normally an honest soul, on one camping trip. A giant mosquito had landed on my arm and he alerted me to some expert advice.

"Flex your arm muscles," he commanded, watching the mosquito fill with my blood. "He'll get stuck in your arm, then he'll explode."

For some reason, I believed him. We both proceeded to watch the mosquito drill countless holes in my arm.

Alas, the unknowing face sabotage from their most trusted companions on camping trips. It can arise at any time, usually in the form of advice from a friendly, honest-looking face, as if to say, "What? How can you doubt me?" After that mosquito episode, I was a little more skeptical of my dear old brother. Then the next day, when another mosquito was nailing me in the back of the neck, out came this gem:

"Hold your breath," he commanded. I instinctively obeyed. "That will freeze the mosquito," he said, "then you can squish him."

But in the time I wasted holding my breath, the little bugger was able to fly off without my having the satisfaction of squishing him. When he got home, he probably told his family, "What a dummy I got to drill today!"

Over the years, I have been duped numerous times with dubious advice:

On a grizzly bear attack: "If he grabs you, tuck your head under the grizzly's chin; then he won't be able to bite you in the head." This made sense to me until the first time I came face-to-face with a nine-foot grizzly 40 yards away. In seconds, I was at the top of a tree, which suddenly seemed to make the most sense.

On coping with animal bites: "If a bear bites you in the arm, don't try to jerk it away. That will just rip up your arm. Instead force your arm deeper into his mouth. He'll lose his grip and will have to open it to get a firmer hold, and right then you can get away." I was told this in the Boy Scouts, and when I was 14, I had a chance to try it out when a friend's dog bit me as I tried to pet it. What happened? When I shoved my arm deeper into his mouth, he bit me about three more times.

On cooking breakfast: "The bacon will curl up every time in a camp frying pan. So make sure you have a bacon stretcher to keep it flat." As a 12-year-old Tenderfoot, I spent two hours looking for the bacon stretcher until I figured out the camp leader had forgotten it. It wasn't for several years until I learned that there is no such thing.

On preventing sore muscles: "If you haven't hiked for a long time and you are facing a rough climb, you can keep from getting sore muscles in your legs, back, and shoulders by practicing the 'Dead Man's Walk.' Simply let your entire body go slack, and then take slow, wobbling steps. This will clear your muscles of lactic acid, which causes them to be so sore after a rough hike." Foonsky pulled this one on me. Rambob and I both bought it and tried it while we were hiking up Mount Whitney, which requires a 6,000-foot elevation gain in six miles. In one 45-minute period, about 30 other hikers passed us and looked at us as if we were suffering from some rare form of mental aberration.

Fish won't bite? No problem: "If the fish are not feeding or will not bite, persistent anglers can still catch dinner with little problem. Keep casting across the current, and eventually, as they hover in the stream, the line will feed across their open mouths. Keep reeling and you will hook the fish right in the side of the mouth. This technique is called 'lining.' Never worry if the fish will not bite, because you can always line 'em." Of course, heh, heh, heh, that explains why so many fish get hooked in the side of the mouth.

How to keep bears away: "To keep bears away, urinate around the borders of your campground. If there are a lot of bears in the area, it is advisable to go right on your sleeping bag." Yeah, surrrrrre.

What to do with trash: "Don't worry about packing out trash. Just bury it. It will regenerate into the earth and add valuable minerals." Bears, raccoons, skunks, and other critters will dig up your trash as soon as you depart, leaving one huge mess for the next camper. Always pack out everything.

Often the advice comes without warning. That was the case after a fishing trip with a female companion, when she outcaught me two to one, the third such trip in a row. I explained this to a shopkeeper, and he nodded, then explained why.

"The male fish are able to detect the female scent on the lure, and thus become aroused into striking."

Of course! That explains everything!

I was just a lad when Foonsky pulled the old snipe-hunt trick on **GETTING** me. It took nearly 30 years to get revenge. **REVENGE**

You probably know about snipe hunting. That is where the victim is led out at night in the woods by a group, then is left holding a bag.

"Stay perfectly still and quiet," Foonsky explained. "You don't want to scare the snipe. The rest of us will go back to camp and let the woods settle down. Then when the snipe are least expecting it, we'll form a line and charge through the forest with sticks, beating bushes and trees, and we'll flush the snipe out right to you. Be ready with the bag. When we flush the snipe out, bag it. But until we start our charge, make sure you don't move or make a sound or you will spook the snipe and ruin everything."

I sat out there in the woods with my bag for hours, waiting for the charge. I waited, waited, and waited. Nothing happened. No charge, no snipe. It wasn't until well past midnight that I figured something was wrong. When I finally returned to camp, everybody was sleeping.

Well, I tell ya, don't get mad at your pals for the tricks they pull on you. Get revenge. Some 25 years later, on the last day of a camping trip, the time finally came.

"Let's break camp early," Foonsky suggested to Mr. Furnai and me. "Get up before dawn, eat breakfast, pack up, and be on the ridge to watch the sun come up. It will be a fantastic way to end the trip."

"Sounds great to me," I replied. But when Foonsky wasn't looking, I turned his alarm clock ahead three hours. So when the alarm sounded at the appointed 4:30 a.m. wake-up time, Mr. Furnai and I knew it was actually only 1:30 a.m.

Foonsky clambered out of his sleeping bag and whistled with a grin. "Time to break camp."

"You go ahead," I answered. "I'll skip breakfast so I can get a little more sleep. At the first sign of dawn, wake me up, and I'll break camp."

"Me, too," said Mr. Furnai.

Foonsky then proceeded to make some coffee, cook a breakfast, and eat it, sitting on a log in the black darkness of the forest, waiting for the sun to come up. An hour later, with still no sign of dawn, he checked his clock. It now read 5:30 a.m. "Any minute now we should start seeing some light," he said.

He made another cup of coffee, packed his gear, and sat there in the middle of the night, looking up at the stars, waiting for dawn. "Anytime now," he said. He ended up sitting there all night long.

Revenge is sweet. Prior to a fishing trip at a lake, I took Foonsky aside and explained that the third member of the party, Jimbobo, was hard of hearing and very sensitive about it. "Don't mention it to him," I advised. "Just talk real loud."

Meanwhile, I had already told Jimbobo the same thing. "Foonsky just can't hear very good."

We had fished less than 20 minutes when Foonsky got a nibble. "GET A BITE?" shouted Jimbobo.

"YEAH!" yelled back Foonsky, smiling. "BUT I DIDN'T HOOK HIM!"

"MAYBE NEXT TIME!" shouted Jimbobo with a friendly grin.

Well, they spent the entire day yelling at each other from the distance of a few feet. They never did figure it out. Heh, heh, heh.

That is, I thought so, until we made a trip salmon fishing. I got a strike that almost knocked my fishing rod out of the boat. When I grabbed the rod, it felt as if Moby Dick were on the other end. "At least a 25-pounder," I said. "Maybe bigger."

The fish dove, ripped off line, and then bulldogged. "It's acting like a 40-pounder," I announced, "Huge, just huge. It's going deep. That's how the big ones fight."

Some 15 minutes later, I finally got the "salmon" to the surface. It turned out to be a coffee can that Foonsky had clipped on the line with a snap swivel. By maneuvering the boat, he made the coffee can fight like a big fish.

This all started with a little old snipe hunt years ago. You never know what your pals will try next. Don't get mad. Get revenge.

## Camp Ethics and Politics

The perfect place to set up a base camp turned out to be not so perfect. In fact, according to Doug Williams of California, it did not even exist.

Williams and his son, James, had driven deep into Angeles National Forest, prepared to set up camp and then explore the surrounding area on foot. But when they reached their destination, no campground existed.

"I wanted a primitive camp in a national forest where I could teach my son some basics," said the senior Williams. "But when we got there, there wasn't much left of the camp and it had been closed. It was obvious that the area had been vandalized."

It turned out not to be an isolated incident. A lack of outdoor ethics practiced by a few people using the unsupervised campgrounds available on national forestland has caused the U.S. Forest Service to close a few of them and make extensive repairs to others.

"There have been sites closed, especially in Angeles and San Bernardino national forests in Southern California," said David Flohr, regional campground coordinator for the U.S. Forest Service. "It's an urban type of thing, affecting forests near urban areas, and not just Los Angeles. They get a lot of urban users and they bring with them a lot of the same ethics they have in the city. They get drinking and they're not afraid

## Keep It Wild Tip 6: Respect Other Users

1.  Horseback riders have priority over hikers. Step to the downhill side of the trail and talk softly when encountering horseback riders.

2.  Hikers and horseback riders have priority over mountain bikers. When mountain bikers encounter other users even on wide trails, they should pass at an extremely slow speed. On very narrow trails they should dismount and get off to the side so hikers or horseback riders can pass without having their trip disrupted.

3.  Mountain bikes aren't permitted on most single-track trails and are expressly prohibited in designated wilderness areas. Mountain bikers breaking these rules should be confronted and told to dismount and walk their bikes until they reach a legal area.

4.  It's illegal for horseback riders to break off branches that may be in the path of wilderness trails.

5.  Horseback riders on overnight trips are prohibited from camping in many areas and are usually required to keep stock animals in specific areas where they can do no damage to the landscape.

to do things. They vandalize and run. Of course, it is a public facility, so they think nobody is getting hurt."

But somebody is getting hurt, starting with the next person who wants to use the campground. And if the ranger district budget doesn't have enough money to pay for repairs, the campground is then closed for the next arrivals. Just ask Doug and James Williams.

In an era of considerable fiscal restraint for the U.S. Forest Service, vandalized campgrounds could face closure instead of repair in the next few years. Williams had just a taste of it, but Flohr, as camping coordinator, gets a steady diet.

"It starts with behavior," Flohr said. "General rowdiness, drinking, partying, and then vandalism. It goes all the way from the felt tip pen things (graffiti) to total destruction, blowing up toilet buildings with dynamite. I have seen toilets destroyed totally with shotguns. They burn up tables, burn barriers. They'll burn up signs for firewood, even the shingles right off the roofs of the bathrooms. They'll shoot anything, garbage cans, signs. It can get a little hairy. A favorite is to remove the stool out of a toilet building. We've had people fall in the open hole."

The National Park Service had a similar problem some years back, especially with rampant littering. Park Director Bill Mott responded by creating an interpretive program that attempts to teach visitors the wise use of natural areas, and to have all park workers set examples by picking up litter and reminding others to do the same.

The U.S. Forest Service has responded with a similar program, making brochures available that detail the wise use of national forests.

The four most popular brochures are titled: "Rules for Visitors to the National Forest," "Recreation in the National Forests," "Is the Water Safe?" and "Backcountry Safety Tips." These include details on campfires, drinking water from lakes or streams, hypothermia, safety, and outdoor ethics. They are available for free by writing to Public Affairs, U.S. Forest Service, Rocky Mountain Regional Office, P.O. Box 25127, Lakewood, CO 80225.

Flohr said even experienced campers sometimes cross over the ethics line unintentionally. The most common example, he said, is when campers toss garbage into the outhouse toilet, rather than packing it out in a plastic garbage bag.

"They throw it in the vault toilet bowls, which just fills them up," Flohr said. "That creates an extremely high cost to pump it. You know why? Because some poor guy has to pick that stuff out piece by piece. It can't be pumped."

At most backcountry sites, the U.S. Forest Service has implemented a program called "Pack it in, pack it out," even posting signs that remind all visitors to do so. But a lot of people don't do it, and others may even uproot the sign and burn it for firewood.

On a trip to a secluded lake near Carson Pass in the Sierra Nevada, I arrived at a small, little-known camp where the picnic table had been spray painted and garbage had been strewn about. A pristine place, the true temple of God, had been defiled.

## GETTING ALONG WITH FELLOW CAMPERS

The most important thing about a camping, fishing, or hunting trip is not where you go, how many fish you catch, or how many shots you fire. It often has little to do with how beautiful the view is, how easy the campfire lights, or how sunny the days are.

Oh yeah? Then what is the most important factor? The answer: The people you are with. It is that simple.

Who would you rather camp with? Your enemy at work or your dream mate in a good mood? Heh, heh. You get the idea. A camping trip is a fairly close-knit experience, and you can make lifetime friends or lifelong enemies in the process. That is why your choice of companions is so important. Your own behavior is equally consequential.

Yet most people spend more time putting together their camping gear than considering why they enjoy or hate the company of their chosen companions. Here are 10 rules of behavior for good camping mates:

1. No whining: Nothing is more irritating than being around a whiner. It goes right to the heart of adventure, since often the only difference between a hardship and an escapade is simply whether or not an individual has the spirit for it. The people who do can turn a rugged day in the outdoors into a cherished memory. Those who don't can ruin it with their incessant sniveling.

*In setting up camp, always be mindful of potential ecological disturbances. Pitch tents and dispose of human waste at least 200 feet from the water's edge. In grizzly bear territory, increase the distance between your tent and your cooking area, food-hang, and the water's edge threefold. In other words, if you're in grizzly country, do all your cooking 200 yards (not feet) downwind of your sleeping area. If you can establish an escape tree nearby, all the better.*

2. **Activities must be agreed upon:** Always have a meeting of the minds with your companions over the general game plan. Then everybody will possess an equal stake in the outcome of the trip. This is absolutely critical. Otherwise they will feel like merely an addendum to your trip, not an equal participant, and a whiner will be born (see No. 1).

3. **Nobody's in charge:** It is impossible to be genuine friends if one person is always telling another what to do, especially if the orders involve simple camp tasks. You need to share the space on the same emotional plane, and the only way to do that is to have a semblance of equality, regardless of differences in experience. Just try ordering your mate around at home for a few days. You'll quickly see the results, and they aren't pretty.

4. **Equal chances at the fun stuff:** It's fun to build the fire, fun to get the first cast at the best fishing spot, and fun to hoist the bagged food for a bear-proof food hang. It is not fun to clean the dishes, collect firewood, or cook every night. So obviously, there must be an equal distribution of the fun stuff and the not-fun stuff, and everybody on the trip must get a shot at the good and the bad.

5. **No heroes:** No awards are bestowed for achievement in the outdoors, yet some guys treat mountain peaks, big fish, and big game as if they are prizes in a trophy competition. Actually, nobody cares how wonderful you are, which is always a surprise to trophy chasers. What people care about is the heart of the adventure, the gut-level stuff.

6. **Agree on a wake-up time:** It is a good idea to agree on a general wake-up time before closing your eyes for the night, and that goes regardless of whether you want to sleep in late or get up at dawn. Then you can proceed on course regardless of what time you crawl out of your sleeping bag in the morning, without the risk of whining (see No. 1).

7. **Think of the other guy:** Be self-aware instead of self-absorbed. A good test is to count the number of times you say, "What do you think?" A lot of potential problems can be solved quickly by actually listening to the answer.

8. **Solo responsibilities:** There are a number of essential camp duties on all trips, and while they should be shared equally, most should be completed solo. That means that when it is time for you to cook, you don't have to worry about me changing the recipe on you. It means that when it is my turn to make the fire, you keep your mitts out of it.

9. **Don't let money get in the way:** Of course everybody should share equally in trip expenses, such as the cost of food, and it should be split up before you head out yonder. Don't let somebody pay extra, because that person will likely try to control the trip. Conversely, don't let somebody weasel out of paying the fair share.

10. **Accordance on the food plan:** Always have complete agreement on what you plan to eat each day. Don't figure that just because you like Steamboat's Sludge, everybody else will, too, especially youngsters. Always, always, always check for food allergies such as nuts, onions, or cheese, and make sure each person brings their own personal coffee brand. Some people drink only decaffeinated; others might gag on anything but Burma monkey beans.

Obviously, it is difficult to find companions who will agree on all of these elements. This is why many campers say that the best camping buddy they'll ever have is their mate, someone who knows all about them and likes them anyway.

## Outdoors with Kids

How do you get a boy or girl excited about the outdoors? How do you compete with the television and remote control? How do you prove to a kid that success comes from persistence, spirit, and logic, which the outdoors teaches, and not from pushing buttons?

The answer is in the **Ten Camping Commandments for Kids.** These are lessons that will get youngsters excited about the outdoors, and will make sure adults help the process along, not kill it. I've put this list together with the help of my own kids, Jeremy and Kris, and their mother, Stephani. Some of the commandments are obvious, some are not, but all are important:

1. Take children to places where there is a guarantee of action. A good example is camping in a park where large numbers of wildlife can be viewed, such as squirrels, chipmunks, deer, and even bears. Other good choices are fishing at a small pond loaded with bluegill, or hunting in a spot where a kid can shoot a .22 at pinecones all day. Boys and girls want action, not solitude.

2. Enthusiasm is contagious. If you aren't excited about an adventure, you can't expect a child to be. Show a genuine zest for life in the outdoors, and point out everything as if it is the first time you have ever seen it.

3. Always, always, always be seated when talking to someone small. This allows the adult and child to be on the same level. That is why fishing in a small boat is perfect for adults and kids. Nothing is worse for youngsters than having a big person look down at them and give them orders. What fun is that?

4. Always *show* how to do something, whether it is gathering sticks for a campfire, cleaning a trout, or tying a knot. Never tell—always show. A button usually clicks to "off" when a kid is lectured. But kids can learn behavior patterns and outdoor skills by watching adults, even when the adults are not aware they are being watched.

5. Let kids be kids. Let the adventure happen, rather than trying to force it within some preconceived plan. If they get sidetracked watching pollywogs, chasing butterflies, or sneaking up on chipmunks, let them be. A youngster can have more fun turning over rocks and looking at different kinds of bugs than sitting in one spot, waiting for a fish to bite.

6. Expect short attention spans. Instead of getting frustrated about it, use it to your advantage. How? By bringing along a bag of candy and snacks. Where there is a lull in the camp activity, out comes the bag. Don't let them know what goodies await, so each one becomes a surprise.

7. Make absolutely certain the child's sleeping bag is clean, dry, and warm. Nothing is worse than discomfort when trying to sleep, but a refreshing sleep makes for a positive attitude the next day. In addition, kids can become quite scared of animals at night. A parent should not wait for any signs of this, but always play the part of the outdoor guardian, the one who will take care of everything.

8. Kids quickly relate to outdoor ethics. They will enjoy eating everything they kill, building a safe campfire, and picking up all their litter, and they will develop a sense of pride that goes with it. A good idea is to bring extra plastic garbage bags to pick up any trash you come across. Kids long remember when they do something right that somebody else has done wrong.

9. If you want youngsters hooked on the outdoors for life, take a close-up photograph of them holding up fish they have caught, blowing on the campfire, or completing other camp tasks. Young children can for-

get how much fun they had, but they never forget if they have a picture of it.

10. The least important word you can ever say to a kid is "I." Keep track of how often you are saying "Thank you" and "What do you think?" If you don't say them very often, you'll lose out. Finally, the most important words of all are: "I am proud of you."

# Predicting Weather

Foonsky climbed out of his sleeping bag, glanced at the nearby meadow, and scowled hard.

"It doesn't look good," he said. "Doesn't look good at all."

I looked at my adventure companion of 20 years, noting his discontent. Then I looked at the meadow and immediately understood why: *"When the grass is dry at morning light, look for rain before the night."*

"How bad you figure?" I asked him.

"We'll know soon enough, I reckon," Foonsky answered. "Short notice, soon to pass. Long notice, long it will last."

When you are out in the wild, spending your days fishing and your nights camping, you learn to rely on yourself to predict the weather. It can make or break you. If a storm hits the unprepared, it can quash the trip and possibly endanger the participants. But if you are ready, a potential hardship can be an adventure.

You can't rely on TV weather forecasters, people who don't even know that when all the cows on a hill are facing north, it will rain that night for sure. God forbid if the cows are all sitting. But what do you expect from TV's talking heads?

Foonsky made a campfire, started boiling some water for coffee and soup, and we started to plan the day. In the process, I noticed the smoke of the campfire: It was sluggish, drifting and hovering.

"You notice the smoke?" I asked, chewing on a piece of homemade jerky.

"Not good," Foonsky said. "Not good." He knew that sluggish, hovering smoke indicates rain.

"You'd think we'd have been smart enough to know last night that this was coming," Foonsky said. "Did you take a look at the moon or the clouds?"

"I didn't look at either," I answered. "Too busy eating the trout we caught." You see, if the moon is clear and white, the weather will be good the next day. But if there is a ring around the moon, the number of stars you can count inside the ring equals the number of days until the next rain. As for clouds, the high, thin clouds called cirrus indicate a change in the weather.

We were quiet for a while, planning our strategy, but as we did so, some terrible things happened: A chipmunk scampered past with his tail high, a small flock of geese flew by very low, and a little sparrow perched on a tree limb quite close to the trunk.

1. Learn about the regulations and issues that apply to the area you're visiting.

2. Avoid heavy-use areas.

3. Obtain all maps and permits.

4. Bring extra garbage bags to pack out any refuse you come across.

"We're in for trouble," I told Foonsky.

"I know, I know," he answered. "I saw 'em, too. And come to think of it, no crickets were chirping last night either."

"Damn, that's right!"

These are all signs of an approaching storm. Foonsky pointed at the smoke of the campfire and shook his head as if he had just been condemned. Sure enough, now the smoke was blowing toward the north, a sign of a south wind. *"When the wind is from the south, the rain is in its mouth."*

"We'd best stay hunkered down until it passes," Foonsky said.

I nodded. "Let's gather as much firewood now as we can, get our gear covered up, then plan our meals."

"Then we'll get a poker game going."

As we accomplished these camp tasks, the sky clouded up, then darkened. Within an hour, we had gathered enough firewood to make a large pile, enough wood to keep a fire going no matter how hard it rained. The day's meals had been separated out of the food bag, so it wouldn't have to be retrieved during the storm. We buttoned two ponchos together, staked two of the corners with ropes to the ground, and tied the other two with ropes to different tree limbs to create a slanted roof/shelter.

As the first raindrop fell with that magic sound on our poncho roof, Foonsky was just starting to shuffle the cards.

"Cut for deal," he said.

Just as I did so, it started to rain a bit harder. I pulled out another piece of beef jerky and started chewing on it. It was just another day in paradise. . . .

Weather lore can be valuable. Small signs provided by nature and wildlife can be translated to provide a variety of weather information. Here is the list I have compiled over the years:

> *When the grass is dry at morning light,*
> *Look for rain before the night.*

> *Short notice, soon to pass.*
> *Long notice, long it will last.*

*When the wind is from the east,*
*'Tis fit for neither man nor beast.*

*When the wind is from the south,*
*The rain is in its mouth.*

*When the wind is from the west,*
*Then it is the very best.*

*Red sky at night, sailors' delight.*
*Red sky in the morning, sailors take warning.*

*When all the cows are pointed north,*
*Within a day rain will come forth.*

*Onion skins very thin, mild winter coming in.*
*Onion skins very tough, winter's going to be very rough.*

*When your boots make the squeak of snow,*
*Then very cold temperatures will surely show.*

*If a goose flies high, fair weather ahead.*
*If a goose flies low, foul weather will come instead.*

- A thick coat on a woolly caterpillar means a big, early snow is coming.
- Chipmunks will run with their tails up before a rain.
- Bees always stay near their hives before a rainstorm.
- When the birds are perched on large limbs near tree trunks, an intense but short storm will arrive.
- On the coast, if groups of seabirds are flying a mile inland, look for major winds.
- If crickets are chirping very loud during the evening, the next day will be clear and warm.
- If the smoke of a campfire at night rises in a thin spiral, good weather is assured for the next day.
- If the smoke of a campfire at night is sluggish, drifting and hovering, it will rain the next day.
- If there is a ring around the moon, count the number of stars inside the ring, and that is how many days until the next rain.
- If the moon is clear and white, the weather will be good the next day.
- High, thin clouds, or cirrus, indicate a change in the weather.

- Oval-shaped lenticular clouds indicate high winds.

- Two levels of clouds moving in different directions indicate changing weather soon.

- Huge, dark, billowing clouds, called cumulonimbus, suddenly forming on warm afternoons in the mountains mean that a short but intense thunderstorm with lightning can be expected.

- When squirrels are busy gathering food for extended periods, it means good weather is ahead in the short term, but a hard winter is ahead in the long term.

- And God forbid if all the cows are sitting down. . . .

## Beating the Time Trap

**Season Passes: For campgrounds that charge additional day-use fees per visit, such as those in the South Park area, you can buy a season pass to save money. Contact the appropriate U. S. Forest Service office for details.**

If the great outdoors is so great, then why don't people enjoy it more? The answer is because of the time trap, and I will tell you exactly how to beat it.

For many, the biggest problem is finding the time to go, whether it is camping, hiking, fishing, boating, backpacking, biking, or even just for a good drive in the country. The solution? Well, believe it or not, the answer is to treat your fun just as you treat your work, and I'll tell you how.

Consider how you treat your job: Always on time? Go there every day you are scheduled? Do whatever it takes to get there and get it done? Right? No foolin' that's right. Now imagine if you took the same approach to the outdoors. Suddenly your life would be a heck of a lot better.

The secret is to schedule all of your outdoor activities. For instance, I go fishing every Thursday evening, hiking every Sunday morning, and on an overnight trip every new moon (when stargazing is best). No matter what, I'm going. Just like going to work, I've scheduled it. The same approach works with longer adventures. The only reason I have been able to complete hikes ranging from 200 to 300 miles was that I scheduled the time to do it. The reason I spend 125 to 150 days a year in the field is that I schedule them. In my top year, I had nearly 200 days where at least part of the day was enjoyed taking part in outdoor recreation.

If you get out your calendar and write in the exact dates you are going, then you'll go. If you don't, you won't. Suddenly, with only a minor change in your life plan, you can be living the life you were previously dreaming about.

See you out there.

—Tom Stienstra

## RESOURCE GUIDE

**Federal Agencies**

- **U.S. Forest Service**, Rocky Mountain Regional Office, P.O. Box 25127, Lakewood, CO 80225, tel. (303) 275-5350
- **Arapaho & Roosevelt National Forests**, 1311 S. College Ave., Fort Collins, CO 80526, tel. (970) 498-2770
- **Grand Mesa, Uncompahgre, & Gunnison National Forests**, 2250 U.S. 50, Delta, CO 81416, tel. (970) 874-6600
- **Routt National Forest**, 925 Weiss Dr., Steamboat Springs, CO 80487, tel. (970) 879-1870
- **Pike & San Isabel National Forests**, 1920 Valley Dr., Pueblo, CO 81108, tel. (719) 545-8737
- **San Juan & Rio Grande National Forests**, 1803 W. Hwy. 160, Monte Vista, CO 81008, tel. (719) 852-5941
- **White River National Forest**, P.O. Box 948, Glenwood Springs, CO 81602, tel. (970) 945-2521
- **National Park Service**, Rocky Mountain Region, P.O. Box 25287, Denver, CO 80225, tel. (303) 969-2000, website: www.nps.gov
- **Bureau of Land Management**, 2850 Youngfield St., Lakewood, CO 80215, tel. (303) 236-2100

**State Agencies**

- **Colorado State Parks**, 1313 Sherman St., Room 618, Denver, CO 80203, tel. (303) 866-3437, website: www.coloradoparks.org
- **Colorado Department of Fish and Wildlife**, 6060 Broadway, Denver, CO 80216, tel. (303) 297-1192

**Private Agencies**

- **Colorado Campground And Lodging Owners Association**, 700 N. Colorado Blvd., Suite 200, Denver, CO 80206, tel. (888) 686-8549
- **Colorado Campground Agency, Inc.**, 5101 Pennsylvania Ave., Boulder, CO 80303, website: www.coloradodirectory.com

**Maps**

- **U.S. Geological Survey**, P.O. Box 25286, Denver Federal Center, Denver, CO 80225, tel. (303) 236-7477

**Road Conditions**

- tel. (303) 639-1111 (metro Denver), tel. (303) 639-1234 (Statewide)

# CAMPING GEAR CHECKLIST

## COOKING GEAR

- Camp fuel
- Camp stove
- Dish soap and scrubber
- Fire-starter cubes or candle
- Itemized food
- Knife, fork
- Matches stored in resealable (such as Ziploc) bags
- Plastic spade
- Pot, pan, cup
- Pot grabber
- Salt, pepper, spices

**Optional Cooking Gear**
- Ax or hatchet
- Can opener
- Clothespins
- Dustpan
- Grill
- Ice chest
- Spatula
- Tablecloth
- Tinfoil
- Whisk broom
- Wood or charcoal for barbecue

## CAMPING CLOTHES

- Cotton/canvas pants
- Cotton shirt
- Hat
- Long-sleeved cotton/wool shirt
- Parka
- Polypropylene underwear
- Rain jacket, pants, or poncho
- Sunglasses
- Vest

**Optional Clothing**
- Gloves
- Seam Lock
- Shorts
- Ski cap
- Swimsuit

## HIKING GEAR

- Backup lightweight shoes
- 80% wool socks
- Gaiters
- Innersole or foot cushion
- Moleskin and medical tape
- Polypropylene socks
- Quality hiking boots
- Strong bootlaces
- Thick cotton socks
- Water-repellent boot treatment

## SLEEPING GEAR

- Sleeping bag
- Insulite or Therm-a-Rest pad
- Ground tarp
- Tent

**Optional Sleeping Gear**
- Air pillow
- Catalytic heater
- Foam pad for truck bed
- Mosquito netting
- Windshield light screen for RV

## FIRST AID

- Ace bandage
- Adhesive bandages
- After-Bite or ammonia
- Aspirin
- Athletic tape
- Biodegradable soap
- Caladryl or Tecnu
- Campho-Phenique gel
- First-aid cream
- Moleskin
- Mosquito repellent
- Neosporin
- Roller gauze
- Sterile gauze pads
- Sunscreen
- Thermometer
- Towelettes
- Tweezers

**Optional First Aid**

- Coins for emergency phone calls
- Extra set of matches
- Mirror for signaling
- Water purification system

## FISHING/RECREATIONAL GEAR

- Fishing reel with fish-line splitshot, snap swivels
- Fishing rod
- Knife
- Pliers

**Optional Recreation Gear**

- Backpacking cribbage board
- Deck of cards
- Knapsack for each person
- Stargazing chart
- Tree identification handbook

## MISCELLANEOUS

- Camera and film
- Compass
- Feminine hygiene products
- Flashlight
- Handkerchief
- Lantern and fuel
- Lip balm
- Maps
- Nylon rope for food hang
- Plastic garbage bags
- Toilet paper
- Toothbrush and toothpaste
- Watch

**Optional Miscellaneous**

- Binoculars
- Notebook and pen
- Towel

# MAP A1

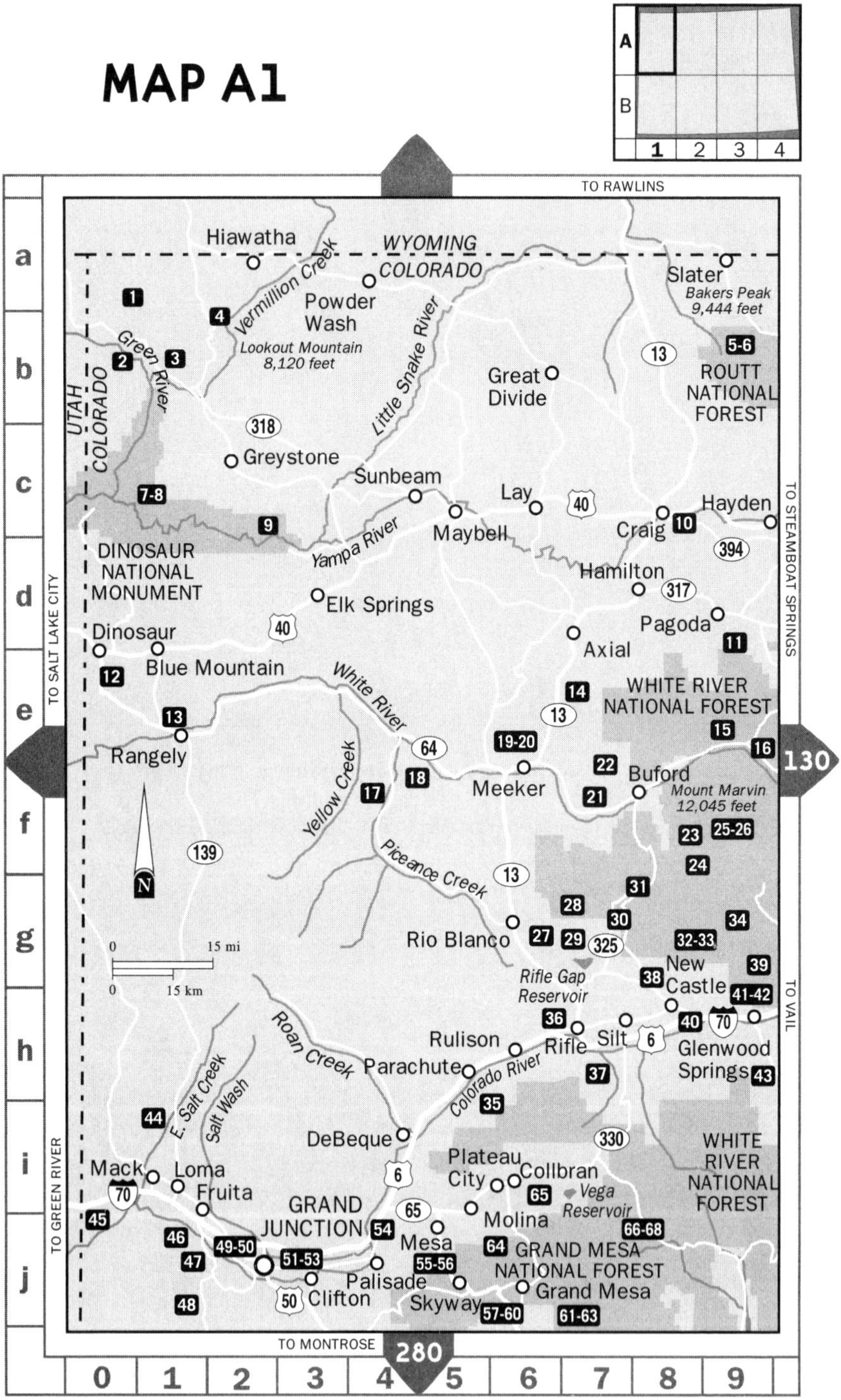

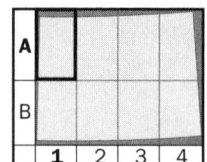

**WYOMING**
**COLORADO**

Hiawatha

1

4

Powder
Wash

*Vermillion Creek*

*Lookout Mountain*
*8,120 feet*

Slater
*Bakers Peak*
*9,444 feet*

13

5-6

ROUTT
NATIONAL
FOREST

2    3

*Green River*

318

Greystone

Sunbeam

Great
Divide

*Little Snake River*

*Yampa River*

Lay

40

Maybell

Hayden

Craig    10

394

UTAH
COLORADO

7-8

9

DINOSAUR
NATIONAL
MONUMENT

Hamilton

317

TO SALT LAKE CITY

TO STEAMBOAT SPRINGS

Dinosaur

40

Elk Springs

Axial

Pagoda

11

12

Blue Mountain

*White River*

WHITE RIVER
NATIONAL
FOREST

13

14

13

15

16    130

Rangely

64

19-20

18

17

Meeker

22    Buford

*Mount Marvin*
*12,045 feet*

21

*Yellow Creek*

139

23    25-26

24

N

*Piceance Creek*

13

31

28

30

34

0        15 mi

Rio Blanco

27    29    325

32-33

39

0        15 km

38    New
Castle

41-42

TO VAIL

*Rifle Gap*
*Reservoir*

40    70

*Roan Creek*

Rulison

36    Silt

6

Glenwood
Springs

Parachute

37

43

*Colorado River*

35

330

WHITE
RIVER
NATIONAL
FOREST

*E. Salt Creek*

*Salt Wash*

44

DeBeque

6

Plateau
City

Collbran

65

*Vega*
*Reservoir*

Mack

TO GREEN RIVER

45    70

Loma
Fruita

GRAND
JUNCTION

54    65

Molina

66-68

46

49-50    51-53

Mesa

64    GRAND MESA
NATIONAL FOREST

47

55-56

Palisade

48    50    Clifton

Skyway

Grand Mesa

57-60    61-63

# CHAPTER A1

## 1 Cold Spring Mountain   7

With more than 2,200 wild acres available for hiking, exploring, and wildlife viewing, Browns Park State Wildlife Area is a little-known mecca for outdoor enthusiasts. The camping area is about as remote and primitive as they come, with simple dirt lots designating the sites, but you're likely to have the place all to yourself. The region might seem stark at first, but take a little time to look around and you'll discover an intricate ecosystem brimming with unique plant and animal life.

**Location:** In Browns Park State Wildlife Area; map A1, grid a1.

**Campsites, facilities:** A primitive dispersed camping area is available. RVs are not recommended. There are no facilities. Leashed pets are permitted.

**Elevation:** 8,000 feet.

**Reservations, fees:** Reservations are not accepted. There is no fee.

**Open:** Year-round.

**Directions:** From U.S. 40 at Maybell, turn north on Hwy. 318 and drive approximately 40 miles. Turn right on County Rd. 10 and drive 17 miles north; then turn left on County Rd. 72 and go nine miles. When you come to a fork, bear left and continue four miles to the camping area.

**Contact:** Colorado Division of Wildlife, 711 Independent Ave., Grand Junction, CO 81505; tel. (970) 255-6100.

## 2 Swinging Bridge     7

Swinging Bridge is a sparse site set amid sagebrush and juniper, and is the smaller and more remote of the two camping areas in the wildlife refuge. Although Browns Park is naturally located in a semiarid setting, water pumped from the adjacent Green River allows it to remain an excellent habitat for more than 200 species of birds, including bald eagles, golden eagles, peregrine falcons, and various waterfowl. The refuge (not to be confused with Browns Park State Wildlife Area) covers 13,455 acres, with recreation ranging from boating and fishing on the Green River to hiking on rough backcountry trails. In the wintertime, visitors may spot moose, elk, deer, and pronghorn antelope.

**Location:** On the Green River in Browns Park National Wildlife Refuge; map A1, grid b0.

**Campsites, facilities:** There are 15 primitive sites for tents and RVs. Vault toilets and a few scattered fire grates are provided, but there is no drinking water. Some sites are wheelchair accessible. Leashed pets are permitted.

**Elevation:** 4,500 feet.

**Reservations, fees:** Reservations are not accepted. There is no fee.

**Open:** Year-round.

**Directions:** From U.S. 40 at Maybell, turn north on Hwy. 318 and drive approximately 63 miles to the Swinging Bridge entrance.

**Contact:** Browns Park National Wildlife Refuge, 1318 Hwy. 318, Maybell, CO 81640; tel. (970) 365-3613.

## **3** Crook      7

Of the two camping areas at Browns Park National Wildlife Refuge, Crook is the more pleasant, set in a leafy grove of cottonwood trees along the banks of the Green River. A variety of activities is available to visitors, including fishing (by bank or by nonmotorized boat, either on the river or at nearby Butch Cassidy Pond), hiking, picnicking, and bird-watching. The campground rarely fills up, with the exception of Memorial Day—and then, look out. The Browns Hole Homemaker's Club holds their annual dance that weekend, and if you want a site, you may just have to produce a quilt square or an apple pie.

**Location:** On the Green River in Browns Park National Wildlife Refuge; map A1, grid b1.

**Campsites, facilities:** There are 20 primitive sites for tents or RVs up to 20 feet long. Vault toilets are provided, but there are no other facilities or drinking water. Some sites are wheelchair accessible. Leashed pets are permitted.

**Elevation:** 4,500 feet.

**Reservations, fees:** Reservations are not accepted. There is no fee.

**Open:** Year-round.

**Directions:** From U.S. 40 at Maybell, turn north on Hwy. 318 and drive approximately 55 miles to the Crook entrance.

**Contact:** Browns Park National Wildlife Refuge, 1318 Hwy. 318, Maybell, CO 81640; tel. (970) 365-3613.

## **4** Irish Canyon     8

After a long, hot drive through the desert, Irish Canyon brushes over you like a cool breeze. The campground is set between the canyon's high granite walls and shaded by tall ponderosa pines. Although the campground is tiny, it is remote enough that you aren't likely to have company, even on summer weekends. Hike a little farther up the canyon and you'll be rewarded with close-up views of ancient petroglyphs all along the canyon walls.

**Location:** Near Browns Park National Wildlife Refuge; map A1, grid b2.

**Campsites, facilities:** There are three sites for tents or RVs up to 30 feet long. Picnic tables and a vault toilet are provided, but there is no drinking water or trash service. Leashed pets are permitted.

**Elevation:** 6,000 feet.

**Reservations, fees:** Reservations are not accepted. There is no fee.

**Open:** Year-round.

**Directions:** From U.S. 40 at Maybell, turn north on Hwy. 318 and drive approximately 45 miles. Turn right on County Rd. 10 and continue about eight miles north to the campground on the west side of the road.

**Contact:** Bureau of Land Management, Little Snake Resource Area, 455 Emerson St., Craig, CO 81625; tel. (970) 826-4000.

## **5** Freeman       7

Freeman Reservoir, a pretty 14-acre lake that provides good fishing for cutthroat trout, is just a short walk away from this campground. Only nonmotorized boating is allowed. Although the water may look mighty inviting after a long day of hiking, don't even think about taking a dunk—this is a high mountain lake and the water is icy, even in late summer. To the north and east are several trails suitable for hiking, horseback riding, and mountain biking.

**Location:** Near Freeman Reservoir in Routt National Forest; map A1, grid b9.

**Campsites, facilities:** There are 17 sites for tents or RVs up to 22 feet long. Drinking water, picnic tables, fire grills, and vault toilets are provided. Leashed pets are permitted.

**Elevation:** 8,800 feet.

**Reservations, fees:** Reservations are not accepted. Sites are $10 a night.

**Open:** June to mid-October.

**Directions:** From U.S. 40 at Craig, turn north on Hwy. 13 and drive 13.5 miles. Turn right on Forest Service Rd. 112 and continue eight miles east to the campground.

**Contact:** Routt National Forest, Hahns Peak-Bears Ears Ranger District, P.O. Box 771212, Steamboat Springs, CO 80477; tel. (970) 824-9438.

## 6 Sawmill Creek     6

Since it's small and fairly remote, this wooded camp avoids heavy traffic most of the year. A trail leads west out of the campground along Sawmill Creek into the Elkhead Mountains, where hikers can hook up with a large network of trails. Mountain bikers can head south along a four-wheel-drive road for about three miles to Angel Spring. Note: Bring plenty of cold-weather gear; the nights are chilly up here throughout the summer.

**Location:** In the Elkhead Mountains in Routt National Forest; map A1, grid b9.

**Campsites, facilities:** There are six sites for tents or RVs up to 22 feet long. Drinking water, picnic tables, fire grills, and vault toilets are provided. Leashed pets are permitted.

**Elevation:** 9,000 feet.

**Reservations, fees:** Reservations are not accepted. Sites are $10 a night.

**Open:** Mid-June to mid-October.

**Directions:** From U.S. 40 at Craig, turn north on Hwy. 13 and drive 13 miles. Turn right on Forest Service Rd. 110 and continue 12 miles north to the campground.

**Contact:** Routt National Forest, Hahns Peak-Bears Ears Ranger District, P.O. Box 771212, Steamboat Springs, CO 80477; tel. (970) 824-9438.

## 7 Gates of Lodore      8

Set in the depths of the spectacular Canyon of Lodore, this spot is best known as a put-in for rafters heading down the Green River. For information on permits or guided rafting trips, contact park headquarters for a list of local outfitters. Fishing on the river is limited; the water is murky, and several endangered species exist here. Check with a ranger first. Although the land surrounding the campground is intriguing, do not veer off marked roads or trails; this ancient, delicate landscape requires a hands-off approach.

**Location:** In Dinosaur National Monument; map A1, grid c1.

**Campsites, facilities:** There are 17 sites for tents or RVs up to 30 feet long. Note: RVs are permitted, but generally not recommended due to rough roads. Drinking water, picnic tables, fire grills, and vault toilets are provided. Leashed pets are permitted.

**Elevation:** 4,900 feet.

**Reservations, fees:** Reservations are not accepted. Sites are $6 a night.

**Open:** Year-round.

**Directions:** From U.S. 40 at Maybell, turn north on Hwy. 318 and drive approximately 40 miles. Look for a sign marked "Gates of Lodore" and turn left on an unpaved road. Continue about 10 miles to the campground. Note: The final access road is rough and can be impassable when wet. A high-clearance vehicle is recommended even in good weather.

**Contact:** Dinosaur National Monument, P.O. Box 210, Dinosaur, CO 81610; tel. (970) 374-3000.

## 🎣 Echo Park      10

Echo Park is one of the more dramatic spots in Dinosaur National Monument, an oasis set at the confluence of the Green and Yampa Rivers amid groves of hardy cottonwoods and backed by towering cliffs. Although access is somewhat difficult (impossible in the rain), it is well worth the drive; this camp is a gateway to some awe-inspiring scenery, as well as being a pristine and peaceful place to relax and enjoy nature's artistry. You can choose from riverside sites or scenic overlook sites that are connected to the river via short footpaths. The few walk-in sites offer more privacy, although you are required to separate from your car. Ask park rangers for tips on hiking trails and rafting trips. While in the park, be sure to head over to the Utah side and visit the famed Dinosaur Quarry, a natural showcase for fossils.

**Location:** In Dinosaur National Monument; map A1, grid c1.

**Campsites, facilities:** There are 14 primitive tent sites. Drinking water, picnic tables, fire grills, and vault toilets are provided. Leashed pets are permitted.

**Elevation:** 5,700 feet.

**Reservations, fees:** Reservations are not accepted. Sites are $6 a night.

**Open:** Memorial Day to Labor Day.

**Directions:** From the town of Dinosaur, travel 1.5 miles east on U.S. 40 to the park entrance. Take Harpers Corner Scenic Rd. for approximately 23 miles to Echo Park Rd. (unpaved), and continue for nine miles. Turn left at the sign for Echo Park and proceed five miles to the campground. Note: In rainy conditions, Echo Park Rd. is often inaccessible to vehicles.

**Contact:** Dinosaur National Monument, P.O. Box 210, Dinosaur, CO 81610; tel. (970) 374-3000.

## 🎣 Deerlodge Park   7

This camp is in one of the most remote and little-used areas of the park. It is set right on the Yampa River, with primitive dirt sites, fishing access, and a few scattered trees. Not much else is out here, but if you're looking for solitude, this is your place.

**Location:** In Dinosaur National Monument; map A1, grid c2.

**Campsites, facilities:** There are 10 primitive tent sites. Picnic tables, fire grills, and vault toilets are provided, but there is no drinking water. Leashed pets are permitted.

**Elevation:** 5,700 feet.

**Reservations, fees:** Reservations are not accepted. There is no fee.

**Open:** Memorial Day to Labor Day.

**Directions:** From Maybell, drive 19 miles west on U.S. 40 and look for a sign indicating Deerlodge Park. Turn right on the unpaved road and continue approximately 15 miles to the campground.

**Contact:** Dinosaur National Monument, P.O. Box 210, Dinosaur, CO 81610; tel. (970) 374-3000.

## 10 Craig KOA  6

The only game in town, this neat, well-kept camp provides the basics and a little more. Sites are dirt lanes separated by patches of grass with little to no shade. Extras include a nice "new frontier" playground, a heated swimming pool (in the summer months), plus an adults-only hot tub and sauna. Tours of area attractions can be arranged on-site. Fishing and golf are nearby.

**Location:** In Craig; map A1, grid c8.

**Campsites, facilities:** There are 17 tent sites and 96 sites for RVs of any length, most with full hookups. Drinking water, picnic tables, fire grills, and bathrooms with hot showers are provided. Laundry facilities, a waste disposal station, recreation room, playground, swimming pool, hot tub, sauna, and public phone are available. Some facilities are wheelchair accessible. Leashed pets are permitted.

**Elevation:** 6,500 feet.

**Reservations, fees:** Reservations are accepted; phone (800) KOA-5095. Sites are $18-24 a night.

**Open:** Year-round.

**Directions:** From the junction of Hwy. 13 N. and U.S. 40 in Craig, drive two miles east on U.S. 40. The campground is on the south side of the highway.

**Contact:** Craig KOA, 2800 E. U.S. 40, Craig, CO 81625; tel. (970) 824-5105.

## 11 Indian Run State Wildlife Refuge      5

Covering more than 2,000 acres of sage flats, spruce forest, and cottonwood-lined creeks, this park gets heavy use from hunters and anglers during hunting season (roughly September through December). In the summer, however, it can be an ideal spot to enjoy crowd-free hiking and wildlife observation. Among the local residents are several species of native birds, as well as elk, deer, blue grouse, and even an occasional bear. You can hike, horseback ride, or mountain bike on old roads that run through the refuge. Some of the creeks border private property, so be on the lookout for signs when you're exploring.

**Location:** South of Craig; map A1, grid d9.

**Campsites, facilities:** Dispersed camping is allowed anywhere in the refuge. Vault toilets are provided, but there are no other facilities or drinking water. A horse corral is available for public use. Leashed pets are permitted.

**Elevation:** 6,500 feet.

**Reservations, fees:** Reservations are not accepted. There is no fee.

**Open:** Year-round.

**Directions:** From U.S. 40 at Craig, turn south on Hwy. 13 and drive 14 miles. Turn left on Hwy. 317 and continue 12 miles east; then turn right on County Rd. 67 and go six more miles south to the park entrance.

**Contact:** Colorado Division of Wildlife, 711 Independent Ave., Grand Junction, CO 81505; tel. (970) 255-6100.

## 12 Blue Mountain Village      3

Although it's hot, dry, and virtually devoid of scenery, this RV park is large and well maintained, with roomy, even sites. It's the first stop past the Utah-Colorado border on U.S. 40, only a few miles from Dinosaur National Monument Headquarters. The Green River, which offers fishing and white-water rafting, is a short drive north.

**Location:** In Dinosaur; map A1, grid e0.

**Campsites, facilities:** There are 100 full-hookup sites for tents or RVs of any length. Drinking water, picnic tables, fire grills, and bathrooms with hot showers are provided. Laundry facilities and a public phone are available. Some facilities are wheelchair accessible. Leashed pets are permitted.

**Elevation:** 5,900 feet.

**Reservations, fees:** Reservations are not necessary. Sites are $16.50 a night.

**Open:** April to November.

**Directions:** From the junction of U.S. 40 and Hwy. 64 in Dinosaur, drive one-half mile east on Hwy. 64. Turn west on 7th St. and continue a short distance to the campground.

**Contact:** Blue Mountain Village, P.O. Box 7, Dinosaur, CO 81610; tel. (970) 374-2747.

## 13 Rangely Camper Park     5

Set in the tiny town of Rangely near the White River, this oft-overlooked camp is an excellent option for folks who require more developed facilities than those offered by the primitive camps in the region. It's cool and fairly quiet despite its proximity to the highway. A small city park is adjacent to the sites, and nearby Kinney Reservoir offers boating and fishing access. If you've been exploring the hot, sometimes mucky territory of Dinosaur National Monument, the showers alone might seem worth the $5-10 fee.

**Location:** South of Dinosaur National Monument; map A1, grid e1.

**Campsites, facilities:** There are 25 sites for tents or RVs of any length. Drinking water and rest rooms with hot showers are provided. Tables and grills are located at the adjacent city park. Electric hookups are available. Leashed pets are permitted.

**Elevation:** 4,800 feet.

**Reservations, fees:** Reservations are not accepted. Sites are $5-10 per night.

**Open:** Open approximately May to November.

**Directions:** From Hwy. 64 in the town of Rangely, turn north at the sign for the Camper Park and continue one block to the park entrance.

**Contact:** Rangely Recreation Center, 611 S. Stanolind Ave., Rangely, CO 81648; tel. (970) 675-8211.

## 14 Jensen State Wildlife Area    5

This 6,000-acre wildlife area is home to several species of game, including deer, elk, blue grouse, and black bear—all ardently chased by hunters in the fall. For those who prefer to shoot with a camera, the open, grassy terrain provides a perfect stage for high plains sunsets and blooming desert wildflowers. Camping is primitive, with plain dirt sites carved out of random spots on the prairie.

**Location:** Northeast of Meeker; map A1, grid e7.

**Campsites, facilities:** Dispersed camping is permitted in designated areas throughout the property. There are no other facilities or drinking water. Leashed pets are permitted.

**Elevation:** 7,500 feet.

**Reservations, fees:** Reservations are not accepted. There is no fee.

**Open:** Mid-July through November.

**Directions:** From Meeker, drive nine miles northeast on Hwy. 13 to the entrance, located at the junction of Hwy. 13 and County Rd. 30.

**Contact:** Colorado Division of Wildlife, 711 Independent Ave., Grand Junction, CO 81505; tel. (970) 255-6100.

## 15 North Fork      7

This pretty, wooded camp is across the road from the North Fork of the White River, an icy, clear stream that provides excellent trout fishing. West of camp is a worthwhile trail that runs along Long Park Creek; to the southwest are numerous trails routed into the Flat Tops Wilderness. All are suitable for hikers and horses, but no mountain bikes are permitted past the wilderness boundary.

**Location:** On the North Fork of the White River in White River National Forest; map A1, grid e9.

**Campsites, facilities:** There are 39 sites for tents or RVs of any length. Picnic tables, fire grills, and vault toilets are provided, but there is no drinking water. Leashed pets are permitted.

**Elevation:** 8,000 feet.

**Reservations, fees:** Reservations are accepted; phone (877) 444-6777. There's an $8.65 reservation fee. You may also reserve sites at website: www.reserveusa.com. Sites are $10 a night.

**Open:** Memorial Day to November.

**Directions:** From Meeker, drive two miles east on Hwy. 13, turn right on County Rd. 8, and drive approximately 34 miles to the campground.

**Contact:** White River National Forest, Blanco Ranger District, 317 E. Market St., Meeker, CO 81641; tel. (970) 878-4039.

## 16 Vaughn Lake      7

Secluded and pretty, Vaughn Lake is set high in the midst of Routt National Forest, just north of the Flat Tops Wilderness. Sites are situated well back from the lake, sheltered by a mixed conifer forest. Trout fishing and a few easy hiking trails are available within walking distance. If you desire a steeper challenge, head a couple miles back north on Forest Hwy. 16, turn right on Forest Service Rd. 967, and you'll end up at a trailhead that winds steeply through the wilderness to several high mountain lakes.

**Location:** West of Yampa in Routt National Forest; map A1, grid e9.

**Campsites, facilities:** There are six sites for tents or RVs up to 22 feet long. Picnic tables, fire grills, and vault toilets are provided, but there is no drinking water. A boat ramp is nearby. Leashed pets are permitted.

**Elevation:** 9,500 feet.

**Reservations, fees:** Reservations are not accepted. Sites are $7 a night.

**Open:** Memorial Day through November.

**Directions:** From Hwy. 131 at Yampa, turn west on County Rd. 132 and drive approximately six miles, turn left on Forest Hwy. 16, and continue about 28 miles to the campground.

**Contact:** Routt National Forest, Yampa Ranger District, P.O. Box 7, Yampa, CO 80483; tel. (970) 638-4516.

## ⬛ Piceance State Wildlife Area     5

Open and wild, Piceance is better known to hunters than to recreational campers, but it's becoming a popular spot for wildlife observation. If you hit it right, you might catch sight of some of the native species: deer, elk, rabbit, blue grouse, sage grouse, dove, and diverse varieties of waterfowl. Camping is basic and primitive, with a number of dispersed areas both in open grassland and forested settings.

**Location:** Southwest of Meeker; map A1, grid f4.

**Campsites, facilities:** Dispersed tent camping is permitted in designated areas. Drinking water and a vault toilet are provided. Leashed pets are permitted.

**Elevation:** 7,700 feet.

**Reservations, fees:** Reservations are not accepted. There is no fee.

**Open:** Year-round.

**Directions:** From Meeker, drive 20 miles west on Hwy. 64 and turn south on County Rd. 5 (Piceance Creek Rd.). Continue seven miles to the Dry Fork turnoff and follow the signs for three miles to the entrance station.

**Contact:** Colorado Division of Wildlife, 711 Independent Ave., Grand Junction, CO 81505; tel. (970) 255-6100.

## ⬛ Rio Blanco Lake
## State Wildlife Area       5

Camping in a parking lot is not my idea of a great wilderness adventure, but in this case, being so close to such a lovely lake just might be worth it. The wildlife area encompasses 383 acres, at the center of which is Rio Blanco Lake, a long, oblong reservoir that offers fishing for a variety of species including largemouth bass, northern pike, channel catfish, and crappie. Power boating is also permitted, so it's a popular spot for waterskiing and PWC riding. The Division of Wildlife has attempted to solve the angler vs. water-skier conflict by prohibiting waterskiing from mid-March to mid-June. Waterfowl hunting is permitted.

**Location:** West of Meeker; map A1, grid f4.

**Campsites, facilities:** Camping is restricted to the parking areas. A vault toilet is provided, but there are no other facilities or drinking water. A boat ramp is available.

Leashed pets are permitted.

**Elevation:** 5,700 feet.

**Reservations, fees:** Reservations are not accepted. There is no fee.

**Open:** Year-round.

**Directions:** From Meeker, drive 20 miles west on Hwy. 64 to the lake.

**Contact:** Colorado Division of Wildlife, 711 Independent Ave., Grand Junction, CO 81505; tel. (970) 255-6100.

## 19 Rimrock Campground   5

Although this camp is right on the edge of noisy Hwy. 64, its saving grace is the view: a gorgeous, sweeping panorama of the rolling, conifer-clad mountains. The sites are smack in the middle of hot, dry, scrub country, with a few cottonwoods and pines providing partial shade.

**Location:** West of Meeker; map A1, grid f6.

**Campsites, facilities:** There are 33 full-hookup sites for tents or RVs of any length. Drinking water, picnic tables, fire grills, and bathrooms with hot showers are provided. Laundry facilities, waste disposal station, and public phone are available. Leashed pets are permitted.

**Elevation:** 6,300 feet.

**Reservations, fees:** Reservations are recommended. Sites are $12-16 a night.

**Open:** April to mid-November.

**Directions:** From Meeker, drive 2.5 miles west on Hwy. 64 to the campground.

**Contact:** Rimrock Campground, 73179 Hwy. 64, Meeker, CO 81641; tel. (970) 878-4486.

## 20 Stagecoach Campground and RV Park      6

Like nearby Rimrock Campground, Stagecoach practically sits on the highway, but at least here the sound of rushing water deflects some of the noise from passing cars. Set directly on the banks of the White River, each campsite is in a grassy area, many with shade trees. Just a short drive away is White River National Forest, with opportunities for hiking, horseback riding, and mountain biking.

**Location:** On the White River; map A1, grid f6.

**Campsites, facilities:** There are 50 sites for tents or RVs of any length. Full hookups are available. Drinking water, picnic tables, fire grills, and bathrooms with hot showers are provided. Also on the property are laundry facilities, a waste disposal station, and cabins. Leashed pets are permitted.

**Elevation:** 6,000 feet.

**Reservations, fees:** Reservations are accepted. Sites are $12-17 a night.

**Open:** Mid-April to November.

**Directions:** From Meeker, drive two miles west on Hwy. 64. The campground is at the junction of Hwy. 13 and Hwy. 64.

**Contact:** Stagecoach Campground and RV Park, P.O. Box 995, Meeker, CO 81641; tel. (970) 878-4334.

**21** Oak Ridge State Wildlife Area     4

The Oak Ridge State Wildlife Area covers 9,325 acres of flat, scrubby land and is home to a variety of huntable wildlife, including deer, elk, rabbit, blue grouse, and dove. The designated camping areas are very primitive, but they provide a decent home base while you enjoy a full day of viewing wildlife or fishing in Sleepy Cat Ponds.

**Location:** East of Meeker; map A1, grid f7.
**Campsites, facilities:** Dispersed camping is permitted in designated areas. Drinking water and a vault toilet are provided. A boat ramp is available. Leashed pets are permitted.
**Elevation:** 6,500 feet.
**Reservations, fees:** Reservations are not accepted. There is no fee.
**Open:** Mid-July to December.
**Directions:** From Meeker, drive two miles northeast on Hwy. 13, turn right on County Rd. 8, and continue 17 miles east to the property boundary.
**Contact:** Colorado Division of Wildlife, 711 Independent Ave., Grand Junction, CO 81505; tel. (970) 255-6100.

**22** Pollard's Ute Lodge       7

For a developed campground, Pollard's provides an amazingly wilderness-like feel, with sites set next to a private alpine lake—a pretty fishing spot nestled in dense spruce and pine forest. Your hosts can arrange for guided fishing or hunting trips if you wish. The camp is just a short drive from trailheads into the Flat Tops Wilderness, where there are over 150 miles of paths for hiking or horseback riding. Mountain biking trails are available.

**Location:** North of the Flat Tops Wilderness; map A1, grid f7.
**Campsites, facilities:** There are 12 full-hookup sites for tents or RVs of any length. Drinking water, picnic tables, fire grills, and bathrooms with hot showers are provided. A waste disposal station and cabins are available. Some facilities are wheelchair accessible. Leashed pets are permitted.
**Elevation:** 8,000 feet.
**Reservations, fees:** Reservations are accepted. Sites are $10-20 a night.
**Open:** Mid-May to November.
**Directions:** From Meeker, drive two miles northeast on Hwy. 13, turn right on County Rd. 8, and drive approximately 27 miles east. Turn north (left) on County Rd. 75 and proceed 1.5 miles to the campground.
**Contact:** Pollard's Ute Lodge, 393 County Rd. 75, Meeker, CO 81641; tel. (888) 414-2022 or (970) 878-4669.

**23** South Fork       10

While many campgrounds are merely one-night stopovers on the way to vacation destinations, others are vacation destinations in their own right. South Fork is definitely the latter. It's beautiful, quiet, and secluded, tucked under towering evergreens next to the South Fork of the White River. Recreation includes fishing in the river (there's a perfect access spot at the campground, with a wheelchair-accessible bridge) or venturing by horse or foot into the Flat Tops Wilderness. One of the best trails in the area runs along the river through scenic South Fork Canyon. One reader alerted me that this campground has become increasingly popular in the past couple of years, so expect plenty of company.

**Location:** On the South Fork of the White River in White River National Forest; map A1, grid f8.

**Campsites, facilities:** There are 18 sites for tents or RVs up to 20 feet long. Drinking water, picnic tables, fire grills, and vault toilets are provided. Some facilities are wheelchair accessible. Leashed pets are permitted.

**Elevation:** 8,000 feet.

**Reservations, fees:** Reservations are not accepted. Sites are $10 a night.

**Open:** Mid-May to mid-November.

**Directions:** From Meeker, drive two miles northeast on Hwy. 13, turn right on County Rd. 8, and continue about 18 miles east. At County Rd. 10, turn south and drive 12 miles to the campground.

**Contact:** White River National Forest, Blanco Ranger District, 317 E. Market St., Meeker, CO 81641; tel. (970) 878-4039.

## **24** Meadow Lake      7

Meadow Lake's biggest draw is its fishing, with superb prospects for brook and rainbow trout. The lake is small, but pretty and clear, ringed by conifers and providing a peaceful place for nonmotorized boating. Campsites are cozy, huddled in a forest just a short walk from the lakeshore. A small boat ramp is located at the U.S. Forest Service fishing access area. To the north are trails routed into the Flat Tops Wilderness.

**Location:** North of Glenwood Springs in White River National Forest; map A1, grid f8.

**Campsites, facilities:** There are 10 sites for tents or RVs up to 16 feet long. Drinking water, picnic tables, fire grills, and a vault toilet are provided. A primitive boat ramp is nearby. Leashed pets are permitted.

**Elevation:** 9,525 feet.

**Reservations, fees:** Reservations are not accepted. Sites are $10 a night.

**Open:** June to September.

**Directions:** From Rifle, drive three miles northeast on Hwy. 13. Turn right on Hwy. 325 and go 6.5 miles; then turn right on County Rd. 225 and continue seven miles. Turn left on Buford-New Castle Rd., drive 18 miles to Hiner Springs, turn right on Forest Service Rd. 601, and continue three miles to Forest Service Rd. 823. Turn right and proceed to the campground.

**Contact:** White River National Forest, Rifle Ranger District, 0094 County Rd. 204, Rifle, CO 81650; tel. (970) 625-2371.

## **25** Marvine       7

Wooded and quiet, this campground is set along Marvine Creek near the northern border of the Flat Tops Wilderness. Two trails run from camp into the wilderness: one heads about five miles and 1,100 feet up to Marvine Lakes (there's good trout fishing), and another veers off to the east where it hooks into a large network of trails. Since it offers special facilities for horses, the camp is an obvious choice for folks planning a wilderness pack trip.

**Location:** East of Meeker in White River National Forest; map A1, grid f9.

**Campsites, facilities:** There are 25 sites for tents or RVs up to 30 feet long. Some sites are adjacent to horse corrals. Drinking water, picnic tables, fire grills, and vault toilets are provided. Leashed pets are permitted.

**Elevation:** 8,200 feet.

**Reservations, fees:** Reservations are not accepted. Sites are $11 a night, plus $5 for a horse corral.

**Open:** June to September.

**Directions:** From Meeker, drive two miles northeast on Hwy. 13, turn right on County Rd. 8, and continue approximately 29 miles east. Turn south on County Rd. 12 (Marvine Creek Rd.) and drive about four miles to the campground.

**Contact:** White River National Forest, Blanco Ranger District, 317 E. Market St., Meeker, CO 81641; tel. (970) 878-4039.

## **26** East Marvine      7

Located just down the road from the Marvine camp, this lesser-known spot is small and pretty, circled by conifers and aspens. Fishing is available in nearby Marvine Creek, and you can ride a horse or hike into the Flat Tops Wilderness via one of the trails out of Marvine.

**Location:** East of Meeker in White River National Forest; map A1, grid f9.

**Campsites, facilities:** There are seven sites for tents or RVs up to 30 feet long. Drinking water, picnic tables, fire grills, and vault toilets are provided. Some sites are adjacent to horse corrals. Leashed pets are permitted.

**Elevation:** 8,200 feet.

**Reservations, fees:** Reservations are not accepted. Sites are $11 a night, plus $5 for a horse corral.

**Open:** June to September.

**Directions:** From Meeker, drive two miles northeast on Hwy. 13, turn right on County Rd. 8, and continue approximately 29 miles east. Turn south on County Rd. 12 (Marvine Creek Rd.) and drive about 4.5 miles to the campground.

**Contact:** White River National Forest, Blanco Ranger District, 317 E. Market St., Meeker, CO 81641; tel. (970) 878-4039.

## **27** West Rifle Creek State Wildlife Area    5

Since camping here is outlawed in the summer, West Rifle Creek gets bypassed by a large proportion of the tourists. September still offers prime camping weather, however, and this may be one of the few spots around that you'll have all to yourself (before hunting season, anyway). Some of Colorado's larger native species, including bobcats, mountain lions, and black bears, have been spotted here (they're routinely hunted on the property). Keep your eyes open, and if you spot one of these gigantic critters, worship from a distance.

**Location:** Near Rifle Gap State Park; map A1, grid g6.

**Campsites, facilities:** Dispersed tent camping is permitted anywhere on the property. There are no facilities. Leashed pets are permitted.

**Elevation:** 5,700 feet.

**Reservations, fees:** Reservations are not accepted. There is no fee.

**Open:** September to December 31.

**Directions:** From Rifle, drive three miles northeast on Hwy. 13 to Hwy. 325. Turn right and continue six miles to County Rd. 252; then turn left and drive past Rifle Gap Reservoir to the wildlife area.

**Contact:** Colorado Division of Wildlife, 711 Independent Ave., Grand Junction, CO 81505; tel. (970) 255-6100.

## 28 Three Forks     7

In the summer, when nearby Rifle Falls State Park is a crowded jam of tourists, Three Forks is likely to be silent and serene. It's set along narrow Three Forks Creek, just past the national forest boundary, with small sites in a mixed conifer and aspen forest. A trail winds north of camp along the creek, with several good fishing access spots.

**Location:** North of Glenwood Springs in White River National Forest; map A1, grid g7.

**Campsites, facilities:** There are four sites for tents or RVs under 16 feet long. Drinking water, picnic tables, fire grills, and vault toilets are provided. Leashed pets are permitted.

**Elevation:** 6,000 feet.

**Reservations, fees:** Reservations are not accepted. Sites are $11 a night.

**Open:** June to September.

**Directions:** From Rifle, drive three miles northeast on Hwy. 13 to Hwy. 325. Turn right and continue 11 miles, through Rifle Falls State Park, to the White River National Forest boundary. Continue north for three miles on Forest Service Rd. 825 to the campground.

**Contact:** White River National Forest, Rifle Ranger District, 0094 County Rd. 204, Rifle, CO 81650; tel. (970) 625-2371.

## 29 Rifle Gap State Park       9

Rifle Gap Reservoir gets its name from the uniquely tapered split in the canyon you drive through to reach it. The reservoir is long and narrow, stretching 360 crystal-clear surface acres from east to west, and is a popular haven for water enthusiasts of all sorts. All boating is allowed, including waterskiing and PWC riding, with often-excellent conditions for sailing and windsurfing. Anglers can choose between cutthroat, rainbow, and brook trout, walleye, or largemouth bass. There are designated fishing access points all along the southern shore. Swimming is best at the beach on the west side of the reservoir where the water is warmer and shallower. The campsites are spread out along the northern shore of the lake and offer wide, open sites and broad mountain views. One drawback: the crowds. The combination of spectacular scenery and unrestricted water sports is relatively rare in Colorado; consequently, the park is often booked to capacity throughout the summer.

**Location:** North of Rifle; map A1, grid g7.

**Campsites, facilities:** There are 46 sites for tents or RVs of any length. Drinking water, picnic tables, fire grills, and vault toilets are provided. A waste disposal station and a boat ramp are available nearby. Leashed pets are permitted.

**Elevation:** 6,200 feet.

**Reservations, fees:** Reservations are accepted. Phone (303) 470-1144 or (800) 678-CAMP (800-678-2267) outside the Denver Metro area; there's a $7 reservation fee. Sites are $10 a night, and there's a $4 entrance fee.

**Open:** Year-round.

**Directions:** From Rifle, drive three miles northeast on Hwy. 13 to Hwy. 325. Turn right and continue six miles to the park entrance.

**Contact:** Rifle Gap State Park, 0050 County Rd. 219, Rifle, CO 81650; tel. (970) 625-1607.

## 30 Rifle Falls State Park      9

After driving through the hot, dry Interstate 70 corridor, Rifle Falls State Park comes as a lush, gorgeous surprise. The park's centerpiece is Rifle Falls, a triple waterfall surrounded by sumptuous, almost tropical greenery. A well-maintained hiking trail links the falls to the campground, which sits to the south along East Rifle Creek. The sites are wide, cool, and grassy, bordered by lots of cottonwoods and native wildflowers in a quiet, serene setting. Trout fishing is available in the creek. This is one of the more beautiful campgrounds in the state and quite popular—reserve well in advance. An inside tip: On the stretch of road between the park and the nearby fish hatchery, keep an eye out for a small dirt parking lot on the right side. From there you can take a short walkway to a perfect view of a cluster of tiny waterfalls.

**Location:** North of Rifle; map A1, grid g7.

**Campsites, facilities:** There are 18 sites for tents or RVs of any length. Drinking water, picnic tables, fire grills, and vault toilets are provided. One campsite is wheelchair accessible. Leashed pets are permitted.

**Elevation:** 6,800 feet.

**Reservations, fees:** Reservations are accepted. Phone (303) 470-1144 or (800) 678-CAMP (800-678-2267) outside the Denver Metro area; there's a $7 reservation fee. Sites are $10 a night, and there's a $4 entrance fee.

**Open:** Year-round.

**Directions:** From Rifle, drive three miles northeast on Hwy. 13 to Hwy. 325. Turn right and continue 10 miles to the park entrance.

**Contact:** Rifle Falls State Park, 0050 County Rd. 219, Rifle, CO 81650; tel. (970) 625-1607.

## 31 Rifle Mountain Park      9

This little-known gem is an excellent alternative to the crowded state park campgrounds in the area. It's simply beautiful, with a choice of open or shaded sites dispersed throughout the park, many of them situated along Rifle Creek. Activities abound, with numerous trails for hiking or horseback riding, jeep roads to explore, and ice caves for spelunkers. Rock climbing on the surrounding canyon walls is rumored to be some of the best in the state. The log-and-stone lodge is often rented for weddings or family parties; it's also perfect for a group camping party or reunion. A word of caution for owners of large RVs: Although there is no length restriction in the campground, turning around in the park's box canyon can be tricky; and be aware that the access road is gravel, not paved.

**Location:** North of Rifle Falls State Park; map A1, grid g7.

**Campsites, facilities:** There are 30 sites available for tents or RVs of any length and one group camping area. Drinking water, vault toilets, picnic tables, and fire rings are provided. A community lodge is available for rent. Leashed pets are permitted.

**Elevation:** 7,250 feet.

**Reservations, fees:** Reservations are not accepted. Single sites are $7; the group camping area is $15-25, depending on the number of cars in your party.

**Open:** Open from mid-February to mid-December.

**Directions:** From Rifle, drive three miles northeast on Hwy. 13 to Hwy. 325. Turn right and continue approximately 14 miles to the park entrance (about four miles past the entrance to Rifle Falls State Park).

**Contact:** City of Rifle, P.O. Box 1908, Rifle, CO 81650; tel. (970) 625-2121.

## 32 Supply Basin     6

Though pleasant, this camp offers only the bare basics and seven tiny sites partially shaded by pine trees. At nearly 11,000 feet, the nights can get mighty chilly, so pack up your thermals and fleece. While you're at it, throw in plenty of drinking water and a few trash bags—neither is available at the campground. Heart Lake is nearby, providing good fishing for brook trout. Bank fishing is difficult due to a shallow shoreline, but nonmotorized boats are permitted.

**Location:** Near Heart Lake in White River National Forest; map A1, grid g8.

**Campsites, facilities:** There are five tent sites and two sites for tents or RVs up to 25 feet long. Picnic tables, fire grills, and a vault toilet are provided, but there is no drinking water or trash service. Leashed pets are permitted.

**Elevation:** 10,760 feet.

**Reservations, fees:** Reservations are not accepted. No fee is required, but a donation of $6 a night is requested.

**Open:** July to September.

**Directions:** From Eagle, drive 12 miles west on Interstate 70 to the Dotsero exit. Turn north on Colorado River Rd. (look for the signs for Sweetwater). Drive about two miles, turn left on Forest Service Rd. 600 (Coffee Pot Rd.), and continue 28 miles to Forest Service Rd. 601. Turn left and continue one mile to the campground.

**Contact:** White River National Forest, Eagle Ranger District, 125 W. 5th St., P.O. Box 720, Eagle, CO 81631; tel. (970) 328-6388.

## 33 Klines Folly    7

This small, tent-only campground is set near the edge of a little pond on the border of a pretty subalpine meadow surrounded by spruce and fir trees. Nice! Nearby Heart Lake is stocked regularly with brook trout and provides decent fishing if you have a small boat. Several four-wheel-drive roads in the area lead into more remote stretches of the forest.

**Location:** Near Heart Lake in White River National Forest; map A1, grid g8.

**Campsites, facilities:** Four tent sites are located just past a central parking area. The parking area is not suitable for RVs. Picnic tables, fire grills, and a vault toilet are provided, but there is no drinking water or trash service. Leashed pets are permitted.

**Elevation:** 10,660 feet.

**Reservations, fees:** Reservations are not accepted. No fee is required, but a donation of $6 a night is requested.

**Open:** July to September.

**Directions:** From Eagle, drive 12 miles west on Interstate 70 to the Dotsero exit. Turn north on Colorado River Rd. (look for the signs for Sweetwater). Drive approximately two miles, turn left on Forest Service Rd. 600 (Coffee Pot Rd.), and continue 28 miles to Forest Service Rd. 601. Turn left and continue one-half mile to the campground.

**Contact:** White River National Forest, Eagle Ranger District, 125 W. 5th St., P.O. Box 720, Eagle, CO 81631; tel. (970) 328-6388.

## 34 Deep Lake      8

The guest register at this site is impressive: Ute hunting parties and pioneer travelers headed to Meeker camped here, and later, a survey group headed by Teddy Roosevelt. Since then a hotel and a U.S. Forest Service station have been built and torn down, but little else has changed—the lake is still a deep mountain blue, and the views of surrounding pristine meadows and Deep Canyon remain as they have for hundreds of years. The campsites, many of them shaded, are set amid scattered spruce and fir, with a few right on the lake's edge for prime trout fishing access. For a scenic hike, head up to the Ute Trail (which doubles as a four-wheel-drive road), located to the north of the lake. In the late 1990s the U.S. Forest Service added drinking water to this site.

**Location:** North of Glenwood Springs in White River National Forest; map A1, grid g9.

**Campsites, facilities:** There are 35 sites for tents or RVs up to 35 feet long. Drinking water, picnic tables, fire grills, and vault toilets are provided. A small boat ramp is available for nonmotorized boats. Leashed pets are permitted.

**Elevation:** 10,580 feet.

**Reservations, fees:** Reservations are not accepted. No fee is required, but a donation of $8 a night is requested.

**Open:** July to September.

**Directions:** From Eagle, drive 12 miles west on Interstate 70 to the Dotsero exit. Turn north on Colorado River Rd. (look for the signs for Sweetwater). Drive approximately two miles, turn left on Forest Service Rd. 600 (Coffee Pot Rd.), and continue 29 miles to the turnoff for the campground on the right.

**Contact:** White River National Forest, Eagle Ranger District, 125 W. 5th St., P.O. Box 720, Eagle, CO 81631; tel. (970) 328-6388.

## 35 Battlement Mesa RV Park

       5

Battlement Mesa RV Park is essentially a year-round residence facility with a smattering of seasonal sites. It's close to the highway, and although the road noise can be intrusive, at least you get a view of the valley and surrounding mountains. The campsites are concrete and gravel pads with full hookups and a few scattered trees. On-site facilities are well maintained but limited; as compensation, the owners provide their guests with access to a recreation center three miles away that offers amenities, including a golf course, fishing access, gym facilities, and a paved walking/biking path. Campers can be shuttled to a nearby activity center that offers a golf course, swimming pool, hot tub, sauna, gym, paved hiking trails, and organized activities ranging from fishing to golf. Phone hookups are available for campers with modems.

**Location:** Near Parachute; map A1, grid i5.

**Campsites, facilities:** There are 110 sites for RVs of any length, most with full hookups, and a separate area for tents. Drinking water, picnic tables, fire grills, and bathrooms with hot showers are provided. Laundry facilities, a waste disposal station, and a public phone are available. The campground facilities are wheelchair accessible. Leashed pets are permitted.

**Elevation:** 5,200 feet.

**Reservations, fees:** Reservations are accepted. Sites are $10-20 a night.

**Open:** Year-round.

**Directions:** From Interstate 70 west of Rifle, take Exit 75 and follow the signs with the RV symbol to the campground.

**Contact:** Battlement Mesa RV Park, P.O. Box 6000, Battlement Mesa, CO 81636; tel. (800) 275-5687 (ask to be connected to the RV Park) or (970) 285-7023.

## 36 6 & 24 Trailer Park

  3

In case you were wondering, 6 & 24 refers to the state highways on which this trailer park is located. Because the park is usually filled with long-term residents, it only allows overnighters when space is available, so it's hit-or-miss if you're passing through. Sites are fenced, surrounded by a liberal sprinkling of shade trees. Restaurants and other amenities are located 1.5 miles away in downtown Rifle, and fishing access is available at the nearby Colorado River.

**Location:** In Rifle; map A1, grid h7.

**Campsites, facilities:** There are 20 sites for RVs of any length. Tents are not permitted. Water and sewer hookups are provided, but no other facilities are available. No pets are permitted.

**Elevation:** 5,345 feet.

**Reservations, fees:** Reservations are not accepted. Sites are $10-15 per night.

**Open:** Year-round.

**Directions:** From Interstate 70 west of Glenwood Springs, take Exit 90 and turn north toward Rifle. Turn west at the stoplight and drive approximately one mile to the park.

**Contact:** 6 & 24 Trailer Park, 24341 Hwy. 6, Unit 27, Rifle, CO 81650; tel. (970) 625-5102.

## **37** Viking RV Park     6

This 50-acre park offers wide, grassy campsites beside the sloping banks of the beautiful Colorado River. Its unique feature is a heron rookery located to the east of the park and easily seen from the grounds. Although the park is only a short distance from the highway, the river blocks much of the traffic noise, ensuring a peaceful night's sleep. There is no formal boat ramp, but small boats can be launched easily from the riverbank. Trout fishing in this section of the Colorado River is rumored to be excellent.

**Location:** On the Colorado River west of Glenwood Springs; map A1, grid h7.

**Campsites, facilities:** There are 20 tent sites and 60 sites for RVs of any length, most with full hookups. Drinking water, picnic tables, fire grills, and bathrooms with hot showers are provided. Laundry facilities and a public phone are available. Leashed pets are permitted.

**Elevation:** 5,400 feet.

**Reservations, fees:** Reservations are accepted. Sites are $15-20 a night.

**Open:** Year-round.

**Directions:** From Interstate 70 west of Glenwood Springs, take the Silt exit (Exit 97) and turn south on the river frontage road. Continue about one-half mile to the campground entrance.

**Contact:** Viking RV Park, P.O. Box 190, Silt, CO 81652; tel. (970) 876-2443.

## **38** New Castle-Glenwood Springs KOA     7

I generally consider "KOA" and "wilderness" contradictory terms, but they work together in this spot. Although well known, the campground is far enough off the highway to seem isolated, with hiking trails into the adjacent forest providing an opportunity for a mini backcountry expedition. The sites are private and comfortable, huddled under lofty firs and flanked by East Elk Creek, a stream that is regularly stocked with trout. Weekend breakfasts and nightly suppers are available at the on-site cafe.

**Location:** North of New Castle; map A1, grid g8.

**Campsites, facilities:** There are 51 sites for tents or RVs of any length. Drinking water, picnic tables, fire grills, and bathrooms with hot showers are provided. Electric hookups, laundry facilities, a waste disposal station, restaurant, and game room are also available. Rental cabins, one of which is wheelchair accessible, are on the property. Leashed pets are permitted.

**Elevation:** 6,000 feet.

**Reservations, fees:** Reservations are accepted; phone (800) KOA-3240. Sites are $20-25 a night.

**Open:** May to September.

**Directions:** From Interstate 70 west of Glenwood Springs, take the Elk Creek exit (Exit 105) and go into the town of New Castle. Turn right on 7th St. and continue 2.5 miles to the campground entrance on the right.

**Contact:** New Castle-Glenwood Springs KOA, 0581 County Rd. 241, New Castle, CO 81647; tel. (970) 984-2240; e-mail: rosrich@rof.net.

## 39 White Owl  8

None of the U.S. Forest Service campgrounds in this area is highly developed, but White Owl is the most primitive of the lot, with nothing more than old fire rings designating half of its dinky sites. The lack of amenities, however, is more than made up for by the pristine quality of adjacent White Owl Lake and the lush green meadow that encompasses part of the campground. The lake is small but stocked with brook trout, perfect for fishing from the shore or a small boat.

**Location:** On White Owl Lake in White River National Forest; map A1, grid g9.

**Campsites, facilities:** There are six sites for tents or RVs up to 30 feet long. Two of the sites have picnic tables, and all have fire grills. One vault toilet is provided. There is no drinking water or trash service. Some facilities are wheelchair accessible. Leashed pets are permitted.

**Elevation:** 10,680 feet.

**Reservations, fees:** Reservations are not accepted. No fee is required, but a donation of $6 a night is requested.

**Open:** July to September.

**Directions:** From Eagle, drive 12 miles west on Interstate 70 to the Dotsero exit. Turn north on Colorado River Rd. (look for the signs for Sweetwater). Drive approximately two miles, turn left on Forest Service Rd. 600 (Coffee Pot Rd.), and continue 27 miles to the turnoff for the campground on the left.

**Contact:** White River National Forest, Eagle Ranger District, 125 W. 5th St., P.O. Box 720, Eagle, CO 81631; tel. (970) 328-6388.

## 40 Burning Mountain RV Park  6

Most of the pleasing, spacious sites in this camp are out in the open beside the rippling Colorado River. Fishing is possible by shore or boat, with wide banks and a small boat ramp that provides excellent access for campers. White-water rafting is also available. Trails for hiking and horseback riding are nearby.

**Location:** On the Colorado River west of Glenwood Springs; map A1, grid h8.

**Campsites, facilities:** There are 72 sites for tents or RVs of any length. Drinking water, picnic tables, fire grills, and wheelchair-accessible bathrooms with hot showers are provided. Electric hookups, a waste disposal station, store, public phone, and nearby boat ramp are also available. Leashed pets are permitted.

**Elevation:** 5,500 feet.

**Reservations, fees:** Reservations are accepted. Sites are $16-18 a night.

**Open:** Year-round.

**Directions:** From Interstate 70 west of Glenwood Springs, take the New Castle exit (Exit 105) and head south on County Rd. 335. Turn east at a signed dirt road and continue about 100 yards.

**Contact:** Burning Mountain RV Park, 7051 County Rd. 335, New Castle, CO 81647; tel. (970) 984-0331.

## 41 Ami's Acres  3

My first view of this park was from the freeway. I looked up out of my window and there it was, sitting on a bluff directly over Interstate 70. As you might guess, it's not the quietest spot around, nor is it the prettiest. Most of the terraced sites are rocky and sparsely vegetated, although they are large enough to accommodate the most massive RVs. You can take comfort in the knowledge that all kinds of great recreation opportunities are within a short drive, including the steaming mineral pools at Glenwood Hot Springs, fishing in the Colorado River, and hiking in White River National Forest.

**Location:** West of Glenwood Springs; map A1, grid h9.

**Campsites, facilities:** There are 60 sites for tents or RVs of any length, many with full hookups. Drinking water, picnic tables, fire grills, and bathrooms with hot showers are provided. Also available are laundry facilities, a public phone, and camping cabins. Leashed pets are permitted.

**Elevation:** 5,700 feet.

**Reservations, fees:** Reservations are accepted. Sites are $18.50-24 a night.

**Open:** April to November.

**Directions:** From Interstate 70 at Glenwood Springs, take Exit 114 and turn west on the frontage road. The campground is about one mile down the road.

**Contact:** Ami's Acres, P.O. Box 1239, West Glenwood Springs, CO 81602; tel. (970) 945-5340.

## 42 Rock Gardens Campground and Rafting

      6

Imagine waking to the sound of rushing water, catching a fresh trout for a pan-fried breakfast, and then hopping into a boat for an exhilarating day of white-water rafting. Sound good? Such a scenario is possible at Rock Gardens, a combination campground/rafting outfitter alongside the Colorado River. The park offers all the features of a full-service campground, including large, grassy sites with hookups and showers, plus guided rafting and float trips (or individual boat rentals if you prefer to go solo). A paved bike trail is also available. Although the camp is squeezed between the freeway and the river, the sites are positioned away from much of the road noise.

**Location:** On the Colorado River, east of Glenwood Springs; map A1, grid h9.

**Campsites, facilities:** There are 74 sites for tents or RVs of any length. Drinking water, picnic tables, fire grills, and bathrooms with hot showers are provided. Electric hookups, a waste disposal station, small store, boat rentals, bike rentals, and public phone are available. Leashed pets are permitted.

**Elevation:** 5,700 feet.

**Reservations, fees:** Reservations are accepted. Sites are $19-23 a night.

**Open:** April to November.

**Directions:** From Interstate 70 at Glenwood Springs, take Exit 119 and turn south on the frontage road to the campground.

**Contact:** Rock Gardens Campground and Rafting, 1308 County Rd. 129, Glenwood Springs, CO 81601; tel. (970) 945-6737; e-mail: therock@sopris.net.

## 43 The Hideout Cabins and Campground      8

Set along little Three Mile Creek, the Hideout makes a perfect layover for travelers on their way to Aspen. Each site is wooded, with plenty of room and privacy and adjacent fishing access. You can take a paved bike path into the town of Glenwood Springs. Other nearby options include hiking, rafting, and mountain biking. If you're feeling decadent, head into town for a visit to Yampah Hot Springs Spa and Vapor Caves, where you can indulge in a full-body mud wrap and massage before strolling across the street to the hot spring pools.

**Location:** South of Glenwood Springs; map A1, grid h9.

**Campsites, facilities:** There are 60 sites for tents or RVs of any length, many with full hookups. Drinking water, picnic tables, fire grills, and bathrooms with hot showers are provided (showers are turned off from December to May). Laundry facilities, a public phone, and cabins are also available. Leashed pets are permitted.

**Elevation:** 5,700 feet.

**Reservations, fees:** Reservations are accepted. Sites are $17-20 a night.

**Open:** Year-round with limited facilities from December to May.

**Directions:** From Interstate 70 at Glenwood Springs, take Exit 116 and turn south on Hwy. 82, driving toward Aspen. Continue over the bridge to the other side of the Colorado River. Proceed under the railroad trestle and go straight through the next two stop signs; then turn west on 27th St. to Midland Avenue. Turn south on Midland Ave. and continue just over one mile to the campground entrance on the right (across from the Texaco station).

**Contact:** The Hideout, 1293 County Rd. 117, Glenwood Springs, CO 81601; tel. (970) 945-5621 or (800) 987-0779.

## 44 Highline State Park           8

The campground at this state park is actually called Bookcliff, named after the dark, towering pillars of striated rock that dominate the eastern horizon. Set near the western shore of Highline Lake, the grassy sites are within walking distance of a large swimming beach and a hiking trail that loops around the southeast side of the lake. A boat ramp on the northwestern shore provides access for water-skiers and fishing boats, although anglers may prefer the quieter atmosphere of adjacent Mack Mesa Lake. This smaller lake is located just steps from the northwest corner of Highline Lake and is stocked with rainbow trout, channel catfish, largemouth bass, and walleye. Boating is prohibited on Mack Mesa from October to February, when waterfowl are permitted to peacefully take over the lake. Swift afternoon winds afford excellent conditions for sailing and windsurfing. Limited hunting is permitted; call the park for details.

**Location:** North of Loma near the Colorado-Utah border; map A1, grid i1.

**Campsites, facilities:** There are 25 sites for tents or RVs of any length. Drinking water, picnic tables, fire grills, and bathrooms with hot showers are provided. A boat ramp is on the opposite side of the lake. Some facilities are wheelchair accessible. Leashed pets are permitted.

**Elevation:** 4,700 feet.

**Reservations, fees:** Reservations are accepted. Phone (303) 470-1144 or (800) 678-CAMP (800-678-2267) outside the Denver Metro area; there's a $7 reservation fee. Sites are $10 a night, and there's a $4 entrance fee.

**Open:** Year-round.

**Directions:** From Interstate 70 west of Grand Junction, take the Loma exit (Exit 15) and head north on Hwy. 139. After about five miles, turn left on Q Rd. and continue one mile to 11.8 Road. Turn north and drive to the park entrance.

**Contact:** Highline State Park, 1800 11.8 Rd., Loma, CO 81524; tel. (970) 858-7208.

## 45 Rabbit Valley     4

A base camp popular with off-road vehicle enthusiasts, this dry, sparsely vegetated camp is located at the trailhead for the Rabbit Valley Interpretive Trail. The trail runs north and south of camp for several miles and is used by hikers and equestrians as well as motor bikers. It's also a decent option if you're simply looking for a cheap place to spend the night on your way west to Utah.

**Location:** East of the Colorado/Utah border; map A1, grid j0.

**Campsites, facilities:** There are eight sites for tents or RVs up to 30 feet long. Vault toilets are provided, but there are no other facilities or drinking water. Leashed pets are permitted.

**Elevation:** 4,500 feet.

**Reservations, fees:** Reservations are not accepted. There is no fee.

**Open:** Year-round.

**Directions:** From Interstate 70 just east of the Colorado/Utah border, take Exit 2 and turn south. The parking area is a short distance south on the access road.

**Contact:** Bureau of Land Management, 2815 H Rd., Grand Junction, CO 81506; tel. (970) 244-3000.

## 46 Fruita Monument RV Park    3

Fruita Monument RV Park's slogan is "A peach of a place to stay," borrowing the fame of the Grand Junction orchards, consistent producers of huge, luscious fruit. Unfortunately, this spot's proximity to the interstate makes it seem more like a highway rest stop than a rural orchard. The park is well maintained, however, with lots of shade trees and friendly folks. A bonus for pet owners is the on-site dog run. Colorado National Monument is just a few miles away.

**Location:** In Fruita; map A1, grid j1.

**Campsites, facilities:** There are 112 sites for tents or RVs of any length, many with full hookups. Drinking water, picnic tables, fire grills, and bathrooms with hot showers are provided. Laundry facilities, a waste disposal station, small store, and public phone are available. Some facilities are wheelchair accessible. Leashed pets are permitted.

**Elevation:** 4,600 feet.

**Reservations, fees:** Reservations are accepted. Sites are $16-22 a night.

**Open:** Year-round.

**Directions:** From Interstate 70 west of Grand Junction, take the Fruita exit (Exit 19) and drive one-quarter mile south on Hwy. 340 to the campground.

**Contact:** Fruita Monument RV Park, 607 Hwy. 340, Fruita, CO 81521; tel. (970) 858-3155 or (888) 977-6777.

## 47 Colorado National Monument       10

Framed by spectacular sandstone cliffs and skyscraping monoliths, Colorado National Monument offers one of the most dramatic and breathtaking views in the state. The campground, which provides modest sites bordered by juniper bushes, makes a peaceful base camp from which to explore this amazingly scenic area. At the edge of the canyon you get a sensational view of sheer stone walls plunging to the floor of the Grand Valley and the edge of the Colorado River. You can tour the park on one of its many hiking, horseback riding, or mountain biking trails (the Window Rock Loop is just a short walk from the campground), or drive along 23-mile Rim Rock Dr., stopping at frequent vista points for mind-blowing views. Be sure to make it to Monument Canyon and Wedding Canyon, where enormous rock formations such as Kissing Couple and Praying Hands appear as natural sculptures sprouting from the ground.

**Location:** West of Grand Junction; map A1, grid j1.

**Campsites, facilities:** There are 80 sites for tents or RVs up to 26 feet long. Drinking water, picnic tables, fire grills, and flush and vault toilets are provided. Some facilities are wheelchair accessible. Leashed pets are permitted in the campground only.

**Elevation:** 5,800 feet.

**Reservations, fees:** Reservations are not accepted. Sites are $10 a night.

**Open:** Year-round.

**Directions:** From Interstate 70 at Fruita, take Exit 19 and turn south on Hwy. 340. Drive two miles to the western entrance of the park and continue four miles on Rim Rock Dr. to the campground.

**Contact:** Colorado National Monument, Fruita, CO 81521; tel. (970) 858-3617.

## 48 Mud Springs    8

This little-known option to the popular Colorado National Monument campground is an excellent choice for budget-minded campers who want privacy and a natural setting. Generously sized and secluded, the sites are surrounded by oak trees, with aspens sprinkled around the camp. Facilities are simple but adequate for the price. Although hiking trails are available in the area, there are no other recreation opportunities immediately available from camp.

**Location:** South of Grand Junction; map A1, grid j1.

**Campsites, facilities:** There are 12 sites for tents or RVs up to 30 feet long. Drinking water, vault toilets, and picnic tables are provided. Leashed pets are permitted.

**Elevation:** 8,000 feet.

**Reservations, fees:** No reservations are accepted. There is no fee.

**Open:** Mid-May to mid-October.

**Directions:** From Interstate 70 at Fruita, take Exit 19 and turn south on Hwy. 340. Drive two miles to the western entrance of Colorado National Monument. If you are planning on visiting the park on your way, you must pay the entrance fee; otherwise, tell the clerk at the entrance booth that you are just passing through to the BLM camp south of the park. Drive south on Rim Rock Dr. until you come to a fork. Bear right on Rd. 16.50 and continue through Glade Park. Go approximately six more miles south to the campground.

**Contact:** Bureau of Land Management, 2815 H Rd., Grand Junction, CO 81506; tel. (970) 244-3000.

## 49 Junction West RV Park     4

If you're stuck on the hot, dry highway with nowhere to go, Junction West offers an adequate layover option. The campground has large, flat sites, some with scattered trees for shade and wide-open views of the surrounding hills. There's not much in the way of recreation at the park, but the owners, in the interest of keeping their guests occupied, have implemented a paperback exchange program—so at least you can curl up with a good read. A central modem hookup is also available for guests who wish to check their e-mail. Recreation in the area includes hiking, fishing, and rafting, all available within a short drive.

**Location:** In Grand Junction; map A1, grid j2.

**Campsites, facilities:** There are 70 full-hookup sites for RVs of any length. No tents are permitted. Drinking water, picnic tables, fire grills, and bathrooms with hot showers are provided. Laundry facilities, a waste disposal station, a small store, and a public phone are also available. Small indoor pets are permitted.

**Elevation:** 4,600 feet.

**Reservations, fees:** Reservations are accepted. Sites are $21 a night.

**Open:** Year-round.

**Directions:** From Interstate 70 at Grand Junction, take Exit 26 and drive one-quarter mile west on U.S. 6. Turn north on 22 Rd. and go one-half mile to the campground.

**Contact:** Junction West RV Park, 793 22 Rd., Grand Junction, CO 81505; tel. (970) 245-8531.

## 50 Mobile City RV Park  2

If you ask me, any campground that boasts of close proximity to the "Biggest Mall in Western Colorado" as its main attraction is worth missing. But if you find yourself desperate for a safe place to sleep for the night, it just may do. The owners are friendly and accommodating, and the facilities are well maintained. Mobile City is plunked in the middle of a mobile home park near downtown Grand Junction and has nice views of the Grand Mesa, with a few trees providing a hint of nature.

**Location:** West of Grand Junction; map A1, grid j2.

**Campsites, facilities:** There are 30 sites with full hookups for RVs of any length. No tents are permitted. Drinking water, picnic tables, fire grills, and bathrooms with hot showers are provided. Laundry facilities and a public phone are available. Leashed pets are permitted.

**Elevation:** 4,500 feet.

**Reservations, fees:** Reservations are accepted but are not usually necessary. Sites are $20 a night.

**Open:** Year-round.

**Directions:** From eastbound Interstate 70, take Exit 26 at Grand Junction, turn south on U.S. 50, and drive 1.5 miles to the campground. From westbound Interstate 70, take Exit 28 at Grand Junction, turn south on Rd. 24, and drive 1.5 miles. Turn right on U.S. 50 and continue one mile to the campground.

**Contact:** Mobile City RV Park, 2322 U.S. 6/50, Grand Junction, CO 81505; tel. (970) 242-9291.

## 51 Big J RV Park   3

The reason this park doesn't accept reservations, the clerk told me, is that they want to inspect each RV That comes through to make sure it "fits in aesthetically" with the park. When I pressed the owner, he admitted that RVs must look well kept and have functioning water and sewer facilities to be admitted. Hmm. If your RV passes muster, you'll enjoy large, grassy sites, a heated pool, and all the comforts of home, including cable TV (for an extra charge).

**Location:** In Grand Junction; map A1, grid j3.

**Campsites, facilities:** There are 110 sites with full hookups for RVs of any length. No tents are permitted. Drinking water, picnic tables, fire grills, and bathrooms with hot showers are provided. Laundry facilities, cable TV, a small store, swimming pool (in summer), and public phone are available. Pets are forbidden.

**Elevation:** 4,600 feet.

**Reservations, fees:** Reservations are not accepted. Sites are $21 a night.

**Open:** Year-round.

**Directions:** From eastbound Interstate 70, take Exit 26 at Grand Junction and drive about seven miles east on U.S. 50 to the campground. From westbound Interstate 70, take Exit 37 east of Grand Junction and drive one mile south to Hwy. 141, turn left, and go five miles south. When you come to U.S. 50, turn west and continue about four miles to the campground.

**Contact:** Big J RV Park, 2819 U.S. 50, Grand Junction, CO 81503; tel. (970) 242-2527.

## 52 Rose Park RV Campground  2

Like many of the campgrounds in this area, Rose Park consists of a sectioned-off area of a mobile home park. It is little more than a parking lot with trees, but it's clean and conveniently close to the highway for on-the-go travelers.

**Location:** In Grand Junction; map A1, grid j3.

**Campsites, facilities:** There are 25 sites with full hookups for RVs of any length. No tents are permitted. Drinking water, picnic tables, and bathrooms with hot showers are provided. Laundry facilities and a waste disposal station are available. Leashed pets are permitted.

**Elevation:** 4,500 feet.

**Reservations, fees:** Reservations are accepted. Sites are $16 a night.

**Open:** Year-round.

**Directions:** From eastbound Interstate 70, take Exit 26 at Grand Junction and drive a short distance southeast on Business Loop 70; then turn left on North Ave. and continue to the campground. From westbound Interstate 70, take Exit 37 east of Grand Junction and drive a short distance southwest on Business Loop 70; then turn right on North Ave. and continue to the campground.

**Contact:** Rose Park RV Campground, 644 29.5 Rd., Grand Junction, CO 81504; tel. (970) 243-1292.

## 53 RV Ranch at Grand Junction    6

This former KOA used to be one of the few campgrounds in the Grand Junction area that was tent-friendly, with spacious, grassy sites and plenty of trees. Tents have since been outlawed, and the grassy sites have been replaced with concrete pads. The new owners have also upgraded the bathrooms and maintained all the previous amenities, including a heated swimming pool and recreation room, plus proximity to Colorado National Monument and Grand Mesa National Forest. In the summertime, an on-site restaurant serves home-style meals.

**Location:** In Clifton; map A1, grid j3.

**Campsites, facilities:** There are 125 sites for RVs of any length, many with full hookups. No tents are permitted. Drinking water, picnic tables, fire grills, and bathrooms with hot showers are provided. Laundry facilities, a waste disposal station, small store, restaurant, swimming pool, cabins, and public phone are available. One bathroom is wheelchair accessible. Leashed pets are permitted.

**Elevation:** 4,600 feet.

**Reservations, fees:** Reservations are accepted; phone (800) 793-0041. Sites are $27-29 a night.

**Open:** Year-round, with limited winter facilities.

**Directions:** From Interstate 70 east of Grand Junction, take Exit 37 and drive one mile southwest on Business Loop 70.

**Contact:** RV Ranch at Grand Junction, 3238 Interstate 70 Business Loop, Clifton, CO 81520; tel. (970) 434-6644.

## 54 Colorado River State Park: Island Acres       8

Since the damming of the Colorado, the island in the middle of the river has disappeared, leaving a single wide, flowing ribbon of water in its place. The campground is set next to the river in colorful DeBeque Canyon, spread out in a large, grassy area within a short walk of four numbered lakes. Each lake features special recreation options: Lake No. 1 provides boating and fishing for catfish, and Lakes No. 3 and 4 are stocked regularly with trout. Lake No. 2 is designated for swimming only, with a large beach on the south side. A hiking trail runs along the riverbanks, allowing additional fishing access along the way.

**Location:** East of Grand Junction; map A1, grid j4.

**Campsites, facilities:** There are 60 sites for tents or RVs of any length. Drinking water, picnic tables, fire grills, and bathrooms with hot showers are provided. Electric hookups and a waste disposal station are available. Leashed pets are permitted.

**Elevation:** 4,700 feet.

**Reservations, fees:** Reservations are accepted. Phone (303) 470-1144 or (800) 678-CAMP (800-678-2267) outside the Denver Metro area; there's a $7 reservation fee. Sites are $10-14 a night, and there's a $4 entrance fee.

**Open:** Year-round.

**Directions:** From Interstate 70 at Palisade, take Exit 47 and drive into the park entrance.

**Contact:** Colorado River State Park, P.O. Box 700, Clifton, CO 81520; tel. (970) 434-3388.

## 55 Jumbo      7

This basic camp features spacious, open sites surrounded by Grand Mesa National Forest. West Bench Trail, one of the most scenic hiking and mountain biking routes in the area, runs west of the campground. Also nearby is Mesa Lakes Lodge, which offers a good restaurant if the fish in Jumbo Reservoir aren't biting. Chances are they will be, though—anglers come from miles around to try their luck at catching one of Jumbo's plump rainbow or brook trout. No boating is permitted on the reservoir, so expect quiet, peaceful camping. Note: This campground may be closed for the 2000 season.

**Location:** On Jumbo Reservoir in Grand Mesa National Forest; map A1, grid j5.

**Campsites, facilities:** There are 26 sites for tents or RVs up to 22 feet long. Drinking water, picnic tables, fire grills, and vault toilets are provided. Leashed pets are permitted.

**Elevation:** 9,800 feet.

**Reservations, fees:** Reservations are not accepted. Sites are $12 a night.

**Open:** July to September. (This campground may be closed for the 2000 season.)

**Directions:** From Interstate 70 east of Grand Junction, take Exit 49 and drive 26 miles east on Hwy. 65. Turn south on Forest Service Rd. 252 and continue a short distance to the campground.

**Contact:** Grand Mesa National Forest, Grand Junction Ranger District, 764 Horizon Dr., Room 115, Grand Junction, CO 81506; tel. (970) 242-8211.

## 56 Spruce Grove    5

Being adjacent to Hwy. 65, this camp can sound as if it's next to an urban freeway, especially in the late summer. The sites are nice and roomy, though, huddled under large spruce and fir trees. Nearby are numerous alpine lakes that provide good fishing opportunities and an often-unexpected drawback: lots and lots of mosquitoes. According to one U.S. Forest Service ranger, the skeeters get so bad by late August that "it feels like Minnesota." Needless to say, bring repellent.

**Location:** Near Mesa Lakes in Grand Mesa National Forest; map A1, grid j5.

**Campsites, facilities:** There are 16 sites for tents or RVs up to 22 feet long. Drinking water, picnic tables, fire grills, and vault toilets are provided. Leashed pets are permitted.

**Elevation:** 9,900 feet.

**Reservations, fees:** Reservations are not accepted. Sites are $10 a night.

**Open:** July to September.

**Directions:** From Interstate 70 east of Grand Junction, take Exit 49 and drive approximately 20 miles east on Hwy. 65 to the campground.

**Contact:** Grand Mesa National Forest, Grand Junction Ranger District, 764 Horizon Dr., Room 115, Grand Junction, CO 81506; tel. (970) 242-8211.

## 57 Island Lake      6

Though not actually on Island Lake, this campground isn't far away—a short hike will get you to one of its superb fishing spots. Highlights include an ATV Trailhead to Granby Reservoirs that is suitable for motor biking, hiking, or mountain biking. If you're easily annoyed by the whine of ATVs, skip this one and head over to the Little Bear or Cobbett Lake camps.

**Location:** Near Island Lake in Grand Mesa National Forest; map A1, grid j6.

**Campsites, facilities:** There are 41 sites for tents or RVs up to 45 feet long. Drinking water, picnic tables, fire grills, and flush and vault toilets are provided. A boat ramp and fish cleaning area are nearby. Some facilities are wheelchair accessible. Leashed pets are permitted.

**Elevation:** 10,300 feet.

**Reservations, fees:** Reservations are not accepted. Sites are $10 a night.

**Open:** July to September.

**Directions:** From Interstate 70 east of Grand Junction, take Exit 49 and drive approximately 34 miles east on Hwy. 65. Turn right on Forest Service Rd. 116 and continue one mile to the campground.

**Contact:** Grand Mesa National Forest, Grand Junction Ranger District, 764 Horizon Dr., Room 115, Grand Junction, CO 81506; tel. (970) 242-8211.

## 58 Little Bear       7

Private, scenic, and right next to the shore of Island Lake, Little Bear is one of the most popular camps in the Grand Junction district. Island Lake is the largest lake in Grand Mesa National Forest and provides opportunities for fishing and boating, with a boat ramp near the camp. Trout fishing is decent, and there are many good hiking and mountain biking trails nearby. A wheelchair-accessible fishing pier is provided.

**Location:** On Island Lake in Grand Mesa National Forest; map A1, grid j6.

**Campsites, facilities:** There are 36 sites for tents or RVs up to 22 feet long. Drinking water, picnic tables, fire grills, and flush and vault toilets are provided. A boat ramp is available. Some facilities are wheelchair accessible. Leashed pets are permitted.

**Elevation:** 10,200 feet.

**Reservations, fees:** Reservations are not accepted. Sites are $10 a night.

**Open:** July to September.

**Directions:** From Interstate 70 east of Grand Junction, take Exit 49 and drive approximately 34 miles east on Hwy. 65. Turn right on Forest Service Rd. 116 and continue one-half mile to the campground.

**Contact:** Grand Mesa National Forest, Grand Junction Ranger District, 764 Horizon Dr., Room 115, Grand Junction, CO 81506; tel. (970) 242-8211.

## 59 Cobbett Lake     7

Newly renamed Cobbett Lake (formerly Carp Lake) is a pretty little pond on Hwy. 65, just across the highway from the Grand Mesa Visitor Center. Sites are wide and private, partially shaded by mixed conifer forest. No boating is allowed, but you can fish for trout from the shoreline. A wheelchair-accessible trail runs from the campground to the visitor center.

**Location:** East of Island Lake in Grand Mesa National Forest; map A1, grid j6.

**Campsites, facilities:** There are 20 sites for tents or RVs up to 30 feet long. Drinking water, picnic tables, fire grills, and vault toilets are provided. Some facilities are wheelchair accessible. Leashed pets are permitted.

**Elevation:** 10,200 feet.

**Reservations, fees:** Reservations are not accepted. Sites are $10 a night.

**Open:** July to September.

**Directions:** From Interstate 70 east of Grand Junction, take Exit 49 and drive approximately 35 miles east on Hwy. 65 to the campground.

**Contact:** Grand Mesa National Forest, Grand Junction Ranger District, 764 Horizon Dr., Room 115, Grand Junction, CO 81506; tel. (970) 242-8211.

## 60 Ward Lake     7

One of several small, clear lakes in the region, Ward offers a primitive boat ramp and good fishing prospects for rainbow trout, brook trout, and splake. The campground stands in fir and spruce forest and offers basic amenities. Check with the Grand Mesa Visitor Center for info on trails and activities nearby.

**Location:** In Grand Mesa National Forest; map A1, grid j6.

**Campsites, facilities:** There are 27 sites for tents or RVs up to 22 feet long. Drinking water, picnic tables, fire grills, and vault toilets are provided. A primitive boat ramp is available. Leashed pets are permitted.

**Elevation:** 10,200 feet.

**Reservations, fees:** Reservations are not accepted. Sites are $12 a night.

**Open:** July to September.

**Directions:** From Interstate 70 east of Grand Junction, take Exit 49 and drive approximately 35 miles east on Hwy. 65. Turn left on Forest Service Rd. 121 and continue a short distance to the campground.

**Contact:** Grand Mesa National Forest, Grand Junction Ranger District, 764 Horizon Dr., Room 115, Grand Junction, CO 81506; tel. (970) 242-8211.

## 61 Kiser Creek     4

Not only is this campground not on Kiser Creek, it's nowhere near Kiser Creek. It's got no trailheads, no scenery, no nothin'. However, it's not far from Eggleston Lake, which has good fishing, a boat ramp, and a campground that's generally much more crowded than this one—so Kiser Creek isn't such a bad option for those who are willing to trade a little traveling for a lot of privacy.

**Location:** South of Eggleston Lake in Grand Mesa National Forest; map A1, grid j7.

**Campsites, facilities:** There are 12 sites for tents or RVs up to 16 feet long. Drinking water, picnic tables, fire grills, and vault toilets are provided. Leashed pets are permitted.

**Elevation:** 10,300 feet.

**Reservations, fees:** Reservations are not accepted. Sites are $10 a night.

**Open:** July to September.

**Directions:** From Interstate 70 east of Grand Junction, take Exit 49 and drive approximately 35 miles east on Hwy. 65. Turn left on Forest Service Rd. 121 and drive three miles east, turn right on Forest Service Rd. 123, and continue a short distance to the campground.

**Contact:** Grand Mesa National Forest, Grand Junction Ranger District, 764 Horizon Dr., Room 115, Grand Junction, CO 81506; tel. (970) 242-8211.

## 62 Eggleston     4

Need a pretty spot for a family reunion trip? Halt your search. This camp is large enough for up to 30 people yet has an intimate feel, with snug sites nestled in conifer forest. And it's off the main highway, so you avoid most of the Hwy. 65 traffic noise. Fish from the shore or launch your boat for the early morning rise of rainbow and brook trout.

**Location:** In Grand Mesa National Forest; map A1, grid j7.

**Campsites, facilities:** There are six sites for tents or RVs up to 30 feet long. The entire campground can also be used as a group site for up to 30 people. Drinking water, picnic tables, fire grills, and vault toilets are provided. A boat ramp is available. Leashed pets are permitted.

**Elevation:** 10,100 feet.

**Reservations, fees:** Reservations are accepted for groups only; phone (877) 444-6777. The reservation fee is $8.65. You may also reserve sites at website: www.reserveusa.com. Group fees vary according to size of party; single-site fees are $10 a night.

**Open:** July to September.

**Directions:** From Interstate 70 east of Grand Junction, take Exit 49 and drive approximately 35 miles east on Hwy. 65. Turn left on Forest Service Rd. 121 and drive four miles east to the campground.

**Contact:** Grand Mesa National Forest, Grand Junction Ranger District, 764 Horizon Dr., Room 115, Grand Junction, CO 81506; tel. (970) 242-8211.

## 63 Crag Crest      7

If you're looking for a single campsite and you've got your eye on Eggleston Lake, pass by Eggleston group camp and pitch your tent here at a lovely, forested waterfront site. To the south you get easy access to the lake and a boat ramp; to the east is the Crag Crest Trailhead, the eastern jump-off point for the beautiful Crag Crest National Recreation Trail. It winds north, then west, passing tiny, glittering lakes and meandering through cool stands of spruce and pine and sprawling alpine meadows.

**Location:** On Eggleston Lake in Grand Mesa National Forest; map A1, grid j7.

**Campsites, facilities:** There are 11 sites for tents or RVs up to 30 feet long. Drinking water, picnic tables, fire grills, and vault toilets are provided. A boat ramp is nearby. Leashed pets are permitted.

**Elevation:** 10,100 feet.

**Reservations, fees:** Reservations are not accepted. Sites are $10 a night.

**Open:** July to September.

**Directions:** From Interstate 70 east of Grand Junction, take Exit 49 and drive approximately 35 miles east on Hwy. 65. Turn left on Forest Service Rd. 121 and drive 3.5 miles east to the campground.

**Contact:** Grand Mesa National Forest, Grand Junction Ranger District, 764 Horizon Dr., Room 115, Grand Junction, CO 81506; tel. (970) 242-8211.

## 64 Cottonwood  7

This campground is set on the first of five Cottonwood Lakes. It's got a boat ramp, good trout fishing, and a trail that runs west into Bull Basin to several sparkling high-altitude lakes. Of the many camps in the immediate area, this is my favorite because it's far enough off the tourist track to feel (almost) as if you're in the wilderness.

**Location:** North of Eggleston Lake in Grand Mesa National Forest; map A1, grid j6.

**Campsites, facilities:** There are 42 sites for tents or RVs up to 30 feet long. Drinking water, picnic tables, fire grills, and vault toilets are provided. Leashed pets are permitted.

**Elevation:** 10,000 feet.

**Reservations, fees:** Reservations are not accepted. Sites are $10 a night.

**Open:** July to September.

**Directions:** From Interstate 70 east of Grand Junction, take Exit 49 and drive approximately 10 miles east on Hwy. 65. Turn left on Hwy. 330 and drive 11 miles to Collbran; turn south on Forest Service Rd. 121 and continue 12 miles. Turn right on Forest Service Rd. 257 and proceed four miles west to the campground.

**Contact:** Grand Mesa National Forest, Grand Junction Ranger District, 764 Horizon Dr., Room 115, Grand Junction, CO 81506; tel. (970) 242-8211.

## 65 Vega State Park  8

Bordered by lush, abundant trees and shrubs, the sparkling blue water of Vega Reservoir is the highlight of this 900-acre state park. Waterskiing, PWC riding, and windsurfing are permitted on the eastern side of the reservoir, but the roped-off western portion is a designated fishing area, stocked seasonally with rainbow, cutthroat, brown, and brook trout. The campground has been renovated, adding a new loop of 34 sites with water and electric hookups, as well as a new shower building. The park has also added a new visitor center, a playground, and a staging area for off-highway vehicles and snowmobiles. A hiking trail runs west from the Marmot camping area to Park Creek Rd., which heads south to a network of trails in Grand Mesa National Forest. Limited hunting is permitted; contact the park for details.

**Location:** Near Collbran; map A1, grid i6.

**Campsites, facilities:** There are 133 sites for tents or RVs of any length and 10 walk-in tent sites. Drinking water, picnic tables, fire grills, and flush and vault toilets are provided. Hot showers (coin-operated), electric hookups, water hookups, a waste disposal station, and boat ramps are available. Some facilities are wheelchair accessible. Leashed pets are permitted.

**Elevation:** 8,000 feet.

**Reservations, fees:** Reservations are accepted. Phone (303) 470-1144 or (800) 678-CAMP (800-678-2267) outside the Denver Metro area; there's a $7 reservation fee. Sites are $10-16 a night, and there's a $4 entrance fee.

**Open:** Year-round.

**Directions:** From Interstate 70 east of Grand Junction, take Exit 49 and drive 10 miles east on Hwy. 65. Turn left on Hwy. 330 and continue 22 miles.

**Contact:** Vega State Park, P.O. Box 186, Collbran, CO 81624; tel. (970) 487-3407.

## 66 Big Creek     7

From 1993 to 1997 there was no water in Big Creek Reservoir—and since a big, dry hole is not a huge camping draw, this site didn't get much use. Now the reservoir is full of clear mountain water and stocked with trout, providing a cool, idyllic setting for a weekend getaway. The campsites are set in conifer forest, not far from a primitive boat ramp (for small boats only).

**Location:** In Grand Mesa National Forest; map A1, grid j7.

**Campsites, facilities:** There are 26 sites for tents or RVs up to 30 feet long. Picnic tables, fire grills, and vault toilets are provided, but there is no drinking water. Leashed pets are permitted.

**Elevation:** 10,000 feet.

**Reservations, fees:** Reservations are not accepted. Sites are $8 a night.

**Open:** July to September.

**Directions:** From Interstate 70 east of Grand Junction, take Exit 49 and drive approximately 10 miles east on Hwy. 65. Turn left on Hwy. 330 and drive 11 miles to Collbran. Turn south on Forest Service Rd. 121 and continue about 14 miles to the campground entrance.

**Contact:** Grand Mesa National Forest, Grand Junction Ranger District, 764 Horizon Dr., Room 115, Grand Junction, CO 81506; tel. (970) 242-8211.

## 67 Twin Lake    4

Of the handful of U.S. Forest Service camps in this region, Twin Lake is the most dilapidated, offering old, run-down facilities and no drinking water. The setting is pleasant, however, with open and shaded sites located just off the main road near Twin Lake No. 2. Boating is not allowed, but fishing from the shoreline is okay. A couple of good hiking trails are available down the road at the Weir and Johnson camp.

**Location:** In Grand Mesa National Forest; map A1, grid j7.

**Campsites, facilities:** There are 13 sites for tents or RVs up to 22 feet long. Picnic tables, fire grills, and a vault toilet are provided, but there is no drinking water. Leashed pets are permitted.

**Elevation:** 10,300 feet.

**Reservations, fees:** Reservations are not accepted. Sites are $8 a night.

**Open:** July to September.

**Directions:** From Interstate 70 east of Grand Junction, take Exit 49 and drive approximately 10 miles east on Hwy. 65. Turn left on Hwy. 330 and drive 11 miles to Collbran. Turn south on Forest Service Rd. 121 and continue about 16 miles. Turn left on Forest Service Rd. 126 and go two miles to the campground.

**Contact:** Grand Mesa National Forest, Grand Junction Ranger District, 764 Horizon Dr., Room 115, Grand Junction, CO 81506; tel. (970) 242-8211.

**68** Weir and Johnson

 7

Located at the remote end of Forest Service Rd. 126, this one gets missed by lots of travelers. The camp is near the open southwestern shore of Weir and Johnson Reservoir, with good fishing for rainbow and brook trout and beautiful mountain views. Two trails begin at the camp: Trail 716 heads north about 1,000 feet up to Leon Peak, and Trail 717 leads west to Leon Lake, which boasts good fishing and access to a network of four-wheel-drive roads.

**Location:** In Grand Mesa National Forest; map A1, grid j7.

**Campsites, facilities:** There are 12 sites for tents or RVs up to 22 feet long. Picnic tables, fire grills, and a vault toilet are provided, but there is no drinking water. Leashed pets are permitted.

**Elevation:** 10,500 feet.

**Reservations, fees:** Reservations are not accepted. Sites are $8 a night.

**Open:** July to September.

**Directions:** From Interstate 70 east of Grand Junction, take Exit 49 and drive about 10 miles east on Hwy. 65. Turn left on Hwy. 330 and drive 11 miles to Collbran; turn south on Forest Service Rd. 121 and continue about 16 miles. Turn left on Forest Service Rd. 126 and go three miles to the campground.

**Contact:** Grand Mesa National Forest, Grand Junction Ranger District, 764 Horizon Dr., Room 115, Grand Junction, CO 81506; tel. (970) 242-8211.

WATERFALL IN SUMMIT COUNTY

# MAP A2

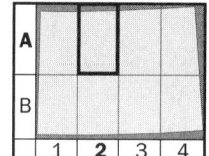

A
B
1
2
3
4

a
b
c
d
e
f
g
h
i
j
0
1
2
3
4
5
6
7
8
9
94
228
332
0
15 mi
0
15 km
N
WYOMING
COLORADO
Continental
Divide
North Platte River
Laramie River
ROOSEVELT NATIONAL FOREST
ROUTT NATIONAL FOREST
ROCKY MOUNTAIN NATIONAL PARK
WHITE RIVER NATIONAL FOREST
PIKE NATIONAL FOREST
Elk River
Yampa River
Colorado River
Blue River
Arkansas River
Middle Fork
Shadow Mountain Reservoir
Lake Granby
Green Mountain Reservoir
Turquoise Lake
Columbine
Hahns Peak
Clark
Cowdrey
Glendevey
Walden
Rustic
Hebron
Coalmont
Gould
Milner
Steamboat Springs
Rand
Estes Park
Oak Creek
Phippsburg
Yampa
Hot Sulphur Springs
Kremmling
Toponas
Granby
Ward
Tabernash
Nederland
Winter Park
Central City
Wolcott
Dotsero
Eagle
Gypsum
Dowd
Vail
Avon
Minturn
Dillon
Georgetown
Echo Lake
Frisco
Redcliff
Breckenridge
Grant
Carbondale
Basalt
Meredith
Jefferson
Como
Leadville
Malta
Fairplay
Aspen
Redstone
Granite
125
127
14
34
40
7
72
134
131
9
70
24
91
285
82
133
1
2
3
6
7-8
9
4-5
10
11
15
16
17-19
30
12-14
38
39-45
23
24
26
27
28-29
31-35
36-37
20-21
22
25
46
50
51
52-53
61-63
48-49
56
57-60
64-68
47
54-55
74
75-78
79
80
81
82-85
69
70
71
72
73
113
114
86-90
91-94
95-97
98
107
117
99
100-106
108
111-112
116
121
109-110
115
118-120
124
125-127
131-134
122
123
128-130
143-148
135
136-137
160-162
149
154-158
163
142
138-141
168-171
174
150-153
159
164
175
176-181
184-185
190
167
172-173
191
182
183
186-187
189
165
166
188
193-196
197
202-203
211
192
198-201
212
204-205
206-208
209
210

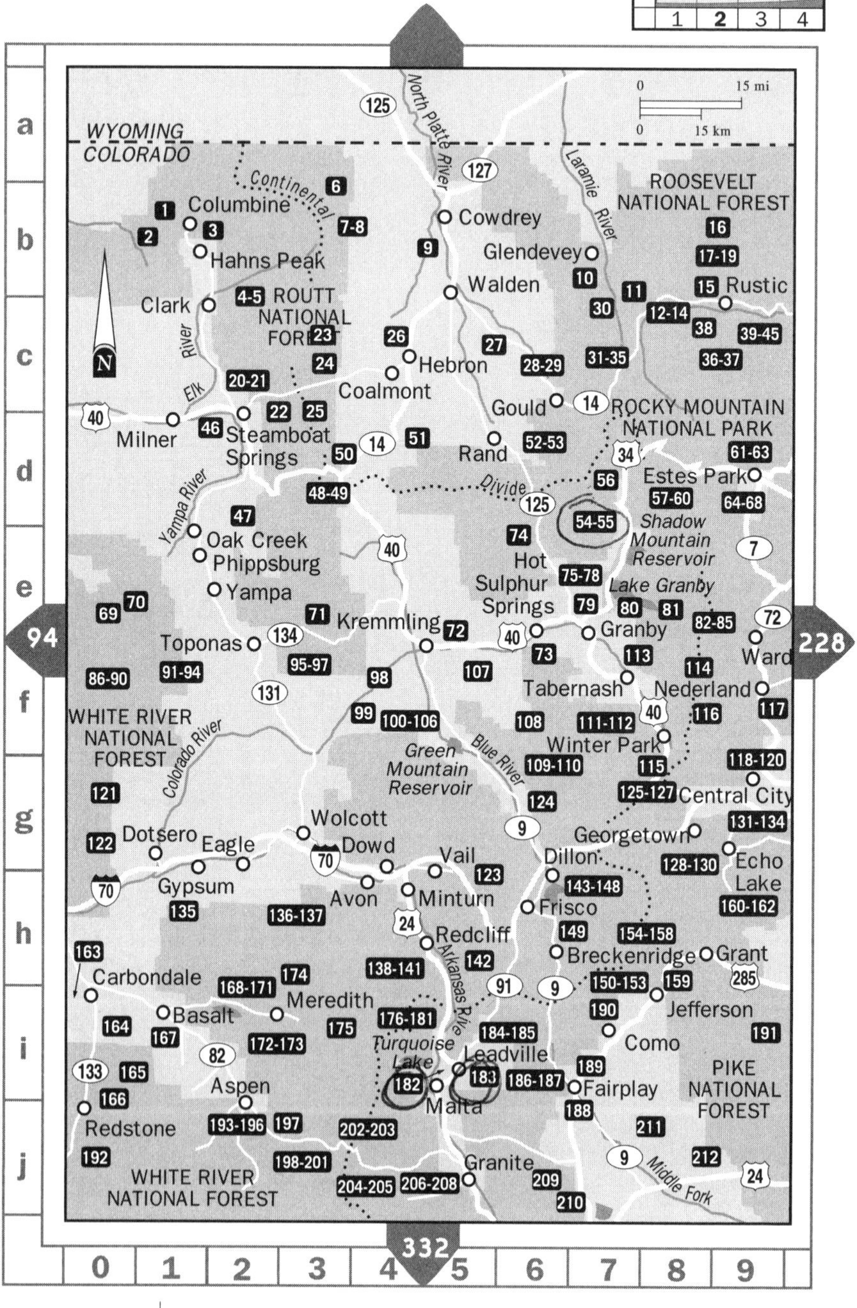

# CHAPTER A2

## ■ Hahns Peak Lake      9

The pristine, wilderness-like quality of this campground makes it one of the most popular destinations in the region. It's perched on the northwestern edge of Hahns Peak Lake with incredibly scenic views and convenient lake access. There are two loops in the campground: the lake loop and the tree loop. The lake loop campsites are the most sought after and provide the most picturesque views, but you can't go wrong with any site at Hahns Peak Lake—they're all lovely. Nonmotorized boating and fishing are permitted in the lake, and adjacent to the campground is a sunny day-use area and several good hiking trails for those who want to explore the surroundings.

**Location:** North of Steamboat Springs in Routt National Forest; map A2, grid b1.

**Campsites, facilities:** There are 25 sites for tents or RVs up to 40 feet long. Drinking water, picnic tables, fire grills, and vault toilets are provided. Leashed pets are permitted.

**Elevation:** 8,500 feet.

**Reservations, fees:** Reservations are accepted; phone (877) 444-6777. There's an $8.65 reservation fee. You may also reserve sites at website: www.reserveusa.com. Sites are $10 a night.

**Open:** June to October.

**Directions:** From Steamboat Springs, drive two miles west on U.S. 40 and turn north on County Rd. 129. Drive approximately 26 miles (you'll pass the entrance to Steamboat Lake State Park). Turn left on Forest Service Rd. 486 and continue 2.5 miles to the campground entrance.

**Contact:** Routt National Forest, Hahns Peak-Bears Ears Ranger District, P.O. Box 771212, Steamboat Springs, CO 80477; tel. (970) 824-9438.

## ■ Steamboat Lake State Park      8

There are two camping areas in the park: Dutch Hill and Sunrise Vista. If you're into boating, consider Dutch Hill, which is adjacent to a boat ramp and marina. Waterskiing and PWC riding are permitted in designated areas, while several coves and the entire southwest portion of the lake are cordoned off for fishing and no-wake boating. The Sunrise Vista area is a bit more secluded, offering striking views of the Continental Divide. Swimming and hiking are two recreational options here, with designated swimming beaches and an interpretive nature trail nearby. Horses can be rented for rides on park trails. Limited hunting is permitted; call for details. In 2000 the park added a new visitor center and year-round camper cabins (contact the marina for details).

**Location:** North of Steamboat Springs; map A2, grid b1.

**Campsites, facilities:** There are 178 sites for tents or RVs of any length, and 20 walk-in tent sites. Picnic tables, fire grills, drinking water, and vault and flush toilets are provided. Hot showers, electric hookups, a waste disposal station, laundry facilities, small store, cabins, public phone, boat ramps, and boat rentals are available. Leashed pets are permitted.

**Elevation:** 8,000 feet.

**Reservations, fees:** Reservations are accepted. Phone (303) 470-1144 or (800) 678-CAMP (800-678-2267) outside the Denver Metro area; there's a $7 reservation fee. Sites are $10-16 a night, and there's a $4 entrance fee.

**Open:** Year-round.

**Directions:** From Steamboat Springs, drive two miles west on U.S. 40 and turn north on County Rd. 129. Drive approximately 25 miles to the park entrance.

**Contact:** Steamboat Lake State Park, P.O. Box 750, Clark, CO 80483; tel. (970) 879-3922.

## 🖪 Pearl Lake State Park       10

You won't find hot showers here. Nor will you find resort-style facilities for speedboats and PWCs. What you will find is a quiet refuge next to a pristine mountain lake, steeped in tranquillity and tucked at the base of spectacular snowcapped mountains and lush conifer forest. The campground is at the north end of Pearl Lake, with a lakeside trail leading around the southern perimeter. Those who desire more extensive hiking can head east to the Mount Zirkel Wilderness, which provides a network of trails. The boat ramp is at the end of the main access road and offers launching for small watercraft (no-wake boating only). Fishing for cutthroat, rainbow, and brook trout is excellent, but there are many special regulations; contact the park office for details, as well as for hunting information. In 2000 the park finished building yurts—woodframed, canvas-walled cabins of Nordic origin—in the campground. Special note: The campground is closed during the winter, but the rest of the park offers fantastic cross-country skiing then.

**Location:** North of Steamboat Springs; map A2, grid b2.

**Campsites, facilities:** There are 38 sites for tents or RVs of any length, plus yurts available for rent. Drinking water, picnic tables, fire grills, and vault and flush toilets are provided. A boat ramp is nearby. Some facilities are wheelchair accessible. Leashed pets are permitted.

**Elevation:** 8,100 feet.

**Reservations, fees:** Reservations are accepted. Phone (303) 470-1144 or (800) 678-CAMP (800-678-2267) outside the Denver Metro area; there's a $7 reservation fee. Sites are $10 a night, and there's a $4 fee.

**Open:** June to October.

**Directions:** From Steamboat Springs, drive two miles west on U.S. 40 and turn north on County Rd. 129. Drive approximately 22 miles, turn right at the sign for Pearl Lake State Park, and continue two miles to the entrance.

**Contact:** Pearl Lake State Park, P.O. Box 750, Clark, CO 80428; tel. (970) 879-3922.

## 🖪 Hinman    8

Set along the Elk River northeast of Steamboat Springs, Hinman is a perfect spot to spend a day or two relaxing. It's far enough off the beaten track to remain quiet and serene, and is known locally for superb river fishing and wildlife viewing. Native critters include elk, deer, a variety of birds, and even—yikes!—an occasional bear or mountain lion. Bring your camera.

**Location:** On the Elk River in Routt National Forest; map A2, grid b2.

**Campsites, facilities:** There are 13 sites for tents or RVs up to 22 feet long. Drinking water, picnic tables, fire grills, and vault toilets are provided. Leashed pets are permitted.

**Elevation:** 7,600 feet.

**Reservations, fees:** Reservations are not accepted. Sites are $10 a night.

**Open:** June to October.

**Directions:** From Steamboat Springs, drive two miles west on U.S. 40 and turn north on County Rd. 129. Drive approximately 17 miles, turn right on Forest Service Rd. 400, and continue about five miles east to the campground.

**Contact:** Routt National Forest, Hahns Peak-Bears Ears Ranger District, P.O. Box 771212, Steamboat Springs, CO 80477; tel. (970) 824-9438.

## 5 Seedhouse      8

Seedhouse is the closest campground to the popular Slavonia Trailhead, a major jump-off point into the Mount Zirkel Wilderness. The sites, set under towering pine trees, border the Elk River; you can fish within walking distance of your site. To the north are more hiking trails and a few excellent mountain biking trails.

**Location:** On the Elk River in Routt National Forest; map A2, grid b2.

**Campsites, facilities:** There are 24 sites for tents or RVs up to 22 feet long, and one large group site for as many as 30 people. Drinking water, picnic tables, fire grills, and vault toilets are provided. Leashed pets are permitted.

**Elevation:** 8,000 feet.

**Reservations, fees:** Reservations are accepted only for the group site; phone (877) 444-6777. There's an $8.65 reservation fee. You may also reserve sites at website: www.reserveusa.com. Fees are $10 a night for single sites; the price for the group site varies according to size of the party.

**Open:** June to October.

**Directions:** From Steamboat Springs, drive two miles west on U.S. 40 and turn north on County Rd. 129. Drive approximately 17 miles, turn right on Forest Service Rd. 400, and continue about eight miles east to the campground.

**Contact:** Routt National Forest, Hahns Peak-Bears Ears Ranger District, P.O. Box 771212, Steamboat Springs, CO 80477; tel. (970) 824-9438.

## 6 Big Creek Lakes        8

Upper Big Creek Lake is a mecca for water sports enthusiasts and hikers. It's one of the few lakes in the region that allow power boating, including waterskiing, while still maintaining a wilderness-like environment. The lake is adjacent to a short interpretive trail, as well as two major trailheads routed into the Mount Zirkel Wilderness. The Beaver Creek Trail meanders west about 10 miles before crossing the northern border of the wilderness; the Seven Lakes Trail heads 2.5 miles south, passing Lower Big Creek Lake and Big Creek Falls before crossing into the wilderness. If you continue south of the lake on Forest Service Rd. 660, you'll come to the Helena Trailhead, another wilderness access point.

**Location:** Northeast of Steamboat Springs in Routt National Forest; map A2, grid b3.

**Campsites, facilities:** There are 54 sites for tents or RVs up to 76 feet long. Drinking water, picnic tables, fire grills, and vault toilets are provided. A boat ramp is available. Leashed pets are permitted.

**Elevation:** 9,000 feet.

**Reservations, fees:** Reservations are accepted; phone (877) 444-6777. There's an $8.65 reservation fee. You may also reserve sites at website: www.reserveusa.com. Sites are $10 a night.

**Open:** June to October.

**Directions:** From the junction of Hwy. 14 and Hwy. 125 just south of Walden, drive approximately eight miles north on Hwy. 125 to Cowdrey. Turn left on County Rd. 6W and drive about 11 miles west to the town of Pearl. Turn left on Forest Service Rd. 600 and continue eight miles southwest to the campground.

**Contact:** Routt National Forest, Parks Ranger District, 100 Main St., P.O. Box 158, Walden, CO 80480; tel. (970) 723-8204.

## 7 Lake John State Wildlife Area      5

It's simple: If you've got an RV, head across the lake to Richard's RV Park. If you're in a tent, stay here. Either way, you're in for a bare-bones camping experience with few amenities. The trade-off, however, is the splendid 560-acre Lake John, a clear, cold jewel brimming with every imaginable variety of trout. Since no motorized boats are permitted on the lake, the atmosphere is relaxed and quiet—so whether you're paddling your canoe or hiking around the lake, the only sound you're likely to hear is the chatter of native birds (aside from the occasional shot from a hunting rifle).

**Location:** Northwest of Walden; map A2, grid b4.

**Campsites, facilities:** Dispersed tent camping is permitted in designated areas. A vault toilet and shade shelters are provided, but there is no drinking water. A boat ramp (nonmotorized craft only) is available nearby. Leashed pets are permitted.

**Elevation:** 7,800 feet.

**Reservations, fees:** Reservations are not accepted. There is no fee.

**Open:** Year-round.

**Directions:** From the junction of Hwy. 14 and Hwy. 125 just south of Walden, go one mile north on Hwy. 125 and turn left on County Rd. 12W. Drive seven miles west, take a right on County Rd. 7, and drive six miles north to the turnoff for Lake John. Turn left and look for the signs designating Division of Wildlife property.

**Contact:** Colorado Division of Wildlife, 317 W. Prospect Ave., Fort Collins, CO 80526; tel. (970) 472-4300.

## 8 Richard's RV Park     5

This place is for self-contained units only, lacking showers and even toilets, and having no room set aside for tents. That said, it's not a bad place to park your rig, with open, treeless sites and excellent views of Lake John and the surrounding distant peaks. Set near the lakeshore, the campground provides easy access to a boat ramp and fishing spots. If you like trout, you'll have your pick: rainbow, brown, brook, or cutthroat. Hiking trails are scattered around the shore, and more hiking is available at nearby Lake John State Wildlife Area.

**Location:** On Lake John; map A2, grid b4.

**Campsites, facilities:** There are 33 sites for RVs of any length, many with full hookups. No tents are permitted. Drinking water, picnic tables, and fire grills are provided, but there are no toilets or showers. A waste disposal station and a boat ramp (nonmotorized craft only) are available. Leashed pets are permitted.

**Elevation:** 8,500 feet.

**Reservations, fees:** Reservations are accepted. Sites are $9-11 a night.

**Open:** Mid-May to October.

**Directions:** From the junction of Hwy. 14 and Hwy. 125 just south of Walden, go one mile north on Hwy. 125 and turn left on County Rd. 12W. Drive seven miles west, take a right on County Rd. 7, and drive six miles north to the turnoff for Lake John. Turn left and continue about four miles around the lake to the campground.

**Contact:** Richard's RV Park, 4521 County Rd. 7A, SR Box 410, Walden, CO 80480; tel. (970) 723-4407 (phone turned off in winter).

## 9 Cowdrey Lake State Wildlife Area     5

The attraction at this state wildlife area is 80-acre Cowdrey Lake, where you can fish for rainbow or brook trout by boat or from the shore. The surrounding land is sparsely vegetated, with few trees and scanty wildlife that draws hunters at various times. Since you're not limited to designated campsites, however, you're free to explore the area's 280 acres to find just the right spot.

**Location:** North of Walden; map A2, grid b5.

**Campsites, facilities:** Dispersed camping is permitted throughout the property. A vault toilet and a boat ramp (no-wake boating only) are provided, but there is no drinking water. Leashed pets are permitted.

**Elevation:** 7,900 feet.

**Reservations, fees:** Reservations are not accepted. There is no fee.

**Open:** Year-round.

**Directions:** From the junction of Hwy. 14 and Hwy. 125 just south of Walden, drive approximately eight miles north on Hwy. 125 to the campground entrance.

**Contact:** Colorado Division of Wildlife, 317 W. Prospect Ave., Fort Collins, CO 80526; tel. (970) 472-4300.

## 10 Browns Park    7

It's a long haul to get here, but you'll be pleased you made the trip. The camp is in a secluded, thickly wooded area on the border of the Rawah Wilderness. Adjacent to camp is the Link McIntyre Trailhead, which heads south into the wilderness for several miles, eventually reaching McIntyre Lake and Rawah Lakes.

**Location:** On Jinks Creek in Roosevelt National Forest; map A2, grid b7.

**Campsites, facilities:** There are 28 sites for tents or RVs up to 30 feet long. A vault toilet is provided, but there are no other facilities or drinking water. Leashed pets are permitted.

**Elevation:** 8,400 feet.

**Reservations, fees:** Reservations are not accepted. Sites are $8 a night.

**Open:** June to November.

**Directions:** From Fort Collins, head west on Hwy. 14 for approximately 70 miles to Chambers Lake. Turn north on County Rd. 103 (Laramie River Rd.) and drive 20 miles to the campground, located just past the old Stub Creek Ranger Station.

**Contact:** Roosevelt National Forest, Canyon Lakes Ranger District, 1311 S. College Ave., Fort Collins, CO 80524; tel. (970) 498-2770.

## 11 Bliss State Wildlife Area    8

Bliss is right. Thick, green stands of trees, a narrow riverbed strewn with huge boulders and sliced by shimmering, crystal-clear water—it's no wonder that Poudre Canyon is one of the most popular camping destinations in Colorado. The wildlife area covers more than 350 acres and straddles the Cache la Poudre River, providing access to miles of pristine backcountry. There are no developed hiking trails, but the adventurous will enjoy exploring the canyon on their own. Keep an eye out for elk and bighorn sheep. Limited hunting is permitted.

**Location:** In Poudre Canyon; map A2, grid b7.

**Campsites, facilities:** Dispersed camping is permitted throughout the property. A vault toilet is provided, but there are no other facilities or drinking water. Leashed pets are permitted. No boat takeouts or put-ins are permitted.

**Elevation:** 7,500 feet.

**Reservations, fees:** Reservations are not accepted. There is no fee.

**Open:** Year-round.

**Directions:** From Fort Collins, turn west on Hwy. 14 and drive approximately 60 miles to the property entrance.

**Contact:** Colorado Division of Wildlife, 317 W. Prospect Ave., Fort Collins, CO 80526; tel. (970) 472-4300.

## 12 Home Moraine Trailer Park     7

Tall, spiny cliffs overlook this RV park tucked along the banks of the rushing Cache la Poudre River. It offers easy access to the river and hiking trails, plus a private stocked trout pond for guests. The sites are large and airy, some shaded by small trees. The campground's proximity to the highway can be a problem in midsummer, when traffic zooms through Poudre Canyon at an alarming rate.

**Location:** On the Cache la Poudre River; map A2, grid b8.

**Campsites, facilities:** There are 20 tent sites and 32 full-hookup sites for RVs of any length. Drinking water, picnic tables, fire grills, and bathrooms with hot showers are provided. Laundry facilities are available. Pets are forbidden.

**Elevation:** 7,500 feet.

**Reservations, fees:** Reservations are accepted. Sites are $12-14 a night.

**Open:** May to October.

**Directions:** From Fort Collins, turn west on Hwy. 14 and drive approximately 50 miles to the campground.

**Contact:** Home Moraine Trailer Park, 37797 Poudre Canyon Dr., Bellvue, CO 80512; tel. (970) 881-2356.

## 13 Big Bend      7

One of the smaller camps in the area, Big Bend offers private, moderately shaded sites adjacent to the river. From the campground you can fish, sunbathe, or simply watch the icy water tumble over the rocks. Up the road about a mile is a hiking trail that runs along the river.

**Location:** On the Cache la Poudre River in Roosevelt National Forest; map A2, grid b8.

**Campsites, facilities:** There are six sites for tents or RVs up to 20 feet long, and three walk-in tent sites. Drinking water, picnic tables, fire grills, and vault toilets are provided. Leashed pets are permitted.

**Elevation:** 7,770 feet.

**Reservations, fees:** Reservations are not accepted. Sites are $9 a night.

**Open:** Year-round.

**Directions:** From Fort Collins, turn west on Hwy. 14 and drive approximately 49 miles to the campground.

**Contact:** Roosevelt National Forest, Canyon Lakes Ranger District, 1311 S. College Ave., Fort Collins, CO 80524; tel. (970) 498-2770.

## 14 Poudre River Resort     6

"Resort" is the key word in this campground's name. It boasts every amenity imaginable, from a hot tub to video rentals to full-service cabins. A thick band of conifers separates the grassy, open sites from the beautiful Cache la Poudre River, where you can fish, hike, or just kick back in your camp chair and watch the water go by. Like many other campgrounds in the area, this one is directly adjacent to the highway.

**Location:** On the Cache la Poudre River; map A2, grid b8.

**Campsites, facilities:** There are six full-hookup RV sites and a separate area for tents. Drinking water, picnic tables, fire grills, and bathrooms with hot showers are provided. Laundry facilities, a waste disposal station, restaurant, and cabins are also available. The bathrooms and bridges are wheelchair accessible. Leashed pets are permitted.

**Elevation:** 7,000 feet.

**Reservations, fees:** Reservations are accepted. Sites are $12-20 a night.

**Open:** Year-round.

**Directions:** From Fort Collins, turn west on Hwy. 14 and drive approximately 45 miles to the campground.

**Contact:** Poudre River Resort, 33021 Hwy. 14, Bellvue, CO 80512; tel. (970) 881-2139.

## 15 North Fork Poudre     7

Since this wooded camp is indeed on the North Fork of the Cache la Poudre River, it's a perfect spot to relax and do a little fishing. Little in more ways than one: You probably won't catch anything but tiny brookies. If you crave more adventurous activity, head across the highway to the Killpecker Trailhead, which leads a few miles south into the forest along Killpecker Creek.

**Location:** On the North Fork of the Cache la Poudre River in Roosevelt National Forest; map A2, grid b8.

**Campsites, facilities:** There are nine sites for tents or RVs up to 30 feet long. Picnic tables, fire grills, and vault toilets are provided, but there is no drinking water. Leashed pets are permitted.

**Elevation:** 9,200 feet.

**Reservations, fees:** Reservations are not accepted. Sites are $7 a night.

**Open:** June to November.

**Directions:** From Fort Collins, drive 21 miles north on U.S. 287 to Livermore. Turn west on County Rd. 74E and continue some 30 miles (seven miles past Red Feather Lakes village) to the campground.

**Contact:** Roosevelt National Forest, Canyon Lakes Ranger District, 1311 S. College Ave., Fort Collins, CO 80524; tel. (970) 498-2770.

## **16** Beaver Meadows Resort Ranch

 9

Set in a scenic spot on this 840-acre ranch, the campground at Beaver Meadows Resort is simple and lovely, with tidy, shaded sites along the North Fork of the Cache La Poudre River. There are sandy areas for tents at each site, and RVs are permitted (although no hookups are available). The camp is in the middle of a full-service resort that offers lodging in its condos, log hotel, or cabins; it also has a restaurant and lounge. The ranch features 22 miles of hiking trails, as well as mountain biking, horseback riding, and fishing in the river or the private, stocked trout ponds. Trail rides and rafting trips can also be arranged. And if you're so inspired by the natural beauty that you must express yourself, karaoke is offered every Saturday in the lounge.

**Location:** Near Red Feather Lakes, map A2, grid b8.

**Campsites, facilities:** There are 50 sites for tents or RVs. Drinking water, picnic tables, fire pits, and vault toilets are provided. Hot showers are available for a fee. Cabins, condos, a restaurant, and a lodge are also available. Leashed pets are permitted.

**Elevation:** 8,500 feet.

**Reservations, fees:** Reservations are accepted. Sites are $15 a night.

**Open:** May to November, depending on snowfall.

**Directions:** From Fort Collins, drive 21 miles north on U.S. 287 to Livermore. Turn left (west) on County Rd. 74E and go 24. 25 miles. Turn right on County Rd. 73C and continue five miles to the ranch entrance.

**Contact:** Beaver Meadows Resort Ranch, 100 Marmot Dr., Unit 1, Red Feather Lakes, CO 80545; tel. (970) 881-2450 or 800-462-5870; e-mail: info@beavermeadows.com.

## **17** Bellaire Lake      8

Bellaire Lake is far enough from the main Red Feather Lakes complex to get missed by most tourists. It's set in dense conifer forest with little clumps of wildflowers scattered about in midsummer. You'll find mediocre trout fishing and a wheelchair-accessible nature trail at the campground. The western trailhead for the Lady Moon Trail is across the road.

**Location:** Southeast of Redfeather Lakes in Roosevelt National Forest; map A2, grid b8.

**Campsites, facilities:** There are 26 sites for tents or RVs up to 60 feet long. Drinking water, picnic tables, fire grills, and vault toilets are provided. Some facilities are wheelchair accessible. Leashed pets are permitted.

**Elevation:** 8,600 feet.

**Reservations, fees:** Reservations are not accepted. Sites are $12 a night.

**Open:** June to November.

**Directions:** From Fort Collins, drive 21 miles north on U.S. 287 to Livermore. Turn west on County Rd. 74E and continue about 23 miles to the town of Red Feather Lakes. Go west another half mile, turn left on Forest Service Rd. 162, and drive two miles to the campground entrance.

**Contact:** Roosevelt National Forest, Canyon Lakes Ranger District, 1311 S. College Ave., Fort Collins, CO 80524; tel. (970) 498-2770.

## 18 West Lake      8

West Lake is a gorgeous little spot in the northern reaches of Roosevelt National Forest near the Red Feather Lakes complex. The campground is on the south side of the lake in a partially shaded setting, with shoreline access for fishing. Backtrack about a mile east on County Rd. 74E to find a trailhead for the Lady Moon Trail.

**Location:** Near Red Feather Lakes in Roosevelt National Forest; map A2, grid b8.

**Campsites, facilities:** There are 29 sites for tents or RVs up to 50 feet long. Drinking water, picnic tables, fire grills, and vault toilets are provided. Leashed pets are permitted.

**Elevation:** 8,200 feet.

**Reservations, fees:** Reservations are accepted; phone (877) 444-6777. There's an $8.65 reservation fee. You may also reserve sites at website: www.reserveusa.com. Sites are $10 a night.

**Open:** Mid-May to September.

**Directions:** From Fort Collins, drive 21 miles north on U.S. 287 to Livermore. Turn west on County Rd. 74E and continue about 22 miles to the campground entrance.

**Contact:** Roosevelt National Forest, Canyon Lakes Ranger District, 1311 S. College Ave., Fort Collins, CO 80524; tel. (970) 498-2770.

## 19 Dowdy Lake      8

Campers enjoy access to no-wake boating and fishing for rainbow, brown, brook, and cutthroat trout at this 120-acre lake. The camp is divided into two areas, one on the south side of the lake and one on the north. Both are situated amid pine trees not far from the shoreline, but the south side is slightly more secluded and is close to the Mount Margaret Trail, leading up to the peak of Mount Margaret (elevation 7,957 feet).

**Location:** Near Red Feather Lakes in Roosevelt National Forest; map A2, grid b8.

**Campsites, facilities:** There are 62 sites for tents or RVs up to 40 feet long. Drinking water, picnic tables, fire grills, and vault toilets are provided. Leashed pets are permitted.

**Elevation:** 8,100 feet.

**Reservations, fees:** Reservations are accepted; phone (877) 444-6777. There's an $8.65 reservation fee. You may also reserve sites at website: www.reserveusa.com. Sites are $10 a night.

**Open:** Mid-May to September.

**Directions:** From Fort Collins, drive 21 miles north on U.S. 287 to Livermore. Turn west on County Rd. 74E and continue about 22 miles. Turn right and proceed past West Lake to the campground entrance.

**Contact:** Roosevelt National Forest, Canyon Lakes Ranger District, 1311 S. College Ave., Fort Collins, CO 80524; tel. (970) 498-2770.

## 20 Dry Lake  8

As the closest U.S. Forest Service campground to Steamboat Springs, Dry Lake gets a lot of use. It's an oval-shaped camp set in aspen and pine forest, with small, well-spaced, private sites. The allure lies mainly in its proximity to town, but it offers a peaceful, pretty environment for those who want to escape civilization as well. There are no designated hiking trails in the immediate area, but here's an insider's tip: Between sites 4 and 5 lies an unmarked trail that leads out of camp to a grassy meadow where the former lake once stood. Another tip: You're within a short drive of beautiful, rustic Strawberry Park Hot Springs—don't miss it!

**Location:** Near Steamboat Springs in Routt National Forest; map A2, grid c2.

**Campsites, facilities:** There are eight sites for tents or RVs up to 16 feet long. Drinking water, picnic tables, fire grills, and a vault toilet are provided. Leashed pets are permitted.

**Elevation:** 8,000 feet.

**Reservations, fees:** Reservations are not accepted. Sites are $10 a night.

**Open:** June to October.

**Directions:** From U.S. 40 in the town of Steamboat Springs, turn east on 7th St. and follow the signs to Strawberry Park Hot Springs. Turn right at the sign for Buffalo Pass and drive approximately three miles to the campground turnoff on your left, across from the day-use parking lot. Note: This route can be confusing. Before you head out, stop at the Steamboat Springs Chamber of Commerce office in town and pick up a free city map, which highlights the roads you'll need to find.

**Contact:** Routt National Forest, Hahns Peak-Bears Ears Ranger District, P.O. Box 771212, Steamboat Springs, CO 80477; tel. (970) 824-9438.

## 21 Summit Lake  9

Take a deep breath of oxygen-depleted air and look around—you're at the top of the Continental Divide. This campground is at the crest of Buffalo Pass across the road from the Wyoming Trailhead, a popular route into the Mount Zirkel Wilderness. Despite—or perhaps because of—its remote location and extremely short season, the camp gets heavy use; it is frequented by mountain bikers heading up and over the pass. The walk-in sites are my favorite; they're just a few bucks, and although you don't get a picnic table or grill, you do get privacy—the sites are well spaced— and pristine views of a small pond. Just to the northwest of camp is scenic Summit Lake, where you can fish and tool around in a cartop boat.

**Location:** East of Steamboat Springs in Routt National Forest; map A2, grid c2.

**Campsites, facilities:** There are 16 tent sites and a few primitive walk-in sites. Drinking water, picnic tables, fire grills, and vault toilets are provided. Leashed pets are permitted.

**Elevation:** 10,300 feet.

**Reservations, fees:** Reservations are not accepted. Fees are $4 a night for walk-in sites, $10 for developed sites.

**Open:** July to August.

**Directions:** From U.S. 40 in the town of Steamboat Springs, turn east on 7th St.

and follow the signs to Strawberry Park Hot Springs. Turn right at the sign for Buffalo Pass and drive approximately 11 miles east to the campground. The roads gets rough past Dry Lake Campground; high-clearance vehicles are recommended. Note: This route can be confusing. Before you head out, stop at the Steamboat Springs Chamber of Commerce office in town and pick up a free city map, which highlights the roads you'll need to find.

**Contact:** Routt National Forest, Hahns Peak-Bears Ears Ranger District, P.O. Box 771212, Steamboat Springs, CO 80477; tel. (970) 824-9438.

## 22 Granite      8

If you can manage to find your way here, you probably won't want to leave. This camp is positioned alongside Fish Creek Reservoir with good fishing access and impressive views of the rocky peaks surrounding Steamboat. The atmosphere is quiet, lush, and green, and you're within easy reach of the Continental Divide and spectacular Fish Creek Falls, the prominent cascade made famous on Coors beer cans.

**Location:** On Fish Creek Reservoir in Routt National Forest; map A2, grid c2.

**Campsites, facilities:** There are four walk-in tent sites and four drive-in sites. Vehicles are not subject to restrictions on length, but you must have a high-clearance vehicle to reach the campground (which rules out most RVs). Picnic tables, fire grills, and vault toilets are provided, but there is no drinking water. Leashed pets are permitted.

**Elevation:** 9,900 feet.

**Reservations, fees:** Reservations are not accepted. Sites are $4 a night.

**Open:** June to October.

**Directions:** From U.S. 40 in the town of Steamboat Springs, turn east on 7th St. and follow the signs to Strawberry Park Hot Springs. Turn right at the sign for Buffalo Pass and drive approximately 11 miles east to Summit Lake Campground; turn south on Forest Service Rd. 310 and continue about four miles to Granite Campground, located on the north side of Fish Creek Reservoir. The roads gets rough past Dry Lake Campground; high-clearance vehicles are recommended. Note: This route can be confusing. Before you head out, stop at the Steamboat Springs Chamber of Commerce office in town and pick up a free city map, which highlights the roads you'll need to find.

**Contact:** Routt National Forest, Hahns Peak-Bears Ears Ranger District, P.O. Box 771212, Steamboat Springs, CO 80477; tel. (970) 824-9438.

## 23 Teal Lake       8

One of the most popular camps in this district, Teal Lake mostly attracts anglers in search of rainbow trout. Only electric powerboats are allowed, but fishing is excellent. Two sites are near the water's edge; the rest are set back in a conifer forest. Although it's true that a couple of sites are wheelchair accessible, the toilets and water are not so easily accessible, so wheelchair campers should call ahead for details. Just a mile or two north on Forest Service Rd. 615 are trails routed into the Mount Zirkel Wilderness, including a 30-mile motorized trail called the Grizzly-Helena Trail, which is frequented by ATV riders.

**Location:** Southwest of Walden in Routt National Forest; map A2, grid c3.

**Campsites, facilities:** There are 17 sites for tents or RVs of any length, and one group site which can accommodate up to seven vehicles. Drinking water, picnic tables, fire grills, and vault toilets are provided. Two sites are wheelchair accessible. Leashed pets are permitted.

**Elevation:** 9,000 feet.

**Reservations, fees:** Reservations are accepted; phone (877) 444-6777. The reservation fee is $8.65. You may also reserve sites at website: www.reserveusa.com. Individual sites are $10 a night; group rates vary according to group size.

**Open:** June to Labor Day.

**Directions:** From Walden, drive approximately 12 miles west on Hwy. 14 to Hebron. Turn right on County Rd. 24 and drive about 10 miles; then turn right on Forest Service Rd. 60 and continue one-half mile to Grizzly Campground. Turn right on Forest Service Rd. 615 and continue four miles north to Teal Lake.

**Contact:** Routt National Forest, Parks Ranger District, 100 Main St., P.O. Box 158, Walden, CO 80480; tel. (970) 723-8204.

## 24 Grizzly Creek    6

You'll probably find solitude here, but not much else. Grizzly Creek is a small, unadorned campground with sites scattered among pine trees. It's just inside the national forest and a few miles south of the Mount Zirkel Wilderness boundary. If you drive north up Forest Service Rd. 615, you'll run into a trailhead bound for several tiny alpine lakes.

**Location:** Southwest of Walden in Routt National Forest; map A2, grid c3.

**Campsites, facilities:** There are 12 sites for tents or RVs up to 18 feet long. Drinking water, picnic tables, fire grills, and vault toilets are provided. Leashed pets are permitted.

**Elevation:** 8,500 feet.

**Reservations, fees:** Reservations are not accepted. Sites are $10 a night.

**Open:** June to October.

**Directions:** From Walden, drive approximately 12 miles west on Hwy. 14 to Hebron. Turn right on County Rd. 24 and drive about 10 miles; turn right on Forest Service Rd. 60 and continue one-half mile to the campground.

**Contact:** Routt National Forest, Parks Ranger District, 100 Main St., P.O. Box 158, Walden, CO 80480; tel. (970) 723-8204.

## 25 Hidden Lakes     7

The secluded and little-used camp is quite pretty. It's in a partially wooded setting with fair views, near a cluster of tiny lakes that offer nonmotorized boating and fair fishing for trout. These lakes are hidden, all right—they're out in the boonies, and except for locals, hardly anyone seems to know they exist.

**Location:** Near Steamboat Springs in Routt National Forest; map A2, grid c3.

**Campsites, facilities:** There are nine sites for tents or RVs up to 22 feet long. Drinking water, picnic tables, fire grills, and vault toilets are provided. Leashed pets are permitted.

**Elevation:** 8,900 feet.

**Reservations, fees:** Reservations are not accepted. Sites are $10 a night.

**Open:** June to October.

**Directions:** From Walden, drive approximately 12 miles west on Hwy. 14 to Hebron. Turn right on County Rd. 24 and drive about 10 miles; turn right on Forest Service Rd. 60 and go 1.5 miles. Turn left on Forest Service Rd. 20 and continue four miles to the campground.

**Contact:** Routt National Forest, Parks Ranger District, 100 Main St., P.O. Box 158, Walden, CO 80480; tel. (970) 723-8204.

## 26 Delaney Butte Lakes State Wildlife Area
    7

As is true of many of the state wildlife areas in this region, the primary attraction here is fishing. You have three lakes to choose from: East Delaney Butte, North Delaney Butte, and South Delaney Butte. North Delaney, the largest of the trio, is renowned as a Gold Medal Water, boasting enormous brown trout (the record is 25 inches, seven pounds). Each has a boat ramp suitable for small craft. The fishing regulations are lengthy and detailed, so be sure to check with the Division of Wildlife before you cast a line. You can camp pretty much anywhere on the property, and with more than 2,600 acres, you should be able to find a nice spot. Much of the land is open mesa, but scattered conifers offer a little shade and privacy. Limited hunting is permitted.

**Location:** West of Walden; map A2, grid c4.

**Campsites, facilities:** Dispersed tent camping is permitted throughout the property. Picnic tables, shade shelters, and vault toilets are provided, but there is no drinking water. Each of the three lakes has a boat ramp (no-wake boating only). Leashed pets are permitted.

**Elevation:** 8,100 feet.

**Reservations, fees:** Reservations are not accepted. There is no fee.

**Open:** Year-round.

**Directions:** From the junction of Hwy. 14 and Hwy. 125 just south of Walden, travel one mile north on Hwy. 125 and turn left on County Rd. 12W. Drive five miles west, turn left on County Rd. 18, and continue west 4.5 miles. At County Rd. 5, turn right and proceed about a mile north to the property entrance.

**Contact:** Colorado Division of Wildlife, 317 W. Prospect Ave., Fort Collins, CO 80526; tel. (970) 472-4300.

## 27 Owl Mountain State Wildlife Area
  4

There just plain isn't much out here. The 920-acre Owl Mountain State Wildlife Area, along with Cohagen and Kemp Draw State Trust Lands to the north, is hunting country. This means that although camping is allowed year-round, you should beware of gun-toting wildlife-chasers during hunting season. Off-season, however, you're practically guaranteed complete solitude and quiet—and sometimes that's all you need. The area supports a diverse variety of plants and wildlife, including deer, elk, and blue grouse.

**Location:** Southeast of Walden; map A2, grid c5.

**Campsites, facilities:** Dispersed camping is permitted throughout the property, which has no facilities. Leashed pets are permitted.

**Elevation:** 9,000 feet.

**Reservations, fees:** Reservations are not accepted. There is no fee.

**Open:** Year-round.

**Directions:** From Walden, drive approximately 13 miles east on Hwy. 14, turn south on County Rd. 25, and continue six miles to the property entrance.

**Contact:** Colorado Division of Wildlife, 317 W. Prospect Ave., Fort Collins, CO 80526; tel. (970) 472-4300.

## 28 North Park KOA     6

So many KOAs are smack-dab in the middle of a town—it hardly seems like you're camping. But this one is off the highway in a grove of pine trees, a full two miles outside the tiny town of Gould. It almost feels like the wilderness, although road noise from Hwy. 14 can pose problems during high traffic season. Generally, though, this is a peaceful, pretty spot, with full facilities to boot. Recreation options include fishing in nearby Michigan Creek Reservoir and exploring Colorado State Forest.

**Location:** Near Gould; map A2, grid c6.

**Campsites, facilities:** There are 35 sites for RVs of any length, many with full hookups, and seven tent sites. Drinking water, picnic tables, fire grills, and bathrooms with hot showers are provided. Laundry facilities, a waste disposal station, store, and public phone are available. Leashed pets are permitted.

**Elevation:** 9,000 feet.

**Reservations, fees:** Reservations are recommended; phone (800) KOA-3596. Sites are $16-22 a night.

**Open:** June to November.

**Directions:** From the town of Gould, drive two miles west on Hwy. 14 to the campground.

**Contact:** North Park KOA, 53337 Hwy. 14, Walden, CO 80480; tel. (970) 723-4310.

## 29 Colorado State Forest        8

Covering more than 70,000 acres and climbing to elevations well over 12,000 feet, this enormous state park offers everything an outdoor enthusiast might want: 50 miles of hiking trails, 100 miles of mountain biking and horseback riding trails, fishing, boating, and, naturally, camping. Campsites have been placed at high-profile spots throughout the park, with the most popular ones at North Michigan Reservoir and Ranger Lakes. I prefer the more remote spots to the south, near American Lakes and the spectacular Nokhu Crags, which loom behind the camp at 12,400 feet. Other highlights in the park include the scenic Ruby Jewel Lake Trail, a local moose herd, and some unique high-altitude sand dunes (you have to hike several miles north into a remote area of the park to see them). Diverse vegetation and wildlife also abound; take advantage of the interpretive programs conducted by park rangers.

**Location:** Near Gould; map A2, grid c6.

**Campsites, facilities:** Spread throughout the park are 104 campsites that can accommodate both tents and RVs up to 35 feet long. Rustic cabins and yurts (wood-frame structures with canvas or plastic walls and ceiling) are also available for rent. Drinking water, picnic tables, fire grills, and vault toilets are provided. A waste disposal station is located near Ranger Lakes. There is a boat ramp at North Michigan Reservoir (no-wake boating only). Wheelchair-accessible facilities are available. Leashed pets are permitted.

**Elevation:** The average campsite elevation is 8,500 feet.

**Reservations, fees:** Reservations are accepted. Phone (303) 470-1144 or (800) 678-CAMP (800-678-2267) outside the Denver Metro area; there's a $7 reservation fee. Sites are $6 a night.

**Open:** June to October.

**Directions:** From the town of Gould, drive approximately 2.5 miles west on Hwy. 14 to the park entrance station on the right.

**Contact:** Colorado State Forest, Star Route, Box 91, Walden, CO 80480; tel. (970) 723-8366.

## 30 Tunnel     8

Named for the Laramie-Poudre Tunnel, which connects Laramie River Rd. to Hwy. 14, this pretty camp has it all. It's a short drive from the highway in a quiet, remote location, with shaded, riverside sites and wilderness access. Slightly to the north is the West Branch Trail leading west into the Rawah Wilderness.

**Location:** On the Laramie River in Roosevelt National Forest; map A2, grid c7.

**Campsites, facilities:** There are 49 sites for tents or RVs up to 50 feet long. Drinking water, picnic tables, fire grills, and vault toilets are provided. A waste disposal station is available. Leashed pets are permitted.

**Elevation:** 8,600 feet.

**Reservations, fees:** Reservations are not accepted. Sites are $10 a night.

**Open:** May to September.

**Directions:** From Fort Collins, follow Hwy. 14 west approximately 70 miles to Chambers Lake. Turn north on County Rd. 103 (Laramie River Rd.) and drive 5.5 miles to the campground.

**Contact:** Roosevelt National Forest, Canyon Lakes Ranger District, 1311 S. College Ave., Fort Collins, CO 80524; tel. (970) 498-2770.

## 31 Chambers Lake     8

An immensely popular campground, Chambers Lake adjoins the southeastern border of the Rawah Wilderness and provides opportunities for cartop boating and fishing. The sites are set back from the highway near the southern shore, with lots of shade and good views of the sparkling blue lake. Fishing tip: If you get skunked at Chambers Lake, Lost Lake (located across Laramie River Rd.) provides an alternative. To the south on Hwy. 14 is the trailhead for the Blue Lake Trail, a spectacularly scenic trek into the Rawah Wilderness.

**Location:** Near the Rawah Wilderness in Roosevelt National Forest; map A2, grid c7.

**Campsites, facilities:** There are 52 sites for tents or RVs up to 30 feet long. Drinking water, picnic tables, fire grills, and vault toilets are provided. Leashed pets are permitted.

**Elevation:** 9,200 feet.

**Reservations, fees:** Reservations are accepted; phone (877) 444-6777. There's an $8.65 reservation fee. You may also reserve sites at website: www.reserveusa.com.

Sites are $12 a night.

**Open:** June to September.

**Directions:** From Fort Collins, follow Hwy. 14 west approximately 70 miles to Chambers Lake. The campground access road is on the right, about one-half mile past the turnoff to County Rd. 103 (Laramie River Road).

**Contact:** Roosevelt National Forest, Canyon Lakes Ranger District, 1311 S. College Ave., Fort Collins, CO 80524; tel. (970) 498-2770.

## 32 Sleeping Elephant   6

The mountain that faces this campground really does look like an elephant—which is a good thing because not much else in the camp is interesting. It's quite pretty, sheltered by lots of tall pine trees, but is set across the highway from the river, with no fishing access or hiking trails in the immediate vicinity. The closest river access point is about a mile away; don't try to explore the private property across the road or you might find angry locals on your tail.

**Location:** On the Cache la Poudre River in Roosevelt National Forest; map A2, grid c7.

**Campsites, facilities:** There are 15 sites for tents or RVs up to 20 feet long. Drinking water, picnic tables, fire grills, and vault toilets are provided. Leashed pets are permitted.

**Elevation:** 7,800 feet.

**Reservations, fees:** Reservations are not accepted. Sites are $9 a night.

**Open:** Mid-May to October.

**Directions:** From Fort Collins, follow Hwy. 14 west approximately 53 miles to the campground.

**Contact:** Roosevelt National Forest, Canyon Lakes Ranger District, 1311 S. College Ave., Fort Collins, CO 80524; tel. (970) 498-2770.

## 33 Sportsman's Lodge    7

Since the main attraction is the lodge, many tourists miss the campground. And that's their loss, as this is a truly beautiful area located across the highway from the river in scenic Poudre Canyon. The campsites are scattered over several acres behind the main lodge, each enclosed by tall pines and aspens, providing privacy and quiet the like of which you'll not find at any other developed campground around. Fishing access is available just across the highway, and other area highlights, including Poudre Falls and Colorado State Forest, are a short drive away.

**Location:** Near the Cache la Poudre River; map A2, grid c7.

**Campsites, facilities:** There are approximately 10 dispersed sites for tents and RVs up to 35 feet long. Drinking water, picnic tables, a fire ring, and bathrooms with hot showers are provided. The lodge operates a restaurant and a store. Cabins and rooms are also available for rent. Leashed pets are permitted.

**Elevation:** 7,800 feet.

**Reservations, fees:** Reservations are recommended. Sites are $17.50 a night.

**Open:** May to November.

**Directions:** From Fort Collins, head west on Hwy. 14 for 54 miles to the campground.

**Contact:** Sportsman's Lodge, 44174 Hwy. 14, Bellvue, CO 80512; tel. (970) 881-2272.

## 34 Big South     7

This tiny, partially wooded camp makes a perfect base for a trip into the Comanche Peak Wilderness. It's located just south of the confluence of the Cache la Poudre River and Joe Wright Creek, with a trailhead that leads south along the river for several miles. Fishing is actually better in Joe Wright Creek than in the river, although the scenery is more dramatic on the Poudre.

**Location:** On the Cache la Poudre River in Roosevelt National Forest; map A2, grid c7.

**Campsites, facilities:** There are four sites for tents or RVs up to 25 feet long. Drinking water, picnic tables, fire grills, and vault toilets are provided. Leashed pets are permitted.

**Elevation:** 8,440 feet.

**Reservations, fees:** Reservations are not accepted. Sites are $7 a night.

**Open:** June to November.

**Directions:** From Fort Collins, follow Hwy. 14 west approximately 65 miles to the campground.

**Contact:** Roosevelt National Forest, Canyon Lakes Ranger District, 1311 S. College Ave., Fort Collins, CO 80524; tel. (970) 498-2770.

## 35 Aspen Glen      8

As Hwy. 14 turns away from the Cache la Poudre River, the road winds narrowly through a section of forest sandwiched between three designated wilderness areas: Rawah, Neota, and Comanche Peak. Aspen Glen lies at the mouth of this beautiful stretch of road, situated along Joe Wright Creek on the west side of the highway. As the name implies, the campsites are under tall, shimmering aspen trees that gleam a lush silver-green in the summer, transforming into warm gold by fall. The only drawback to this camp is its proximity to the highway—the road noise can be distracting. The creekside sites offer excellent fishing access, and nearby you'll find numerous trailheads routed into the three wilderness areas. The closest is the Big South Trail, located to the north at Big South campground.

**Location:** On Joe Wright Creek in Roosevelt National Forest; map A2, grid c7.

**Campsites, facilities:** There are eight sites for tents or RVs up to 30 feet long. Drinking water, picnic tables, fire grills, and vault toilets are provided. Leashed pets are permitted.

**Elevation:** 8,660 feet.

**Reservations, fees:** Reservations are not accepted. Sites are $8 a night.

**Open:** May to November.

**Directions:** From Fort Collins, follow Hwy. 14 west approximately 66 miles to the campground.

**Contact:** Roosevelt National Forest, Canyon Lakes Ranger District, 1311 S. College Ave., Fort Collins, CO 80524; tel. (970) 498-2770.

## 36 Grandview     9

Few folks know about this one. It's in a prime spot, along the far eastern shore of pretty Long Draw Reservoir on a tiny finger of national forest land pressed between the

Neota Wilderness and Rocky Mountain National Park. The fishing in the reservoir is decent, but the real attraction is hiking. If you continue to the end of the road, you'll come to the La Poudre Pass Trailhead at the base of the Continental Divide and leading south to a network of trails in Rocky Mountain National Park. Tip: At 10,220 feet elevation, it can snow even in the height of summer, so come prepared with warm gear.

**Location:** On Long Draw Reservoir in Roosevelt National Forest; map A2, grid c8.

**Campsites, facilities:** There are eight tent sites. Drinking water, picnic tables, fire grills, and vault toilets are provided. Leashed pets are permitted.

**Elevation:** 10,220 feet.

**Reservations, fees:** Reservations are not accepted. Sites are $8 a night.

**Open:** July to November.

**Directions:** From Fort Collins, follow Hwy. 14 west approximately 72 miles to Forest Service Rd. 156 (about two miles past the Laramie River Rd. turnoff). Turn left and drive about 11 miles southeast, passing the Long Draw camp, to the campground.

**Contact:** Roosevelt National Forest, Canyon Lakes Ranger District, 1311 S. College Ave., Fort Collins, CO 80524; tel. (970) 498-2770.

## 37 Long Draw     8

Here is an enchanted little spot in a dense grove of conifers. It's well off the main road, tucked between the southern boundary of the Comanche Peak Wilderness and the northern border of Rocky Mountain National Park. The Corral Creek Trail leads about a mile east of camp before splitting to the north and south, following the Cache la Poudre River through the wilderness. Long Draw Reservoir a few miles south provides good fishing.

**Location:** Near Long Draw Reservoir in Roosevelt National Forest; map A2, grid c8.

**Campsites, facilities:** There are 25 sites for tents or RVs up to 30 feet long. Drinking water, picnic tables, fire grills, and vault toilets are provided. Leashed pets are permitted.

**Elevation:** 10,030 feet.

**Reservations, fees:** Reservations are not accepted. Sites are $8 a night.

**Open:** July to November.

**Directions:** From Fort Collins, follow Hwy. 14 west approximately 72 miles to Forest Service Rd. 156 (about two miles past the Laramie River Rd. turnoff). Turn left and drive about eight miles southeast to the campground.

**Contact:** Roosevelt National Forest, Canyon Lakes Ranger District, 1311 S. College Ave., Fort Collins, CO 80524; tel. (970) 498-2770.

## 38 Glen Echo Resort    7

If you're looking for a family-oriented, full-service hot spot, stop your search. This place has lots of creature comforts, including a restaurant, store, and playground for kids. The sites are wide and shady, lined up side by side along the banks of the river, so you can easily get a few casts in before dinner. It's a lovely spot, but the downside is that your experience is apt to be marred by road noise and/or crowds. If quiet and solitude are what you want, try one of the more low-key spots in the canyon (see Sportsman's Lodge).

**Location:** On the Cache la Poudre River; map A2, grid c8.

**Campsites, facilities:** There are 50 full-hookup sites for RVs of any length and a few tent sites. Drinking water, picnic tables, fire grills, and bathrooms with hot showers are provided. Laundry facilities, a restaurant, store, public phone, and cabins are available. Leashed pets are permitted.

**Elevation:** 7,000 feet.

**Reservations, fees:** Reservations are recommended; phone (800) 348-2208. Sites are $15-21 a night.

**Open:** May to November.

**Directions:** From Fort Collins, follow Hwy. 14 west approximately 41 miles to the campground.

**Contact:** Glen Echo Resort, 31503 Poudre Canyon Hwy., Bellvue, CO 80512; tel. (970) 881-2208.

## 39 Stove Prairie     8

For years Stove Prairie remained a charming, if slightly dilapidated, campground. In 1996, however, it was reconstructed and now sports improved roads and sites along with modernized vault toilets. In addition, it's one of the few campgrounds in the area to stay open year-round. The partially shaded sites are near the river, offering excellent access to fishing and a few hiking trails.

**Location:** On the Cache la Poudre River in Roosevelt National Forest; map A2, grid c9.

**Campsites, facilities:** There are seven sites for tents or RVs up to 30 feet long, and two walk-in tent sites. Drinking water, picnic tables, fire grills, and vault toilets are provided. Leashed pets are permitted.

**Elevation:** 6,000 feet.

**Reservations, fees:** Reservations are not accepted. Sites are $10 a night.

**Open:** Year-round.

**Directions:** From Fort Collins, follow Hwy. 14 west approximately 26 miles to the campground.

**Contact:** Roosevelt National Forest, Canyon Lakes Ranger District, 1311 S. College Ave., Fort Collins, CO 80524; tel. (970) 498-2770.

## 40 Mountain Park     9

As the most developed U.S. Forest Service campground in Poudre Canyon, Mountain Park is nearly always packed full. It's simply beautiful, situated slightly back from the highway underneath tall pines on the banks of the Cache la Poudre River, near the border of the Cache la Poudre Wilderness. The sites are close to premium access for fishing and hiking. A trail leads south up to the top of Mount McConnell, where you'll find exceptional views of the river canyon. There's even a little playground for kids at the camp.

**Location:** On the Cache la Poudre River in Roosevelt National Forest; map A2, grid c9.

**Campsites, facilities:** There are 55 sites for tents or RVs up to 50 feet long. Drinking water, picnic tables, fire grills, and bathrooms with hot showers are provided. Electric hookups are available. Leashed pets are permitted.

**Elevation:** 6,500 feet.

**Reservations, fees:** Reservations are accepted; phone (877) 444-6777. There's an $8.65 reservation fee. You may also reserve sites at website: www.reserveusa.com. Sites are $12-14 a night.

**Open:** Memorial Day to Labor Day.

**Directions:** From Fort Collins, follow Hwy. 14 west approximately 33 miles to the campground.

**Contact:** Roosevelt National Forest, Canyon Lakes Ranger District, 1311 S. College Ave., Fort Collins, CO 80524; tel. (970) 498-2770.

## 41 Mountain Park Group Camp     7

Large parties can set up camp at this group facility located adjacent to the immensely popular Mountain Park Campground. It's near the river and puts you within easy reach of fishing and hiking opportunities.

**Location:** On the Cache la Poudre River in Roosevelt National Forest; map A2, grid c9.

**Campsites, facilities:** A large area with walk-in tent sites can accommodate up to 30 people. The central parking area has room for RVs up to 50 feet long. Drinking water, picnic tables, a large community fire grill, and vault toilets are provided. Leashed pets are permitted.

**Elevation:** 6,500 feet.

**Reservations, fees:** Reservations are required; phone (877) 444-6777. There's an $8.65 reservation fee. You may also reserve sites at website: www.reserveusa.com. Sites are $75 a night.

**Open:** Memorial Day to Labor Day.

**Directions:** From Fort Collins, follow Hwy. 14 west approximately 33 miles to the campground.

**Contact:** Roosevelt National Forest, Canyon Lakes Ranger District, 1311 S. College Ave., Fort Collins, CO 80524; tel. (970) 498-2770.

## 42 Kelly Flats     7

Yet another in the long line of U.S. Forest Service campgrounds along the Cache la Poudre River, Kelly Flats offers partially shaded sites, beautiful streamside views, and superb fishing access. There are some good trailheads within a short drive; consult a U.S. Forest Service map for details.

**Location:** On the Cache la Poudre River in Roosevelt National Forest; map A2, grid c9.

**Campsites, facilities:** There are 23 sites for tents or RVs up to 40 feet long. Drinking water, picnic tables, fire grills, and vault toilets are provided. Leashed pets are permitted.

**Elevation:** 6,600 feet.

**Reservations, fees:** Reservations are not accepted. Sites are $9 a night.

**Open:** Mid-May to October.

**Directions:** From Fort Collins, follow Hwy. 14 west approximately 37 miles to the campground.

**Contact:** Roosevelt National Forest, Canyon Lakes Ranger District, 1311 S. College Ave., Fort Collins, CO 80524; tel. (970) 498-2770.

## 43 Narrows     8

The rustic nature of this campground seems to add to, rather than detract from, its beauty. Boasting shaded sites overlooking the spectacular Cache la Poudre River and excellent hiking trails in the area, the camp remains one of the most popular in the region. Direct fishing access is available.

**Location:** On the Cache la Poudre River in Roosevelt National Forest; map A2, grid c9.

**Campsites, facilities:** There are five sites for tents or RVs up to 30 feet long, and four walk-in tent sites. Vault toilets are provided, but there is no drinking water. Leashed pets are permitted.

**Elevation:** 6,400 feet.

**Reservations, fees:** Reservations are not accepted. Sites are $7 a night.

**Open:** Year-round.

**Directions:** From Fort Collins, follow Hwy. 14 west approximately 37 miles to the campground.

**Contact:** Roosevelt National Forest, Canyon Lakes Ranger District, 1311 S. College Ave., Fort Collins, CO 80524; tel. (970) 498-2770.

## 44 Jack's Gulch      7

Jack's Gulch, the Estes-Poudre District's newest campground, is unique in that it was designed to accommodate campers using various methods of transportation: car, RV, horse, or wheelchair. There is a short wheelchair-accessible trail that loops around the camp, as well as nearby hiking and horseback riding trails heading off in all directions. The most scenic are routed west into the Comanche Peak Wilderness.

**Location:** West of Fort Collins in Roosevelt National Forest; map A2, grid c9.

**Campsites, facilities:** There are 50 sites for tents or RVs up to 50 feet long, 20 walk-in tent sites, and five equestrian sites with horse corrals. Drinking water, picnic tables, fire grills, and vault toilets are provided. Some sites have electric hookups. Some facilities are wheelchair accessible. Leashed pets are permitted.

**Elevation:** 8,100 feet.

**Reservations, fees:** Reservations are not accepted. Sites are $12 a night.

**Open:** May to October.

**Directions:** From Fort Collins, follow Hwy. 14 west approximately 36 miles. Turn left on County Rd. 63E (Pingree Park Rd.) and drive about seven miles to the campground.

**Contact:** Roosevelt National Forest, Canyon Lakes Ranger District, 1311 S. College Ave., Fort Collins, CO 80524; tel. (970) 498-2770.

## 45 Jack's Gulch Group Camp     7

Basically an addition to the main Jack's Gulch Campground, this place was intended especially for groups. It's located in a pretty, partially wooded setting. See the Jack's Gulch Campground trip notes for recreation options.

**Location:** West of Fort Collins in Roosevelt National Forest; map A2, grid c9.

**Campsites, facilities:** One large group area can accommodate up to 60 people in tents or RVs up to 50 feet long. Drinking water, picnic tables, fire grills, and vault toilets are provided. Leashed pets are permitted.

**Elevation:** 8,100 feet.

**Reservations, fees:** Reservations are required; phone (877) 444-6777. There's an $8.65 reservation fee. You may also reserve sites at website: www.reserveusa.com. Sites are $100 a night.

**Open:** May to October.

**Directions:** From Fort Collins, follow Hwy. 14 west approximately 36 miles, turn left on County Rd. 63E (Pingree Park Rd.), and drive about seven miles to the campground.

**Contact:** Roosevelt National Forest, Canyon Lakes Ranger District, 1311 S. College Ave., Fort Collins, CO 80524; tel. (970) 498-2770.

## 46 Steamboat Springs KOA       7

Unique to this huge campground is its "tent island," an actual island in the middle of the Yampa River where all the tent sites are located. Many of the mainland sites are streamside as well, however, so RVers aren't left out. The campground has all the amenities: a pool and hot tub, miniature golf course, playground, sports facilities (basketball and volleyball courts), and fishing in the Yampa River. There's so much to do, in fact, that you may not feel a need to even leave the place—but trust me, there's more out there. While you're in Steamboat, don't miss Strawberry Park Hot Springs or Fish Creek Falls. These destinations require a rough drive and a steep hike, respectively, but they're worth the effort.

**Location:** On the Yampa River; map A2, grid d2.

**Campsites, facilities:** There are 135 sites for RVs of any length, many with full hookups, and a separate area for tents. Drinking water, picnic tables, fire grills, a waste disposal station, and bathrooms with hot showers are provided. Laundry facilities, a store, public phone, miniature golf, sports facilities, hot tub, and swimming pool are also available. Leashed pets are permitted.

**Elevation:** 6,800 feet.

**Reservations, fees:** Reservations are recommended; phone (800) KOA-7549. Sites are $19-25 a night.

**Open:** Year-round.

**Directions:** From Steamboat Springs, drive two miles west on U.S. 40 to the campground.

**Contact:** Steamboat Springs KOA, 29135 W. U.S. 40, Steamboat Springs, CO 80487; tel. (970) 879-0273.

## 47 Stagecoach State Park  9

Seven hundred-acre Stagecoach Lake is the crown jewel of this lush setting, glimmering quietly against a background of green, rolling hills. The lake is open to all water sports, including waterskiing, PWC riding, sailing, windsurfing, and, naturally, fishing. Available species include rainbow and cutthroat trout, kokanee salmon, splake, whitefish, and northern pike. The lake is divided into separate sections for fishing and waterskiing, keeping both anglers and skiers happy.

There are also several miles of trails for hiking, mountain biking, and horseback riding, as well as a swimming beach on the northern side of the lake, near the campground. The campsites are grouped in four clusters near the northwestern shore, many with prime lakeside views. Add to that lush displays of wildflowers and spectacular alpine sunsets, and you've got a virtual mountain paradise. Limited hunting is permitted.

**Location:** South of Steamboat Springs; map A2, grid d2.

**Campsites, facilities:** There are 100 sites for tents or RVs of any length. Drinking water, picnic tables, fire grills, and bathrooms with hot showers are provided. Electric hookups, a waste disposal station, boat ramps, and wheelchair-accessible facilities also are available. Leashed pets are permitted.

**Elevation:** 7,500 feet.

**Reservations, fees:** Reservations are accepted. Phone (303) 470-1144 or (800) 678-CAMP (800-678-2267) outside the Denver Metro area; there's a $7 reservation fee. Sites are $10-14 a night, and there's a $4 entrance fee.

**Open:** Year-round.

**Directions:** From Steamboat Springs, drive south on U.S. 40 to the junction with Hwy. 131, turn right, and continue five miles south. Turn left on County Rd. 14 and proceed seven miles to the park entrance.

**Contact:** Stagecoach State Park, P.O. Box 98, Oak Creek, CO 80467; tel. (970) 736-2436.

## 48 Meadows   9

It's rare to find a camp along the highway that offers privacy and quiet, but this one satisfies both requirements. It's simply beautiful, located near Rabbit Ears Pass in a densely wooded setting that allows each site complete privacy and shelter from road noise. If you happen to visit in midsummer, you'll be treated to a display of bright green grasses and wildflowers blooming between groves of aspens and pines.

**Location:** South of Steamboat Springs in Routt National Forest; map A2, grid d3.

**Campsites, facilities:** There are 30 sites for tents or RVs up to 40 feet long. Drinking water, picnic tables, fire grills, and vault toilets are provided. Leashed pets are permitted.

**Elevation:** 9,300 feet.

**Reservations, fees:** Reservations are not accepted. Sites are $10 a night.

**Open:** July to November.

**Directions:** From Steamboat Springs, drive approximately 15 miles southeast on U.S. 40 to the campground.

**Contact:** Routt National Forest, Hahns Peak-Bears Ears Ranger District, P.O. Box 771212, Steamboat Springs, CO 80477; tel. (970) 824-9438.

## 49 Walton Creek     8

Although not quite as secluded as the nearby Meadows camp, this one's still a gem. It's got a pretty creek running through the middle of the campground, with decent fishing for small but plentiful native brook trout. Road noise can be annoying during tourist season; choose a site near the creek if possible. The camp is thickly wooded, and several unmarked trails are good for short hikes into the surrounding forest.

**Location:** South of Steamboat Springs in Routt National Forest; map A2, grid d3.

**Campsites, facilities:** There are 14 sites for tents or RVs of any length. Drinking water, picnic tables, fire grills, and vault toilets are provided. Leashed pets are permitted.

**Elevation:** 9,400 feet.

**Reservations, fees:** Reservations are not accepted. Sites are $10 a night.

**Open:** June to October.

**Directions:** From Steamboat Springs, drive approximately 17 miles southeast on U.S. 40 to the campground.

**Contact:** Routt National Forest, Hahns Peak-Bears Ears Ranger District, P.O. Box 771212, Steamboat Springs, CO 80477; tel. (970) 824-9438.

## 50 Dumont Lake       8

Dumont Lake is well off U.S. 40 and consequently gets missed by most highway travelers. Their loss—it's a lovely, open, sprawling campground laced with trees and neighboring a pretty alpine lake. Cartop boating and fishing are permitted, with good shoreline access and an adjacent picnic area. Nearby are four-wheel-drive roads to explore, and to the northwest a trail for hikers and mountain bikers that leads up to Rabbit Ears Peak (elevation 10,654 feet).

**Location:** South of Steamboat Springs in Routt National Forest; map A2, grid d4.

**Campsites, facilities:** There are 22 sites for tents or RVs of any length. Drinking water, picnic tables, fire grills, and vault toilets are provided. Leashed pets are permitted.

**Elevation:** 9,500 feet.

**Reservations, fees:** Reservations are not accepted. Sites are $10 a night.

**Open:** June to October.

**Directions:** From Steamboat Springs, drive approximately 19 miles southeast on U.S. 40 to the turnoff for Dumont Lake. Turn left and continue about a mile to the campground.

**Contact:** Routt National Forest, Hahns Peak-Bears Ears Ranger District, P.O. Box 771212, Steamboat Springs, CO 80477; tel. (970) 824-9438.

## 51 Seymour Lake State Wildlife Area    3

Talk about no-man's-land. Seymour Lake is the biggest draw here, and it isn't much. Little more than a pond at 30 surface acres, it provides mediocre fishing for rainbow trout or perhaps a chance to practice paddling your canoe. You can camp just about anyplace, but if you end up anywhere near the water, be sure to slather on the bug repellent—the mosquitoes look like birds around here.

**Location:** South of Walden; map A2, grid d5.

**Campsites, facilities:** Dispersed camping is permitted throughout the property. A vault toilet and a boat ramp are provided, but there are no other facilities or drinking water. Leashed pets are permitted.

**Elevation:** 8,400 feet.

**Reservations, fees:** Reservations are not accepted. There is no fee.

**Open:** Year-round.

**Directions:** From Walden, drive 14 miles southwest on Hwy. 14 to County Rd. 28. Turn left and continue one mile to County Rd. 11. Then turn right and go three miles to County Rd. 288. Turn west and continue one-half mile to the property entrance.

**Contact:** Colorado Division of Wildlife, 317 W. Prospect Ave., Fort Collins, CO 80526; tel. (970) 472-4300.

## 52 Pines     7

Back from the road and deep inside Routt National Forest, this campground is often passed by unnoticed by travelers on their way to visit Colorado State Forest. It's on the banks of the South Fork of the Michigan River, a prime spot for a day of fishing. It's also a great base camp if you're planning on doing some backpacking. To the south you'll find four-wheel-drive roads and trailheads, including one that follows the South Fork of the Michigan River east into the mystically beautiful Never Summer Wilderness.

**Location:** On the South Fork of the Michigan River in Routt National Forest; map A2, grid d6.

**Campsites, facilities:** There are 11 sites for tents or RVs up to 22 feet long. Drinking water, picnic tables, fire grills, and vault toilets are provided. Leashed pets are permitted.

**Elevation:** 9,200 feet.

**Reservations, fees:** Reservations are not accepted. Sites are $10 a night.

**Open:** June to October.

**Directions:** From Hwy. 14 just west of the town of Gould, turn south on Forest Service Rd. 740 and drive one mile to the campground entrance.

**Contact:** Routt National Forest, Parks Ranger District, 100 Main St., P.O. Box 158, Walden, CO 80480; tel. (970) 723-8204.

## 53 Aspen    7

Here's a tiny, no-frills camp near Hwy. 14 in a quiet, wooded setting. It provides access for fishing on the South Fork of the Michigan River as well as an alternative to the better-known (and more crowded) camps at nearby Colorado State Forest.

**Location:** On the South Fork of the Michigan River in Routt National Forest; map A2, grid d6.

**Campsites, facilities:** There are seven sites for tents or RVs up to 22 feet long. Drinking water, picnic tables, fire grills, and vault toilets are provided. Leashed pets are permitted.

**Elevation:** 8,920 feet.

**Reservations, fees:** Reservations are not accepted. Sites are $10 a night.

**Open:** June to October.

**Directions:** From Hwy. 14 just west of the town of Gould, turn south on Forest Service Rd. 740 and drive approximately four miles to the campground entrance.

**Contact:** Routt National Forest, Parks Ranger District, 100 Main St., P.O. Box 158, Walden, CO 80480; tel. (970) 723-8204.

## 54 Winding River Resort Village     7

This is like sleep-away summer camp for the whole family. Organized activities include hayrides, Frisbee golf, sports—all that's missing is arts and crafts. The campground is only one part of the 150-acre ranch, which is home to a variety of livestock, plus a little petting farm for children. The ranch is quite community oriented, and you'll undoubtedly be roped into a few of the daily events, such as large group breakfasts, dinners, and socials. Horse and mountain bike rentals are available for those who want to break away and have their own adventures. Since the ranch is well off any main road, the atmosphere is quiet and peaceful.

**Location:** Near Rocky Mountain National Park; map A2, grid d7.

**Campsites, facilities:** There are 150 sites for RVs of any length, many with full hookups, and a separate area for tents. Drinking water, picnic tables, fire grills, and bathrooms with hot showers are provided. Laundry facilities, a waste disposal station, public phone, and cabins are also available. Some facilities are wheelchair accessible. Leashed pets are permitted.

**Elevation:** 8,700 feet.

**Reservations, fees:** Reservations are recommended. Sites are $20-24 a night.

**Open:** Mid-May to October.

**Directions:** From the town of Grand Lake, drive one mile north on U.S. 34 and turn left on County Rd. 491 (at the Kawuneeche Visitor Center). Continue 1.5 miles to the campground.

**Contact:** Winding River Resort Village, Box 629, Grand Lake, CO 80447; tel. (970) 627-3215 or (800) 282-5121.

## 55 Elk Creek Campground     6

This campground outside the northwestern entrance to Rocky Mountain National Park provides a good option for folks who want both proximity to the mountains and access to all the amenities (there are no showers at the national park camps). The grounds are well maintained, and each site is shaded, providing a little privacy. They even offer a private stocked trout pond where guests can fish.

**Location:** Near the west entrance of Rocky Mountain National Park; map A2, grid d7.

**Campsites, facilities:** There are 70 sites for tents or RVs of any length, many with full hookups. Drinking water, picnic tables, fire grills, and bathrooms with hot showers are provided. Laundry facilities, a waste disposal station, small store, public phone, and cabins are available. Some facilities are wheelchair accessible. Leashed pets are permitted.

**Elevation:** 8,500 feet.

**Reservations, fees:** Reservations are strongly advised. Sites are $18-22 a night.

**Open:** Year-round with limited winter facilities.

**Directions:** From the town of Grand Lake, drive a short distance south to U.S. 34, turn north, and go one-quarter mile. Turn left on Golf Course Rd. (County Rd. 48) and continue one-quarter mile west to the campground.

**Contact:** Elk Creek Campground, P.O. Box 549, Grand Lake, CO 80447; tel. (970) 627-8502 or (800) 355-2733; e-mail: elkcreek@rkymtnhi.com.

## 56 Timber Creek  7

Nestled in the beautiful Kawuneeche Valley, Timber Creek is the park's easternmost developed campground. The campsites are separated by tall clusters of lodgepole pine, and the Colorado River flows nearby, with good fishing prospects. The premium riverside sites are the finest in the camp, but arrive early to stake your claim. You'll find a network of trails winding through the valley—be sure to stop by Never Summer Ranch, which has visitor information and guides.

**Location:** North of Grand Lake in Rocky Mountain National Park; map A2, grid d7.

**Campsites, facilities:** There are 100 sites for tents or RVs up to 30 feet long. Drinking water, flush and vault toilets, picnic tables, and fire grills are provided. A waste disposal station and public phone are available. Leashed pets are permitted. Horseback riding is permitted on designated trails in the park.

**Elevation:** 8,900 feet.

**Reservations, fees:** Reservations are not accepted. Sites are $16 a night.

**Open:** Year-round with limited winter facilities.

**Directions:** From the town of Grand Lake, drive north on U.S. 34 to the park entrance. Timber Creek Campground is approximately 10 miles north of Grand Lake. If you're coming from Estes Park, follow U.S. 34 (Trail Ridge Rd.) for about 34 miles through the park to the campground. Note: Trail Ridge Rd. is the highest continuous paved highway in the country, climbing to over 12,000 feet, and is only open from about June to October, depending on snowfall.

**Contact:** Rocky Mountain National Park, Estes Park, CO 80517; tel. (970) 586-1206.

## 57 Glacier Basin  7

Glacier Basin is the park's most popular campground, perhaps because of its proximity to Bear Lake, a clear, pristine jewel that offers spectacular views of the Continental Divide. The campground is, in fact, next to the parking area for the Bear Lake Shuttle, which whisks visitors four miles down the road to the lake and trailheads. Fishing is prohibited in Bear Lake, so if you're itching to cast a line, try little Glacier Creek next to the campground.

**Location:** Southwest of Estes Park in Rocky Mountain National Park; map A2, grid d8.

**Campsites, facilities:** There are 150 sites for tents or RVs up to 27 feet long, and one large group camp that can accommodate 10 to 50 people. Drinking water, flush and vault toilets, picnic tables, and fire grills are provided. A waste disposal station and public phone are available. Leashed pets are permitted. Horseback riding is permitted on designated trails in the park.

**Elevation:** 8,600 feet.

**Reservations, fees:** Reservations are required; phone (800) 365-2267. Sites are $16 a night.

**Open:** June to September.

**Directions:** From Estes Park, take U.S. 36 west, past park headquarters, to the Beaver Meadows entrance. Turn left on Bear Lake Road. The campground is approximately six miles from headquarters.

**Contact:** Rocky Mountain National Park, Estes Park, CO 80517; tel. (970) 586-1206.

## 58 Moraine Park  7

The largest of the park's five developed campgrounds, Moraine Park can resemble a giant tent city in the summer. It's not far from Estes Park, making it the first campground many visitors come to, and it's quite a pretty spot, a collection of wide sites sprinkled with tall ponderosa pines. Nearby is a livery stable for horses, an amphitheater with regular summer programs, and several hiking and horseback riding trails, including the popular Cub Lake Trail.

**Location:** Southwest of Estes Park in Rocky Mountain National Park; map A2, grid d8.

**Campsites, facilities:** There are 247 sites for tents or RVs up to 35 feet long. Drinking water, picnic tables, fire grills, and flush and vault toilets are provided. A waste disposal station and public phone are available. Leashed pets are permitted.

**Elevation:** 8,100 feet.

**Reservations, fees:** Reservations are required in the summer months; phone (800) 365-2267. The rest of the year no reservations are accepted. Sites are $16 a night.

**Open:** Year-round with limited winter facilities.

**Directions:** From Estes Park, take U.S. 36 west, past park headquarters, to the Beaver Meadows entrance. Turn left on Bear Lake Road. The campground is approximately three miles from headquarters.

**Contact:** Rocky Mountain National Park, Estes Park, CO 80517; tel. (970) 586-1206.

## 59 Aspenglen  9

Popular and often crowded, Aspenglen is in an open meadow bordered by shimmering aspen trees, right next to the Fall River. You can fish for trout in the river or explore one of several trails in the area. A good one is the route up to Deer Mountain (over 9,500 feet) and Horseshoe Park, which offers prime viewing of bighorn sheep in the summer and elk during the rut in September and October.

**Location:** West of Estes Park in Rocky Mountain National Park; map A2, grid d8.

**Campsites, facilities:** There are 54 sites for tents or RVs up to 30 feet long. Drinking water, picnic tables, fire grills, and flush toilets are provided. A waste disposal station and a public phone are available. Leashed pets are permitted. Horseback riding is permitted on designated trails in the park.

**Elevation:** 8,200 feet.

**Reservations, fees:** Reservations are not accepted. Sites are $16 a night.

**Open:** June to September.

**Directions:** From Estes Park, drive west on U.S. 34 to the Fall River entrance. The campground is just past the entrance, a total of five miles from Estes Park.

**Contact:** Rocky Mountain National Park, Estes Park, CO 80517; tel. (970) 586-1206.

## 60 Longs Peak  7

If you're camping here, you're most likely planning on climbing Longs Peak, one of Colorado's most popular 14ers (a peak with a summit over 14,000 feet). It's a grueling endeavor, 16 miles round-trip with an elevation gain of nearly 5,000 feet—definitely not for the weak-hearted or limp-legged. Most people start climbing at around 3 a.m. in order to reach the top and head back down by early afternoon. If you're not up for such exertion, you might try the hike up to Chasm Lake, a lovely alpine oasis at the foot of the mountain. It's not exactly a cakewalk either—4.2 miles one way, with an elevation gain of 2,400 feet-but you'll be rewarded with dramatic mountain views.

**Location:** South of Estes Park in Rocky Mountain National Park; map A2, grid d8.

**Campsites, facilities:** There are 26 tent sites. Drinking water, flush and vault toilets, picnic tables, and fire grills are provided. A public phone is available nearby at the ranger station. Leashed pets are permitted. Horseback riding is permitted on designated trails in the park.

**Elevation:** 9,400 feet.

**Reservations, fees:** Reservations are not accepted. Sites are $2 a night.

**Open:** Year-round with limited winter facilities.

**Directions:** From Estes Park, follow Hwy. 7 south approximately 10 miles to the Longs Peak turnoff. The campground is one mile up the road.

**Contact:** Rocky Mountain National Park, Estes Park, CO 80517; tel. (970) 586-1206.

## 61 National Park Resort Campground and Cabins   5

Pine and aspen trees shade the roomy sites at this developed campground. It's right beside Rocky Mountain National Park's most popular entrance, so you get easy access to the mountains as well as to the sights in Estes Park. Some highlights: Trail Ridge Rd. in Rocky Mountain National Park, the highest continuous paved highway in the United States; the Stanley Hotel, which inspired Stephen King's novel *The Shining;* and if you're here in the fall, the annual Scottish-Irish Festival, where you can sample aged Scotch whisky and watch a re-creation of the Scottish Games.

**Location:** Near Rocky Mountain National Park; map A2, grid d9.

**Campsites, facilities:** There are 100 sites for tents or RVs of any length, many with full hookups. Drinking water, picnic tables, fire grills, and bathrooms with hot showers are provided. Laundry facilities, a waste disposal station, small store, and cabins are available. Leashed pets are permitted.

**Elevation:** 8,300 feet.

**Reservations, fees:** Reservations are recommended. Sites are $25-27 a night.

**Open:** May to October.

**Directions:** From Estes Park, drive approximately five miles west on U.S. 34 to the campground, located next to the Fall River entrance to Rocky Mountain National Park.

**Contact:** National Park Resort Campground and Cabins, 3501 Fall River Rd., Estes Park, CO 80517; tel. (970) 586-4563.

## 62 Manor RV Park   6

At first glance, this campground looks like a big RV parking lot, but look up—you'll be astounded by the breathtaking mountain views. The daunting amount of concrete in the park is countered by an abundance of trees and grass surrounding the campsites, and the Big Thompson Reservoir River runs adjacent. The stretch of river next to the campground gets extra fish stocks, so the fishing is usually very good.

**Location:** Near Estes Park; map A2, grid d9.

**Campsites, facilities:** There are 110 full-hookup sites for RVs of any length. No tents are permitted. Drinking water, picnic tables, a community grill, and bathrooms with hot showers are provided. A motel, laundry facilities, and store are also available. Leashed pets are permitted with approval.

**Elevation:** 7,600 feet.

**Reservations, fees:** Reservations are required. Sites are $27 a night.

**Open:** Mid-May to October.

**Directions:** From the junction of U.S. 36 and U.S. 34 in Estes Park, turn south on Crags Dr. and go a short distance to Riverside Drive. Turn right and continue to the campground entrance on your right.

**Contact:** Manor RV Park, 815 E. Riverside Dr., Moraine Rte., Estes Park, CO 80517; tel. (970) 586-3251.

## 63 Estes Park KOA       6

Set on a hillside, this extremely clean campground offers large sites with wonderful views of Lake Estes and the mountains to the west. Sites are large, level, and well-shaded, some with private decks. The facilities include a playground, basketball court, and television lounge with games, and boating, biking, and fishing across the road at Lake Estes and horse rentals next door. It's just a short hop to downtown Estes Park, where you'll find a variety of antique stores and good restaurants.

**Location:** Near Lake Estes; map A2, grid d9.

**Campsites, facilities:** There are 84 sites for tents or RVs of any length, many with full hookups. Drinking water, picnic tables, fire grills, and bathrooms with hot showers are provided. Laundry facilities, a waste disposal station, small store, playground, and public phone are available. Tepees are also available for rent. Some facilities are wheelchair accessible. Leashed pets are permitted.

**Elevation:** 8,200 feet.

**Reservations, fees:** Reservations are recommended; phone (800) KOA-1887. Sites are $22-30 a night.

**Open:** Late April through late October.

**Directions:** From the junction of U.S. 34 and U.S. 36 in Estes Park, drive two miles east on U.S. 34 to the campground.

**Contact:** Estes Park KOA, 2051 Big Thompson Ave., Estes Park, CO 80517; tel. (970) 586-2888; e-mail: estesparkkoa@compuserve.com.

## 64 Blue Arrow Campground     6

Since it's slightly off the beaten track, you may not have to fight the same crowds you would at campgrounds closer to Estes Park, but you still get easy access to Rocky Mountain National Park and other recreation options in the area. The well-maintained campground covers 33 acres, with access to hiking trails, and offers full facilities.

**Location:** Near Estes Park; map A2, grid d9.

**Campsites, facilities:** There are 170 sites for tents or RVs of any length, many with full hookups. Drinking water, picnic tables, fire grills, and bathrooms with hot showers are provided. Laundry facilities, a recreation room, and store are available. Some facilities are wheelchair accessible. Leashed pets are permitted. **Elevation:** 8,000 feet.

**Reservations, fees:** Reservations are recommended; phone (800) 582-5342. Sites are $18-25 a night.

**Open:** Year-round.

**Directions:** From the junction of U.S. 36 and Hwy. 66 west of Estes Park, turn southwest on Hwy. 66 and drive one-quarter mile to the campground.

**Contact:** Blue Arrow Campground, 1665 Hwy. 66, Estes Park, CO 80517; tel. (970) 586-5342.

## 65 Paradise Travel Park     7

If you want to stay here, reserve well in advance so you can get a streamside site. They cost a little more but are well worth it—it's so peaceful to drift into sleep to the sound of rushing water, and if you were any closer to the river, you'd be in it. Best of all for anglers, you can fish right from these sites. The other sites are also quite nice, carpeted with grass and nestled under tall pine trees. Both Estes Park and Rocky Mountain National Park are just minutes away.

**Location:** On the Big Thompson River; map A2, grid d9.

**Campsites, facilities:** There are 30 full-hookup sites for tents or RVs up to 32 feet long. Drinking water, picnic tables, fire grills, and bathrooms with hot showers are provided. Laundry facilities and a public phone are available. Pets are forbidden.

**Elevation:** 7,500 feet.

**Reservations, fees:** Reservations are recommended. Sites are $18-25 a night.

**Open:** May to October.

**Directions:** From the junction of U.S. 36 and Hwy. 66 west of Estes Park, turn southwest on Hwy. 66 and drive one-half mile to the campground.

**Contact:** Paradise Travel Park, 1836 Moraine Rd., Estes Park, CO 80517; tel. (970) 586-5513.

## 66 Estes Park Campground     6

With so many campgrounds scrambling to accommodate oversize RVs, it's nice to find a place now and then that caters to smaller rigs and tents. This is one of those places. It doesn't offer hookups, but it does furnish a quiet, woodsy setting that's off the main drag. You can hike and horseback ride on nearby trails, or drive a short distance into Rocky Mountain National Park.

**Location:** Near Estes Park; map A2, grid d9.

**Campsites, facilities:** There are 68 sites for tents or RVs up to 28 feet long, all without hookups. Drinking water, picnic tables, fire grills, and bathrooms with hot showers are provided. Leashed pets are permitted.

**Elevation:** 8,200 feet.

**Reservations, fees:** Reservations are recommended. Sites are $17.50-22.50 a night.

**Open:** June to September.

**Directions:** From the junction of U.S. 36 and Hwy. 66 west of Estes Park, turn southwest on Hwy. 66 and drive three miles to the campground.

**Contact:** Estes Park Campground, Box 3517, Estes Park, CO 80517; tel. (970) 586-4188; e-mail: epcampground@estes-park.com.

## 67 Mary's Lake Campground     8

Snuggled in a tiny valley backed by striking peaks, Mary's Lake is one of the hidden jewels of Larimer County. Although the lake receives a heavy amount of traffic in the summer months, a ban on all water sports—including boating—helps keep it pristine. You can still fish from the shoreline, though—right from your site if you're lucky enough to get a waterside spot. Campsites are within walking distance of the lake, with excellent views of the Rocky Mountains. For campers who can't live without their computers, there are three dedicated e-mail work centers.

**Location:** Near Estes Park; map A2, grid d9.

**Campsites, facilities:** There are 150 sites for RVs of any length, many with full hookups, and a separate area for tents. Drinking water, picnic tables, fire grills, and bathrooms with hot showers are provided. Laundry facilities, a waste disposal station, and a swimming pool are available. Some facilities are wheelchair accessible. Leashed pets are permitted.

**Elevation:** 8,100 feet.

**Reservations, fees:** Reservations are recommended; phone (800) 445-6279. Sites are $19-25 a night.

**Open:** Mid-May to October.

**Directions:** From Estes Park, drive two miles west on U.S. 36 and turn left on Mary's Lake Road. Continue 1.5 miles to the campground.

**Contact:** Mary's Lake Campground, Box 2514, Estes Park, CO 80517; tel. (970) 586-4411; e-mail: maryslake@aol.com.

## 68 Spruce Lake RV Park    7

Water lovers rejoice: Not only do you have the icy, clear Big Thompson River rushing by, you also get access to a private, fish-laden lake. Add in the miniature golf course and swimming pool, and you may never want to leave. Sites are gravel and grass, separated by fences. The campground hosts are warm and accommodating, and they love to organize community suppers and group excursions. Modem access is also available.

**Location:** Near Estes Park; map A2, grid d9.

**Campsites, facilities:** There are 110 sites for RVs of any length, most with full hookups. No tents are permitted. Drinking water, picnic tables, a community fire ring, and bathrooms with hot showers are provided. Laundry facilities, a waste disposal station, swimming pool, miniature golf, and restaurant are available. Leashed pets are permitted.

**Elevation:** 7,700 feet.

**Reservations, fees:** Reservations are strongly recommended. Sites are $22-31 a night.

**Open:** March to November.

**Directions:** From Estes Park, drive two miles west on U.S. 36 and turn left on Mary's Lake Road. Continue a short distance to the campground.

**Contact:** Spruce Lake RV Park, 1050 Mary's Lake Rd., Estes Park, CO 80517; tel. (970) 586-2889; e-mail: sprucelake@estes-park.com

## 69 Sheriff Reservoir     8

You're camped next to a tranquil, trout-laden mountain lake, about to head off on a multi-day backpacking trip into a spectacular wilderness area. Sound like paradise? I agree. Sheriff Reservoir is primitive and beautiful, virtually teetering on the edge of wildlands. You can fish, boat, or choose from one of two excellent hiking trails routed south into the Flat Tops Wilderness.

**Location:** West of Yampa in Routt National Forest; map A2, grid e0.

**Campsites, facilities:** There are six tent sites. Fire grills and vault toilets are provided, but there are no tables or drinking water. Leashed pets are permitted.

**Elevation:** 9,800 feet.

**Reservations, fees:** Reservations are not accepted. Sites are $5 a night.

**Open:** June to October.

**Directions:** From Yampa, drive five miles north on County Rd. 17 to Forest Hwy. 16 (Dunckley Scenic Byway). Turn left and drive approximately nine miles west. Turn south on Forest Service Rd. 959/960 and continue four miles to the campground.

**Contact:** Routt National Forest, Yampa Ranger District, P.O. Box 7, Yampa, CO 80483; tel. (970) 638-4516.

## 70 Chapman Reservoir     8

Remote and little-used, this primitive camp is situated near the shore of Chapman Reservoir, a perfect setting for a weekend fishing trip. The reservoir is too small for anything but a rowboat or canoe, but the fishing is said to be quite good, and the surrounding forest provides a natural, serene environment.

**Location:** West of Yampa in Routt National Forest; map A2, grid e1.

**Campsites, facilities:** There are 12 tent sites. Fire grills and vault toilets are provided, but there are no tables or drinking water. Leashed pets are permitted.

**Elevation:** 9,400 feet.

**Reservations, fees:** Reservations are not accepted. Sites are $5 a night.

**Open:** June to October.

**Directions:** From Yampa, drive five miles north on County Rd. 17 to Forest Hwy. 16 (Dunckley Scenic Byway). Turn left and drive approximately six miles west. Turn south on Forest Service Rd. 940 and continue 1.5 miles to the campground.

**Contact:** Routt National Forest, Yampa Ranger District, P.O. Box 7, Yampa, CO 80483; tel. (970) 638-4516.

## 71 Lynx Pass       7

The draw to this camp is the Morrison Divide Trail, a rugged hike that leads several miles west, eventually connecting to a web of other backcountry trails. Various nearby roads and trails also provide good opportunities for mountain biking. The camp offers partially shaded sites and basic amenities.

**Location:** East of Yampa in Routt National Forest; map A2, grid e3.

**Campsites, facilities:** There are 11 sites for tents or RVs up to 18 feet long. Drinking water, picnic tables, fire grills, and vault toilets are provided. Leashed pets are permitted. Horseback riding is permitted on designated trails in the park.

**Elevation:** 8,900 feet.

**Reservations, fees:** Reservations are not accepted. Sites are $10 a night.

**Open:** June to October.

**Directions:** From Kremmling, drive six miles northwest on U.S. 40. Turn left on Hwy. 134 and drive approximately 15 miles, over Gore Pass, to Forest Service Rd. 270. Turn right and continue three miles north to the campground.

**Contact:** Routt National Forest, Yampa Ranger District, P.O. Box 7, Yampa, CO 80483; tel. (970) 638-4516.

## 72 Red Mountain RV Park      5

Dry, open, and flat—that pretty much sums up Kremmling. It's not an ideal vacation destination, perhaps, but isn't a bad place to stop for the night either. This campground is very well maintained, with even sites divided by scattered trees and shrubs. Nearby recreation options include fishing and rafting on the Colorado River.

**Location:** In Kremmling; map A2, grid e5.

**Campsites, facilities:** There are 18 tent sites and 45 full-hookup sites for RVs of any length. Drinking water, picnic tables, and bathrooms with hot showers are provided. Laundry facilities, a waste disposal station, and public phone are available. Some facilities are wheelchair accessible. Leashed pets are permitted.

**Elevation:** 7,500 feet.

**Reservations, fees:** Reservations are accepted. Sites are $12-17 a night.

**Open:** Year-round.

**Directions:** From the junction of U.S. 40 and Hwy. 9 in Kremmling, drive 1.5 miles east on U.S. 40, turn north on County Rd. 22, and go one block to the campground.

**Contact:** Red Mountain RV Park, Box 532, Kremmling, CO 80459; tel. (970) 724-9593.

## 73 Hot Sulphur Springs State Wildlife Area    7

Everyone's first question is, "So, where are the hot springs?" Answer: Not on this property. The only hot springs around are a few miles away in the tiny town of Hot Sulphur Springs, at Hot Sulphur Springs Mineral Baths and Motel. What you'll find instead at this wildlife area are rustic campsites next to a pristine stretch of the Colorado River, perfect for fishing, bird-watching, some hunting, and relaxing. The sites are rugged and simple—and you probably won't have much company save for a few native riparian critters.

**Location:** East of Kremmling; map A2, grid e6.

**Campsites, facilities:** Campsites are scattered throughout the property. Vault toilets and campfire rings are provided, but there are no other facilities. Leashed pets are permitted.

**Elevation:** 7,800 feet.

**Reservations, fees:** Reservations are not accepted. There is no fee.

**Open:** Year-round.

**Directions:** From the town of Hot Sulphur Springs, drive three miles west on U.S. 40 to the Colorado River bridge; then turn south at the east end of the bridge to reach the campsites. Or continue another half mile past the bridge to access more campsites.

**Contact:** Colorado Division of Wildlife, 317 W. Prospect Ave., Fort Collins, CO 80526; tel. (970) 472-4300.

## 74 Denver Creek   5

The best that can be said about this camp is that it's isolated. There's not much out here except for a few willows and some scrub brush. However, if you happen to arrive in the middle of summer, one look at the crowded tent cities around nearby Lake Granby may send you running in this direction.

**Location:** Northwest of Granby in Arapaho National Forest; map A2, grid e6.

**Campsites, facilities:** There are 22 sites for tents or RVs up to 32 feet long. Half are on the north side of the highway, half on the south. Drinking water, picnic tables, fire grills, and vault toilets are provided. Leashed pets are permitted.

**Elevation:** 8,800 feet.

**Reservations, fees:** Reservations are not accepted. Sites are $10 a night.

**Open:** Memorial Day to Labor Day.

**Directions:** From Granby, drive 16 miles northwest on Hwy. 125.

**Contact:** Arapaho National Forest, Sulphur Ranger District, 9 Ten Mile Dr., P.O. Box 10, Granby, CO 80446; tel. (970) 887-4100.

## 75 Sawmill Gulch    6

Of the many campgrounds in the immediate area, this is one of the least used. It's just a few miles from Lake Granby and has both open and wooded sites. Fish nearby in Willow Creek.

**Location:** On Willow Creek in Arapaho National Forest; map A2, grid e7.

**Campsites, facilities:** There are six sites for tents or RVs up to 32 feet long. Drinking water, picnic tables, fire grills, and vault toilets are provided. Leashed pets are permitted.

**Elevation:** 8,780 feet.

**Reservations, fees:** Reservations are not accepted. Sites are $9 a night.

**Open:** Memorial Day to Labor Day.

**Directions:** From the town of Granby, drive 13 miles north on U.S. 34.

**Contact:** Arapaho National Forest, Sulphur Ranger District, 9 Ten Mile Dr., P.O. Box 10, Granby, CO 80446; tel. (970) 887-4100.

## 76 Stillwater       8

Since it's the only U.S. Forest Service campground around that offers amenities like showers and flush toilets, this camp fills up quickly in the summer. It's on the western shoreline of Lake Granby, close to a boat ramp and marina facilities. All water sports are permitted, including waterskiing, PWC riding, and fishing, but at over 8,000 feet elevation, the water is generally too chilly for swimming. Most of the campsites have excellent views of the lake.

**Location:** On Lake Granby in Arapaho National Forest; map A2, grid e7.

**Campsites, facilities:** There are 127 sites for tents or RVs up to 32 feet long. Drinking water, picnic tables, fire grills, flush toilets, and hot showers are provided. Electric hookups are available. A boat ramp and an amphitheater are nearby. Leashed pets are permitted.

**Elevation:** 8,300 feet.

**Reservations, fees:** Reservations are accepted; phone (877) 444-6777. There's an

$8.65 reservation fee. You may also reserve sites at website: www.reserveusa.com. Sites are $15-20 a night.

**Open:** Memorial Day to Labor Day.

**Directions:** From the town of Granby, drive 10 miles north on U.S. 34 to the campground entrance.

**Contact:** Arapaho National Forest, Sulphur Ranger District, 9 Ten Mile Dr., P.O. Box 10, Granby, CO 80446; tel. (970) 887-4100.

## 77 River Pines RV Park and Cabins     7

The lofty lodgepole pine trees that surround each site nearly dwarf this tiny campground, which is next to a string of alpine cabins. Although it offers only a few sites—sadly, none for tents—the camp is near lots of recreation options, including fishing on the adjacent Colorado River and hiking and mountain biking on nearby trails. Be warned that these sites are for self-contained RVs only—that means no outside showers, sewer hookups, or other facilities.

**Location:** On the North Fork of the Colorado River; map A2, grid e7.

**Campsites, facilities:** There are 12 sites for self-contained RVs up to 35 feet long. No tents are permitted. Drinking water, picnic tables, and barbecues are provided. Electric and water hookups, a hot tub, and cabins are available. Leashed pets are permitted.

**Elevation:** 8,300 feet.

**Reservations, fees:** Reservations are recommended. Sites are $16 a night.

**Open:** June to October.

**Directions:** From the town of Grand Lake, drive three miles south on U.S. 34 to the campground.

**Contact:** River Pines RV Park, 12082 U.S. 34, Grand Lake, CO 80447; tel. (970) 627-3632.

## 78 Green Ridge      8

This is a prime camping spot, snuggled between the headwaters of the Colorado River and the southern end of Shadow Mountain Reservoir. Since it's off the main road, it maintains a quiet atmosphere, with gorgeous views to boot. It's possibly the most popular campground in the Sulphur Ranger District, so reserve well in advance. Tip: The choice sites are on Loop B—they're closer to the river and very lush. A boat ramp, fishing access, and hiking trails are nearby. Within walking distance is an "interpretive barn" where the U.S. Forest Service presents interpretive and wildlife viewing programs.

**Location:** On Shadow Mountain Reservoir in Arapaho National Forest; map A2, grid e7.

**Campsites, facilities:** There are 78 sites for tents or RVs up to 32 feet long. Drinking water, picnic tables, fire grills, and flush toilets are provided. A boat ramp is available. Leashed pets are permitted.

**Elevation:** 8,360 feet.

**Reservations, fees:** Reservations are accepted; phone (877) 444-6777. There's an $8.65 reservation fee. You may also reserve sites at website: www.reserveusa.com. Sites are $12 a night.

**Open:** Memorial Day to Labor Day.

**Directions:** From the town of Grand Lake, drive four miles south on U.S. 34.

**Contact:** Arapaho National Forest, Sulphur Ranger District, 9 Ten Mile Dr., P.O. Box 10, Granby, CO 80446; tel. (970) 887-4100.

## **79** Willow Creek     7

Long, narrow Willow Creek Reservoir borders this campground in Arapaho National Recreation Area. Nearby is a boat ramp for small watercraft (only no-wake boating is allowed). The campground is open and sunny, sprinkled with lodgepole pine trees, and tends to fill up very quickly on summer weekends, so plan to arrive early in the day.

**Location:** On Willow Creek Reservoir in Arapaho National Forest; map A2, grid e7.

**Campsites, facilities:** There are 35 sites for tents or RVs up to 32 feet long. Drinking water, picnic tables, fire grills, and vault toilets are provided. A small boat launch is available. Leashed pets are permitted.

**Elevation:** 8,130 feet.

**Reservations, fees:** Reservations are not accepted. Sites are $10 a night.

**Open:** Memorial Day to Labor Day.

**Directions:** From the town of Granby, drive six miles north on U.S. 34 to County Rd. 40. Turn left and continue 2.5 miles west to the campground entrance.

**Contact:** Arapaho National Forest, Sulphur Ranger District, 9 Ten Mile Dr., P.O. Box 10, Granby, CO 80446; tel. (970) 887-4100.

## **80** Sunset Point     8

Because the demand for campsites on Lake Granby is so high, the U.S. Forest Service converted this former picnic area to a campground in the late 1990s, providing campers with an option to the crowded Arapaho Bay Campground. It's just off U.S. 34 on the southwest side of the lake, with a boat ramp near the sites. Sites are small but scenic, with excellent views of the lake.

**Location:** On Lake Granby in Arapaho National Forest; map A2, grid e7.

**Campsites, facilities:** There are 25 sites for tents or RVs up to 35 feet long. Drinking water, picnic tables, fire grills, and vault toilets are provided. A boat ramp is nearby. Leashed pets are permitted.

**Elevation:** 8,300 feet.

**Reservations, fees:** Reservations are not accepted. Sites are $15 a night

**Open:** Memorial Day to Labor Day.

**Directions:** From the town of Granby, drive six miles north on U.S. 34, turn right on County Rd. 6, and continue a short distance to the campground.

**Contact:** Arapaho National Forest, Sulphur Ranger District, 9 Ten Mile Dr., P.O. Box 10, Granby, CO 80446; tel. (970) 887-4100.

## **81** Arapaho Bay       8

You get the best of two worlds here: To the west lies huge Lake Granby and water sports galore, and to the east is the Indian Peaks Wilderness, where you can hook up with a network of outstanding hiking trails. The sites are enveloped in a private forest of Engelmann spruce, fir, and pine, and are close to a boat ramp.

**Location:** On Lake Granby in Arapaho National Forest; map A2, grid e8.

**Campsites, facilities:** There are 84 sites for tents or RVs up to 32 feet long. Drinking water, picnic tables, fire grills, and vault toilets are provided. A boat ramp is nearby. Leashed pets are permitted.

**Elevation:** 8,320 feet.

**Reservations, fees:** Reservations are accepted; phone (877) 444-6777. There's an $8.65 reservation fee. You may also reserve sites at website: www.reserveusa.com. Sites are $12 a night.

**Open:** Memorial Day to Labor Day.

**Directions:** From the town of Granby, drive six miles north on U.S. 34, turn right on County Rd. 6, and continue nine miles east.

**Contact:** Arapaho National Forest, Sulphur Ranger District, 9 Ten Mile Dr., P.O. Box 10, Granby, CO 80446; tel. (970) 887-4100.

## 82 Pawnee      8

My first experience camping at Brainard Lake occurred in the middle of winter, when the snow was piled up to the roofs of the toilet shelters. We had enjoyed an exhilarating backcountry ski in and I was thrilled by the sensational sunset over Indian Peaks, but as soon as that sun dropped, I was miserable, damp, and shivering in my minus-20-degree bag all night. Happily, conditions are significantly more pleasant in the summer months, with clear blue water, great fishing, good hiking trails, and lots of greenery—and the sunsets are just as spectacular.

**Location:** On Brainard Lake in Roosevelt National Forest; map A2, grid e8.

**Campsites, facilities:** There are 55 sites for tents or RVs up to 45 feet long. Drinking water, picnic tables, fire grills, and vault toilets are provided. Leashed pets are permitted.

**Elevation:** 10,400 feet.

**Reservations, fees:** Reservations are accepted; phone (877) 444-6777. There's an $8.65 reservation fee. You may also reserve sites at website: www.reserveusa.com. Sites are $12 a night.

**Open:** July to October.

**Directions:** From Nederland, drive approximately 11 miles north on Hwy. 72 (Peak to Peak Hwy.) to Ward. Turn left at the sign for Brainard Lake and continue six miles west to the campground.

**Contact:** Roosevelt National Forest, Boulder Ranger District, 2140 Yarmouth Ave., Boulder, CO 80301; tel. (303) 444-6600.

## 83 Olive Ridge    6

One of the biggest draws of Olive Ridge is its proximity to Rocky Mountain National Park. It's near the southeastern border, not far from trailheads that lead into the park and beyond into the Indian Peaks Wilderness. The sites are partially open and partially shaded, set in ponderosa pine forest. If possible, try to avoid the sites closer to the road (it can sound like a freeway in the summer).

**Location:** Near Estes Park in Roosevelt National Forest; map A2, grid e8.

**Campsites, facilities:** There are 56 sites for tents or RVs up to 30 feet long. Drinking water, picnic tables, fire grills, and vault toilets are provided. Leashed pets are permitted.

**Elevation:** 8,350 feet.

**Reservations, fees:** Reservations are accepted; phone (877) 444-6777. There's an $8.65 reservation fee. You may also reserve sites at website: www.reserveusa.com. Sites are $12 a night.

**Open:** Mid-May to October.

**Directions:** From Nederland, drive approximately 26 miles north on Hwy. 72 (Peak to Peak Hwy.) to the campground on the west (left) side of the road.

**Contact:** Roosevelt National Forest, Boulder Ranger District, 2140 Yarmouth Ave., Boulder, CO 80301; tel. (303) 444-6600.

## 84 Peaceful Valley      6

Peaceful Valley is anything but peaceful on busy summer days. The campground is right next to the highway and near a trailhead into the Indian Peaks Wilderness. Between campers and day hikers, the crowds can make you feel that you're in downtown Denver. If you're lucky enough to get a site away from the road, you'll be better off, buffered from the noise by tall ponderosa pines. Nearby is Middle St. Vrain Creek, a good fishing stream.

**Location:** Near Middle St. Vrain Creek in Roosevelt National Forest; map A2, grid e8.

**Campsites, facilities:** There are 17 sites for tents or RVs up to 55 feet long. Drinking water, picnic tables, fire grills, and vault toilets are provided. Some facilities are wheelchair accessible. Leashed pets are permitted.

**Elevation:** 8,500 feet.

**Reservations, fees:** Reservations are accepted; phone (877) 444-6777. There's an $8.65 reservation fee. You may also reserve sites at website: www.reserveusa.com. Sites are $12 a night.

**Open:** Mid-May to October.

**Directions:** From Nederland, drive approximately 17 miles north on Hwy. 72 (Peak to Peak Hwy.) to the campground.

**Contact:** Roosevelt National Forest, Boulder Ranger District, 2140 Yarmouth Ave., Boulder, CO 80301; tel. (303) 444-6600.

## 85 Camp Dick       7

If you have a choice between a site at Camp Dick or a site at Peaceful Valley, go for Camp Dick. It's set back off the road and adjacent to Middle St. Vrain Creek, a crystal-cold, bubbling stream where you can cast your fishing line in the evening or dunk your feet after a long day of hiking. Behind the camp is a four-wheel-drive road that doubles as a mountain bike trail, heading up about five miles to the border of the Indian Peaks Wilderness, where you'll find a little bridge and a trailhead.

**Location:** Near Middle St. Vrain Creek in Roosevelt National Forest; map A2, grid e8.

**Campsites, facilities:** There are 41 sites for tents or RVs up to 55 feet long. Drinking water, picnic tables, fire grills, and vault toilets are provided. Some facilities are wheelchair accessible. Leashed pets are permitted.

**Elevation:** 8,650 feet.

**Reservations, fees:** Reservations are accepted; phone (877) 444-6777. There's an

$8.65 reservation fee. You may also reserve sites at website: www.reserveusa.com. Sites are $12 a night.

**Open:** Mid-May to October.

**Directions:** From Nederland, drive approximately 17 miles north on Hwy. 72 (Peak to Peak Hwy.) to the campground entrance. Continue past Peaceful Valley Campground to reach the campsites.

**Contact:** Roosevelt National Forest, Boulder Ranger District, 2140 Yarmouth Ave., Boulder, CO 80301; tel. (303) 444-6600.

## 86 Himes Peak      9

Set next to a thin strip of road that splits the Flat Tops Wilderness, Himes Peak is an isolated, thickly wooded spot that's makes a great base camp for backpackers and equestrians. The adjacent trailhead leads in the direction of a tangle of trails routed south, passing by several alpine lakes, streams, and meadows.

**Location:** Near Trappers Lake in White River National Forest; map A2, grid f0.

**Campsites, facilities:** There are nine sites for tents or RVs up to 25 feet long. Drinking water, picnic tables, fire grills, and vault toilets are provided. A hitch rack for horses is at the adjacent trailhead. Some facilities are wheelchair accessible. Leashed pets are permitted.

**Elevation:** 9,500 feet.

**Reservations, fees:** Reservations are not accepted. Sites are $10 a night.

**Open:** June to November.

**Directions:** From Meeker, drive two miles east on Hwy. 13, turn right on County Rd. 8, and drive approximately 37 miles. Turn south on Forest Service Rd. 205 and continue five miles to the campground.

**Contact:** White River National Forest, Blanco Ranger District, 317 E. Market St., Meeker, CO 81641; tel. (970) 878-4039.

## 87 Shepherd's Rim      9

Of all the camps clustered near Trappers Lake, this one is most popular with tent campers and equestrians planning a pack trip into the Flat Tops Wilderness. The sites are small and cozy, some with convenient tent pads. A few special sites have accommodations for horses, and it's just a short walk or ride to the nearest trailhead. In 1999 additional horse corrals were constructed north of the camping areas. Fishing is available at Trappers Lake as well as many small lakes and streams in the area.

**Location:** Near Trappers Lake in White River National Forest; map A2, grid f0.

**Campsites, facilities:** There are 20 sites for tents or RVs up to 40 feet long, and a special area for campers with horses. Drinking water, picnic tables, fire grills, and vault toilets are provided. Some facilities are wheelchair accessible. Leashed pets are permitted.

**Elevation:** 9,800 feet.

**Reservations, fees:** Reservations are not accepted. Sites are $11 a night.

**Open:** Mid-June to November.

**Directions:** From Meeker, drive two miles east on Hwy. 13, turn right on County Rd. 8, and drive approximately 37 miles. Turn south on Forest Service Rd. 205 and continue eight miles to the campground.

**Contact:** White River National Forest, Blanco Ranger District, 317 E. Market St., Meeker, CO 81641; tel. (970) 878-4039.

## 88 Bucks       9

Bucks is in a dense grove of spindly pines, not far from the road. It's the smallest of five camps in the area, with easy access to Trappers Lake and numerous wilderness trails.

**Location:** Near Trappers Lake in White River National Forest; map A2, grid f0.

**Campsites, facilities:** There are 10 sites for tents or RVs up to 40 feet long. Drinking water, picnic tables, fire grills, and vault toilets are provided. Leashed pets are permitted.

**Elevation:** 9,800 feet.

**Reservations, fees:** Reservations are not accepted. Sites are $11 a night.

**Open:** Mid-June to November.

**Directions:** From Meeker, drive two miles east on Hwy. 13, turn right on County Rd. 8, and drive approximately 37 miles. Turn south on Forest Service Rd. 205 and continue eight miles to the campground.

**Contact:** White River National Forest, Blanco Ranger District, 317 E. Market St., Meeker, CO 81641; tel. (970) 878-4039.

## 89 Cutthroat      9

Named for the dinker-sized fish in nearby Trappers Lake, this camp is pretty close to the boundary of the Flat Tops Wilderness. A short footpath leads to the lake, and there are several hiking/horseback-riding trails to the south.

**Location:** Near Trappers Lake in White River National Forest; map A2, grid f0.

**Campsites, facilities:** There are 14 sites for tents or RVs up to 40 feet long. Drinking water, picnic tables, fire grills, and vault toilets are provided. Leashed pets are permitted.

**Elevation:** 9,800 feet.

**Reservations, fees:** Reservations are not accepted. Sites are $11 a night.

**Open:** Mid-June to November.

**Directions:** From Meeker, drive two miles east on Hwy. 13, turn right on County Rd. 8, and drive approximately 37 miles. Turn south on Forest Service Rd. 205 and continue eight miles to the campground.

**Contact:** White River National Forest, Blanco Ranger District, 317 E. Market St., Meeker, CO 81641; tel. (970) 878-4039.

## 90 Trapline       9

As the closest camp to Trappers Lake, Trapline has some of the most sought-after sites. It is also the closest to major wilderness trailheads, including one that meanders south past a natural rock amphitheater and up to several high mountain lakes. If you arrive in midsummer, you'll be treated to colorful expanses of native wildflowers including paintbrush, gentian, and columbine.

**Location:** Near Trappers Lake in White River National Forest; map A2, grid f0.

**Campsites, facilities:** There are 13 sites for tents or RVs up to 40 feet long. Drinking water, picnic tables, fire grills, and vault toilets are provided. Leashed pets are permitted.

**Elevation:** 9,800 feet.

**Reservations, fees:** Reservations are not accepted. Sites are $11 a night.

**Open:** Mid-June to November.

**Directions:** From Meeker, drive two miles east on Hwy. 13, turn right on County Rd. 8, and drive approximately 37 miles to Forest Service Rd. 205. Turn south and continue eight miles to the campground.

**Contact:** White River National Forest, Blanco Ranger District, 317 E. Market St., Meeker, CO 81641; tel. (970) 878-4039.

## 91 Bear River Dispersed Sites    8

Primitive and plain, these sites offer little more than a place to park (and maybe a fishing hole), but you may be grateful for that if you can't find a spot at one of the nearby developed camps during the high season. The first sites after the Forest Boundary are along the river; the last ones sit high above the river past Bear Lake Campground. No water is available, so bring your own or a filter for river water.

**Location:** Near Stillwater Reservoir in Routt National Forest; map A2, grid f1.

**Campsites, facilities:** There are several primitive sites scattered along County Rd. 7. Fire rings are provided, but no drinking water or toilets are available. Leashed pets are permitted.

**Elevation:** From 9,300 to 10,200 feet.

**Reservations, fees:** Reservations are not accepted. Sites are $3 a night.

**Open:** June to October.

**Directions:** From Yampa on Hwy. 131, turn south on County Rd. 7 (Forest Service Rd. 900) and drive to the National Forest Boundary. Sites are located randomly along the road from this point to above Bear Lake Campground.

**Contact:** Routt National Forest, Yampa Ranger District, P.O. Box 7, Yampa, CO 80483; tel. (970) 638-4516.

## 92 Cold Springs     8

This partially wooded campground makes an excellent base camp for backpacking excursions into the Flat Tops Wilderness. You can take a trail south from nearby Stillwater Reservoir up to Keener Lake, a beautiful high mountain lake with good fishing for rainbow trout. If you don't want to venture quite so far, the fishing in Stillwater Reservoir is quite good, and you can get even better access with a boat (nonmotorized craft only).

**Location:** Near Stillwater Reservoir in Routt National Forest; map A2, grid f1.

**Campsites, facilities:** There are five sites for tents or RVs up to 22 feet long. Drinking water, picnic tables, fire grills, and vault toilets are provided. Leashed pets are permitted.

**Elevation:** 10,200 feet.

**Reservations, fees:** Reservations are not accepted. Sites are $10 a night.

**Open:** June to October.

**Directions:** From Yampa on Hwy. 131, turn south on County Rd. 7 (Forest Service Rd. 900) and drive approximately 17 miles to the campground.

Contact: Routt National Forest, Yampa Ranger District, P.O. Box 7, Yampa, CO 80483; tel. (970) 638-4516.

## 93 Horseshoe    7

Just a mile up the road from the Cold Springs camp, Horseshoe also sits near the border of the Flat Tops Wilderness. Starting from the northwest side of Stillwater Reservoir, you can follow a trail that leads west into the wilderness, skirting literally hundreds of tiny alpine lakes and streams. The wildflower displays in this area are overwhelming during the summer months, but unfortunately, so are the mosquitoes—be sure to bring plenty of insect repellent.

**Location:** Near Stillwater Reservoir in Routt National Forest; map A2, grid f1.

**Campsites, facilities:** There are seven sites for tents or RVs up to 18 feet long. Drinking water, picnic tables, fire grills, and vault toilets are provided. Leashed pets are permitted.

**Elevation:** 10,000 feet.

**Reservations, fees:** Reservations are not accepted. Sites are $10 a night.

**Open:** June to October.

**Directions:** From Yampa on Hwy. 131, turn south on County Rd. 7 (Forest Service Rd. 900) and drive approximately 16 miles to the campground.

**Contact:** Routt National Forest, Yampa Ranger District, P.O. Box 7, Yampa, CO 80483; tel. (970) 638-4516.

## 94 Bear Lake     7

An alternative to nearby Horseshoe and Cold Springs, this is the largest of the three camps in the area. It's near the eastern shore of Yampa Reservoir (also known as Upper Stillwater Reservoir) and accesses a trailhead that leads west into the Flat Tops Wilderness up to the Mandall Lakes area. Fishing and nonmotorized boating are allowed in Yampa Reservoir.

**Location:** Near Yampa Reservoir in Routt National Forest; map A2, grid f1.

**Campsites, facilities:** There are 29 sites for tents or RVs up to 30 feet long. Drinking water, picnic tables, fire grills, and vault toilets are provided. Leashed pets are permitted.

**Elevation:** 9,600 feet.

**Reservations, fees:** Reservations are not accepted. Sites are $10 a night.

**Open:** June to October.

**Directions:** From Yampa on Hwy. 131, turn south on County Rd. 7 (Forest Service Rd. 900) and drive approximately 14 miles to the campground.

**Contact:** Routt National Forest, Yampa Ranger District, P.O. Box 7, Yampa, CO 80483; tel. (970) 638-4516.

## 95 Rock Creek State Wildlife Area     6

Rock Creek provides a decent opportunity for fishing and bird-watching, but there isn't much else out here. The terrain is rugged and beautiful, good for hiking—but there aren't any developed trails, so brush up on your orienteering skills if you plan to explore. If you climb up high enough, you'll be rewarded with spectacular views of the Gore Range to the east. Limited hunting is permitted.

**Location:** West of Kremmling; map A2, grid f3.

**Campsites, facilities:** Dispersed camping is permitted throughout the property. Vault toilets are provided, but there are no other facilities or drinking water. Leashed pets are permitted.

**Elevation:** 7,700 feet.

**Reservations, fees:** Reservations are not accepted. There is no fee.

**Open:** Year-round.

**Directions:** From Kremmling, drive six miles northwest on U.S. 40. Turn left on Hwy. 134 and drive approximately 12 miles, over Gore Pass, to Forest Service Rd. 206. Turn left and continue 2.5 miles to the property boundary.

**Contact:** Colorado Division of Wildlife, 317 W. Prospect Ave., Fort Collins, CO 80526; tel. (970) 472-4300.

## 96 Blacktail Creek    7

This simple camp beside the banks of a bubbling little creek affords a serene atmosphere and decent fishing. The sites are mostly shaded, and there's a sunny picnic area adjacent to camp. A short distance west off Forest Service Rd. 206 is the Wells Fargo Stage Stop, a historic reminder of folks who once camped here by necessity.

**Location:** West of Kremmling in Routt National Forest; map A2, grid f3.

**Campsites, facilities:** There are eight sites for tents or RVs up to 18 feet long. Drinking water, picnic tables, fire grills, and vault toilets are provided. Leashed pets are permitted.

**Elevation:** 9,100 feet.

**Reservations, fees:** Reservations are not accepted. Sites are $10 a night.

**Open:** June to October.

**Directions:** From Kremmling, drive six miles northwest on U.S. 40. Turn left on Hwy. 134 and drive approximately 11 miles, over Gore Pass, to the campground.

**Contact:** Routt National Forest, Yampa Ranger District, P.O. Box 7, Yampa, CO 80483; tel. (970) 638-4516.

## 97 Gore Pass    8

This popular camp lies at the base of the spectacular Gore Range, adjacent to several good hiking trails. It's often packed on summer weekends, but the views of the surrounding peaks are worth the crowds. Each site is sheltered by looming pine trees, with aspens scattered in between. Look closely in midsummer for bunches of the delicate purple columbine that grow wild at the base of the aspens.

**Location:** West of Kremmling in Routt National Forest; map A2, grid f3.

**Campsites, facilities:** There are 12 sites for tents or RVs up to 22 feet long. Drinking water, picnic tables, fire grills, and vault toilets are provided. Leashed pets are permitted.

**Elevation:** 9,600 feet.

**Reservations, fees:** Reservations are not accepted. Sites are $10 a night.

**Open:** June to October.

**Directions:** From Kremmling, drive six miles northwest on U.S. 40. Turn left on Hwy. 134 and drive approximately 10 miles, over Gore Pass, to the campground.

**Contact:** Routt National Forest, Yampa Ranger District, P.O. Box 7, Yampa, CO 80483; tel. (970) 638-4516.

## 98 Radium State Wildlife Area      7

Rumor has it there's a natural hot spring around here along the Colorado River, but you have to climb down a steep embankment to reach it, and it's completely unmarked. They say it's definitely worth a shot, though. If you can't find it, there's always fishing—this stretch of the Colorado is clear and unsullied, offering good prospects for rainbow trout. For those who enjoy rock climbing, outcroppings in the area present challenging opportunities for bouldering and climbing. Limited hunting is permitted.

**Location:** Southwest of Kremmling; map A2, grid f4.

**Campsites, facilities:** Dispersed camping is permitted throughout the property. Vault toilets are provided, but there are no other facilities. Leashed pets are permitted.

**Elevation:** 7,500 feet.

**Reservations, fees:** Reservations are not accepted. There is no fee.

**Open:** Year-round.

**Directions:** From Kremmling, drive 2.5 miles south on Hwy. 9 and turn right on County Rd. 1 (Trough Road). Continue 12 miles southwest to the property entrance.

**Contact:** Colorado Division of Wildlife, 317 W. Prospect Ave., Fort Collins, CO 80526; tel. (970) 472-4300.

## 99 Pumphouse    8

By midsummer, this popular spot is more often than not taken over by raucous groups of kayakers and white-water rafters. It's set alongside the Colorado River, with roomy sites and the sound of rushing water to lull you to sleep. All the basics are provided, including water and toilets. If you hit it before prime rafting season, you'll be more likely to be rewarded with quiet and some excellent bird-watching.

**Location:** On the Colorado River; map A2, grid f4.

**Campsites, facilities:** There are 14 sites for tents or RVs up to 30 feet long. Drinking water, picnic tables, vault toilets, and fire rings are provided. The toilets are wheelchair accessible. Leashed pets are permitted.

**Elevation:** 7,000 feet.

**Reservations, fees:** Reservations are not accepted. There is no fee.

**Open:** April to November.

**Directions:** From Kremmling, drive 2.5 miles south on Hwy. 9 and turn right on County Rd. 1 (Trough Road). Continue approximately 15 miles southwest to the camp.

**Contact:** Bureau of Land Management, P.O. Box 8, Kremmling, CO 80459; tel. (970) 724-3437.

## 100 Willows       6

An open, bare-bones camping area, Willows doesn't offer any luxuries—just plain, treeless dirt sites—but it's free and has excellent lake access. You can launch boats from the sloping shoreline and swim at the nearby beach. All water sports, including waterskiing and windsurfing, are allowed.

**Location:** On Green Mountain Reservoir in Arapaho National Forest; map A2, grid f4.

**Campsites, facilities:** Dispersed tent and RV camping is permitted within designated areas. Vault toilets are provided, but there are no other facilities. Leashed pets are permitted.

**Elevation:** 8,500 feet.

**Reservations, fees:** Reservations are not accepted. There is no fee.

**Open:** June to November.

**Directions:** From Interstate 70 at Silverthorne, take Exit 205 and drive approximately 24 miles north on Hwy. 9 to an unmarked dirt road at the north end of the reservoir. Turn left. The campground is on the immediate left.

**Contact:** Arapaho National Forest, Dillon Ranger District, 680 Blue River Parkway, P.O. Box 620, Silverthorne, CO 80498; tel. (970) 468-5400.

## 101 Elliott Creek      6

Elliott Creek is situated in a large, primitive area on Green Mountain Reservoir's westernmost arm. You have to pack in your own water and pack out your trash, but as a reward you get fantastic views of the Gore Range along with superb fishing and swimming access.

**Location:** On Green Mountain Reservoir in Arapaho National Forest; map A2, grid f4.

**Campsites, facilities:** There are 60 primitive sites for tents or RVs up to 22 feet long. Vault toilets are provided, but there are no other facilities. Leashed pets are permitted.

**Elevation:** 8,300 feet.

**Reservations, fees:** Reservations are not accepted. There is no fee.

**Open:** June to November.

**Directions:** From Interstate 70 at Silverthorne, take Exit 205 and drive approximately 24 miles north on Hwy. 9 to an unmarked dirt road at the north end of the reservoir. Turn left and continue about three miles past the Willows camping area to Elliott Creek, located on the westernmost arm of the reservoir.

**Contact:** Arapaho National Forest, Dillon Ranger District, 680 Blue River Parkway, P.O. Box 620, Silverthorne, CO 80498; tel. (970) 468-5400.

## 102 Cataract Creek     8

Situated southwest of Green Mountain Reservoir, this tiny camp is near the northern edge of the Eagles Nest Wilderness. A short walk to the end of the road will take you to a trailhead that leads into the wilderness and on to Lower Cataract Lake, where fishing is poor but possible. You'll have wonderful views of the spiky Gore Range peaks from this camp, but expect company; it's a popular spot and is nearly always full.

**Location:** Southwest of Green Mountain Reservoir in Arapaho National Forest; map A2, grid f4.

**Campsites, facilities:** There are four sites for tents or RVs of any length. Drinking water, picnic tables, and fire rings are provided. Leashed pets are permitted.

**Elevation:** 8,300 feet.

**Reservations, fees:** Reservations are not accepted. Sites are $5 a night, and there's a $5 daily entrance fee.

**Open:** June to November.

**Directions:** From Interstate 70 at Silverthorne, take Exit 205 and drive approximately 16 miles north on Hwy. 9 to an unmarked dirt road on the left side of the highway, just south of Green Mountain Reservoir. Turn left and drive about five miles. Then turn left on County Rd. 1725 and continue about two miles more to the campground.

**Contact:** Arapaho National Forest, Dillon Ranger District, 680 Blue River Parkway, P.O. Box 620, Silverthorne, CO 80498; tel. (970) 468-5400.

## **103** Cow Creek      6

Easily accessible from Hwy. 9, Cow Creek offers rustic camping in a dry, scrubby lot with direct shoreline access for fishing, swimming, and windsurfing. This site is commonly used by day-trippers for swimming and picnicking, so if it's privacy you seek, you're better off at Elliott Creek Campground.

**Location:** On Green Mountain Reservoir in Arapaho National Forest; map A2, grid f4.

**Campsites, facilities:** Dispersed tent and RV camping is available at designated areas. Vault toilets are provided, but there are no other facilities or drinking water. Leashed pets are permitted.

**Elevation:** 8,400 feet.

**Reservations, fees:** Reservations are not accepted. There is no fee.

**Open:** June to November.

**Directions:** From Interstate 70 at Silverthorne, take Exit 205 and drive approximately 22 miles north on Hwy. 9 to the campground entrance on the left.

**Contact:** Arapaho National Forest, Dillon Ranger District, 680 Blue River Parkway, P.O. Box 620, Silverthorne, CO 80498; tel. (970) 468-5400.

## **104** McDonald Flats      6

As the only developed campground on the main body of huge Green Mountain Reservoir, McDonald Flats gets a lot of use. The boat ramp makes it popular with anglers and water-skiers alike, and this area can become quite congested on sunny summer afternoons. The adjacent day-use area offers picnicking and swimming access.

**Location:** On Green Mountain Reservoir in Arapaho National Forest; map A2, grid f4.

**Campsites, facilities:** There are 13 sites for tents or RVs up to 20 feet long. Drinking water, picnic tables, and vault toilets are provided. A boat launch is adjacent to the campground. Leashed pets are permitted.

**Elevation:** 8,200 feet.

**Reservations, fees:** Reservations are not accepted. Sites are $7 a night.

**Open:** June to November.

**Directions:** From Interstate 70 at Silverthorne, take Exit 205 and drive approximately 16 miles north on Hwy. 9 to an unmarked dirt road on the left side of the highway just south of Green Mountain Reservoir. Turn left and continue about two miles to the campground.

**Contact:** Arapaho National Forest, Dillon Ranger District, 680 Blue River Parkway, P.O. Box 620, Silverthorne, CO 80498; tel. (970) 468-5400.

## 105 Prairie Point    6

Prairie Point is located at the merging point of the Blue River and Green Mountain Reservoir. The campsites offer some shade, but most are open and sunny. You can reach the river via a short walk. Since it's right on the highway, this camp fills up quickly on summer weekends.

**Location:** On Green Mountain Reservoir in Arapaho National Forest; map A2, grid f4.

**Campsites, facilities:** There are 33 sites for tents or RVs up to 20 feet long. Drinking water, picnic tables, and vault toilets are provided. Leashed pets are permitted.

**Elevation:** 8,200 feet.

**Reservations, fees:** Reservations are not accepted. Sites are $7 a night.

**Open:** June to November.

**Directions:** From Interstate 70 at Silverthorne, take Exit 205 and drive approximately 18 miles north on Hwy. 9 to the campground entrance on the left.

**Contact:** Arapaho National Forest, Dillon Ranger District, 680 Blue River Parkway, P.O. Box 620, Silverthorne, CO 80498; tel. (970) 468-5400.

## 106 Davis Springs    6

Tiny Davis Springs is a more primitive (and private) alternative to Prairie Point across the river. It offers little more than a place to park your tent, but as a bonus you get a short trail that leads down to the river and a perfect little fishing access spot.

**Location:** On Green Mountain Reservoir in Arapaho National Forest; map A2, grid f4.

**Campsites, facilities:** There are seven sites for tents or RVs up to 20 feet long. Vault toilets are available, but there are no other facilities or drinking water. Leashed pets are permitted.

**Elevation:** 8,600 feet.

**Reservations, fees:** Reservations are not accepted. There is no fee.

**Open:** June to November.

**Directions:** From Interstate 70 at Silverthorne, take Exit 205 and drive approximately 16 miles north on Hwy. 9 to an unmarked dirt road on the left side of the highway just south of Green Mountain Reservoir. Turn left and continue about a mile to the campground.

**Contact:** Arapaho National Forest, Dillon Ranger District, 680 Blue River Parkway, P.O. Box 620, Silverthorne, CO 80498; tel. (970) 468-5400.

## 107 Williams Fork Reservoir     5

The sparse, open campsites at 1800-acre Williams Fork Reservoir are divided between the east and west shores of the reservoir. Each site has a gravel pad, a picnic table, and a fire ring, but not much else is available. Bring your own firewood and drinking water. The landscape is wide and open, with views of the reservoir and the distant Williams Fork Mountains to the south. Stocked with rainbow trout, brown trout, and kokanee salmon, the reservoir offers good chances for an evening fish fry. Although motorized boating is allowed, water skiing and PWCs are prohibited, as is swimming. Windsurfing, however, is permitted, with nice, swift winds sweeping through the basin on summer afternoons.

**Location:** West of Granby; map A2, grid f5.

**Campsites, facilities:** There are approximately 24 sites for tents or RVs of any length. Vault toilets, picnic tables, and fire rings are provided. There is no drinking water. Two boat ramps are available. Leashed pets are permitted.

**Elevation:** 7,800 feet.

**Reservations, fees:** Reservations are not accepted. There is no fee.

**Open:** Year-round.

**Directions:** From Parshall on U.S. 40, turn south on County Rd. 3 and continue approximately four miles to the reservoir. Campsites are available near the west boat ramp (first turnoff) or the east boat ramp (second turnoff).

**Contact:** Denver Water District, 1600 W. 12th Ave., Denver, CO 80254; tel. (303) 628-6526.

## 108 Horseshoe    7

This small campground is popular with off-road-vehicle enthusiasts, who enjoy exploring dirt trails in the Williams Fork Valley. The camp is set in mixed conifer and aspen forest on the Williams Fork River, with fairly dismal fishing prospects. Williams Fork Reservoir is a few miles north.

**Location:** On the Williams Fork River in Arapaho National Forest; map A2, grid f6.

**Campsites, facilities:** There are seven sites for tents or RVs up to 35 feet long. Drinking water, picnic tables, fire grills, and vault toilets are provided. Leashed pets are permitted.

**Elevation:** 8,700 feet.

**Reservations, fees:** Reservations are not accepted. Sites are $9 a night.

**Open:** Memorial Day to Labor Day.

**Directions:** From Silverthorne on Interstate 70, take Exit 205 and drive 15 miles north on Hwy. 9. Turn right on County Rd. 15 and continue approximately nine miles, turn left on Forest Service Rd. 138, and proceed three miles north to the campground.

**Contact:** Arapaho National Forest, Sulphur Ranger District, 9 Ten Mile Dr., P.O. Box 10, Granby, CO 80446; tel. (970) 887-4100.

## 109 South Fork     7

Situated near the trailhead of a popular wilderness trail, this camp is frequented by both hikers and equestrians. Corrals are available for campers who bring their horses along. Sites are cozy, nestled under thickly clustered pine trees, and the Williams Fork River is a short jaunt away.

**Location:** North of Silverthorne in Arapaho National Forest; map A2, grid f6.

**Campsites, facilities:** There are 21 sites for tents or RVs up to 35 feet long. Drinking water, picnic tables, fire grills, and vault toilets are provided. Horse corrals are available. Leashed pets are permitted.

**Elevation:** 9,000 feet.

**Reservations, fees:** Reservations are not accepted. Sites are $10 a night.

**Open:** Memorial Day to Labor Day.

**Directions:** From Silverthorne on Interstate 70, take Exit 205 and drive 15 miles north on Hwy. 9. Turn right on County Rd. 15 and continue approximately nine miles. Turn right on Forest Service Rd. 138 and proceed six miles south to the campground.

**Contact:** Arapaho National Forest, Sulphur Ranger District, 9 Ten Mile Dr., P.O. Box 10, Granby, CO 80446; tel. (970) 887-4100.

## 110 Sugarloaf      7

Located just down the road from South Fork Campground, Sugarloaf is the only wheelchair-accessible campground for miles around. Some sites and toilets accommodate wheelchairs, along with a short trail routed near the Williams Fork River. Other options include horseback riding and hiking on area trails.

**Location:** North of Silverthorne in Arapaho National Forest; map A2, grid f6.

**Campsites, facilities:** There are 11 sites for tents or RVs up to 35 feet long. Drinking water, picnic tables, fire grills, and vault toilets are provided. Some facilities are wheelchair accessible. Leashed pets are permitted.

**Elevation:** 9,000 feet.

**Reservations, fees:** Reservations are not accepted. Sites are $10 a night.

**Open:** Memorial Day to Labor Day.

**Directions:** From Silverthorne on Interstate 70, take Exit 205 and drive 15 miles north on Hwy. 9. Turn right on County Rd. 15 and continue approximately nine miles, turn right on Forest Service Rd. 138, and proceed six miles south to the campground.

**Contact:** Arapaho National Forest, Sulphur Ranger District, 9 Ten Mile Dr., P.O. Box 10, Granby, CO 80446; tel. (970) 887-4100.

## 111 Byers Creek     9

The land surrounding this tiny campground comprises the Fraser Experimental Forest, a special area set aside in the 1940s by the U.S. Forest Service for the purpose of collecting data on soil erosion, water, and timber practices. The camp itself is very heavily wooded and secluded, not far from St. Louis Creek. Its biggest draw is being close to an extensive network of trails for hiking and mountain biking; in fact, the majority of people who frequent the camp are cyclists in search of challenging terrain.

**Location:** Near Fraser in Arapaho National Forest; map A2, grid f7.

**Campsites, facilities:** There are six sites for tents or RVs up to 32 feet long. Drinking water, picnic tables, fire grills, and vault toilets are provided. Leashed pets are permitted.

**Elevation:** 9,360 feet.

**Reservations, fees:** Reservations are not accepted. Sites are $10 a night.

**Open:** Memorial Day to Labor Day.

**Directions:** From the town of Fraser on U.S. 40, turn west on County Rd. 73 and drive approximately seven miles to the campground.

**Contact:** Arapaho National Forest, Sulphur Ranger District, 9 Ten Mile Dr., P.O. Box 10, Granby, CO 80446; tel. (970) 887-4100.

**112** St. Louis Creek     7

Of the two campgrounds in the Fraser Experimental Forest (the other being Byers Creek), this one gets the heaviest use, probably because it's the first one you come to on the road from Fraser. It's also larger, with three times the number of sites. There are excellent hiking and mountain biking trails in the region; contact the Sulphur Ranger District for details. St. Louis Creek runs adjacent to camp.

**Location:** Near Fraser in Arapaho National Forest; map A2, grid f7.

**Campsites, facilities:** There are 18 sites for tents or RVs up to 32 feet long. Drinking water, picnic tables, fire grills, and vault toilets are provided. Leashed pets are permitted.

**Elevation:** 8,900 feet.

**Reservations, fees:** Reservations are not accepted. Sites are $10 a night.

**Open:** Memorial Day to Labor Day.

**Directions:** From the town of Fraser on U.S. 40, turn west on County Rd. 73 and drive approximately four miles to the campground.

**Contact:** Arapaho National Forest, Sulphur Ranger District, 9 Ten Mile Dr., P.O. Box 10, Granby, CO 80446; tel. (970) 887-4100.

**113** YMCA Snow Mountain Ranch     10

Until now, this spot has remained an undiscovered treasure in the realm of Colorado campgrounds. Not only is it one of the few developed campgrounds near Winter Park, it's simply beautiful: Picture quiet, private sites sitting far back from the road in a lush thicket of trees, with a pretty little trout pond shimmering nearby and stunning views of snowcapped peaks. The campground is just one small part of this 5,000-acre YMCA ranch, which also offers cabin rentals and full recreation facilities, including a private stocked lake for fishing and canoeing. Other activities are roller skating, miniature golf, volleyball, basketball, tennis, hiking, mountain biking, and horseback riding on private trails. The managers also organize family-oriented entertainment such as square dancing, arts and crafts, and hayrides. Adjacent to the property is an 18-hole golf course. All this, and believe it or not, it's hardly ever full.

**Location:** Near Winter Park; map A2, grid f7.

**Campsites, facilities:** There are 13 tent sites and 42 sites for RVs up to 40 feet long, many with full hookups. Drinking water, picnic tables, fire grills, and bathrooms with hot showers are provided. Laundry facilities, a grocery store, restaurant, swimming pool, sports facilities, miniature golf, horse and mountain bike rentals, canoe rentals, and cabins are available. Leashed pets are permitted.

**Elevation:** 8,800 feet.

**Reservations, fees:** Reservations are accepted. Sites are $17-21 a night. If you are not a YMCA member, there is a small additional charge for a guest membership.

**Open:** Memorial Day to Labor Day.

**Directions:** From Winter Park, drive 12 miles northwest on U.S. 40 to the ranch entrance.

**Contact:** Snow Mountain Ranch, P.O. Box 169, Winter Park, CO 80482; tel. (970) 887-2152, or from the Denver Metro area (303) 443-4743.

## 114 Rainbow Lakes     7

Tourists often miss this one. It's far off the main road on a rough, rocky route that is only five miles long but takes about 45 minutes to navigate. Trailers are not recommended. If you enjoy four-wheeling, there are several other suitable roads in the area to explore (they make good mountain biking trails, too). A trailhead here leads about a mile west to the string of little lakes for which the camp was named, and then on to Glacier Rim in the Indian Peaks Wilderness. Fishing is best at those lakes, but it's possible—when water levels are high in late spring—to fish in the small drainage that follows the trail.

**Location:** Near Nederland in Roosevelt National Forest; map A2, grid f8.

**Campsites, facilities:** There are 16 tent sites. Drinking water, picnic tables, fire grills, and vault toilets are provided. Leashed pets are permitted.

**Elevation:** 10,000 feet.

**Reservations, fees:** Reservations are not accepted. Sites are $6 a night.

**Open:** July to October.

**Directions:** From Nederland, drive approximately 6.5 miles north on Hwy. 72 (Peak to Peak Hwy.). Turn left on County Rd. 116 and drive one-half mile to a fork. Bear left and continue about five miles to the camp.

**Contact:** Roosevelt National Forest, Boulder Ranger District, 2140 Yarmouth Ave., Boulder, CO 80301; tel. (303) 444-6600.

## 115 Idlewild     6

If you camp here, you're going to have company. This campground is convenient to Winter Park, a popular tourist destination, and right on the highway, so it's often the first spot travelers try. It's in a pretty, forested setting, with a nice biking trail running adjacent. There are several other excellent biking and hiking trails in the surrounding forest; contact the Sulphur Ranger District for information.

**Location:** Near Winter Park in Arapaho National Forest; map A2, grid g8.

**Campsites, facilities:** There are 26 sites for tents or RVs up to 32 feet long. Drinking water, picnic tables, fire grills, and vault toilets are provided. Leashed pets are permitted.

**Elevation:** 9,000 feet.

**Reservations, fees:** Reservations are not accepted. Sites are $10 a night.

**Open:** Memorial Day to Labor Day.

**Directions:** From Winter Park, drive one mile south on U.S. 40.

**Contact:** Arapaho National Forest, Sulphur Ranger District, 9 Ten Mile Dr., P.O. Box 10, Granby, CO 80446; tel. (970) 887-4100.

## 116 Buckingham   9

Perched on the southeastern border of the Indian Peaks Wilderness, this tiny, rocky campground attracts an alarming number of visitors in the summer. Its popularity is due to its proximity to the Fourth of July Trailhead, a popular jump-off point for backpackers headed into the wilderness. In an area of jam-packed, expensive campgrounds, the fact that Buckingham is free doesn't hurt either. It's beautiful, tucked near the edge of a grove of tall conifers, but quite rustic. You must bring your own water and pack out your trash. No ground fires are permitted, so if you've got your heart set on s'mores, either toast your marshmallow over your stove flame, or find an alternate spot.

**Location:** Northwest of Nederland; map A2, grid f8.

**Campsites, facilities:** There are six sites for tents only. Picnic tables and a vault toilet are provided, but there is no drinking water. Leashed pets are permitted.

**Elevation:** 10,100 feet.

**Reservations, fees:** Reservations are not accepted. There is no fee.

**Open:** Year-round.

**Directions:** From Nederland, drive south on Hwy. 119 to County Rd. 130 (the road to Eldora Ski Area). Turn west and drive approximately five miles. When the road forks, bear right on Rd. 111 and continue about five miles to the campground.

**Contact:** Boulder County Parks and Recreation, P.O. Box 791, Boulder, CO 80306; tel. (303) 441-3408.

## 117 Kelly Dahl     7

When I first moved to Colorado, Kelly Dahl served as my temporary home for a few days while I searched for an apartment. It was a perfect location, actually—an easy 20-minute drive from Boulder, located in a wooded, peaceful environment on a hill not far from the little mountain community of Nederland. A short trail leads east from camp to some old mining caves (of historical interest only—they're not safe to enter). If you want more extensive hiking trails, head back down the road toward Nederland and turn left on the road to Eldora. Go through the little town and you'll eventually come to the Hessie Trailhead, which takes you up along a pretty stream into the Indian Peaks Wilderness.

**Location:** Near Nederland in Roosevelt National Forest; map A2, grid f9.

**Campsites, facilities:** There are 46 sites for tents or RVs up to 40 feet long. Drinking water, picnic tables, fire grills, and vault toilets are provided. Leashed pets are permitted.

**Elevation:** 8,600 feet.

**Reservations, fees:** Reservations are accepted; phone (877) 444-6777. There's an $8.65 reservation fee. You may also reserve sites at website: www.reserveusa.com. Sites are $12 a night.

**Open:** May to October.

**Directions:** From Nederland, drive three miles south on Hwy. 119 to the campground on the east side of the road.

**Contact:** Roosevelt National Forest, Boulder Ranger District, 2140 Yarmouth Ave., Boulder, CO 80301; tel. (303) 444-6600.

## 118 Cold Springs     7

Even though it's easily accessible from Interstate 70, this campground still maintains a wilderness feel. The sites have been placed in wide groves of aspen and lodgepole pine, with a short vista trail nearby that leads up to a magnificent view of Mount Evans. It's also just minutes from Black Hawk and Central City.

**Location:** Near Central City in Arapaho National Forest; map A2, grid f9.

**Campsites, facilities:** There are 38 sites for tents or RVs up to 50 feet long.

Drinking water, picnic tables, fire grills, and vault toilets are provided. Leashed pets are permitted.

**Elevation:** 9,200 feet.

**Reservations, fees:** Reservations are accepted; phone (877) 444-6777. There's an $8.65 reservation fee. You may also reserve sites at website: www.reserveusa.com. Sites are $11 a night.

**Open:** Memorial Day to Labor Day.

**Directions:** From Black Hawk, drive five miles north on Hwy. 119 to the campground.

**Contact:** Arapaho National Forest, Clear Creek Ranger District, 101 Chicago Creek, P.O. Box 3307, Idaho Springs, CO 80452; tel. (303) 567-2901.

## 119 Central City/Black Hawk KOA    5

Las Vegas in the mountains—that's what Central City and Black Hawk look like these days. Big-name limited-stakes gambling saloons have taken over both towns, slapped on false fronts, and transformed them from quaint, historical mining communities into rollicking tourist traps. Fortunately, this campground is a bit outside of town, high up in the mountains in a pretty, wooded setting. The sites are surrounded by aspens and conifers in a quiet, pleasant environment.

**Location:** Northeast of Black Hawk; map A2, grid f9.

**Campsites, facilities:** There are 30 sites for tents or RVs of any length. Drinking water, picnic tables, fire grills, and bathrooms with hot showers are provided. Laundry facilities, a small store, swimming pool, and cabins are available. Leashed pets are permitted.

**Elevation:** 9,200 feet.

**Reservations, fees:** Reservations are recommended; phone (800) KOA-1620. Sites are $20-26 a night.

**Open:** Year-round.

**Directions:** From Black Hawk, drive five miles north on Hwy. 119, turn right on Hwy. 46, and drive one-half mile east to the campground.

**Contact:** Central City/Black Hawk KOA, 661 Hwy. 46, Golden, CO 80403; tel. (303) 582-9979.

## 120 Pickle Gulch Group Camp  7

These group sites offer only basic amenities, but they're in an attractive, wooded setting and are near an amphitheater that can be used for group functions. Next to the campground is a large picnic area with horseshoe pits and a volleyball court; you must bring your own horseshoes and net.

**Location:** Near Central City in Arapaho National Forest; map A2, grid f9.

**Campsites, facilities:** Five group sites can accommodate up to 30 people each, and one smaller group site holds up to 15 people. You must walk between 300 to 600 feet from the parking area to the sites. Drinking water, picnic tables, fire grills, and vault toilets are provided. Leashed pets are permitted.

**Elevation:** 9,100 feet.

**Reservations, fees:** Reservations are required; phone (877) 444-6777. There's an $8.65 reservation fee. You may also reserve sites at website: www.reserveusa.com. Nightly fees vary according to group size.

**Open:** Memorial Day to Labor Day.

**Directions:** From Black Hawk, drive three miles north on Hwy. 119 to the campground entrance on the west side of the road.

**Contact:** Arapaho National Forest, Clear Creek Ranger District, 101 Chicago Creek, P.O. Box 3307, Idaho Springs, CO 80452; tel. (303) 567-2901.

## 121 Sweetwater       8

Located on the south end of Sweetwater Lake, this campground is close to excellent fishing for rainbow trout and kokanee salmon, with access at the shoreline, the dock, or by hand-powered boat. The partly shaded sites offer good lake views and direct access to three trailheads open to hikers and horseback riders. The most scenic is the Cross Creek Trail, which travels through more than six miles of sagebrush, aspen, and wildflowers to meet up with the Sweetwater Trail. If you're looking for a shorter trek, try the Scenic Overlook Trail, which goes about 500 yards up to a view of the lake and a small waterfall.

**Location:** On Sweetwater Lake in White River National Forest; map A2, grid g0.

**Campsites, facilities:** There are 10 sites for tents or RVs up to 30 feet long. Picnic tables, fire grills, and vault toilets are provided. There is no drinking water at the campground, but a hydrant is available on the roadside one-quarter mile up the road. A fishing dock is nearby. Leashed pets are permitted.

**Elevation:** 7,740 feet.

**Reservations, fees:** Reservations are not accepted. No fee is required, but a donation of $6 a night is requested.

**Open:** May to November.

**Directions:** From Interstate 70 west of Eagle, take the Dotsero exit (Exit 133) and turn north on Colorado River Road. (Follow the signs for Sweetwater/Burns.) Drive seven miles to the Sweetwater Lake turnoff and continue a short distance to the campground.

**Contact:** White River National Forest, Eagle Ranger District, 125 W. 5th St., P.O. Box 720, Eagle, CO 81631; tel. (970) 328-6388.

## 122 Coffee Pot Springs    8

This lovely campground borders a forest of spruce, aspen, and fir and faces a high subalpine meadow backed by fantastic mountain vistas. You get a choice of open or shaded sites near little French Creek. There are no hiking trails directly adjacent to camp, but if you head three miles up the road to Broken Rib Spring (the nearest water source), you'll come to the Broken Rib Trail, which heads southwest about three miles before connecting with the No Name Trail. One mile back down Coffee Pot Rd. are two short trails that lead to dramatic overlooks of Deep Creek Canyon.

**Location:** West of Eagle in White River National Forest; map A2, grid g0.

**Campsites, facilities:** There are nine sites for tents or RVs up to 30 feet long. Picnic tables, fire grills, and vault toilets are provided, but there is no drinking water or trash service. Water is available about three miles up the road at Broken Rib Spring, but you must purify it. Leashed pets are permitted.

**Elevation:** 10,100 feet.

**Reservations, fees:** Reservations are not accepted. No fee is required, but a donation of $6 a night is requested.

**Open:** June to October.

**Directions:** From Interstate 70 west of Eagle, take the Dotsero exit (Exit 133) and turn north on Colorado River Road. (Follow the signs for Sweetwater/Burns.) Drive about two miles north, turn left on Forest Service Rd. 600 (Coffee Pot Rd.), and drive 16.5 miles west to the campground.

**Contact:** White River National Forest, Eagle Ranger District, 125 W. 5th St., P.O. Box 720, Eagle, CO 81631; tel. (970) 328-6388.

## **123** Gore Creek       7

Alas, this wooded camp is situated very close to Interstate 70, so you're subject to the buzz and whine of traffic at night. You can easily escape, however, by heading east into the Eagles Nest Wilderness via one of several trails in the vicinity. Adjacent to camp is the Vail Pass-10 Mile Canyon Trail, which is suitable for hiking or mountain biking. Fish at Gore Creek near the campsites or at any of several mountain lakes within hiking distance.

**Location:** Near Vail in White River National Forest; map A2, grid g5.

**Campsites, facilities:** There are seven walk-in tent sites and 25 sites for tents or RVs up to 25 feet long. Drinking water, picnic tables, fire grills, and vault toilets are provided. Some facilities are wheelchair accessible. Leashed pets are permitted.

**Elevation:** 8,760 feet.

**Reservations, fees:** Reservations are not accepted. Sites are $12 a night.

**Open:** June to September.

**Directions:** From Interstate 70 east of Vail, take Exit 180 and drive 2.5 miles east on the frontage road to the campground entrance.

**Contact:** White River National Forest, Holy Cross Ranger District, P.O. Box 190, Minturn, CO 81645; tel. (970) 827-5715.

## **124** Blue River     7

Squeezed between Hwy. 9 and the Blue River, this pretty campground is sheltered from the road by thick clusters of trees. It bumps right up against the riverbank, with good fishing access and views of lush farmland and rolling hills. There are some excellent mountain biking trails nearby off Hwy. 9.

**Location:** Near Green Mountain Reservoir in Arapaho National Forest; map A2, grid g6.

**Campsites, facilities:** There are 20 sites for tents or RVs up to 32 feet long. Drinking water, picnic tables, fire grills, and vault toilets are provided. Leashed pets are permitted.

**Elevation:** 8,400 feet.

**Reservations, fees:** Reservations are not accepted. Sites are $10 a night.

**Open:** June to November.

**Directions:** From Interstate 70 at Silverthorne, take Exit 205 and drive six miles north on Hwy. 9 to the campground on the right.

**Contact:** Arapaho National Forest, Dillon Ranger District, 680 Blue River Parkway, P.O. Box 620, Silverthorne, CO 80498; tel. (970) 468-5400.

## 125 Rollers Roost    8

Amazingly, this camp often gets passed by unnoticed by travelers on their way to Winter Park. Lucky for you—it's a great spot, set at the base of Berthoud Pass and the Continental Divide with spectacular mountain vistas. It's far enough back from the highway to feel remote, and a thick wall of trees keeps the road noise out. About a half mile to the south is a hiking trail that leads up to the top of Berthoud Pass (elevation 11,315 feet).

**Location:** Near Winter Park in Arapaho National Forest; map A2, grid g8.

**Campsites, facilities:** There are 11 sites for tents or RVs up to 32 feet long. Drinking water, picnic tables, fire grills, and vault toilets are provided. Leashed pets are permitted.

**Elevation:** 9,826 feet.

**Reservations, fees:** Reservations are not accepted. Sites are $10 a night.

**Open:** June to Labor Day.

**Directions:** From Winter Park, drive five miles south on U.S. 40 to the campground entrance on the east side of the highway.

**Contact:** Arapaho National Forest, Sulphur Ranger District, 9 Ten Mile Dr., P.O. Box 10, Granby, CO 80446; tel. (970) 887-4100.

## 126 Mountain Meadow Campground    7

Here is a little-known jewel of a spot, with easy access off Interstate 70 and a quiet, natural setting. The sites are positioned under tall pines at the base of Berthoud Pass and near hiking trails.

**Location:** Near Empire; map A2, grid g8.

**Campsites, facilities:** There are 50 sites for tents or RVs of any length, many with full hookups. Drinking water, picnic tables, fire grills, and bathrooms with hot showers are provided. A waste disposal station and a public phone are available. Leashed pets are permitted.

**Elevation:** 8,700 feet.

**Reservations, fees:** Reservations are accepted. Sites are $14.50-19.50 a night.

**Open:** June to October.

**Directions:** From Interstate 70 west of Idaho Springs, take the Empire exit (Exit 232) and drive three miles northwest on U.S. 40.

**Contact:** Mountain Meadow Campground, P.O. Box 2, Empire, CO 80438; tel. (303) 569-2424.

## 127 Mizpah   7

Because it was built in the 1950s, before the advent of large RVs, this campground has tiny sites, just big enough for tents. It's nestled in dense spruce and fir forest near the West Fork of Clear Creek, which runs adjacent to the camp and offers excellent fishing. Picnic grounds on either side of the campground furnish a little sun and more fishing access.

**Location:** On the West Fork of Clear Creek in Arapaho National Forest; map A2, grid g8.

**Campsites, facilities:** There are 10 tent sites. Drinking water, picnic tables, fire grills, and vault toilets are provided. Leashed pets are permitted.

**Elevation:** 9,600 feet.

**Reservations, fees:** Reservations are not accepted. Sites are $10 a night.

**Open:** Memorial Day to Labor Day.

**Directions:** From Winter Park, drive 18 miles south on U.S. 40 to the campground.

**Contact:** Arapaho National Forest, Clear Creek Ranger District, 101 Chicago Creek, P.O. Box 3307, Idaho Springs, CO 80452; tel. (303) 567-2901.

## 128 Clear Lake     8

Although the drive down Guanella Pass Scenic Byway can be a bit hairy, with steep switchbacks and slippery gravel, making it to this campground is worth the effort. It's got private sites scattered amid aspen and lodgepole pine next to the South Fork of Clear Creek, which offers excellent fishing. Anglers who prefer lake fishing can head a mile back up the road to Clear Lake and fish from the shoreline. About two miles south of the campground is a trailhead for the Silver Dollar Lake Trail, a three-mile round-trip hike that starts off at 11,000 feet and climbs up to a pretty alpine lake at 12,200 feet.

**Location:** On the South Fork of Clear Creek in Arapaho National Forest; map A2, grid g8.

**Campsites, facilities:** There are eight tent sites. Drinking water, picnic tables, fire grills, and vault toilets are provided. Leashed pets are permitted.

**Elevation:** 10,100 feet.

**Reservations, fees:** Reservations are not accepted. Sites are $8 a night.

**Open:** Memorial Day to Labor Day.

**Directions:** From Interstate 70 at Georgetown, take Exit 228 and drive approximately five miles south on Forest Service Rd. 381 (Guanella Pass Scenic Byway).

**Contact:** Arapaho National Forest, Clear Creek Ranger District, 101 Chicago Creek, P.O. Box 3307, Idaho Springs, CO 80452; tel. (303) 567-2901.

## 129 Guanella Pass     7

One of the more popular campgrounds in the immediate vicinity, this site is perched on the border of the Mount Evans Wilderness in a densely wooded setting. There's good fishing in the nearby South Fork of Chicago Creek, as well as several hiking trails to the south, over Guanella Pass.

**Location:** On the South Fork of Chicago Creek in Arapaho National Forest; map A2, grid g8.

**Campsites, facilities:** There are 18 sites for tents or RVs up to 35 feet long. Picnic tables, fire grills, and vault toilets are provided, but there is no drinking water. Leashed pets are permitted.

**Elevation:** 10,900 feet.

**Reservations, fees:** Reservations are accepted; phone (877) 444-6777. There's an $8.65 reservation fee. You may also reserve sites at website: www.reserveusa.com. Sites are $11 a night.

**Open:** Memorial Day to Labor Day.

**Directions:** From Interstate 70 at Georgetown, take Exit 228 and drive approximately nine miles south on Forest Service Rd. 381 (Guanella Pass Scenic Byway).

**Contact:** Arapaho National Forest, Clear Creek Ranger District, 101 Chicago Creek, P.O. Box 3307, Idaho Springs, CO 80452; tel. (303) 567-2901.

## 130 Echo Lake     6

These campsites aren't actually on Echo Lake, which is owned by Denver Mountain Parks and is not open to camping. The lake is close by, however, and offers good fishing for rainbow and cutthroat trout (but no boating). Near the campground are three major trailheads routed into the Mount Evans Wilderness. If you'd rather ride than hike, you can drive 14 miles up a toll road to the top of Mount Evans. At over 14,200 feet, it's the highest road in North America.

**Location:** South of Idaho Springs in Arapaho National Forest; map A2, grid g8.

**Campsites, facilities:** There are 18 sites for tents or RVs up to 20 feet long. Drinking water, picnic tables, fire grills, and vault toilets are provided. Leashed pets are permitted.

**Elevation:** 10,600 feet.

**Reservations, fees:** Reservations are accepted; phone (877) 444-6777. There's an $8.65 reservation fee. You may also reserve sites at website: www.reserveusa.com. Sites are $10 a night.

**Open:** June to Labor Day.

**Directions:** From Interstate 70 at Idaho Springs, take Exit 240 and drive 14 miles south on Hwy. 103.

**Contact:** Arapaho National Forest, Clear Creek Ranger District, 101 Chicago Creek, P.O. Box 3307, Idaho Springs, CO 80452; tel. (303) 567-2901.

## 131 Cottonwood RV Campground   6

It's hard to believe that Cottonwood RV is only a mile or so from a major interstate. Quiet and calm, it's a lush little oasis. The grounds are beautifully landscaped, with a virtual forest of trees encircling the sites. Chicago Creek runs adjacent to the camp, providing easy fishing access and the soothing sound of running water. It would be perfect for tent camping—but alas, they don't have bathrooms or showers and thus don't allow tenters.

**Location:** Near Idaho Springs; map A2, grid g9.

**Campsites, facilities:** There are 20 sites for RVs of any length, many with full hookups. No tents are permitted. A waste disposal station is provided, but there are no other facilities. Leashed pets are permitted.

**Elevation:** 8,000 feet.

**Reservations, fees:** Reservations are recommended during the summer. Sites are $16.25-20.50 a night.

**Open:** Year-round.

**Directions:** From Interstate 70 at Idaho Springs, take Exit 240 and drive 1.5 miles south on Hwy. 103 to the campground.

**Contact:** Cottonwood RV Campground, 1485 Hwy. 103, Idaho Springs, CO 80452; tel. (303) 567-2617.

## 132 Indian Springs Resort      4

Ahh—camping next to a hot spring! Imagine slipping into your tent under a star-studded sky, peacefully reflecting on a day spent hiking, biking, or perhaps rafting, and then indulging in an extravagant soak in the mineral baths next door. Sadly, however, your relaxation is likely to be spoiled by the roar of diesel engines—you could throw a rock from here and hit the freeway. Here's a tip: Try to get a site far from the entrance, close to the little creek that runs by the resort. The rushing water diffuses the road noise a bit and you might even catch a fish or two.

**Location:** Near Idaho Springs; map A2, grid g9.

**Campsites, facilities:** There are 32 sites for tents or RVs of any length. Drinking water, picnic tables, and bathrooms with hot showers are provided. Electric hookups, a waste disposal station, public phone, restaurant, swimming pool, hot mineral springs, and motel rooms are available. Leashed pets are permitted.

**Elevation:** 7,600 feet.

**Reservations, fees:** Reservations are not accepted. Sites are $18 a night.

**Open:** Year-round.

**Directions:** From Interstate 70 at Idaho Springs, take Exit 240 and drive north on Hwy. 103 to Miner Street. Turn east and drive one-half mile to Soda Creek Road. Turn south and continue a short distance to the campground.

**Contact:** Indian Springs Resort, 302 Soda Creek Rd., Idaho Springs, CO 80452; tel. (303) 989-6666.

## 133 Columbine   5

Although it's named for Colorado's state flower, you're not likely to see much flora at this camp. The area is a mecca for four-wheel-drive vehicle enthusiasts, and they often use Columbine as a base camp. Unless you're not bothered by the whine of ATVs, skip this one.

**Location:** Near Central City in Arapaho National Forest; map A2, grid g9.

**Campsites, facilities:** There are 47 sites for tents or RVs up to 20 feet long. Drinking water, picnic tables, fire grills, and vault toilets are provided. Leashed pets are permitted.

**Elevation:** 9,200 feet.

**Reservations, fees:** Reservations are accepted; phone (877) 444-6777. There's an $8.65 reservation fee. You may also reserve sites at website: www.reserveusa.com. Sites are $10 a night.

**Open:** Memorial Day to Labor Day.

**Directions:** From Black Hawk, turn west on Hwy. 279 toward Central City and continue approximately three miles to the campground.

**Contact:** Arapaho National Forest, Clear Creek Ranger District, 101 Chicago Creek, P.O. Box 3307, Idaho Springs, CO 80452; tel. (303) 567-2901.

## 134 West Chicago Creek     7

The draw to this campground is the Hells Hole Trail, a moderately difficult hike into the Mount Evans Wilderness, winding through aspen groves and beaver ponds and culminating at a luxuriant meadow at 11,200 feet. If you're more inclined to take it easy, there are several wide pullouts on the banks of West Chicago Creek that provide good fishing access (the fishing is said to be superb) or simply a spot to sit in your camp chair and relax.

**Location:** South of Idaho Springs in Arapaho National Forest; map A2, grid g9.

**Campsites, facilities:** There are 16 sites for tents or RVs up to 30 feet long. Drinking water, picnic tables, fire grills, and vault toilets are provided. Leashed pets are permitted.

**Elevation:** 9,600 feet.

**Reservations, fees:** Reservations are accepted; phone (877) 444-6777. There's an $8.65 reservation fee. You may also reserve sites at website: www.reserveusa.com. Sites are $9 a night.

**Open:** Memorial Day to Labor Day.

**Directions:** From Interstate 70 at Idaho Springs, take Exit 240 and drive 6.5 miles south on Hwy. 103. Turn right on Forest Service Rd. 188 (W. Chicago Creek Rd.) and continue three miles to the campground.

**Contact:** Arapaho National Forest, Clear Creek Ranger District, 101 Chicago Creek, P.O. Box 3307, Idaho Springs, CO 80452; tel. (303) 567-2901.

## 135 Sylvan Lake State Park     9

Sylvan Lake State Park is one of those out-of-the-way spots that is often overlooked by highway travelers. At 8,500 feet elevation, the park reveals a stunning high-mountain scene, with vast lodgepole pine and fir forests bordering green, grassy meadows. The lake covers more than 40 acres and since no motorized boating is permitted, it remains calm and peaceful even in the busy summer months—perfect for sailing or canoeing. A boat ramp is located near the Fisherman's Paradise campsites, and a mile-long hiking trail follows the perimeter of the lake.

**Location:** South of Eagle; map A2, grid h1.

**Campsites, facilities:** There are 50 sites for tents or RVs of any length. Drinking water, picnic tables, fire grills, and vault toilets are provided. Electric hookups and a boat ramp are available. Leashed pets are permitted.

**Elevation:** 8,500 feet.

**Reservations, fees:** Reservations are accepted. Phone (303) 470-1144 or (800) 678-CAMP (800-678-2267) outside the Denver Metro area; there's a $7 reservation fee. Sites are $10-14 a night, and there's a $4 entrance fee.

**Open:** Year-round.

**Directions:** From Interstate 70 at Eagle, take Exit 147 and drive south on Main St. until you reach W. Brush Creek Road. Turn right and continue approximately 15 miles to the park entrance.

**Contact:** Sylvan Lake State Park, 0050 Rd. 219, Rifle, CO 81650; tel. (970) 625-1607.

## 136 Yeoman Park      8

This camp offers roomy sites sheltered by tall spruce trees, with picturesque views of Craig Peak and streamside fishing in little Brush Creek, which runs through the campground. It sits on the edge of a pretty wetland meadow, a perfect spot for bird-watching. A wheelchair-accessible hiking trail, the Yeoman Discovery

Trail, extends 200 yards from the campground.

**Location:** Southeast of Eagle in White River National Forest; map A2, grid h3.

**Campsites, facilities:** There are 23 sites for tents or RVs up to 30 feet long. Drinking water, picnic tables, fire grills, and vault toilets are provided. Several sites have tent platforms. Some facilities are wheelchair accessible. Leashed pets are permitted.

**Elevation:** 9,000 feet.

**Reservations, fees:** Reservations are not accepted. No fee is required, but a donation of $8 a night is requested.

**Open:** June to November.

**Directions:** From Interstate 70 at Eagle, take Exit 147 and turn south on Brush Creek Road. Drive 10 miles, turn left on Forest Service Rd. 415 (E. Brush Creek Rd.), and continue 5.5 miles to the campground.

**Contact:** White River National Forest, Eagle Ranger District, 125 W. 5th St., P.O. Box 720, Eagle, CO 81631; tel. (970) 328-6388.

## 137 Fulford Cave     8

Aspen, fir, and spruce trees screen the tiny, intimate sites at this campground, located high above East Brush Creek, where anglers fish for dinky rainbow and brook trout. Nearby Fulford Cave is open for exploration, but follow safety precautions and make sure you have adequate spelunking knowledge and equipment before you head too far in. Nearby is the Iron Edge Trail, a hiking/equestrian trail that heads up to Lake Charles, passing by the Peter Estin Hut (a popular winter stopover for backcountry skiers) on the way.

**Location:** Southeast of Eagle in White River National Forest; map A2, grid h3.

**Campsites, facilities:** There are seven tent sites. Drinking water, picnic tables, fire grills, and vault toilets are provided. Leashed pets are permitted.

**Elevation:** 9,400 feet.

**Reservations, fees:** Reservations are not accepted. No fee is required, but a donation of $8 a night is requested.

**Open:** June to October.

**Directions:** From Interstate 70 at Eagle, take Exit 147 and turn south on Brush Creek Road. Drive 10 miles, turn left on Forest Service Rd. 415 (E. Brush Creek Rd.), and continue seven miles to the campground. Note: The last mile on E. Brush Creek Rd. is very narrow and rocky. Trailers and low-clearance vehicles are not recommended.

**Contact:** White River National Forest, Eagle Ranger District, 125 W. 5th St., P.O. Box 720, Eagle, CO 81631; tel. (970) 328-6388.

## 138 Tigiwon     8

Remote and rustic, Tigiwon is an excellent choice for those who value a pristine environment over modern conveniences. The campsites border an alpine meadow with striking views of the Gore Range. At the end of Tigiwon Rd. are two trails, Half Moon Pass and Fall Creek, that begin at over 10,000 feet and climb steeply into the wilderness, providing unique views of "the cross" on Mount of the Holy Cross (elevation 14,005 feet). Insider's tip: If camp food is wearing you down, scoot up to the wonderful little Mexican restaurant in the town of Redcliff. It's a local tradition for hikers (and backcountry skiers in the winter) to stop here after a long day in the wilderness.

**Location:** On Homestake Creek in White River National Forest; map A2, grid h4.

**Campsites, facilities:** There are nine sites for tents or RVs up to 25 feet long. Picnic tables, fire grills, and vault toilets are provided, but there is no drinking water or trash service. Leashed pets are permitted.

**Elevation:** 8,800 feet.

**Reservations, fees:** Reservations are not accepted. Sites are $8 a night.

**Open:** June to September.

**Directions:** From Interstate 70 west of Vail, take Exit 171 and turn south on U.S. 24. Drive approximately three miles, turn right on Forest Service Rd. 707 (Tigiwon Rd.), and continue six miles southwest to the campground.

**Contact:** White River National Forest, Holy Cross Ranger District, P.O. Box 190, Minturn, CO 81645; tel. (970) 827-5715.

## 139 Hornsilver       7

This wooded campground is positioned along the banks of Homestake Creek on the eastern border of the Holy Cross Wilderness. It's especially beautiful in September, when the surrounding aspen groves turn a deep yellow. Fishing is decent in Homestake Creek and even better at Homestake Reservoir, a long, finger-shaped lake to the southwest. There are no hiking trails leaving from camp, but if you travel down Homestake Rd., you'll find several trailheads for hiking or horseback riding, as well as four-wheel-drive roads that double as biking trails.

**Location:** On Homestake Creek in White River National Forest; map A2, grid h4.

**Campsites, facilities:** There are 12 sites for tents or RVs up to 30 feet long. Drinking water, picnic tables, fire grills, and vault toilets are provided. Leashed pets are permitted.

**Elevation:** 8,800 feet.

**Reservations, fees:** Reservations are not accepted. Sites are $10 a night.

**Open:** June to September.

**Directions:** From Interstate 70 west of Vail, take Exit 171 and turn south on U.S. 24. Drive approximately 12 miles to the campground.

**Contact:** White River National Forest, Holy Cross Ranger District, P.O. Box 190, Minturn, CO 81645; tel. (970) 827-5715.

## 140 Blodgett       7

Located at the entrance to Homestake Canyon, this intimate, wooded camp has sites within walking distance of Homestake Creek. Farther down Homestake Rd. you'll find several hiking trails routed into the Holy Cross Wilderness; Homestake Reservoir to the south provides opportunities for fishing and cartop boating.

**Location:** On the Eagle River in White River National Forest; map A2, grid h4.

**Campsites, facilities:** There are six sites for tents or RVs up to 30 feet long. Drinking water, picnic tables, fire grills, and vault toilets are provided. Leashed pets are permitted.

**Elevation:** 8,900 feet.

**Reservations, fees:** Reservations are not accepted. Sites are $10 a night.

**Open:** June to September.

**Directions:** From Interstate 70 west of Vail, take Exit 171 and turn south on U.S. 24. Drive approximately 14 miles to Forest Service Rd. 703 (Homestake Rd.). Turn right and continue a short distance to the campground on the left.

**Contact:** White River National Forest, Holy Cross Ranger District, P.O. Box 190, Minturn, CO 81645; tel. (970) 827-5715.

## 141 Gold Park      8

Campers at Gold Park, just three miles north of Homestake Reservoir, enjoy fishing in Homestake Creek and convenient access to the Holy Cross Wilderness. Across the highway, a designated four-wheel-drive road (and they mean it—passenger cars won't make it) leads west to the ruins of Holy Cross City, a historic mining town. You can also access wilderness trails from that road, including an incredibly scenic route that climbs up to Seven Sisters Lakes for a great view of Mount of the Holy Cross.

**Location:** On Homestake Creek in White River National Forest; map A2, grid h4.

**Campsites, facilities:** There are 11 sites for tents or RVs up to 40 feet long. Drinking water, picnic tables, fire grills, and vault toilets are provided. Leashed pets are permitted.

**Elevation:** 9,300 feet.

**Reservations, fees:** Reservations are not accepted. Sites are $10 a night.

**Open:** June to September.

**Directions:** From Interstate 70 west of Vail, take Exit 171 and turn south on U.S. 24. Drive approximately 14 miles to Forest Service Rd. 703 (Homestake Rd.). Turn right and continue about seven miles to the campground.

**Contact:** White River National Forest, Holy Cross Ranger District, P.O. Box 190, Minturn, CO 81645; tel. (970) 827-5715.

## 142 Camp Hale Memorial      7

This developed recreation area was established partly as a tribute to the men of the U.S. Army's 10th Mountain Division, who were trained here in mountaineering and skiing techniques before being sent off to fight in Italy during World War II. The campsites are set among spindly lodgepole pines, not far from the headwaters of the Eagle River. There is no direct fishing or hiking access from camp, but that doesn't mean that there are no recreation possibilities. There are numerous lakes, streams, and hiking trails in the surrounding forest that provide options; consult the Holy Cross Ranger District office for details.

**Location:** On the East Fork of the Eagle River in White River National Forest; map A2, grid h5.

**Campsites, facilities:** There are 21 sites for tents or RVs up to 60 feet long. Drinking water, picnic tables, fire grills, and vault toilets are provided. Some facilities are wheelchair accessible. Leashed pets are permitted.

**Elevation:** 9,240 feet.

**Reservations, fees:** Reservations are accepted; phone (877) 444-6777. There's an $8.65 reservation fee. You may also reserve sites at website: www.reserveusa.com. Sites are $10 a night.

**Open:** June to September.

**Directions:** From Interstate 70 west of Vail, take Exit 171 and turn south on U.S. 24. Drive approximately 17 miles to the main Camp Hale entrance. Turn left and pass through the stone pillars. Turn right at the first road and proceed to the campground.

**Contact:** White River National Forest, Holy Cross Ranger District, P.O. Box 190, Minturn, CO 81645; tel. (970) 827-5715.

## 143 Heaton Bay        7

This camp is on the western edge of Dillon Reservoir, a 3,300-acre sparkling jewel stretched along the south side of Interstate 70 between Dillon and Frisco. The campground is heavily wooded with easy access to fishing and picnic areas as well as a paved bike path that traces the perimeter of the lake. Tip: Try to get a site on Loop B or D—they're closer to the shore and you get great views of the lake and the Continental Divide. Boat ramps and rentals are available at Frisco and Dillon Marinas.

**Location:** On Dillon Reservoir in Arapaho National Forest; map A2, grid h7.

**Campsites, facilities:** There are 72 sites for tents or RVs up to 32 feet long. Drinking water, picnic tables, fire grills, and vault toilets are provided. One site is wheelchair accessible. Leashed pets are permitted.

**Elevation:** 9,100 feet.

**Reservations, fees:** Reservations are accepted; phone (877) 444-6777. There's an $8.65 reservation fee. You may also reserve sites at website: www.reserveusa.com. Sites are $11 a night.

**Open:** June to October.

**Directions:** From Interstate 70 at Frisco, take Exit 203. Turn south at the end of the off-ramp and head toward Frisco; turn left on Dillon Dam Rd. and continue a little over a mile to the campground.

**Contact:** Arapaho National Forest, Dillon Ranger District, 680 Blue River Parkway, P.O. Box 620, Silverthorne, CO 80498; tel. (970) 468-5400.

## 144 Peak One     7

One of my favorite memories of this area is sailing with my husband, Ben, and his family on Dillon Reservoir. The combination of sun, wind, water, and mountain vistas makes for an experience that is both exhilarating and peaceful. Since Peak One is the closest campground to Frisco Marina, it's a perfect base camp for those who wish to include boating in their camping adventure. The folks at the marina are very accommodating and will set you up with anything from a fishing boat to a pontoon.

**Location:** On Dillon Reservoir in Arapaho National Forest; map A2, grid h7.

**Campsites, facilities:** There are 79 sites for tents or RVs up to 32 feet long. Drinking water, picnic tables, fire grills, and flush toilets are provided. A boat ramp and marina facilities are nearby. Leashed pets are permitted.

**Elevation:** 9,100 feet.

**Reservations, fees:** Reservations are accepted; phone (877) 444-6777. There's an $8.65 reservation fee. You may also reserve sites at website: www.reserveusa.com. Sites are $11 a night.

**Open:** June to October.

**Directions:** From Interstate 70 at Frisco, take Exit 203. Turn south at the end of the off-ramp onto Hwy. 9 and drive 2.5 miles, through Frisco, to the campground entrance on the left.

**Contact:** Arapaho National Forest, Dillon Ranger District, 680 Blue River Parkway, P.O. Box 620, Silverthorne, CO 80498; tel. (970) 468-5400.

## 145 Pine Cove     8

Tucked between Dillon Reservoir's main body and the Blue River arm, Pine Cove feels a bit more remote than some of the other campgrounds in the area. It faces the reservoir to the east, with spectacular views of snowcapped peaks on the Continental Divide. Since there's a ramp adjacent to camp, this is a prime spot for campers with their own boats.

**Location:** On Dillon Reservoir in Arapaho National Forest; map A2, grid h7.

**Campsites, facilities:** There are 55 sites for tents or RVs up to 32 feet long. Drinking water, picnic tables, fire grills, and vault toilets are provided. A boat ramp is available. Leashed pets are permitted.

**Elevation:** 9,100 feet.

**Reservations, fees:** Reservations are not accepted. Sites are $8 a night.

**Open:** June to October.

**Directions:** From Interstate 70 at Frisco, take Exit 203. Turn south at the end of the off-ramp onto Hwy. 9 and drive 2.5 miles, through Frisco, to the campground entrance on the left.

**Contact:** Arapaho National Forest, Dillon Ranger District, 680 Blue River Parkway, P.O. Box 620, Silverthorne, CO 80498; tel. (970) 468-5400.

## 146 Prospector      7

Prospector is one of Dillon Reservoir's largest campgrounds, set far off the highway on the eastern shore. Nearby is the Sapphire Point Overlook, which offers a short hiking trail and a vista point. If you happen to be here on the Fourth of July weekend, it's a perfect spot from which to watch the city's fireworks displays.

**Location:** On Dillon Reservoir in Arapaho National Forest; map A2, grid h7.

**Campsites, facilities:** There are 107 sites for tents or RVs up to 32 feet long. Drinking water, picnic tables, fire grills, and vault toilets are provided. Some facilities are wheelchair accessible. Leashed pets are permitted.

**Elevation:** 9,100 feet.

**Reservations, fees:** Reservations are accepted; phone (877) 444-6777. There's an $8.65 reservation fee. You may also reserve sites at website: www.reserveusa.com. Sites are $10 a night.

**Open:** June to October.

**Directions:** From Interstate 70 at Frisco, take Exit 203. Turn south at the end of the off-ramp onto Hwy. 9 and drive approximately four miles, through Frisco, to Swan Mountain Road. Turn left and continue about three miles to the campground entrance on the left.

**Contact:** Arapaho National Forest, Dillon Ranger District, 680 Blue River Parkway, P.O. Box 620, Silverthorne, CO 80498; tel. (970) 468-5400.

**147** Lowry     7

This place is relatively unknown to the thousands of campers who flock to Dillon Reservoir each year. That's because it's not right at the reservoir, sitting instead on a hill amid the trees off Swan Mountain Rd., across from the entrance to Prospector Campground. You still get easy access to the reservoir, however, and since it's the only U.S. Forest Service camp in the vicinity that offers electric hookups, it's a good option for RVers.

**Location:** Near Dillon Reservoir in Arapaho National Forest; map A2, grid h7.

**Campsites, facilities:** There are 29 sites for tents or RVs up to 25 feet long. Drinking water, picnic tables, fire grills, and vault toilets are provided. Electric hookups are available. Some facilities are wheelchair accessible. Leashed pets are permitted.

**Elevation:** 9,100 feet.

**Reservations, fees:** Reservations are accepted; phone (877) 444-6777. There's an $8.65 reservation fee. You may also reserve sites at website: www.reserveusa.com. Sites are $10-15 a night.

**Open:** June to October.

**Directions:** From Interstate 70 at Frisco, take Exit 203. Turn south at the end of the off-ramp onto Hwy. 9 and drive approximately four miles, through Frisco, to Swan Mountain Road. Turn left and continue about three miles to the campground entrance on the left.

**Contact:** Arapaho National Forest, Dillon Ranger District, 680 Blue River Parkway, P.O. Box 620, Silverthorne, CO 80498; tel. (970) 468-5400.

**148** Windy Point Group Camp     7

As Dillon Reservoir's only group camp, Windy Point makes a perfect site for a family reunion or party. It's situated under tall pine trees next to the Snake River arm of the reservoir, with excellent shoreline access for anglers.

**Location:** On Dillon Reservoir in Arapaho National Forest; map A2, grid h7.

**Campsites, facilities:** There are 72 sites that can accommodate up to 200 people in tents or RVs up to 32 feet long. Drinking water, picnic tables, fire grills, and vault toilets are provided. Some facilities are wheelchair accessible. Leashed pets are permitted.

**Elevation:** 9,100 feet.

**Reservations, fees:** Reservations are required; phone (877) 444-6777. There's an $8.65 reservation fee. You may also reserve sites at website: www.reserveusa.com. Nightly fees vary according to group size.

**Open:** June to October.

**Directions:** From Interstate 70 at Frisco, take Exit 203. Turn south at the end of the off-ramp onto Hwy. 9 and drive approximately four miles, through Frisco, to Swan Mountain Road. Turn left and continue about three miles to the campground entrance on the left. The group camp is at the end of the road past the Prospector camp.

**Contact:** Arapaho National Forest, Dillon Ranger District, 680 Blue River Parkway, P.O. Box 620, Silverthorne, CO 80498; tel. (970) 468-5400.

**149** Tiger Run Resort  8

This immaculate RV park is framed by picturesque mountain views and a pretty alpine stream. It's well off the main highway and stays quiet and peaceful, yet is just minutes from Breckenridge and Dillon Reservoir. The sites are grassy and open, set on beautifully landscaped grounds with every possible luxury available. The community clubhouse has an indoor pool and hot tub, and is adjacent to tennis courts. Your hosts will gladly arrange local tours or give you advice on the best spots to hike, bike, and raft. Nearby is an 18-hole golf course.

**Location:** Near Breckenridge; map A2, grid h7.

**Campsites, facilities:** There are 150 full-hookup sites for RVs of any length. No tents are allowed. Drinking water, picnic tables, fire grills, and bathrooms with hot showers are provided. Laundry facilities, restaurant, small store, public phone, swimming pool, hot tub, sports facilities, horse and bike rentals, and cabins are available. Some facilities are wheelchair accessible. Leashed pets are permitted.

**Elevation:** 9,200 feet.

**Reservations, fees:** Reservations are recommended. Sites are $29-49 a night.

**Open:** Year-round.

**Directions:** From Interstate 70 at Frisco, take Exit 203 and drive 6.5 miles south on Hwy. 9 to the resort entrance on the left.

**Contact:** Tiger Run Resort, 85 Tiger Run Rd., Box 815, Breckenridge, CO 80424; tel. (970) 453-9690; e-mail: tiger@colorado.net.

**150** Lodgepole  7

This is the first campground you come to on the road up to Jefferson Lake, a 145-acre lake that offers boating and fishing for rainbow and Mackinaw trout. Trees scattered around the sites provide a little seclusion and shade. To the north are hiking trails routed into the surrounding forest.

**Location:** Near Jefferson Lake in Pike National Forest; map A2, grid h7.

**Campsites, facilities:** There are 35 sites for tents or RVs up to 25 feet long. Drinking water, picnic tables, fire grills, and vault toilets are provided. Leashed pets are permitted.

**Elevation:** 9,900 feet.

**Reservations, fees:** Reservations are not accepted. Sites are $10 a night, plus $3 for a day-use permit (charged only once per visit).

**Open:** May to October.

**Directions:** From Jefferson on U.S. 285, turn north at the sign for Jefferson Lake and drive 3.75 miles, following the signs to the campground.

**Contact:** Pike National Forest, South Park Ranger District, P.O. Box 219, Fairplay, CO 80440; tel. (719) 836-2031.

**151** Aspen  7

The second in the line of campgrounds that lead up to Jefferson Lake, this one provides a smaller, more intimate alternative to Lodgepole. It's often full, however, because it is commonly used as a stopping point for hikers on the Colorado Trail, which runs adjacent to camp. Other hiking trails are nearby, as is Jefferson Lake, a good place to boat and fish.

**Location:** Near Jefferson Lake in Pike National Forest; map A2, grid h7.

**Campsites, facilities:** There are 12 sites for tents or RVs up to 25 feet long. Drinking water, picnic tables, fire grills, and vault toilets are provided. Leashed pets are permitted.

**Elevation:** 9,900 feet.

**Reservations, fees:** Reservations are not accepted. Sites are $10 a night, plus $3 for a day-use permit (charged only once per visit).

**Open:** May to October.

**Directions:** From Jefferson on U.S. 285, turn north at the sign for Jefferson Lake and drive four miles, following the signs to the campground.

**Contact:** Pike National Forest, South Park Ranger District, P.O. Box 219, Fairplay, CO 80440; tel. (719) 836-2031.

## **152** Jefferson Creek      7

The closest you'll get to camping at Jefferson Lake is right here, where you're only about a mile down the road. Consequently, Jefferson Creek is the most popular camp of the three in the immediate area, so expect plenty of company. At over 10,000 feet elevation, it gets chilly even in late summer, so be sure to bring warm clothes and equipment—and don't forget the bug repellent.

**Location:** Near Jefferson Lake in Pike National Forest; map A2, grid h7.

**Campsites, facilities:** There are 17 sites for tents or RVs up to 25 feet long. Drinking water, picnic tables, fire grills, and vault toilets are provided. Leashed pets are permitted.

**Elevation:** 10,100 feet.

**Reservations, fees:** Reservations are not accepted. Sites are $10 a night, plus $3 for a day-use permit (charged only once per visit).

**Open:** May to October.

**Directions:** From Jefferson on U.S. 285, turn north at the sign for Jefferson Lake and drive 5.25 miles, following the signs to the campground.

**Contact:** Pike National Forest, South Park Ranger District, P.O. Box 219, Fairplay, CO 80440; tel. (719) 836-2031.

## **153** Michigan Creek     7

This remote, quiet spot offers shaded sites, solitude, and a chance to fish in Michigan Creek. If you continue up the road past the campground, you'll come to a trailhead leading up to Georgia Pass (elevation 11,585 feet).

**Location:** Near Jefferson in Pike National Forest; map A2, grid h7.

**Campsites, facilities:** There are 13 sites for tents or RVs up to 25 feet long. Drinking water, picnic tables, fire grills, and vault toilets are provided. Leashed pets are permitted.

**Elevation:** 10,000 feet.

**Reservations, fees:** Reservations are not accepted. Sites are $7 a night.

**Open:** May to October.

**Directions:** From Jefferson on U.S. 285, turn north at the sign for Jefferson Lake and stay on that road (don't turn toward the lake) for approximately four miles until you reach the campground.

**Contact:** Pike National Forest, South Park Ranger District, P.O. Box 219, Fairplay, CO 80440; tel. (719) 836-2031.

## **154** Handcart    5

This small, remote camp is tucked into a stand of scattered ponderosa pine and Douglas fir trees. Nearby is the North Fork of the South Platte River, which offers dubious fishing prospects. To the north are a couple of primitive U.S. Forest Service roads that double as mountain biking trails.

**Location:** Northwest of Grant in Pike National Forest; map A2, grid h8.

**Campsites, facilities:** There are 10 tent sites. Drinking water, picnic tables, fire grills, and vault toilets are provided. Leashed pets are permitted.

**Elevation:** 9,800 feet.

**Reservations, fees:** Reservations are not accepted. Sites are $10 a night.

**Open:** May to October.

**Directions:** From Grant, take U.S. 285 southwest approximately two miles to County Rd. 60. Turn right and drive about four miles northwest to the campground.

**Contact:** Pike National Forest, South Platte Ranger District, 1913 Goddard Ranch Ct., Morrison, CO 80465; tel. (303) 275-5610.

## **155** Hall Valley     6

Just a mile past Handcart Campground is yet another isolated little spot, Hall Valley. There's not a whole lot happening out here, but you do get a picture-perfect view of the Continental Divide and exquisite summer sunsets. Nearby is the Gibson Lake Trail, which heads about three miles up to a tiny alpine lake with decent fishing.

**Location:** Northwest of Grant in Pike National Forest; map A2, grid h8.

**Campsites, facilities:** There are nine sites that will accommodate tents or RVs up to 20 feet long; however, RVs and trailers are not recommended due to the rough road in. Drinking water, picnic tables, fire grills, and vault toilets are provided. Leashed pets are permitted.

**Elevation:** 9,900 feet.

**Reservations, fees:** Reservations are not accepted. Sites are $10 a night.

**Open:** May to October.

**Directions:** From Grant, take U.S. 285 south approximately two miles to County Rd. 60. Turn right and drive about five miles northwest to the campground.

**Contact:** Pike National Forest, South Platte Ranger District, 1913 Goddard Ranch Ct., Morrison, CO 80465; tel. (303) 275-5610.

## **156** Geneva Park     8

If you really want to avoid the crowds, this camp is a good bet. It's far enough from the main road to get missed by most people and offers quiet and solitude in a natural, open setting. You can fish in nearby Geneva Creek or take the trail to Shelf Lake, which climbs about three miles to the base of the Continental Divide.

**Location:** Northwest of Grant in Pike National Forest; map A2, grid h8.

**Campsites, facilities:** There are 26 sites for tents or RVs up to 16 feet long.

Drinking water, picnic tables, fire grills, and vault toilets are provided. Leashed pets are permitted.

**Elevation:** 9,800 feet.

**Reservations, fees:** Reservations are not accepted. Sites are $10 a night.

**Open:** Memorial Day to Labor Day.

**Directions:** From Grant, drive approximately seven miles north on County Rd. 62 (Guanella Pass Rd.), turn left on Forest Service Rd. 119, and continue a short distance to the campground.

**Contact:** Pike National Forest, South Platte Ranger District, 1913 Goddard Ranch Ct., Morrison, CO 80465; tel. (303) 275-5610.

## 157 Whiteside    7

Whiteside sits beside little Geneva Creek (I'm told there's fishing, but it's poor) on the border of the Mount Evans Wilderness. The camp is shaded and tiny, just big enough for a few tents, and is the more primitive of the two camps in the area. There is no drinking water provided, so pack in your own. It makes a perfect base camp for a wilderness trip—the Three Mile Creek Trailhead is about a mile north of camp.

**Location:** Northwest of Grant in Pike National Forest; map A2, grid h8.

**Campsites, facilities:** There are five tent sites. Picnic tables, fire grills, and vault toilets are provided, but there is no drinking water. Leashed pets are permitted.

**Elevation:** 8,900 feet.

**Reservations, fees:** Reservations are not accepted. Sites are $10 a night.

**Open:** May to October.

**Directions:** From Grant, turn north on County Rd. 62 (Guanella Pass Rd.) and drive approximately two miles to the campground.

**Contact:** Pike National Forest, South Platte Ranger District, 1913 Goddard Ranch Ct., Morrison, CO 80465; tel. (303) 275-5610.

## 158 Burning Bear    7

If Whiteside Campground is too rustic for you, keep going another three miles up the road to this camp. It's got drinking water and is also the site of the Abyss Lake Trailhead, which climbs up to a pretty alpine lake halfway between Mount Bierstadt (14,060 feet) and Mount Evans (14,264 feet), two of Colorado's stunning 14ers. Enjoys the majestic views from the lake, or if you're the ambitious type, go ahead and climb one of the mountains—either one will provide a challenging ascent for even the most seasoned hiker.

**Location:** Northwest of Grant in Pike National Forest; map A2, grid h8.

**Campsites, facilities:** There are 13 sites for tents or RVs up to 16 feet long. Drinking water, picnic tables, fire grills, and vault toilets are provided. Leashed pets are permitted.

**Elevation:** 9,500 feet.

**Reservations, fees:** Reservations are not accepted. Sites are $10 a night.

**Open:** May to October.

**Directions:** From Grant, turn north on County Rd. 62 (Guanella Pass Rd.) and drive approximately five miles to the campground.

**Contact:** Pike National Forest, South Platte Ranger District, 1913 Goddard Ranch Ct., Morrison, CO 80465; tel. (303) 275-5610.

## 159 Kenosha Pass   8

In autumn this place is simply spectacular, as the aspen leaves at the top of the pass turn shades of yellow and orange, casting a golden glow on everything below them. In summer the trees are lush and green, creating a bright, thriving environment in which to relax and enjoy nature's pleasures. The Colorado Trail runs nearby and draws an astounding number of day hikers and campers. Since the U.S. Forest Service doesn't take reservations here, you're well advised to arrive early to claim a spot.

**Location:** On Kenosha Pass in Pike National Forest; map A2, grid h8.

**Campsites, facilities:** There are 25 sites for tents or RVs up to 16 feet long. Drinking water, picnic tables, fire grills, and vault toilets are provided. Leashed pets are permitted.

**Elevation:** 10,000 feet.

**Reservations, fees:** Reservations are not accepted. Sites are $10 a night.

**Open:** June to September.

**Directions:** From Grant, drive approximately six miles south on U.S. 285 to the campground at the top of Kenosha Pass.

**Contact:** Pike National Forest, South Platte Ranger District, 1913 Goddard Ranch Ct., Morrison, CO 80465; tel. (303) 275-5610.

## 160 Deer Creek   7

If it's hiking you want, look no further. Two trailheads, Tanglewood and Rosalie, are adjacent to camp and will lead you into the depths of the Mount Evans Wilderness, each following pretty mountain streams along the way. There's fishing in Deer Creek just a short walk from the conifer-shaded campsites.

**Location:** Northwest of Bailey in Pike National Forest; map A2, grid h9.

**Campsites, facilities:** There are 13 sites for tents or RVs up to 16 feet long. Drinking water, picnic tables, fire grills, and vault toilets are provided. Leashed pets are permitted.

**Elevation:** 9,000 feet.

**Reservations, fees:** Reservations are not accepted. Sites are $10 a night.

**Open:** May to October.

**Directions:** From Bailey, drive approximately two miles north on U.S. 285 and turn right on County Rd. 43. Continue about seven miles northwest to the campground.

**Contact:** Pike National Forest, South Platte Ranger District, 1913 Goddard Ranch Ct., Morrison, CO 80465; tel. (303) 275-5610.

## 161 Meridian 5

Although it offers a good trailhead into the Mount Evans Wilderness, this camp is unfortunately close to Highland Park, a housing subdivision. One look at the rows of cookie-cutter homes and suddenly your nature experience may seem decidedly unnatural. Simply turn your back, though, and you've got majestic views of several mountain peaks to the west.

**Location:** Northwest of Bailey in Pike National Forest; map A2, grid h9.

**Campsites, facilities:** There are 18 sites for tents or RVs up to 16 feet long. Drinking water, picnic tables, fire grills, and vault toilets are provided. Leashed pets are permitted.

**Elevation:** 9,000 feet.

**Reservations, fees:** Reservations are not accepted. Sites are $10 a night.

**Open:** May to September.

**Directions:** From Bailey, drive approximately two miles north on U.S. 285 and turn right on County Rd. 43. Drive six miles northwest, turn north on County Rd. 47, and continue about a mile to the campground.

**Contact:** Pike National Forest, South Platte Ranger District, 1913 Goddard Ranch Ct., Morrison, CO 80465; tel. (303) 275-5610.

## 162 Mount Evans State Wildlife Area     9

Primitive, rugged, and beautiful, this wildlife area provides a unique opportunity to camp in a wilderness-like setting without being hemmed in by hundreds of tourists. There are no developed facilities, but the trade-off is being in a backcountry paradise: virgin timber and lush meadows full of alpine wildflowers, laced with discernible trails that stretch west into the Mount Evans Wilderness. In addition to the standard high-alpine species of wildlife (deer, rabbits, a variety of birds), you might catch a glimpse of elk or bighorn sheep. Some hunting is permitted.

**Location:** Southeast of Idaho Springs; map A2, grid h9.

**Campsites, facilities:** Camping is permitted at designated areas only. No facilities are provided. Leashed pets are permitted.

**Elevation:** 9,500 feet.

**Reservations, fees:** Reservations are not accepted. There is no fee. The maximum stay is five days.

**Open:** Mid-June through August.

**Directions:** From Interstate 70 west of Denver, take the El Rancho exit (Exit 252 if westbound, Exit 251 eastbound) and drive six miles south on Hwy. 74. At Evergreen Lake, turn right on Upper Bear Creek Rd. and drive 6.5 miles. Then turn right on County Rd. 480 and continue three miles to the property entrance.

**Contact:** Colorado Division of Wildlife, 6060 Broadway, Denver, CO 80216; tel. (303) 297-1192.

## 163 Sopris RV Park      6

Since this RV park takes weekly and monthly renters, sometimes there's not a space to be had for short-term RV campers. (Always call ahead of time.) Tenters have no such worries, however, with separate sites set among the trees near the Roaring Fork River. You get superb access to the river, with a small, private boat ramp providing a convenient drop-in point for your fishing boat or canoe.

**Location:** On the Roaring Fork River; map A2, grid i0.

**Campsites, facilities:** There are 45 sites for RVs of any length, many with full hookups, and a separate area for tents. Drinking water, picnic tables, fire grills, and bathrooms with hot showers are provided. Laundry facilities, a waste disposal station, small store, public phone, and cabins are available. A boat ramp (nonmotorized watercraft only) is adjacent to camp. Some facilities are wheelchair accessible. Leashed pets are permitted.

**Elevation:** 6,500 feet.

**Reservations, fees:** Reservations are accepted. Sites are $14-20 a night.

**Open:** Year-round.

**Directions:** From Carbondale, drive 1.5 miles north on Hwy. 82. Then turn left on County Rd. 106 and continue a mile to the campground.

**Contact:** Sopris RV Park, P.O. Box 218, Carbondale, CO 81623; tel. (970) 963-0163.

## 164 B-R-B Crystal River Resort      7

Although it's very near a noisy, well-traveled highway, this campground has much to offer in the way of natural delights: shaded riverside sites, prime stream fishing, an outdoor pool, and a hot tub. The Glenwood Hot Springs resort is a half-hour drive away, but if you'd enjoy a more primitive setting for your soak, here's a secret: About nine miles south of the campground on Hwy. 133 is Penny Hot Springs, a primitive spring that is accessible via a short hike down from the road. There's no sign, just a pull-out on the east side of the highway. Since it's undeveloped, it's free (and clothing optional) but is often jammed with people.

**Location:** South of Carbondale; map A2, grid i0.

**Campsites, facilities:** There are 55 sites for tents or RVs of any length. Electric hookups, drinking water, picnic tables, fire grills, and bathrooms with hot showers are provided. Laundry facilities, a waste disposal station, hot tub and swimming pool, small store, public phone, and cabins are available. Leashed pets are permitted.

**Elevation:** 6,200 feet.

**Reservations, fees:** Reservations are recommended. Sites are $13.50-19.50 a night.

**Open:** Year-round.

**Directions:** From Carbondale, drive six miles south on Hwy. 133.

**Contact:** B-R-B Crystal River Resort, 7202 Hwy. 133, Carbondale, CO 81623; tel. (970) 963-2341 or (800) 963-2341.

## 165 Avalanche     9

Avalanche Creek is adjacent to this lovely camp situated in a mixed forest of conifers and deciduous trees. The access road is not well signed and consequently gets missed by many travelers, which means that there is almost always a site to be found. Many of the sites are directed on the creek, and anglers can find fishing access within walking distance. The camp also is next to a major trailhead into the Maroon Bells-Snowmass Wilderness, which follows the creek south for several miles.

**Location:** South of Carbondale in White River National Forest; map A2, grid i0.

**Campsites, facilities:** There are 13 sites for tents or RVs up to 16 feet long. Drinking water, picnic tables, fire grills, and vault toilets are provided. Leashed pets are permitted.

**Elevation:** 6,800 feet.

**Reservations, fees:** Reservations are not accepted. Sites are $10 a night.

**Open:** June to September.

**Directions:** From Carbondale, drive nine miles south on Hwy. 133 and turn left on County Rd. 310. Continue two miles down the rutted dirt road to the campground.

**Contact:** White River National Forest, Sopris Ranger District, 620 Main St., P.O. Box 309, Carbondale, CO 81623; tel. (970) 963-2266.

## 166 Redstone     6

As one of the few U.S. Forest Service campgrounds to offer such luxuries as flush toilets and showers, Redstone gets a lot of use. It's near the Crystal River on Hwy. 133, just west of the Maroon Bells-Snowmass Wilderness boundary. The Allgier and Osgood Loops are more scenic and designed for large RVs; the Mechau Loop is better suited for tents, although at some spots the only place to erect your tent is in the gravel. There are no hiking trails in the immediate vicinity, but you can reach trailheads within minutes by car.

**Location:** South of Carbondale in White River National Forest; map A2, grid i0.

**Campsites, facilities:** There are 19 sites for tents and RVs of any length. Drinking water, picnic tables, fire grills, bathrooms with flush toilets and hot showers, and vault toilets are provided. Electric hookups are available. Leashed pets are permitted.

**Elevation:** 7,200 feet.

**Reservations, fees:** Reservations are accepted; phone (877) 444-6777. There's an $8.65 reservation fee. You may also reserve sites at website: www.reserveusa.com. Sites are $15-22 a night.

**Open:** June to September.

**Directions:** From Carbondale, drive 13 miles south on Hwy. 133 and turn left on the campground access road.

**Contact:** White River National Forest, Sopris Ranger District, 620 Main St., P.O. Box 309, Carbondale, CO 81623; tel. (970) 963-2266.

## 167 Aspen-Basalt Campground       7

If you're looking for a full-service campground near Aspen, this is the closest one you'll find. The large, grassy sites are thickly wooded and allow anglers quick access to the Roaring Fork River, a designated Gold Medal Water. Nearby are hiking trails, white-water rafting outfitters, and in the winter, of course, alpine skiing.

**Location:** On the Roaring Fork River; map A2, grid i1.

**Campsites, facilities:** There are 85 sites for tents or RVs of any length, many with full hookups. Drinking water, picnic tables, fire grills, and bathrooms with hot showers are provided. Laundry facilities, a waste disposal station, a small store, a public phone, a swimming pool, and a hot tub are available. Leashed pets are permitted.

**Elevation:** 6,200 feet.

**Reservations, fees:** Reservations are recommended. Sites are $20-29 a night.

**Open:** Year-round.

**Directions:** From Basalt, drive two miles west on Hwy. 82 to the campground.

**Contact:** Aspen-Basalt Campground, 20640 Hwy. 82, Basalt, CO 81621; tel. (800) 567-2773 e-mail: abc@sopris.net.

**168** Little Maud       8

As you approach Ruedi Reservoir, this large, square campground is the first one you'll encounter. Since it's the only camp on the lake with a dump station, it's a good choice for RVs. The sites are near the northwestern shore of the reservoir, with a boat ramp just to the east of the marina and access to several hiking trails and four-wheel-drive roads to the north.

**Location:** On Ruedi Reservoir in White River National Forest; map A2, grid i2.

**Campsites, facilities:** There are 22 sites for tents or RVs up to 32 feet long. Drinking water, picnic tables, fire grills, and flush toilets are provided. A waste disposal station is available. Some facilities are wheelchair accessible. Leashed pets are permitted.

**Elevation:** 7,800 feet.

**Reservations, fees:** Reservations are not accepted. Sites are $14 a night.

**Open:** June to September.

**Directions:** From Basalt on Hwy. 82, turn east on Forest Service Rd. 105 (Fryingpan River Rd.) and drive approximately 16 miles to the campground.

**Contact:** White River National Forest, Sopris Ranger District, 620 Main St., P.O. Box 309, Carbondale, CO 81623; tel. (970) 963-2266.

**169** Mollie X       8

Mollie B, which is right in the middle of the cluster of four campgrounds next to Ruedi Reservoir, offers roomy sites sheltered by willow and aspen trees, all within walking distance of the lakeshore. This is the only campground here that allows you to reserve sites, so it's the one to stay at if you want a guaranteed spot. Boating facilities, fishing access, and hiking trails are available nearby.

**Location:** On Ruedi Reservoir in White River National Forest; map A2, grid i2.

**Campsites, facilities:** There are 26 sites for tents or RVs up to 32 feet long. Drinking water, picnic tables, fire grills, and flush toilets are provided. Some facilities are wheelchair accessible. Leashed pets are permitted.

**Elevation:** 7,800 feet.

**Reservations, fees:** Reservations are accepted; phone (877) 444-6777. There's an $8.65 reservation fee. You may also reserve sites at website: www.reserveusa.com. Sites are $14 a night.

**Open:** June to September.

**Directions:** From Basalt on Hwy. 82, turn east on Forest Service Rd. 105 (Fryingpan River Rd.) and drive approximately 16 miles to the campground.

**Contact:** White River National Forest, Sopris Ranger District, 620 Main St., P.O. Box 309, Carbondale, CO 81623; tel. (970) 963-2266.

**170** Little Mattie        8

With smaller sites than the Little Maud or Mollie B campgrounds, this camp is best suited for people with tents. It's right next to the marina, with full boating facilities available. Hiking trails are located to the west and north.

**Location:** On Ruedi Reservoir in White River National Forest; map A2, grid i2.

**Campsites, facilities:** There are 20 sites for tents or RVs up to 22 feet long.

Drinking water, picnic tables, fire grills, and vault toilets are provided. Some facilities are wheelchair accessible. Leashed pets are permitted.

**Elevation:** 7,800 feet.

**Reservations, fees:** Reservations are not accepted. Sites are $10 a night.

**Open:** June to September.

**Directions:** From Basalt on Hwy. 82, turn east on Forest Service Rd. 105 (Fryingpan River Rd.) and drive approximately 16 miles to the campground.

**Contact:** White River National Forest, Sopris Ranger District, 620 Main St., P.O. Box 309, Carbondale, CO 81623; tel. (970) 963-2266.

## 171 Ruedi Marina RV Camp     6

This place consists of little more than a large RV parking area adjacent to a marina. Since there are no tables, water, or bathroom facilities, it's best for folks with self-contained units. The marina provides a ramp, boat storage, and boat rentals. Should you need water or a dump station, you can find both at nearby Little Maud Campground.

**Location:** On Ruedi Reservoir in White River National Forest; map A2, grid i2.

**Campsites, facilities:** There are five sites for RVs of any length. Tents are prohibited. No water, bathrooms, or other camping facilities are provided. A marina with full boating access and supplies is next door. The marina facilities are wheelchair accessible. Leashed pets are permitted.

**Elevation:** 7,800 feet.

**Reservations, fees:** Reservations are not accepted. Sites are $10 a night.

**Open:** June to September.

**Directions:** From Basalt on Hwy. 82, turn east on Forest Service Rd. 105 (Fryingpan River Rd.) and drive approximately 16 miles to the campground.

**Contact:** White River National Forest, Sopris Ranger District, 620 Main St., P.O. Box 309, Carbondale, CO 81623; tel. (970) 963-2266.

## 172 Dearhammer     8

Dearhammer is a great camp for anglers, with spacious sites nestled in mixed conifer forest between Ruedi Reservoir and the Fryingpan River. It's an out-of-the-way option for campers who want to be next to the lake but away from the crowds. A boat ramp is available on the far western side of the lake, with shoreline fishing access points within walking distance of camp.

**Location:** On the Fryingpan River in White River National Forest; map A2, grid i2.

**Campsites, facilities:** There 13 sites for tents or RVs up to 32 feet long. Drinking water, picnic tables, fire grills, and vault toilets are provided. Leashed pets are permitted.

**Elevation:** 7,800 feet.

**Reservations, fees:** Reservations are not accepted. Sites are $11 a night.

**Open:** June to September.

**Directions:** From Basalt on Hwy. 82, turn east on Forest Service Rd. 105 (Fryingpan River Rd.) and drive approximately 23 miles to the campground.

**Contact:** White River National Forest, Sopris Ranger District, 620 Main St., P.O. Box 309, Carbondale, CO 81623; tel. (970) 963-2266.

## 173 Chapman     8

The lower section of the Fryingpan River is designated as a Gold Medal Water by the Colorado Division of Wildlife, making this camp a superb base for a fishing trip. It's a lovely setting, with large sites beneath tall Lodgepole pines at the base of a lush, sprawling valley. A short distance to the south are hiking trails routed into the Hunter-Fryingpan Wilderness.

**Location:** On the Fryingpan River in White River National Forest; map A2, grid i2.

**Campsites, facilities:** There are 84 sites for tents or RVs up to 45 feet long. Drinking water, picnic tables, fire grills, and vault toilets are provided. Leashed pets are permitted.

**Elevation:** 8,800 feet.

**Reservations, fees:** Reservations are accepted; phone (877) 444-6777. There's an $8.65 reservation fee. You may also reserve sites at website: www.reserveusa.com. Sites are $11 a night.

**Open:** June to September.

**Directions:** From Basalt on Hwy. 82, turn east on Forest Service Rd. 105 (Fryingpan River Rd.) and drive approximately 29 miles to the campground.

**Contact:** White River National Forest, Sopris Ranger District, 620 Main St., P.O. Box 309, Carbondale, CO 81623; tel. (970) 963-2266.

## 174 Elk Wallow      7

This camp is often passed by in favor of the more scenic and developed sites at Chapman Campground. It's adjacent to the North Fork of the Fryingpan River with good fishing access, although the fishing is much better on the lower stretches of the main fork to the south. At the end of Forest Service Rd. 501 is a short but steep trail to Savage Lakes in the Holy Cross Wilderness.

**Location:** Near the North Fork of the Fryingpan River in White River National Forest; map A2, grid h3.

**Campsites, facilities:** There are seven sites for tents or RVs up to 22 feet long. Picnic tables, fire grills, and vault toilets are provided, but there is no drinking water. Leashed pets are permitted.

**Elevation:** 9,000 feet.

**Reservations, fees:** Reservations are not accepted. No fee is required, but donations are requested.

**Open:** June to September.

**Directions:** From Basalt on Hwy. 82, turn east on Forest Service Rd. 105 (Fryingpan River Rd.) and drive approximately 27 miles to Forest Service Rd. 501. Turn left and continue about two miles to the campground.

**Contact:** White River National Forest, Sopris Ranger District, 620 Main St., P.O. Box 309, Carbondale, CO 81623; tel. (970) 963-2266.

## 175 Coke Oven State Wildlife Area      7

At just over 300 acres, this property is small by Division of Wildlife standards. That doesn't mean, however, that it's lacking in recreation opportunities. The terrain is rugged and heavily forested, but if you head north far enough you can hook up with U.S. Forest Service trails that trace a network of tiny alpine streams. On the drive in you pass Ruedi Reservoir, which offers full facilities for boating, camping, and fishing. Limited hunting is permitted.

**Location:** East of Ruedi Reservoir; map A2, grid i3.

**Campsites, facilities:** Dispersed camping is permitted throughout the property. There are no facilities. Leashed pets are permitted.

**Elevation:** 9,000 feet.

**Reservations, fees:** Reservations are not accepted. There is no fee.

**Open:** Year-round.

**Directions:** From Basalt on Hwy. 82, turn east on Forest Service Rd. 105 (Fryingpan River Rd.) and drive approximately 33 miles to the property boundary.

**Contact:** Colorado Division of Wildlife, 6060 Broadway, Denver, CO 80216; tel. (303) 297-1192.

## 176 May Queen      8

Once an old mining site, May Queen is now the most remote and isolated of all the campgrounds on Turquoise Lake. Both open and shaded sites are available. The camp is near several trailheads, including those for the Timberline Lake Trail and the Colorado Trail. A lakeside trail also begins at this camp, leading east along the northern shoreline. Since it's near the inlet side of the lake, it is a prime spot for fishing; to the east are facilities for boating and more fishing access points.

**Location:** On Turquoise Lake in San Isabel National Forest; map A2, grid i4.

**Campsites, facilities:** There are 27 sites for tents or RVs up to 32 feet long. Drinking water, picnic tables, fire grills, and vault toilets are provided. Leashed pets are permitted.

**Elevation:** 9,900 feet.

**Reservations, fees:** Reservations are available; phone (877) 444-6777. There's an $8.65 reservation fee. You may also reserve sites at website: www.reserveusa.com. Sites are $12 a night.

**Open:** June to September.

**Directions:** From U.S. 24 in Leadville, turn west on 6th St. and drive approximately four miles (as you leave town, the road becomes County Rd. 4). Then turn right on Forest Service Rd. 104 and drive about six miles north and west to the campground, located on the far western shore of the lake.

**Contact:** San Isabel National Forest, Leadville Ranger District, 2015 N. Poplar St., Leadville, CO 80461; tel. (719) 486-0752.

## 177 Father Dyer       8

They named this camp for a Methodist missionary who earned his distinction as the first man to ski in Colorado and the first mail carrier to brave Mosquito Pass (elevation 13,186 feet). Set on the edge of a conifer forest, the sites are partially shaded. Nearby is the Tabor Boat Ramp and fishing access points. If you keep going past the campground on Forest Service Rd. 104, you'll come to two vista points with fantastic views of the lake and the mountains to the south.

**Location:** On Turquoise Lake in San Isabel National Forest; map A2, grid i4.

**Campsites, facilities:** There are 25 sites for tents or RVs up to 32 feet long. Drinking water, picnic tables, fire grills, flush toilets, and sinks are provided. Leashed pets are permitted.

**Elevation:** 9,900 feet.

**Reservations, fees:** Reservations are accepted; phone (877) 444-6777. There's an $8.65 reservation fee. You may also reserve sites at website: www.reserveusa.com. Sites are $12 a night.

**Open:** June to September.

**Directions:** From U.S. 24 in Leadville, turn west on 6th St. and drive approximately four miles (as you leave town, the road becomes County Rd. 4). Then turn right on Forest Service Rd. 104 and drive about 2.5 miles north to the campground.

**Contact:** San Isabel National Forest, Leadville Ranger District, 2015 N. Poplar St., Leadville, CO 80461; tel. (719) 486-0752.

## 178 Baby Doe      8

Here's yet another wooded, developed camp on Turquoise Lake. Elizabeth McCourt Doe, better known as Baby Doe, caused a flurry of scandal after her arrival in 1880, when she won the heart of infamous mining mogul Horace Tabor, prompting him to divorce his wife to marry her. A short distance to the south is the Matchless Boat Ramp, a tribute to Baby Doe's death in 1935; she froze in a nearby mine when she had no matches to build a fire. Other points of recreational interest in the area include the Turquoise Lake Trail and several fishing access sites.

**Location:** On Turquoise Lake in San Isabel National Forest; map A2, grid i4.

**Campsites, facilities:** There are 50 sites for tents or RVs up to 32 feet long. Drinking water, picnic tables, fire grills, flush toilets, and sinks are provided. Leashed pets are permitted.

**Elevation:** 9,900 feet.

**Reservations, fees:** Reservations are accepted; phone (877) 444-6777. There's an $8.65 reservation fee. You may also reserve sites at website: www.reserveusa.com. Sites are $12 a night.

**Open:** June to September.

**Directions:** From U.S. 24 in Leadville, turn west on 6th St. and drive approximately four miles (as you leave town, the road becomes County Rd. 4). Then turn right on Forest Service Rd. 104 and drive about two miles north to the campground.

**Contact:** San Isabel National Forest, Leadville Ranger District, 2015 N. Poplar St., Leadville, CO 80461; tel. (719) 486-0752.

## 179 Belle of Colorado     8

One of a back-to-back string of lovely national forest campgrounds along the eastern shore of Turquoise Lake, this camp is next to an old mine. The sites have excellent lake views and put you within easy reach of hiking, boating, and fishing.

**Location:** On Turquoise Lake in San Isabel National Forest; map A2, grid i4.

**Campsites, facilities:** There are 19 tent sites. Drinking water, picnic tables, fire grills, flush toilets, and sinks are provided. Leashed pets are permitted.

**Elevation:** 9,900 feet.

**Reservations, fees:** Reservations are not accepted. Sites are $12 a night.

**Open:** June to September.

**Directions:** From U.S. 24 in Leadville, turn west on 6th St. and drive approximately four miles (as you leave town, the road becomes County Rd. 4). Then turn right on Forest Service Rd. 104 and drive about two miles north to the campground.

**Contact:** San Isabel National Forest, Leadville Ranger District, 2015 N. Poplar St., Leadville, CO 80461; tel. (719) 486-0752.

## 180 Molly Brown      8

Anyone who's seen the movie *Titanic* knows who Molly Brown is—the sassy, "unsinkable" heroine who mingled with the rich and survived the ship's disaster. She was a Leadville legend who, like many, came into wealth during the mining boom. The camp is set near the banks of Turquoise Lake, with an adjacent nature trail and boating and fishing facilities nearby.

**Location:** On Turquoise Lake in San Isabel National Forest; map A2, grid i4.

**Campsites, facilities:** There are 49 sites for tents or RVs up to 32 feet long. Drinking water, picnic tables, fire grills, flush toilets, and sinks are provided. A waste disposal station is available. Leashed pets are permitted.

**Elevation:** 9,900 feet.

**Reservations, fees:** Reservations are accepted; phone (877) 444-6777. There's an $8.65 reservation fee. You may also reserve sites at website: www.reserveusa.com. Sites are $12 a night.

**Open:** June to September.

**Directions:** From U.S. 24 in Leadville, turn west on 6th St. and drive approximately four miles (as you leave town, the road becomes County Rd. 4). Then turn right on Forest Service Rd. 104 and drive about a mile north to the campground.

**Contact:** San Isabel National Forest, Leadville Ranger District, 2015 N. Poplar St., Leadville, CO 80461; tel. (719) 486-0752.

## 181 Silver Dollar      8

This is the first camp you come to as you head up the road along the eastern shore of Turquoise Lake. The sites are scenic and heavily wooded. Nearby are the Matchless Boat Ramp and the Turquoise Lake Trail. The site is named after local mining tycoon Horace Tabor's daughter, Rosemary Echo Silverdollar Tabor.

**Location:** On Turquoise Lake in San Isabel National Forest; map A2, grid i4.

**Campsites, facilities:** There are 43 sites for tents or RVs up to 22 feet long. Drinking water, picnic tables, fire grills, flush toilets, and sinks are provided. Leashed pets are permitted.

**Elevation:** 9,900 feet.

**Reservations, fees:** Reservations are accepted; phone (877) 444-6777. There's an $8.65 reservation fee. You may also reserve sites at website: www.reserveusa.com. Sites are $12 a night.

**Open:** June to September.

**Directions:** From U.S. 24 in Leadville, turn west on 6th St. and drive approximately four miles (as you leave town, the road becomes County Rd. 4). Then turn right on Forest Service Rd. 104 and drive a short distance north to the campground entrance. Turn left and continue to the campground at the end of the road.

**Contact:** San Isabel National Forest, Leadville Ranger District, 2015 N. Poplar St., Leadville, CO 80461; tel. (719) 486-0752.

## 182 Sugar Loafin' RV/Campground

With everything from ice cream socials to gold panning in the river to slide shows of the Leadville region, this full-service campground is a good choice for those who want an activity-oriented camping experience. The sites are grassy, set near the Arkansas River amid tall pines with majestic views of frosted peaks, including Mount Elbert, Colorado's highest mountain at 14,433 feet. Recreation options in the area include hiking, mountain biking, gold panning, horseback riding, and boating and fishing in nearby Turquoise Lake. Recent improvements to the campground include upgraded service buildings (including showers and bathrooms), and a 24-hour "interface station" where campers can hook up their laptops to the public phone and surf the net or check their e-mail.

**Location:** On the Arkansas River near Leadville; map A2, grid i5.

**Campsites, facilities:** There are 95 sites for tents or RVs of any length, many with full hookups. Drinking water, picnic tables, fire grills, and bathrooms with hot showers are provided. Laundry facilities, a waste disposal station, store, public phone, and bike rentals are available. Leashed pets are permitted.

**Elevation:** 9,700 feet.

**Reservations, fees:** Reservations are recommended. Sites are $20-23 a night. (Note: You must be a senior citizen, mention your affiliation with AAA or Good Sam, or say "I Love Camping" to get this "discounted" rate).

**Open:** Late May to October.

**Directions:** From U.S. 24 in Leadville, turn west on 6th St. and drive approximately 3.5 miles to the campground. As you leave town, the road becomes County Rd. 4.

**Contact:** Sugar Loafin' RV/Campground, 303 Hwy. 300, Leadville, CO 80461; tel. (719) 486-1031; e-mail: sugarloafin@sni.net.

## 183 Leadville RV Corral  6

If you have to set up camp in the middle of a town, high-altitude Leadville's not a bad place to do it. Although it's dilapidated and in need of a good backyard cleanup, this campground offers basic, adequate amenities coupled with spectacular panoramic views of the surrounding snowcapped peaks. The restaurants and quaint shops of Leadville are within walking distance, and there is no shortage of recreation opportunities in the nearby mountains.

**Location:** In Leadville; map A2, grid i5.

**Campsites, facilities:** There are 33 full-hookup sites for tents or RVs of any length, many with full hookups. Drinking water, picnic tables, fire grills, and bathrooms with hot showers are provided. Laundry facilities, a waste disposal station, and public phone are available. Leashed pets are permitted.

**Elevation:** 10,400 feet.

**Reservations, fees:** Reservations are recommended. Sites are $15-20 a night.

**Open:** Year-round.

**Directions:** From U.S. 24 in downtown Leadville, turn west on W. 2nd St. and proceed a short distance to the campground.

**Contact:** Leadville RV Corral, 135 W. 2nd St., Leadville, CO 80461; tel. (719) 486-3111.

## 184 Kite Lake    9

This little diamond-shaped lake offers a scenic camping spot and mediocre fishing, but campers usually come here for one thing: mountaineering. The four 14ers surrounding Kite Lake—Lincoln, Bross, Cameron, and Democrat Peaks—are linked by a single trail and can be climbed in one day. It's a long day, but how often do you get a chance to bag four peaks at once? Just don't make the mistake that my friend Marisa and I did. For some reason, we decided it would be a good idea to stop in Breckenridge for a huge pancake breakfast about a half hour before our climb; an hour later, at around 13,000 feet, we felt as if we had stomachs full of lead.

**Location:** Northwest of Alma in Pike National Forest; map A2, grid i6.

**Campsites, facilities:** There are seven tent sites. Picnic tables, fire grills, and vault toilets are provided, but there is no drinking water. Leashed pets are permitted.

**Elevation:** 12,000 feet.

**Reservations, fees:** Reservations are not accepted. Sites are $7 a night, and there's a $3 day-use fee (charged only once per visit).

**Open:** May to October.

**Directions:** From Breckenridge, drive approximately 14 miles south on Hwy. 9 to Alma. Turn right on County Rd. 8 (watch closely for the sign—it's hard to see) and drive 5.5 miles up a rough, rocky road to the campground.

**Contact:** Pike National Forest, South Park Ranger District, P.O. Box 219, Fairplay, CO 80440; tel. (719) 836-2031.

## 185 Alma State Wildlife Area    7

This is a little-known alternative to the expensive and overcrowded U.S. Forest Service campgrounds in the area. There are no developed facilities, but hey—you get what you pay for. Actually, you get a lot more: Recreation options in the area include fishing on the South Platte River, hiking, or climbing (several 14ers are accessible within a short drive). To the west is the Bristlecone Pine Scenic Area, where you can hike and view uniquely gnarled, thousand-year-old trees.

**Location:** On the South Platte River, west of Alma; map A2, grid i6.

**Campsites, facilities:** A few primitive campsites along the river are designated by fire rings. Vault toilets are provided, but there are no other facilities or drinking water. Leashed pets are permitted.

**Elevation:** 11,500 feet.

**Reservations, fees:** Reservations are not accepted. There is no fee.

**Open:** Year-round.

**Directions:** From Breckenridge, drive approximately 12 miles south on Hwy. 9 and turn right on County Rd. 4 (about 1.5 miles north of Alma). The property line is approximately one-quarter mile down the road.

**Contact:** Colorado Division of Wildlife, 6060 Broadway, Denver, CO 80216; tel. (303) 297-1192.

## 186 Horseshoe     7

At this sparsely wooded site you get both easy access to hiking trails and fantastic views of the Mosquito Range. It has remained largely undiscovered up to now and maintains a remote, peaceful quality while still providing all the basics. Several hiking trails in the area are routed into the surrounding national forest. You can also try your luck at fishing in nearby Fourmile Creek.

**Location:** West of Fairplay in Pike National Forest; map A2, grid i6.

**Campsites, facilities:** There are 19 sites for tents or RVs up to 25 feet long. Drinking water, picnic tables, fire grills, and vault toilets are provided. Leashed pets are permitted.

**Elevation:** 10,560 feet.

**Reservations, fees:** Reservations are not accepted. Sites are $9 a night.

**Open:** May to October.

**Directions:** From Fairplay, drive 1.5 miles south on U.S. 285, turn right on County Rd. 18, and continue seven miles west to the campground entrance road.

**Contact:** Pike National Forest, South Park Ranger District, P.O. Box 219, Fairplay, CO 80440; tel. (719) 836-2031.

## 187 Fourmile     7

Even though it's only a few miles off the state highway, this little campground feels as if it's in the wilderness. It's simple and pretty, set on Fourmile Creek with a postcard-quality view of Mount Sherman to the northwest.

**Location:** West of Fairplay in Pike National Forest; map A2, grid i6.

**Campsites, facilities:** There are 14 sites for tents or RVs up to 22 feet long. Drinking water, picnic tables, fire grills, and vault toilets are provided. Leashed pets are permitted.

**Elevation:** 10,760 feet.

**Reservations, fees:** Reservations are not accepted. Sites are $9 a night.

**Open:** May to October.

**Directions:** From Fairplay, drive 1.5 miles south on U.S. 285, turn right on County Rd. 18, and continue eight miles west to the campground.

**Contact:** Pike National Forest, South Park Ranger District, P.O. Box 219, Fairplay, CO 80440; tel. (719) 836-2031.

## 188 South Park Lodge   6

Although downtown Fairplay isn't exactly an adventurer's paradise, consider that you're still in the midst of a region that offers a plethora of outdoor activities: fishing on the South Platte River, hiking in nearby Pike National Forest, climbing 14ers, rafting on the Arkansas River to the south. With simple, unadorned sites and great mountain vistas, this park makes a decent layover spot between excursions.

**Location:** In Fairplay; map A2, grid i7.

**Campsites, facilities:** There are 40 sites for tents or RVs of any length, many with full hookups. Drinking water and bathrooms with hot showers are provided. A waste disposal station and motel rooms are available. Leashed pets are permitted.

**Elevation:** 10,000 feet.

**Reservations, fees:** Reservations are accepted. Sites are $15-22 a night.

**Open:** Year-round.

**Directions:** From downtown Fairplay, head south on Hwy. 9 to the campground on the south end of town.

**Contact:** South Park Lodge, P.O. Box 149, Fairplay, CO 80440; tel. (719) 836-3278.

## 189 Western Inn Motel and RV Park   4

This camp is located just outside of Fairplay on U.S. 285, adjacent to a motel. The sites are positioned in a large gravel parking area devoid of vegetation, with an endless view of the eastern horizon. If you're in a tent, you must pay full price for a (rather uncomfortable) gravel site, or you can pitch your tent in back of the motel for half the price. Road noise can be a problem during busy summer months.

**Location:** Near Fairplay; map A2, grid i7.

**Campsites, facilities:** There are 10 full-hookup sites for tents or RVs of any length. Drinking water, picnic tables, and bathrooms with hot showers are provided. A waste disposal station is available. Leashed pets are permitted.

**Elevation:** 10,000 feet.

**Reservations, fees:** Reservations are accepted. Sites are $10-20 a night.

**Open:** Year-round.

**Directions:** From the junction of Hwy. 9 and U.S. 285 south of Fairplay, drive a short distance north on U.S. 285.

**Contact:** Western Inn Motel and RV Park, P.O. Box 187, Fairplay, CO 80440; tel. (719) 836-2026.

## 190 Selkirk     8

Bordering Tarryall Creek near a pretty meadow, this spot often goes unnoticed by tourists cruising over Boreas Pass Road. It's a prime camp, however, secluded and remote with great wildflower displays in midsummer. You also get easy access to Boreas Pass Rd., which makes a great mountain bike ride: Head up and over the pass (elevation 11,482 feet) and continue all the way down (about eight miles) into Breckenridge. (Make sure you have a car waiting at the bottom, or you'll have a grueling ride back up.)

**Location:** North of Como in Pike National Forest; map A2, grid i7.

**Campsites, facilities:** There are 15 sites for tents or RVs up to 25 feet long. Picnic tables, fire grills, and vault toilets are provided, but there is no drinking water. Leashed pets are permitted.

**Elevation:** 10,500 feet.

**Reservations, fees:** Reservations are not accepted. Sites are $7 a night.

**Open:** May to October.

**Directions:** From U.S. 285 south of Jefferson, take the Como turnoff and drive approximately four miles to County Rd. 50. Turn left and go about three-quarters of a mile. Turn northwest on County Rd. 33 and continue two miles to the campground.

**Contact:** Pike National Forest, South Park Ranger District, P.O. Box 219, Fairplay, CO 80440; tel. (719) 836-2031.

## 191 Lost Park    10

In recent years this area has become a highly popular destination for day hikers and backpackers. Since the campground is next to a major trailhead for the Lost Creek Wilderness, it gets a lot of use. A few years ago, I headed off with a group of friends one fall weekend for a short backpacking trip and found myself awestruck by the eerie beauty around me. A light gray mist and leaves of gold and red signaled the advent of autumn, but a kaleidoscope of hundreds of tiny wildflowers remained as a reminder of spring and summer. The trail from camp crisscrosses Lost Creek and provides a perfect vantage point from which to observe the region's astonishingly diverse population of flowers, grasses, trees, and wildlife.

**Location:** Southeast of Jefferson in Pike National Forest; map A2, grid i9.

**Campsites, facilities:** There are 12 sites for tents or RVs up to 22 feet long. Drinking water, picnic tables, fire grills, and vault toilets are provided. Leashed pets are permitted.

**Elevation:** 10,000 feet.

**Reservations, fees:** Reservations are not accepted. Sites are $7 a night, plus $3 for a day-use permit (charged only once per visit).

**Open:** May to October.

**Directions:** From Jefferson, drive one mile north on U.S. 285 and turn right on County Rd. 56. Continue 20 miles east to the campground.

**Contact:** Pike National Forest, South Park Ranger District, P.O. Box 219, Fairplay, CO 80440; tel. (719) 836-2031.

## 192 Bogan Flats     8

Flanking the Crystal River, this camp offers beautiful, wooded sites and fantastic views of peaks in the Maroon Bells-Snowmass Wilderness to the east. Its scenic appeal and proximity to two wilderness areas (the other is the Raggeds Wilderness, located to the south) make this camp one of the most popular in the area. For a rewarding day trip, take Forest Service Rd. 314 east of Marble along the Crystal River (the road is very rough, accessible to four-wheel-drive vehicles only) for a view of the historic Crystal River Mill, a spectacularly beautiful and frequently photographed spot near the old Crystal City mining operation.

**Location:** On the Crystal River in White River National Forest; map A2, grid j0.

**Campsites, facilities:** There are 37 sites for tents and RVs up to 45 feet long. Drinking water, picnic tables, fire grills, and vault toilets are provided. Leashed pets are permitted.

**Elevation:** 7,600 feet.

**Reservations, fees:** Reservations are accepted; phone (877) 444-6777. There's an $8.65 reservation fee. You may also reserve sites at website: www.reserveusa.com. Sites are $11 a night.

**Open:** June to September.

**Directions:** From Carbondale, drive 21 miles south on Hwy. 133, turn left on Forest Service Rd. 314 (the turnoff for Marble), and continue 1.5 miles to the campground.

**Contact:** White River National Forest, Sopris Ranger District, 620 Main St., P.O. Box 309, Carbondale, CO 81623; tel. (970) 963-2266.

## **193** Silver Bar    9

This tiny, incredibly scenic campground is the first in a line of three campgrounds along Maroon Creek. It's wooded and lush, with fishing in the adjacent creek and good hiking in the area. There's a short nature trail in the camp, and the Maroon Creek Trail runs nearby on its way to the Maroon Bells-Snowmass Wilderness. The mountain vistas to the west are absolutely breathtaking. Don't forget your camera.

**Location:** Southwest of Aspen in White River National Forest; map A2, grid j2.

**Campsites, facilities:** There are four tent sites. Drinking water, picnic tables, fire grills, and vault toilets are provided. Leashed pets are permitted.

**Elevation:** 8,460 feet.

**Reservations, fees:** Reservations are accepted; phone (877) 444-6777. There's an $8.65 reservation fee. You may also reserve sites at website: www.reserveusa.com. Sites are $12 a night.

**Open:** June to October.

**Directions:** From Hwy. 82 west of Aspen, turn west on Maroon Creek Rd. and drive five miles to the campground. Note: During the summer, Maroon Creek Rd. is closed to all vehicles except those with campground passes. You may obtain a pass at the entrance station across from Silver Bar Campground.

**Contact:** White River National Forest, Aspen Ranger District, 806 W. Hallam St., Aspen, CO 81611; tel. (970) 925-3445.

## **194** Silver Bell    9

Like the two other camps in this vicinity, Silver Bell is immensely popular, usually booked up all season long. It's easy to see why, with shaded sites set beneath aspen trees a stone's throw from a pretty creek, incredible mountain views, and prime hiking access. From mid-June through September, the adjacent road is closed from 8:30 a.m. to 4:30 p.m. to all traffic except for campers with a vehicle pass and a local shuttle bus, keeping the area quiet and peaceful.

**Location:** Southwest of Aspen in White River National Forest; map A2, grid j2.

**Campsites, facilities:** There are four tent sites. Picnic tables, fire grills, and vault toilets are provided. There is no drinking water at the camp, but you can obtain water at nearby Silver Bar Campground. Leashed pets are permitted.

**Elevation:** 8,490 feet.

**Reservations, fees:** Reservations are accepted; phone (877) 444-6777. There's an $8.65 reservation fee. You may also reserve sites at website: www.reserveusa.com. Sites are $12 a night.

**Open:** June to October.

**Directions:** From Hwy. 82 west of Aspen, turn west on Maroon Creek Rd. and drive five miles to the campground. Note: During the summer, Maroon Creek Rd. is closed to all vehicles except those with campground passes. You may obtain a pass at the entrance station across from Silver Bar Campground.

**Contact:** White River National Forest, Aspen Ranger District, 806 W. Hallam St., Aspen, CO 81611; tel. (970) 925-3445.

## 195 Silver Queen    10

As the closest developed campground to the Maroon Bells-Snowmass Wilderness, this is one of the most sought-after spots in the state. The views are spectacular and the sites are partially shaded, some set right next to the creek. (Try for astoundingly scenic site 50.) You're also close to a major trailhead that leads south to hook up with a web of trails deep in the wilderness. If you're up for a real challenge, take the Maroon Trail up and over Copper Pass and Triangle Pass; then jog north and follow Conundrum Creek about a mile. It's a gut-thumper of a hike, but the reward is enchanting Conundrum Hot Springs, remote, primitive, natural springs near a wildflower-filled meadow high in the mountains. Amazingly, despite the arduous treks in (it's a shorter but equally difficult hike coming from the other direction), the springs are nearly always jammed with people.

**Location:** Southwest of Aspen in White River National Forest; map A2, grid j2.

**Campsites, facilities:** There are six tent sites. Drinking water, picnic tables, fire grills, and vault toilets are provided. Leashed pets are permitted.

**Elevation:** 8,680 feet.

**Reservations, fees:** Reservations are accepted; phone (877) 444-6777. There's an $8.65 reservation fee. You may also reserve sites at website: www.reserveusa.com. Sites are $12 a night.

**Open:** June to October.

**Directions:** From Hwy. 82 west of Aspen, turn west on Maroon Creek Rd. and drive 5.5 miles to the campground. Note: During the summer, Maroon Creek Rd. is closed to all vehicles except those with campground passes. You may obtain a pass at the entrance station across from Silver Bar Campground.

**Contact:** White River National Forest, Aspen Ranger District, 806 W. Hallam St., Aspen, CO 81611; tel. (970) 925-3445.

## 196 Difficult     7

Set along the Roaring Fork River just off Hwy. 82, Difficult offers easy access to both Aspen and the adjacent Collegiate Peaks Wilderness. The sites offer distant mountain views and are isolated from each other by thick clumps of trees. Fishing access is available within walking distance. A two-mile trail leads south from camp into the wilderness.

**Location:** On the Roaring Fork River in White River National Forest; map A2, grid j2.

**Campsites, facilities:** There are 47 sites for tents or RVs up to 40 feet long. Drinking water, picnic tables, fire grills, and vault toilets are provided. Leashed pets are permitted.

**Elevation:** 8,180 feet.

**Reservations, fees:** Reservations are accepted; phone (877) 444-6777. There's an $8.65 reservation fee. You may also reserve sites at website: www.reserveusa.com. Sites are $12 a night.

**Open:** June to October.

**Directions:** From Aspen, drive five miles southeast on Hwy. 82.

**Contact:** White River National Forest, Aspen Ranger District, 806 W. Hallam St., Aspen, CO 81611; tel. (970) 925-3445.

## 197 Weller  7

Here is another camp located between Hwy. 82 and the Roaring Fork River, on the border of the Collegiate Peaks Wilderness with access to hiking trails. Sites are well shaded and cozy, perfect for tents or pop-up campers. Weller Lake, located just over the wilderness boundary, offers good fishing for rainbow trout.

**Location:** On the Roaring Fork River in White River National Forest; map A2, grid j3.

**Campsites, facilities:** There are 11 sites for tents or RVs up to 16 feet long. Drinking water, picnic tables, fire grills, and vault toilets are provided. Leashed pets are permitted.

**Elevation:** 9,400 feet.

**Reservations, fees:** Reservations are not accepted. Sites are $9 a night.

**Open:** June to mid-September.

**Directions:** From Aspen, drive nine miles southeast on Hwy. 82.

**Contact:** White River National Forest, Aspen Ranger District, 806 W. Hallam St., Aspen, CO 81611; tel. (970) 925-3445.

## 198 Lincoln Gulch  8

Located just south of the confluence of the Roaring Fork River and Lincoln Creek, this campground has excellent fishing access. It's set back off the road in a quiet, wooded setting, adjoining the Collegiate Peaks Wilderness. Down the road about three miles, off Forest Service Rd. 107, is a beautiful trail that follows New York Creek into the wilderness, skirting several spectacular peaks on the way.

**Location:** Southeast of Aspen in White River National Forest; map A2, grid j3.

**Campsites, facilities:** There are seven sites for tents or RVs up to 16 feet long. Drinking water, picnic tables, fire grills, and vault toilets are provided. Leashed pets are permitted.

**Elevation:** 9,600 feet.

**Reservations, fees:** Reservations are not accepted. Sites are $9 a night.

**Open:** Mid-June to mid-September.

**Directions:** From Aspen, drive 11 miles southeast on Hwy. 82. Turn right on Forest Service Rd. 106 (Lincoln Creek Rd.) and continue one-half mile southeast to the campground.

**Contact:** White River National Forest, Aspen Ranger District, 806 W. Hallam St., Aspen, CO 81611; tel. (970) 925-3445.

## 199 Lincoln Creek Dispersed Sites  8

If you don't mind roughing it, these campsites are ideal. They're sprinkled near Lincoln Creek along Lincoln Creek Rd., marked only by fire rings. You have to bring your own water and pack out your trash, but in return you get gorgeous views with access to great fishing and nearby hiking trails—and it's all free.

**Location:** Southeast of Aspen in White River National Forest; map A2, grid j3.

**Campsites, facilities:** There are 28 designated tent sites dispersed along the roadside. No facilities are available. Leashed pets are permitted.

**Elevation:** 9,800 feet.

**Reservations, fees:** Reservations are not accepted. There is no fee.

**Open:** Mid-June to mid-November.

**Directions:** From Aspen, drive 11 miles southeast on Hwy. 82 and turn right on Forest Service Rd. 106 (Lincoln Creek Rd.). The campgrounds are dispersed along the road, starting just past Lincoln Gulch Campground.

**Contact:** White River National Forest, Aspen Ranger District, 806 W. Hallam St., Aspen, CO 81611; tel. (970) 925-3445.

## 200 Portal      8

Remote and virtually unknown, this little wooded camp lies on a tiny sliver of U.S. Forest Service land tucked between the Collegiate Peaks and Sawatch Wilderness areas. A trail from camp climbs steeply to the east and south, following Grizzly Creek to where it pours into Grizzly Lake.

**Location:** Southeast of Aspen in White River National Forest; map A2, grid j3.

**Campsites, facilities:** There are seven sites for tents or RVs up to 16 feet long. Drinking water, picnic tables, fire grills, and vault toilets are provided. Leashed pets are permitted.

**Elevation:** 10,550 feet.

**Reservations, fees:** Reservations are not accepted. Sites are $9 a night.

**Open:** July to mid-October.

**Directions:** From Aspen, drive 11 miles southeast on Hwy. 82. Turn right on Forest Service Rd. 106 (Lincoln Creek Rd.) and continue seven miles southeast to the campground.

**Contact:** White River National Forest, Aspen Ranger District, 806 W. Hallam St., Aspen, CO 81611; tel. (970) 925-3445.

## 201 Lost Man      8

Located along Hwy. 82 a few miles west of Independence Pass, this camp provides shaded sites not far from the Roaring Fork River (fishing access is within walking distance). Across the highway is a trailhead for a trail that heads north along Lostman Creek into the Hunter-Fryingpan Wilderness and up to South Fork Pass.

**Location:** Southeast of Aspen in White River National Forest; map A2, grid j3.

**Campsites, facilities:** There are 10 sites for tents or RVs up to 16 feet long. Drinking water, picnic tables, fire grills, and vault toilets are provided. Leashed pets are permitted.

**Elevation:** 10,500 feet.

**Reservations, fees:** Reservations are not accepted. Sites are $9 a night.

**Open:** July to mid-September.

**Directions:** From Aspen, drive 14.5 miles southeast on Hwy. 82.

**Contact:** White River National Forest, Aspen Ranger District, 806 W. Hallam St., Aspen, CO 81611; tel. (970) 925-3445.

## 202 Elbert Creek     8

The Colorado Trail, a 400-mile trek that winds from Denver to Durango, runs directly through this camp. It's right at the boundary of the Mount Massive Wilderness, next to a pretty, wooded creek with fishing and scenic views. Since it's used as a layover for hikers on the Colorado Trail, the camp is often full.

**Location:** Southwest of Leadville in San Isabel National Forest; map A2, grid j4.

**Campsites, facilities:** There are 17 sites for tents or RVs up to 16 feet long. Drinking water, picnic tables, fire grills, and vault toilets are provided. A waste disposal station is provided. Leashed pets are permitted.

**Elevation:** 9,500 feet.

**Reservations, fees:** Reservations are not accepted. Sites are $9 a night.

**Open:** June to September.

**Directions:** From Leadville, drive approximately four miles south on U.S. 24 to Forest Service Rd. 300. Turn right and drive west about three-quarters of a mile. Turn south on Forest Service Rd. 110 and continue about 6.5 miles to the campground.

**Contact:** San Isabel National Forest, Leadville Ranger District, 2015 N. Poplar St., Leadville, CO 80461; tel. (719) 486-0752.

## 203 Halfmoon      8

Unlike nearby Elbert Creek, which is right on the Colorado Trail, this camp is a short distance from major trailheads and consequently doesn't get quite as much use. It's in a forested setting, with two separate groups of sites along little Halfmoon Creek. Recreation options include fishing and hiking.

**Location:** Southwest of Leadville in San Isabel National Forest; map A2, grid j4.

**Campsites, facilities:** There are 22 sites for tents or RVs up to 16 feet long. Drinking water, picnic tables, fire grills, and vault toilets are provided. A waste disposal station is provided. Leashed pets are permitted.

**Elevation:** 9,500 feet.

**Reservations, fees:** Reservations are not accepted. Sites are $9 a night.

**Open:** June to September.

**Directions:** From Leadville, drive approximately four miles south on U.S. 24 to Forest Service Rd. 300. Turn right and drive west about three-quarters of a mile. Turn south on Forest Service Rd. 110 and continue about 5.5 miles to the campground.

**Contact:** San Isabel National Forest, Leadville Ranger District, 2015 N. Poplar St., Leadville, CO 80461; tel. (719) 486-0752.

## 204 Twin Peaks      9

The spectacular view of Mount Elbert makes this camp one of the best choices in the area. Here's your opportunity to climb a 14er—the nearby Black Cloud Trail will lead you all the way up to the top of the peak (elevation 14,433 feet). If you continue west on Hwy. 82, you'll reach scenic Independence Pass (12,095 feet), a thickly wooded area that's squeezed between the borders of the Mount Massive and Hunter-Fryingpan Wilderness areas and is particularly popular during the change of fall colors.

**Location:** On Lake Creek in San Isabel National Forest; map A2, grid j4.

**Campsites, facilities:** There are 39 sites for tents or RVs up to 32 feet long. Drinking water, picnic tables, fire grills, and vault toilets are provided. Leashed pets are permitted.

**Elevation:** 9,500 feet.

**Reservations, fees:** Reservations are not accepted. Sites are $10 a night.

**Open:** June to September.

**Directions:** From Leadville, drive approximately 12 miles south on U.S. 24 to Hwy. 82. Turn right and drive west, past Twin Lakes Reservoir, until you come to the campground, located a short distance past the Parry Peak camp.

**Contact:** San Isabel National Forest, Leadville Ranger District, 2015 N. Poplar St., Leadville, CO 80461; tel. (719) 486-0752.

## **205** Parry Peak     8

Here is an out-of-the-way alternative to the crowded lakeside camps at Twin Lakes Reservoir. It's not far from the village of Twin Lakes, a charming hamlet steeped in mining history. A trailhead adjacent to camp leads south to Hope Pass; it also hooks up with the Colorado Trail. You can fish in Lake Creek, and full boating and fishing facilities are available nearby at Twin Lakes Reservoir.

**Location:** On Lake Creek in San Isabel National Forest; map A2, grid j4.

**Campsites, facilities:** There are 26 sites for tents or RVs up to 32 feet long. Drinking water, picnic tables, fire grills, and vault toilets are provided. Leashed pets are permitted.

**Elevation:** 9,500 feet.

**Reservations, fees:** Reservations are not accepted. Sites are $10 a night.

**Open:** June to September.

**Directions:** From Leadville, drive approximately 12 miles south on U.S. 24 to Hwy. 82. Turn right and drive west, past Twin Lakes Reservoir, until you come to the campground.

**Contact:** San Isabel National Forest, Leadville Ranger District, 2015 N. Poplar St., Leadville, CO 80461; tel. (719) 486-0752.

## **206** Whitestar     8

Whitestar is the largest and most developed camp on Twin Lakes Reservoir, offering lakeshore sites with stunning views and good fishing access. Directly across the lake is the Inter Laken Historical Site, where a grand hotel once hosted elite guests from all over the world. To the north are hiking trails that lead up to Mount Elbert and the Mount Massive Wilderness.

**Location:** On Twin Lakes Reservoir in San Isabel National Forest; map A2, grid j4.

**Campsites, facilities:** There are 68 sites for tents or RVs up to 32 feet long. Drinking water, picnic tables, fire grills, and vault toilets are provided. A waste disposal station is provided. Leashed pets are permitted.

**Elevation:** 9,500 feet.

**Reservations, fees:** Reservations are accepted; phone (877) 444-6777. There's an $8.65 reservation fee. You may also reserve sites at website: www.reserveusa.com. Sites are $10 a night.

**Open:** June to September.

**Directions:** From Leadville, drive approximately 12 miles south on U.S. 24 to Hwy. 82. Turn right and drive west along the north side of the lake until you reach the campground entrance on the north shore.

**Contact:** San Isabel National Forest, Leadville Ranger District, 2015 N. Poplar St., Leadville, CO 80461; tel. (719) 486-0752.

## 207 Lakeview  8

This camp is adjacent to a major trailhead for the Colorado Trail, which circumnavigates the lake between two wilderness areas. The sites are set back from the road in a pretty, wooded area near the Mount Elbert Hydroelectric Plant. Two fishing access points are just across the road on the lakeshore, and there are hiking trails to the north, including one that's routed to the top of Mount Elbert.

**Location:** On Twin Lakes Reservoir in San Isabel National Forest; map A2, grid j4.

**Campsites, facilities:** There are 59 sites for tents or RVs up to 32 feet long. Drinking water, picnic tables, fire grills, and vault toilets are provided. Leashed pets are permitted.

**Elevation:** 9,500 feet.

**Reservations, fees:** Reservations are accepted; phone (877) 444-6777. There's an $8.65 reservation fee. You may also reserve sites at website: www.reserveusa.com. Sites are $10 a night.

**Open:** June to September.

**Directions:** From Leadville, drive approximately 12 miles south on U.S. 24 to Hwy. 82. Turn right and drive west along the north side of the lake until you reach the campground entrance on the north shore.

**Contact:** San Isabel National Forest, Leadville Ranger District, 2015 N. Poplar St., Leadville, CO 80461; tel. (719) 486-0752.

## 208 Dexter  8

Set along the eastern shore of Twin Lakes Reservoir, Dexter is a great spot for boaters and anglers. A picnic area and a boat ramp are adjacent, with a fishing access point nearby. The Colorado Trail skirts this camp before heading south into the Collegiate Peaks Wilderness.

**Location:** On Twin Lakes Reservoir in San Isabel National Forest; map A2, grid j4.

**Campsites, facilities:** There are 24 sites for tents or RVs up to 37 feet long. Drinking water, picnic tables, fire grills, and vault toilets are provided. A boat ramp is available. Leashed pets are permitted.

**Elevation:** 9,500 feet.

**Reservations, fees:** Reservations are not accepted. Sites are $10 a night.

**Open:** June to September.

**Directions:** From Leadville, drive approximately 12 miles south on U.S. 24 to Hwy. 82. Turn right and drive west along the north side of the lake until you reach the campground on the east shore.

**Contact:** San Isabel National Forest, Leadville Ranger District, 2015 N. Poplar St., Leadville, CO 80461; tel. (719) 486-0752.

## 209 Weston Pass  7

This campground is on the South Fork of the South Platte River (you can fish here, but success rates are not great). It's next to the trailhead for the Buffalo Meadows Trail and the Rich Creek-Tumble Creek Trail, which together form a challenging 12-mile loop. If you continue past the campground up County Rd. 22, you'll eventually come to Weston Pass (elevation 11,921 feet), which affords magnificent views of the surrounding mountains.

**Location:** South of Fairplay in Pike National Forest; map A2, grid j6.

**Campsites, facilities:** There are 14 sites for tents or RVs up to 25 feet long. Drinking water, picnic tables, fire grills, and vault toilets are provided. Leashed pets are permitted.

**Elevation:** 10,200 feet.

**Reservations, fees:** Reservations are not accepted. Sites are $9 a night.

**Open:** May to October.

**Directions:** From Fairplay, drive 4.5 miles south on U.S. 285, turn right on County Rd. 5, and drive seven miles to County Rd. 22. Turn right and continue four miles to the campground.

**Contact:** Pike National Forest, South Park Ranger District, P.O. Box 219, Fairplay, CO 80440; tel. (719) 836-2031.

## 210 Buffalo Springs      5

Set just off the highway in a sparsely vegetated, windswept region, Buffalo Springs makes a decent stopover for U.S. 285 travelers. Farther west on Forest Service Rd. 431 are trailheads for an extensive network of hiking and mountain biking routes. To the southeast is Antero Reservoir, which offers boating and excellent fishing.

**Location:** South of Fairplay in Pike National Forest; map A2, grid j6.

**Campsites, facilities:** There are 17 sites for tents or RVs up to 25 feet long. Drinking water, picnic tables, fire grills, and vault toilets are provided. Leashed pets are permitted.

**Elevation:** 9,000 feet.

**Reservations, fees:** Reservations are not accepted. Sites are $9 a night.

**Open:** May to October.

**Directions:** From Fairplay, drive 10.5 miles south on U.S. 285 and turn west on Forest Service Rd. 431. Continue a short distance to the campground.

**Contact:** Pike National Forest, South Park Ranger District, P.O. Box 219, Fairplay, CO 80440; tel. (719) 836-2031.

## 211 Tarryall Reservoir State Wildlife Area       5

This wildlife area offers a no-cost alternative to Spruce Grove, the only other campground for miles around, but you might end up trading your privacy in the bargain. The primary attraction is trout fishing, and it's pretty much guaranteed that you'll be keeping company with a dozen or so local anglers on any given day. Fishing is allowed by shoreline or boat, with gravel boat ramps on the southeastern and northeastern banks. Other recreation options include wildlife observation and some hunting—this is a good spot to view elk in the fall—and hiking in the surrounding forest. The area is mostly grassy, with scattered trees to the east.

**Location:** East of Fairplay; map A2, grid j8.

**Campsites, facilities:** Dispersed camping is permitted throughout the property. Vault toilets are provided, but there are no other facilities or drinking water. Fishing piers and two boat ramps are available. Leashed pets are permitted.

**Elevation:** 8,800 feet.

**Reservations, fees:** Reservations are not accepted. There is no fee.

**Open:** Year-round.

**Directions:** From Jefferson on U.S. 285, turn southeast on County Rd. 77 and drive 15 miles to the reservoir.

**Contact:** Colorado Division of Wildlife, 6060 Broadway, Denver, CO 80216; tel. (303) 297-1192.

## 2 1 2 Spruce Grove     8

As yet only insiders (like you) know about this secret spot, which is part of what makes it so great. The camp borders Tarryall Creek, about a mile from the western edge of the Lost Creek Wilderness. The fishing in the creek, as well as at Tarryall Reservoir to the north, is said to be excellent. There are also several hiking trails in the region; consult the South Park Ranger District for information. The camp can accommodate both tents and RVs, but if you have a tent, I recommend trying one of the walk-in sites, which offer a little extra privacy.

**Location:** Near the Lost Creek Wilderness in Pike National Forest; map A2, grid j8.

**Campsites, facilities:** There are 27 sites for tents or RVs up to 35 feet long. A few of the sites require walking in a short distance. Drinking water, picnic tables, fire grills, and vault toilets are provided. Leashed pets are permitted.

**Elevation:** 8,600 feet.

**Reservations, fees:** Reservations are not accepted. Sites are $9 a night.

**Open:** May to October.

**Directions:** From Jefferson on U.S. 285, turn southeast on County Rd. 77 and drive approximately 25 miles, past Tarryall Reservoir, to the campground.

**Contact:** Pike National Forest, South Park Ranger District, P.O. Box 219, Fairplay, CO 80440; tel. (719) 836-2031.

TWO CAMPERS ON THE TRAIL

# MAP A3

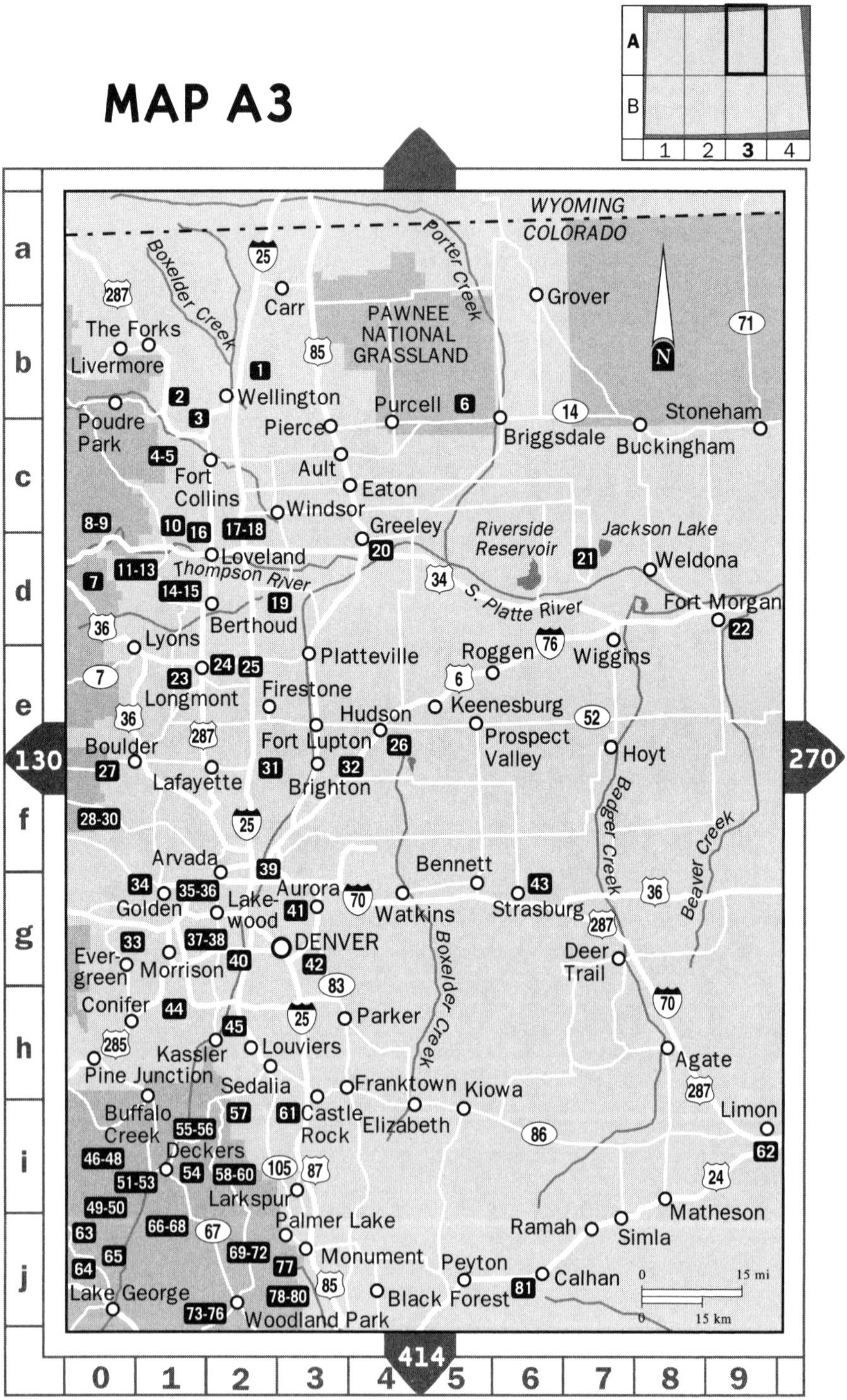

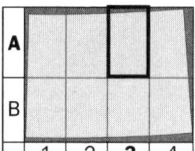

A
B
1 2 **3** 4

*WYOMING*
*COLORADO*

Porter Creek

**287**

The Forks
Livermore

Boxelder Creek

**25**

Carr

PAWNEE
NATIONAL
GRASSLAND

Grover

**71**

Poudre
Park

**1**

**85**

Wellington

Pierce

Purcell **6**

**14**

Briggsdale

Stoneham

Buckingham

**2**

**3**

**4-5**

Fort
Collins

Ault

Eaton

Windsor

Greeley

*Riverside
Reservoir*

*Jackson Lake*

**8-9**

**10** **16**

**17-18**

**20**

**21**

Weldona

Loveland

*Thompson River*

**11-13**

**14-15**

Berthoud

*S. Platte River*

Fort Morgan

**7**

**19**

**34**

**76**

**22**

**36**

Lyons

Platteville

Roggen

Wiggins

**7**

**23** **24** **25**

Longmont

Firestone

**6**

Keenesburg

**52**

**36**

**287**

Hudson

Prospect
Valley

Hoyt

Boulder

Fort Lupton

**26**

**27**

Lafayette

**31**

**32**

Brighton

*Badger Creek*

*Beaver Creek*

**28-30**

**25**

Arvada

**39**

Bennett

**43**

**34**

**35-36**

Aurora

**70**

Strasburg

**36**

Golden

Lake-
wood

**41**

Watkins

**287**

Ever-
green

**33**

**37-38**

**40**

**DENVER**

**42**

Deer
Trail

Morrison

**83**

**70**

Conifer

**44**

**25**

Parker

**285**

**45**

Louviers

Kassler

Pine Junction

Sedalia

Franktown

Kiowa

Agate

**287**

Buffalo
Creek

**55-56**

**57**

**61**

Castle
Rock

Elizabeth

Limon

**46-48**

**51-53**

Deckers

**54**

**58-60**

**105**

**87**

**86**

**62**

**49-50**

Larkspur

**24**

**63**

**66-68**

**67**

Palmer Lake

**65**

**69-72**

**77**

Monument

Ramah

Simla

Matheson

**64**

Lake George

**73-76**

**78-80**

**85**

Black Forest

Peyton

Calhan

**81**

Woodland Park

0      15 mi
0      15 km

130

270

414

a b c d e f g h i j

0 1 2 3 4 5 6 7 8 9

# CHAPTER A3

## ◘ Fort Collins North KOA    3

Although this camp is close to the interstate, you do get a nice view of the mountains on the northeastern border of the Indian Peaks Wilderness. The sites are set in a large, open, grassy area, and many have shade trees.

**Location:** Northeast of Fort Collins; map A3, grid b2.

**Campsites, facilities:** There are 75 sites for tents or RVs of any length, many with full hookups. Drinking water, picnic tables, fire grills, and bathrooms with hot showers are provided. Laundry facilities, a waste disposal station, store, public phone, and swimming pool are available. Leashed pets are permitted.

**Elevation:** 4,800 feet.

**Reservations, fees:** Reservations are accepted; phone (800) KOA-8142. Sites are $19-25 a night.

**Open:** Year-round.

**Directions:** From Interstate 25 north of Fort Collins, take Exit 281 and drive one-quarter mile east on County Rd. 5 to the campground.

**Contact:** Fort Collins North KOA, Box 130, Wellington, CO 80549; tel. (970) 568-7486.

## ◙ Fort Collins Mile High KOA    5

This campground at the entrance to the scenic Poudre River Canyon is easily accessible from Fort Collins and close to a multitude of regional outdoor activities, including hiking and fishing. The sites are enclosed in a grove of conifers, with plenty of shade and views of scrub-covered foothills. The camp is set a short distance back from U.S. 287, so you'll have to endure a lot of road noise in the summer.

**Location:** North of Fort Collins; map A3, grid b1.

**Campsites, facilities:** There are 20 tent sites and 45 sites for RVs of any length, many with full hookups. Drinking water, picnic tables, fire grills, and bathrooms with hot showers are provided. Laundry facilities, a waste disposal station, store, public phone, and swimming pool are available. Leashed pets are permitted.

**Elevation:** 4,800 feet.

**Reservations, fees:** Reservations are accepted; phone (800) KOA-2648. Sites are $19-25 a night.

**Open:** May to mid-October.

**Directions:** From Fort Collins, drive 10 miles north on U.S. 287 to the campground on the right.

**Contact:** Fort Collins Mile High KOA, Box 600, 6670 N. Hwy. 287, LaPorte, CO 80535; tel. (970) 493-9758.

## ◘ Blue Spruce RV Park  4

Located between Fort Collins and LaPorte, Blue Spruce is basically a roadside mobile home park that sets aside a few spots for overnighters. The facilities are designed for self-contained vehicles only, with no showers (or even water at the electric-only sites). The sites are shaded by drooping willow trees, with patches of grass here and there.

**Location:** Northwest of Fort Collins; map A3, grid c1.

**Campsites, facilities:** There are approximately 10 sites for RVs of any length, some with full hookups. No tents are permitted. There are no facilities. Pets are prohibited.

**Elevation:** 4,800 feet.

**Reservations, fees:** Reservations are accepted. Sites are $15 a night.

**Open:** Year-round.

**Directions:** From Fort Collins, drive three miles north on U.S. 287 to the corner of U.S. 287 and Shields Street.

**Contact:** Blue Spruce RV Park, 2730 N. Shields St., Fort Collins, CO 80524; tel. (970) 221-3723.

## ◪ Watson Lake State Wildlife Area     6

Set slightly south of the Cache la Poudre River, Watson Lake is a no-cost alternative to the more developed campgrounds in the region. The campsites are within walking distance of the lake and offer pleasant views and limited shade. Fishing is permitted by shore or inflatable boat, with decent prospects for rainbow, brown, and brook trout. There's a nature trail encircling the lake and opportunities for bird-watching and wildlife observation.

**Location:** North of Fort Collins; map A3, grid c1.

**Campsites, facilities:** A large area holds several designated campsites for tents or RVs of any length. Vault toilets are provided, but there is no drinking water. Leashed pets are permitted.

**Elevation:** 5,100 feet.

**Reservations, fees:** Reservations are not accepted. There is no fee.

**Open:** Year-round.

**Directions:** From Fort Collins, drive seven miles north on U.S. 287, turn left on Rist Canyon Rd., and continue one mile west to the property.

**Contact:** Colorado Division of Wildlife, 317 W. Prospect Ave., Fort Collins, CO 80526; tel. (970) 472-4300.

## ◱ Horsetooth Reservoir     7

Long, narrow Horsetooth Reservoir covers nearly 2,000 acres and is more than six miles long. It's a local water sports mecca, offering facilities for waterskiing, windsurfing, fishing, and scuba diving. Fishing is excellent, with good prospects for trout, bass, perch, and walleye, and designated fishing access points all around the shore. The campsites are clustered on the reservoir's southern end, with a few sites on the north end at Satanka Cove, where you'll find a boat ramp and picnic facilities. Swimming is best at South Bay Landing near the southern campsites; limited supplies and services are available there as well. The park has 26 miles of trails for hiking, mountain biking, and horseback riding, including a scenic hike from the Horsetooth Dam a couple of miles south to the Dixon Canyon Dam. Other options include rock climbing and photography (there are several excellent vista points on the south and eastern shores).

**Location:** Near Fort Collins; map A3, grid c1.

**Campsites, facilities:** There are five tent sites and 100 sites for RVs up to 30 feet long. Drinking water, picnic tables, fire grills, and vault toilets are provided. Electric hookups, a waste disposal station, small store, public phone, and marina with a boat ramp, docks, and boat rentals are available. Some facilities are wheelchair accessible. Leashed pets are permitted.

**Elevation:** 5,400 feet.

**Reservations, fees:** Reservations are not accepted. Sites are $7 a night, and there's a $6 park use fee.

**Open:** Year-round with limited winter facilities.

**Directions:** From Interstate 25 south of Fort Collins, take Exit 265 and drive seven miles west on Hwy. 68 (Harmony Road). Turn right onto County Rd. 19 (Taft Hill Rd.) and drive one mile north. Turn left on County Rd. 38E and continue to the reservoir.

**Contact:** Larimer County Parks, 1800 S. County Rd. 31, Loveland, CO 80537; tel. (970) 679-4570.

## 6 Crow Valley Recreation Area     8

This small, quiet campground is set under tall elm trees on the high plains east of Fort Collins. Pawnee National Grassland covers 193,000 acres of level prairie, providing recreation opportunities and a safe habitat for a variety of native wildlife, including nearly 300 species of birds. An interpretive birding trail begins at the campground and runs 36 miles to the far reaches of the grasslands. Also at the campground is a historic display of farming equipment once used in the region.

**Location:** In Pawnee National Grassland; map A3, grid b5.

**Campsites, facilities:** There are seven single-family sites (accommodating up to five people each) and three double sites (for up to 10 people each) for tents or RVs up to 35 feet long. There are also three group camps that can accommodate up to 30 people each. Drinking water, picnic tables, fire grills, and vault toilets are provided. Some facilities are wheelchair accessible. Leashed pets are permitted.

**Elevation:** 4,800 feet.

**Reservations, fees:** Reservations are accepted for group sites only; phone (970) 353-5004 for information and fees. Individual sites are $8 a night; double sites are $12 a night.

**Open:** May to October.

**Directions:** From Interstate 25 near Fort Collins, take Exit 269 and drive approximately 30 miles east on Hwy. 14 to the town of Briggsdale. Turn left on County Rd. 77 and continue one-half mile north to the campground.

**Contact:** Pawnee National Grassland, 660 O St., Suite A, Greeley, CO 80631; tel. (970) 353-5004.

## 7 Yogi Bear's Jellystone Park of Estes     7

Like all the parks in the Yogi's Jellystone chain, this camp is a full-service destination resort, firmly family oriented. The park is huge, covering 35 acres, with hiking trails and wagon rides providing means for exploration. A thick line of trees separates the sites from the road, and most sites are protected by trees that afford privacy and shade, with majestic views of a large mountain meadow and high rocky peaks in the background. The atmosphere can get quite raucous—each summer weekend features a theme celebration, complete with contests and games. Examples include the Fabulous 50s Weekend, the Who-Dun-It Mystery Weekend, and State Appreciation Weekends (drivers from surrounding states receive a 20% discount).

**Location:** East of Estes Park; map A3, grid d0.

**Campsites, facilities:** There are 20 tent sites and 90 sites for RVs of any length, many with full hookups. Drinking water, picnic tables, fire grills, and bathrooms with hot showers are provided. Laundry facilities, a waste disposal station, a store, a public phone, a swimming pool, and cabins are available. Some facilities are wheelchair accessible. Leashed pets are permitted.

**Elevation:** 7,800 feet.

**Reservations, fees:** Reservations are accepted. Sites are $21-30 a night.

**Open:** May to late September.

**Directions:** From the junction of U.S. 36 and U.S. 34 in Estes Park, drive four miles southeast on U.S. 36 to the campground.

**Contact:** Yogi Bear's Jellystone Park of Estes, 5495 U.S. 36, Estes Park, CO 80517; tel. (970) 586-4230 or (800) 722-2928.

## 🖪 Seven Pines Campground and Cabins   8

Most of these beautiful, shaded sites sit on the rocky banks of the Big Thompson River, with fishing access just a cast away. Since it's next to the highway, Seven Pines is subject to a fair amount of road noise from tourist traffic; nonetheless, the camp is extremely popular and usually is full from spring to fall. Reservations aren't officially required, but I strongly suggest calling well ahead of time. Rocky Mountain National Park and Estes Park are within a short drive.

**Location:** Near Estes Park; map A3, grid c0.

**Campsites, facilities:** There are 25 full-hookups sites for RVs up to 40 feet long. No tents are permitted. Drinking water, picnic tables, fire grills, and bathrooms with hot showers are provided. A waste disposal station and cabins are available. Leashed pets are permitted.

**Elevation:** 7,200 feet.

**Reservations, fees:** Reservations are accepted. Sites are $27 a night.

**Open:** Mid-May to September.

**Directions:** From the junction of U.S. 36 and U.S. 34 in Estes Park, drive seven miles east on U.S. 34 to the campground.

**Contact:** Seven Pines Campground and Cabins, 2137 U.S. 34, Drake, CO 80515; tel. (970) 586-3809.

## 🖪 River Bend Campground    8

Tourists who wish to be closer to Rocky Mountain National Park typically bypass this camp. That's their loss (and your gain), since the park is just as pretty as those in Estes Park, only less crowded and less expensive. The sites are well back from the road and are sheltered from highway noise. Tent campers are settled in a grassy area about 10 feet from the banks of the Big Thompson River, with larger RV sites under trees nearby.

**Location:** Between Loveland and Estes Park; map A3, grid c0.

**Campsites, facilities:** There are 10 tent sites and 30 sites for RVs up to 25 feet long.

Drinking water, picnic tables, fire grills, and bathrooms with hot showers are provided. Electric hookups and a small store are available. Leashed pets are permitted.

**Elevation:** 7,500 feet.

**Reservations, fees:** Reservations are not accepted. Sites are $15-18 a night.

**Open:** May to September.

**Directions:** From Loveland, drive 16 miles west on U.S. 34. The campground is exactly halfway between Loveland and Estes Park.

**Contact:** River Bend Campground, 1520 U.S. 34, Loveland, CO 80537; tel. (970) 667-3641.

## **10** Riverview RV Park and Campground    7

Only a half hour's drive from Estes Park, this friendly camp provides an alternative to the cluster of more crowded, expensive facilities near Rocky Mountain National Park. The close-set, shaded sites are near the banks of the Big Thompson River, with the most desirable sites overlooking the water. Hiking trails are available nearby.

**Location:** On the Big Thompson River; map A3, grid c1.

**Campsites, facilities:** There are 34 tent sites and 130 full-hookup sites for RVs of any length. Drinking water, picnic tables, fire grills, and bathrooms with hot showers are provided. Laundry facilities, a waste disposal station, store, sports facilities, and public phone are available. Leashed pets are permitted.

**Elevation:** 5,100 feet.

**Reservations, fees:** Reservations are accepted; phone (800) 447-9910. Sites are $17.50-25.50 a night.

**Open:** Year-round.

**Directions:** From Loveland, drive six miles west on U.S. 34 to the park.

**Contact:** Riverview RV Park and Campground, 7806 W. U.S. 34, Loveland, CO 80537; tel. (970) 667-9910; e-mail: rivlland@aol.com.

## **11** Pinewood Reservoir      7

One hundred-acre Pinewood Reservoir is a simple, clear mountain lake known well by locals but overlooked by most tourists. The shoreline is partly wooded, with secluded tent sites in the trees and larger open sites close to shore. Wakeless boating is permitted; anglers can expect decent fishing for rainbow trout.

**Location:** Southwest of Loveland; map A3, grid d1.

**Campsites, facilities:** There are eight tent sites and 22 sites for RVs of any length. Drinking water, picnic tables, fire grills, and vault toilets are provided. A small boat ramp is available. Some facilities are wheelchair accessible. Leashed pets are permitted.

**Elevation:** 6,600 feet.

**Reservations, fees:** Reservations are not accepted. Sites are $7 a night, and there's a $6 day use fee.

**Open:** Year-round.

**Directions:** From Loveland, turn west on U.S. 34 and drive six miles. Turn left on County Rd. 29 and head two miles south. Then turn right on County Rd. 18E and continue a little more than six miles to the reservoir.

**Contact:** Larimer County Parks, 1800 S. County Rd. 31, Loveland, CO 80537; tel. (970) 679-4570.

## 12 Flatiron Reservoir    7

Flatiron Reservoir, covering 50 surface acres, is a popular local fishing hole. No boating or swimming is allowed, but shoreline fishing can be excellent, as the lake is stocked regularly with rainbow trout. The campground is enveloped in deciduous forest, within walking distance of the shore. The large, adjacent picnic area affords beautiful views and is a popular weekend destination, so the park receives heavy use throughout summer.

**Location:** Southwest of Loveland; map A3, grid d1.

**Campsites, facilities:** There are 31 sites for tents or RVs of any length. Drinking water, picnic tables, fire grills, and vault toilets are provided. Leashed pets are permitted.

**Elevation:** 5,400 feet.

**Reservations, fees:** Reservations are not accepted. Sites are $7 a night, and there's a $6 day use fee.

**Open:** Year-round.

**Directions:** From Interstate 25 south of Fort Collins, take Exit 257B and drive approximately 10 miles west on U.S. 34. Turn left on County Rd. 29 and drive two miles south. Turn west on County Rd. 18E and continue two more miles to the reservoir.

**Contact:** Larimer County Parks, 1800 S. County Rd. 31, Loveland, CO 80537; tel. (970) 679-4570.

## 13 Carter Valley Campground   7

This camp is at its best in late spring and early summer, when the winter snowmelt and cool rains have turned the surrounding valley and hills a deep, fresh green infused with patches of wildflowers. The sites are set on grassy pads dotted with shade trees and provide a quiet, lesser-known alternative to more developed RV resort campgrounds in the area. Carter Lake is a short drive to the south.

**Location:** Southwest of Loveland; map A3, grid d1.

**Campsites, facilities:** There are 56 full-hookup sites for tents or RVs up to 40 feet long. Drinking water, picnic tables, fire grills, and bathrooms with hot showers are provided. Laundry facilities, a waste disposal station, a store, and a public phone are available. Leashed pets are permitted.

**Elevation:** 5,200 feet.

**Reservations, fees:** Reservations are accepted. Sites are $14-18 a night.

**Open:** Year-round.

**Directions:** From Loveland, drive seven miles west on U.S. 34. Turn south on County Rd. 29 and continue one-half mile.

**Contact:** Carter Valley Campground, 1326 N. Carter Lake Rd., Loveland, CO 80537; tel. (970) 663-3131.

## 14 Carter Lake          8

Carter Lake is a popular local swimming hole, with 1,100 surface acres and facilities for all manner of water sports. Waterskiing, sailing, and windsurfing are among the activities of choice, and there's a good swimming beach near Dam Two on the east shore (a lifeguard is on duty during the high-use season). In addition, there are four miles of trails for hiking, horseback riding, and mountain biking, plus various rock outcroppings for technical climbing. Fishing—for trout, largemouth bass, perch, and kokanee salmon—is said to be quite good. The campsites are spread north to south along the tree-studded eastern shore; the western shore remains largely undeveloped.

**Location:** Southwest of Loveland; map A3, grid d1.

**Campsites, facilities:** There are 190 sites for tents or RVs of any length. Drinking water, picnic tables, fire grills, and flush toilets are provided. A waste disposal station, small store, public phone, and marina with a boat ramp, docks, and boat rentals are available. Some facilities are wheelchair accessible. Leashed pets are permitted.

**Elevation:** 5,700 feet.

**Reservations, fees:** Reservations are not accepted. Sites are $7 a night, and there's a $6 park use fee.

**Open:** Year-round.

**Directions:** From Interstate 25 south of Loveland, take Exit 250 and drive nine miles west, through Berthoud, on Hwy. 56. After the highway veers sharply right, turn left on County Rd. 8E and continue about four miles west to the park entrance.

**Contact:** Larimer County Parks, 1800 S. County Rd. 31, Loveland, CO 80537; tel. (970) 679-4570.

## 15 Lon Hagler State Wildlife Area      6

No-wake boating and fishing are the sports of choice at this somewhat murky-looking lake where prospects for rainbow trout, channel catfish, tiger muskie, and largemouth bass are excellent. The designated sites are basic, charmless dirt clearings, but they provide a simple, inexpensive base from which to explore the reservoir and the wildlife area. A nature trail runs adjacent to the lake.

**Location:** South of Loveland; map A3, grid d1.

**Campsites, facilities:** A large area holds several designated campsites for tents or RVs of any length. A vault toilet and a boat ramp are provided, but there is no drinking water. Leashed pets are permitted.

**Elevation:** 5,400 feet.

**Reservations, fees:** Reservations are not accepted. A $3 use permit is required to enter, but there are no additional camping fees.

**Open:** Year-round.

**Directions:** From Loveland, drive three miles south on U.S. 287 to Campion. Turn west on County Rd. 14 (Hwy. 60) and drive three miles. Turn north on County Rd. 21, and continue one-half mile to the Hagler Reservoir entrance.

**Contact:** Colorado Division of Wildlife, 317 W. Prospect Ave., Fort Collins, CO 80526; tel. (970) 472-4300.

## 16 Fireside Motel   5

This camp is adjacent to a small motel a few miles outside of Loveland. It's clean and offers shaded gravel sites. Although not far from the Big Thompson River (you can't see the water from your site, but you can hear it rushing by), there is no direct river access from the camp, so you must drive about a half mile down the road if you want to fish. (Note: Fishing in the Big Thompson is catch-and-release only.) There are some decent undeveloped hiking trails nearby. The downside: The camp is on the busy U.S. 34 corridor, the highway used by Interstate 25 travelers en route to Rocky Mountain National Park.

**Location:** West of Loveland; map A3, grid c2.

**Campsites, facilities:** There are 38 full-hookup sites for RVs up to 40 feet long. Drinking water, picnic tables, and bathrooms with hot showers are provided. Laundry facilities, a store, hot tub, and motel rooms are available. Leashed pets are permitted.

**Elevation:** 5,000 feet.

**Reservations, fees:** Reservations are accepted. Sites are $16-20 a night.

**Open:** Year-round.

**Directions:** From Loveland, drive five miles west on U.S. 34.

**Contact:** Fireside Motel, 6850 W. U.S. 34, Loveland, CO 80537; tel. (970) 667-2903; e-mail: alan@oneimage.com.

## 17 Boyd Lake State Park

8

Two hundred-acre Boyd Lake State Park is a perfect camping destination. The campsites are settled around the western shore of Boyd Lake in a grassy, partially shaded area within walking distance of facilities for boating, fishing, and swimming. The lake is 1,800 surface acres, with plenty of room for waterskiing, sailing, and fishing. Waterskiing is limited to the south half of the lake, leaving the northern half peaceful and wake-free for anglers. There is a large swimming beach with a snack bar and lifeguard and a full-service marina that rents sailboats, pontoons, fishing boats, and ski boats. A hiking/bicycling trail traces the western shore for three miles, eventually meandering south to hook up with a network of regional trails. This is a prime area to view the lake's population of birds, including pelicans, snowy egrets, blue herons, and eagles. Facilities are limited to the west side of the lake, so the eastern shore remains pristine and undeveloped with boundless views of the eastern plains. Limited hunting is permitted; contact the park for details.

**Location:** East of Loveland; map A3, grid c2.

**Campsites, facilities:** There are 148 sites for tents or RVs up to 32 feet long. Drinking water, picnic tables, fire grills, and bathrooms with hot showers are provided. Laundry facilities and a waste disposal station are also available. Electric hookups may be added in 2000. A full-service marina with docks and boat rentals is located north of the camping area. Some facilities are wheelchair accessible. Leashed pets are permitted.

**Elevation:** 4,900 feet.

**Reservations, fees:** Reservations are accepted. Phone (303) 470-1144 or (800) 678-CAMP (800-678-2267) outside the Denver Metro area; there's a $7 reservation fee. Sites are $10 a night, and there's a $4 entrance fee. Electric hookups will add an extra $4 to the camping fee).

**Open:** Year-round.

**Directions:** From Interstate 25 south of Fort Collins, take Exit 257B and drive four miles west on U.S. 34. Turn right on Madison Ave. and go 1.5 miles north. Then

turn east on County Rd. 24E and continue one mile to the park.
**Contact:** Boyd Lake State Park, 3720 N. County Rd. 11C, Loveland, CO 80538; tel. (970) 669-1739.

## 18 Loveland RV Village   7

On any given day, you're bound to encounter some sort of social event at this campground. The hosts take an active interest in community and family involvement, and encourage their guests to attend "village" gatherings, which range from home-style pancake breakfasts, potluck dinners, and parties to festivals for Father's Day and the yearly corn harvest. The campsites are wide and grassy, set side-by-side, and surrounded by lots of trees.

**Location:** East of Loveland; map A3, grid c2.

**Campsites, facilities:** There are 40 tent sites and 160 sites for RVs of any length, most with full hookups. Drinking water, picnic tables, fire grills, and bathrooms with hot showers are provided. Laundry facilities, a waste disposal station, store, public phone, sports facilities, miniature golf, and swimming pool are available. Leashed pets are permitted.

**Elevation:** 5,000 feet.

**Reservations, fees:** Reservations are recommended in the summer; phone (888) 571-3350. Sites are $18-26 a night.

**Open:** Year-round.

**Directions:** From Interstate 25 south of Fort Collins, take Exit 257B and drive one mile west on U.S. 34 to the park.

**Contact:** Loveland RV Village, 4421 E. U.S. 34, Loveland, CO 80538; tel. (970) 667-1204.

## 19 Johnson's Corner Campground     5

Located exactly halfway between Cheyenne, Wyoming, and Denver, this camp is a well-maintained, comfortable stopover for Interstate 25 travelers. The RV sites are landscaped and even, with grass and a few trees, and the tent sites have privacy barriers and covered tables. The barriers serve the added purpose of blocking road noise from Interstate 25, which is unfortunately close by. Good views of the mountains are to the west.

**Location:** Southeast of Loveland; map A3, grid d3.

**Campsites, facilities:** There are eight tent sites and 135 full-hookup sites for RVs of any length. Drinking water, picnic tables, fire grills, and bathrooms with hot showers are provided. Laundry facilities, a waste disposal station, a store, a public phone, a swimming pool, miniature golf, sports facilities, and cabins are available. Some facilities are wheelchair accessible. Small, leashed pets are permitted (for a fee).

**Elevation:** 5,000 feet.

**Reservations, fees:** Reservations are accepted; phone (800) 322-5416. Sites are $14-22 a night.

**Open:** Year-round.

**Directions:** From Interstate 25 south of Loveland, take Exit 254 and drive one-half mile south on the frontage road.

**Contact:** Johnson's Corner Campground, 3618 S.E. Frontage Rd., Loveland, CO 80537; tel. (970) 669-8400.

## 20 Greeley RV Park   7

Located in the midst of one of the largest agricultural regions in the country, Greeley is ripe with lush farmland and abundant livestock. Although limited recreation options have kept the area from becoming a vacation destination, you may find its tranquil, pastoral flavor soothing. This camp is set on several acres of level grassland, sprinkled liberally with shade trees. Many of the sites are occupied by long-term seasonal campers, but nightly sites are almost always available. One word of warning: If a strong wind kicks up (a common occurrence), prepare to be overwhelmed by the distinct aroma of manure—a pungent by-product of all that agriculture.

**Location:** East of Greeley; map A3, grid d4.

**Campsites, facilities:** There are 80 full-hookup sites for tents or RVs of any length. Drinking water, picnic tables, fire grills, and bathrooms with hot showers are provided. Laundry facilities, a small store, and a sports field are available. Leashed pets are permitted.

**Elevation:** 4,600 feet.

**Reservations, fees:** Reservations are accepted. Sites are $15-26 a night.

**Open:** Year-round.

**Directions:** From the junction of U.S. 85 and U.S. 34 in Greeley, drive three-quarters of a mile east on U.S. 34, turn north on the frontage road, and continue one-half mile to the campground (follow the camping signs).

**Contact:** Greeley RV Park, 501 E. 27th St., Greeley, CO 80631; tel. (970) 353-6476.

## 21 Jackson Lake State Park     8

The campsites at this state park are divided into seven loops, most along the western shore of Jackson Lake. Some are on the beach; others rest under shady groves of cottonwoods. The best sites are at the Dunes Loop on the southern shore, where campers enjoy beautiful mountain views, private swimming access, and secluded sites. Waterskiing, sailing, and windsurfing are permitted, as is fishing for trout, catfish, bass, and crappie. (Note: Fishing is prohibited in the winter months.) Large sandy beaches and clear water on the west and south shores are perfect for swimming. There aren't any developed trails in the park, but would-be hikers can head up to Jackson Lake State Wildlife Area, which borders the northeastern shore and is a good place for viewing wildlife. Bird-watching is also popular, with species including great blue heron, eagles, hawks, and a variety of waterfowl.

**Location:** East of Greeley; map A3, grid d7.

**Campsites, facilities:** There are 250 sites for tents or RVs of any length. Drinking water, picnic tables, fire grills, and bathrooms with hot showers are provided. Electric hookups, laundry facilities, a waste disposal station, and a marina with a boat ramp, docks, and boat rentals are available. Some facilities are wheelchair accessible. Leashed pets are permitted.

**Elevation:** 4,700 feet.

**Reservations, fees:** Reservations are accepted. Phone (303) 470-1144 or (800) 678-

CAMP (800-678-2267) outside the Denver Metro area; there's a $7 reservation fee. Sites are $10-14 a night, and there's a $4 entrance fee.

**Open:** Year-round.

**Directions:** From Interstate 76 west of Fort Morgan, take Exit 66 and drive seven miles north on Hwy. 39. Turn left on County Rd. Y5 and continue 2.5 miles west to the park.

**Contact:** Jackson Lake State Park, 26363 County Rd. 3, Orchard, CO 80649; tel. (970) 645-2551.

## 22 Wayward Wind Campground   3

Wayward Wind is near downtown Fort Morgan, squeezed between a motel and a gas station. Although a bit dusty and run-down, it's quite well kept, with clean bathrooms, large shade trees, and a little plot of grass at each site. There's also a swimming pool and a wading pool, and there's a playground and a video arcade.

**Location:** In Fort Morgan; map A3, grid d9.

**Campsites, facilities:** There are 18 full-hookup sites for RVs of any length. Drinking water, picnic tables, and bathrooms with hot showers are provided. Laundry facilities, a public phone, a playground, and a swimming pool are available. Leashed pets are permitted.

**Elevation:** 4,300 feet.

**Reservations, fees:** Reservations are accepted. Sites are $17-19 a night.

**Open:** Year-round.

**Directions:** From Interstate 76 at Fort Morgan, take Exit 75. Go over the overpass and follow the road to the right. Look for the campground between the Quality Inn and the Loaf N' Jug service station.

**Contact:** Wayward Wind Campground, P.O. Box 51, Fort Morgan, CO 80701; tel. (970) 867-8948.

## 23 Boulder County Fairgrounds   5

Dry and dusty, this campground offers little more than a parking lot with side-by-side spaces to park an RV or pitch a tent. A few trees dot the camp, but it's generally wide open, which means it gets hot in the summer. To cool down, take a look at the panoramic mountain view to the west, where you can catch sight of snow-capped peaks well into August.

**Location:** North of Boulder; map A3, grid e1.

**Campsites, facilities:** There are 20 tent sites and 71 sites for RVs up to 40 feet long. Drinking water, picnic tables, electric hookups, bathrooms with hot showers, and a community barbecue area are available. Pets are permitted.

**Elevation:** 5,400 feet.

**Reservations, fees:** Reservations are accepted. Sites are $10-13 a night.

**Open:** All year.

**Directions:** From Boulder, head northeast on Hwy. 119 (the Diagonal Hwy.) for approximately nine miles to Nelson Road. Turn right and proceed two blocks west to the fairground entrance. The campground is on the southeast side of the complex.

**Contact:** Boulder County Fairgrounds Campground, 9595 Nelson Rd., Longmont, CO 80501; tel. (303) 678-1525.

## 24 Westwood Inn Campground  4

Set next to a motel on a busy street in downtown Longmont, this camp makes a fair stopover for travelers who want to get off the interstate—but not too far off—for a night or two. You get close proximity to restaurants and shops, plus majestic views of Longs Peak looming to the west. The sites are within a stone's throw of the road, but the enormous elm trees that shade each site help absorb some of the noise.

**Location:** In Longmont; map A3, grid e2.

**Campsites, facilities:** There are 15 full-hookup sites for RVs up to 30 feet long. No tents are permitted. Drinking water, picnic tables, and bathrooms with hot showers are provided. Laundry facilities and motel rooms are available. Pets are forbidden.

**Elevation:** 5,000 feet.

**Reservations, fees:** Reservations are accepted. Sites are $20 a night.

**Open:** Year-round.

**Directions:** The campground is located in downtown Longmont at 1550 N. Main St. (U.S. 287).

**Contact:** Westwood Inn Campground, 1550 N. Main St., Longmont, CO 80501; tel. (303) 776-2185.

## 25 Barbour Ponds State Park      7

Barbour Ponds State Park encompasses three camping areas placed around four fishing ponds. Used mostly for fishing (they are well stocked with trout, catfish, and crappie), the somewhat mucky ponds are also used for sailing, canoeing, and other types of nonmotorized boating. Deciduous trees border the ponds, creating shade and a hushed, intimate environment for campers. A small nature trail near the entrance station provides opportunities for viewing aquatic plants and wildlife, plus a wide variety of bird species including songbirds, waterfowl, great blue herons, and, rarely, the black-crowned night heron. To the west you'll see distant views of the Indian Peaks; to the east are miles and miles of high plains.

**Location:** East of Longmont; map A3, grid e2.

**Campsites, facilities:** There are 60 sites for tents or RVs of any length. Drinking water, picnic tables, fire grills, and vault toilets are provided. A waste disposal station is available. Some facilities are wheelchair accessible. Leashed pets are permitted.

**Elevation:** 5,000 feet.

**Reservations, fees:** Reservations are accepted. Phone (303) 470-1144 or (800) 678-CAMP (800-678-2267) outside the Denver Metro area; there's a $7 reservation fee. Sites are $10 a night, and there's a $4 entrance fee.

**Open:** Year-round.

**Directions:** From Interstate 25 near Longmont, take Exit 240 and drive one mile west on Hwy. 119. Turn right on County Rd. 7 and continue north to the park.

**Contact:** Barbour Ponds State Park, 3720 N. County Rd. 11C, Loveland, CO 80538; tel. (303) 678-9402.

## 26 Denver Northeast/Hudson KOA    4

Wilderness it's not, but this camp makes an adequate stopover for travelers heading toward the mountains. It's right in downtown Hudson, just off Interstate 76, and offers a decent respite from the hot, dusty highway. Large, grassy sites are sprinkled with trees (some pretty flowering ones) and are adjacent to a swimming pool and a big recreation room with arcade games. Restaurants and supplies are within walking distance.

**Location:** In Hudson; map A3, grid e4.

**Campsites, facilities:** There are 75 sites for tents or RVs of any length, many with full hookups. Drinking water, picnic tables, and bathrooms with hot showers are provided. Laundry facilities, a waste disposal station, grocery store, swimming pool, and public phone are available. Some facilities are wheelchair accessible. Leashed pets are permitted.

**Elevation:** 5,000 feet.

**Reservations, fees:** Reservations are accepted; phone (800) KOA-4793. Sites are $18-25 a night.

**Open:** Year-round.

**Directions:** From Interstate 76 at Hudson, take Exit 31 and drive one block east on Hwy. 52. Turn south on the frontage road and go another block. At 5th Ave., turn west and continue one block to the campground.

**Contact:** Denver Northeast/Pepper Pod KOA, Box 445, Hudson, CO 80642; tel. (303) 536-4763.

## 27 Boulder Mountain Lodge     7

As the only campground in the popular college town of Boulder, you'd think this spot would get heavy use; in truth, it's often passed by unnoticed. It's set along a pretty little creek in Boulder Canyon between Boulder and Nederland, with shaded, cozy sites, easy access, and tons of recreation options nearby. Points of interest include Boulder Falls, Castle Rock (for technical rock climbing), and mountain biking in the adjacent foothills.

**Location:** On Boulder Creek; map A3, grid f0.

**Campsites, facilities:** There are 25 sites for tents or RVs up to 25 feet long, some with full hookups. Drinking water, picnic tables, fire grills, and bathrooms with hot showers are provided. A swimming pool, hot tub, and rooms are available. Leashed pets are permitted.

**Elevation:** 5,400 feet.

**Reservations, fees:** Reservations are not accepted. Sites are $14 a night.

**Open:** Year-round.

**Directions:** From Boulder, turn west on Hwy. 119 (Canyon Blvd.) and drive four miles. Turn right on Four Mile Canyon Rd., go about two hundred feet north, and turn left into the campground entrance.

**Contact:** Boulder Mountain Lodge, 91 Four Mile Canyon Rd., Boulder, CO 80302; tel. (303) 444-0882.

## 28 Reverends Ridge      7

As Golden Gate Canyon's most developed campground, Reverends Ridge bears the lion's share of summer traffic. It's the best choice for RV campers who want electricity, since it's the sole camp in the park that offers hookups. It's also fully wheelchair accessible and is the only camp with flush toilets and showers, so if those are important considerations for you, look no further. The camp is tucked in the northwest corner of the park, close to several hiking trails. One of the more popular trails leads up to Panorama Point, which offers unmatched views of the Continental Divide and is a favorite spot for summer weddings. You can also take the Elk Trail south for several miles, along the park's western boundary, to meet up with a web of other scenic trails. Limited hunting is permitted; call for details.

**Location:** Northwest of Denver in Golden Gate Canyon State Park; map A3, grid f0.

**Campsites, facilities:** There are 106 sites for tents or RVs of any length. Electric hookups, drinking water, picnic tables, fire grills, and bathrooms with hot showers are provided. Laundry facilities are available. The facilities are wheelchair accessible. Leashed pets are permitted.

**Elevation:** 9,200 feet.

**Reservations, fees:** Reservations are accepted. Phone (303) 470-1144 or (800) 678-CAMP (800-678-2267) outside the Denver Metro area; there's a $7 reservation fee. Sites are $10-14 a night, and there's a $4 entrance fee.

**Open:** Year-round.

**Directions:** From the junction of Hwy. 119 and Hwy. 46 (about four miles north of Black Hawk and 10 miles south of Nederland), drive five miles east on Hwy. 46 to the park's western entrance. Continue a short distance east on Gap Rd. to the campground on the left. If you're coming from the Denver area, drive west on Interstate 70 and take Exit 265 (Hwy. 58). Continue about five miles west toward Golden, turn north on Hwy. 93, and drive two miles to the stoplight at Golden Gate Canyon Road. Turn left and drive approximately 15 miles north to the southern park entrance.

**Contact:** Golden Gate Canyon State Park, 3873 Hwy. 46, Golden, CO 80025; tel. (303) 582-3707.

## 29 Aspen Meadow      9

Simply beautiful, this camp is in an intimate stand of aspen and pine trees in the northwestern region of the park. With special facilities for campers with horses, it's a prime headquarters for day rides (or hikes). A short access trail heads west to hook up with the Mule Deer Trail, which then heads south to Frazer Meadow, one of the park's most magical spots—a lush meadow with tons of wildflowers, aspen groves, and spectacular mountain vistas. Anglers can check out the Snow Hare Trail, which travels east to a tiny fishing hole that holds a few dinker-sized trout. Even if you don't catch anything, the scenic hike is worth the trip. Limited hunting is permitted; call for details. Special note: Besides the three drive-to campgrounds covered here, the park offers a number of backcountry sites and primitive shelters for those who prefer to camp in the wilderness. Contact park headquarters for details.

**Location:** Northwest of Denver in Golden Gate Canyon State Park; map A3, grid f0.

**Campsites, facilities:** There are 35 sites for tents only and a separate loop designated for equestrian campers, with extra space for horse trailers. Drinking water, picnic tables, fire grills, and vault toilets are provided. Leashed pets are permitted.

**Elevation:** 9,200 feet.

**Reservations, fees:** Reservations are accepted. Phone (303) 470-1144 or (800) 678-CAMP (800-678-2267) outside the Denver Metro area; there's a $7 reservation fee. Sites are $10 a night, and there's a $4 entrance fee.

**Open:** Year-round.

**Directions:** From the junction of Hwy. 119 and Hwy. 46 (about four miles north of Black Hawk and 10 miles south of Nederland), drive five miles east on Hwy. 46 to the park's western entrance. Continue approximately 2.5 miles east on Gap Rd. to the campground on the right.

If you're coming from the Denver area, drive west on Interstate 70 and take Exit 265 (Hwy. 58). Continue about five miles west toward Golden, turn north on Hwy. 93, and drive two miles to the stoplight at Golden Gate Canyon Road. Turn left and drive approximately 15 miles north to the southern park entrance.

**Contact:** Golden Gate Canyon State Park, 3873 Hwy. 46, Golden, CO 80025; tel. (303) 582-3707.

## 30 Rifleman Phillips Group Camp     7

Located in a Lodgepole pine forest just south of the convergence of the Snowshoe Hare and Buffalo Trails, this camp includes simple facilities divided into three sections, each with its own large fire pit for cooking. It's not far from Nott Creek, which offers decent fishing access (albeit dubious prospects) and spectacular scenery. Since the camp is positioned almost exactly in the middle of the park, most trails and points of interest are easily accessible. Limited hunting is permitted; call for details.

**Location:** Northwest of Denver in Golden Gate Canyon State Park; map A3, grid f0.

**Campsites, facilities:** A large group area can accommodate up to 75 people in tents. Drinking water, picnic tables, fire grills, and vault toilets are provided. Leashed pets are permitted.

**Elevation:** 9,000 feet.

**Reservations, fees:** Reservations are required. Phone (303) 470-1144 or (800) 678-CAMP (800-678-2267) outside the Denver Metro area; there's a $7 reservation fee. Fees vary depending on group size, and each vehicle must pay a $4 entrance fee.

**Open:** June to September.

**Directions:** From the junction of Hwy. 119 and

Hwy. 46 (about four miles north of Black Hawk and 10 miles south of Nederland), drive five miles east on Hwy. 46 to the park's western entrance. Continue approximately three miles east on Gap Rd. to the campground on the right. If you're coming from the Denver area, drive west on Interstate 70 and take Exit 265 (Hwy. 58). Continue about five miles west on Hwy. 58 toward Golden, turn north on Hwy. 93, and drive two miles to the stoplight at Golden Gate Canyon Road. Turn left and drive approximately 15 miles north to the southern park entrance.

**Contact:** Golden Gate Canyon State Park, 3873 Hwy. 46, Golden, CO 80025; tel. (303) 582-3707.

## 31 Denver North Campground    4

Just off Interstate 25, this city campground has large sites with grassy patios and dappled shade. The hosts are down-to-earth and friendly, offering daily pancake breakfasts in the summer and advice on area attractions. The swimming pool is a welcome bonus in the summer, when temperatures can reach the upper 90s.

**Location:** In Broomfield; map A3, grid f2.

**Campsites, facilities:** There are 25 tent sites and 125 sites for RVs of any length, many with full hookups. Drinking water, picnic tables, fire grills, and bathrooms with hot showers are provided. Laundry facilities, a waste disposal station, grocery store, swimming pool, and public phone are available. Leashed pets are permitted.

**Elevation:** 5,300 feet.

**Reservations, fees:** Reservations are accepted. Sites are $20-26 a night.

**Open:** Year-round.

**Directions:** From Interstate 25 north of Denver, take Exit 229 and drive a short distance east on the frontage road to the corner of Washington Boulevard.

**Contact:** Denver North Campground, 16700 N. Washington Blvd., Broomfield, CO 80020; tel. (303) 452-4120.

## 32 Barr Lake RV Park    5

This camp actually sits a full two miles from Barr Lake, on a flat, dry lot with grassy sites and a smattering of shade trees. The highlight of the area is Barr Lake State Park, a day-use-only fishing mecca that doubles as a nationally known wildlife observation area. The Colorado Bird Observatory operates an office there, and the staff will happily give advice on the best locations and times to spot the park's hundreds of species of birds, including egrets, herons, hawks, and raptors. Hiking, biking, and nonmotorized boating are allowed at the state park. Denver International Airport is just a few miles to the southeast.

**Location:** In Brighton; map A3, grid f3.

**Campsites, facilities:** There are 98 sites for tents or RVs of any length, most with full hookups. Drinking water, picnic tables, fire grills, and bathrooms with hot showers are provided. Laundry facilities, a waste disposal station, grocery store, swimming pool, and public phone are available. Pets are forbidden.

**Elevation:** 5,000 feet.

**Reservations, fees:** Reservations are accepted. Sites are $19-27 a night.

**Open:** Year-round.

**Directions:** From Denver, drive 20 miles northeast on Interstate 76 to 136th Ave., turn west, and drive about 50 yards to the campground entrance.

**Contact:** Barr Lake RV Park, 17180 E. 136th Ave., Brighton, CO 80601; tel. (303) 659-6180 or (800) 654-7988.

## 33 Chief Hosa     8

Once you're inside the confines of this densely wooded campground, it's hard to believe the interstate is a couple hundred feet away. It's the ultimate family campground, just 20 minutes from Denver, with a swimming pool, sports field for impromptu games, and plenty of hiking trails nearby. Restaurants and supplies are available a mile to the west at the Evergreen exit. If you come on a summer weekend, chances are good that you'll see a wedding reception or family reunion: the park's popular historic lodge is often rented out for large events.

**Location:** Near Evergreen; map A3, grid g0.

**Campsites, facilities:** There are 150 sites for tents or RVs of any length, many with full hookups. Drinking water, picnic tables, fire grills, and bathrooms with hot showers are provided. Laundry facilities, a waste disposal station, swimming pool, sports field, and public phone are available. Pets are forbidden.

**Elevation:** 7,700 feet.

**Reservations, fees:** Reservations are accepted. Sites are $16-20 a night.

**Open:** Memorial Day to Labor Day.

**Directions:** From Interstate 70 west of Denver, take Exit 253 and turn south, crossing under the interstate to the campground entrance.

**Contact:** Chief Hosa Lodge, 27661 Genessee Dr., Golden, CO 80401; tel. (303) 526-0364.

## 34 Golden Clear Creek RV Park       7

Set back from the road in the town of Golden, this park features partially shaded paved sites and streamside fishing access. Clear Creek parallels the park, with several sites along the banks. A paved trail runs along the creek to the shops and restaurants of downtown Golden, and there are more trails around Lookout Mountain to the south. About 200 feet from camp is a city recreation center that contains a gym, swimming pool, and sports facilities.

**Location:** In Golden; map A3, grid g1.

**Campsites, facilities:** There are 38 sites for tents or RVs of any length, many with full hookups. Drinking water, picnic tables, fire grills, and bathrooms with hot showers are provided. Laundry facilities, a waste disposal station, and a public phone are available. Some facilities are wheelchair accessible. Leashed pets are permitted.

**Elevation:** 5,300 feet.

**Reservations, fees:** Reservations are not accepted. Sites are $18-26 a night.

**Open:** Year-round.

**Directions:** From the junction of Washington Ave. and Hwy. 58 in Golden, drive three blocks south on Washington Ave., turn right on 10th St., and continue one-quarter mile to the park entrance at the end of the road.

**Contact:** Clear Creek RV Park, 1400 10th St., Golden, CO 80401; tel. (303) 278-1437.

## 35 Golden Terrace South RV Resort  6

Golden Terrace is a decent metro campground that provides easy access to both the city and the mountains. The sites are concrete and gravel pads, with a few patches of green and small trees distributed throughout the property. Buses to the casinos in Central City and Black Hawk leave regularly; the camp is also on a city bus route for easy access to shops, restaurants, and local points of interest (tours of the Coors Brewery are popular). To the west are vistas of the foothills of Golden; to the east, the Denver skyline.

**Location:** East of Golden; map A3, grid g1.

**Campsites, facilities:** There are 90 sites for RVs of any length, most with full hookups. Drinking water, picnic tables, and bathrooms with hot showers are provided. Laundry facilities, a waste disposal station, and public phone are available. Small, leashed pets are permitted.

**Elevation:** 5,300 feet.

**Reservations, fees:** Reservations are accepted; phone (800) 638-6279. Sites are $27 a night.

**Open:** Year-round.

**Directions:** From westbound Interstate 70, take Exit 262 and drive 1.5 miles west on Colfax Avenue. From eastbound Interstate 70, take Exit 259 and drive one mile east on Colfax.

**Contact:** Golden Terrace South, 17801 W. Colfax Ave., Golden, CO 80401; tel. (303) 279-6279.

## 36 Dakota Ridge RV Park   3

This RV-only campground resembles an exclusive suburban community, complete with a pillared entrance and impeccable, landscaped lots. It's situated between Denver and Golden, not far from the interstate, and offers easy access to both city and mountains, plus basic supplies at the on-site store. Computer work areas with dedicated phone lines are available for Internet surfers. Since it's so close to the interstate, road noise can be a problem at any time of the year.

**Location:** East of Golden; map A3, grid g1.

**Campsites, facilities:** There are 141 full-hookup sites for RVs of any length. No tents are permitted. Drinking water, picnic tables, fire grills, and bathrooms with hot showers are provided. Laundry facilities, a waste disposal station, small store, and public phone are available. Some facilities are wheelchair accessible. Leashed pets are permitted.

**Elevation:** 5,300 feet.

**Reservations, fees:** Reservations are accepted. Sites are $28.50 a night.

**Open:** Year-round.

**Directions:** From westbound Interstate 70, take Exit 262 and drive two miles west on Colfax Avenue. From eastbound Interstate 70, take Exit 259 and drive one-half mile east on Colfax.

**Contact:** Dakota Ridge RV Park, 17700 W. Colfax Ave., Golden, CO 80401; tel. (303) 279-1625 or (800) 398-1625; e-mail: dakotardge@aol.com.

## 37 Prospect RV Park      7

Unless you were looking for it, you'd probably never notice this low-profile RV park. It's set back from the road, hidden behind a row of buildings on busy

44th Avenue. Past the park's entrance lies another world, where concrete streets give way to lush, green lawns and which extends west to a huge expanse of open, grassy meadow—city open-space property—and endless views of foothills to the west. There are trees, picnic spots, hiking and biking trails, and even a little stream for fishing. With quick access from Interstate 70, it's a perfect overnight stop if you're stuck in the city.

**Location:** West of Denver; map A3, grid g1.

**Campsites, facilities:** There are 72 sites for RVs of any length, many with full hookups. No tents are permitted. Drinking water, picnic tables, and bathrooms with hot showers are provided. Laundry facilities, a waste disposal station, and a public phone are available. Some facilities are wheelchair accessible. Leashed pets are permitted.

**Elevation:** 5,400 feet.

**Reservations, fees:** Reservations are accepted. Sites are $24-28.50 a night.

**Open:** Year-round.

**Directions:** From Interstate 70 west of Denver, take Exit 266 and drive south on Ward Rd. to 44th Avenue. Turn east and continue 200 yards to the campground.

**Contact:** Prospect RV Park, P.O. Box 626, Wheat Ridge, CO 80033; tel. (303) 344-5702 or (800) 344-5702.

## 38 Bear Creek Lake Park       7

Settled east of the foothills in a high prairie setting, Bear Creek Lake Park is a hidden sanctuary on the border of the Denver Metro area. The park encompasses two fishing lakes stocked with rainbow trout and tiger muskie, plus several miles of trails for hiking and mountain biking. Nonmotorized boating is permitted on Soda Lake, and Bear Creek Lake has facilities for motorized (but wakeless) boating. Camping is available in open, grassy, pull-through sites with western views of the foothills. Use is generally light, except for those nights when there are performances at nearby Red Rocks Amphitheater, when happy, noisy concert goers, intoxicated by music—and various other substances—take over the place.

**Location:** In Lakewood; map A3, grid g1.

**Campsites, facilities:** There are 52 sites for tents or RVs of any length. Drinking water, picnic tables, fire grills, and vault toilets are provided. Electric hookups, a marina with boat rentals, and public phone are available. Some facilities are wheelchair accessible. Leashed pets are permitted.

**Elevation:** 5,400 feet.

**Reservations, fees:** Reservations are not accepted. Sites are $10-13 a night.

**Open:** Mid-April to mid-October.

**Directions:** From the junction of Interstate 70 and Hwy. 470 west of Denver, follow Hwy. 470 east. Take the Morrison Rd. exit and go one-quarter mile east to the park entrance.

**Contact:** Bear Creek Lake Park, c/o City of Lakewood, 777 S. Wadsworth Blvd., Lakewood, CO 80226; tel. (303) 697-6159.

## 39 Delux RV Park  4

This downtown RV park is a good bet for those who have come to Denver to see the city sights: Mile High Stadium, Coors Field, the Denver Mint, and the Denver Zoo are all a short drive away. The campsites provide a bit of relief in summer from the hot concrete, with towering shade trees and large grassy areas. Warning: Delux RV Park is smack in between two major interstates, so be prepared for road noise, especially at sites near the front of the park.

**Location:** In Denver; map A3, grid g2.

**Campsites, facilities:** There are 35 sites for RVs up to 38 feet long, most with full hookups. No tents are allowed. Drinking water, picnic tables, fire grills, and bathrooms with hot showers are provided. Laundry facilities, a waste disposal station, and a public phone are available. Leashed pets are permitted.

**Elevation:** 5,300 feet.

**Reservations, fees:** Reservations are accepted. Sites are $23 a night.

**Open:** Year-round.

**Directions:** From Interstate 70 in Denver, take Exit 272 and drive three-quarters of a mile north on Federal Boulevard. The campground is just north of 55th Avenue.

**Contact:** Delux RV Park, 5520 N. Federal Blvd., Denver, CO 80221; tel. (303) 433-0452.

## 40 Flying Saucer RV Park     3

Flying Saucer campground doubles as a mobile home park, with big sites, grassy lawns, and plots of colorful flowers supplied by year-round residents. Although near a busy metro area, it's clean and quiet, and some sites flank Bear Creek. Fishing is best about a block away, at the confluence of Bear Creek and the Platte River. A paved bike path is nearby, as are shops, restaurants, and a golf course.

**Location:** On Bear Creek; map A3, grid g2.

**Campsites, facilities:** There are 120 full-hookup sites for RVs of any length. No tents are permitted. Drinking water and bathrooms with hot showers are provided. Laundry facilities and a public phone are available. Pets are forbidden.

**Elevation:** 5,200 feet.

**Reservations, fees:** Reservations are not accepted. Sites are $24 a night.

**Open:** Year-round.

**Directions:** From Interstate 25, take Exit 201 and drive west on U.S. 285 to Federal Boulevard. Turn left and go about 100 yards south, staying in the left lane. Turn left on eastbound U.S. 285 (Hampden Ave.) and continue one block to the campground.

**Contact:** Flying Saucer RV Park, 2500 W. Hampden Ave., Englewood, CO 80110; tel. (303) 789-1707.

## 41 Denver Meadows RV Park   5

The camp is near the middle of Denver, seven miles from downtown and 13 miles from Denver International Airport. Sites are dirt lanes, with a choice of shade or sun. Toll Gate Creek runs next to the park; the sight and sound of water may be pleasant, but nary a fish has been caught, according to the owner. The campground hosts offer RV storage, propane, and even computer access for those who need an e-mail fix from the road.

**Location:** In Aurora; map A3, grid g3.

**Campsites, facilities:** There are 278 full-hookup sites for RVs up to 40 feet long.

Drinking water, picnic tables, and bathrooms with hot showers are provided. Laundry facilities, a community barbecue area, swimming pool, recreation room with a big screen TV, and public phone are available. Leashed pets are permitted.

**Elevation:** 5,300 feet.

**Reservations, fees:** Reservations are accepted in summer. Sites are $25 a night.

**Open:** Year-round.

**Directions:** From Interstate 225 in Aurora, take Exit 10 (Colfax Ave.) and drive west on Colfax to Potomac Street. Turn right and continue one-half mile north to the campground.

**Contact:** Denver Meadows RV Park, 2075 Potomac St., Aurora, CO 80011; tel. (303) 364-9483 or (800) 364-9487; e-mail: info@denvermeadows.com.

## 42 Cherry Creek State Park  8

Although it's only a 20-minute drive from Denver, this park feels eons from the sweltering concrete of the city. On any given summer day you can see white sailboats dotting the water or kids splashing on the northeastern shore's large swimming beach. The campground is just east of that beach, across the access road in a partially shaded setting. Cherry Creek is a popular spot for scuba diving; groups and schools often train here before heading off to more exotic locales. On the opposite side of the lake is a special area for windsurfing, with boat ramps and a full-service marina slightly to the north. All water sports, including waterskiing and PWC riding, are allowed. Fishing is excellent for bass, trout, crappie, pike, perch, catfish, tiger muskie, and carp.

**Location:** South of Aurora; map A3, grid g3.

**Campsites, facilities:** There are 102 sites for tents or RVs of any length, and three group camping areas. Drinking water, picnic tables, fire grills, and bathrooms with hot showers are provided. A small number of electric hookups are available, as are laundry facilities, a waste disposal station, public phone, horse rentals, snack bar, and full-service marina with boat ramps, docks, and rentals. Some facilities are wheelchair accessible. Leashed pets are permitted.

**Elevation:** 5,500 feet.

**Reservations, fees:** Reservations are accepted. Phone (303) 470-1144 or (800) 678-CAMP (800-678-2267) outside the Denver Metro area; there's a $7 reservation fee. Sites are $10-14 a night, and there's a $5 entrance fee.

**Open:** Year-round.

**Directions:** From Interstate 225 south of Aurora, take Exit 4 (Parker Rd.) and drive one mile south to the park entrance.

**Contact:** Cherry Creek State Park, 4201 S. Parker Rd., Aurora, CO 80014; tel. (303) 699-3860.

## 43 Denver East/Strasburg KOA    3

Set on the high plains east of Denver, this KOA offers an inviting bit of green in the dry eastern Colorado terrain. The sites are level and spacious, with patchy grass lawns and tall shade trees, plus clean facilities and friendly hosts. It's a quick hop off the interstate and just a short drive from Denver International Airport.

**Location:** East of Denver; map A3, grid g6.

**Campsites, facilities:** There are 75 sites for tents or RVs of any length, many with full hookups. Drinking water, picnic tables, fire grills, and bathrooms with hot showers are provided. Laundry facilities, a waste disposal station, store, swimming pool, sports field, and public phone are available. Leashed pets are permitted.

**Elevation:** 5,300 feet.

**Reservations, fees:** Reservations are accepted; phone (800) KOA-6538. Sites are $17-22 a night.

**Open:** Year-round.

**Directions:** From Interstate 70 east of Denver, take Exit 310 and turn north toward Strasburg, crossing under the freeway. Turn right onto the frontage road and continue one-quarter mile east to the campground.

**Contact:** Denver East/Strasburg KOA, Box 597, Strasburg, CO 80136; tel. (303) 622-9274.

## 44 Stage Stop Campground      7

Set in a thick grove of pine, fir, aspen, and cottonwoods, this quiet campground is easily accessible from U.S. 285 yet provides a sense of deep seclusion, with private, well-spaced sites placed far back from the road. Established in the mid-1960s, the camp is maintained by its original owners, who live here year-round and will happily point you in the direction of whichever recreational option you choose. Among local attractions are rock climbing, hiking, horseback riding, and mountain biking. Red Rocks Amphitheater, about five minutes away, features big-name concerts throughout summer, and the quaint town of Morrison offers antique shops and restaurants. Note: This campground may be closed due to road construction in 2000.

**Location:** In Morrison; map A3, grid h1.

**Campsites, facilities:** There are 20 sites for tents or RVs up to 24 feet long. Drinking water, picnic tables, fire grills, and bathrooms with hot showers are provided. Electric hookups and a waste disposal station are available. Leashed pets are permitted.

**Elevation:** 7,500 feet.

**Reservations, fees:** Reservations are accepted. Sites are $16-19 a night.

**Open:** Memorial Day to Labor Day; this campground may be closed due to road construction in 2000.

**Directions:** From the junction of Interstate 25 and U.S. 285 in Denver, drive about 20 miles southwest on U.S. 285. The park is five miles north of Conifer.

**Contact:** Stage Stop Campground, 8884 S. U.S. 285, Morrison, CO 80465; tel. (303) 697-4901.

## 45 Chatfield State Park      8

Boomerang-shaped Chatfield Reservoir is the main attraction at this state park, with 1,500 acres and facilities for all types of water sports. The campground areas are set on the inner curve of the southern shore near the marina, in a grassy, partially shaded setting. Boating includes waterskiing, sailing, windsurfing, and fishing, with separate areas for powerboats and fishing boats. Resident fish include bass, trout, walleye, perch, catfish, and crappie. Chatfield is especially known for its incredible resident population of birds, ranging from blue herons (bring binoculars to check out the unique rookery on the southern arm of the reservoir) and osprey to eagles and hawks. There are multiple varieties of grasses, flowers, and trees; the most diverse concentration can be seen at the Chatfield Arboretum on the northwestern side of the park. More than 25 miles of trails are perfect for viewing the flora and fauna; all trails are accessible by foot, wheelchair, bike, or horse. Swimming is restricted to a large beach on the southwest portion of lake, where power boating is prohibited.

**Location:** Near Denver; map A3, grid h2.

**Campsites, facilities:** There are 193 sites for tents or RVs up to 35 feet long. Drinking water, picnic tables, fire grills, and bathrooms with hot showers are provided. Electric hookups, laundry facilities, a waste disposal station, a small store, a public phone, and a marina with a boat ramp, docks, and boat rentals are available. Some facilities are wheelchair accessible. Leashed pets are permitted. **Elevation:** 5,400 feet.

**Reservations, fees:** Reservations are accepted. Phone (303) 470-1144 or (800) 678-CAMP(800-678-2267) outside the Denver Metro area; there's a $7 reservation fee. Sites are $10-14 a night, and there's a $4 entrance fee.

**Open:** Year-round.

**Directions:** There are two entrances to the park. The campground is closest to the south entrance: From the junction of Hwy. 470 and U.S. 85 (Santa Fe Dr.) south of Littleton, drive four miles south on U.S. 85. Turn right on Titan Rd. and go one mile. At Roxborough Park Rd., turn right and continue about 1.5 miles to the campground. Alternatively, you can enter from the west: From Denver, drive south on Hwy. 121 (Wadsworth Blvd.) and cross Hwy. 470; the entrance is about a mile past this crossing, off Hwy. 121.

**Contact:** Chatfield State Park, 11500 N. Roxborough Park Rd., Littleton, CO 80125; tel. (303) 791-7275.

## 46 Buffalo      8

Nestled under pine and fir forest between a lush mountain meadow and pretty Buffalo Creek, this scenic campground offers easy access to multiple recreation options. Buffalo Creek is stocked with fish, and there's streamside access from camp. The Colorado Trail runs right next to camp, heading south and eventually connecting with a network of trails that make up the Buffalo Mountain Biking Area, with more than 40 miles of trails.

**Location:** On Buffalo Creek in Pike National Forest; map A3, grid i0.

**Campsites, facilities:** There are 41 sites for tents or RVs up to 20 feet long. Drinking water, picnic tables, fire grills, and vault toilets are provided. Leashed pets are permitted. **Elevation:** 7,400 feet.

**Reservations, fees:** Reservations are accepted; phone (877) 444-6777. There's an

$8.65 reservation fee. You may also reserve sites at website: www.reserveusa.com. Sites are $10 a night.

**Open:** Mid-May to September.

**Directions:** From Pine Junction on U.S. 285, turn south on Hwy. 126 and drive nine miles. Turn right on Forest Service Rd. 543 and continue five miles southwest. At Forest Service Rd. 550, turn left and continue a short distance to the campground.

**Contact:** Pike National Forest, South Platte Ranger District, 19316 Goddard Ranch Ct., Morrison, CO 80465; tel. (303) 275-5610.

## 47 Meadows Group Camp     8

You get a choice of settings at the two spacious group sites in this camp: Site 1 is in an open meadow, with lots of sun, grass, and wildflowers; Site 2 is set farther back in a secluded grove of mixed conifers. Either one will accommodate a large group, and both have access to fishing in Buffalo Creek and mountain biking on nearby trails.

**Location:** On the South Fork of Buffalo Creek in Pike National Forest; map A3, grid i0.

**Campsites, facilities:** Two large sites can accommodate up to 150 people each. Drinking water, picnic tables, fire grills, and vault toilets are provided. Leashed pets are permitted.

**Elevation:** 7,600 feet.

**Reservations, fees:** Reservations are required; phone (877) 444-6777. There's an $8.65 reservation fee. You may also reserve sites at website: www.reserveusa.com. Fees vary according to group size.

**Open:** Mid-May to September.

**Directions:** From Pine Junction on U.S. 285, turn south on Hwy. 126 and drive nine miles. Turn right onto Forest Service Rd. 543 and continue about 5.5 miles southwest to the campground.

**Contact:** Pike National Forest, South Platte Ranger District, 19316 Goddard Ranch Ct., Morrison, CO 80465; tel. (303) 275-5610.

## 48 Green Mountain    8

This tiny, remote-feeling campground is in a beautiful, wooded spot along the South Fork of Buffalo Creek. Since it gets less use than some of the larger camps to the north, it's a good option if you're looking for seclusion. Fishing is possible in the creek adjacent to the western sites. If you prefer to hike, keep going south on Forest Service Rd. 543 to Forest Service Rd. 560; head north, and you'll come to trailheads that provide access to the east side of the Lost Creek Wilderness. The Colorado Trail and trails in the Buffalo Mountain Biking Area are a few miles north.

**Location:** On the South Fork of Buffalo Creek in Pike National Forest; map A3, grid i0.

**Campsites, facilities:** There are six tent sites. Drinking water, picnic tables, fire grills, and vault toilets are provided. Leashed pets are permitted.

**Elevation:** 7,600 feet.

**Reservations, fees:** Reservations are not accepted. Sites are $10 a night.

**Open:** Mid-May to September.

**Directions:** From Pine Junction on U.S. 285, turn south on Hwy. 126 and drive nine miles. Turn right on Forest Service Rd. 543 and continue about seven miles southwest to the campground.

**Contact:** Pike National Forest, South Platte Ranger District, 19316 Goddard Ranch Ct., Morrison, CO 80465; tel. (303) 275-5610.

## 49 Molly Gulch      7

An isolated camp near the eastern border of the Lost Creek Wilderness, Molly Gulch offers access to fishing and hiking, with Goose Creek and Cheesman Reservoir nearby, plus wilderness trailheads to the south. The sites are partially shaded by pine and fir trees, set slightly back from the road for privacy.

**Location:** Near the Lost Creek Wilderness in Pike National Forest; map A3, grid i0.

**Campsites, facilities:** There are 15 sites for tents or RVs up to 16 feet long. Drinking water, picnic tables, fire grills, and vault toilets are provided. Leashed pets are permitted.

**Elevation:** 7,400 feet.

**Reservations, fees:** Reservations are not accepted. Sites are $10 a night.

**Open:** Mid-May to September.

**Directions:** From the town of Lake George, drive one mile west on U.S. 24, turn right on Forest Service Rd. 77, and go six miles northwest. Turn right on Matukat Rd. (Forest Service Rd. 211) and continue about 14 miles north to the campground.

**Contact:** Pike National Forest, South Platte Ranger District, 19316 Goddard Ranch Ct., Morrison, CO 80465; tel. (303) 275-5610.

## 50 Goose Creek     7

This popular spot is the closest camp to the eastern edge of the Lost Creek Wilderness, with easy access to the Hankins Pass Trail and the Goose Creek Trail. No reservations are taken, and use is quite heavy, so it's advisable to arrive early in the day to claim a site. Bring your fishing gear: a few miles north is the South Platte River, and to the east is Cheesman Reservoir.

**Location:** Near the Lost Creek Wilderness in Pike National Forest; map A3, grid i0.

**Campsites, facilities:** There are 10 sites for tents or RVs up to 16 feet long. Drinking water, picnic tables, fire grills, and vault toilets are provided. Leashed pets are permitted.

**Elevation:** 7,800 feet.

**Reservations, fees:** Reservations are not accepted. Sites are $10 a night.

**Open:** Mid-May to September.

**Directions:** From the town of Lake George, drive one mile west on U.S. 24, turn right on Forest Service Rd. 77, and drive six miles northwest. Turn right on Matukat Rd. (Forest Service Rd. 211) and continue about 12 miles north to the campground.

**Contact:** Pike National Forest, South Platte Ranger District, 19316 Goddard Ranch Ct., Morrison, CO 80465; tel. (303) 275-5610.

## 51 Kelsey        7

Although this camp doesn't offer much on-site recreation, it's within minutes of every outdoor activity imaginable—hiking, fishing, backpacking, and horseback riding among the most popular—and is generally packed to capacity. Also appealing is its scenic locale, a private, wooded spot encircled by pines and aspens just off Hwy. 126 between the Rampart Range and the Lost Creek Wilderness. Nearby is a vista point with sprawling views of the Rampart Range, and to the east, fishing in the Platte River. Trailheads into the Lost Creek Wilderness are located to the west off Forest Service Rd. 550 and Forest Service Rd. 543.

**Location:** South of Pine Junction in Pike National Forest; map A3, grid i1.

**Campsites, facilities:** There are 17 sites for tents and RVs up to 16 feet long. Drinking water, picnic tables, fire grills, and vault toilets are provided. Leashed pets are permitted.

**Elevation:** 8,000 feet.

**Reservations, fees:** Reservations are accepted; phone (877) 444-6777. There's an $8.65 reservation fee. You may also reserve sites at website: www.reserveusa.com. Sites are $10 a night.

**Open:** Mid-May to September.

**Directions:** From Pine Junction on U.S. 285, turn south on Hwy. 126 and drive 16 miles to the campground.

**Contact:** Pike National Forest, South Platte Ranger District, 19316 Goddard Ranch Ct., Morrison, CO 80465; tel. (303) 275-5610.

## 52 Wigwam     8

Set near the confluence of Wigwam Creek and the South Platte River, this pleasing, partially wooded spot makes a great base camp for a fishing trip, either on the adjacent streams (the South Platte River is a Gold Medal Water, with sections designated as Wild Trout Water) or at nearby Cheesman Reservoir, where you can take your pick of trout, pike, or kokanee salmon.

**Location:** Near Deckers in Pike National Forest; map A3, grid i1.

**Campsites, facilities:** There are 10 tent sites. Drinking water, picnic tables, fire grills, and vault toilets are provided. Some facilities are wheelchair accessible. Leashed pets are permitted.

**Elevation:** 6,600 feet.

**Reservations, fees:** Reservations are not accepted. Sites are $10 a night.

**Open:** May to October.

**Directions:** From Pine Junction on U.S. 285, turn south on Hwy. 126 and drive approximately 21 miles to the campground.

**Contact:** Pike National Forest, South Platte Ranger District, 19316 Goddard Ranch Ct., Morrison, CO 80465; tel. (303) 275-5610.

## 53 Lone Rock      8

One of several popular camps along the South Platte River, Lone Rock is set in an open, sunny area along the riverbanks, with superb fishing access and scenic views of the river and surrounding forest. A special campsite provides comfortable access for campers in wheelchairs.

**Location:** On the South Platte River in Pike National Forest; map A3, grid i1.

**Campsites, facilities:** There are 20 sites for tents or RVs up to 16 feet long. Drinking water, picnic tables, fire grills, and vault toilets are provided. Some facilities are wheelchair accessible. Leashed pets are permitted.

**Elevation:** 6,500 feet.

**Reservations, fees:** Reservations are accepted; phone (877) 444-6777. There's an $8.65 reservation fee. You may also reserve sites at website: www.reserveusa.com. Sites are $10 a night.

**Open:** May to September.

**Directions:** From Pine Junction on U.S. 285, turn south on Hwy. 126 and drive approximately 23 miles to the campground.

**Contact:** Pike National Forest, South Platte Ranger District, 19316 Goddard Ranch Ct., Morrison, CO 80465; tel. (303) 275-5610.

## 54 Platte River       8

A more developed alternative to nearby Ouzel and Osprey, Platte River offers open sites with little shade and great fishing. Trail 695, adjacent to camp, is accessible by foot, bike, horse, or motorcycle and heads north for several miles before meeting the Colorado Trail.

**Location:** On the South Platte River in Pike National Forest; map A3, grid i1.

**Campsites, facilities:** There are 10 tent sites. Drinking water, picnic tables, fire grills, and vault toilets are provided. Leashed pets are permitted.

**Elevation:** 6,400 feet.

**Reservations, fees:** Reservations are not accepted. Sites are $10 a night.

**Open:** May to October.

**Directions:** From Conifer, drive one mile south on U.S. 285, turn left on Forest Service Rd. 97, and continue approximately 22 miles southeast to the campground.

**Contact:** Pike National Forest, South Platte Ranger District, 19316 Goddard Ranch Ct., Morrison, CO 80465; tel. (303) 275-5610.

## 55 Osprey   7

This campground, along with Ouzel to the south, was originally designated as an overflow area, but the demand for sites along the South Platte became so great that the U.S. Forest Service was compelled to make official campgrounds of them. They remain quite primitive, with no water, tables, or even toilets—not exactly a bargain for the price tag. The sites are partially shaded, some set along the river, with excellent fishing access.

**Location:** On the South Platte River in Pike National Forest; map A3, grid i1.

**Campsites, facilities:** There are 14 primitive tent sites. Fire rings are provided, but there are no other facilities or drinking water. Leashed pets are permitted.

**Elevation:** 6,200 feet.

**Reservations, fees:** Reservations are not accepted. Sites are $9 a night.

**Open:** May to October.

**Directions:** From Conifer, drive one mile south on U.S. 285, turn left on Forest Service Rd. 97, and continue approximately 17 miles southeast to the campground.

**Contact:** Pike National Forest, South Platte Ranger District, 19316 Goddard Ranch Ct., Morrison, CO 80465; tel. (303) 275-5610.

## 56 Ouzel   7

Like the nearby Osprey camp, Ouzel is in a lovely, though primitive (and expensive) setting. Fishing access is outstanding; hence there's a fair amount of traffic from day-trippers casting their lines alongside those of campers. Considering that you can get full facilities for the same price down the road at Platte River Campground, this spot isn't the greatest deal, but if you're facing a cluster of full campgrounds without a reservation, it's not a bad option.

**Location:** On the South Platte River in Pike National Forest; map A3, grid i1.

**Campsites, facilities:** There are 13 primitive tent sites. Fire rings are provided, but there are no other facilities or drinking water. Leashed pets are permitted.

**Elevation:** 6,400 feet.

**Reservations, fees:** Reservations are not accepted. Sites are $9 a night.

**Open:** May to October.

**Directions:** From Conifer, drive one mile south on U.S. 285. Turn left on Forest Service Rd. 97 and continue approximately 20 miles southeast to the campground.

**Contact:** Pike National Forest, South Platte Ranger District, 19316 Goddard Ranch Ct., Morrison, CO 80465; tel. (303) 275-5610.

## 57 Indian Creek     6

Bordering a popular trailhead at the north end of the Rampart Range Motorcycle Area, this camp gets heavy use all season, especially from equestrian campers. The sites are just off the main road in a grove of ponderosa pine and fir trees, with some open sites. The Rampart Range tract is also a favorite with ATV riders; beware of high-speed motorbikes when hiking or riding.

**Location:** In the Rampart Range Motorcycle Area in Pike National Forest; map A3, grid i2.

**Campsites, facilities:** There are 11 sites for tents or RVs up to 16 feet long. Drinking water, picnic tables, fire grills, and vault toilets are provided. Leashed pets are permitted.

**Elevation:** 7,540 feet.

**Reservations, fees:** Reservations are not accepted. Sites are $10 a night.

**Open:** Mid-May to September.

**Directions:** From Interstate 25 just north of Castle Rock, take Exit 183 and drive six miles west on U.S. 85 to Sedalia. Turn left on Hwy. 67 and drive 10 miles southwest. Turn right on Forest Service Rd. 512 and continue one-quarter mile north to the campground.

**Contact:** Pike National Forest, South Platte Ranger District, 19316 Goddard Ranch Ct., Morrison, CO 80465; tel. (303) 275-5610.

## 58 Flat Rocks   6

This wooded camp lies at the foot of the Rampart Range between two popular trailheads, part of a network of several miles of well-developed routes. The scenic trails would be ideal for hiking, but sadly, have been overtaken by dirt bikes and ATV riders. In the words of one South Platte ranger: "Unless you want to take your life in your hands, don't hike here."

**Location:** In the Rampart Range Motorcycle Area in Pike National Forest; map A3, grid i2.

**Campsites, facilities:** There are 20 sites for tents or RVs up to 16 feet long. Drinking water, picnic tables, fire grills, and vault toilets are provided. Leashed pets are permitted.

**Elevation:** 8,000 feet.

**Reservations, fees:** Reservations are not accepted. Sites are $10 a night.

**Open:** Mid-May to September.

**Directions:** From Interstate 25 just north of Castle Rock, take Exit 183 and drive six miles west on U.S. 85 to Sedalia. Turn left on Hwy. 67 and drive 10 miles southwest. Turn left on Rampart Range Rd. and continue five miles to the campground.

**Contact:** Pike National Forest, South Platte Ranger District, 19316 Goddard Ranch Ct., Morrison, CO 80465; tel. (303) 275-5610.

## 59 Devil's Head    7

The last of three wooded campgrounds you pass going south on Rampart Range Rd., Devil's Head sits at the base of Devil's Head Peak (elevation 9,748 feet), the highest point in the Rampart Range. When viewed from the south, the peak does indeed resemble a demonic face, complete with horns. Devil's Head National Recreation Trail—the only hikable trail in the Rampart Range Motorcycle Area— leads 1.5 miles south up to Devil's Head Lookout, where Helen Dow, the U.S. Forest Service's first female fire lookout, once lived and worked. Vistas from the lookout are beautiful, with dramatic panoramic views of peaks to the west and plains to the east.

**Location:** In the Rampart Range Motorcycle Area in Pike National Forest; map A3, grid i2.

**Campsites, facilities:** There are 22 sites for tents or RVs up to 16 feet long. Drinking water, picnic tables, fire grills, and vault toilets are provided. Leashed pets are permitted.

**Elevation:** 8,800 feet.

**Reservations, fees:** Reservations are not accepted. Sites are $10 a night.

**Open:** Mid-May to September.

**Directions:** From Interstate 25 just north of Castle Rock, take Exit 183 and drive six miles west on U.S. 85 to Sedalia. Turn left on Hwy. 67 and drive 10 miles southwest. Turn left on Rampart Range Rd. and continue nine miles south to the campground entrance road.

**Contact:** Pike National Forest, South Platte Ranger District, 19316 Goddard Ranch Ct., Morrison, CO 80465; tel. (303) 275-5610.

## 60 Jackson Creek   7

Just south of the Rampart Range Motorcycle Area on Jackson Creek is this semi-wooded camp, a quieter alternative to the ATV camps to the north. The rough access road is popular with four-wheel-drive enthusiasts, who often continue beyond the camp to explore more primitive roads to the east. There are no hiking trails directly adjacent to camp, but there are several nearby, including Trail 649, a beautiful 6.2-mile loop that starts across Rampart Range Rd. from the Jackson Creek turnoff and circles back to the road, crossing Trout Creek on the way.

**Location:** Southwest of Castle Rock in Pike National Forest; map A3, grid i2.

**Campsites, facilities:** The nine sites are for tents only. Drinking water, picnic tables, fire grills, and vault toilets are provided. Leashed pets are permitted.

**Elevation:** 8,200 feet.

**Reservations, fees:** Reservations are not accepted. Sites are $10 a night.

**Open:** Mid-May to September.

**Directions:** From Interstate 25 just north of Castle Rock, take Exit 183 and drive six miles west on U.S. 85 to Sedalia. Turn left on Hwy. 67 and drive 10 miles southwest. Turn left on Rampart Range Rd. and continue approximately 14 miles south. Turn left on Jackson Creek Rd. and continue about two miles to the campground. Note: During wet weather, Jackson Creek Rd. may only be accessible by four-wheel-drive vehicle.

**Contact:** Pike National Forest, South Platte Ranger District, 19316 Goddard Ranch Ct., Morrison, CO 80465; tel. (303) 275-5610.

## 61 Castle Rock KOA    5

You can't miss this camp from the highway; simply look for the bright red train caboose at the entrance. The campground is located at the base of a sloping hill, with sunny RV sites close to the interstate and more secluded sites up the hill in the trees. Things can get pretty crowded in the middle of the summer, when the annual Renaissance Festival in Larkspur draws crowds of thousands to the area. Colorado Springs and Garden of the Gods provide day-trip options to the south.

**Location:** South of Castle Rock; map A3, grid i3.

**Campsites, facilities:** There are 90 sites for tents or RVs of any length, most with full hookups. Drinking water, picnic tables, fire grills, and bathrooms with hot showers are provided. Laundry facilities, a waste disposal station, a store, a swimming pool, and a sports field are available. Leashed pets are permitted.

**Elevation:** 6,200 feet.

**Reservations, fees:** Reservations are accepted; phone (800) KOA-3102. Sites are $18.50-23.50 a night.

**Open:** Mid-March to November.

**Directions:** From Castle Rock, drive seven miles south on Interstate 25 and take Exit 174. Turn west on Tomah Rd. and continue two blocks to the campground.

**Contact:** Castle Rock KOA, 6527 S. Interstate 25, Castle Rock, CO 80104; tel. (303) 681-2568.

## 62 Limon KOA    3

With long, orderly lines of RVs parked side by side and a few lots graced with patchy grass and scraggly shade trees, this campground resembles a mobile home park. The property is flat and open, with a sports field and recreation hall providing on-site activities, and is convenient to shops, restaurants, and Interstate 70.

**Location:** In Limon; map A3, grid i9.

**Campsites, facilities:** There are 70 sites for tents or RVs of any length, many with full hookups. Drinking water, picnic tables, fire grills, and bathrooms with hot showers are provided. Laundry facilities, a waste disposal station, a grocery store, swimming pool, sports field, and public phone are available. Leashed pets are permitted.

**Elevation:** 5,300 feet.

**Reservations, fees:** Reservations are accepted; phone (800) KOA-2129. Sites are $16.50-20.50 a night.

**Open:** April to November.

**Directions:** From Interstate 70 just east of Limon, take Exit 361 and drive one-half mile west on U.S. 24. Turn right at the KOA sign on Colorado Ave. and continue two blocks north to the campground.

**Contact:** Limon KOA, 575 Colorado Ave., Limon, CO 80828; tel. (719) 775-2151.

## 63 Twin Eagle Trailhead    7

Located near Tarryall Creek, this small trailhead camp is frequented by climbers and hikers headed into the Lost Creek Wilderness. The camp is primitive, with no fresh drinking water available, but it makes a perfectly adequate base camp.

**Location:** North of Lake George in Pike National Forest; map A3, grid j0.

**Campsites, facilities:** There are nine sites for tents or RVs up to 22 feet long. Vault toilets, picnic tables, and fire rings are provided, but there is no drinking water. Leashed pets are permitted.

**Elevation:** 8,600 feet.

**Reservations, fees:** Reservations are not accepted. Sites are $9 a night, and there's a $3 day use fee.

**Open:** May to October.

**Directions:** From the town of Lake George, drive one mile northwest on U.S. 24, turn right on Forest Service Rd. 77, and continue approximately 13 miles to the campground.

**Contact:** Pike National Forest, South Park Ranger District, P.O. Box 219, Fairplay, CO 80440; tel. (719) 836-2031.

## 64 Round Mountain   6

With easy access from the highway, this private camp gets a lot of traffic from folks who are simply driving by, looking for a place to plant their tent for the night. It's set in open forest, so shade is limited. There's not much at the camp itself, but opportunities for fishing, hiking, and biking are available within a short drive.

**Location:** Northwest of Lake George in Pike National Forest; map A3, grid j0.

**Campsites, facilities:** There are 17 sites for tents or RVs up to 30 feet long. Drinking water, picnic tables, fire grills, and vault toilets are provided. Leashed pets are permitted.

**Elevation:** 8,500 feet.

**Reservations, fees:** Reservations are not accepted. Sites are $9 a night.

**Open:** May to October.

**Directions:** From the town of Lake George, drive 6.5 miles northwest on U.S. 24 to the campground.

**Contact:** Pike National Forest, South Park Ranger District, P.O. Box 219, Fairplay, CO 80440; tel. (719) 836-2031.

## **65** Happy Meadows     7

Locally known as a great tubing put-in, this popular campground near the banks of the South Platte River has sites under tall cottonwood trees. Fishing is superb on this stretch of the river; the campsites are often used as day-use areas by anglers. Up the road is a trail that leads north along the river, providing beautiful scenery and a less crowded option for fishing.

**Location:** On the South Platte River in Pike National Forest; map A3, grid j0.

**Campsites, facilities:** There are seven sites for tents or RVs up to 22 feet long. Drinking water, picnic tables, fire grills, and vault toilets are provided. Leashed pets are permitted.

**Elevation:** 7,900 feet.

**Reservations, fees:** Reservations are not accepted. Sites are $9 a night.

**Open:** May to October.

**Directions:** From the town of Lake George, drive one mile northwest on U.S. 24, turn right on Forest Service Rd. 77, and drive one mile. Then turn right on Forest Service Rd. 112 and continue three-quarters of a mile to the campground.

**Contact:** Pike National Forest, South Park Ranger District, P.O. Box 219, Fairplay, CO 80440; tel. (719) 836-2031.

## **66** Trail Creek   7

Located next to little Trail Creek is this small and rustic camp, one of the few in the area offering an opportunity for solitude—and it's free. The sites are tiny and cozy, set well apart, and sheltered by trees. You have to haul in your own water and pack out your own trash, but that's a small price to pay for what seems like a custom-made retreat, right? Here's the catch: The peace is often unexpectedly marred by the persistent buzz of motorcycles and ATVs that roam nearby roads and trails. It's a crapshoot, though; sometimes they're there and sometimes they're not. Take your chances.

**Location:** Northwest of Woodland Park in Pike National Forest; map A3, grid j1.

**Campsites, facilities:** There are five tent sites and two sites for RVs up to 16 feet long. Picnic tables, fire grills, and vault toilets are provided, but there is no drinking water or trash service. Leashed pets are permitted.

**Elevation:** 7,800 feet.

**Reservations, fees:** Reservations are not accepted. Sites are $5 a night.

**Open:** May to October.

**Directions:** From Florissant on U.S. 24, turn north on County Rd. 3 and drive approximately 14 miles to the campground. Note: The access road is narrow and bumpy, not suitable for large trailers or RVs.

**Contact:** Pike National Forest, Pikes Peak Ranger District, 601 S. Weber St., Colorado Springs, CO 80903; tel. (719) 636-1602.

## **67** Wildhorn       6

A slightly more developed alternative to Trail Creek to the north, Wildhorn is most popular with ATV users who enjoy following the multi-use trail that begins at camp. The trail is also suitable for hikers and mountain bikers, but you run the risk of being mowed down by a high-speed motorbike. Although the camp technically closes in October, the gate remains open for those who wish to snow camp and cross-country ski in the winter.

**Location:** Northwest of Woodland Park in Pike National Forest; map A3, grid j1.

**Campsites, facilities:** There are nine sites for tents or RVs up to 23 feet long. Drinking water, picnic tables, fire grills, and vault toilets are provided, but there is no trash service, so you must pack out all refuse. Leashed pets are permitted.

**Elevation:** 9,100 feet.

**Reservations, fees:** Reservations are not accepted. Sites are $9 a night.

**Open:** May to October.

**Directions:** From Florissant on U.S. 24, turn north on County Rd. 3 and drive approximately eight miles to the campground. Note: The access road is narrow and bumpy, not suitable for large trailers or RVs.

**Contact:** Pike National Forest, Pikes Peak Ranger District, 601 S. Weber St., Colorado Springs, CO 80903; tel. (719) 636-1602.

## 68 Painted Rocks      7

Though a bit off the beaten path, this camp still provides easy access to the popular Manitou Lake area, which offers a variety of opportunities for fishing, hiking, and biking. The sites are secluded and wooded, set well back from the main road. Since you can't see the camp from Hwy. 67, many tourists miss this one, and it tends to get slightly less use than other camps in the region. To the west are a number of roads that double as mountain bike trails—but watch out for noisy motorcyclists who use them for racetracks.

**Location:** Northwest of Woodland Park in Pike National Forest; map A3, grid j1.

**Campsites, facilities:** There are 18 sites for tents or RVs up to 30 feet long. Drinking water, picnic tables, fire grills, and vault toilets are provided. Leashed pets are permitted.

**Elevation:** 7,800 feet.

**Reservations, fees:** Reservations are accepted; phone (877) 444-6777. There's an $8.65 reservation fee. You may also reserve sites at website: www.reserveusa.com. Sites are $10 a night.

**Open:** May to October.

**Directions:** From the junction of U.S. 24 and Hwy. 67 in Woodland Park, turn north on Hwy. 67 and drive six miles. Then turn left on Forest Service Rd. 78 and continue one-half mile to the campground.

**Contact:** Pike National Forest, Pikes Peak Ranger District, 601 S. Weber St., Colorado Springs, CO 80903; tel. (719) 636-1602.

## 69 Colorado      7

As the closest campground to Manitou Lake (where no overnight stays are permitted), this site gets fairly heavy use in summer and early fall. It's set in a dense stand of conifers, with interpretive programs in the summer. Manitou

Lake is a 16-acre blue jewel, surrounded by vibrant green grasses and colorful wildflowers, with good shoreline fishing for rainbow and cutthroat trout. A paved hiking/mountain biking trail runs north from camp to the lake.

**Location:** Northwest of Woodland Park in Pike National Forest; map A3, grid j2.

**Campsites, facilities:** There are 81 sites for tents or RVs up to 30 feet long. Drinking water, picnic tables, fire grills, and vault toilets are provided. A waste disposal station is available nearby at Pike Community Group Camp. Leashed pets are permitted.

**Elevation:** 7,800 feet.

**Reservations, fees:** Reservations are accepted; phone tel. (877) 444-6777. There's an $8.65 reservation fee. You may also reserve sites at website: www.reserveusa.com. Sites are $12 a night.

**Open:** May to October.

**Directions:** From the junction of U.S. 24 and Hwy. 67 in Woodland Park, turn north on Hwy. 67 and drive about six miles to the campground on the right.

**Contact:** Pike National Forest, Pikes Peak Ranger District, 601 S. Weber St., Colorado Springs, CO 80903; tel. (719) 636-1602.

## 70 Pike Community Group Camp   7

Easily accessible from Colorado Springs, this wooded camp is a perfect spot for a weekend family reunion or company retreat. There is a small amphitheater for presentations or meetings; a baseball field and horseshoe pit set the stage for a little friendly competition. The surrounding area offers something for everyone, from hiking or biking to fishing and four-wheel driving. See a U.S. Forest Service map for detailed information.

**Location:** Northwest of Woodland Park in Pike National Forest; map A3, grid j2.

**Campsites, facilities:** One large group area can accommodate up to 150 people. Drinking water, picnic tables, fire grills, and vault toilets are provided. A waste disposal station and a baseball field are available. Leashed pets are permitted.

**Elevation:** 7,700 feet.

**Reservations, fees:** Reservations are required; phone (877) 444-6777. There's an $8.65 reservation fee. You may also reserve sites at website: www.reserveusa.com. Fees vary depending on group size.

**Open:** May to October.

**Directions:** From the junction of U.S. 24 and Hwy. 67 in Woodland Park, turn north on Hwy. 67 and drive about five miles to the campground.

**Contact:** Pike National Forest, Pikes Peak Ranger District, 601 S. Weber St., Colorado Springs, CO 80903; tel. (719) 636-1602.

## 71 South Meadows      7

As the Pikes Peak Ranger District's only year-round campground, South Meadows is a great introduction to winter snow camping. It's a relatively short drive from Colorado Springs, and basic facilities are maintained through all seasons. The sites are roomy, with concrete pads and lots of pine trees. The Centennial Trail, a 4.2-mile paved hiking/mountain biking trail, begins at South Meadows, continuing on to Colorado Campground and ending at Manitou Lake. In the winter, it makes a great cross-country ski trail.

**Location:** Northwest of Woodland Park in Pike National Forest; map A3, grid j2.

**Campsites, facilities:** There are 64 sites for tents or RVs up to 30 feet long. Drinking water, picnic tables, fire grills, and vault toilets are provided. A waste disposal station is available nearby at Pike Community Group Camp. Leashed pets are permitted.

**Elevation:** 8,000 feet.

**Reservations, fees:** Reservations are accepted; phone (877) 444-6777. There's an $8.65 reservation fee. You may also reserve sites at website: www.reserveusa.com. Sites are $12 a night.

**Open:** Year-round.

**Directions:** From the junction of U.S. 24 and Hwy. 67 in Woodland Park, turn north on Hwy. 67 and drive about four miles to the campground on the left.

**Contact:** Pike National Forest, Pikes Peak Ranger District, 601 S. Weber St., Colorado Springs, CO 80903; tel. (719) 636-1602.

## 72 Red Rocks Group Camp   7

Slightly more rustic than the Pike Community Group Camp to the north (no baseball diamond or dump station here), Red Rocks still offers easy access from U.S. 24 and convenient proximity to lots of recreation options. The sites are just off the highway, set back in a grove of ponderosa pines.

**Location:** Northwest of Woodland Park in Pike National Forest; map A3, grid j2.

**Campsites, facilities:** One large group area can accommodate up to 125 people. Drinking water, picnic tables, fire grills, and vault toilets are provided. Leashed pets are permitted.

**Elevation:** 8,200 feet.

**Reservations, fees:** Reservations are required; phone (877) 444-6777. There's an $8.65 reservation fee. You may also reserve sites at website: www.reserveusa.com. Fees vary depending on group size.

**Open:** May to October.

**Directions:** From the junction of U.S. 24 and Hwy. 67 in Woodland Park, turn north on Hwy. 67 and drive about four miles to the campground on the right.

**Contact:** Pike National Forest, Pikes Peak Ranger District, 601 S. Weber St., Colorado Springs, CO 80903; tel. (719) 636-1602.

## 73 Diamond Campground and RV     7

In an area packed with campgrounds of every sort, from full-service resorts to dirt parking lots, Diamond Campground provides a happy medium. It has showers and even a place to do your laundry, but the heavily wooded sites, nestled beneath sturdy pine and spruce trees, afford an aura of backcountry seclusion. Hiking, biking, and fishing are all possible within a short drive, off Hwy. 67.

**Location:** North of Woodland Park; map A3, grid j1.

**Campsites, facilities:** There are 150 full-hookup sites for tents or RVs of any length. Drinking water, picnic tables, fire grills, and bathrooms with hot showers are provided. Laundry facilities, a waste disposal station, and a public phone are available. Leashed pets are permitted.

**Elevation:** 6,800 feet.

**Reservations, fees:** Reservations are accepted. Sites are $20 a night.

**Open:** May to October.

**Directions:** From the junction of U.S. 24 and Hwy. 67 in Woodland Park, drive three-quarters of a mile north on Hwy. 67.

**Contact:** Diamond Campground and RV, 900 N. Hwy. 67, Woodland Park, CO 80863; tel. (719) 687-9684.

## 74 Campground at Woodland Park     7

Tucked under a sun-dappled grove of tall pines and aspens, this camp feels as though it's much farther from the city than it really is. The environment is serene and quiet, with hiking trails nearby and a bike path running adjacent to the camp, plus miniature golf and a pool for those with more urban tastes. It's set near the beginning of the scenic Hwy. 67 corridor—a heavily visited tourist destination—but gets passed over by many campers on their way up to the U.S. Forest Service recreation areas. Nevertheless, you're likely to have plenty of company here, especially in July and August. On-site attractions include nightly movies and group activities.

**Location:** North of Woodland Park; map A3, grid j1.

**Campsites, facilities:** There are 40 tent sites and 85 sites for RVs of any length, many with full hookups. Drinking water, picnic tables, fire grills, and bathrooms with hot showers are provided. Laundry facilities, a waste disposal station, swimming pool, store, miniature golf course, and public phone are available. Leashed pets are permitted.

**Elevation:** 8,500 feet.

**Reservations, fees:** Reservations are accepted; phone (800) 808-2267. Sites are $18-23.50 a night.

**Open:** May to October.

**Directions:** From the junction of U.S. 24 and Hwy. 67 in Woodland Park, drive one-half mile north on Hwy. 67. Turn left on Bowman Ave. and continue 300 yards to the campground.

**Contact:** Campground at Woodland Park, P.O. Box 725, Woodland Park, CO 80866; tel. (719) 687-7575.

## 75 Town and Country Resort  7

It's a shame this park doesn't allow tent camping, because it would be a perfect spot to toss your sleeping bag on the ground and gaze up at the stars. The sites are adjacent to a small motel, on an incline covered with green grass and scattered trees. Each site has shaded picnic tables and level, concrete pads. If you're feeling lucky, you can hop on a shuttle to Cripple Creek for some low-stakes gambling, or stick around for one of the camp's nightly poker tournaments.

**Location:** North of Woodland Park; map A3, grid j1.

**Campsites, facilities:** There are 50 full-hookup sites for or RVs of any length. No tents are permitted. Drinking water, picnic tables, fire grills, and bathrooms with hot showers are provided. Laundry facilities, a waste disposal station, small store, motel rooms, and public phone are available. Leashed pets are permitted.

**Elevation:** 8,500 feet.

**Reservations, fees:** Reservations are accepted. Sites are $22-24.50 a night.

**Open:** Year-round.

**Directions:** From the junction of U.S. 24 and Hwy. 67 in Woodland Park, drive one-half mile north on Hwy. 67.

**Contact:** Town and Country Resort, P.O. Box 368, Woodland Park, CO 80866; tel. (719) 687-9518 or (800) 600-0399.

## 76 Coachlight RV Park and Motel    6

Set at the base of the hills surrounding Pikes Peak, Coachlight offers terraced, well-spaced sites and striking mountain views. The camp is enveloped in aspen, pine, and spruce trees, with hiking trails beckoning beyond into the neighboring hills and valleys. One drawback: It is on busy U.S. 24, and road noise can be a problem in the summer. Try to get a site far back off the road, so you'll be buffered by trees.

**Location:** In Woodland Park; map A3, grid j1.

**Campsites, facilities:** There are 60 sites for tents or RVs of any length, many with full hookups. Drinking water, picnic tables, fire grills, and bathrooms with hot showers are provided. Laundry facilities, a waste disposal station, motel rooms, and a public phone are available. Leashed pets are permitted.

**Elevation:** 8,400 feet.

**Reservations, fees:** Reservations are accepted. Sites are $15-20 a night.

**Open:** Year-round.

**Directions:** From the junction of U.S. 24 and Hwy. 67 in Woodland Park, drive one mile southeast on U.S. 24.

**Contact:** Coachlight RV Park and Motel, 19253 Hwy. 24, Woodland Park, CO 80863; tel. (719) 687-8732.

## 77 Lake of the Rockies Resort  8

Perched on the edge of a beautiful mountain lake, this full-service resort offers developed camping in a forested setting and opportunities for nonmotorized boating and fishing. Regular stocks of rainbow and cutthroat trout, channel catfish, and largemouth bass make for excellent fishing prospects. Hiking trails crisscross the property. Organized activities include Frisbee golf tournaments, miniature golf challenges, and basketball games. There's a swimming pool and hot tub for those who prefer to relax.

**Location:** On Monument Lake; map A3, grid j3.

**Campsites, facilities:** There are 70 tent sites and 185 sites for RVs of any length, many with full hookups. Drinking water, picnic tables, and bathrooms with hot showers are provided. Laundry facilities, a waste disposal station, store, swimming pool and hot tub, miniature golf, cabins, and boat rentals are available. Leashed pets are permitted.

**Elevation:** 6,900 feet.

**Reservations, fees:** Reservations are recommended. Sites are $14.50-28 a night.

**Open:** April to November.

**Directions:** From Interstate 25 at Monument, take Exit 161 and drive one-quarter mile south on County Rd. 5. Turn right on 3rd St. and go one-half mile west. At Front St., take a left and drive one block south. Then turn right on 2nd St., proceed west to Mitchell Ave., turn left, and continue one block south to the campground.

**Contact:** Lake of the Rockies Resort, 99 Mitchell Ave., Monument, CO 80132; tel. (719) 481-4227 or (800) 429-4228; e-mail: lor@rmi.net.

## 78 Springdale     7

Springdale, a lesser-known alternative to the popular camps at Rampart Reservoir, is easy to reach and offers basic amenities. The sites are pleasant and shady, set in a stand of ponderosa pine. A short drive away, the reservoir provides opportunities to fish, boat, and hike.

**Location:** Near Rampart Reservoir in Pike National Forest; map A3, grid j3.

**Campsites, facilities:** There are 14 tent sites. Picnic tables, fire grills, and vault toilets are provided, but there is no drinking water. Leashed pets are permitted.

**Elevation:** 9,100 feet.

**Reservations, fees:** Reservations are not accepted. Sites are $9 a night.

**Open:** Mid-May to mid-September.

**Directions:** From U.S. 24 at Woodland Park, turn east on Forest Service Rd. 22 and drive four miles. Then turn right on Forest Service Rd. 300 (Rampart Range Rd.) and continue one mile to the campground.

**Contact:** Pike National Forest, Pikes Peak Ranger District, 601 S. Weber St., Colorado Springs, CO 80903; tel. (719) 636-1602.

## 79 Thunder Ridge      7

Thunder Ridge overlooks the southern edge of Rampart Reservoir and is far enough away from the developed day-use facilities to feel remote and private. It's a wheelchair-friendly campground, with three sites developed specifically for the special needs of wheelchair users (see Meadow Ridge below for more wheelchair-accessible facilities). The relatively short camping season has city folks from Colorado Springs scrambling for sites on summer weekends; it's advisable to make a reservation well in advance. Boats (no-wake boating only) can be launched nearby, and fishing for rainbow trout is said to be quite good. Hiking trails trace the entire perimeter of the reservoir.

**Location:** On Rampart Reservoir in Pike National Forest; map A3, grid j3.

**Campsites, facilities:** There are 21 sites for tents or RVs up to 30 feet long. Drinking water, picnic tables, fire grills, and vault toilets are provided. A boat ramp and docks are available. Some facilities are wheelchair accessible. Leashed pets are permitted.

**Elevation:** 9,200 feet.

**Reservations, fees:** Reservations are accepted; phone (877) 444-6777. There's an $8.65 reservation fee. You may also reserve sites at website: www.reserveusa.com. Sites are $10 a night.

**Open:** June to September.

**Directions:** From U.S. 24 at Woodland Park, turn east on Forest Service Rd. 22 and drive four miles. Turn right on Forest Service Rd. 300 (Rampart Range Rd.) and continue four miles to the lake entrance. Follow signs to the campground.

**Contact:** Pike National Forest, Pikes Peak Ranger District, 601 S. Weber St., Colorado Springs, CO 80903; tel. (719) 636-1602.

## 80 Meadow Ridge       7

This camp sits high above Rampart Reservoir in a dense grove of ponderosa pine, not far from the Thunder Ridge camp. Southeast of the campground is the Business and Professional Women's Nature Trail, a short wheelchair-accessible interpretive trail that offers signs in Braille. Also nearby is Trail 700, which heads down to the reservoir and continues along the shoreline, with fishing access along the way. Keep heading east and you'll come to the Dikeside Boat Ramp and two scenic vista points.

**Location:** On Rampart Reservoir in Pike National Forest; map A3, grid j3.

**Campsites, facilities:** There are 19 sites for tents or RVs up to 30 feet long. Drinking water, picnic tables, fire grills, and vault toilets are provided. A boat ramp and docks are nearby. Some facilities are wheelchair accessible. Leashed pets are permitted.

**Elevation:** 9,200 feet.

**Reservations, fees:** Reservations are accepted; phone (877) 444-6777. There's an $8.65 reservation fee. You may also reserve sites at website: www.reserveusa.com. Sites are $10 a night.

**Open:** June to September.

**Directions:** From U.S. 24 at Woodland Park, turn east on Forest Service Rd. 22 and drive four miles. Then turn right on Forest Service Rd. 300 (Rampart Range Rd.) and continue four miles to the lake entrance. Follow signs to the campground.

**Contact:** Pike National Forest, Pikes Peak Ranger District, 601 S. Weber St., Colorado Springs, CO 80903; tel. (719) 636-1602.

## 81 Cadillac Jack's  3

Here in the dusty, dry plains of eastern Colorado, Cadillac Jack's provides a little relief from the sun, with a few leafy shade trees sprinkled among level, graveled campsites. The sites are adjacent to a conglomeration of shops—the owners call it a "trading post"—that include an antique store, pawnshop, and liquor store. Considering your other options (cheap roadside motels), it's not a bad overnight stop for highway travelers heading into or out of Colorado Springs.

**Location:** In Calhan; map A3, grid j6.

**Campsites, facilities:** There are 35 full-hookup sites for RVs of any length. No tents are allowed. Drinking water, picnic tables, fire grills, and flush toilets are provided. A waste disposal station, store, and public phone are available. Leashed pets are permitted.

**Elevation:** 6,400 feet.

**Reservations, fees:** Reservations are recommended. Sites are $18-20 a night.

**Open:** Year-round.

**Directions:** The campground is located on U.S. 24 on the western edge of Calhan.

**Contact:** Cadillac Jack's Campground, U.S. 24, Calhan, CO 80808; tel. (719) 347-2000.

PRICKLY PEAR CACTUS

# MAP A4

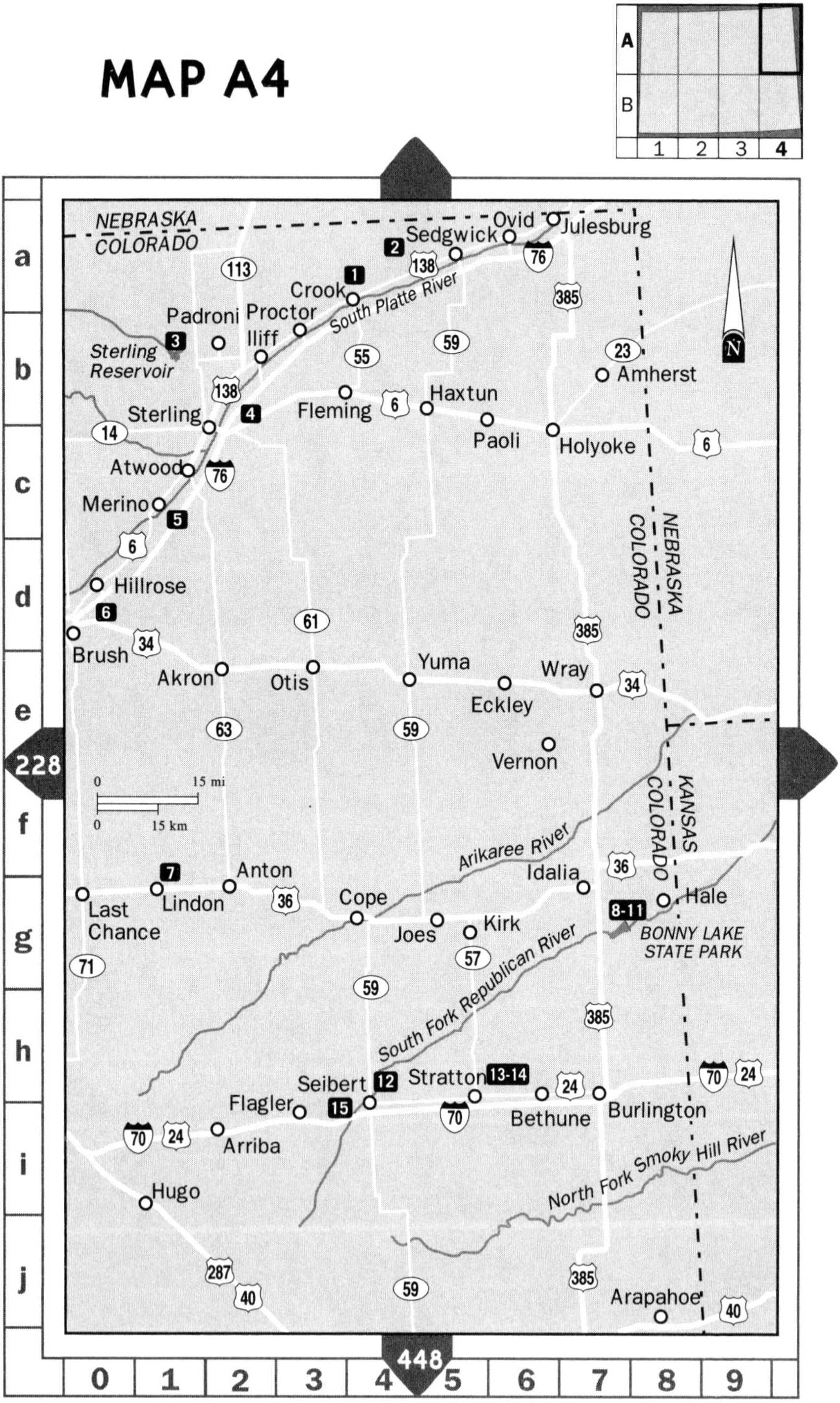

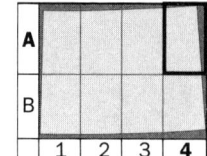

NEBRASKA
COLORADO

Ovid
Sedgwick
**2**
Julesburg
138
76
113
Crook
**1**
385
Proctor
Padroni
Iliff
South Platte River
**3**
55
59
23
Sterling
Reservoir
138
Amherst
b
Fleming
6
Haxtun
**4**
Sterling
Paoli
14
Holyoke
6
Atwood
76
Merino
**5**
6
Hillrose
**6**
385
Brush
34
61
Akron
Otis
Yuma
Wray
Eckley
34
63
59
Vernon

228

0        15 mi
0        15 km

Arikaree River
Idalia
**7**
Anton
36
Last
Lindon
36
Cope
Hale
**8-11**
Chance
Joes
Kirk
BONNY LAKE
STATE PARK
71
57
59
385
South Fork Republican River

Seibert
**12**
Stratton
**13-14**
70
24
Flagler
**15**
70
24
70
Bethune
Burlington
Arriba
North Fork Smoky Hill River
Hugo

287
40
59
385
Arapahoe
40

448

NEBRASKA
COLORADO

KANSAS
COLORADO

N

# CHAPTER A4

## ◼ Tamarack Ranch State Wildlife Area    2

This primitive wildlife area occupies a long, narrow section of the South Platte River bottom. Considered too shallow for most boating, it is visited primarily by hunters of small game and waterfowl. If it's fishing you're after, bypass the river; the only decent prospects in the wildlife area are at Tamarack Ranch Pond, where the fortunate angler might come away with a smallmouth bass or two. The "camping area" is really no more than a dirt parking lot, but there is nowhere else to camp for miles, so it makes a decent stopover if you plan to explore the wildlife area or just need a quiet spot to throw down your tent as you pass through eastern Colorado.

**Location:** On the South Platte River; map A4, grid a4.

**Campsites, facilities:** Dispersed camping is allowed in the dirt lot next to the check-in station. A vault toilet is provided, but there are no other facilities or drinking water. Leashed pets are permitted.

**Elevation:** 3,500 feet.

**Reservations, fees:** Reservations are not accepted. There is no fee.

**Open:** Year-round.

**Directions:** From Interstate 76, take the Crook exit and turn north on Hwy. 55. Continue approximately one-half mile to the park entrance.

**Contact:** Colorado Division of Wildlife, 6060 Broadway, Denver, CO 80216; tel. (303) 297-1192.

## ◻ Jumbo State Wildlife Area       3

Jumbo Reservoir covers more than 1,700 acres in high, dry sagebrush country. It is one of the few lakes in the eastern part of the state that allows waterskiing, PWC riding, and swimming. This means it can get fairly crowded in the summertime; however, it is so easily accessible that folks from neighboring towns simply come for the day and leave before sunset, so it's usually not too hard to find a camping spot. Anglers can try their hand at fishing for warm-water species including bass, crappie, and catfish.

**Location:** On Jumbo Reservoir; map A4, grid a4.

**Campsites, facilities:** Dispersed camping is allowed anywhere in the wildlife area. (Note: Do not drive off of designated roads.) Vault toilets and trash bins are provided, but there are no other facilities or drinking water. A boat ramp is available. Leashed pets are permitted.

**Elevation:** 3,500 feet.

**Reservations, fees:** Reservations are not accepted. The entrance fee is $3.

**Open:** Year-round.

**Directions:** From Interstate 76, take the Red Lion exit and head three miles north on County Rd. 93 to U.S. 138. Drive approximately one mile, turn northeast on County Rd. 95, and continue for two miles to the reservoir.

**Contact:** Colorado Division of Wildlife, 6060 Broadway, Denver, CO 80216; tel. (303) 297-1192.

## 3 North Sterling Reservoir State Park  4

This easy-access state park is a popular vacation destination for thousands of visitors annually. Its centerpiece is North Sterling Reservoir, a 3,000-acre gem set in the high eastern plains with expansive views of the surrounding vast prairie and high bluffs. Water sports are the preferred activities, with waterskiing, PWC riding, sailing, and swimming particularly popular during the summer months. Fishing is permitted year-round. The developed campsites are open and sparse— if you want a little more shade, head down to the primitive area south of the dam, where you can set up your tent amid groves of cottonwood trees. Limited hunting is permitted; call the park for details.

**Location:** On North Sterling Reservoir; map A4, grid b1.

**Campsites, facilities:** There are 50 developed sites for tents or RVs of any length. Drinking water, picnic tables, fire grills, shade shelters, and vault toilets are provided. Electric hookups and a waste disposal station are available. A more primitive (and less expensive) dispersed camping area is located south of the dam. Boat ramps and a full-service marina are available. Some facilities are wheelchair accessible. Leashed pets are permitted.

**Elevation:** 4,000 feet.

**Reservations, fees:** Reservations are accepted. Phone (303) 470-1144 or (800) 678-CAMP (800-678-2267) outside the Denver Metro area; there's a $7 reservation fee. Fees are $6 a night for primitive sites and $10-14 a night for developed sites, and there's a $4 entrance fee.

**Open:** Year-round.

**Directions:** From Interstate 76, take the Sterling exit. Go over a viaduct and through the first stoplight. At the second light, turn left on a one-way street and drive north to Main Street. Turn right on Main and proceed to North 7th Avenue. Turn right and continue 12 miles, following the signs to the park entrance.

**Contact:** North Sterling Reservoir State Park, 24005 County Rd. 330, Sterling, CO 80751; tel. (970) 522-3657.

## 4 Yogi Bear's Jellystone Park of Sterling    2

This place can look like Disneyland at the peak of the summer tourist season when dozens of kids cluster around the large pool, joyfully shrieking as they cannonball into the water. The rest of the resort resembles a kiddie park as well, complete with a playground, a game room, and a miniature golf course. As with all the Jellystone Park camps, this one offers a multitude of organized activities for families. Sites are large and well shaded by cottonwood and elm trees, and they are within walking distance of a large store that carries groceries and goodies.

**Location:** Near Sterling; map A4, grid b3.

**Campsites, facilities:** There are 90 sites for tents or RVs of any length, most with full hookups. Drinking water, picnic tables, fire grills, and bathrooms with hot showers are provided. Also on the grounds are laundry facilities, a waste disposal station, store, arcade, swimming pool, movie theater, and miniature golf course. Leashed pets are permitted.

**Elevation:** 4,000 feet.

**Reservations, fees:** Reservations are accepted; phone (800) 569-1824. Sites are $18-24.50 a night.

**Open:** Year-round.

**Directions:** From Interstate 76, take the Sterling exit and turn east on U.S. 6. The park is one-quarter mile down the road.

**Contact:** Yogi Bear's Jellystone Park of Sterling, 22018 U.S. 6, Sterling, CO 80751; tel. (970) 522-2233; e-mail: yogibearpark@yahoo.com.

## 5 Prewitt Reservoir State Wildlife Area     4

Although it's not much to look at, Prewitt is one of the only places around to find a bit of relief from the summer's heat and dry, brown plains. The reservoir, covering 2,500 acres, is used primarily as an irrigation facility but also permits no-wake boating and fishing for bass and walleye. Camping is limited to the western side of the reservoir; most of the eastern shore borders private property. The best spots are at the southwestern end, where groves of cottonwoods provide a little shade and privacy. In the fall, the place is usually overrun by small game hunters.

**Location:** Northeast of Brush; map A4, grid c1.

**Campsites, facilities:** Dispersed camping is permitted anywhere along the western shore of the reservoir. A vault toilet is provided, but there are no other facilities or drinking water. A boat ramp is available. Leashed pets are permitted.

**Elevation:** 4,000 feet.

**Reservations, fees:** Reservations are not accepted. The entrance fee is $3.

**Open:** Year-round.

**Directions:** From Interstate 76 just east of Fort Morgan, take Exit 92 and turn east on U.S. 6. Drive 15 miles to a signed access road and continue one mile to the entrance.

**Contact:** Colorado Division of Wildlife, 6060 Broadway, Denver, CO 80216; tel. (303) 297-1192.

## 6 Brush Memorial Campground      5

Set in the middle of a city park, the sites at this campground are roomy and shaded, set in soft grass surrounded by large trees. A golf course, tennis courts, basketball courts, and a softball field are available to those with athletic inclinations, along with a swimming pool and sunbathing area for those who prefer to lounge. If you're just planning a single night's stopover along Interstate 76, this is a perfect choice. How many campgrounds offer all amenities, including hot showers, for free?

**Location:** In Brush; map A4, grid d0.

**Campsites, facilities:** There are 10 tent sites and 24 sites with electric hookups for RVs of any length. Picnic tables, drinking water, a waste disposal station, bathrooms with hot showers, and a swimming pool are provided. Some facilities are wheelchair accessible. Leashed pets are permitted.

**Elevation:** 3,700 feet.

**Reservations, fees:** Reservations are not accepted. The first night is free; there is a $10 fee for every night thereafter.

**Open:** Memorial Day through October.

**Directions:** From Interstate 76 east of Fort Morgan, take Exit 89A toward Brush and turn south on U.S. 34 (Colorado Avenue). Drive to Edison St. and go through the stop sign. Turn right on North Railway Street. Go to Clayton St. and turn south, cross the railroad tracks, and continue two blocks to the park entrance.

**Contact:** Brush Memorial Campground, P.O. Box 363, Brush, CO 80723; tel. (970) 842-5001.

## ■ Meadowlark RV Park  4

Basic and clean, this simple campground provides a decent layover for highway travelers. The RV sites are grassy and orderly, set next to a motel and home-style cafe, with tent sites in a large adjacent field. No fire grills or barbecues are provided because according to the owner, "everyone wants to eat in the cafe anyway." A few pine trees dot the property, but there's no shade to speak of.

**Location:** In Lindon; map A4, grid g1.

**Campsites, facilities:** There are 12 sites for RVs of any length, most with full hookups, and a separate area for tents. Drinking water, a few picnic tables, a community fire pit, and bathrooms with hot showers are provided. Laundry facilities, a waste disposal station, a cafe, public phone, and motel rooms are available. Leashed pets are permitted.

**Elevation:** 4,800 feet.

**Reservations, fees:** Reservations are accepted. Sites are $8-21 a night.

**Open:** May to September.

**Directions:** From U.S. 36 in Lindon, turn north on County Rd. S and drive 400 feet to the campground.

**Contact:** Meadowlark RV Park, 12120 County Rd. S, Lindon, CO 80740; tel. (970) 383-2298.

## ■ Foster Grove        7

Encircled by lush wetlands, Bonny Lake is a lovely, flourishing oasis in the dry plains of eastern Colorado. Of the four campgrounds on the lake, Foster Grove is the quietest and most secluded. Set back from the water's edge on the northwest side of the lake, the camp is sheltered from the buzz of water traffic, and most sites are shady and secluded. This is also the best spot on the lake for viewing the park's abundant wildlife; campers may be visited by deer, badgers, rabbits, coyotes, or some of the park's 250 species of birds, including wood ducks, prairie falcons, osprey, and bald eagles. Limited hunting is permitted; call the park for details.

**Location:** In Bonny Lake State Park, near the Kansas border; map A4, grid g7.

**Campsites, facilities:** There are 49 sites for tents or RVs of any length. Drinking water, picnic tables, fire grills, vault toilets, and bathrooms with flush toilets and hot showers are provided. A waste disposal station is available. Leashed pets are permitted.

**Elevation:** 3,700 feet.

**Reservations, fees:** Reservations are required. Phone (303) 470-1144 or (800) 678-CAMP (800-678-2267) outside the Denver Metro area; there's a $7 reservation fee.

Sites are $10 a night, and there's a $4 entrance fee.

**Open:** Year-round with limited winter facilities.

**Directions:** From Interstate 70 east of Denver, take the Burlington exit and turn north on U.S. 385. Drive approximately 24 miles, turn right on County Rd. 2, and continue east to the park entrance.

**Contact:** Bonny Lake State Park, 30010 County Rd. 3, Idalia, CO 80735; tel. (970) 354-7306.

## 🖥 Wagon Wheel         7

Wagon Wheel is the most developed campground on Bonny Lake, the only one with electric hookups for RVs and wheelchair-accessible facilities. It offers good views of the 1,900-acre lake and is close to the marina and main boat docks, making it attractive to campers with boats. The camp sits right on the lake's south shore, with plenty of shade trees sprinkled among the sites. Limited hunting is permitted.

**Location:** In Bonny Lake State Park, near the Kansas border; map A4, grid g7.

**Campsites, facilities:** There are 87 sites for tents or RVs of any length. Drinking water, picnic tables, fire grills, vault toilets, and bathrooms with flush toilets and hot showers are provided. Electric hookups, a waste disposal station, a swimming beach, a boat ramp, and a marina are available. Some facilities are wheelchair accessible. Leashed pets are permitted.

**Elevation:** 3,700 feet.

**Reservations, fees:** Reservations are required. Phone (303) 470-1144 or (800) 678-CAMP (800-678-2267) outside the Denver Metro area; there's a $7 reservation fee. Sites are $10-14 a night, and there's a $4 entrance fee.

**Open:** Year-round with limited winter facilities.

**Directions:** From Interstate 70 east of Denver, take the Burlington exit and turn north on U.S. 385. Drive approximately 24 miles, turn right on County Rd. 2, and continue east to the park entrance.

**Contact:** Bonny Lake State Park, 30010 County Rd. 3, Idalia, CO 80735; tel. (970) 354-7306.

## 🔟 North Cove         8

Set next to a boat ramp on a quiet, remote northern finger of Bonny Lake, North Cove is best known as "the fisherman's campground." Although waterskiing is permitted on the main body of the lake, it is prohibited in this area, so anglers and swimmers can take advantage of calm, quiet waters. Bonny offers excellent prospects for bass, walleye, wiper, and northern pike as well as abundant bluegill and crappie. Limited hunting is permitted; call for details. Each campsite has a beautiful view of the lake, and just north of camp is a short self-guided nature hike where you can enjoy spectacular native wildflower displays in late spring and summer.

**Location:** In Bonny Lake State Park, near the Kansas border; map A4, grid g7.

**Campsites, facilities:** There are 21 sites for tents or RVs of any length, as well as a large group area. Drinking water, picnic tables, fire grills, and vault toilets are provided. Leashed pets are permitted.

**Elevation:** 3,700 feet.

**Reservations, fees:** Reservations are required. Phone (303) 470-1144 or (800) 678-CAMP (800-678-2267) outside the Denver Metro area; there's a $7 reservation fee. Sites are $10 a night, and there's a $4 entrance fee.

**Open:** Year-round.

**Directions:** From Interstate 70 east of Denver, take the Burlington exit and turn north on U.S. 385. Drive approximately 24 miles, turn right on County Rd. 2, and continue east to the park entrance.

**Contact:** Bonny Lake State Park, 30010 County Rd. 3, Idalia, CO 80735; tel. (970) 354-7306.

## **11** East Beach          6

This camp is most attractive to boaters and families who want to be near the beach. There is a large swimming beach adjacent to the campground, and boaters can park their craft right on the shoreline. The sites are mostly open and sunny; the shadiest spots are in the tent-only area. Hikers can hop on the nearby road and walk an eight-mile loop around the lake. Limited hunting is permitted.

**Location:** In Bonny Lake State Park, near the Kansas border; map A4, grid g7.

**Campsites, facilities:** There are 26 sites for tents or RVs of any length, and 12 sites for tents only. Drinking water, picnic tables, fire grills, and vault toilets are provided. Leashed pets are permitted.

**Elevation:** 3,700 feet.

**Reservations, fees:** Reservations are required. Phone (303) 470-1144 or (800) 678-CAMP (800-678-2267) outside the Denver Metro area; there's a $7 reservation fee. Sites are $10 a night, and there's a $4 entrance fee.

**Open:** Year-round.

**Directions:** From Interstate 70 east of Denver, take the Burlington exit and turn north on U.S. 385. Drive approximately 24 miles, turn right on County Rd. 2, and continue east to the park entrance.

**Contact:** Bonny Lake State Park, 30010 County Rd. 3, Idalia, CO 80735; tel. (970) 354-7306.

## **12** Gorton's Shady Grove RV Park   3

Although this camp offers pleasant, grassy sites sheltered by large elm trees, its proximity to Interstate 70 often precludes a peaceful night's sleep. Gorton's is the only game in town, though, and with spotless facilities and friendly owners, it's a convenient and adequate spot to spend the night.

**Location:** In Seibert; map A4, grid h4.

**Campsites, facilities:** There are six tent sites and 32 sites for RVs of any length, most with full hookups. Drinking water, picnic tables, fire grills, and bathrooms with hot showers are provided. Laundry facilities, a waste disposal station, a hot tub, cabins, and a public phone are available. Leashed pets are permitted.

**Elevation:** 4,700 feet.

**Reservations, fees:** Reservations are accepted. Sites are $11-18 a night.

**Open:** May to September.

**Directions:** From Interstate 70 in Seibert, take Exit 405 and drive one block north on Hwy. 59 to the campground entrance.

**Contact:** Gorton's Shady Grove RV Park, P.O. Box 178, Seibert, CO 80834; tel. (970) 664-2218.

## ⓭ Marshall Ash Village RV Park   4

This campground is attached to a car/tractor/truck museum and craft shop. Not perhaps your ideal camping experience? It's really not so bad. Most of the graveled sites are shaded, and there's a little park next door, with a playground, covered picnic tables, and grass. In the spring, the surrounding wheat fields can be quite lovely if you don't mind looking past the freeway to see them. One weird feature: The showers are located inside the adjacent convenience store, so you'll have to expose your towel-turbaned head to truckers and tourists passing through.

**Location:** In Stratton; map A4, grid h6.

**Campsites, facilities:** There are 33 full-hookup sites for tents or RVs of any length. Drinking water, picnic tables, bathrooms with hot showers are provided. A convenience store, laundry facilities, gas station, gift shop, and public phone are available. Leashed pets are permitted.

**Elevation:** 4,500 feet.

**Reservations, fees:** Reservations are accepted; phone (800) 577-5795. Sites are $12-22 a night.

**Open:** Year-round.

**Directions:** From Interstate 70 at Stratton, take Exit 419 and follow the signs to Marshall Ash Village.

**Contact:** Marshall Ash Village RV Park, 818 Colorado Ave., Stratton, CO 80836; tel. (719) 348-5141.

## ⓮ Trail's End Campground    2

Trail's End, a campground on the outskirts of Stratton, makes a decent stopover for Interstate 70 travelers. The 30 sites, many of which are shaded by tall elm trees, are patchworked with scraggly grass, and the atmosphere is quiet and calm. In the summertime, the hosts deliver home-baked cookies nightly—yum. And hey, they have a hot tub—a welcome sight after a long day of driving.

**Location:** In Stratton; map A4, grid h6.

**Campsites, facilities:** There are 30 sites for tents or RVs of any length, most with full hookups. Drinking water, picnic tables, fire grills, and bathrooms with hot showers are provided. Laundry facilities, a waste disposal station, small store, swimming pool and hot tub, miniature golf course, and camping cabins are also available. Leashed pets are permitted.

**Elevation:** 4,500 feet.

**Reservations, fees:** Reservations are recommended. Sites are $14-18 a night.

**Open:** Year-round.

**Directions:** From Interstate 70 east of Denver, take the Stratton exit and drive one block north. Turn right on 7th St. and continue to the corner of 7th and New York Streets.

**Contact:** Trail's End Campground, P.O. Box 419, Stratton, CO 80836; tel. (719) 348-

5529 or (800) 777-6042; e-mail: tctravis@ria.net

## 15 Flagler State Wildlife Area      4

Like many of the state's wildlife areas, Flagler has a remote, even desolate feel upon first examination, but once you experience the spectacular sunsets and sunrises you may deem it paradise. Formerly a state park, Flagler is now a primitive region used mainly for fishing and hunting. Picnic shelters and old campsites are all that remain of the developed state park facilities, but the Colorado Division of Wildlife now maintains vault toilets and water service. The reservoir is small, just 150 acres, but is stocked regularly with smallmouth and largemouth bass and is a popular spot for anglers in the fall. Since it is used as an irrigation facility, the reservoir's water levels can fluctuate; boaters should watch for submerged hazards. Only no-wake boating is allowed.

**Location:** On Flagler Reservoir; map A4, grid i4.

**Campsites, facilities:** There are a few primitive campsites just past the entrance station. Drinking water, picnic tables with shade shelters, and vault toilets are provided. A boat ramp is available. Leashed pets are permitted.

**Elevation:** 4,500 feet.

**Reservations, fees:** Reservations are not accepted. There is no fee.

**Open:** Year-round.

**Directions:** From Flagler, drive five miles east on County Rd. 4 to the reservoir.

**Contact:** Colorado Division of Wildlife, 6060 Broadway, Denver, CO 80216; tel. (303) 297-1192.

FALL ASPENS

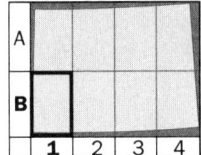

**94**

**332**

Whitewater

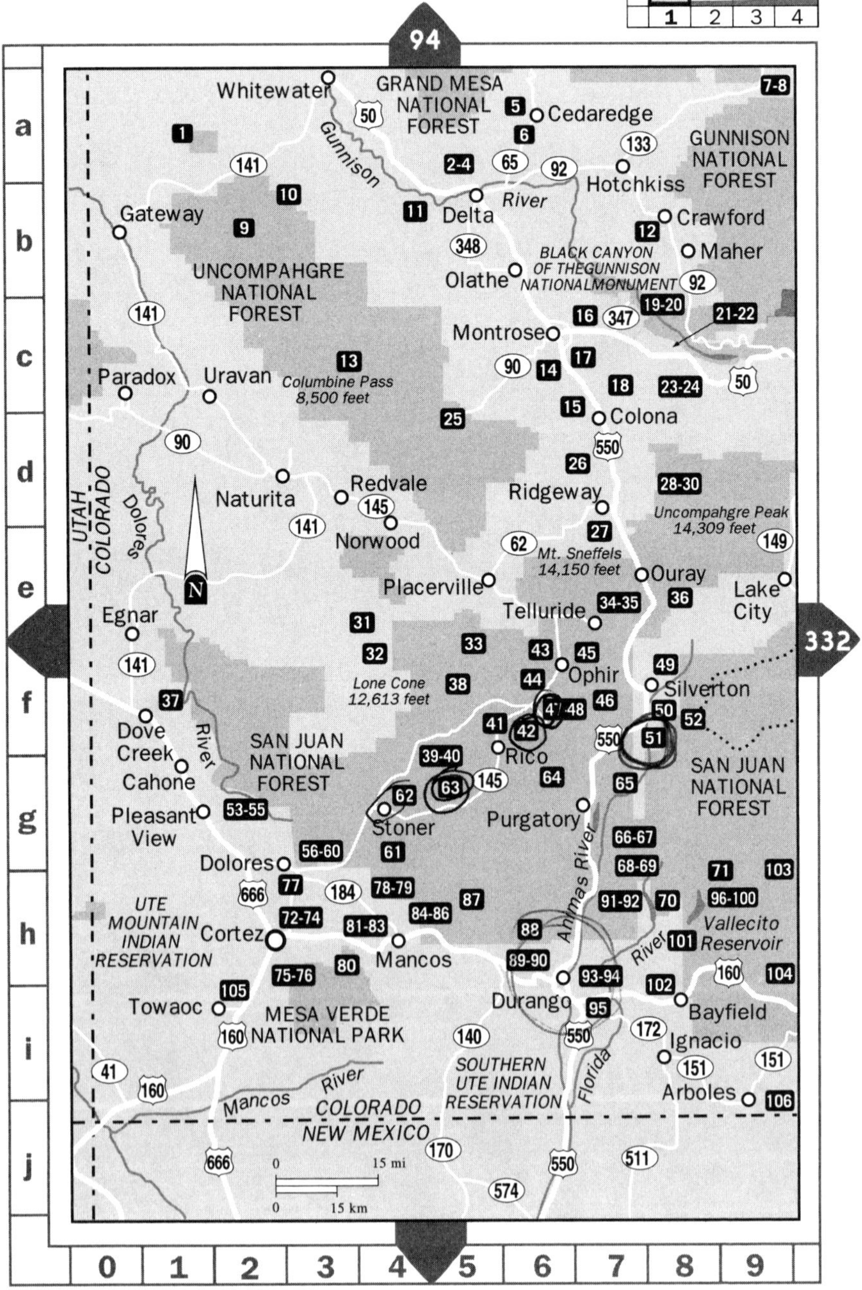

GRAND MESA NATIONAL FOREST

7-8

1

5

Cedaredge

6

133

GUNNISON NATIONAL FOREST

141

2-4

65

92

Hotchkiss

10

11

Delta

*River*

Gateway

9

12

Crawford

Maher

UNCOMPAHGRE NATIONAL FOREST

348

Olathe

BLACK CANYON OF THE GUNNISON NATIONAL MONUMENT

92

141

16

347

19-20

21-22

Montrose

90

17

14

50

Paradox

Uravan

13

Columbine Pass 8,500 feet

18

23-24

15

Colona

90

25

26

550

28-30

Naturita

Redvale

145

Ridgeway

Uncompahgre Peak 14,309 feet

149

141

Norwood

27

62

Mt. Sneffels 14,150 feet

Ouray

Lake City

Egnar

Placerville

Telluride

34-35

36

141

31

32

33

43

45

49

Silverton

52

37

38

44

Ophir

46

Dove Creek

Lone Cone 12,613 feet

41

47

48

50

Cahone

42

51

Pleasant View

39-40

Rico

64

65

SAN JUAN NATIONAL FOREST

Dolores

62

63

145

53-55

Stoner

61

Purgatory

66-67

56-60

68-69

71

103

77

184

78-79

91-92

70

96-100

UTE MOUNTAIN INDIAN RESERVATION

666

72-74

81-83

84-86

87

88

101

Vallecito Reservoir

Cortez

Mancos

89-90

93-94

102

160

104

75-76

80

105

Durango

95

172

Bayfield

Towaoc

160

MESA VERDE NATIONAL PARK

140

550

Ignacio

151

SOUTHERN UTE INDIAN RESERVATION

151

41

160

*River*

Arboles

106

Mancos

COLORADO

NEW MEXICO

666

170

0     15 mi

0     15 km

550

574

511

280 Colorado Camping

# CHAPTER B1

**❶ Haypress**  7

This camp covers a tiny square of national forest land south of Grand Junction, adjacent to one of three tiny reservoirs in the Fruita Division. It's so remote and primitive that it gets little use from anyone but die-hard anglers casting their lines in search of elusive rainbow trout. The area is quite hot in the summer, relieved only in spots by scrubby piñon pines. The little reservoir offers a bit of coolness, but be sure to bring your own drinking water.

**Location:** On Little Fruita Reservoir No. 3 in Grand Mesa National Forest; map B1, grid a1.

**Campsites, facilities:** There are 11 sites for tents or RVs up to 16 feet long. Picnic tables, fire grills, and vault toilets are provided, but there is no drinking water. Leashed pets are permitted.

**Elevation:** 9,300 feet.

**Reservations, fees:** Reservations are not accepted. There is no fee.

**Open:** June to November.

**Directions:** From Grand Junction, turn west on Hwy. 340 and drive 10 miles. Turn left on County Rd. 400 and continue 20 miles south to the campground.

**Contact:** Grand Mesa National Forest, Grand Junction Ranger District, 764 Horizon Dr., Room 115, Grand Junction, CO 81506; tel. (970) 242-8211.

**❷ Riverwood Inn and RV Park**  6

These sites are in a large thicket of shade trees, squeezed between a tiny fishing pond and the banks of the Gunnison River. Adjacent to camp is a small motel with full facilities and friendly hosts. If possible, try to reserve a site close to the river to block out traffic noise. Guided rafting trips are available nearby through several local outfitters. Kayaking and tubing are also popular on this stretch of river.

**Location:** On the Gunnison River; map B1, grid a5.

**Campsites, facilities:** There are 40 sites for tents or RVs of any length, most with full hookups. Drinking water, picnic tables, fire grills, and bathrooms with hot showers are provided. Laundry facilities, motel rooms, and a public phone are available. Leashed pets are permitted.

**Elevation:** 5,000 feet.

**Reservations, fees:** Reservations are accepted. Sites are $11-21.50 a night.

**Open:** Year-round.

**Directions:** From the junction of U.S. 50 and Hwy. 92 in Delta, drive one-half mile north on U.S. 50.

**Contact:** Riverwood Inn and RV Park, 677N. U.S. 50, Delta, CO 81416; tel. (970) 874-5787.

**❸ Flying A Motel and RV Park**  6

Like its neighbor the Riverwood Inn, this camp also offers riverside sites and fishing access. The sites are well maintained and grassy, shaded by robust willows and adjacent to a hiking trail that runs along the river. Launch your own boat or kayak right from camp, or let the hosts arrange a guided rafting trip for a group of any size. A night's stay includes two free passes to the nearby recreation center at Confluence Park, where you can use the swimming pool, take exercise classes, or enjoy a hot tub and sauna.

**Location:** On the Gunnison River; map B1, grid a5.

**Campsites, facilities:** There are 35 sites for tents or RVs of any length, most with full hookups. Drinking water, picnic tables, fire grills, and bathrooms with hot showers are provided. Laundry facilities, a waste disposal station, small store, motel rooms, and boat dock with a ramp are available. Leashed pets are permitted (for a fee).

**Elevation:** 5,000 feet.

**Reservations, fees:** Reservations are accepted. Sites are $16-24 a night.

**Open:** Year-round.

**Directions:** From the junction of U.S. 50 and Hwy. 92 in Delta, drive one-half mile north on U.S. 50.

**Contact:** Flying A Motel and RV Park, 676N. U.S. 50, Delta, CO 81416; tel. (970) 874-9659 or (888) 340-4689; e-mail: flyinga@wic.net.

## 🔟 Delta-Grand Mesa KOA     5

Offering easy access to hiking and exploring on the Grand Mesa, this KOA is a full-service alternative for highway travelers. Sites are level, with and without shade, and the facilities are clean and modern. The hot tub is an especially welcome treat after a long day of trekking around the Grand Mesa.

**Location:** Near the Grand Mesa; map B1, grid a5.

**Campsites, facilities:** There are 50 sites for tents or RVs of any length, most with full hookups. Drinking water, picnic tables, fire grills, and bathrooms with hot showers are provided. Laundry facilities, a waste disposal station, small store, swimming pool and hot tub, and public phone are available. Leashed pets are permitted.

**Elevation:** 5,000 feet.

**Reservations, fees:** Reservations are accepted; phone (800) KOA-3351. Sites are $18-25 a night.

**Open:** April to October.

**Directions:** From the junction of U.S. 50 and Hwy. 92 in Delta, drive one mile east on Hwy. 92. Turn left at the Ferrell Gas Gasamat and continue one block north.

**Contact:** Delta-Grand Mesa KOA, 1675 Hwy. 92, Delta, CO 81416; tel. (970) 874-3918.

## 🔟 Aspen Trails Campground    7

Aspen Trails has roomy sites in a meadow of scraggly grass, some with willows for shade. Youngs Creek runs nearby, providing a pleasing ambience but no fish (excellent fishing is available, however, at several mountain lakes and streams within driving distance). Highway 65 is also called the Grand Mesa Scenic Byway; if you take it north, you'll be treated to views of cool forests and sparkling alpine lakes, plus beautiful mountain views in Grand Mesa National Forest.

**Location:** Near Cedaredge; map B1, grid a6.

**Campsites, facilities:** There are 30 sites for tents or RVs of any length, many with full hookups. Drinking water, picnic tables, fire grills, and bathrooms with hot showers are provided. A waste disposal station, a swimming pool, a snack bar, a store, and a public phone are available. Leashed pets are permitted.

**Elevation:** 6,800 feet.

**Reservations, fees:** Reservations are accepted. Sites are $14-19.50 a night.

**Open:** Year-round.

**Directions:** From Cedaredge, drive three miles north on Hwy. 65.

**Contact:** Aspen Trails Campground, 1997 Hwy. 65, Cedaredge, CO 81413; tel. (970) 856-6321 or (888) 856-1101.

## 6 Shady Creek RV Park    7

Strictly adults only (the owner described it as a "senior park"), this camp features 16 gravel sites, each shaded by mature trees. Surface Creek runs through the camp, providing excellent fishing. Shops and restaurants in Cedaredge are within walking distance, and an 18-hole golf course is nearby.

**Location:** In Cedaredge; map B1, grid a6.

**Campsites, facilities:** There are 16 full-hookup sites for RVs of any length. Tents are not allowed Drinking water, picnic tables, and bathrooms with hot showers are provided. Pets are permitted, but children are not.

**Elevation:** 6,200 feet.

**Reservations, fees:** Reservations are accepted. Sites are $18.75 a night.

**Open:** Year-round.

**Directions:** The park is located in Cedaredge at 205 N. Grand Mesa Dr. (Hwy. 65).

**Contact:** Shady Creek RV Park, 205 N. Grand Mesa Dr., Cedaredge, CO 81413; tel. (970) 856-7522.

## 7 Crystal Meadows Ranch     9

As you turn off Hwy. 133 on the rugged road to Crested Butte, you enter a wonderful, craggy wilderness, at the entrance of which is Crystal Meadows Ranch. The ranch is sprawled on the floor of a beautiful valley backed by a tree-covered mountainside and cut through by cold, clear Anthracite Creek (excellent fishing). The campsites are located well back from the road; many are shaded by conifers, while others are open and sunny. The ranch also boasts a full-service but down-to-earth resort, with cabins, restaurant, and private fishing pond. Hiking trails are adjacent to the campground, and the Raggeds Wilderness is accessible within a short drive.

**Location:** Near Somerset; map B1, grid a9.

**Campsites, facilities:** There are 25 sites for tents or RVs of any length, most with full hookups. Drinking water, picnic tables, fire grills, and bathrooms with hot showers are provided. Laundry facilities, a store, cafe, public phone, and cabins are available. Leashed pets are permitted.

**Elevation:** 6,300 feet.

**Reservations, fees:** Reservations are accepted. Sites are $16-21 a night.

**Open:** June to November.

**Directions:** From Somerset, drive six miles east on Hwy. 133. Turn right on County Rd. 12 and continue one-half mile south to the campground.

**Contact:** Crystal Meadows Ranch, 30682 County Rd. 12, Somerset, CO 81434; tel. (970) 929-5656.

## 8 Paonia State Park      9

You must bring all your own supplies, including drinking water, to this primitive camp, but the extra work is well worth it. Long, finger-shaped Paonia Reservoir covers more than 300 surface acres, though it feels much smaller and private, with huge bordering mountains and lush vegetation providing a sense of deep seclusion. Seven campsites are near the northeastern shore not far from the boat ramp, and eight more lie on the opposite side of the reservoir near a small stream. All are shaded by tall spruce trees and offer convenient access to the water. Every type of boating is allowed—the long, thin lake corridor is especially popular with speed-demon water-skiers—and fishing for rainbow trout and northern pike is excellent. There are no formal trails in the park, but you can hike or ride horseback along much of the shoreline, which is virtually covered with wildflowers in midsummer.

**Location:** Near the Raggeds Wilderness; map B1, grid a9.

**Campsites, facilities:** There are 15 sites for tents or RVs up to 40 feet long. Drinking water, picnic tables, fire grills, and vault toilets are provided. A boat ramp is nearby. Leashed pets are permitted.

**Elevation:** 6,500 feet.

**Reservations, fees:** Reservations are accepted; phone (303) 470-1144 or (800) 678-CAMP (800-678-2267) outside the Denver Metro area; there's a $7 reservation fee. Sites are $10 a night, and there's a $4 entrance fee.

**Open:** Year-round.

**Directions:** From Carbondale, drive 45 miles south on Hwy. 133.

**Contact:** Paonia State Park, P.O. Box 147, Crawford, CO 81415; tel. (970) 921-5721.

## 9 Divide Fork   6

Divide Fork is a basic but pleasant U.S. Forest Service campground in the remote reaches of Uncompahgre National Forest. Some sites are in an open meadow; others are back in a forest of pine brightened with a few aspens. Use is fairly light and there's no charge, so if you simply need a quiet spot to spend the night, the camp is a bargain.

**Location:** South of Grand Junction in Uncompahgre National Forest; map B1, grid b2.

**Campsites, facilities:** There are 11 sites for tents or RVs up to 16 feet long. Drinking water, picnic tables, fire grills, and vault toilets are provided. Leashed pets are permitted.

**Elevation:** 9,200 feet.

**Reservations, fees:** Reservations are not accepted. There is no fee.

**Open:** June to October.

**Directions:** From Grand Junction, drive approximately seven miles south on U.S. 50 to Whitewater. Turn right on Hwy. 141 and drive 13 miles southwest. Then turn left on Forest Service Rd. 402 and continue 15 miles southwest to the campground.

**Contact:** Uncompahgre National Forest, Grand Junction Ranger District, 764 Horizon Dr., Room 115, Grand Junction, CO 81506; tel. (970) 242-8211.

## 🔟 Big Dominguez    6

No one ends up here by accident. This is a strictly do-it-yourself spot: you need to pack in your own water and toilet paper and pack out your trash. If you can handle that, you'll be rewarded with some lovely hiking and good fishing in Big Dominguez Creek. Follow a trail up the canyon for the best fishing spots.

**Location:** South of Grand Junction; map B1, grid b3.

**Campsites, facilities:** There are nine tent sites. There are a few primitive fire rings, but no other facilities.

**Elevation:** 7,500 feet.

**Reservations, fees:** Reservations are not accepted. There is no fee.

**Open:** Mid-May to mid-October.

**Directions:** From Grand Junction, drive approximately seven miles south on U.S. 50 to Whitewater. Turn right on Hwy. 141 and drive about seven miles southwest. Turn left on Rd. 24.4 and continue about four miles to the campground.

**Contact:** Bureau of Land Management, 2815 H Rd., Grand Junction, CO 81506; tel. (970) 244-3000.

## 1️⃣1️⃣ Escalante State Wildlife Area     7

Fishing the Gunnison River is the primary draw of this state wildlife area that boasts outstanding access and exquisite scenery. Camping is remote and primitive, with a few rough clearings on the south side of the river and opportunities for hiking, bird-watching, and wildlife observation (look for deer, elk, and waterfowl). Limited hunting is permitted.

**Location:** On the Gunnison River; map B1, grid b4.

**Campsites, facilities:** Dispersed camping is permitted throughout the property. There are no other facilities or drinking water. Leashed pets are permitted.

**Elevation:** 5,000 feet.

**Reservations, fees:** Reservations are not accepted. There is no fee.

**Open:** June to October.

**Directions:** From Delta, drive 12 miles northwest on U.S. 50. Turn left on Escalante Canyon Rd. and drive three miles to the Gunnison River. Cross the river and continue a mile upstream on a rough dirt road to the property.

**Contact:** Colorado Division of Wildlife, 2300 S. Townsend Ave., Montrose, CO 81401; tel. (970) 252-6000.

## 1️⃣2️⃣ Crawford State Park  8

Renovated in 1997, this formerly rustic state campground now offers showers and RV hookups. The sites are divided into three loops along the east side of Crawford Reservoir, just off Hwy. 92 in a pleasant grassy area. A swimming beach and a boat ramp are next to the northern loops; there's a dump station at the middle loop. The shoreline is sunny and open, with few trees and sprawling vistas of rolling green farmland in spring and early summer and crisp, cold breezes in the fall. Waterskiing is a pleasure in the clear, cool water and is allowed in designated areas during the summer months, with year-round fishing in all other areas. Prospects are good for warm-water species including largemouth bass, perch, and catfish. Hike on the quarter-mile Indian Fire Nature Trail, a short but scenic trail from which to view wildlife and birds. The remote reaches of Black Canyon of the Gunnison National Park are conveniently close, with the North Rim entrance some 15 miles south via N. Rim Road. Limited hunting is permitted; contact the park for details.

**Location:** East of the Black Canyon of the Gunnison; map B1, grid b8.

**Campsites, facilities:** There are 44 sites for tents or RVs of any length. Drinking water, picnic tables, fire grills, and bathrooms with hot showers are provided. Electric hookups, a waste disposal station, and boat ramp are available. The rest rooms are wheelchair accessible. Leashed pets are permitted.

**Elevation:** 6,600 feet.

**Reservations, fees:** Reservations are accepted; phone (303) 470-1144 or (800) 678-CAMP (800-678-2267) outside the Denver Metro area; there's a $7 reservation fee. Sites are $10-16 a night, and there's a $4 entrance fee.

**Open:** Year-round.

**Directions:** From Delta, turn east on Hwy. 92 and drive approximately 17 miles to Hotchkiss. Continue about 10 miles southeast on Hwy. 92 to Crawford. The park entrance is about one mile south of Crawford on Hwy. 92.

**Contact:** Crawford State Park, P.O. Box 147, Crawford, CO 81415; tel. (970) 921-5721.

## 13 Columbine  6

People on a tight budget will appreciate this small camp, a simple but pleasing spot tucked under pine trees. Although it's the only campground around for miles, few people know of it, so your chances of solitude are good. A short trail leads south from here through the forest, along a small creek.

**Location:** West of Delta in Uncompahgre National Forest; map B1, grid c3.

**Campsites, facilities:** There are six sites for tents or RVs up to 32 feet long. Picnic tables, fire grills, and vault toilets are provided, but there is no drinking water. Leashed pets are permitted.

**Elevation:** 9,500 feet.

**Reservations, fees:** Reservations are not accepted. There is no fee, but donations are requested.

**Open:** June to September.

**Directions:** From Delta, turn west on County Rd. 214 and drive 30 miles. Turn south on Forest Service Rd. 402 and continue one mile.

**Contact:** Uncompahgre National Forest, Ouray Ranger District, 2505 S. Townsend St., Montrose, CO 81401; tel. (970) 240-5300.

## 14 The Hangin' Tree  4

Legend has it that an outlaw of some sort was hanged from the large tree in front of this camp, hence the name. The camp is just outside of Montrose, set behind a gas station/convenience store with grassy sites, plenty of shade, and nice views of the valley to the east. There are a fair number of seasonal long-term campers in the summer months. Hiking trails and the Ute Indian Museum are nearby.

**Location:** South of Montrose; map B1, grid c6.

**Campsites, facilities:** There are 25 sites for tents or RVs of any length, most with full hookups. Drinking water, picnic tables, fire grills, and bathrooms with hot showers are provided. Laundry facilities, a waste disposal station, small store, and public phone are available. Some facilities are wheelchair accessible. Leashed pets are permitted.

**Elevation:** 5,800 feet.

**Reservations, fees:** Reservations are accepted. Sites are $15.50-21.50 a night.

**Open:** Year-round.

**Directions:** From the junction of U.S. 50 and U.S. 550 in Montrose, drive approximately 3.5 miles south on U.S. 550.

**Contact:** The Hangin' Tree, 17250 U.S. 550, Montrose, CO 81401; tel. (970) 249-9966.

## 15 Centennial RV Park     6

Surrounded by 20 sprawling acres of hay fields, Centennial RV Park makes a nice stopover between Montrose and Ouray on Hwy. 550. Although a bit close to the road, most sites are set far enough back to be reasonably quiet and are large and immaculately kept. Trees are few and far between, but you'll get scenic views of the San Juan Mountains peeking out from the south, with a fishing pond on-site and a bevy of recreational activities to choose from in the region, including hiking, biking, fishing, and four-wheel driving.

**Location:** South of Montrose; map B1, grid c6

**Campsites, facilities:** There are 10 tent sites and 50 full-hookup sites for RVs of any length. Drinking water, picnic tables, fire rings, and bathrooms with hot showers are provided. A waste disposal station, laundry facilities, a playground, cabins, and public phones are available. The facilities are wheelchair accessible. Leashed pets are permitted.

**Elevation:** 6,000 feet.

**Reservations, fees:** Reservations are accepted. Sites are $14-20 a night.

**Open:** May to November.

**Directions:** From the junction of U.S. 50 and U.S. 550 in Montrose, drive ten miles south on U.S. 550. The campground is on the west side of the highway.

**Contact:** Centennial RV Park, 23449 U.S. 550, Montrose, CO 81401; tel. (970) 240-3832.

## 16 Montrose RV Resort    4

Formerly a KOA campground, this basic but adequate facility is located near downtown Montrose in a graveled lot with trees. It's a good central spot for day trips to Blue Mesa Reservoir or Telluride.

**Location:** Near Montrose; map B1, grid c7.

**Campsites, facilities:** There are 39 sites for tents or RVs of any length, some with full hookups. Drinking water, picnic tables, fire grills, and bathrooms with hot showers are provided. Laundry facilities, a waste disposal station, store, cafe, swimming pool, and public phone are available. Leashed pets are permitted.

**Elevation:** 5,800 feet.

**Reservations, fees:** Reservations are accepted. Sites are $18-23 a night.

**Open:** Mid-April to mid-October.

**Directions:** From the junction of U.S. 50 and U.S. 550 in Montrose, drive three-quarters of a mile east on U.S. 50. Turn north on Cedar Ave. and continue to the campground on the right.

**Contact:** Montrose KOA, 200 N. Cedar Ave., Montrose, CO 81401; tel. (970) 249-9177.

## **17** Cedar Creek RV Park   5

One of a smattering of RV campgrounds in Montrose, this place has the bonus of creekside sites on little Cedar Creek. The sites are grassy and relatively quiet, set back from the street. Shops and restaurants in downtown Montrose are a short distance away.

**Location:** On Cedar Creek near Montrose; map B1, grid c7.

**Campsites, facilities:** There are 50 sites for tents or RVs of any length, many with full hookups. Drinking water, picnic tables, fire grills, and bathrooms with hot showers are provided. Laundry facilities, a waste disposal station, miniature golf course, small store, and public phone are available. Leashed pets are permitted.

**Elevation:** 5,800 feet.

**Reservations, fees:** Reservations are accepted. Sites are $15-21 a night.

**Open:** Year-round.

**Directions:** From the junction of U.S. 50 and U.S. 550 in Montrose, drive a little over a mile east on U.S. 50 and turn south on Rose Lane (Village Dr.). The campground is behind Gibson's building.

**Contact:** Cedar Creek RV Park, 126 Rose Lane, Montrose, CO 81401; tel. (970) 249-3884; e-mail: ccreekinc@aol.com.

## **18** Billy Creek State Wildlife Area     7

The Billy Creek State Wildlife Area covers more than 900 acres and is split into four separate tracts of land. The best area for camping and recreation is the Billy Creek Tract, which straddles Billy Creek for about five miles before running into the Uncompahgre National Forest boundary. Fishing is excellent, with a hiking trail running parallel to the creek providing superb access. Near the stream are a few leveled areas with primitive campfire rings, perfect for tents. Remember to practice no-trace camping methods: always camp at least 200 feet from major water sources and naturalize the area you've used when you leave. Limited hunting is permitted.

**Location:** South of Montrose; map B1, grid c7.

**Campsites, facilities:** Dispersed camping is permitted throughout the property. There are no other facilities or drinking water. Leashed pets are permitted.

**Elevation:** 5,600 feet.

**Reservations, fees:** Reservations are not accepted. There is no fee.

**Open:** May to October.

**Directions:** From the junction of U.S. 50 and U.S. 550 in Montrose, drive 16 miles south on U.S. 550. Turn left at the State Wildlife House and proceed into the property.

**Contact:** Colorado Division of Wildlife, 2300 S. Townsend Ave., Montrose, CO 81401; tel. (970) 252-6000.

## 🔢 North Rim      9

North Rim is the more remote and primitive of the Black Canyon's two campgrounds, set in piñon pine and juniper forest near the canyon's edge. The park encompasses the 14 most dramatic miles of the 53-mile-long canyon, which drops abruptly to depths of nearly 2,000 feet, and some of the most fantastic vistas can be seen from two hiking trails—Chasm View Nature Trail and North Vista Trail—located adjacent to the campground. Other options in the park include fishing and rafting in the Gunnison River; contact park headquarters for regulations and services.

**Location:** East of Montrose in Black Canyon of the Gunnison National Park; map B1, grid c7.

**Campsites, facilities:** There are 13 sites for tents or RVs up to 22 feet long. Drinking water, picnic tables, and vault toilets are provided. Leashed pets are permitted.

**Elevation:** 8,200 feet.

**Reservations, fees:** Reservations are not accepted. Sites are $10 a night.

**Open:** Mid-April to October.

**Directions:** From Delta, turn east on Hwy. 92 and drive approximately 17 miles to Hotchkiss. Continue about 10 miles southeast on Hwy. 92 to Crawford. From Crawford, follow the signs for Black Canyon of the Gunnison for about 12 miles (on gravel roads) to the campground.

**Contact:** Black Canyon of the Gunnison National Park, 102 Elk Creek Rd., Gunnison, CO 81230; tel. (970) 641-2337.

## 🔢 South Rim    9

If developed facilities and plenty of company appeal to you, you'll prefer this campground to North Rim. It's got a little restaurant and store nearby and a visitor center with information about the park. Also in the vicinity are picnic areas and several short hiking trails that lead to vista points, including the Rim Rock Trail, which leaves the campground to head north to Tomichi Point at the canyon rim. A highlight: Continue north on the access road to Dragon Point, where you'll get a spectacular view of the Painted Wall, a sheer 2,300-foot face inlaid with light-colored bands of molten granite. In the summer/fall of 2000, the park plans to renovate this campground, adding new sites and lengthening existing ones.

**Location:** East of Montrose in Black Canyon of the Gunnison National Park; map B1, grid c7.

**Campsites, facilities:** There are 103 sites for tents or RVs up to 22 feet long. Drinking water, picnic tables, and vault toilets are provided. A snack bar and limited supplies are located nearby at the Rim House. Leashed pets are permitted.

**Elevation:** 8,200 feet.

**Reservations, fees:** Reservations are not accepted. Sites are $10 a night.

**Open:** Mid-April to October.

**Directions:** From Montrose, drive six miles east on U.S. 50. Turn north on Hwy. 347 and continue five miles to the campground.

**Contact:** Black Canyon of the Gunnison National Park, 102 Elk Creek Rd., Gunnison, CO 81230; tel. (970) 641-2337.

## 21 East Portal   8

East Portal Rd. leads you on a narrow, twisting journey down to the bottom of the Black Canyon, where, in a stand of box elders just above the Gunnison River, sits pretty East Portal campground. A short trail leads down to the river, where you'll find excellent canyon views and fishing access. A few brave souls launch kayaks here, but park officials do not advise boating—even if you're an expert. This stretch of river tends to be unforgiving and has claimed more than one life. Nearby is the historic Gunnison River Diversion Tunnel.

**Location:** East of Montrose in Curecanti National Recreation Area; map B1, grid c8.

**Campsites, facilities:** The 15 sites are for tents. Drinking water, picnic tables, fire grills, and vault toilets are provided. A visitor center is nearby. Leashed pets are permitted.

**Elevation:** 7,500 feet.

**Reservations, fees:** Reservations are not accepted. Sites are $10 a night.

**Open:** Year-round with limited access and facilities from mid-September to mid-May.

**Directions:** From Montrose, drive six miles east on U.S. 50, turn north on Hwy. 347, and drive five miles. Turn right on East Portal Rd. and continue five steep, winding miles down to the campground. Note: East Portal Rd. is closed to RVs and vehicles with trailers.

**Contact:** Curecanti National Recreation Area, 102 Elk Creek Rd., Gunnison, CO 81230; tel. (970) 641-2337.

## 22 Cimarron      7

One of the more developed camps in Curecanti National Recreation Area, Cimarron is quite popular and will likely be crowded. It offers easy access from U.S. 50, set above Morrow Point Dam on the western edge of Morrow Point Lake. An on-site historic train exhibit has cars and engines from the late 1800s, and tours of the Morrow Point Dam power station are available nearby. A mile beyond the campground is the 1.5-mile Mesa Creek Trail, which crosses a footbridge high over the Gunnison River and provides excellent views of the sheer, narrow canyon walls, plus fishing access to Crystal Lake.

**Location:** East of Montrose in Curecanti National Recreation Area; map B1, grid c8.

**Campsites, facilities:** There are 22 sites for tents or RVs of any length. Drinking water, picnic tables, fire grills, and flush toilets are provided. A waste disposal station, restaurant, and visitor center are available. Some facilities are wheelchair accessible. Leashed pets are permitted.

**Elevation:** 6,900 feet.

**Reservations, fees:** Reservations are not accepted. Sites are $10 a night.

**Open:** Year-round with limited access and facilities from mid-September to mid-May.

**Directions:** From Montrose, drive 20 miles east on U.S. 50 to the campground.

**Contact:** Curecanti National Recreation Area, 102 Elk Creek Rd., Gunnison, CO 81230; tel. (970) 641-2337.

## 23 Pleasant Valley Campground    7

This lovely, well-kept campground features grassy sites under clusters of cottonwood trees. Adjacent to the sites is the Little Cimarron River, a stream that unfortunately offers poor fishing prospects. The camp is surrounded by a gorgeous valley dotted with working ranches. Proximity to Black Canyon of the Gunnison National Park and Curecanti National Recreation Area keep this camp packed throughout the summer.

**Location:** On the Little Cimarron River; map B1, grid c8.

**Campsites, facilities:** There are 13 sites for tents or RVs of any length, most with full hookups. Drinking water, picnic tables, fire grills, and bathrooms with hot showers are provided. Laundry facilities, a grocery store, cabins, and a public phone are available. Small, leashed pets are permitted.

**Elevation:** 7,500 feet.

**Reservations, fees:** Reservations are accepted. Sites are $13.50-16.50 a night.

**Open:** May to November.

**Directions:** From Cimarron, drive three miles east on U.S. 50.

**Contact:** Pleasant Valley Campground, P.O. Box 127, Cimarron, CO 81220; tel. (970) 249-8330.

## 24 Black Canyon RV Park     7

Black Canyon RV Park is on the floor of the scenic Cimarron Valley, with a spectacular 360-degree view of distant peaks including Sheep Mountain and Ute Peak. The sites are open, offering little shade but lots and lots of green grass. RV sites are large and well maintained, and tenters have a choice of a "bungalow" (a grassy site with a three-sided wind shelter), an open meadow site (these have no tables or grills), or a standard site with grass and electricity. Black Canyon of the Gunnison National Park is a short drive away, as are Silver Jack Reservoir and Beaver Lake, where fishing prospects are good.

**Location:** East of Cimarron; map B1, grid c8.

**Campsites, facilities:** There are three tent sites with wind shelters, plus a grassy field for unlimited tent camping. Forty-five full-hookup sites for RVs of any length are also available. Drinking water, picnic tables, fire grills, and bathrooms with hot showers are provided. Laundry facilities, a small store, public phone, and cabins are available. Leashed pets are permitted.

**Elevation:** 7,500 feet.

**Reservations, fees:** Reservations are accepted. Sites are $14-19 a night.

**Open:** January to November.

**Directions:** From Cimarron, drive five miles east on U.S. 50.

**Contact:** Black Canyon RV Park, P.O. Box 128, Cimarron, CO 81220; tel. (970) 249-1147.

## 25 Iron Springs     7

Shaded and quiet, this rarely used campground is quite a find for budget-minded adventurers. The campsites are intimate, set beneath pine trees at the top of a plateau. Four-wheel-drive roads and rustic trails in the immediate area provide opportunities for hiking and mountain biking.

**Location:** Southwest of Montrose in Uncompahgre National Forest; map B1, grid d5.

**Campsites, facilities:** There are 12 sites for tents or RVs up to 32 feet long. Picnic tables, fire grills, and vault toilets are provided, but there is no drinking water. Leashed pets are permitted.

**Elevation:** 9,500 feet.

**Reservations, fees:** Reservations are not accepted. There is no fee, but donations are requested.

**Open:** June to September.

**Directions:** From Montrose, drive 25 miles southwest on Hwy. 90.

**Contact:** Uncompahgre National Forest, Ouray Ranger District, 2505 S. Townsend St., Montrose, CO 81401; tel. (970) 240-5300.

## 26 Ridgway State Park  8

The campground is divided into three large loops, each with its own distinct features. The first loop you come to from Ridgway is the Pa-Co-Chu-Puk Loop, which is near the Uncompahgre River and a good choice for anglers, with hiking trails that lead down to the riverbanks for perfect access. The Dakota Terraces Loop has open sites near the edge of Ridgway Reservoir (perfect for campers with boats), and the Elk Ridge Loop offers pine-shaded sites high on a bluff overlooking the reservoir (great views of the San Juan Range). Ridgway Reservoir is a dammed-up section of the Uncompahgre River that has been developed into a recreation paradise, complete with a full-service marina and a large swimming beach. Waterskiing is permitted in designated areas, along with sailing and windsurfing, and anglers have their own no-wake zone for fishing, with good prospects for rainbow and brown trout, plus kokanee salmon in the winter. The park is well known for its wheelchair accessibility, including a special trail to the swimming area and concrete pads at all sites for easy mobility.

**Location:** North of Ridgway; map B1, grid d6.

**Campsites, facilities:** There are 283 sites for tents or RVs of any length. Drinking water, picnic tables, fire grills, and bathrooms with hot showers are provided. Electric hookups, laundry facilities, and a waste disposal station are available. At the reservoir there's a marina with a boat ramp, docks, boat rentals, and a snack bar. The facilities are wheelchair accessible. Leashed pets are permitted.

**Elevation:** 6,900 feet.

**Reservations, fees:** Reservations are accepted; phone (303) 470-1144 or (800) 678-CAMP (800-678-2267) outside the Denver Metro area; there's a $7 reservation fee. Sites are $10-16 a night, and there's a $4 entrance fee.

**Open:** May to October.

**Directions:** From Ridgway, drive five miles north on U.S. 550. The Pa-Co-Chu-Puk sites are accessible from the first entrance; access Dakota Terraces and Elk Ridge from the second entrance a short distance south.

**Contact:** Ridgway State Park, 28555 U.S. 550, Ridgway, CO 81432; tel. (970) 626-5822.

## **27** Weber's Campground   6

You'll find the campground just south of the town of Ridgway, directly off the highway. Though the facilities appear a bit run down, the camp offers large, grassy sites and good views of the adjacent lush ranch land. Large trees help shield sites from road noise; to further ensure quiet, try for a site down the hill, far from the entrance (you also get the best views from these sites). The San Juan Mountains provide an impressive backdrop.

**Location:** Near Ridgway; map B1, grid d7.

**Campsites, facilities:** There are 45 sites for tents or RVs of any length, many with full hookups. Drinking water, picnic tables, fire grills, and bathrooms with hot showers are provided. Laundry facilities, a waste disposal station, and public phone are available. Leashed pets are permitted.

**Elevation:** 7,200 feet.

**Reservations, fees:** Reservations are accepted. Sites are $15-19 a night.

**Open:** May to October.

**Directions:** From Ridgway, drive 2.5 miles south on U.S. 550.

**Contact:** Weber's Campground, 20725 U.S. 550, Ridgway, CO 81432; tel. (970) 626-5383.

## **28** Big Cimarron     7

Big Cimarron is on the scenic drive south to Silver Jack Reservoir, snuggled between Big Cimarron Rd. and the Cimarron River. It offers only basic amenities (no drinking water) but is pretty and pleasant, with cozy sites shaded by spruce trees. The river and fishing access points are within walking distance. Hiking trails are available to the south, near Silver Jack Reservoir.

**Location:** On the Cimarron River in Uncompahgre National Forest; map B1, grid d8.

**Campsites, facilities:** There are 12 sites for tents or RVs up to 20 feet long. Picnic tables, fire grills, and vault toilets are provided, but there is no drinking water. Leashed pets are permitted.

**Elevation:** 8,750 feet.

**Reservations, fees:** Reservations are not accepted. Sites are $6 a night.

**Open:** Memorial Day to Labor Day.

**Directions:** From Montrose, drive 20 miles east on U.S. 50, turn right on Big Cimarron Rd. (Forest Service Rd. 858) and drive 20 miles south to the campground.

**Contact:** Uncompahgre National Forest, Ouray Ranger District, 2505 S. Townsend St., Montrose, CO 81401; tel. (970) 240-5300.

## **29** Beaver Lake      7

Just down the road from Big Cimarron, this camp is similar in ambience but has the added luxuries of drinking water and wheelchair accessibility. Beaver Lake is little more than a pond, but rumor has it there are rainbow trout in there, dinky though they may be. If you want better odds, hop down the road to Silver Jack Reservoir, which offers nonmotorized boating access. There is a wheelchair-accessible hiking trail with fishing piers around Beaver Lake.

**Location:** Near Silver Jack Reservoir in Uncompahgre National Forest; map B1, grid d8.

**Campsites, facilities:** There are 11 sites for tents or RVs up to 20 feet long. Drinking water, picnic tables, fire grills, and vault toilets are provided. Some facilities are wheelchair accessible. Leashed pets are permitted.

**Elevation:** 8,800 feet.

**Reservations, fees:** Reservations are not accepted. Sites are $8 a night.

**Open:** Memorial Day to Labor Day.

**Directions:** From Montrose, drive 20 miles east on U.S. 50, turn right on Big Cimarron Rd. (Forest Service Rd. 858), and drive 20.5 miles south to the campground.

**Contact:** Uncompahgre National Forest, Ouray Ranger District, 2505 S. Townsend St., Montrose, CO 81401; tel. (970) 240-5300.

## 30 Silver Jack       9

The region around 300-acre Silver Jack Reservoir epitomizes everything campers come to Colorado to see: stunning mountain views, lush forest bordering a vast wilderness, and fantastic fishing—all of it centered on a pristine alpine lake. Silver Jack camp is simply beautiful, set high in an aspen grove overlooking the reservoir. The campground is divided into three loops, with the most scenic sites on the far eastern ends of the Ouray Loop and the Sapinero Loop. (Hint: Try for sites 48 or 49.) Nearby is a picturesque overlook that provides a striking view of Silver Jack Reservoir, with picnic areas and excellent wheelchair access. Nonmotorized boating is permitted, and to the south are hiking trails routed into the Big Blue Wilderness.

**Location:** Near Silver Jack Reservoir in Uncompahgre National Forest; map B1, grid d8.

**Campsites, facilities:** There are 60 sites for tents or RVs up to 30 feet long. Drinking water, picnic tables, fire grills, and vault toilets are provided. Some facilities are wheelchair accessible. Leashed pets are permitted.

**Elevation:** 8,900 feet.

**Reservations, fees:** Reservations are accepted; phone (877) 444-6777. There's an $8.65 reservation fee. You may also reserve sites at website: www.reserveusa.com. Sites are $10 a night.

**Open:** Memorial Day to Labor Day.

**Directions:** From Montrose, drive 20 miles east on U.S. 50, turn right on Big Cimarron Rd. (Forest Service Rd. 858), and drive 22 miles south to the campground.

**Contact:** Uncompahgre National Forest, Ouray Ranger District, 2505 S. Townsend St., Montrose, CO 81401; tel. (970) 240-5300.

## 31 Miramonte Reservoir State Wildlife Area       8

It's quite rare to find a free campground with developed facilities—much less access to a big lake—and this one is simply a treasure. The campsites are bare and mostly treeless but are close to the shoreline, with beautiful views of the reservoir and surrounding mountains. Four hundred-acre Miramonte Reservoir is rumored to produce some of the biggest rainbow trout around, with prime fishing access by shore or boat and special areas separating water-skiers from anglers. All boating is allowed, including sailing and windsurfing. Rough hiking trails head off to the north and south, providing opportunities to view some of the area's native songbirds and waterfowl. Limited hunting is permitted.

**Location:** South of Norwood; map B1, grid e3.

**Campsites, facilities:** There are approximately 50 sites for tents or RVs of any length. Drinking water, picnic tables, fire grills, and vault toilets are provided. A waste disposal station and a boat ramp are available. Leashed pets are permitted.

**Elevation:** 7,800 feet.

**Reservations, fees:** Reservations are not accepted. There is no fee.

**Open:** Year-round.

**Directions:** From Norwood, drive 1.5 miles east on Hwy. 145, turn south on the Dolores-Norwood Rd. (Forest Service Rd. 610), and continue 17 miles to the reservoir.

**Contact:** Colorado Division of Wildlife, 2300 S. Townsend Ave., Montrose, CO 81401; tel. (970) 252-6000.

## 32 Lone Cone State Wildlife Area      7

Morrison Creek snakes through this remote tract, offering a lesser-known fishing alternative to the West Dolores River, which is often swarming with eager anglers. Horse corrals are provided for equestrian campers, with hiking and riding limited to rambling, crude cross-country trails. You may camp anywhere in the wildlife area, but since campers are naturally drawn to water, you're likely to find a few good previously cleared tent sites with established fire rings near the stream. A word of warning: This is bear country. Be sure to hang your food bag high—and never keep edibles in your tent. Limited hunting is permitted.

**Location:** South of Norwood; map B1, grid e4.

**Campsites, facilities:** Dispersed camping is permitted throughout the property. Horse corrals are provided, but there are no other facilities. Leashed pets are permitted.

**Elevation:** 8,000 feet.

**Reservations, fees:** Reservations are not accepted. There is no fee.

**Open:** Year-round.

**Directions:** From Norwood, drive 1.5 miles east on Hwy. 145, turn south on the Dolores-Norwood Rd. (Forest Service Rd. 610), and continue 24 miles to the property.

**Contact:** Colorado Division of Wildlife, 2300 S. Townsend Ave., Montrose, CO 81401; tel. (970) 252-6000.

## 33 Woods Lake    8

Small and simple Woods Lake is a former hidden treasure that recently underwent a face-lift. Originally it was a primitive, no-fee dispersed site, known to few but locals and folks who accidentally bumped into it—then the U.S. Forest Service decided to make it a developed campground, adding picnic tables and fire pits and generally improving the sites. Although this means the camp gets more use, it's still a lovely spot, set in aspen and spruce forest with a striking view of Sunshine Peak. Fishing in Woods Lake is permitted with artificial flies and lures only; bait fishing is allowed at Fall Creek, which runs out of the lake to the west. A rough trail leads south of camp into the Lizard Head Wilderness, where there are more scenic hiking trails and spectacular wildflower displays. Note: This campground may be closed for the 2000 season.

**Location:** Near the Lizard Head Wilderness in Uncompahgre National Forest; map B1, grid e5.

**Campsites, facilities:** Several designated tent sites are near the lakeshore. Picnic tables, fire grills, and vault toilets are provided, but there is no drinking water. Leashed pets are permitted.

**Elevation:** 9,400 feet.

**Reservations, fees:** Reservations are not accepted. Sites are $14 a night.

**Open:** May to October. (This campground may be closed for the 2000 season.)

**Directions:** From the junction of Hwy. 62 and Hwy. 145, turn east on Hwy. 145 (toward Telluride) and drive three miles; then turn right on Forest Service Rd. 618 and continue approximately seven miles. Turn right on Forest Service Rd. 621 and continue about a mile south to the campground.

**Contact:** Uncompahgre National Forest, Norwood Ranger District, P.O. Box 388, Norwood, CO 81423; tel. (970) 327-4261.

## 34 Ouray KOA 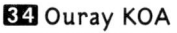     8

Tourists swarm to this beautiful mountain campground like bees to honey—and it's no wonder. Set at the base of the San Juan Mountains, it's reasonably priced and offers a full range of amenities including showers and a hot tub, plus on-site outdoor activities. The camp is off the main highway in a quiet, wooded environment and is adjacent to hiking trails and river fishing spots. The sites, some of which are next to the river, are large and well maintained, with lush green grass and optional shade. Pancake breakfasts and communal barbecues are held in the summer.

**Location:** On the Uncompahgre River; map B1, grid e7.

**Campsites, facilities:** There are 116 sites for tents or RVs of any length, many with full hookups. Drinking water, picnic tables, fire grills, and bathrooms with hot showers are provided. Laundry facilities, a waste disposal station, a hot tub, a store, and a public phone are available. Leashed pets are permitted.

**Elevation:** 7,800 feet.

**Reservations, fees:** Reservations are accepted; phone (800) KOA-8026. Sites are $19-24.50 a night.

**Open:** May to September.

**Directions:** From Ouray, drive four miles north on U.S. 550, turn west on County Rd. 23, and continue one-quarter mile to the campground.

**Contact:** Ouray KOA, P.O. Box J, Ouray, CO 81427; tel. (970) 325-4736.

## 35 4 J + 1 + 1 RV Park     7

This camp is just off the main drag in Ouray, backed against a hillside covered with tall spruce trees. While the RV sites are nice and roomy, the tent spots leave a bit to be desired, with sites crammed together side-by-side on scraggly grass and gravel lanes. The Uncompahgre River runs along the camp boundary, with good fishing access not far from camp, and the steaming mineral pools at Ouray Hot Springs (not to be missed) are within walking distance. Restaurants and businesses in Ouray are also nearby. In case you were wondering, the campground's name refers to the owners' family, which started out with four members then grew by two.

**Location:** On the Uncompahgre River in Ouray; map B1, grid e7.

**Campsites, facilities:** There are 80 sites for tents or RVs of any length, many with full hookups. Drinking water, picnic tables, fire grills, and bathrooms with hot showers are provided. Laundry facilities are available. Some facilities are wheelchair accessible. Leashed pets are permitted.

**Elevation:** 7,800 feet.

**Reservations, fees:** Reservations are accepted. Sites are $16-22 a night.

**Open:** May to October.

**Directions:** From U.S. 550 in Ouray, turn west on 7th Ave. and drive three blocks.

**Contact:** 4 J + 1 + 1 RV Park, P.O. Box F, Ouray, CO 81427; tel. (970) 325-4418.

## 36 Amphitheater    8

This immensely popular campground features small sites hooded by tall spruce trees, not far from a natural rock amphitheater. The camp overlooks Ouray and features panoramic mountain views. The Cascade Falls Trail begins at the campground, leading several miles up to the Chief Ouray Mine. The hike is a long, steep, two- to three-hour trek, but at the top you'll be rewarded with breathtaking views of the Upper Cascade Falls and colorful rock formations around Ouray.

**Location:** Near the Big Blue Wilderness in Uncompahgre National Forest; map B1, grid e8.

**Campsites, facilities:** There are 30 sites for tents or RVs up to 20 feet long. Drinking water, picnic tables, fire grills, and vault toilets are provided. Leashed pets are permitted.

**Elevation:** 9,000 feet.

**Reservations, fees:** Reservations are accepted; phone (877) 444-6777. There's an $8.65 reservation fee. You may also reserve sites at website: www.reserveusa.com. Sites are $14 a night.

**Open:** May to September.

**Directions:** From Ouray, drive one-half mile south on U.S. 550, turn left on Forest Service Rd. 885, and proceed one-half mile to the campground.

**Contact:** Uncompahgre National Forest, Ouray Ranger District, 2505 S. Townsend St., Montrose, CO 81401; tel. (970) 240-5300.

## 37 Mountain Sheep Point      8

This area is a gateway to recreational paradise, with mountain bikers, hikers, and river rafters arriving from the far reaches of the state to sample the wonders of the Dolores River Canyon area. The sites are simple but provide the necessities (except for water—bring your own). Contact the Bureau of Land Management for details on hiking and biking trails and boat access.

**Location:** On the Dolores River; map B1, grid f1.

**Campsites, facilities:** There are three sites for tents or RVs up to 30 feet long. Picnic tables, fire grills, and a vault toilet are provided, but there is no drinking water. Leashed pets are permitted.

**Elevation:** 6,100 feet.

**Reservations, fees:** Reservations are not accepted. There is no fee.

**Open:** April to November.

**Directions:** From the town of Dove Creek, drive one mile south on U.S. 666, turn left on J Rd., and drive one mile east. Turn left on Rd. 10 and continue approximately three miles to the campground.

**Contact:** Bureau of Land Management, 2465 S. Townsend Ave., Montrose, CO 81401; tel. (970) 240-5300.

## 38 Groundhog Reservoir State Wildlife Area       7

If you're looking for a bargain, you've found it. Groundhog Reservoir offers rustic sites, basic amenities, and facilities for nonmotorized boating in a pretty, wooded area—all for free. It's west of the scenic Dolores River Valley and close to a network of backcountry roads that make great mountain biking trails, with a few undesignated hiking trails branching off to the north along feeder creeks. Fishing for rainbow and cutthroat trout is excellent. Limited hunting is permitted.

**Location:** North of Dolores; map B1, grid f5.

**Campsites, facilities:** There are 13 sites for tents or RVs of any length. Drinking water and vault toilets are provided. A boat ramp and a small store are available. Leashed pets are permitted.

**Elevation:** 8,700 feet.

**Reservations, fees:** Reservations are not accepted. There is no fee.

**Open:** Year-round.

**Directions:** From Hwy. 145 in Dolores, turn north on 11th St. (once out of town, the road becomes Forest Service Rd. 526) and drive 26 miles. Turn right on Forest Service Rd. 533 and continue five miles east to the reservoir.

**Contact:** Colorado Division of Wildlife, 2300 S. Townsend Ave., Montrose, CO 81401; tel. (970) 252-6000.

## 39 Mavreeso     8

Set in a breathtaking region, this lovely camp is situated alongside the West Dolores River with stunning mountain vistas and a pleasing mix of aspens and evergreens interspersed with wildflower-studded meadows. The sites are large and level, and many are shaded by spruce trees. River fishing is excellent; this spot is a popular day-use area for local anglers.

**Location:** On the West Dolores River in San Juan National Forest; map B1, grid f4.

**Campsites, facilities:** There are 14 sites for tents or RVs up to 35 feet long. Drinking water, picnic tables, fire grills, a waste disposal station, and vault toilets are provided. One site is wheelchair accessible. Leashed pets are permitted.

**Elevation:** 7,800 feet.

**Reservations, fees:** Reservations are not accepted. Sites are $10 a night.

**Open:** June to September.

**Directions:** From Dolores, drive 13 miles north on Hwy. 145, turn left on West Dolores Rd. (Forest Service Rd. 535), and continue six miles northeast to the campground.

Contact: San Juan National Forest, Dolores Ranger District, P.O. Box 210, Dolores, CO 81323; tel. (970) 882-7296.

## 40 West Dolores     8

The West Dolores River runs alongside this 10-acre camp, which has pleasant sites tucked under mature spruce and fir trees. The river is stocked regularly with catchable-sized trout, and there are several good fishing perches near camp. Despite its scenic location and easy access, this camp is known to few and is rarely full, even on busy weekends. For more recreation options, continue up West Dolores Rd., where you'll pass several dirt roads that provide access to trails into the backcountry. If you keep going, eventually you'll come to the tiny town of Dunton, and from there, you can take Forest Service Trail 648, which leads up to Colorado's only known active geyser. North of Dunton is a spectacularly scenic area called the Meadows, a patchwork quilt of lush grasses richly carpeted with wildflowers.

**Location:** On the West Dolores River in San Juan National Forest; map B1, grid f4.

**Campsites, facilities:** There are 13 sites for tents or RVs up to 35 feet long. Drinking water, picnic tables, fire grills, a waste disposal station, and vault toilets are provided. One site is wheelchair accessible. Leashed pets are permitted.

**Elevation:** 7,600 feet.

**Reservations, fees:** Reservations are not accepted. Sites are $10 a night.

**Open:** June to September.

**Directions:** From Dolores, drive 13 miles north on Hwy. 145, turn left on West Dolores Rd. (Forest Service Rd. 535), and continue seven miles northeast to the campground.

**Contact:** San Juan National Forest, Dolores Ranger District, P.O. Box 210, Dolores, CO 81323; tel. (970) 882-7296

## 41 Burro Bridge      8

These airy sites are sprinkled with trees and set on a steep hill overlooking the West Dolores River, with a precipitous trail leading down to the banks for fishing access. This is a good base for trips into the Lizard Head Wilderness. From camp, continue about a mile up West Dolores Rd. to access the Navajo Lake Trail, which traces the West Dolores River deep into the wilderness, culminating at its headwaters in the Navajo Basin.

**Location:** Near the West Dolores River in San Juan National Forest; map B1, grid f5.

**Campsites, facilities:** There are 15 sites for tents or RVs up to 35 feet long. Drinking water, picnic tables, fire grills, and vault toilets are provided. One site is wheelchair accessible. Leashed pets are permitted.

**Elevation:** 9,000 feet.

**Reservations, fees:** Reservations are not accepted. Sites are $10 a night.

**Open:** June to September.

**Directions:** From Dolores, drive 13 miles north on Hwy. 145, turn left on West Dolores Rd. (Forest Service Rd. 535), and continue 24 miles northeast to the campground.

**Contact:** San Juan National Forest, Dolores Ranger District, P.O. Box 210, Dolores, CO 81323; tel. (970) 882-7296.

## 42 Cayton     8

One of the most popular campgrounds along the Dolores River, Cayton offers lightly shaded sites near the riverbanks. (Tip: The lower loop has the best sites, with level ground and river access. Sites on the upper loop are on a sloping hillside.) This is a great camp for hikers interested in day hikes or longer forays into the backcountry, with several trails in the area. If you continue up Barlow Creek Rd., you'll eventually come to Bolam Pass, which affords panoramic mountain vistas and access to the Colorado Trail.

**Location:** On the Dolores River in San Juan National Forest; map B1, grid f6.

**Campsites, facilities:** There are 27 sites for tents or RVs up to 45 feet long. Drinking water, picnic tables, fire grills, a waste disposal station, and vault toilets are provided. Leashed pets are permitted.

**Elevation:** 9,400 feet.

**Reservations, fees:** Reservations are not accepted. Sites are $10 a night.

**Open:** June to September.

**Directions:** From Telluride, drive about 20 miles southwest on Hwy. 145, turn east on Barlow Creek Rd. (Forest Service Rd. 578), and continue one-half mile to the campground.

**Contact:** San Juan National Forest, Dolores Ranger District, P.O. Box 210, Dolores, CO 81323; tel. (970) 882-7296.

## 43 Sunshine   7

This camp offers easy access to Telluride, but since it's not on a main thoroughfare, it's often overlooked by tourists. You'll find Sunshine just off Hwy. 145 in a conifer forest, not far from the Lizard Head Wilderness. During the annual Telluride Bluegrass Festival, when as many as 40,000 people flock to Telluride's tiny valley, the camp provides a quieter escape from the hordes of campers that line the valley floor. Note: This campground may be closed for the 2000 season.

**Location:** Southwest of Telluride in Uncompahgre National Forest; map B1, grid f6.

**Campsites, facilities:** There are 15 sites for tents or RVs up to 25 feet long. Drinking water, picnic tables, fire grills, and vault toilets are provided. Leashed pets are permitted.

**Elevation:** 9,500 feet.

**Reservations, fees:** Reservations are not accepted. Sites are $10 a night.

**Open:** May to September. (This campground may be closed for the 2000 season.)

**Directions:** From Telluride, drive eight miles southwest on Hwy. 145.

**Contact:** Uncompahgre National Forest, Norwood Ranger District, P.O. Box 388, Norwood, CO 81423; tel. (970) 327-4261.

## 44 Sheep Corrals   8

Sheep Corrals (also known as Illium Valley) is a beautiful and little-known spot, set in a large meadow adjacent to the South Fork of the San Miguel River. Sites are open and airy, with spectacular views of Wilson and Sunshine Peaks. Fishing on this stretch of river is said to be excellent.

**Location:** On the South Fork of the San Miguel River in Uncompahgre National

Forest; map B1, grid f6.

**Campsites, facilities:** There are eight walk-in tent sites. Picnic tables, fire grills, and vault toilets are provided, but there is no drinking water. Leashed pets are permitted.

**Elevation:** 9,500 feet.

**Reservations, fees:** Reservations are not accepted. Sites are $10 a night.

**Open:** June to September.

**Directions:** From Telluride, drive about 11 miles southwest on Hwy. 145, turn west on Forest Service Rd. 625 (Illium Valley Rd.), and continue three miles to the campground.

**Contact:** Uncompahgre National Forest, Norwood Ranger District, P.O. Box 388, Norwood, CO 81423; tel. (970) 327-4261.

## 45 Alta Lakes     8

Although the difficult access keeps many folks away, the extra work to get here is worth it. High and primitive, the camp is set partly in spruce and pine forest, partly in sagebrush meadow, adjacent to tiny, crystal-clear Alta Lakes. Fishing is decent, and the views are magnificent, with the San Miguel Mountains to the west and the San Juans to the northeast.

**Location:** Near the Lizard Head Wilderness in Uncompahgre National Forest; map B1, grid f7.

**Campsites, facilities:** Dispersed camping is permitted anywhere around the lakes. Vault toilets are provided, but there are no other facilities. Leashed pets are permitted.

**Elevation:** 11,200 feet.

**Reservations, fees:** Reservations are not accepted. There is no fee.

**Open:** June to September.

**Directions:** From Telluride, drive nine miles southwest on Hwy. 145, turn east on Forest Service Rd. 632, and continue four miles to the campground. Note: The access road is steep and rough. Trailers are not recommended.

**Contact:** Uncompahgre National Forest, Norwood Ranger District, P.O. Box 388, Norwood, CO 81423; tel. (970) 327-4261.

## 46 South Mineral    7

Level, private sites surrounded by abundant bushy vegetation are featured at this pleasant U.S. Forest Service camp, set below the highway along the South Fork of Mineral Creek. Some sites are available along the creek banks. Fishing from this camp is a sublimely scenic experience, worth the trouble even if you end up getting skunked.

**Location:** On the South Fork of Mineral Creek in San Juan National Forest; map B1, grid f7.

**Campsites, facilities:** There are 26 sites for tents or RVs up to 45 feet long. Drinking water, picnic tables, fire grills, and vault toilets are provided. Leashed pets are permitted.

**Elevation:** 9,800 feet.

**Reservations, fees:** Reservations are not accepted. Sites are $10 a night.

**Open:** Year-round with limited winter services.

**Directions:** From Silverton, drive two miles northwest on U.S. 550, turn left on Forest Service Rd. 585, and continue four miles to the campground.

**Contact:** San Juan National Forest, Columbine Ranger District, Durango Office, 701 Camino del Rio, Durango, CO 81301; tel. (970) 247-4874.

##  Matterhorn   7

As the most modern and developed of all the U.S. Forest Service camps in the Telluride area, Matterhorn is very popular with tourists, especially RV campers. Sites are set in pine forest, with views of peaks near the Lizard Head Wilderness to the west. Trout Lake, located a couple miles south, provides excellent fishing and stunning views of Yellow Peak, Vermilion Peak, and Sheep Mountain, plus colorful stands of aspens in the fall.

**Location:** Near the Lizard Head Wilderness in Uncompahgre National Forest; map B1, grid f6.

**Campsites, facilities:** There are three walk-in tent sites, eight full-hookup RV sites, and 17 sites that can accommodate either tents or RVs of any length. Drinking water, picnic tables, fire grills, and bathrooms with hot showers are provided. Leashed pets are permitted.

**Elevation:** 9,500 feet.

**Reservations, fees:** Reservations are not accepted. Sites are $10-14 a night.

**Open:** June to September.

**Directions:** From Telluride, drive 12 miles southwest on Hwy. 145.

**Contact:** Uncompahgre National Forest, Norwood Ranger District, P.O. Box 388, Norwood, CO 81423; tel. (970) 327-4261.

## 48 Priest Lake   7

Priest Lake is a rustic yet pleasing alternative to Matterhorn. It's set in stands of spruce and aspen trees next to a large, beautiful meadow surrounding Priest Lake. Fishing in the lake is limited; chances are better at Trout Lake, about a mile to the south.

**Location:** Near the Lizard Head Wilderness in Uncompahgre National Forest; map B1, grid f6.

**Campsites, facilities:** Dispersed camping is permitted anywhere around the lake. Vault toilets are provided, but there are no other facilities. Leashed pets are permitted.

**Elevation:** 9,800 feet.

**Reservations, fees:** Reservations are not accepted. There is no fee.

**Open:** Memorial Day to Labor Day.

**Directions:** From Telluride, drive 12 miles southwest on Hwy. 145. Turn at the entrance to Matterhorn campground and continue about a mile past the camp to Priest Lake.

**Contact:** Uncompahgre National Forest, Norwood Ranger District, P.O. Box 388, Norwood, CO 81423; tel. (970) 327-4261.

## 49 Red Mountain Motel and RV Park   7

Spacious, open sites at this camp allow clear views of high peaks to the southeast. The campground is adjacent to a charming, old west-style motel on the main drag in Silverton, with mini-golf next door. Nearby recreation options include hiking and horseback riding in the Weminuche Wilderness, fishing and rafting on the Animas River, and exploring jeep trails in the surrounding mountains.

**Location:** In Silverton; map B1, grid f8.

**Campsites, facilities:** There are five tent sites and 15 full-hookup sites for RVs of any length. Drinking water, picnic tables, and bathrooms with hot showers are provided. Laundry facilities, a waste disposal station, miniature golf course, sports field, and motel rooms are available. Leashed pets are permitted.

**Elevation:** 9,300 feet.

**Reservations, fees:** Reservations are accepted. Sites are $11-16 a night.

**Open:** Mid-April to October.

**Directions:** From the junction of Hwy. 110 and U.S. 550 in Silverton, drive one block north on Hwy. 110.

**Contact:** Red Mountain Motel and RV Park, P.O. Box 346, Silverton, CO 81433; tel. (970) 387-5512.

## 50 Silverton Lakes Campground       7

Open, riverside sites with dramatic views of snowcapped peaks and access to every outdoor activity imaginable make this spot perfect for a weekend adventure. It's across the road from an old mine north of town and flanked by quaint, old-fashioned buildings. There are no Silverton Lakes, just a couple of stocked trout ponds where you can cast your line if the Animas River doesn't produce. Other activities include hiking, horseback riding, and exploring historic sites around Silverton.

**Location:** On the Animas River; map B1, grid f8.

**Campsites, facilities:** There are 20 tent sites and 50 sites for RVs of any length, many with full hookups. Drinking water, picnic tables, fire grills, and bathrooms with hot showers are provided. Laundry facilities, a waste disposal station, store, public phone, and jeep rentals are available. Leashed pets are permitted.

**Elevation:** 9,300 feet.

**Reservations, fees:** Reservations are accepted. Sites are $16 a night.

**Open:** May to November.

**Directions:** From U.S. 550 in Silverton, turn east on Greene St. and drive one block. Then turn east on Hwy. 110 and drive one-quarter mile to the campground.

**Contact:** Silverton Lakes Campground, P.O. Box 126, Silverton, CO 81433; tel. (970) 387-5721.

## 51 Molas Lake Park      10

A more primitive option to the developed RV parks in Silverton, this large camp is a gem hidden away in the woods. It's pretty and private, nestled next to Big Molas Lake at the base of several spectacularly beautiful mountains. The views are truly jaw dropping—Ouray may be known as the "Little Switzerland" of the United States, but I think this spot is far more beautiful. For the best view, head up the highway a short distance to the scenic vista parking area. Molas Lake offers good fishing and nonmotorized boating, and a hiking trail begins south of the campground and heads east for several miles into the Weminuche Wilderness.

**Location:** South of Silverton; map B1, grid f8.

**Campsites, facilities:** There are 60 sites for tents or RVs up to 45 feet long. Drinking water, picnic tables, fire grills, and vault toilets are provided. A waste disposal station and a small store are available. Leashed pets are permitted.

**Elevation:** 9,000 feet.

**Reservations, fees:** Reservations are accepted. Sites are $15 a night.

**Open:** Mid-May to September.

**Directions:** From Silverton, drive five miles south on U.S. 550.

**Contact:** Molas Lake Park, Silverton, CO 81433; tel. (970) 387-5848.

## 52 Silver Summit RV Park      7

One of several developed RV parks near downtown Silverton, Silver Summit offers sunny, level sites with instant access to riverside fishing, hiking trails, and hundreds of miles of four-wheel-drive roads. You can rent a jeep at the campground, or—if you can afford to splurge—arrange a helicopter tour for a unique view of the breathtaking mountain scenery. This is one of the only campgrounds around with a hot tub, a real luxury after a long day of hiking or riding.

**Location:** In Silverton; map B1, grid f8.

**Campsites, facilities:** There are 40 full-hookup sites for tents or RVs of any length. Drinking water, picnic tables, fire grills, and bathrooms with hot showers are provided. Laundry facilities, a hot tub, store, public phone, and jeep rentals are available. Some facilities are wheelchair accessible. Leashed pets are permitted.

**Elevation:** 9,300 feet.

**Reservations, fees:** Reservations are accepted. Sites are $15-20 a night.

**Open:** May to November.

**Directions:** From the junction of Hwy. 110 and U.S. 550 in Silverton, drive one block north on Hwy. 110. Turn east on 7th St. and continue two blocks to the campground.

**Contact:** Silver Summit RV Park, 640 Mineral St., Silverton, CO 81433; tel. (970) 387-0240 or (800) 352-1637; e-mail: slvrsmmt@frontier.net.

## 53 Bradfield      7

Although technically owned by the Bureau of Land Management, this popular camp on the Dolores River next to the Bradfield Bridge is administered by the U.S. Forest Service. It's a common put-in for rafting trips on the river, with a designated beach for launching boats. The campsites are not far from the water, partially shaded by cottonwoods and piñon pines. This stretch of river is a designated Gold Medal Water and provides excellent catch-and-release fishing.

**Location:** On the Dolores River in San Juan National Forest; map B1, grid g2.

**Campsites, facilities:** There are 22 sites for tents or RVs up to 22 feet long. Drinking water, picnic tables, fire grills, and vault toilets are provided. Some facilities are wheelchair accessible. Leashed pets are permitted.

**Elevation:** 6,500 feet.

**Reservations, fees:** Reservations are not accepted. Sites are $10 a night.
**Open:** May to November.
**Directions:** From Cortez, drive 20 miles north on U.S. 666 to Pleasant View. Continue one mile north, turn right on County Rd. DD, and drive one mile east. Turn left on County Rd. 16 and drive three miles north; turn right on the access road to the Bradfield Bridge. The campground is just before the bridge.
**Contact:** San Juan National Forest, Dolores Ranger District, P.O. Box 210, Dolores, CO 81323; tel. (970) 882-7296.

## 54 Cabin Canyon     7

Featuring fully accessible sites and a concrete nature trail along the river, this barrier-free camp is an excellent choice for campers in wheelchairs. Cottonwood, ponderosa pine, piñon pine, and juniper trees shelter the sites. Anglers will be pleased to know there's Gold Medal fishing in the Dolores River. One-tenth of a mile east of camp is a waste disposal station for RVs.
**Location:** On the Dolores River in San Juan National Forest; map B1, grid g2.
**Campsites, facilities:** There are 11 sites for tents or RVs up to 22 feet long. Drinking water, picnic tables, fire grills, and vault toilets are provided. A waste disposal station is nearby. Some facilities are wheelchair accessible. Leashed pets are permitted.
**Elevation:** 6,500 feet.
**Reservations, fees:** Reservations are not accepted. Sites are $10 a night.
**Open:** May to November.
**Directions:** From Cortez, drive 20 miles north on U.S. 666 to Pleasant View. Continue one mile north, turn right on County Rd. DD, and drive one mile east. Turn left on County Rd. 16 and drive three miles north. Then turn right on the access road to the Bradfield Bridge, cross the bridge, and continue four miles to the campground.
**Contact:** San Juan National Forest, Dolores Ranger District, P.O. Box 210, Dolores, CO 81323; tel. (970) 882-7296.

## 55 Ferris Canyon     7

Oak, cottonwood, and pine trees ring this barrier-free camp, set next to a meadow along the Dolores River. Fishing is particularly good on this Gold Medal stretch of water, with several excellent access points. Lots of local anglers flock here for day use, so you may have to battle for a spot. At 6,500 feet, temperatures can get steaming in midsummer.
**Location:** On the Dolores River in San Juan National Forest; map B1, grid g2.
**Campsites, facilities:** There are six sites for tents or RVs up to 22 feet long. Drinking water, picnic tables, fire grills, and vault toilets are provided. Some facilities are wheelchair accessible. Leashed pets are permitted.
**Elevation:** 6,500 feet.
**Reservations, fees:** Reservations are not accepted. Sites are $10 a night.
**Open:** May to October.
**Directions:** From Cortez, drive 20 miles north on U.S. 666 to Pleasant View. Continue one mile north, turn right on County Rd. DD, and drive one mile east. Turn left on County Rd. 16 and drive three miles north. Turn right on the access road to the

Bradfield Bridge, cross the bridge, and continue seven miles to the campground.
**Contact:** San Juan National Forest, Dolores Ranger District, P.O. Box 210, Dolores, CO 81323; tel. (970) 882-7296.

## 56 House Creek       8

Although not as developed as the McPhee camp, House Creek may be a better choice for campers whose primary interests are boating or swimming. It's in a large, grassy area near the reservoir's shoreline, with a four-lane boat ramp and a swimming beach nearby. Cottonwoods and juniper trees provide limited shade.
**Location:** On McPhee Reservoir in San Juan National Forest; map B1, grid g3.
**Campsites, facilities:** There are five walk-in tent sites and 55 sites for tents or RVs up to 35 feet long. Two adjacent group camping areas can accommodate up to 30 people each. Drinking water, picnic tables, fire grills, and flush toilets are provided, and a waste disposal station is available. A boat ramp is nearby. Some facilities are wheelchair accessible. Leashed pets are permitted.
**Elevation:** 6,900 feet.
**Reservations, fees:** Reservations are accepted for some single sites and required for group sites; phone (877) 444-6777. There's an $8.65 reservation fee. You may also reserve sites at website: www.reserveusa.com. Single-site fees are $12 a night; group fees vary depending on size of the party.
**Open:** May to October.
**Directions:** From Hwy. 145 in Dolores, turn north on 11th St. and drive six miles (once out of town, the road becomes Forest Service Rd. 526). Turn left on House Creek Rd. (Forest Service Rd. 528) and continue 5.5 miles southeast to the campground.
**Contact:** San Juan National Forest, Dolores Ranger District, P.O. Box 210, Dolores, CO 81323; tel. (970) 882-7296.

## 57 McPhee       8

Perched high on a bluff overlooking McPhee Reservoir, this is one of the most developed campgrounds on the San Juan National Forest and gets extremely heavy use. The sites are large, partially shaded by piñon and juniper trees, with electric hookups, flush toilets, and even hot showers (for a fee). The walk-in sites are especially scenic, located in a separate area with good vistas of the reservoir and surrounding hills. All water sports are allowed on the reservoir, including waterskiing, sailing, swimming (best across the lake at House Creek Recreation Area), and fishing for McConaughy trout, kokanee salmon, crappie, catfish, bass, and perch.
**Location:** On McPhee Reservoir in San Juan National Forest; map B1, grid g3.
**Campsites, facilities:** There are 12 walk-in tent sites and 64 sites for tents or RVs of any length. Two adjacent group camping areas can accommodate up to 30 people each. Drinking water, picnic tables, fire grills, and flush toilets are provided. Electric hookups, laundry facilities, a waste disposal station, and showers are available. A boat ramp is nearby. Some facilities are wheelchair accessible. Leashed pets are permitted.
**Elevation:** 6,900 feet.

**Reservations, fees:** Reservations are accepted for some single sites and required for group sites; phone (877) 444-6777. There's an $8.65 reservation fee. You may also reserve sites at website: www.reserveusa.com. Single-site fees are $12-14 a night; group fees vary depending on size of the party.
**Open:** May to October.
**Directions:** From Dolores, drive two miles southwest on Hwy. 145, turn west on Hwy. 184, and continue approximately four miles. Turn right on Forest Service Rd. 271 and continue about two miles north to the campground.
**Contact:** San Juan National Forest, Dolores Ranger District, P.O. Box 210, Dolores, CO 81323; tel. (970) 882-7296.

## 58 McPhee RV Park    7

Located on a high plateau across from McPhee Reservoir, this camp offers scenic, grassy sites inside a mobile home park. The sites are huge and provide a viable alternative for folks whose extra-long RVs won't fit in the nearby U.S. Forest Service camps. The reservoir is within walking distance, with facilities for fishing, boating, and picnicking.
**Location:** West of Dolores; map B1, grid g3.
**Campsites, facilities:** There are 50 full-hookup sites for RVs of any length. No tents are permitted. Drinking water, picnic tables, fire grills, and bathrooms with hot showers are provided. Laundry facilities and a public phone are available. Leashed pets are permitted.
**Elevation:** 6,800 feet.
**Reservations, fees:** Reservations are accepted. Sites are $17-20 a night.
**Open:** May to October.
**Directions:** From the junction of Hwy. 145 and Hwy. 184 west of Dolores, drive four miles west on Hwy. 184. The camp is across the road from the entrance to McPhee Reservoir.
**Contact:** McPhee RV Park, 24990 Hwy. 84 West, Dolores, CO 81323; tel. (970) 882-4901.

## 59 Outpost RV Park      7

Although it's close to downtown Dolores, this small camp retains a natural, cozy feel, with well-kept, shaded sites next to the Dolores River. There is a large grassy area for picnics or Frisbee tossing, and a fishing platform overlooking the river. Recreation options in the area include fishing and boating on McPhee Reservoir, hiking in the nearby national forest, or rafting on the river.
**Location:** On the Dolores River; map B1, grid g3.
**Campsites, facilities:** There are 15 full-hookup sites for RVs of any length. No tents are permitted. Drinking water, picnic tables, fire grills, and bathrooms with hot showers are provided. Laundry facilities, motel rooms, and a public phone are available. Leashed pets are permitted.
**Elevation:** 6,800 feet.
**Reservations, fees:** Reservations are accepted. Sites are $18.50 a night.
**Open:** Year-round.
**Directions:** The campground is in Dolores, at 1800 Hwy. 145.

**Contact:** Outpost RV Park, P.O. Box 295, Dolores, CO 81323; tel. (970) 882-7271 or (800) 382-4892.

## 60 Dolores River RV Park     7

This full-service resort caters to both tent campers and RVers with large rigs. The main camping area is paved and open, with strips of grass marking each site, while the most sought-after sites are shaded, in grassy areas facing the river. Direct fishing access is available in the river or at the campground's private pond, and there is a riverside trail at the camp's edge for walking or biking.

**Location:** On the Dolores River; map B1, grid g3.

**Campsites, facilities:** There are 100 sites for tents or RVs of any length, many with full hookups. Drinking water, picnic tables, fire grills, and bathrooms with hot showers are provided. Laundry facilities, a waste disposal station, store, snack bar, public phone, and cabins are available. Leashed pets are permitted.

**Elevation:** 7,200 feet.

**Reservations, fees:** Reservations are accepted; phone (800) 200-2399. Sites are $11-20 a night.

**Open:** April to November.

**Directions:** From Dolores, drive 2.5 miles northeast on Hwy. 145.

**Contact:** Dolores River RV Park, 18680 Hwy. 145, Dolores, CO 81223; tel. (970) 882-7761.

## 61 Transfer      8

Covering four acres of land, the camp is situated in a beautiful aspen grove with level, partially shaded sites next to a large picnic area. There is a half-mile wheelchair-accessible hiking trail leading up to a vista point that provides expansive views of the canyon below. The Transfer Trail, just across the road from the campground, drops steeply for nearly a mile before running into the West Mancos River, where you'll find superb fishing access. If you want easier access, head a mile south of the campground to the Box Canyon Trail; it's only half a mile long with a more moderate grade.

**Location:** On the West Mancos River in San Juan National Forest; map B1, grid g4.

**Campsites, facilities:** There are 12 sites for tents or RVs up to 45 feet long. Drinking water, picnic tables, fire grills, and vault toilets are provided. Some facilities are wheelchair accessible. Leashed pets are permitted.

**Elevation:** 8,500 feet.

**Reservations, fees:** Reservations are not accepted. Sites are $10 a night.

**Open:** Memorial Day to Labor Day.

**Directions:** From Mancos, drive one-quarter mile north on Hwy. 184, turn east on West Mancos Rd. (Forest Service Rd. 561), and continue 12 miles to the campground.

**Contact:** San Juan National Forest, Dolores Ranger District, P.O. Box 210, Dolores, CO 81323; tel. (970) 882-7296.

## 62 Stoner Creek RV Park     7

Settled between little Stoner Creek and the Dolores River, this wooded camp is a perfect home base for a fishing trip in the Dolores River Valley. The sites are far enough off the main road to remain quiet and secluded, and most are sheltered by large ponderosa pines. A road leads north along Stoner Creek and ends at a trailhead that continues paralleling the creek for several miles north into the national forest.

**Location:** Northeast of Dolores; map B1, grid g4.

**Campsites, facilities:** There are 45 sites for tents or RVs of any length, most with full hookups. Drinking water, picnic tables, fire grills, and bathrooms with hot showers are provided. Laundry facilities, a waste disposal station, store, cafe, public phone, and cabins are available. Leashed pets are permitted.

**Elevation:** 7,500 feet.

**Reservations, fees:** Reservations are accepted. Sites are $12.50-19 a night.

**Open:** Mid-May to mid-November.

**Directions:** From Dolores, drive approximately 15.5 miles northeast on Hwy. 145 to the campground, located in the middle of Stoner.

**Contact:** Stoner Creek RV Park, 25113 Hwy. 145, Dolores, CO 81323; tel. (970) 882-2204.

## 63 Priest Gulch Campground and RV Park    7

This camp offers the best of two worlds—a private, quiet forest setting combined with all the comforts of the urban realm. Each site is spacious enough for large RVs, either open and sunny or shaded by large pine, spruce, and aspen trees. There are leveled fishing spots along the rocky riverbanks and hiking and horseback riding trails on the camp's property.

**Location:** On the Dolores River; map B1, grid g5.

**Campsites, facilities:** There are 93 sites for tents or RVs of any length, most with full hookups. Drinking water, picnic tables, fire grills, and bathrooms with hot showers are provided. Laundry facilities, a waste disposal station, a store, and cabins are available. Leashed pets are permitted.

**Elevation:** 8,100 feet.

**Reservations, fees:** Reservations are accepted. Sites are $18-23 a night.

**Open:** Mid-April to mid-November.

**Directions:** From Dolores, drive 23 miles northeast on Hwy. 145.

**Contact:** Priest Gulch Campground and RV Park, 26750 Hwy. 145, Dolores, CO 81323; tel. (970) 562-3810; e-mail: gulch@fone.net.

## 64 Sig Creek     7

About a quarter mile from the East Fork of Hermosa Creek—in which there is excellent fishing for rainbow and brook trout—this campground is on a gently sloping hillside in an open forest of spruce and fir. Since it's south facing, it gets plenty of sun, although temperatures remain fairly cool throughout the summer at this elevation. If you continue a little way up the road, you'll come to the Hermosa Creek Trail, an excellent mountain bike route with scenic vistas.

**Location:** Near the East Fork of Hermosa Creek in San Juan National Forest; map B1, grid g6.

**Campsites, facilities:** There are nine sites for tents or RVs up to 35 feet long.

Drinking water, picnic tables, fire grills, and vault toilets are provided. Leashed pets are permitted.

**Elevation:** 9,400 feet.

**Reservations, fees:** Reservations are not accepted. Sites are $8 a night.

**Open:** Year-round with limited winter services.

**Directions:** From Durango, drive 26 miles north on U.S. 550 to Purgatory Ski Resort. Turn west on Hermosa Creek Rd. (Forest Service Rd. 578) and continue six miles to the campground.

**Contact:** San Juan National Forest, Columbine Ranger District, Durango Office, 701 Camino del Rio, Durango, CO 81301; tel. (970) 247-4874.

## 65 Purgatory    7

Although its proximity to the road makes Purgatory a potentially noisy campground, it's an excellent base camp if you're planning a backpacking trip into the Weminuche Wilderness. The sites are not large, best suited for small vehicles with tents, and shaded by plenty of spruce and fir trees. A trail starts at camp and follows Cascade Creek to the Animas River, where you can cross a small bridge and continue into the wilderness.

**Location:** Near Purgatory Ski Resort in San Juan National Forest; map B1, grid g7.

**Campsites, facilities:** There are 14 sites for tents or RVs up to 25 feet long. Drinking water, picnic tables, fire grills, and vault toilets are provided. Leashed pets are permitted.

**Elevation:** 8,800 feet.

**Reservations, fees:** Reservations are not accepted. Sites are $10 a night.

**Open:** Memorial Day to Labor Day.

**Directions:** From Durango, drive 26 miles north on U.S. 550 to Purgatory Ski Resort. The campground is across the road from the resort.

**Contact:** San Juan National Forest, Columbine Ranger District, Durango Office, 701 Camino del Rio, Durango, CO 81301; tel. (970) 247-4874.

## 66 Haviland Lake     8

With the Hermosa Cliffs looming dramatically above the lake, this easy-to-reach pine-shaded camp makes a great scenic weekend getaway. It's a popular spot for fishing (by shore or inflatable boat) for rainbow and cutthroat trout. There is no hiking directly from the lake, but about a mile south of here is the trailhead for the Goulding Creek Trail, a steep but incredibly scenic hike.

**Location:** North of Durango in San Juan National Forest; map B1, grid g7.

**Campsites, facilities:** There are 45 sites for tents or RVs up to 35 feet long. Drinking water, picnic tables, fire grills, and vault toilets are provided. Leashed pets are permitted.

**Elevation:** 8,100 feet.

**Reservations, fees:** Reservations are not accepted. Sites are $10 a night.

**Open:** Year-round with limited winter facilities and access.

**Directions:** From Durango, drive 18 miles north on U.S. 550, turn right on Forest Service Rd. 671, and drive one mile to the lake.

**Contact:** San Juan National Forest, Columbine Ranger District, Durango Office, 701 Camino del Rio, Durango, CO 81301; tel. (970) 247-4874.

## 67 Chris Park Group  6

Chris Park's claim to fame is that in the late 1800s it was a stop on the Animas-Silverton Wagon Trail, the only route available until the railroad opened in 1882. The camp is large and open, dotted with ponderosa pines and with plenty of space for a big family reunion or party.

**Location:** Near Haviland Lake in San Juan National Forest; map B1, grid g7.

**Campsites, facilities:** Three large sites can accommodate up to 75 people each. Drinking water, picnic tables, fire grills, and vault toilets are provided. Leashed pets are permitted.

**Elevation:** 8,500 feet.

**Reservations, fees:** Reservations are required; phone (877) 444-6777. There's an $8.65 reservation fee. You may also reserve sites at website: www.reserveusa.com. Fees vary depending on size of group.

**Open:** Year-round with limited winter facilities and access.

**Directions:** From Durango, drive 18 miles north on U.S. 550, turn right on Forest Service Rd. 166, and go two miles.

**Contact:** San Juan National Forest, Columbine Ranger District, Durango Office, 701 Camino del Rio, Durango, CO 81301; tel. (970) 247-4874.

## 68 Transfer Park    8

Since it's adjacent to the Burnt Timber Trailhead, Transfer Park is a popular base camp for backpackers. Set on 11 acres between Lemon Reservoir and the Weminuche Wilderness, the camp offers large sites in a mix of conifer and aspen forest. The upper loop is better for large RVs; the lower loop, with smaller sites near the river, is best for tents.

**Location:** North of Lemon Reservoir in San Juan National Forest; map B1, grid g7.

**Campsites, facilities:** There are 25 sites for tents or RVs up to 45 feet long. Drinking water, picnic tables, fire grills, and vault toilets are provided. Leashed pets are permitted.

**Elevation:** 8,600 feet.

**Reservations, fees:** Reservations are not accepted. Sites are $10 a night.

**Open:** Year-round with limited winter facilities and access.

**Directions:** From Durango, drive approximately 15 miles east on Florida Rd. (County Rd. 240), turn left on Forest Service Rd. 596, and continue approximately eight miles north, passing Lemon Reservoir, to the campground.

**Contact:** San Juan National Forest, Columbine Ranger District, Bayfield Office, P.O. Box 439, Bayfield, CO 81122; tel. (970) 884-2512.

## 69 Florida      7

Florida is about two miles north of Lemon Reservoir in a brilliant forest of aspen, blue spruce, and fir. Sites are level and roomy, with a few good tent sites along the riverbanks. Across from the campground entrance, E. Florida Rd. climbs steeply to the east, providing access to the Lost Lake and Stump Lake Trails, a couple of short, gentle hikes into the backcountry. Boating and fishing are within a short drive at Lemon Reservoir.

**Location:** On the Florida River in San Juan National Forest; map B1, grid g7.

**Campsites, facilities:** There are 20 sites for tents or RVs up to 45 feet long, and a large group area for up to 100 people. Drinking water, picnic tables, fire grills, and vault toilets are provided. Leashed pets are permitted.

**Elevation:** 8,100 feet.

**Reservations, fees:** Reservations are required for group sites; phone (877) 444-6777. There's an $8.65 reservation fee. You may also reserve sites at website: www.reserveusa.com. The fee varies depending on group size. Reservations are not accepted for single sites, which are $10 a night.

**Open:** Year-round with limited winter facilities and access.

**Directions:** From Durango, drive approximately 15 miles east on Florida Rd. (County Rd. 240), turn left on Forest Service Rd. 596, and continue approximately seven miles north, passing Lemon Reservoir, to the campground.

**Contact:** San Juan National Forest, Columbine Ranger District, Bayfield Office, P.O. Box 439, Bayfield, CO 81122; tel. (970) 884-2512.

## 70 Miller Creek     7

At this little campground across the road from Lemon Reservoir you have a choice of sunny or shaded sites along Miller Creek. It's the closest campground to the reservoir, although access is limited due to the steep shoreline. A boat ramp is nearby, and a little more than a mile up the road there's a day-use area with picnic facilities and fishing access. Prospects are best for rainbow trout and kokanee salmon.

**Location:** Near Lemon Reservoir in San Juan National Forest; map B1, grid h8.

**Campsites, facilities:** There are 11 sites for tents or RVs up to 35 feet long. Drinking water, picnic tables, fire grills, and vault toilets are provided. A boat ramp is just north of the campground. Leashed pets are permitted.

**Elevation:** 8,100 feet.

**Reservations, fees:** Reservations are not accepted. Sites are $10 a night.

**Open:** Year-round with limited winter facilities and access.

**Directions:** From Durango, drive approximately 15 miles east on Florida Rd. (County Rd. 240), turn left on Forest Service Rd. 596, and continue approximately three miles north to the campground.

**Contact:** San Juan National Forest, Columbine Ranger District, Bayfield Office, P.O. Box 439, Bayfield, CO 81122; tel. (970) 884-2512.

## 71 Vallecito      8

With convenient access to Vallecito Reservoir and the Weminuche Wilderness, this large campground is one of the most popular in the region. It's spread over several acres of level, conifer-covered terrain offering spacious sites, including a few coveted spots next to the creek. Fishing in Vallecito Creek is rumored to be even better than at Vallecito Reservoir, with good prospects for native trout. Adjacent to camp is the trailhead for the Vallecito Creek Trail, which meanders north for several miles into the depths of the Weminuche Wilderness. The trailhead is a favorite with folks on horse packing trips, with facilities nearby for animal loading and unloading.

**Location:** On Vallecito Creek in San Juan National Forest; map B1, grid g8.

**Campsites, facilities:** There are 80 sites for tents or RVs up to 45 feet long. Drinking water, picnic tables, fire grills, and vault toilets are provided. Leashed pets are permitted.

**Elevation:** 8,000 feet.

**Reservations, fees:** Reservations are not accepted. Sites are $10 a night.

**Open:** Year-round with limited winter facilities and access.

**Directions:** From U.S. 160 at Bayfield, turn north on County Rd. 501 (Forest Service Rd. 600) and drive approximately 23 miles, passing along the western shore of Vallecito Reservoir, to the campground.

**Contact:** San Juan National Forest, Columbine Ranger District, Bayfield Office, P.O. Box 439, Bayfield, CO 81122; tel. (970) 884-2512.

## 72 Sundance RV Park    6

Plunked right in the middle of Cortez, this park is one of the town's newest, specializing in extra-large spaces for big RVs. You get well-kept, shady sites with basic amenities and easy access to the shops and restaurants in town. Across the street is a city park with a visitor center, swimming pool, playground, and tennis courts.

**Location:** In Cortez; map B1, grid h3.

**Campsites, facilities:** There are 68 full-hookup sites for RVs of any length,. Drinking water, picnic tables, fire grills, and bathrooms with hot showers are provided. Laundry facilities and a public phone are available, and a grocery store and restaurant are next door. Leashed pets are permitted.

**Elevation:** 6,200 feet.

**Reservations, fees:** Reservations are accepted; phone (800) 880-9413. Sites are $22 a night.

**Open:** Year-round.

**Directions:** The camp is located in downtown Cortez at 815 E. Main Street.

**Contact:** Sundance RV Park, 815 E. Main St., Cortez, CO 81321; tel. (970) 565-0997.

## 73 La Mesa RV Park   6

Set near the eastern edge of Cortez, La Mesa offers convenient access to all the amenities in town. The sites are mostly open, with a few large shade trees at some, and all have clear mountain views. The Spanish-speaking hosts are friendly and helpful, happy to offer advice, directions, or even local tours.

**Location:** In Cortez; map B1, grid h3.

**Campsites, facilities:** There are 40 sites for tents or RVs of any length, most with full hookups. Drinking water, picnic tables, fire grills, and bathrooms with hot showers are provided. Laundry facilities, a waste disposal station, and a public phone are available. Leashed pets are permitted.

**Elevation:** 6,200 feet.

**Reservations, fees:** Reservations are accepted. Sites are $15-19 a night.

**Open:** Year-round.

**Directions:** The park is located in Cortez, on U.S. 160 at its junction with Hwy. 145.

**Contact:** La Mesa RV Park, 2430 E. Main St., Cortez, CO 81321; tel. (970) 565-3610.

## 74 Lazy G Campground     5

Although this camp is next to a large motel, it's quite pleasant, with fully developed facilities and convenient access to the Mesa Verde area and San Juan National Forest. The sites are even and open, with a few trees sprinkled here and there, and the restaurant, swimming pool, and hot tub feel like luxuries after an arduous day of hiking and exploring.

**Location:** In Cortez; map B1, grid h3.

**Campsites, facilities:** There are 80 sites for tents or RVs of any length, many with full hookups. Drinking water, picnic tables, fire grills, and bathrooms with hot showers are provided. Laundry facilities, a waste disposal station, swimming pool and hot tub, restaurant, public phone, and sports field are available. Some facilities are wheelchair accessible. Leashed pets are permitted.

**Elevation:** 6,200 feet.

**Reservations, fees:** Reservations are accepted. Sites are $19.50-25.50 a night.

**Open:** Year-round.

**Directions:** In Cortez, drive to the junction of U.S. 160 and Hwy. 145. The campground is to the north on Hwy. 145, adjacent to the Days Inn.

**Contact:** Lazy G Campground, c/o Days Inn, P.O. Box 1048, Cortez, CO 81321; tel. (970) 565-8577.

## 75 Cortez-Mesa Verde KOA    7

The best sites at this camp are the deluxe tent sites set in nice, grassy areas with picture-perfect views of the Mesa Verde Mountains and Sleeping Ute Mountain. RV sites are placed side-by-side on gravel pads, with scattered trees. Full services in downtown Cortez are nearby, with Mesa Verde National Park only a few miles away.

**Location:** East of Cortez; map B1, grid h3.

**Campsites, facilities:** There are 90 sites for tents or RVs of any length, many with full hookups. Drinking water, picnic tables, fire grills, and bathrooms with hot showers are provided. Laundry facilities, a waste disposal station, a store, a swimming pool and hot tub, and a public phone are available. Leashed pets are permitted.

**Elevation:** 6,200 feet.

**Reservations, fees:** Reservations are accepted; phone (800) KOA-3901. Sites are $20-25 a night.

**Open:** Mid-April to mid-October.

**Directions:** From Cortez, drive one-half mile east on U.S. 160.

**Contact:** Cortez-Mesa Verde KOA, 27432 E. U.S. 160, Cortez, CO 81321; tel. (970) 565-9301.

## 76 Mesa Oasis Campground    7

The large, sparsely grassed sites at this camp provide superb views of Ute Mountain and Mesa Verde to the southeast. The Ute Mountain Tribal Park is located to the south, with opportunities for hiking and exploring Anasazi ruins (you'll need a reservation to visit; phone (970) 565-3751, extension 330). At the other end of the spectrum, just a few miles south in Towaoc, you'll find the Ute Mountain Casino, touted as the largest casino in the Four Corners region.

**Location:** South of Cortez; map B1, grid h3.

**Campsites, facilities:** There are 40 tent sites and 52 sites for RVs of any length, some with full hookups. Drinking water, picnic tables, fire grills, and bathrooms with hot showers are provided. Laundry facilities, a waste disposal station, store, and public phone are available. Leashed pets are permitted.

**Elevation:** 6,200 feet.

**Reservations, fees:** Reservations are accepted. Sites are $15-20 a night.

**Open:** Year-round.

**Directions:** From Cortez, drive four miles south on U.S. 160.

**Contact:** Mesa Oasis Campground, 5608 U.S. 160, Cortez, CO 81321; tel. (970) 565-8716.

## 77 Cozy Comfort RV Park    6

on highway, small weeping willows, silver maples, in canyon, Dolores River walking distance, fishing, McPhee Res. mile away. graveled, tent sites grasses trees shading, patio slab for tables. Set within a forest of young silver maples and delicate weeping willow trees in the Dolores River Canyon, this tents-only camp offers easy access from the highway. Fishing access points along the Dolores River are within walking distance, and McPhee Reservoir, a mile away, provides another option for anglers. Sites are a mixture of gravel and grass, each with a small concrete patio and table.

**Location:** In Dolores; map B1, grid h3.

**Campsites, facilities:** There are two tent sites and 12 full-hookup sites. Drinking water, picnic tables, fire grills (at tent sites only), and bathrooms with hot showers are provided. Laundry facilities and a waste disposal station are available. Leashed pets are permitted.

**Elevation:** 6,000 feet.

**Reservations, fees:** Reservations are accepted. Sites are $12.50-16.50 a night.

**Open:** Year-round.

**Directions:** From Hwy. 160 at Cortez, drive nine miles north on Hwy. 145. The park is on the west side of the highway.

**Contact:** Cozy Comfort RV Park, P.O. Box 1327, Dolores, CO 81323; tel. (970) 882-2483.

## 78 Summit Reservoir State Wildlife Area     6

The highlight of this reservoir is diverse warm-water fishing for species including smallmouth and largemouth bass, channel catfish, walleye, northern pike, and crappie. No-wake boating is permitted, and there's a rough boat ramp on the northwestern shore, close to several campsites. Sites are generally small but level, spread randomly near the open shoreline. Waterfowl hunting is permitted.

**Location:** North of Mancos; map B1, grid h4.

**Campsites, facilities:** Camping is permitted in several designated campsites around the reservoir. Vault toilets and a boat ramp are provided, but there is no drinking water. Leashed pets are permitted.

**Elevation:** 7,300 feet.

**Reservations, fees:** Reservations are not accepted. There is no fee.

**Open:** Year-round.

**Directions:** From Mancos, drive nine miles northeast on Hwy. 184.

**Contact:** Colorado Division of Wildlife, 2300 S. Townsend Ave., Montrose, CO 81401; tel. (970) 252-6000.

## **79** Joe Moore Reservoir State Wildlife Area    6

Joe Moore, a modest-sized reservoir at 33 acres, lies a few miles north of Mancos, providing a primitive alternative to the several U.S. Forest Service camps and private RV parks in the vicinity. Sites are simple and basic, mostly rough clearings with well-used fire rings. No-wake boating is permitted, and prospects for rainbow and brown trout and largemouth bass are good. To the west are rough U.S. Forest Service roads reaching to the edges of the scenic Lost Canyon. Waterfowl hunting is permitted.

**Location:** North of Mancos; map B1, grid h4.

**Campsites, facilities:** Dispersed camping is permitted throughout the property. Vault toilets and a boat ramp are provided, but there are no other facilities or drinking water. Leashed pets are permitted.

**Elevation:** 7,500 feet.

**Reservations, fees:** Reservations are not accepted. There is no fee.

**Open:** Year-round.

**Directions:** From Mancos, drive five miles northeast on Hwy. 184, turn north on County Rd. 40, and continue four miles to the reservoir.

**Contact:** Colorado Division of Wildlife, 2300 S. Townsend Ave., Montrose, CO 81401; tel. (970) 252-6000.

## **80** Morefield     8

This privately operated camp is set in the midst of Mesa Verde National Park, a natural showcase for the ruins of dozens of pre-Columbian cliff dwellings and remnants of ancient Anasazi culture. High points include the Step House and the Spruce Tree House as well as the Cliff Palace, the largest known cliff dwelling in the world. You can tour the park by car, but this intricate environment is best appreciated on foot. The campground, in contrast to the park's primitive nature, is well developed and offers such niceties as RV hookups, hot showers, and laundry facilities.

**Location:** In Mesa Verde National Park; map B1, grid h3.

**Campsites, facilities:** There are 450 sites for tents or RVs of any length, some with full hookups. Drinking water, picnic tables, fire grills, and bathrooms with hot showers are provided. Laundry facilities, a waste disposal station, store, and public phone are available. Guided bus tours leave the campground regularly. Some facilities are wheelchair accessible. Leashed pets are permitted.

**Elevation:** 8,000 feet.

**Reservations, fees:** Reservations are not accepted. Sites are $11-18 a night.

**Open:** May to mid-October.

**Directions:** From Mancos, drive seven miles west on U.S. 160, turn south on the

Mesa Verde National Park access road, and continue four miles to the park entrance. **Contact:** Morefield Campground, Mesa Verde National Park, CO 81330; tel. (970) 529-4421.

## **81** A & A Mesa Verde Resort     7

This full-service option to the Morefield camp offers convenient access to Mesa Verde National Park and a choice of sites unobstructed or shaded by piñon pine trees. The managers boast of a "million-dollar view" of Mesa Verde and lots of group activities, including ice cream socials, nightly bonfires, fossil hunts, and wagon rides for the kids. A swimming pool, hot tub, and baseball field round out the facilities. A mile-long hiking trail is also available on the property, and if you should want to spend the day hiking at Mesa Verde, the owners will even pet sit for you (no dogs are allowed on the national park trails).

**Location:** Near Mesa Verde National Park; map B1, grid h3.

**Campsites, facilities:** There are 25 tent sites and 55 sites for RVs of any length, many with full hookups. Drinking water, picnic tables, fire grills, and bathrooms with hot showers are provided. Laundry facilities, a waste disposal station, store, cabins, sports facilities, mini golf, swimming pool and hot tub, and public phone are available. Leashed pets are permitted.

**Elevation:** 7,000 feet.

**Reservations, fees:** Reservations are accepted; phone (800) 972-6620. Sites are $19-25 a night.

**Open:** Year-round.

**Directions:** From Mancos, drive seven miles west on U.S. 160, turn north opposite the entrance to Mesa Verde National Park, and drive one block. Turn east on the frontage road and continue two blocks to the resort.

**Contact:** A & A Mesa Verde Resort, 34979 U.S. 160, Mancos, CO 81328; tel. (970) 565-3517.

## **82** Mesa Verde Point Kampark    6

One of several RV parks in the Mesa Verde area, this popular camp provides grassy sites, some shaded and some open, with an unobstructed view of Mesa Verde and the bonus of a swimming pool and hot tub. Mesa Verde National Park is a short drive away.

**Location:** Near Mesa Verde National Park; map B1, grid h3.

**Campsites, facilities:** There are 42 sites for tents or RVs of any length, many with full hookups. Drinking water, picnic tables, fire grills, and bathrooms with hot showers are provided. Laundry facilities, a waste disposal station, swimming pool and hot tub, store, and public phone are available. Leashed pets are permitted.

**Elevation:** 7,000 feet.

**Reservations, fees:** Reservations are accepted. Sites are $22.50-25.50 a night.

**Open:** April to October.

**Directions:** From Mancos, drive six miles west on U.S. 160.

**Contact:** Mesa Verde Point Kampark, 35303 U.S. 160, Mancos, CO 81328; tel. (970) 533-7421 or (800) 776-7421.

## 83 Wild Wild Rest     6

This graveled campground may lack ambience—it's right on the highway, adjacent to a convenience store—but it offers basic facilities at a reasonable rate. The sites are treeless and level, most set tolerably far back from the highway, with a little trout pond providing on-site fishing. Guided horseback rides are available. The entrance to Mesa Verde National Park is about a mile to the east.

**Location:** Near Mesa Verde National Park; map B1, grid h3.

**Campsites, facilities:** There are six tent sites and nine full-hookup sites for RVs of any length. Drinking water, picnic tables, fire grills, and bathrooms with hot showers are provided. Laundry facilities, a waste disposal station, store, public phone, and horse rentals are available. Leashed pets are permitted.

**Elevation:** 8,000 feet.

**Reservations, fees:** Reservations are accepted. Sites are $15-19 a night.

**Open:** Year-round.

**Directions:** From Mancos, drive seven miles west on U.S. 160.

**Contact:** Wild Wild Rest, P.O. Box 689, Mancos, CO 81328; tel. (970) 533-9747.

## 84 Mancos State Park     8

Mancos State Park is organized around Mancos Reservoir, a quiet, serene 200-acre lake bordered by pine and fir trees with spectacular views of the La Plata Mountains. Nonmotorized boating and fishing are permitted throughout the lake, with easy access and good prospects for rainbow trout. All campsites are wooded and level, but the larger loop on the south shore is best suited for large RVs, while tent campers tend to prefer the more secluded sites on the north shore. Near that area is the park's only designated hiking trail, the Chicken Creek Trail, which starts at West Side Rd. and heads north into the national forest.

**Location:** Northeast of Mancos; map B1, grid h4.

**Campsites, facilities:** There are nine tent sites and 24 sites for tents or RVs up to 45 feet long. Drinking water, picnic tables, fire grills, and vault toilets are provided. A waste disposal station is available. Leashed pets are permitted.

**Elevation:** 7,800 feet.

**Reservations, fees:** Reservations are accepted. Phone (303) 470-1144 or (800) 678-CAMP (800-678-2267) outside the Denver Metro area; there's a $7 reservation fee. Sites are $10 a night, and there's a $4 entrance fee.

**Open:** May to October.

**Directions:** From Mancos, drive one-quarter mile north on Hwy. 184, turn right on County Rd. 42, and drive four miles northwest. Turn left into the park entrance. The main camping loop is on the southeast shore of the reservoir; the nine tent sites are on the northwest edge.

**Contact:** Mancos State Park, P.O. Box 1697, Arboles, CO 81121; tel. (970) 434-6862.

## 85 Echo Basin Dude Ranch Resort       8

This 650-acre cattle-ranch-turned-resort successfully melds urban and rural worlds, creating a peaceful backcountry environment with lots of creature comforts. The campsites are set beneath towering pine and spruce trees, adjacent to the main resort complex. Fish from the banks of the Mancos River or at the resort's own private stocked ponds. Other options include hiking or horseback riding through alpine meadows and forest.

**Location:** Northeast of Mancos; map B1, grid h4.

**Campsites, facilities:** There are 110 sites for tents or RVs of any length, many with full hookups. Drinking water, picnic tables, fire grills, and bathrooms with hot showers are provided. Laundry facilities, a waste disposal station, store, restaurant, public phone, swimming pool, cabins, and sports facilities are available. Leashed pets are permitted.

**Elevation:** 7,800 feet.

**Reservations, fees:** Reservations are accepted; phone (800) 426-1890. Sites are $17-25 a night.

**Open:** Year-round.

**Directions:** From Mancos, drive two miles east on U.S. 160, turn left on Echo Basin Rd. (County Rd. 44), and drive three miles north to the resort.

**Contact:** Echo Basin Dude Ranch Resort, 43747 Rd. M, Mancos, CO 81328; tel. (970) 533-7000.

## 86 Target Tree      8

This camp's name was inspired by nearby ponderosa pines that bear marks made by the Ute Native Americans, who used the trees for target practice with rifles and bows and arrows. The sites sit atop a sunny hillside above the scenic Cherry Creek Valley, providing a perfect perch from which to view the area's resident population of birds, including red-tailed hawks, eagles, and a variety of native songbirds. The Narrow Gauge Trail starts at camp and leads nearly a mile up to the old railroad site. Mesa Verde Park is just a short drive south.

**Location:** East of Mancos in San Juan National Forest; map B1, grid h4.

**Campsites, facilities:** There are 25 sites for tents or RVs up to 45 feet long. Drinking water, picnic tables, fire grills, and vault toilets are provided. Some facilities are wheelchair accessible. Leashed pets are permitted.

**Elevation:** 7,800 feet.

**Reservations, fees:** Reservations are not accepted. Sites are $10 a night.

**Open:** May to November.

**Directions:** From Mancos, drive seven miles east on U.S. 160 to the campground.

**Contact:** San Juan National Forest, Dolores Ranger District, P.O. Box 210, Dolores, CO 81323; tel. (970) 882-7296.

## 87 Kroeger     8

Set in the beautiful La Plata Canyon, this camp provides easy access to the river and cool sites shaded by a diverse mixture of aspen, fir, spruce, and cottonwood trees. A hiking trail leads west of camp into the La Plata Mountains, crossing tiny backcountry creeks along the way. Fishing is available across the road from camp in the La Plata River, but heavy competition has lowered success rates. To the north you'll find more remote river access and several good hiking trails.

**Location:** Near the La Plata River in San Juan National Forest; map B1, grid h5.

**Campsites, facilities:** There are 11 sites for tents or RVs up to 35 feet long. Drinking water, picnic tables, fire grills, and vault toilets are provided. Leashed pets are permitted.

**Elevation:** 9,000 feet.

**Reservations, fees:** Reservations are not accepted. Sites are $8 a night.

**Open:** Year-round with limited winter facilities and access.

**Directions:** From Durango, drive 12 miles west on U.S. 160, turn right on La Plata Canyon Rd. (Forest Service Rd. 571), and drive six miles north to the campground.

**Contact:** San Juan National Forest, Columbine Ranger District, Durango Office, 701 Camino del Rio, Durango, CO 81301; tel. (970) 247-4874.

## **88** Junction Creek      7

Only five miles from Durango, Junction Creek is a great choice for those who wish to camp in a wilderness-like setting and still have convenient access to shops and restaurants in town. The camp is large, set on 38 acres with roomy sites well screened by ponderosa pines. Although there are no creekside sites, you can reach the creek via a short downhill trail. Fishing prospects are so-so near camp; a better bet, if you have the time, is to hike farther upstream where there are fewer people and less fishing pressure. The southern end of the Colorado Trail is about a mile south of camp, beginning at the national forest boundary at the end of the pavement. To the north is the wheelchair-accessible Animas Overlook, which provides interpretive information and sprawling vistas of the Animas Valley and peaks to the east.

**Location:** Northwest of Durango in San Juan National Forest; map B1, grid h6.

**Campsites, facilities:** There are 34 sites for tents or RVs of any length. Drinking water, picnic tables, fire grills, and vault toilets are provided. Some facilities are wheelchair accessible. Leashed pets are permitted.

**Elevation:** 7,500 feet.

**Reservations, fees:** Reservations are not accepted. Sites are $10 a night.

**Open:** Year-round with limited winter facilities and access.

**Directions:** From U.S. 550 in Durango, turn west on 25th St. and follow it for 3.5 miles (25th St. becomes Junction Creek Rd. outside of town). Continue 1.5 miles west on Forest Service Rd. 171 to the campground.

**Contact:** San Juan National Forest, Columbine Ranger District, Durango Office, 701 Camino del Rio, Durango, CO 81301; tel. (970) 247-4874.

## **89** Lightner Creek Campground      8

With easy access off the picturesque San Juan Skyway, Lightner Creek provides comfortable camping in a beautiful, forested setting. Many sites are next to the rocky banks of the icy, clear mountain creek; others have direct access to hiking trails that wind throughout the resort's 25 acres. All have ample room for large vehicles and plenty of shade. A grocery store and large bathrooms offer modern conveniences.

**Location:** West of Durango; map B1, grid h6.

**Campsites, facilities:** There are 98 sites for tents or RVs of any length, many with full hookups. Drinking water, picnic tables, fire grills, and bathrooms with hot showers are provided. Laundry facilities, a waste disposal station, store, public phone, swimming pool, camping cabins, lodge rooms, and sports facilities are available. Some facilities are wheelchair accessible. Leashed pets are permitted.

**Elevation:** 7,200 feet.

**Reservations, fees:** Reservations are accepted. Sites are $22-28 a night.

**Open:** May to October.

**Directions:** From Durango, drive two miles west on U.S. 160, turn right on Lightner Creek Rd., and continue 1.5 miles north to the campground.

**Contact:** Lightner Creek Campground, 1567 County Rd. 207, Durango, CO 81301; tel. (970) 247-5406.

## **90** Cottonwood RV Park    7

This pleasing camp sits on a large, level lot at the base of a wooded hill, adjacent to Lightner Creek. Direct fishing access is available at the creek; the nearby Animas River also offers decent prospects. The sites are mostly open, with a little shade closer to the hill. Downtown Durango and the Durango and Silverton Narrow Gauge Railroad are within walking distance.

**Location:** In Durango; map B1, grid h6.

**Campsites, facilities:** There are 73 full-hookup sites for tents or RVs of any length. Drinking water, picnic tables, fire grills, and bathrooms with hot showers are provided. A waste disposal station, public phone, and camping cabins are available. Leashed pets are permitted.

**Elevation:** 7,000 feet.

**Reservations, fees:** Reservations are accepted. Sites are $22 a night.

**Open:** Year-round with limited winter facilities.

**Directions:** From the junction of U.S. 160 and U.S. 550 in Durango, drive one-quarter mile west on U.S. 160.

**Contact:** Cottonwood RV Park, 21636 U.S. 160, Durango, CO 81301; tel. (970) 247-1977.

## **91** Durango North KOA      8

One of several camps beside the Animas River along U.S. 550, this KOA is in a particularly beautiful setting with a brilliant mixture of conifers and deciduous trees, stately mountain views, and great fishing access. There are hiking trails nearby and a small fishpond on site (you must pay to fish), plus a well-stocked grocery store and a cafe. Swim in the heated pool; braver souls can dunk in the chilly river water.

**Location:** On the Animas River; map B1, grid h7.

**Campsites, facilities:** There are 20 tent sites and 130 sites for RVs of any length, many with full hookups. Drinking water, picnic tables, fire grills, and bathrooms with hot showers are provided. Laundry facilities, a waste disposal station, store, cafe, public phone, and swimming pool are available. Leashed pets are permitted.

**Elevation:** 7,000 feet.

**Reservations, fees:** Reservations are accepted; phone (800) KOA-2792. Sites are $20.50-28 a night.

**Open:** May to mid-October.

**Directions:** From Durango, drive 10 miles north on U.S. 550, turn right on County Rd. 250, and continue into the campground.

**Contact:** Durango North KOA, 13391 County Rd. 250, Durango, CO 81301; tel. (970) 247-4499.

## 92 Hermosa Meadows Campground     8

Enormous willow and cottonwood trees droop over the grassy, riverside sites at this camp. The Animas River runs the length of the property, providing superb fishing access and the peaceful sound of rushing water. The park also offers stocked trout ponds that virtually guarantee success. Hiking trails are available to the northeast and west in the San Juan National Forest.

**Location:** On the Animas River; map B1, grid h7.

**Campsites, facilities:** There are 75 tent sites and 75 sites for RVs of any length, many with full hookups. Drinking water, picnic tables, fire grills, and bathrooms with hot showers are provided. Laundry facilities, a waste disposal station, store, public phone, and sports facilities are available. Leashed pets are permitted.

**Elevation:** 6,600 feet.

**Reservations, fees:** Reservations are accepted; phone (800) 748-2853. Sites are $18-26 a night.

**Open:** Year-round.

**Directions:** From Durango, drive seven miles north on U.S. 550, turn right on Hermosa Meadows Rd., and continue one-quarter mile east.

**Contact:** Hermosa Meadows Campground, 31420 U.S. 550, Unit 24, Durango, CO 81301; tel. (970) 247-3055; e-mail: hermosameadowscamperpark@compuserve.com.

## 93 Alpen Rose RV Park      7

Scenic mountain views and large sites shaded by deciduous trees are featured at this park on the floor of the lush Animas Valley. Although the Animas River runs nearby, there is no public fishing access at the camp; instead, the owners furnish a privately stocked fishing pond for guests. Hiking and horseback riding are possible to the north in the San Juan National Forest. During the summer, homemade pancake breakfasts are available.

**Location:** North of Durango; map B1, grid h7.

**Campsites, facilities:** There are 108 full-hookup sites for RVs of any length. No tents are permitted. Drinking water, picnic tables, fire grills, and bathrooms with hot showers are provided. Laundry facilities, a waste disposal station, store, public phone, swimming pool, and sports facilities are available. Some facilities are wheelchair accessible. Leashed pets are permitted.

**Elevation:** 6,700 feet.

**Reservations, fees:** Reservations are accepted. Sites are $28.50 a night.

**Open:** Mid-April to mid-October.

**Directions:** From Durango, drive 1.5 miles north on U.S. 550.

**Contact:** Alpen Rose RV Park, 27847 U.S. 550 North, Durango, CO 81301; tel. (970) 247-5540.

## 94 United Campground of Durango  8

Located at the entrance to the Animas Valley, this beautiful campground sits on 80 acres of natural forest and meadow, with miles of hiking trails and a close-up view of the historic Durango and Silverton Narrow Gauge Railroad. The sites are well shaded by pine trees and have gorgeous views of the sprawling green hills surrounding the valley. Fishing is available on the Animas River. The camp is on a local bus route, so you can easily get to Durango without having to disrupt your campsite.

**Location:** North of Durango; map B1, grid h7.

**Campsites, facilities:** There are 90 tent sites and 103 sites for RVs of any length, many with full hookups. Drinking water, picnic tables, fire grills, and bathrooms with hot showers are provided. Laundry facilities, a waste disposal station, a store, a public phone, and a swimming pool are available. Some facilities are wheelchair accessible. Leashed pets are permitted.

**Elevation:** 6,500 feet.

**Reservations, fees:** Reservations are accepted. Sites are $17-28 a night.

**Open:** April to November.

**Directions:** From Durango, drive one-half mile north on U.S. 550, turn right on Animas View Dr., and continue a short distance to the campground.

**Contact:** United Campground of Durango, 1322 Animas View Dr., Durango, CO 81301; tel. (970) 247-3853.

## 95 Durango East KOA  6

Set on a dry, sloping mesa just outside of Durango, this KOA offers piñon-shaded, private sites and lovely, unspoiled mountain views. The campground hosts keep things activity oriented, with amusements including nightly ice cream socials and big group pancake breakfasts. Most tourist attractions In and around Durango are within a short drive.

**Location:** Near Durango; map B1, grid h7.

**Campsites, facilities:** There are 30 tent sites and 90 sites for RVs of any length, many with full hookups. Drinking water, picnic tables, fire grills, and bathrooms with hot showers are provided. Laundry facilities, a waste disposal station, store, public phone, and swimming pool are available. Some facilities are wheelchair accessible. Leashed pets are permitted.

**Elevation:** 7,000 feet.

**Reservations, fees:** Reservations are accepted; phone (800) KOA-0793. Sites are $20-27 a night.

**Open:** Mid-April to mid-October.

**Directions:** From the junction of U.S. 160 and U.S. 550 in Durango, drive three miles east on U.S. 160 to the campground on the right.

**Contact:** Durango East KOA, 30090 U.S. 160, Durango, CO 81301; tel. (970) 247-0783.

## 96 Middle Mountain     7

The last in the line of four campgrounds along Vallecito Reservoir's eastern shore, Middle Mountain is a slightly more out-of-the-way alternative. It's just past the Los Pinos River and has easy access to both the stream and the reservoir. The south-facing sites stay sunny most of the day, with a few aspen and ponderosa pine trees providing scattered shade. The marina and boat ramp are to the south of camp. All boating is permitted, including waterskiing and windsurfing; fishing for brown trout and northern pike is excellent.

**Location:** On Vallecito Reservoir in San Juan National Forest; map B1, grid h9.

**Campsites, facilities:** There are 24 sites for tents or RVs up to 35 feet long. Drinking water, picnic tables, fire grills, and vault toilets are provided. A full-service marina with a boat ramp and rentals is nearby. Leashed pets are permitted.

**Elevation:** 7,900 feet.

**Reservations, fees:** Reservations are not accepted. Sites are $10 a night.

**Open:** Year-round with limited winter facilities and access.

**Directions:** From U.S. 160 at Bayfield, turn north on County Rd. 501 (Forest Service Rd. 600) and drive approximately 15 miles to the Vallecito Dam. Turn right on Forest Service Rd. 603 and drive 4.5 miles northwest Then turn left on Forest Service Rd. 602 and continue one-quarter mile west to the campground.

**Contact:** San Juan National Forest, Columbine Ranger District, Bayfield Office, P.O. Box 439, Bayfield, CO 81122; tel. (970) 884-2512.

## 97 Pine Point       8

Pine Point is the most rustic campground on Vallecito Reservoir, providing shady sites with clear views of the lake and high peaks to the northwest, but no drinking water. A few sites are near the shore, but boating access is limited; the boat ramp and access to all water sports is about a half mile north. Private resorts nearby offer limited supplies and amenities. The East Creek Trail, suitable for both hikers and horses, begins near camp and heads east for several miles into the backcountry, eventually meeting other trails routed north into the Weminuche Wilderness.

**Location:** On Vallecito Reservoir in San Juan National Forest; map B1, grid h9.

**Campsites, facilities:** There are 30 sites for tents or RVs up to 35 feet long. Picnic tables, fire grills, and vault toilets are provided, but there is no drinking water. A full-service marina with a boat ramp and rentals is nearby. Leashed pets are permitted.

**Elevation:** 7,900 feet.

**Reservations, fees:** Reservations are not accepted. Sites are $10 a night.

**Open:** Year-round with limited winter facilities and access.

**Directions:** From U.S. 160 at Bayfield, turn north on County Rd. 501 (Forest Service Rd. 600) and drive approximately 15 miles to the Vallecito Dam. Turn right on Forest Service Rd. 603 and drive 4.5 miles northwest to the campground.

**Contact:** San Juan National Forest, Columbine Ranger District, Bayfield Office, P.O. Box 439, Bayfield, CO 81122; tel. (970) 884-2512.

## 98 Five Branches Camper Park  9

The most developed of the several campgrounds on the east side of Vallecito Reservoir, this beautifully landscaped park provides direct lake access and unparalleled views of the water and mountains to the west. Wide-open RV spaces sit just feet from the lakeshore, while the tent sites and additional RV spots are farther back, shaded by enormous mature pines. A large marina comes complete with a modern boat ramp, docks, and boat rentals, plus gas and snacks. The Los Pinos River is just north of the campground, providing easy access to more fishing and hiking/horseback riding trails. Rafting trips and mountain bike rentals can also be arranged at the camp.

**Location:** On Vallecito Reservoir; map B1, grid h9.

**Campsites, facilities:** There are 20 tent sites and 95 full-hookup sites for RVs of any length. Drinking water, picnic tables, fire grills, and bathrooms with hot showers are provided. Laundry facilities, a waste disposal station, store, public phone, cabins, and full-service marina with a boat ramp and rentals are available. Some facilities are wheelchair accessible. Leashed pets are permitted.

**Elevation:** 7,650 feet.

**Reservations, fees:** Reservations are accepted; phone (800) 582-9580. Sites are $15-25 a night.

**Open:** May to October.

**Directions:** From U.S. 160 at Bayfield, turn north on County Rd. 501 (Forest Service Rd. 600) and drive 20 miles. Turn right on the graveled access road and continue about four miles southeast to the campground.

**Contact:** Five Branches Camper Park, 4677 County Rd. 501A, Bayfield, CO 81122; tel. (970) 884-2582.

## 99 North Canyon       7

The smallest of the four campgrounds in the immediate area, North Canyon is often used as an overflow camp in the summer. It's open and airy, with large, level sites dotted with mature ponderosa pines. Access to Vallecito Reservoir is nearby, and there's a good hiking/equestrian trail routed east from camp along North Canyon Creek.

**Location:** On Vallecito Reservoir in San Juan National Forest; map B1, grid h9.

**Campsites, facilities:** There are 21 sites for tents or RVs up to 35 feet long. Drinking water, picnic tables, fire grills, and vault toilets are provided. A full-service marina with a boat ramp and rentals is nearby. Leashed pets are permitted.

**Elevation:** 7,900 feet.

**Reservations, fees:** Reservations are not accepted. Sites are $10 a night.

**Open:** Memorial Day to Labor Day.

**Directions:** From U.S. 160 at Bayfield, turn north on County Rd. 501 (Forest Service Rd. 600) and drive approximately 15 miles to the Vallecito Dam. Turn right on Forest Service Rd. 603 and drive four miles northwest to the campground.

**Contact:** San Juan National Forest, Columbine Ranger District, Bayfield Office, P.O. Box 439, Bayfield, CO 81122; tel. (970) 884-2512.

## 100 Graham Creek     8

Since it's the only camp that has its own boat ramp, Graham Creek is a good choice if you're hauling your own craft. The ramp is a primitive one, best suited for small boats, but using it means you won't have to wait in line at the larger concrete ramp to the north. The campsites are on a gently sloping hill above the shoreline, many open and sunny and a few with large shade trees overhead. The Graham Creek Trail heads uphill about half a mile east, providing a great view of the reservoir below.

**Location:** On Vallecito Reservoir in San Juan National Forest; map B1, grid h9.

**Campsites, facilities:** There are 25 sites for tents or RVs up to 45 feet long. Drinking water, picnic tables, fire grills, and vault toilets are provided. A primitive boat ramp is adjacent to the campground. Leashed pets are permitted.

**Elevation:** 7,900 feet.

**Reservations, fees:** Reservations are not accepted. Sites are $10 a night.

**Open:** Memorial Day to Labor Day.

**Directions:** From U.S. 160 at Bayfield, turn north on County Rd. 501 (Forest Service Rd. 600) and drive approximately 15 miles to the Vallecito Dam. Turn right on Forest Service Rd. 603 and drive 3.5 miles northwest to the campground.

**Contact:** San Juan National Forest, Columbine Ranger District, Bayfield Office, P.O. Box 439, Bayfield, CO 81122; tel. (970) 884-2512.

## 101 Vallecito Resort     7

Square dancing seems to be the primary focus at this camp, so if you're not sure how to swing your partner, you'd better be prepared to learn. Lessons and raucous dances are held regularly. The camp offers a surprising selection of services and activities, ranging from beauty specialists and aerobic classes to card games and church services. If you prefer more traditional camping pastimes, there are also hiking trails and access to fishing on the Los Pinos River. The sites are basic, with grass pads and tall ponderosa pines.

**Location:** On the Los Pinos River; map B1, grid h8.

**Campsites, facilities:** There are 210 full-hookup sites for tents or RVs of any length. Drinking water, picnic tables, fire grills, and bathrooms with hot showers are provided. Laundry facilities, cabins, a store, and public phone are available. Leashed pets are permitted.

**Elevation:** 7,600 feet.

**Reservations, fees:** Reservations are accepted. Sites are $13.50-18 a night.

**Open:** May to October.

**Directions:** From U.S. 160 at Bayfield, turn north on County Rd. 501 (Forest Service Rd. 600) and drive 13 miles to the campground.

**Contact:** Vallecito Resort, 13030 County Rd. 501, Bayfield, CO 81122; tel. (970) 884-9458 or (800) 258-9458.

## 102 Riverside RV Park     7

This attractive spot is a good alternative to the crowded camps at Vallecito Reservoir to the north. Sites are large and grassy, shaded by tall cottonwoods.

Fish in the Los Pinos River or the park's private pond. A short nature trail follows the river, providing opportunities to view native birds and wildlife.

**Location:** On the Los Pinos River; map B1, grid h8.

**Campsites, facilities:** There are five tent sites and 80 sites for RVs of any length, many with full hookups. Drinking water, picnic tables, fire grills, and bathrooms with hot showers are provided. Laundry facilities, a waste disposal station, and public phone are available. Some facilities are wheelchair accessible. Leashed pets are permitted.

**Elevation:** 6,900 feet.

**Reservations, fees:** Reservations are accepted. Sites are $12-20 a night.

**Open:** April to November.

**Directions:** From Bayfield, drive one-quarter mile west on U.S. 160.

**Contact:** Riverside RV Park, P.O. Box 919, Bayfield, CO 81122; tel. (970) 884-2475.

## **103** Pine River     8

Set adjacent to a major trailhead (the Pine River Trail), this campground is most commonly used as a base camp for backpackers headed into the Weminuche Wilderness. The sites are tiny, just big enough for tents or small RVs, and offer gorgeous views of the Los Pinos River Valley and the surrounding forest. The land bordering this section of the Los Pinos River is private, so there is no river access, but if you don't mind hiking, you'll find plenty of backcountry lakes and streams in the region that provide good fishing prospects.

**Location:** Northeast of Vallecito Reservoir in San Juan National Forest; map B1, grid h9.

**Campsites, facilities:** There are six sites for tents or RVs up to 16 feet long. Picnic tables, fire grills, and vault toilets are provided, but there is no drinking water. Leashed pets are permitted.

**Elevation:** 8,100 feet.

**Reservations, fees:** Reservations are not accepted. Sites are $8 a night.

**Open:** Year-round with limited winter facilities and access.

**Directions:** From U.S. 160 at Bayfield, turn north on County Rd. 501 (Forest Service Rd. 600) and drive approximately 15 miles to the Vallecito Dam. Turn right on Forest Service Rd. 603 and drive 4.5 miles northwest. Then turn right on Forest Service Rd. 602 and continue four miles east to the campground.

**Contact:** San Juan National Forest, Columbine Ranger District, Bayfield Office, P.O. Box 439, Bayfield, CO 81122; tel. (970) 884-2512.

## **104** Lower Piedra      8

Located on the shady west bank of the Piedra River, this camp offers prime river access in a private, wooded setting. This section of river gets a fair amount of fishing pressure; your chances for success may increase as you move farther upstream. Lower Piedra is also a stopping point for rafters and kayakers on the river (contact the district ranger office for information on guides). Nearby points of interest include the Chimney Rock Archaeological Area to the south, where you can tour an ancient Ute pueblo, and several hot spring resorts in the town of Pagosa Springs.

**Location:** On the Piedra River in San Juan National Forest; map B1, grid h9.

**Campsites, facilities:** There are 17 sites for tents or RVs up to 35 feet long. Picnic tables, fire grills, and vault toilets are provided, but there is no drinking water. Leashed pets are permitted.

**Elevation:** 7,200 feet.

**Reservations, fees:** Reservations are not accepted. Sites are $6 a night.

**Open:** June to October.

**Directions:** From Bayfield, drive 18 miles east on U.S. 160, turn north on Forest Service Rd. 621, and continue one mile to the campground.

**Contact:** San Juan National Forest, Pagosa Ranger District, P.O. Box 310, Pagosa Springs, CO 81147; tel. (970) 264-2268.

## 105 Sleeping Ute RV Park and Campground     7

Don't let the adjacent casino scare you away—this pleasant bargain-priced camp is far enough from the casino's parking lot (and the highway) to remain quiet and peaceful. The sites are graveled and open, sprinkled with grass, flowers, and small globe willow and aspen trees, and are close to a heated swimming pool. Behind the camp is a sweeping expanse of farmland and high desert terrain backed by an unobstructed view of Sleeping Ute Mountain. If you wish to try your luck at the casino tables, you can take a footbridge and walk up or hop on a free shuttle. The camp is also modem-friendly, with online access for campers.

**Location:** In Towaoc; map B1, grid i2.

**Campsites, facilities:** There are 84 sites for tents or RVs of any length, many with full hookups. Drinking water, picnic tables, fire grills, and bathrooms with hot showers are provided. Laundry facilities, a waste disposal station, store, swimming pool and sauna, and public phone are available. A casino and restaurant are next door. Some facilities are wheelchair accessible. Leashed pets are permitted.

**Elevation:** 6,200 feet.

**Reservations, fees:** Reservations are accepted. Sites are $11-14 a night.

**Open:** Year-round.

**Directions:** From Cortez, drive 11 miles south on U.S. 160.

**Contact:** Sleeping Ute RV Park and Campground, P.O. Box 269, Towaoc, CO 81334; tel. (970) 565-6544 or (800) 889-5072; website: www.utemountaincasino.com.

## 106 Navajo State Park       7

Originally built as a water source for the Navajo Indian Reservation, Navajo Reservoir has become one of Colorado and New Mexico's premier water sports destinations. All boating, including windsurfing, sailing, and waterskiing, is allowed on the 15,500-acre reservoir, with plenty of small, quiet coves for anglers in search of trout, bass, and kokanee salmon. The main campground is on the northeast shore and provides clear, pure views across the water to the New Mexico mountains, as well as easy access and full services. If you can live with the bare basics, the primitive areas offer a more secluded option, with no designated sites—just open areas to pitch a tent or park an RV. There is no hiking to speak of at the park, but it's an excellent site for bird-watching; many species of waterfowl and songbirds can be seen during summer evenings. Limited hunting is available; contact the park for details.

**Location:** Near the New Mexico border; map B1, grid j9.

**Campsites, facilities:** There are three primitive camping areas and a large developed campground with 71 sites for tents or RVs of any length. The primitive areas have vault toilets, but no drinking water or other facilities. At the developed campground, electric hookups, drinking water, picnic tables, fire grills, and bathrooms with hot showers are provided. A waste disposal station, a public phone, and a full-service marina with a boat ramp and rentals are available. Some facilities are wheelchair accessible. Leashed pets are permitted.

**Elevation:** 6,100 feet.

**Reservations, fees:** Reservations are accepted. Phone (303) 470-1144 or (800) 678-CAMP (800-678-2267) outside the Denver Metro area; there's a $7 reservation fee. Sites are $6 a night for primitive sites and $10-14 for developed sites, and there's a $4 entrance fee.

**Open:** Year-round.

**Directions:** From Arboles, drive two miles southeast on County Rd. 982.

**Contact:** Navajo State Park, P.O. Box 1697, Arboles, CO 81121; tel. (970) 883-2208.

# MAP B2

A
B
1
2
3
4
130
280
414
Mt.Crested Butte
Crested Butte
GUNNISON NATIONAL FOREST
Almont
Gunnison
Ohio City
Pitkin
Parlin
Doyleville
Sargents
Monarch
Taylor Park Reservoir
Buena Vista
Nathrop
Antero Junction
PIKE NATIONAL FOREST
Arkansas River
Salida
Howard
Cotopaxi
Alder Creek
Villa Grove
Mineral Hot Springs
Saguache
Blue Mesa Reservoir
San Luis Peak 14,014 feet
Crestone Peak 14,294 feet
Continental Divide
RIO GRANDE NATIONAL FOREST
GREAT SAND DUNES NATIONAL MONUMENT
Creede
Wagon Wheel Gap
Center
Hooper
Mosca
South Fork
Del Norte
Rio Grande
Monte Vista
Alamosa
Platoro Reservoir
Conejos River
Pagosa Springs
SAN JUAN NATIONAL FOREST
Capulin
La Jara
Sanford
Romeo
Manassa
Antonito
Mogote
Chromo
COLORADO
NEW MEXICO
0 15 mi
0 15 km
a
b
c
d
e
f
g
h
i
j
0 1 2 3 4 5 6 7 8 9

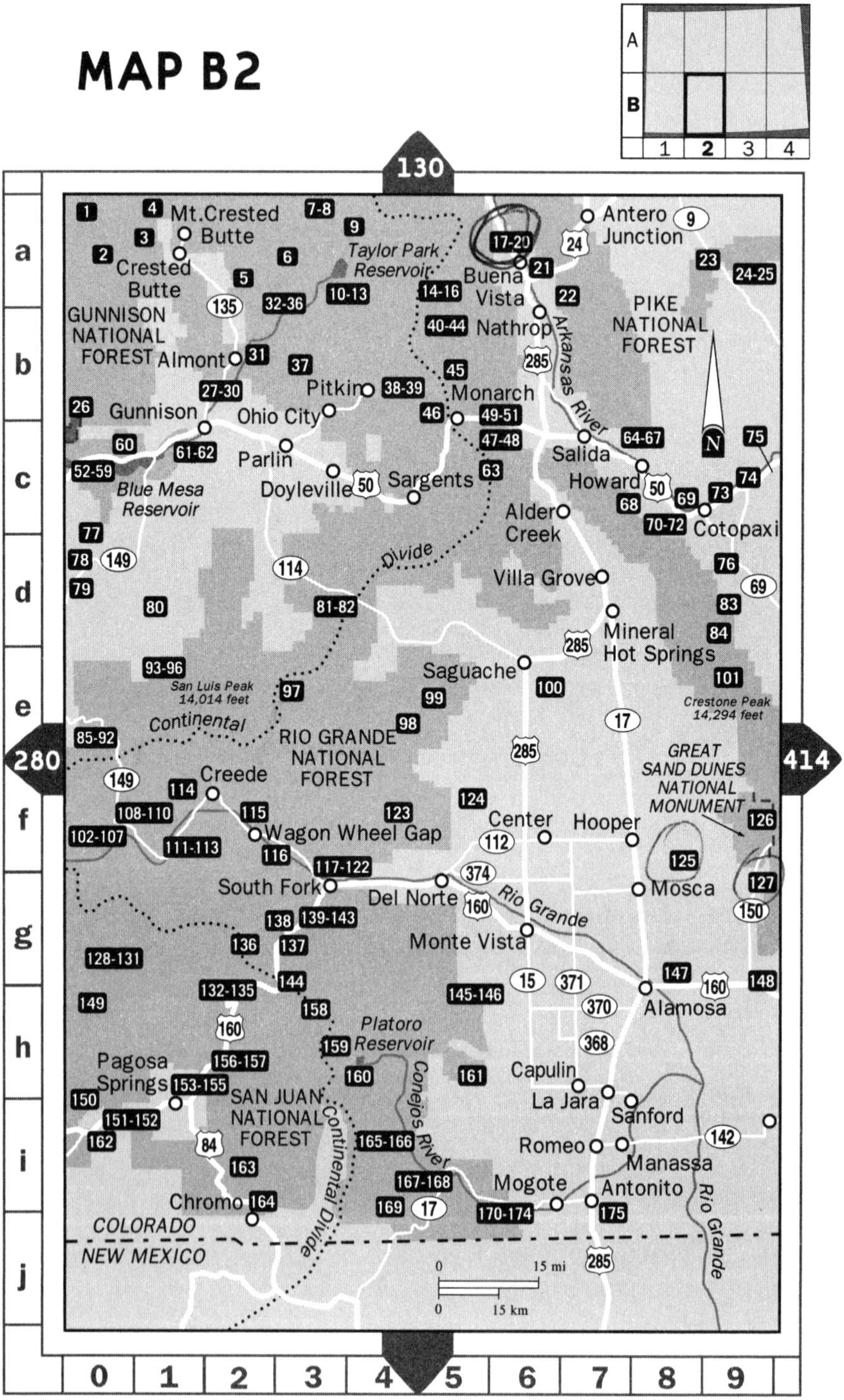

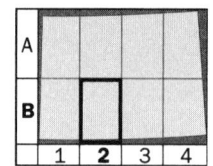

# CHAPTER B2

## ■ Erickson Springs      7

The scenic area northwest of Crested Butte encompasses a fistful of basic campgrounds, including Erickson Springs. Located along the banks of Anthracite Creek near the southwestern boundary of the scenic Raggeds Wilderness, the camp puts you within easy reach of mediocre fishing and spectacular hiking. A popular wilderness trailhead (Dark Canyon Trailhead) starts at camp and leads east along Anthracite Creek before climbing steeply up the precipitous rock steps known as the Devil's Staircase. A few miles to the west is Paonia State Park, where you can fish and boat.

**Location:** On Anthracite Creek in Gunnison National Forest; map B2, grid a0.

**Campsites, facilities:** There are 18 sites for tents or RVs of any length. Drinking water, picnic tables, fire grills, and vault toilets are provided. One toilet is wheelchair accessible. Leashed pets are permitted.

**Elevation:** 6,800 feet.

**Reservations, fees:** Reservations are not accepted. Sites are $8 a night.

**Open:** June to September.

**Directions:** From Crested Butte, turn west on County Rd. 12 (Kebler Pass Rd.) and drive approximately 24 miles to the campground.

**Contact:** Gunnison National Forest, Paonia Ranger District, P.O. Box 1030, Paonia, CO 81428; tel. (970) 527-4131.

## ■ Lost Lake      8

Moderately priced and very scenic, this hiking base camp is set in groves of aspen and oak (especially beautiful in the fall) next to little Lost Lake Slough. Fishing for rainbow and brook trout is decent, but the hiking is better: A trail loops gradually uphill to Lost Lake and Dollar Lake, continuing south over Beckwith Pass into the West Elk Wilderness.

**Location:** West of Crested Butte in Gunnison National Forest; map B2, grid a0.

**Campsites, facilities:** There are 11 sites for tents or RVs up to 16 feet long. Picnic tables, fire grills, and vault toilets are provided, but there is no drinking water or trash service. Leashed pets are permitted.

**Elevation:** 9,600 feet.

**Reservations, fees:** Reservations are not accepted. Sites are $8 a night.

**Open:** June to September.

**Directions:** From Crested Butte, turn west on County Rd. 12 (Kebler Pass Rd.) and drive approximately 15 miles. Turn left on Forest Service Rd. 706 and continue three miles south to the campground.

**Contact:** Gunnison National Forest, Paonia Ranger District, P.O. Box 1030, Paonia, CO 81428; tel. (970) 527-4131.

## ■ Lake Irwin      8

Hundred-acre Lake Irwin, an excellent trout fishing water, is the draw at this camp. Sitting at the base of the Ruby Mountains, the lake is a cool, clear blue, surrounded by mixed conifer forest in a quiet, pristine valley. The camp is within walking distance of the shoreline, providing shady sites and excellent views to the west. A trail leads west and north into the Raggeds Wilderness, crossing several high alpine streams with more good fishing.

**Location:** West of Crested Butte in Gunnison National Forest; map B2, grid a1.

**Campsites, facilities:** There are 32 sites for tents or RVs up to 35 feet long. Drinking water, picnic tables, fire grills, and vault toilets are provided. Leashed pets are permitted.

**Elevation:** 10,300 feet.

**Reservations, fees:** Reservations are accepted; phone (877) 444-6777. There's an $8.65 reservation fee. You may also reserve sites at website: www.reserveusa.com. Sites are $10 a night.

**Open:** June to September.

**Directions:** From Crested Butte, turn west on County Rd. 12 (Kebler Pass Rd.) and drive seven miles. Turn right on Forest Service Rd. 826 and continue 2.5 miles north to the campground.

**Contact:** Gunnison National Forest, Gunnison Ranger District, 216 N. Colorado St., Gunnison, CO 81230; tel. (970) 641-0471.

## ◢ Gothic  8

Just north of a beautiful valley lies this tiny camp, pristine and primitive. Nearby is the historic town of Gothic—maintained by the Rocky Mountain Biological Laboratory—which has morphed from mining town to biological playground, providing fodder for hundreds of studies of regional plants and wildlife. If you have a sturdy four-wheel-drive vehicle, continue past the campground over Scofield Pass for prime westward views of a bevy of peaks with delicious-sounding names: Purple Mountain, Oh-Be-Joyful Peak, and Cinnamon Mountain.

**Location:** North of Crested Butte in Gunnison National Forest; map B2, grid a1.

**Campsites, facilities:** There are four tent sites. Picnic tables, fire grills, and vault toilets are provided, but there is no drinking water or trash service. Leashed pets are permitted.

**Elevation:** 9,600 feet.

**Reservations, fees:** Reservations are not accepted. Sites are $8 a night.

**Open:** June to September.

**Directions:** From Crested Butte, turn north on County Rd. 317 (Gothic Rd.) and drive approximately 9.5 miles to the campground.

**Contact:** Gunnison National Forest, Gunnison Ranger District, 216 N. Colorado St., Gunnison, CO 81230; tel. (970) 641-0471.

## ◢ Cement Creek  8

These sites are positioned alongside a pretty stream in a beautiful valley, with great views of the Elk Mountains. Although it's less than an hour from Gunnison, the camp feels remote and serene, as if you're in the middle of the wilderness. Fishing is possible in Cement Creek, although prospects are reported to be slim. Nearby is a trail that heads north into the surrounding national forest, where you'll cross numerous streams with better fishing potential. Continue a mile up Forest

Service Rd. 470 and you'll come to Cement Creek Ranch, which offers a single rustic cabin and a private hot spring pool (the catch: you have to rent the cabin to get access to the springs).

**Location:** North of Almont in Gunnison National Forest; map B2, grid a2.

**Campsites, facilities:** There are 13 sites for tents or RVs up to 28 feet long. Drinking water, picnic tables, fire grills, and vault toilets are provided. Leashed pets are permitted.

**Elevation:** 9,000 feet.

**Reservations, fees:** Reservations are not accepted. Sites are $10 a night.

**Open:** June to September.

**Directions:** From Gunnison, drive 21 miles north on Hwy. 135, turn right on Forest Service Rd. 740, and continue four miles east to the campground.

**Contact:** Gunnison National Forest, Gunnison Ranger District, 216 N. Colorado St., Gunnison, CO 81230; tel. (970) 641-0471.

## 6 Mosca     8

This secluded camp is nestled in a thick forest of spruce and fir next to pretty Spring Creek Reservoir. Trout fishing is superb, by shore or nonmotorized boat, and your enjoyment will be amplified by the gorgeous mountain setting—high snowcapped peaks in the distance, brisk alpine breezes, and icy, clear water. Adjacent to camp is a designated wildlife area, with opportunities for viewing deer, elk, and birds.

**Location:** On Spring Creek Reservoir in Gunnison National Forest; map B2, grid a3.

**Campsites, facilities:** There are 16 sites for tents or RVs up to 35 feet long. Drinking water, picnic tables, fire grills, and vault toilets are provided. A small boat ramp is available. Leashed pets are permitted.

**Elevation:** 10,000 feet.

**Reservations, fees:** Reservations are not accepted. Sites are $8 a night.

**Open:** July to September.

**Directions:** From Gunnison, drive 11 miles north on Hwy. 135 to Almont, turn right on Taylor River Rd., and continue seven miles east. Turn left on Forest Service Rd. 744 and proceed 12 miles north.

**Contact:** Gunnison National Forest, Gunnison Ranger District, 216 N. Colorado St., Gunnison, CO 81230; tel. (970) 641-0471.

## 7 Dorchester     7

Way up in the boonies near the Taylor River, Dorchester is becoming an increasingly popular base camp for backpackers heading into the Collegiate Peaks Wilderness. There are no trails starting at camp, but go back about a mile on Taylor River Rd. and you can hop on a rough trail that leads north into the wilderness.

**Location:** Near the Collegiate Peaks Wilderness in Gunnison National Forest; map B2, grid a3.

**Campsites, facilities:** There are 10 sites for tents or RVs up to 35 feet long. Drinking water, picnic tables, fire grills, and vault toilets are provided. Leashed pets are permitted.

**Elevation:** 9,800 feet.

**Reservations, fees:** Reservations are not accepted. Sites are $8 a night.

**Open:** July to September.

**Directions:** From Gunnison, drive 11 miles north on Hwy. 135 to Almont, turn right on Taylor River Rd., and continue 40 miles east to the campground.

**Contact:** Gunnison National Forest, Gunnison Ranger District, 216 N. Colorado St., Gunnison, CO 81230; tel. (970) 641-0471.

## ⑧ Dinner Station     7

Located several miles above Taylor Park Reservoir along the Taylor River, Dinner Station has some sites in open meadow, others in spruce and fir forest, with good fishing access. If you head up the road a little over a mile and turn right on Forest Service Rd. 724.8H, you'll come to the northern trailhead for the Timberline Trail, which skirts the western border of the Collegiate Peaks Wilderness for several miles before connecting with the Texas Creek Trail and heading east over the wilderness boundary.

**Location:** On the Taylor River in Gunnison National Forest; map B2, grid a3.

**Campsites, facilities:** There are 22 sites for tents or RVs up to 35 feet long. Drinking water, picnic tables, fire grills, and vault toilets are provided. Leashed pets are permitted.

**Elevation:** 9,600 feet.

**Reservations, fees:** Reservations are accepted; phone (877) 444-6777. There's an $8.65 reservation fee. You may also reserve sites at website: www.reserveusa.com. Sites are $8 a night.

**Open:** June to September.

**Directions:** From Gunnison, drive 11 miles north on Hwy. 135 to Almont, turn right on Taylor River Rd., and continue 33 miles east to the campground.

**Contact:** Gunnison National Forest, Gunnison Ranger District, 216 N. Colorado St., Gunnison, CO 81230; tel. (970) 641-0471.

## ⑨ Rivers End     8

A less-used alternative to Lakeview, Rivers End offers sunny, treeless sites amid sagebrush, next to the lakeshore with beautiful views of the Sawatch Range on the Continental Divide. There is no boat ramp nearby, but the shoreline is perfect for fishing, with good prospects for rainbow, cutthroat, and brown trout, plus Mackinaw and northern pike.

**Location:** Near Taylor Park Reservoir in Gunnison National Forest; map B2, grid a3.

**Campsites, facilities:** There are 15 sites for tents or RVs up to 35 feet long. Drinking water, picnic tables, fire grills, and vault toilets are provided. A waste disposal station is located four miles east of Taylor Park Reservoir. Leashed pets are permitted.

**Elevation:** 9,400 feet.

**Reservations, fees:** Reservations are not accepted. Sites are $8 a night.

**Open:** June to September.

**Directions:** From Gunnison, drive 11 miles north on Hwy. 135 to Almont, turn right on Taylor River Rd., and continue 28 miles east to the campground.

**Contact:** Gunnison National Forest, Gunnison Ranger District, 216 N. Colorado St., Gunnison, CO 81230; tel. (970) 641-0471.

## 🔟 Lakeview      9

Overlooking the southern shore of 2,000-acre Taylor Park Reservoir, Lakeview lives up to its name, with sweeping vistas of the sparkling blue lake backed by jagged, snowcapped peaks. The camp lies in a cozy forest of spruce and fir trees, not far from a boat ramp. Shoreline fishing access is within walking distance.

**Location:** On Taylor Park Reservoir in Gunnison National Forest; map B2, grid a3.

**Campsites, facilities:** There are 46 sites for tents or RVs up to 35 feet long. Drinking water, picnic tables, fire grills, and vault toilets are provided. A waste disposal station is located four miles east of Taylor Park Reservoir. Some facilities are wheelchair accessible. Leashed pets are permitted.

**Elevation:** 9,400 feet.

**Reservations, fees:** Reservations are accepted; phone (877) 444-6777. There's an $8.65 reservation fee. You may also reserve sites at website: www.reserveusa.com. Sites are $12 a night.

**Open:** June to September.

**Directions:** From Gunnison, drive 11 miles north on Hwy. 135 to Almont, turn right on Taylor River Rd., and continue 24 miles east to the campground.

**Contact:** Gunnison National Forest, Gunnison Ranger District, 216 N. Colorado St., Gunnison, CO 81230; tel. (970) 641-0471.

## 🔟🔟 Lodgepole     8

One of several camps in scenic Taylor Canyon, Lodgepole is among the more popular, with space for RVs and excellent fishing access. The sites are encircled by aspen, spruce, and fir trees, set back far enough from the road that the river overpowers any road noise that might otherwise be bothersome. About a mile to the west you can jump on the Summerville Trail, which heads south for 12 miles, passing into the Fossil Ridge Wilderness and eventually connecting with the Fossil Ridge Trail.

**Location:** On the Taylor River in Gunnison National Forest; map B2, grid a3.

**Campsites, facilities:** There are 16 sites for tents or RVs up to 35 feet long. Drinking water, picnic tables, fire grills, and vault toilets are provided. Leashed pets are permitted.

**Elevation:** 8,800 feet.

**Reservations, fees:** Reservations are accepted; phone (877) 444-6777. There's an $8.65 reservation fee. You may also reserve sites at website: www.reserveusa.com. Sites are $8 a night.

**Open:** June to September.

**Directions:** From Gunnison, drive 11 miles north on Hwy. 135 to Almont, turn right on Taylor River Rd., and continue 14.5 miles east to the campground.

**Contact:** Gunnison National Forest, Gunnison Ranger District, 216 N. Colorado St., Gunnison, CO 81230; tel. (970) 641-0471.

## 12 Cold Spring    8

If you like the looks of the Lodgepole camp but find it's fully occupied (as it often is), continue down the road to this small camp, a primitive but equally scenic option. The camp is close to the stream, with excellent fishing access, and the sites are tiny and snug, perfect for tents. Hiking trails are located within a couple of miles east or west on Taylor River Road.

**Location:** On the Taylor River in Gunnison National Forest; map B2, grid a3.

**Campsites, facilities:** There are six tent sites. Picnic tables, fire grills, and vault toilets are provided, but there is no drinking water. Leashed pets are permitted.

**Elevation:** 9,800 feet.

**Reservations, fees:** Reservations are not accepted. Sites are $6 a night.

**Open:** June to September.

**Directions:** From Gunnison, drive 11 miles north on Hwy. 135 to Almont, turn right on Taylor River Rd., and continue 16 miles east to the campground.

**Contact:** Gunnison National Forest, Gunnison Ranger District, 216 N. Colorado St., Gunnison, CO 81230; tel. (970) 641-0471.

## 13 Lottis Creek      8

Just up the road from the Cold Spring camp is another developed alternative in Taylor Canyon, Lottis Creek. Unlike most of the other camps nearby, this one is across the road from the Taylor River, not alongside it; however, little Lottis Creek runs nearby and provides a fishing option. The South Lottis Trail starts at camp, heading several miles south into the Fossil Ridge Wilderness and over Gunsight Pass, where you'll find spectacular mountain views. The trail eventually ends up at the Gold Creek camp, so you can make a multi-day trek out of it.

**Location:** Near the Taylor River in Gunnison National Forest; map B2, grid a3.

**Campsites, facilities:** There are 27 sites for tents or RVs up to 35 feet long, and one group site for up to 50 people. Drinking water, picnic tables, fire grills, and vault toilets are provided. Some facilities are wheelchair accessible. Leashed pets are permitted.

**Elevation:** 9,000 feet.

**Reservations, fees:** Reservations are not accepted for single sites but are required for the group site; phone (877) 444-6777. There's an $8.65 reservation fee. You may also reserve sites at website: www.reserveusa.com. Single-site fees are $10 a night; group fees vary depending on size of party.

**Open:** June to September.

**Directions:** From Gunnison, drive 11 miles north on Hwy. 135 to Almont, turn right on Taylor River Rd., and continue 17.5 miles east to the campground.

**Contact:** Gunnison National Forest, Gunnison Ranger District, 216 N. Colorado St., Gunnison, CO 81230; tel. (970) 641-0471.

## 14 Mirror Lake     9

Remote and beautiful, this little lake is so far out that most people don't even know it's here. The high elevation makes for cold temperatures and a short season, but the reward comes in beautiful views and a pristine environment, with sites surrounded by mixed conifer forest and a sprinkling of aspen trees. The road is rarely accessible before July, and the tiny 25-acre lake maintains glacial temperatures during its short thaw, but provides good fishing for rainbow and brown trout. A trail north of camp leads up through Garden Basin into the surrounding national forest. Point of interest: On the way in, you'll pass through the historic mining town of Tincup, said to be named after an eccentric prospector who carried his gold dust with him in a little tin mug.

**Location:** Near Taylor in Gunnison National Forest; map B2, grid a5.

**Campsites, facilities:** There are 10 sites for tents or RVs up to 16 feet long. Picnic tables, fire grills, and vault toilets are provided. No piped water or trash service is available, but the U.S. Forest Service may haul in tanks of drinking water; call ahead for information. A waste disposal station is located four miles east of Taylor Park Reservoir. Leashed pets are permitted.

**Elevation:** 10,900 feet.

**Reservations, fees:** Reservations are not accepted. Sites are $6 a night.

**Open:** July to September.

**Directions:** From Gunnison, drive 11 miles north on Hwy. 135 to Almont, turn right on Taylor River Rd., and continue 25 miles east. Turn right on Forest Service Rd. 765 and go eight miles. Then turn left on Forest Service Rd. 767 and continue three miles to the campground.

**Contact:** Gunnison National Forest, Gunnison Ranger District, 216 N. Colorado St., Gunnison, CO 81230; tel. (970) 641-0471.

## 15 Collegiate Peaks     8

Set near the southwestern border of the Collegiate Peaks Wilderness between two trailheads, this is a great base camp for a backpacking expedition. About a mile to the west is the Denny Creek Trailhead; to the east is a more popular trailhead for the Colorado Trail. If fishing is more to your taste, don't try Cottonwood Creek—access is poor and prospects are dubious anyway. You've got Cottonwood Lake just a few miles to the south, however, and various lakes and streams available by hiking south into the surrounding national forest. And no matter which activity you choose, the steaming pools at Cottonwood Hot Springs (a few miles east on County Rd. 306) are a perfect balm for tired muscles. Warning: With several 14ers (peaks over 14,000 feet) in the region, this camp is extremely popular—make reservations well in advance.

**Location:** On Cottonwood Creek in San Isabel National Forest; map B2, grid a5.

**Campsites, facilities:** There are 56 sites for tents or RVs up to 35 feet long. Drinking water, picnic tables, fire grills, and vault toilets are provided. Leashed pets are permitted.

**Elevation:** 9,800 feet.

**Reservations, fees:** Reservations are accepted; phone (877) 444-6777. There's an $8.65 reservation fee. You may also reserve sites at website: www.reserveusa.com. Sites are $10 a night.

**Open:** May to October.

**Directions:** From Buena Vista, drive 11 miles west on County Rd. 306.

**Contact:** San Isabel National Forest, Salida Ranger District, 325 W. Rainbow Blvd., Salida, CO 81201; tel. (719) 539-3591.

## 16 Cottonwood Lake      7

Cottonwood Lake is best known for fishing; anglers flock here to compete for healthy-sized rainbow and cutthroat trout. A boat ramp is provided for small nonmotorized boats, with good shoreline access for landlubbers. This cozy spot also makes an excellent camping destination, with roomy sites within walking distance of the lake's north shore. To the north are trails routed into the Collegiate Peaks Wilderness, and on the access road in you'll pass by the rustic Cottonwood Hot Springs.

**Location:** Southwest of Buena Vista in San Isabel National Forest; map B2, grid a5.

**Campsites, facilities:** There are 28 sites for tents or RVs up to 40 feet long. Drinking water, picnic tables, fire grills, and vault toilets are provided. A small boat ramp is available. Leashed pets are permitted.

**Elevation:** 9,600 feet.

**Reservations, fees:** Reservations are not accepted. Sites are $10 a night.

**Open:** May to October.

**Directions:** From Buena Vista, drive seven miles west on County Rd. 306, turn left on County Rd. 344, and continue four miles to the campground.

**Contact:** San Isabel National Forest, Salida Ranger District, 325 W. Rainbow Blvd., Salida, CO 81201; tel. (719) 539-3591.

## 17 Crazy Horse Resort    7

Situated well back from the highway in an open, ranch-like setting, this full-scale resort spares no energy organizing group activities. Ice cream socials, guided trail rides, buffalo barbecues, and jeep tours are standard procedure. If you prefer to explore on your own, the staff will cheerfully advise you on where to go, what to do, and how to do it. Some sites are shaded, some sunny, most with good mountain views of the Collegiate Peaks to the west.

**Location:** North of Buena Vista; map B2, grid a6.

**Campsites, facilities:** There are 100 sites for tents or RVs of any length, many with full hookups. Drinking water, picnic tables, fire grills, and bathrooms with hot showers are provided. Laundry facilities, a waste disposal station, store, public phone, swimming pool, miniature golf, horse and jeep rentals, and cabins are available. Leashed pets are permitted.

**Elevation:** 8,000 feet.

**Reservations, fees:** Reservations are accepted. Sites are $18-25 a night.

**Open:** Mid-April to October.

**Directions:** From the northern edge of Buena Vista, drive four miles north on U.S. 24.

**Contact:** Crazy Horse Resort, 33975 N. U.S. 24, Buena Vista, CO 81211; tel. (719) 395-2323 or (800) 888-7320; e-mail: crazyhorse@sni.net.

## 18 Arkansas River Rim Campground      7

One of several roadside campgrounds along U.S. 24 north of Buena Vista, this one offers easy access to Buena Vista and the Arkansas River, plus scenic views of grassy hills and plains to the east. The sites sit between scattered piñon pine and juniper trees on a hill overlooking the Arkansas River. There are trails leading down to fishing access points. No rafting is available from the camp, but several licensed outfitters are located nearby.

**Location:** North of Buena Vista; map B2, grid a6.

**Campsites, facilities:** There are 27 tent sites and 38 full-hookup sites for RVs of any length. Drinking water, picnic tables, fire grills, and bathrooms with hot showers are provided. Laundry facilities, a waste disposal station, and public phone are available. Some facilities are wheelchair accessible. Leashed pets are permitted.

**Elevation:** 8,000 feet.

**Reservations, fees:** Reservations are accepted. Sites are $13-19 a night.

**Open:** May to October.

**Directions:** From the junction of U.S. 24 and Cottonwood Pass Rd. (County Rd. 306) in Buena Vista, drive three miles north on U.S. 24.

**Contact:** Arkansas River Rim Campground, 33198 N. U.S. 24, Buena Vista, CO 81211; tel. (719) 395-8883.

## **19** Snowy Peaks RV and Mobile Park   7

Since changing hands in 1997, this park has seen some significant improvements: the new owners cleaned up the somewhat dilapidated place, fully winterized their RV sites, and added a modern exercise room and rec room, plus modem hookups so campers can access the Internet. They've also come up with plans for group meals and activities, including movies, games, and tours. All this, plus spectacular mountain views, make for a pleasant night's stay.

**Location:** North of Buena Vista; map B2, grid a6.

**Campsites, facilities:** There are 10 tent sites and 60 sites for RVs of any length, most with full hookups. Drinking water, picnic tables, fire grills, and bathrooms with hot showers are provided. Laundry facilities, a waste disposal station, exercise room, and public phone are available. Leashed pets are permitted.

**Elevation:** 8,000 feet.

**Reservations, fees:** Reservations are accepted. Sites are $10-17 a night.

**Open:** Year-round.

**Directions:** From the northern edge of Buena Vista, drive 1.5 miles north on U.S. 24.

**Contact:** Snowy Peaks RV and Mobile Park, 30430 N. U.S. 24, Buena Vista, CO 81211; tel. (719) 395-8481; e-mail: snowypks@chaffee.net.

## **20** Mount Princeton RV Park    6

This camp is a bare-basics overnight option, with open, sparsely grassed sites shaded by a smattering of pine trees and clear views of snowcapped peaks in the distance. Unfortunately, it's close to the highway and gets inundated by tourist traffic during the summer. You do have close access to rafting and fishing on the Arkansas River, however, or hiking and horseback riding in San Isabel National Forest. Note: This RV park is strictly adults only, so families with kids should steer toward Buena Vista KOA or Crazy Horse.

**Location:** North of Buena Vista; map B2, grid a6.

**Campsites, facilities:** There are 45 sites for tents or RVs of any length, most with

full hookups. Drinking water, picnic tables, and bathrooms with hot showers are provided. Laundry facilities and a public phone are available. Some facilities are wheelchair accessible. Children are not allowed. Leashed pets are permitted.
**Elevation:** 8,000 feet.
**Reservations, fees:** Reservations are accepted. Sites are $18-20 a night.
**Open:** Year-round with limited winter facilities.
**Directions:** From the northern edge of Buena Vista, drive one mile north on U.S. 24, turn right on County Rd. 383, and continue east to the campground.
**Contact:** Mount Princeton RV Park, 30380 County Rd. 383, Buena Vista, CO 81211; tel. (719) 395-6206 or (888) 642-9203.

## 21 Buena Vista KOA        7

A family-oriented campground with a western flavor, this spot is an excellent choice for folks who desire a single base camp for a week-long (or longer) trip. The sites are mostly open with a few scrubby shade trees, set at the base of a juniper-covered hillside. The resort offers activities ranging from guided horseback rides to ice cream socials, plus mountain biking trails and a roomy outdoor hot tub. You hardly need to leave the place to find outdoor activities, but just a few miles away are Mount Princeton Hot Springs, rafting trips on the Arkansas River, and hiking and mountaineering in the popular Collegiate Peaks Wilderness.
**Location:** South of Buena Vista; map B2, grid a6.
**Campsites, facilities:** There are 100 sites for tents or RVs of any length, many with full hookups. Drinking water, picnic tables, fire grills, and bathrooms with hot showers are provided. Laundry facilities, a waste disposal station, restaurant, small store, hot tub, sports field, horse rentals, guest horse stables, cabins, and public phone are available. Leashed pets are permitted.
**Elevation:** 8,000 feet.
**Reservations, fees:** Reservations are accepted; phone (800) KOA-2672. Sites are $20-26 a night.
**Open:** Year-round.
**Directions:** From the junction of U.S. 24 and U.S. 285 south of Buena Vista, drive one-quarter mile east on U.S. 285, turn left on County Rd. 303, and continue north to the campground.
**Contact:** Buena Vista KOA, 27700 County Rd. 303, Buena Vista, CO 81211; tel. (719) 395-8318.

## 22 Brown's Campground       7

Many of the pretty, private sites at this camp are nestled under mature cottonwoods along the banks of rushing Chalk Creek. The name comes from Brown's Canyon, a Class II-III section of the Arkansas River that has become one of the most popular river rafting runs in the state. An outfitter is located right across the highway, ready to set you up with paddles and life jackets. Other side trips include Mount Princeton Hot Springs, a five-minute drive away, and the Colorado Trail, which runs north and south near the border of San Isabel National Forest.
**Location:** On Chalk Creek; map B2, grid a7.

**Campsites, facilities:** There are 65 sites for tents or RVs of any length, some with full hookups. Drinking water, picnic tables, fire grills, and bathrooms with hot showers are provided. Laundry facilities, a waste disposal station, and a small store are available. Leashed pets are permitted.

**Elevation:** 7,900 feet.

**Reservations, fees:** Reservations are accepted; phone (800) 880-0299. Sites are $16-19.50 a night.

**Open:** Year-round.

**Directions:** From Buena Vista, drive two miles south to the junction of U.S. 24 and U.S. 285. Continue four miles south on U.S. 285, turn left on County Rd. 197, and continue one block east to the campground.

**Contact:** Brown's Campground, P.O. Box 39, Nathrop, CO 81236; tel. (719) 395-8301.

## 23 Eleven Mile State Park       7

The centerpiece of this state park is long, finger-shaped Elevenmile Canyon Reservoir, covering 3,400 surface acres but nowhere near 11 miles long—it's actually closer to seven. The campsites are spread around the reservoir's perimeter, most open and treeless (a few ponderosa pines are sprinkled here and there) with unobstructed views of the granite-lined shores and surrounding grassland. Large, smooth lumps of granite bedrock occupy much of the shoreline and provide an excellent perch from which to fish for Mackinaw, Snake River cutthroat, rainbow, and brown trout, and kokanee salmon. RV campers are best off at the Rocky Ridge area, the only spot with electric hookups, but if you're up for a little backpacking, I recommend the walk-in (or boat-in) campsites around the eastern shore. They're primitive, with no facilities, but extremely scenic and quite private. No-wake boating is popular, especially sailing, with steady winds common in summer. Designated hiking trails are limited, but you may traverse the park's grasslands. Limited hunting is permitted; contact the park for details.

**Location:** West of Colorado Springs; map B2, grid a8.

**Campsites, facilities:** There are 350 sites for tents or RVs of any length, plus 25 walk-in campsites. Drinking water, picnic tables, fire grills, and bathrooms with hot showers are provided. Electric hookups, laundry facilities, waste disposal stations, phones, and boat ramps are available. Some facilities are wheelchair accessible. Leashed pets are permitted.

**Elevation:** 8,600 feet.

**Reservations, fees:** Reservations are accepted. Phone (303) 470-1144 or (800) 678-CAMP (800-678-2267) outside the Denver Metro area; there's a $7 reservation fee. Sites are $10-16 a night, and there's a $4 entrance fee.

**Open:** Year-round.

**Directions:** From Colorado Springs, turn west on U.S. 24 and drive approximately 40 miles Turn south on County Rd. 90 (there's a sign indicating Eleven Mile State Park), and continue 10 miles to the park entrance.

**Contact:** Eleven Mile State Park, 4229 County Rd. 92, Lake George, CO 80827; tel. (719) 748-3401.

## 24 Cove  7

This tiny camp, set amid ponderosa pines and big rocks, provides a lesser-known option to the popular campgrounds at Eleven Mile State Park. It's located about a mile east of the reservoir's eastern shore, so you're still close to fishing and boating on Elevenmile Canyon Reservoir. Fishing is excellent on the South Platte River. Nearby is a trailhead for the Overlook Trail.

**Location:** On the South Platte River in Pike National Forest; map B2, grid a9.

**Campsites, facilities:** There are four sites for tents or RVs up to 16 feet long. Drinking water, picnic tables, fire grills, and a vault toilet are provided. Leashed pets are permitted.

**Elevation:** 8,400 feet.

**Reservations, fees:** Reservations are not accepted. Sites are $10 a night, and there's a $3 use fee.

**Open:** May to October.

**Directions:** From Colorado Springs, turn west on U.S. 24 and drive approximately 39 miles. Then turn south on County Rd. 96 and drive nine miles to the campground.

**Contact:** Pike National Forest, South Park Ranger District, P.O. Box 219, Fairplay, CO 80440; tel. (719) 836-2031.

## 25 Spillway  7

Of the two U.S. Forest Service camps near Elevenmile Canyon Reservoir, Spillway is the largest and best suited for campers with RVs. It's surrounded by ponderosa pines, not far from the eastern shore of the reservoir, with convenient access to the Overlook Trail, which provides superb vistas of the park's natural features. A fishing access point is nearby.

**Location:** On the South Platte River in Pike National Forest; map B2, grid a9.

**Campsites, facilities:** There are 23 sites for tents or RVs up to 25 feet long. Drinking water, picnic tables, fire grills, and a vault toilet are provided. Leashed pets are permitted.

**Elevation:** 8,500 feet.

**Reservations, fees:** Reservations are not accepted. Sites are $10 a night, and there's a $3 use fee.

**Open:** May to October.

**Directions:** From Colorado Springs, turn west on U.S. 24 and drive approximately 39 miles. Turn south on County Rd. 96 and drive 10 miles to the campground.

**Contact:** Pike National Forest, South Park Ranger District, P.O. Box 219, Fairplay, CO 80440; tel. (719) 836-2031.

## 26 Soap Creek  7

A lesser-known alternative to popular Ponderosa camp in Curecanti National Recreation Area, this remote camp is just as friendly to horses as to campers, with special equestrian facilities and the bonus of a trailhead routed east into the West Elk Wilderness. Sites are cool and well shaded, near the banks of Soap Creek, with fishing access and excellent prospects for brook trout. Boating and more fishing are available to the south at Blue Mesa Reservoir.

**Location:** North of Blue Mesa Reservoir in Gunnison National Forest; map B2, grid b0.

**Campsites, facilities:** There are 21 sites for tents or RVs up to 35 feet long. Drinking water, picnic tables, fire grills, and vault toilets are provided. Horse corrals are available. Leashed pets are permitted.

**Elevation:** 7,700 feet.

**Reservations, fees:** Reservations are not accepted. Sites are $10 a night.

**Open:** June to September.

**Directions:** From Gunnison, drive 27 miles west on U.S. 50 and turn right on Hwy. 92. Go one-half mile past the Blue Mesa Dam, turn right on Soap Creek Rd., and travel 7.5 miles north. Turn right on Forest Service Rd. 824 and continue one-half mile to the campground. Note: Soap Creek Rd. can be nearly impassable when muddy. Trailers and RVs are not recommended during rainy periods.

**Contact:** Gunnison National Forest, Gunnison Ranger District, 216 N. Colorado St., Gunnison, CO 81230; tel. (970) 641-0471.

## **27** Shady Island Resort    7

The sprawling, shaded sites at this camp are perfect for fishing, set at the edge of rocky banks that slope gently to meet the cool currents of the Gunnison River. Although the sites are near the highway, large cottonwoods and the rushing of the river absorb much of the road noise, and you get quick, convenient access to supplies and services in downtown Gunnison. The camp hosts can also arrange white-water rafting trips from camp.

**Location:** On the Gunnison River; map B2, grid b2.

**Campsites, facilities:** There are 42 full-hookup sites for RVs of any length. No tents are permitted. Drinking water, picnic tables, fire grills, and vault toilets are provided. A waste disposal station, miniature golf, cabins, and a public phone are available. Leashed pets are permitted.

**Elevation:** 7,700 feet.

**Reservations, fees:** Reservations are accepted. Sites are $19 a night.

**Open:** May to mid-November.

**Directions:** From Gunnison, drive 2.5 miles north on Hwy. 135 to the campground entrance on the right.

**Contact:** Shady Island Resort, 2776 Hwy. 135, Gunnison, CO 81230; tel. (970) 641-0416.

## **28** Tall Texan Campground      8

Set far back from the highway, this place maintains a serene, quiet atmosphere, with the Gunnison River charging past most of the cottonwood-shaded sites. Towering trees enclose the entire camp, making it feel like a private forest, and excellent hiking and horseback riding trails begin nearby. A private fishing pond is available in addition to the river.

**Location:** On the Gunnison River; map B2, grid b2.

**Campsites, facilities:** There are six tent sites and 110 sites for RVs of any length, many with full hookups. Drinking water, picnic tables, fire grills, and bathrooms with hot showers are provided. Laundry facilities, a waste disposal

station, store, and public phone are available. Leashed pets are permitted.
**Elevation:** 7,700 feet.
**Reservations, fees:** Reservations are accepted. Sites are $14-20 a night.
**Open:** Mid-April to mid-November.
**Directions:** From Gunnison, drive two miles north on Hwy. 135, turn right on County Rd. 11, and continue one-quarter mile to the campground.
**Contact:** Tall Texan Campground, 2460 Hwy. 135, Gunnison, CO 81230; tel. (970) 641-2927.

## 29 Rockey River Resort  7

Set on the pleasing green banks of the Gunnison River, these sites are grassy and treeless, with fishing access alongside. Since it's well away from the road, the camp is a quieter option to those right beside Hwy. 135. Continue north up Hwy. 135 to access Gunnison National Forest and scenic Taylor Canyon.
**Location:** On the Gunnison River; map B2, grid b2.
**Campsites, facilities:** There are 27 full-hookup sites for RVs of any length. No tents are permitted. Drinking water, picnic tables, fire grills, and bathrooms with hot showers are provided. A waste disposal station and cabins are available. Leashed pets are permitted.
**Elevation:** 7,800 feet.
**Reservations, fees:** Reservations are not accepted. Sites are $19 a night.
**Open:** May to November.
**Directions:** From Gunnison, drive approximately six miles north on Hwy. 135, turn right on County Rd. 10, and continue one-quarter mile to the campground.
**Contact:** Rockey River Resort, 4359 County Rd. 10, Gunnison, CO 81230; tel. (970) 641-0174.

## 30 Almont  7

Almont is a great choice for bargain-seeking campers, providing basic amenities in the center of a variety of recreation options for only six bucks. The small, wooded camp is located just south of the town of Almont, off Hwy. 135 along the Gunnison River and a short drive from the popular Taylor Canyon. A trail starts at camp, following the Gunnison River south, with fishing access along the way. Fishing is also possible a couple of miles north on both the East River and the Taylor River.
**Location:** On the Gunnison River in Gunnison National Forest; map B2, grid b2.
**Campsites, facilities:** There are 10 sites for tents or RVs up to 28 feet long. Drinking water, picnic tables, fire grills, and vault toilets are provided. Leashed pets are permitted.
**Elevation:** 8,000 feet.
**Reservations, fees:** Reservations are not accepted. Sites are $6 a night.
**Open:** June to September.
**Directions:** From Gunnison, drive 10 miles north on Hwy. 135.
**Contact:** Gunnison National Forest, Gunnison Ranger District, 216 N. Colorado St., Gunnison, CO 81230; tel. (970) 641-0471.

## 31 Three Rivers Resort     8

This pretty, open camp is located in Taylor Canyon near the confluence of—yep, you guessed it—three rivers: the point where the Taylor and East Rivers combine to form the Gunnison. Fishing is phenomenal, and the campground hosts moonlight as river rafting guides, which means you can take an afternoon or overnight trip right from your site. The sites are within walking distance of the river.

**Location:** North of Gunnison; map B2, grid b3.

**Campsites, facilities:** There are 48 sites for tents or RVs up to 35 feet long, many with full hookups. Drinking water, picnic tables, fire grills, and bathrooms with hot showers are provided. Laundry facilities, a waste disposal station, store, cabins, and public phone are available. Leashed pets are permitted.

**Elevation:** 8,000 feet.

**Reservations, fees:** Reservations are accepted. Sites are $16-18 a night.

**Open:** Year-round.

**Directions:** From Gunnison, drive 10 miles north on Hwy. 135, turn right on County Rd. 742, and continue east to the campground.

**Contact:** Three Rivers Resort, P.O. Box 339, Almont, CO 81210; tel. (970) 641-1303 or (888) 761-3474.

## 32 Spring Creek     8

When the camps in Taylor Canyon are packed to capacity, Spring Creek offers a secluded alternative. You sacrifice the on-site access to the Taylor River that the other camps offer, but in return you get a quiet, serene spot amid spruce and aspen trees, next to silvery Spring Creek.

**Location:** North of the Taylor River in Gunnison National Forest; map B2, grid b3.

**Campsites, facilities:** There are 12 sites for tents or RVs up to 35 feet long. Drinking water, picnic tables, fire grills, and vault toilets are provided. Leashed pets are permitted.

**Elevation:** 8,600 feet.

**Reservations, fees:** Reservations are not accepted. Sites are $8 a night.

**Open:** June to September.

**Directions:** From Gunnison, drive 11 miles north on Hwy. 135 to Almont, turn right on Taylor River Rd., and continue seven miles east. Turn left on Forest Service Rd. 744 and proceed two miles north.

**Contact:** Gunnison National Forest, Gunnison Ranger District, 216 N. Colorado St., Gunnison, CO 81230; tel. (970) 641-0471.

## 33 North Bank       8

One of several camps in Taylor Canyon, North Bank is a basic but scenic choice, set in mixed conifer and aspen forest next to the Taylor River, with good fishing access. A trail follows a small creek north from camp through Browns Gulch.

**Location:** On the Taylor River in Gunnison National Forest; map B2, grid b3.

**Campsites, facilities:** There are 17 sites for tents or RVs up to 35 feet long. Drinking water, picnic tables, fire grills, and vault toilets are provided. Some facilities are wheelchair accessible. Leashed pets are permitted.

**Elevation:** 8,600 feet.

**Reservations, fees:** Reservations are not accepted. Sites are $8 a night.

**Open:** June to September.

**Directions:** From Gunnison, drive 11 miles north on Hwy. 135 to Almont, turn right on Taylor River Rd., and continue eight miles east to the campground on the left.

**Contact:** Gunnison National Forest, Gunnison Ranger District, 216 N. Colorado St., Gunnison, CO 81230; tel. (970) 641-0471.

## 34 Taylor Canyon     8

Scenic Taylor Canyon is an annual vacation destination for hundreds of campers and anglers, who are drawn by its pleasing mix of fir, spruce, and aspen trees, rocky canyon walls, and spectacular fishing on the Taylor River. Taylor Canyon Campground is the first of several U.S. Forest Service sites in the canyon and remains quite popular despite its lack of water or developed facilities. The sites are cozy, just big enough for a tent, with river views and fishing access. To the south is a trail routed along Beaver Creek.

**Location:** On the Taylor River in Gunnison National Forest; map B2, grid b3.

**Campsites, facilities:** There are seven walk-in tent sites near a central parking area. Picnic tables, fire grills, and vault toilets are provided, but there is no drinking water. Leashed pets are permitted.

**Elevation:** 8,600 feet.

**Reservations, fees:** Reservations are not accepted. Sites are $4 a night.

**Open:** June to September.

**Directions:** From Gunnison, drive 11 miles north on Hwy. 135 to Almont, turn right on Taylor River Rd., and continue 7.5 miles east to the campground on the right.

**Contact:** Gunnison National Forest, Gunnison Ranger District, 216 N. Colorado St., Gunnison, CO 81230; tel. (970) 641-0471.

## 35 Onemile       8

Since it's the only U.S. Forest Service camp around with electric hookups, Onemile is quite popular with RV campers. In fact, all the sites come with electricity, whether you want it or not, so even if you're in a tent, you can plug in your portable espresso machine. Like other camps in the canyon, these sites are enveloped in aspen, fir, and spruce trees, with the river winding its way through the camp for superb fishing access. Other recreation options include hiking and mountain biking on rough four-wheel-drive roads in the area. (Tip: Forest Service Rd. 414 leads to the border of the Fossil Ridge Wilderness.)

**Location:** On the Taylor River in Gunnison National Forest; map B2, grid b3.

**Campsites, facilities:** There are 25 sites for tents or RVs up to 35 feet long. Electric hookups, drinking water, picnic tables, fire grills, and vault toilets are provided. Some facilities are wheelchair accessible. Leashed pets are permitted.

**Elevation:** 8,600 feet.

**Reservations, fees:** Reservations are accepted; phone (877) 444-6777. There's an $8.65 reservation fee. You may also reserve sites at website: www.reserveusa.com. Sites are $14 a night.

**Open:** June to September.

**Directions:** From Gunnison, drive 11 miles north on Hwy. 135 to Almont, turn right on Taylor River Rd., and continue eight miles east to the campground on the right.

**Contact:** Gunnison National Forest, Gunnison Ranger District, 216 N. Colorado St., Gunnison, CO 81230; tel. (970) 641-0471.

## 36 Rosy Lane      8

Of the long string of camps beside the Taylor River in Taylor Canyon, Rosy Lane is possibly the best choice for campers in wheelchairs, with a special accessible site and a barrier-free trail along the river. Sites are large and shady, with fishing access nearby.

**Location:** On the Taylor River in Gunnison National Forest; map B2, grid b3.

**Campsites, facilities:** There are 20 sites for tents or RVs up to 35 feet long. Drinking water, picnic tables, fire grills, and vault toilets are provided. One site is wheelchair accessible. Leashed pets are permitted.

**Elevation:** 8,600 feet.

**Reservations, fees:** Reservations are accepted; phone (877) 444-6777. There's an $8.65 reservation fee. You may also reserve sites at website: www.reserveusa.com. Sites are $10 a night.

**Open:** June to September.

**Directions:** From Gunnison, drive 11 miles north on Hwy. 135 to Almont, turn right on Taylor River Rd., and continue 8.5 miles east to the campground on the right.

**Contact:** Gunnison National Forest, Gunnison Ranger District, 216 N. Colorado St., Gunnison, CO 81230; tel. (970) 641-0471.

## 37 Gold Creek    7

Though small and primitive, this wooded camp is quite popular, probably due to its proximity to a significant wilderness trailhead. The south end of the South Lottis Trail begins here, heading several miles north through the Fossil Ridge Wilderness to Lottis Creek campground in Taylor Canyon. Fishing is available in Gold Creek.

**Location:** North of Ohio City in Gunnison National Forest; map B2, grid b3.

**Campsites, facilities:** There are six tent sites. Picnic tables, fire grills, and vault toilets are provided, but there is no drinking water or trash service. Leashed pets are permitted.

**Elevation:** 10,000 feet.

**Reservations, fees:** Reservations are not accepted. Sites are $6 a night.

**Open:** June to September.

**Directions:** From Gunnison, turn east on U.S. 50 and drive 11 miles to Parlin. Turn left on County Rd. 3101 (look for a sign indicating Ohio City and Pitkin) and continue nine miles northeast to Ohio City. Turn left on Forest Service Rd. 771 and continue eight miles north to the campground.

**Contact:** Gunnison National Forest, Gunnison Ranger District, 216 N. Colorado St., Gunnison, CO 81230; tel. (970) 641-0471.

## 38 Pitkin     8

Located along Quartz Creek in the national forest east of Gunnison, Pitkin is steeped in history, surrounded by dozens of old mines and mining towns in various states of disrepair. The camp is secluded among spruce and fir trees, with fishing access nearby. Peaks on the Continental Divide provide stunning views to the east.

**Location:** On Quartz Creek in Gunnison National Forest; map B2, grid b4.

**Campsites, facilities:** There are 22 sites for tents or RVs up to 16 feet long. Drinking water, picnic tables, fire grills, and vault toilets are provided. Leashed pets are permitted.

**Elevation:** 9,400 feet.

**Reservations, fees:** Reservations are not accepted. Sites are $10 a night.

**Open:** June to September.

**Directions:** From Gunnison, turn east on U.S. 50 and drive 11 miles to Parlin. Turn left on County Rd. 3101 (look for a sign indicating Ohio City and Pitkin) and continue 15 miles northeast to the town of Pitkin. Continue two miles east on Forest Service Rd. 765 to the campground.

**Contact:** Gunnison National Forest, Gunnison Ranger District, 216 N. Colorado St., Gunnison, CO 81230; tel. (970) 641-0471.

## 39 Quartz     8

This camp lies in the middle of the pretty Quartz Valley, along little North Quartz Creek in a dispersed conifer forest. Fishing for brook trout is said to be quite good. An excellent side trip: Continue north on Forest Service Rd. 765 to Cumberland Pass (12,000 feet) for spectacular views of the Sawatch Range on the Continental Divide. The road eventually descends to the historic mining town of Tincup.

**Location:** On N. Quartz Creek in Gunnison National Forest; map B2, grid b4.

**Campsites, facilities:** There are 10 sites for tents or RVs up to 16 feet long. Drinking water, picnic tables, fire grills, and vault toilets are provided. Leashed pets are permitted.

**Elevation:** 9,800 feet.

**Reservations, fees:** Reservations are not accepted. Sites are $8 a night.

**Open:** June to September.

**Directions:** From Gunnison, turn east on U.S. 50 and drive 11 miles to Parlin. Turn left on County Rd. 3101 (look for a sign indicating Ohio City and Pitkin) and continue 15 miles northeast to the town of Pitkin. Continue four miles northeast on Forest Service Rd. 765 to the campground.

**Contact:** Gunnison National Forest, Gunnison Ranger District, 216 N. Colorado St., Gunnison, CO 81230; tel. (970) 641-0471.

## 40 Iron City      8

This camp requires a bit of a haul in and consequently gets slightly less traffic than the other camps along County Rd. 162. It's worth the drive, though, with secluded sites near the banks of Chalk Creek and an adjacent trailhead. The trail is suitable for hikers, horses, or mountain bikes, and heads north through Poplar

Gulch, eventually connecting with a four-wheel-drive road that leads to Cottonwood Lake. Points of interest: The historic mining town of St. Elmo is located a short distance west of camp, and you'll pass Mount Princeton Hot Springs as you drive up County Rd. 162.

**Location:** On Chalk Creek in San Isabel National Forest; map B2, grid b5.

**Campsites, facilities:** There are 17 sites for tents or RVs up to 35 feet long. Drinking water, picnic tables, fire grills, and vault toilets are provided. Leashed pets are permitted.

**Elevation:** 9,900 feet.

**Reservations, fees:** Reservations are not accepted. Sites are $10 a night.

**Open:** June to October.

**Directions:** From Buena Vista, drive two miles south to the junction of U.S. 24 and U.S. 285 and continue five miles south on U.S. 285 to Nathrop. Turn right on County Rd. 162, drive 15 miles west, turn right on Forest Service Rd. 292, and proceed about half a mile.

**Contact:** San Isabel National Forest, Salida Ranger District, 325 W. Rainbow Blvd., Salida, CO 81201; tel. (719) 539-3591.

## 41 Boot Leg  8

Located near the banks of Chalk Creek with good views of the craggy white Chalk Cliffs and Mount Princeton to the north, Boot Leg is a perfect choice for campers armed with a tent and a sense of adventure. There is an activity in every direction: To the south is a trailhead for the Colorado Trail; to the north is a 14er (Mount Princeton, 14,197 feet); Mount Princeton Hot Springs is just a few miles east; across the road is a pretty interpretive nature trail; and back across the main highway you'll find several outfitters ready to set you up for a rafting trip on the Arkansas River. The drawbacks: You have to pack in your own water and pack out your trash. Also, since this is the first campground that travelers encounter on County Rd. 162, it often fills up quickly (although many continue down the road in search of a camp with drinking water). Try one of the four camps to the west if that's the case.

**Location:** Near Chalk Creek in San Isabel National Forest; map B2, grid b5.

**Campsites, facilities:** There are six tent sites. Picnic tables, fire grills, and a vault toilet are provided, but there is no drinking water or trash service. Leashed pets are permitted.

**Elevation:** 8,400 feet.

**Reservations, fees:** Reservations are not accepted. Sites are $5 a night.

**Open:** May to October.

**Directions:** From Buena Vista, drive two miles south to the junction of U.S. 24 and U.S. 285. Continue five miles south on U.S. 285 to Nathrop, turn right on County Rd. 162, and drive six miles west to the campground.

**Contact:** San Isabel National Forest, Salida Ranger District, 325 W. Rainbow Blvd., Salida, CO 81201; tel. (719) 539-3591.

## 42 Mount Princeton  8

A larger, more developed alternative to Boot Leg, this camp has open sites big enough for full-size RVs. Its name must certainly come from the picturesque view of Mount Princeton you get from the road; to the west, you'll find a trailhead leading up to the 14,197-foot peak. Other options include the Colorado Trail and Mount Princeton Hot Springs.

**Location:** Near Chalk Creek in San Isabel National Forest; map B2, grid b5.

**Campsites, facilities:** There are 17 sites for tents or RVs up to 40 feet long. Drinking water, picnic tables, fire grills, and vault toilets are provided. Leashed pets are permitted.

**Elevation:** 8,000 feet.

**Reservations, fees:** Reservations are accepted; phone (877) 444-6777. There's an $8.65 reservation fee. You may also reserve sites at website: www.reserveusa.com. Sites are $10 a night.

**Open:** May to October.

**Directions:** From Buena Vista, drive two miles south to the junction of U.S. 24 and U.S. 285. Drive five miles south on U.S. 285 to Nathrop, turn right on County Rd. 162, and continue seven miles west to the campground.

**Contact:** San Isabel National Forest, Salida Ranger District, 325 W. Rainbow Blvd., Salida, CO 81201; tel. (719) 539-3591.

## 43 Chalk Lake     8

With just three surface acres, Chalk Lake qualifies better as a pond than a lake, but don't let its tiny size fool you—-there are plentiful (though small) rainbow trout to be caught. The campsites ring the eastern side of the lake and are backed by national forest land to the south. Across the road is a trail that leads north along Cascade Creek to Agnes Vaille Falls, with interpretive information along the way. Back east on the access road is Mount Princeton Hot Springs.

**Location:** South of Mount Princeton in San Isabel National Forest; map B2, grid b5.

**Campsites, facilities:** There are 21 sites for tents or RVs up to 35 feet long. Drinking water, picnic tables, fire grills, and vault toilets are provided. Leashed pets are permitted.

**Elevation:** 8,700 feet.

**Reservations, fees:** Reservations are accepted; phone (877) 444-6777. There's an $8.65 reservation fee. You may also reserve sites at website: www.reserveusa.com. Sites are $12 a night.

**Open:** May to October.

**Directions:** From Buena Vista, drive two miles south to the junction of U.S. 24 and U.S. 285. Drive five miles south on U.S. 285 to Nathrop, turn right on County Rd. 162, and continue 7.5 miles west to the campground.

**Contact:** San Isabel National Forest, Salida Ranger District, 325 W. Rainbow Blvd., Salida, CO 81201; tel. (719) 539-3591.

## 44 Cascade    7

Of the four camps on Chalk Creek, this is the only one with good fishing access, although prospects are only fair. It's the best choice for travelers with extra-large RVs; most U.S. Forest Service camps don't allow lengths much past 40 feet, and these sites go up to 60. See the trip notes for Boot Leg (campground number 42) for recreation suggestions.

**Location:** On Chalk Creek in San Isabel National Forest; map B2, grid b5.

**Campsites, facilities:** There are 23 sites for tents or RVs up to 60 feet long. Drinking water, picnic tables, fire grills, and vault toilets are provided. Leashed pets are permitted.

**Elevation:** 9,000 feet.

**Reservations, fees:** Reservations are accepted; phone (877) 444-6777. There's an $8.65 reservation fee. You may also reserve sites at website: www.reserveusa.com. Sites are $10 a night.

**Open:** May to October.

**Directions:** From Buena Vista, drive two miles south to the junction of U.S. 24 and U.S. 285. Continue five miles south on U.S. 285 to Nathrop, turn right on County Rd. 162, and continue 8.5 miles west to the campground.

**Contact:** San Isabel National Forest, Salida Ranger District, 325 W. Rainbow Blvd., Salida, CO 81201; tel. (719) 539-3591.

## 45 Middle Quartz    8

Secluded and primitive, Middle Quartz is settled at the eastern base of the Continental Divide, with access to fishing and four-wheel-drive roads. The remote location and lack of facilities keeps many would-be campers away, so your chances of solitude are good. For an interesting day trip, jog north to Forest Service Rd. 839, where you can follow a rough dirt road for a view of part of the historic Alpine Tunnel, an impressive 1,800-foot-long railroad thoroughfare bored through the base of the Continental Divide in 1880.

**Location:** Near Middle Quartz Creek in Gunnison National Forest; map B2, grid b5.

**Campsites, facilities:** There are seven sites for tents or RVs up to 16 feet long. Picnic tables, fire grills, and vault toilets are provided, but there is no drinking water. Leashed pets are permitted.

**Elevation:** 10,200 feet.

**Reservations, fees:** Reservations are not accepted. Sites are $6 a night.

**Open:** June to September.

**Directions:** From Gunnison, turn east on U.S. 50 and drive 11 miles to Parlin. Turn left on County Rd. 3101 (look for a sign indicating Ohio City and Pitkin) and continue 15 miles northeast to the town of Pitkin. Continue two miles east on Forest Service Rd. 765, turn right on Forest Service Rd. 767, and go six miles east to the campground.

**Contact:** Gunnison National Forest, Gunnison Ranger District, 216 N. Colorado St., Gunnison, CO 81230; tel. (970) 641-0471.

## 46 Snowblind    7

Snowblind is a simple, bare-bones camp set on Canyon Creek, with fishing access and a peaceful environment. The sites are cozy, surrounded by spruce and fir forest, and there's little noise aside from the squawks of resident blue jays.

**Location:** On Canyon Creek in Gunnison National Forest; map B2, grid b5.

**Campsites, facilities:** There are 23 sites for tents or RVs up to 16 feet long. Drinking water, picnic tables, fire grills, and vault toilets are provided. Leashed pets are permitted.

**Elevation:** 9,800 feet.

**Reservations, fees:** Reservations are not accepted. Sites are $10 a night.

**Open:** June to September.

**Directions:** From Gunnison, turn east on U.S. 50 and drive 31 miles to Forest Service Rd. 888 (one mile past Sargents). Turn left and continue five miles north to the campground.

**Contact:** Gunnison National Forest, Gunnison Ranger District, 216 N. Colorado St., Gunnison, CO 81230; tel. (970) 641-0471.

## 47 Monarch Park     7

This camp is situated in a heavily wooded area, with easy access to the South Arkansas River. To the east is Monarch Pass, where you can find fantastic mountain vistas and tour Monarch Ski Area in the summer. Across the highway from the access road is a trailhead for a two-mile hike to Waterdog Lakes.

**Location:** On the South Arkansas River in San Isabel National Forest; map B2, grid c6.

**Campsites, facilities:** There are 38 sites for tents or RVs up to 40 feet long. Drinking water, picnic tables, fire grills, and vault toilets are provided. Leashed pets are permitted.

**Elevation:** 10,500 feet.

**Reservations, fees:** Reservations are accepted; phone (877) 444-6777. There's an $8.65 reservation fee. You may also reserve sites at website: www.reserveusa.com. Sites are $10 a night.

**Open:** June to October.

**Directions:** From Salida, drive 21 miles west on U.S. 50, turn left on Forest Service Rd. 231, and continue one mile south to the campground.

**Contact:** San Isabel National Forest, Salida Ranger District, 325 W. Rainbow Blvd., Salida, CO 81201; tel. (719) 539-3591.

## 48 Garfield   7

East of the base of Monarch Pass, this pretty campground offers private, well-shaded sites near the banks of the South Arkansas River. Highway noise can pose problems during busy summer months. If you want to escape it, simply hop in your four-wheel-drive vehicle and head up across U.S. 50 on Forest Service Rd. 235, where you can access several high-mountain lakes and wildflower-strewn meadows.

**Location:** Near the South Arkansas River in San Isabel National Forest; map B2, grid c6.

**Campsites, facilities:** There are 11 sites for tents or RVs up to 35 feet long. Drinking water, picnic tables, fire grills, and vault toilets are provided. Leashed pets are permitted.

**Elevation:** 10,000 feet.

**Reservations, fees:** Reservations are not accepted. Sites are $9 a night.

**Open:** June to October.

**Directions:** From Salida, drive 18 miles west on U.S. 50.

**Contact:** San Isabel National Forest, Salida Ranger District, 325 W. Rainbow Blvd., Salida, CO 81201; tel. (719) 539-3591.

## 49 Angel of Shavano     8

Since it's a stopover point on the Colorado Trail, Angel of Shavano gets a lot of use from backpackers. It sits along the banks of the North Fork of the South Arkansas River, with fishing access available nearby. Directly north of camp you can see two 14ers: Tabeguache Peak (14,155 feet) and Mount Shavano (14,229 feet).

**Location:** On the North Fork of the South Arkansas River in San Isabel National Forest; map B2, grid b6.

**Campsites, facilities:** There are 20 sites for tents or RVs up to 45 feet long. Drinking water, picnic tables, fire grills, and vault toilets are provided. Leashed pets are permitted.

**Elevation:** 9,200 feet.

**Reservations, fees:** Reservations are not accepted. Sites are $10 a night.

**Open:** June to October.

**Directions:** From Salida, drive 11 miles west on U.S. 50 to Maysville, turn right on County Rd. 240, and continue four miles north.

**Contact:** San Isabel National Forest, Salida Ranger District, 325 W. Rainbow Blvd., Salida, CO 81201; tel. (719) 539-3591.

## 50 North Fork Reservoir    8

The bumpy, cramped access road keeps many folks away, so you're almost always likely to find a spot here. The sites are set at a breathtaking 11,000 feet near the eastern shore of the reservoir, with excellent shoreline fishing for cutthroat and rainbow trout. Fishing is also available back down the road on the North Fork of the South Arkansas River. A bonus at this camp is the view: to the west, you can see several 13,000-foot peaks, including Shawnee Peak and Monumental Peak.

**Location:** Near the North Fork of the South Arkansas River in San Isabel National Forest; map B2, grid b6.

**Campsites, facilities:** There are eight sites for tents or RVs up to 25 feet long. Picnic tables, fire grills, and vault toilets are provided, but there is no drinking water or trash service. Leashed pets are permitted.

**Elevation:** 11,000 feet.

**Reservations, fees:** Reservations are not accepted. Sites are $6 a night.

**Open:** June to September.

**Directions:** From Salida, drive 11 miles west on U.S. 50 to Maysville, turn right on County Rd. 240, and continue 10 miles north. Note: The last five miles or so on County Rd. 240 are rough and narrow; trailers and low-clearance vehicles are not recommended.

**Contact:** San Isabel National Forest, Salida Ranger District, 325 W. Rainbow Blvd., Salida, CO 81201; tel. (719) 539-3591.

## 51 Heart of the Rockies Campground     7

Stationed at the base of the Continental Divide east of Monarch Pass, this colorful, full-facility camp offers shaded or sunny sites surrounded by groves of conifers. On-site facilities include a swimming pool and a miniature golf course, plus horses for forays into the forest. You're also close to rafting and fishing on the Arkansas

River and hiking in San Isabel National Forest.

**Location:** Near Monarch Pass; map B2, grid b6.

**Campsites, facilities:** There are 20 tent sites and 45 sites for RVs of any length, many with full hookups. Drinking water, picnic tables, fire grills, and bathrooms with hot showers are provided. Laundry facilities, a waste disposal station, store, swimming pool, miniature golf, and horse rentals are available. Leashed pets are permitted.

**Elevation:** 8,300 feet.

**Reservations, fees:** Reservations are accepted. Sites are $17-23 a night.

**Open:** May to September 30.

**Directions:** From Salida, drive 10 miles west on U.S. 50.

**Contact:** Heart of the Rockies Campground, 16105 U.S. 50, Salida, CO 81201; tel. (719) 539-4051 or (800) 496-2245.

## 52 Gateview     8

Located at the southernmost tip of the Lake Fork arm of Blue Mesa Reservoir, this camp sits in a high, narrow canyon and is the most remote of all the Curecanti National Recreation Area campgrounds. Fishing access is available nearby. Although it's a long haul to get here, the camp is cool, quiet (almost eerily so), and, best of all, free.

**Location:** On Blue Mesa Reservoir in Curecanti National Recreation Area; map B2, grid c0.

**Campsites, facilities:** There are seven sites for tents or RVs up to 22 feet long. Drinking water, picnic tables, fire grills, and vault toilets are provided. Leashed pets are permitted.

**Elevation:** 7,600 feet.

**Reservations, fees:** Reservations are not accepted. Sites are $10 a night.

**Open:** Year-round with limited access and facilities from mid-September to mid-May.

**Directions:** From Gunnison, drive approximately 10 miles west on U.S. 50 to Hwy. 149. Turn left and cross the Lake City Bridge. Continue approximately 20 miles south to a signed gravel road, turn right, and continue six miles north to the campground.

**Contact:** Curecanti National Recreation Area, 102 Elk Creek Rd., Gunnison, CO 81230; tel. (970) 641-2337.

## 53 Stevens Creek      7

Set close to the lakeshore with a small boat ramp and basic facilities, Stevens Creek has open sites amid sagebrush, with views of the reservoir and surrounding mesa country. Since access is quite easy from the highway, the camp tends to fill up quickly.

**Location:** On Blue Mesa Reservoir in Curecanti National Recreation Area; map B2, grid c0.

**Campsites, facilities:** There are 54 sites for tents or RVs of any length. Drinking water, picnic tables, fire grills, and vault toilets are provided. A boat ramp for small boats is available. Some facilities are wheelchair accessible. Leashed pets are permitted.

**Elevation:** 7,500 feet.

**Reservations, fees:** Reservations are not accepted. Sites are $10 a night.

**Open:** Year-round with limited access and facilities from mid-September to mid-May.

**Directions:** From Gunnison, drive 12 miles west on U.S. 50.

**Contact:** Curecanti National Recreation Area, 102 Elk Creek Rd., Gunnison, CO 81230; tel. (970) 641-2337.

## 54 Elk Creek       7

Elk Creek is the park's most developed camp, with flush toilets, showers, and a full-service marina offering everything from meals to private boat tours. It's ideal for water-skiers and others who need full boating facilities. Sites are treeless, set in scattered sagebrush, with excellent lake views. Like other camps along U.S. 50, this one fills up quickly.

**Location:** On Blue Mesa Reservoir in Curecanti National Recreation Area; map B2, grid c0.

**Campsites, facilities:** There are 16 walk-in tent sites and 183 sites for tents or RVs of any length. Drinking water, picnic tables, fire grills, flush and vault toilets, and hot showers are provided. A waste disposal station is available. A visitor center and a full-service marina with a restaurant, boat rentals, ramp, and docks are adjacent to the campground. Some facilities are wheelchair accessible. Leashed pets are permitted.

**Elevation:** 7,500 feet.

**Reservations, fees:** Reservations are not accepted. Sites are $10 a night.

**Open:** Year-round with limited access and facilities from mid-September to mid-May.

**Directions:** From Gunnison, drive 16 miles west on U.S. 50.

**Contact:** Curecanti National Recreation Area, 102 Elk Creek Rd., Gunnison, CO 81230; tel. (970) 641-2337.

## 55 East Elk Creek Group Camp   7

Basic and picturesque, these large group sites sit under cottonwood trees on the northern shore of Blue Mesa Reservoir, not far from the Bay of Chickens, a popular windsurfing jump-off point. When the others in the string of camps along U.S. 50 are packed to capacity, this one is often empty—probably because you need at least 10 people to reserve it.

**Location:** On Blue Mesa Reservoir in Curecanti National Recreation Area; map B2, grid c0.

**Campsites, facilities:** There are two group sites that can accommodate up to 50 people each. Drinking water, picnic tables, fire grills, and vault toilets are provided. Leashed pets are permitted.

**Elevation:** 7,500 feet.

**Reservations, fees:** Reservations are required; phone (970) 641-2337. Sites are $2 per person with a $20 nightly minimum.

**Open:** Year-round with limited access and facilities from mid-September to mid-May.

**Directions:** From Gunnison, drive 16.5 miles west on U.S. 50.

**Contact:** Curecanti National Recreation Area, 102 Elk Creek Rd., Gunnison, CO 81230; tel. (970) 641-2337.

## 56 Dry Gulch  6

Because it's across the highway from Blue Mesa Reservoir instead of on the shore and offers no direct access to the water, this camp is slightly less pleasing than the others in Curecanti. That said, it's an adequate option, with roomy sites shaded by leafy cottonwood trees. The nearest boat ramp is at the Elk Creek camp, where you'll also find a restaurant and showers.

**Location:** On Blue Mesa Reservoir in Curecanti National Recreation Area; map B2, grid c0.

**Campsites, facilities:** There are 10 sites for tents or RVs of any length. Drinking water, picnic tables, fire grills, and vault toilets are provided. Leashed pets are permitted.

**Elevation:** 7,500 feet.

**Reservations, fees:** Reservations are not accepted. Sites are $10 a night.

**Open:** Year-round with limited access and facilities from mid-September to mid-May.

**Directions:** From Gunnison, drive 17 miles west on U.S. 50.

**Contact:** Curecanti National Recreation Area, 102 Elk Creek Rd., Gunnison, CO 81230; tel. (970) 641-2337.

## 57 Red Creek  7

This tiny but popular camp is just north of U.S. 50 near the northern banks of Blue Mesa Reservoir. Sites are in the shade, under cottonwoods, with access to fishing in Red Creek. About a mile west on U.S. 50 is the Dillon Pinnacles Trail, a steep two-mile hike that leads 600 feet up through sagebrush and conifers to a cluster of weirdly eroded volcanic formations.

**Location:** On Blue Mesa Reservoir in Curecanti National Recreation Area; map B2, grid c0.

**Campsites, facilities:** There are seven sites for tents or RVs up to 22 feet long. Drinking water, picnic tables, fire grills, and vault toilets are provided. Leashed pets are permitted.

**Elevation:** 7,500 feet.

**Reservations, fees:** Reservations are not accepted. Sites are $10 a night.

**Open:** Year-round with limited access and facilities from mid-September to mid-May.

**Directions:** From Gunnison, drive 19 miles west on U.S. 50.

**Contact:** Curecanti National Recreation Area, 102 Elk Creek Rd., Gunnison, CO 81230; tel. (970) 641-2337.

## 58 Lake Fork ⛵ 🎣 🚣 ♿ 🚐 🏕 7

Aside from Elk Creek, Lake Fork is the best option for campers traveling with boats, with sites large enough for long trailers and an adjacent marina. The camp is cool and well shaded, set on the south shore of Blue Mesa Reservoir just west of the Lake Fork arm.

**Location:** On Blue Mesa Reservoir in Curecanti National Recreation Area; map B2, grid c0.

**Campsites, facilities:** There are five walk-in tent sites and 82 sites for RVs of any length. Drinking water, picnic tables, fire grills, flush and vault toilets, and showers are provided. A waste disposal station is available. A visitor center and a full-service marina with boat rentals, a ramp, and docks are adjacent to the campground. Some facilities are wheelchair accessible. Leashed pets are permitted.

**Elevation:** 7,500 feet.

**Reservations, fees:** Reservations are not accepted. Sites are $10 a night.

**Open:** Year-round with limited access and facilities from mid-September to mid-May.

**Directions:** From Gunnison, drive 27 miles west on U.S. 50.

**Contact:** Curecanti National Recreation Area, 102 Elk Creek Rd., Gunnison, CO 81230; tel. (970) 641-2337.

## 59 Ponderosa       8

Ponderosa is an excellent camp for equestrians, offering special facilities for horses and a 1.5-mile trail suitable for hikers or horses. The catch: You can't bring a horse trailer up here when it rains; the dirt road becomes soggy and deeply rutted, impossible even for some passenger cars. Hope for sun. The sites are mostly open, with scattered pine trees. A boat ramp offers access to the Soap Creek arm of Blue Mesa Reservoir, with excellent prospects for kokanee salmon.

**Location:** On Blue Mesa Reservoir in Curecanti National Recreation Area; map B2, grid c0.

**Campsites, facilities:** There are nine walk-in tent sites and 20 sites for tents or RVs up to 22 feet long. Drinking water, picnic tables, fire grills, and vault toilets are provided. A boat ramp and a horse corral are available. Leashed pets are permitted.

**Elevation:** 7,600 feet.

**Reservations, fees:** Reservations are not accepted. Sites are $10 a night.

**Open:** Year-round with limited access and facilities from mid-September to mid-May.

**Directions:** From Gunnison, drive 27 miles west on U.S. 50 and turn right on Hwy. 92. Go one-half mile past the Blue Mesa Dam, turn right on Soap Creek Rd., and continue seven miles north to the campground. Note: Soap Creek Rd. can be nearly impassable when muddy. Trailers and RVs are not recommended during rainy periods.

**Contact:** Curecanti National Recreation Area, 102 Elk Creek Rd., Gunnison, CO 81230; tel. (970) 641-2337.

## 60 Sunnyside Campground     7

With 120 sites, this campground may sound huge, but beware—it's often almost completely filled with residents in mobile homes. Although the place looks rather hot and dry with just a few shade trees and a bit of grass, you get unobstructed views of rolling green hills, and in the foreground, huge Blue Mesa Reservoir. The sites are on a bluff overlooking the water, a perfect spot for watching summer sunsets. Nearby is a boat ramp and full facilities for fishing, plus access to hiking and mountain biking trails.

**Location:** Near Blue Mesa Reservoir; map B2, grid c1.

**Campsites, facilities:** There are 25 tent sites and 95 full-hookup sites for RVs of any length. Drinking water, picnic tables, and bathrooms with hot showers are provided. Laundry facilities, a store, and a sports field are available. Leashed pets are permitted.

**Elevation:** 7,700 feet.

**Reservations, fees:** Reservations are accepted. Sites are $10-18 a night.

**Open:** April to November.

**Directions:** From Gunnison, drive 12 miles west on U.S. 50.

**Contact:** Sunnyside Campground, 28357 W. U.S. 50, Gunnison, CO 81230; tel. (970) 641-0477.

## **61** Mesa Campground     6

Located near the Gunnison River in a huge cottonwood grove, Mesa Campground is a quiet alternative to the crowded camps at Curecanti National Recreation Area. The park is often filled near capacity with long-term occupants, resulting in a subdued, community-like atmosphere. Most sites are well shaded and grassy. The Gunnison River is minutes away, providing opportunities for fishing and rafting.

**Location:** West of Gunnison; map B2, grid c1.

**Campsites, facilities:** There are 35 tent sites and 100 full-hookup sites for RVs of any length. Drinking water, picnic tables, fire grills, and bathrooms with hot showers are provided. Laundry facilities, a waste disposal station, store, and public phone are available. Leashed pets are permitted.

**Elevation:** 7,700 feet.

**Reservations, fees:** Reservations are not accepted. Sites are $16-22 a night.

**Open:** May to November.

**Directions:** From Gunnison, drive three miles west on U.S. 50.

**Contact:** Mesa Campground, 36128 W. U.S. 50, Gunnison, CO 81230; tel. (970) 641-3186 or (800) 482-8384.

## **62** Gunnison KOA      8

The open, grassy sites at this immaculate camp are next to a wide stretch of the Gunnison River. The water is calm enough for boating; the campground rents little paddleboats for fishing or exploring, and there's even a nice wooden swing from which to watch the water flow by. The sites and the surrounding landscaping are beautifully manicured, with plentiful grass and planted flowers. Weekly communal barbecues are offered, and hiking and rafting are available nearby.

**Location:** On the Gunnison River; map B2, grid c1.

**Campsites, facilities:** There are 45 tent sites and 80 sites for RVs of any length, many with full hookups. Drinking water, picnic tables, fire grills, and bathrooms with hot showers are provided. Laundry facilities, a waste disposal station, store, public phone, sports field, and paddleboat and bike rentals are available. Leashed pets are permitted.

**Elevation:** 7,700 feet.

**Reservations, fees:** Reservations are accepted; phone (800) KOA-1248. Sites are $17-24 a night.

**Open:** May to mid-November.

**Directions:** From Gunnison, drive one mile west on U.S. 50, turn left on County Rd. 38, and continue one-half mile south to the campground.

**Contact:** Gunnison KOA, P.O. Box 1144, Gunnison, CO 81230; tel. (970) 641-1358.

## 63 O'Haver Lake      7

Fourteen-acre O'Haver Lake is a popular local fishing spot, with good chances for rainbow and cutthroat trout by boat (nonmotorized only) or shore. The campground is pleasant, with a choice of sunny or shaded sites along the lake's eastern shore. More fishing access is available on Poncha Creek, along Forest Service Rd. 200. Nearby U.S. Forest Service roads to the south provide access to the popular, well-developed Rainbow Trail.

**Location:** Southwest of Salida in San Isabel National Forest; map B2, grid c5.

**Campsites, facilities:** There are 29 sites for tents or RVs up to 35 feet long. Drinking water, picnic tables, fire grills, and vault toilets are provided. Leashed pets are permitted.

**Elevation:** 9,200 feet.

**Reservations, fees:** Reservations are accepted; phone (877) 444-6777. There's an $8.65 reservation fee. You may also reserve sites at website: www.reserveusa.com. Sites are $10 a night.

**Open:** May to October.

**Directions:** From the junction of U.S. 50 and U.S. 285 in Poncha Springs, drive five miles south on U.S. 285, turn right on Forest Service Rd. 200, and drive 4.5 miles. Turn left on Forest Service Rd. 202 and continue one-quarter mile west to the campground.

**Contact:** San Isabel National Forest, Salida Ranger District, 325 W. Rainbow Blvd., Salida, CO 81201; tel. (719) 539-3591.

## 64 Four Seasons RV Park      7

This simple RV park boasts "the best fishing on the Arkansas River," with direct access to the Gold Medal Water. Sites are lovely—grassy and well shaded by poplar, cottonwood, and elm trees, with great views of the river and surrounding mountains. White-water rafting trips are available from several outfitters in town. The nearby Salida Hot Springs Aquatic Center has a large indoor mineral pool and private tubs.

**Location:** On the Arkansas River; map B2, grid c8.

**Campsites, facilities:** There are 60 full-hookup sites for tents or RVs of any length. Drinking water, picnic tables, and bathrooms with hot showers are provided. Laundry facilities and a waste disposal station are available. Leashed pets are permitted.

**Elevation:** 7,000 feet.

**Reservations, fees:** Reservations are accepted. Sites are $14.50-20.50 a night.

**Open:** Year-round.

**Directions:** From Salida, drive two miles east on U.S. 50.

**Contact:** Four Seasons RV Park, 4305 U.S. 50, Salida, CO 81201; tel. (719) 539-3084.

## 65 Pleasant Valley RV Park      8

Sprawled on 10 acres, with access to nearly three miles of river frontage, this RV park is a destination in itself. The riverside sites are beautiful—grassy and fringed with cottonwood, elm, blue spruce, and ponderosa pine trees, with excellent views of the Sangre de Cristo Range. Hiking trails and tourist attractions (Salida Hot Springs, the Royal Gorge Bridge) are within a short drive, and a rafting company offering day trips and kayak lessons is nearby.

**Location:** On the Arkansas River; map B2, grid c8.

**Campsites, facilities:** There are 10 tent sites and 53 full-hookup sites for RVs of any length. Drinking water, picnic tables, and bathrooms with hot showers are provided. Laundry facilities and a public phone are available. Leashed pets are permitted.

**Elevation:** 6,700 feet.

**Reservations, fees:** Reservations are accepted. Sites are $14-20 a night.

**Open:** Year-round.

**Directions:** From U.S. 50 at the eastern edge of Howard, turn north on County Rd. 47 and cross the Arkansas River. Continue one-quarter mile to the campground.

**Contact:** Pleasant Valley RV Park, 0018 County Rd. 47, Howard, CO 81233; tel. (719) 942-3484.

## 66 Sugarbush Campground    8

This scenic camp boasts the only grocery store in town, a quaint log cabin-style building backed by imposing views of the Sangre de Cristo Mountains. Well shaded by conifer forest, the intimate tent and RV sites are set behind the store and divided by a small creek—a diversion from the Arkansas River, which runs about 400 yards away. A private trail connects the camp to the river and prime fishing access points.

**Location:** Near the Arkansas River; map B2, grid c8.

**Campsites, facilities:** There are 18 tent sites and 12 sites for tents or RVs of any length, some with full hookups. Drinking water, picnic tables, fire grills, and bathrooms with hot showers are provided. Laundry facilities, a waste disposal station, store, and public phone are available. Leashed pets are permitted.

**Elevation:** 7,000 feet.

**Reservations, fees:** Reservations are accepted. Sites are $12-18 a night.

**Open:** May to October, with a few winterized sites.

**Directions:** From Salida, drive approximately 10 miles east on U.S. 50. The camp is located in downtown Howard at 9229 U.S. 50.

**Contact:** Sugarbush Campground, 9229 U.S. 50, Howard, CO 81233; tel. (719) 942-3363.

## 67 Broken Arrow Campground     7

One of a handful of campgrounds in Howard, Broken Arrow is adjacent to a motel and restaurant, with large, terraced sites shaded by deciduous trees and prime mountain views. The Arkansas River is across the highway from camp, with the nearest fishing access about a half mile away. Contact any of the several rafting outfitters along U.S. 50 to arrange a trip on the river.

**Location:** On the Arkansas River; map B2, grid c8.

**Campsites, facilities:** There are 16 full-hookup sites for tents or RVs of any length. Drinking water, picnic tables, fire grills, and bathrooms with hot showers are provided. Laundry facilities, a waste disposal station, a restaurant, and motel rooms are available. Leashed pets are permitted.

**Elevation:** 6,800 feet.

**Reservations, fees:** Reservations are accepted. Sites are $12-16 a night.

**Open:** April to November.

**Directions:** From Salida, drive 10 miles east on U.S. 50.

**Contact:** Broken Arrow Campground, 7528 U.S. 50, Howard, CO 81233; tel. (719) 942-3450.

## 68 Rincon      7

One in a string of camps along U.S. 50, Rincon provides basic amenities and great river access to the Arkansas River as it flows toward Cañon City. As a designated boating put-in/take-out, it gets fairly heavy use from mid-May through September from rafters and kayakers floating their way toward the Royal Gorge, a tumultuous Class IV whitewater adventure. Trout fishing is also excellent along this stretch of river. Want a less popular pastime? Try gold panning—it's rumored that folks have actually had some luck around here.

**Location:** On the Arkansas River; map B2, grid c7.

**Campsites, facilities:** There are 10 tent sites. Picnic tables, fire grills, and vault toilets are provided, but there is no drinking water. Leashed pets are permitted.

**Elevation:** 6,800 feet.

**Reservations, fees:** Reservations are not accepted. Fees are $1 per person, per night.

**Open:** Year-round.

**Directions:** From Salida, drive 12 miles east on U.S. 50.

**Contact:** Bureau of Land Management, 3170 E. Main St., Cañon City, CO 81212; tel. (719) 269-8500.

## 69 Lazy J Resort and Rafting      7

An ideal destination spot, this full-service resort is run by a top-notch rafting company that offers daily trips in season. The sites are on two levels and are carpeted with soft grass—some shaded and some sunny—with outstanding views of the Sangre de Cristo Mountains to the west. The camp caters primarily to tenters, with two types of sites: basic tent sites with tables and barbecues, and deluxe sites with special shelters. The restaurant serves yummy burritos and deli-style sandwiches, as well as snacks and drinks. You can fish near the camp, but since the stretch bordering the resort gets heavy pressure, your chances are better at other access points upstream. Horseback riding tours are also available.

**Location:** On the Arkansas River; map B2, grid c8.

**Campsites, facilities:** There are 32 tent sites and six sites for RVs of any length, some with full hookups. Drinking water, picnic tables, fire grills, and bathrooms with hot showers are provided. Laundry facilities, a waste disposal station, restaurant,

swimming pool, cabins, and public phone are available. Leashed pets are permitted.
**Elevation:** 6,200 feet.
**Reservations, fees:** Reservations are accepted. Sites are $12-20 a night.
**Open:** April to November.
**Directions:** From Salida, drive approximately 16 miles east on U.S. 50. The camp is located on the east side of Coaldale at 16373 U.S. 50.
**Contact:** Lazy J Resort and Rafting, P.O. Box 109, Coaldale, CO 81222; tel. (719) 942-4274 or (800) 678-4274.

## **70** Hidden Valley Ranch      8

The sites at this camp face southwest, with wonderful views of the Sangre de Cristo Mountains peeking over the tops of tall shade trees. Fishing is available in Cottonwood Creek, which runs through the property, as well as at the ranch's privately stocked fishing ponds, which—they claim—hold trophy-size trout. Nearby recreation options include hiking in San Isabel National Forest and rafting (trips can be arranged on-site). On weekends, the camp hosts country-and-western dances, complete with lessons.
**Location:** Southeast of Coaldale; map B2, grid c8.
**Campsites, facilities:** There are 46 sites for tents or RVs of any length, some with full hookups. Drinking water, picnic tables, fire grills, and bathrooms with hot showers are provided. Laundry facilities, a waste disposal station, a small store, and cabins are available. Leashed pets are permitted.
**Elevation:** 7,000 feet.
**Reservations, fees:** Reservations are accepted. Sites are $15.50-20.50 a night.
**Open:** Year-round.
**Directions:** From Coaldale, drive one mile east on U.S. 50, turn south on County Rd. 40, and continue one-half mile to the campground.
**Contact:** Hidden Valley Ranch, P.O. Box 220, Coaldale, CO 81222; tel. (719) 942-4171.

## **71** Coaldale     7

Just inside the national forest boundary, this camp provides a rustic option to the developed camps along U.S. 50. The sites are along Hayden Creek, with nearby access to hiking trails. Other recreation options include rafting or fishing on the Arkansas River.
**Location:** On Hayden Creek in San Isabel National Forest; map B2, grid c8.
**Campsites, facilities:** There are 11 sites for tents or RVs up to 20 feet long. Picnic tables, fire grills, and vault toilets are provided, but there is no drinking water or trash service. Leashed pets are permitted.
**Elevation:** 8,500 feet.
**Reservations, fees:** Reservations are not accepted. Sites are $6 a night.
**Open:** May to October.
**Directions:** From Coaldale, turn west on County Rd. 6 and drive four miles to the campground.
**Contact:** San Isabel National Forest, Salida Ranger District, 325 W. Rainbow Blvd., Salida, CO 81201; tel. (719) 539-3591.

**72 Hayden Creek**    7

A major trailhead for the Rainbow Trail is adjacent to this camp, so it gets a fair amount of pressure from hikers and backpackers. The sites are mostly open, with excellent views of the Sangre de Cristo Mountains to the west.

**Location:** Southwest of Coaldale in San Isabel National Forest; map B2, grid c8.

**Campsites, facilities:** There are 11 sites for tents or RVs up to 35 feet long. Drinking water, picnic tables, fire grills, and vault toilets are provided. Leashed pets are permitted.

**Elevation:** 8,000 feet.

**Reservations, fees:** Reservations are not accepted. Sites are $8 a night.

**Open:** May to October.

**Directions:** From Coaldale, turn west on County Rd. 6 and drive five miles to the campground.

**Contact:** San Isabel National Forest, Salida Ranger District, 325 W. Rainbow Blvd., Salida, CO 81201; tel. (719) 539-3591.

**73 Arkansas River KOA**     6

Fishing is the highlight here, with 1,600 feet of river frontage and great access. The camp is adjacent to a motel and surrounded by rocky, scrubby hills. Highway traffic is obnoxious in the summer, when a steady stream of vehicles zoom by on their way to the mountains. A swimming pool and mini golf course (no charge to play) are on site, and to the west are spectacular rafting waters in the Royal Gorge.

**Location:** Near Cotopaxi; map B2, grid c9.

**Campsites, facilities:** There are 80 sites for tents or RVs of any length, many with full hookups. Drinking water, picnic tables, fire grills, and bathrooms with hot showers are provided. Laundry facilities, a waste disposal station, store, public phone, swimming pool, miniature golf, motel rooms, and cabins are available. Leashed pets are permitted.

**Elevation:** 6,300 feet.

**Reservations, fees:** Reservations are accepted; phone (800) KOA-2686. Sites are $18-23 a night.

**Open:** Mid-April to November.

**Directions:** From Cotopaxi, drive 1.5 miles east on U.S. 50.

**Contact:** Arkansas River KOA, 21435 U.S. 50, Cotopaxi, CO 81223; tel. (719) 275-9309.

**74 Whispering Pines Campground**     7

This basic, highwayside camp may not have a swimming pool or video games, but it sure has a view that makes up for all the rest. The Sangre de Cristo Mountains dip and roll against the eastern horizon, rising steeply to meet boundless skies. The campsites are grassy, treeless spaces on the banks of the Arkansas River, next to a small motel and several cabins. The camp also offers guided river rafting trips. A footbridge provides access to both sides of the river for a total of more than 1,000 feet of shoreline access.

**Location:** On the Arkansas River; map B2, grid c9.

**Campsites, facilities:** There are 160 tent sites and 26 sites for RVs of any length, many with full hookups. Drinking water, picnic tables, fire grills, and bathrooms with hot showers are provided. A waste disposal station, motel rooms, and cabins are available. Leashed pets are permitted.

**Elevation:** 7,000 feet.

**Reservations, fees:** Reservations are accepted. Sites are $9-16 a night.

**Open:** April to October.

**Directions:** From Texas Creek, drive two miles west on U.S. 50.

**Contact:** Whispering Pines Campground, 24871 U.S. 50, Texas Creek, CO 81223; tel. (719) 275-3827.

## 75 Five Points       7

This unassuming camp is on a popular stretch of highway that parallels the Arkansas River west of Cañon City. The camp is set back from the river, but close enough to allow access to fishing and river rafting. Contact the BLM for details on hiking trails in the vicinity.

**Location:** Near the Arkansas River; map B2, grid c9.

**Campsites, facilities:** There are 12 sites for tents or RVs up to 35 feet long. Picnic tables, fire grills, and vault toilets are provided, but there is no drinking water. Leashed pets are permitted.

**Elevation:** 6,000 feet.

**Reservations, fees:** Reservations are not accepted. Fees are $1 per person per night.

**Open:** Year-round.

**Directions:** From Cañon City, drive approximately 18 miles west on U.S. 50. The campground is on the south side of the highway, just east of Texas Creek.

**Contact:** Bureau of Land Management, 3170 E. Main St., Cañon City, CO 81212; tel. (719) 269-8500.

## 76 Lake Creek      7

As a major trailhead for the popular Rainbow Trail, which runs north and south of camp along the forest's edge, this camp gets heavy use. It's surrounded by ponderosa pine and spruce trees at the base of the Sangre de Cristo Mountains, with a small stream running between the sites. The access road continues west, passing several high mountain lakes (Balman Reservoir, Rainbow Lake, Silver Lake) that offer excellent fishing.

**Location:** West of Hillside in San Isabel National Forest; map B2, grid c9.

**Campsites, facilities:** There are 11 sites for tents or RVs up to 30 feet long. Drinking water, picnic tables, fire grills, and vault toilets are provided. Leashed pets are permitted.

**Elevation:** 8,200 feet.

**Reservations, fees:** Reservations are not accepted. Sites are $9 a night.

**Open:** May to October.

**Directions:** From Cañon City, drive approximately 25 miles west on U.S. 50 to Texas Creek, turn south on Hwy. 69, and drive 11 miles. Turn right on County Rd. 198 and continue three miles west to the campground.

**Contact:** San Isabel National Forest, San Carlos Ranger District, 3170 E. Main St., Cañon City, CO 81212; tel. (719) 269-8500.

## Red Bridge  7

Primitive and sparse, Red Bridge is an alternative to Gateview Campground at Blue Mesa Reservoir, which is located a few miles up the road. When you compare the two, this camp isn't much of a bargain; Red Bridge charges five bucks for little more than a toilet, while Gateview is free and offers drinking water to boot. It's a bit farther to drive, though. Fishing is possible on the Lake Fork of the Gunnison River, as are rafting and kayaking.

**Location:** South of Blue Mesa Reservoir; map B2, grid d0.

**Campsites, facilities:** There are seven sites for tents or RVs up to 30 feet long. Picnic tables and a vault toilet are provided, but there is no drinking water or trash service. Some facilities are wheelchair accessible. Leashed pets are permitted.

**Elevation:** 7,800 feet.

**Reservations, fees:** Reservations are not accepted. Sites are $5 a night.

**Open:** June to September.

**Directions:** From Gunnison, drive approximately 10 miles west on U.S. 50 to Hwy. 149. Turn left and cross the Lake City Bridge. Continue approximately 20 miles south to a signed gravel road, turn right, and continue about two miles north to the campground.

**Contact:** Bureau of Land Management, 216 N. Colorado St., Gunnison, CO 81230; tel. (970) 641-0471.

## The Gate  7

This small, rustic camp makes a pleasant stop for campers cruising the lush valley between Lake City and Hwy. 50. It's set near the Gunnison River, with fishing access within walking distance of camp. Because it's alongside the highway, road noise can be disturbing during the high season. Barrier-free access is a bonus for wheelchair campers.

**Location:** North of Lake City; map B2, grid d0.

**Campsites, facilities:** There are eight sites for tents or RVs up to 30 feet long. Picnic tables and a vault toilet are provided, but there is no drinking water or trash service. Some facilities are wheelchair accessible Leashed pets are permitted.

**Elevation:** 8,000 feet.

**Reservations, fees:** Reservations are not accepted. Sites are $5 a night.

**Open:** June to September.

**Directions:** From Lake City, drive 12 miles north on Hwy. 149.

**Contact:** Bureau of Land Management, 216 N. Colorado St., Gunnison, CO 81230; tel. (970) 641-0471.

## Big Blue  7

Set in spruce and fir forest near the border of the Big Blue Wilderness and the Alpine Plateau, this remote tent-only camp is quiet and little-used, a perfect base camp for backpackers. A trail starts here and heads south along Big Blue Creek for several miles, eventually hooking up with a trail that leads to the top of Uncompahgre Peak (14,309 feet).

**Location:** Near the Big Blue Wilderness in Gunnison National Forest; map B2, grid d0.

**Campsites, facilities:** There are 11 tent sites. Picnic tables, fire grills, and vault toilets are provided, but there is no water or trash service. Leashed pets are permitted.

**Elevation:** 9,800 feet.

**Reservations, fees:** Reservations are not accepted. Sites are $6 a night.

**Open:** June to September.

**Directions:** From Lake City, drive 10 miles north on Hwy. 149, turn left on Forest Service Rd. 868, and continue nine miles west to the campground.

**Contact:** Gunnison National Forest, Gunnison Ranger District, 216 N. Colorado St., Gunnison, CO 81230; tel. (970) 641-0471.

## 80 Cebolla Creek   7

If you don't mind a bare minimum of facilities, or if you think seclusion is worth packing in your own water and packing out your trash, you've found your campsite. As indicated by its name, this tiny camp is positioned along the banks of Cebolla Creek, with fishing access and greenery all around. Don't forget bug repellent: the mosquitoes can swarm thickly in early summer evenings.

**Location:** Northeast of Lake City; map B2, grid d1.

**Campsites, facilities:** There are three tent sites. A vault toilet is provided, but there is no drinking water or trash service. Leashed pets are permitted.

**Elevation:** 8,000 feet.

**Reservations, fees:** Reservations are not accepted. There is no fee.

**Open:** June to September.

**Directions:** From Gunnison, drive approximately 10 miles west on U.S. 50 to Hwy. 149, turn left, and cross the Lake City Bridge. Continue approximately 13 miles south to the Powderhorn turnoff (Rd. 27). Turn left and proceed seven miles to the campground.

**Contact:** Gunnison National Forest, Gunnison Ranger District, 216 N. Colorado St., Gunnison, CO 81230; tel. (970) 641-0471.

## 81 Buffalo Pass   7

Nestled at the base of the Continental Divide, this camp is far enough off the highway to avoid most traffic noise. The sites, settled in a mixed conifer forest, are quiet and scenic. A bargain.

**Location:** Near East Pass Creek in Rio Grande National Forest; map B2, grid d3.

**Campsites, facilities:** There are 26 sites for tents or RVs up to 20 feet long. Drinking water, picnic tables, fire grills, and vault toilets are provided. Leashed pets are permitted.

**Elevation:** 9,100 feet.

**Reservations, fees:** Reservations are not accepted. Sites are $5 a night.

**Open:** May to October.

**Directions:** From Saguache, drive 26 miles northwest on Hwy. 114 to the campground entrance.

**Contact:** Rio Grande National Forest, Saguache Ranger District, P.O. Box 67, Saguache, CO 81149; tel. (719) 655-2553.

## 82 Luders Creek     7

This small camp is located at the foot of Cochetopa Pass on the Continental Divide not far from Luders Creek. Its well-spaced sites sit beneath a thick, dark forest of pine, spruce, and fir. Although somewhat primitive, the camp is peaceful and receives relatively little use, which means you could have the place to yourself. And it's free. Fishing and hiking are possible within a short drive.

**Location:** Northwest of Saguache in Rio Grande National Forest; map B2, grid d3.

**Campsites, facilities:** There are six sites for tents or RVs up to 20 feet long. Picnic tables, fire grills, and a vault toilet are provided, but there is no drinking water. Leashed pets are permitted.

**Elevation:** 9,900 feet.

**Reservations, fees:** Reservations are not accepted. There is no fee, but donations are requested.

**Open:** May to October.

**Directions:** From Saguache, drive 21 miles northwest on Hwy. 114, turn left on County Rd. NN14, and continue approximately eight miles west to the campground.

**Contact:** Rio Grande National Forest, Saguache Ranger District, P.O. Box 67, Saguache, CO 81149; tel. (719) 655-2553.

## 83 Middle Taylor Creek State Wildlife Area     7

Set near the border of San Isabel National Forest, this camp provides a no-cost alternative to the U.S. Forest Service camps in the area. Middle Taylor Creek is the central attraction of the property, with several good established campsites along its banks. The creek is regularly stocked with rainbow trout and offers reliable success rates, but only dinker-sized fish. Terrain is open and hilly, with excellent mountain views. The road that follows the creek west eventually winds its way up into the Sangre de Cristo Range, crossing several excellent hiking trails on the way. Limited hunting is permitted.

**Location:** Near Westcliffe; map B2, grid d9.

**Campsites, facilities:** Dispersed camping is permitted throughout the property. Vault toilets and picnic tables are provided, but there is no drinking water. Leashed pets are permitted.

**Elevation:** 9,000 feet.

**Reservations, fees:** Reservations are not accepted. There is no fee.

**Open:** Year-round.

**Directions:** From Westcliffe, turn west on Hermit Lakes Rd. and drive eight miles to the property.

**Contact:** Colorado Division of Wildlife, 2126 N. Weber St., Colorado Springs, CO 80907; tel. (719) 227-5200.

## 84 Alvarado     7

Like the Lake Creek camp to the north, Alvarado is popular with backpackers trekking on the Rainbow Trail. The camp is near the banks of Alvarado Creek, which doesn't offer much in the way of fishing but provides a serene environment and an alternate source of drinking water (purify it first, of course). Sites are wooded, with ponderosa pine and spruce trees above and grassland below, as you head east. From the adjacent trailhead you can also travel west along Venable Creek to Venable Falls, and beyond to Venable Peak.

**Location:** On Alvarado Creek in San Isabel National Forest; map B2, grid d9.

**Campsites, facilities:** There are 47 sites for tents or RVs up to 35 feet long. Drinking water, picnic tables, fire grills, and vault toilets are provided. Leashed pets are permitted.

**Elevation:** 9,000 feet.

**Reservations, fees:** Reservations are not accepted. Sites are $9 a night.

**Open:** May to October.

**Directions:** From Westcliffe, turn west on Hermit Rd. and drive two miles, turn left on County Rd. 137, and go one mile south. Turn right on County Rd. 150 and go another mile west. Turn left on County Rd. 141 and continue two miles south. Turn right on County Rd. 140 and proceed two miles west to the campground.

**Contact:** San Isabel National Forest, San Carlos Ranger District, 3170 E. Main St., Cañon City, CO 81212; tel. (719) 269-8500.

## 85 Henson Creek RV Park     8

Many of these pretty, grassy sites are on the banks of gorgeous Henson Creek, rimmed by tall shade trees and surrounded by the bustling tourist town of Lake City. The camp was full to the brim when I arrived—not surprising given its proximity to the highway. Fishing and hiking are possible directly from camp, and shops and restaurants are within walking distance.

**Location:** In Lake City; map B2, grid e0.

**Campsites, facilities:** There are 33 sites for tents or RVs of any length, most with full hookups. Drinking water, picnic tables, fire grills, and bathrooms with hot showers are provided. Laundry facilities, a waste disposal station, store, and public phone are available. Leashed pets are permitted.

**Elevation:** 8,700 feet.

**Reservations, fees:** Reservations are accepted. Sites are $20 a night.

**Open:** Mid-May to October.

**Directions:** Eastbound from Montrose on U.S. 50, turn south on County Rd. 25 (just west of Blue Mesa Reservoir—look for the sign indicating Lake City). Drive approximately 14 miles south, turn right on Hwy. 149, and continue about 17 miles southwest to Lake City. Westbound on U.S. 50, turn south on Hwy. 149 (at the east end of Blue Mesa Reservoir) and drive approximately 37 miles to Lake City. The campground is located on the south edge of Lake City, at 110 Hwy. 149.

**Contact:** Henson Creek RV Park, P.O. Box 621, Lake City, CO 81235; tel. (970) 944-2394.

## 86 Woodlake Park    7

Located on scenic Hwy. 149, these sites are close to the Lake Fork of the Gunnison River, which rushes by with such force that it drowns most of the road noise that might otherwise bother you. Each site has a lawn of patchy grass, and shade trees are near, if not directly over, most spaces. The park is activity oriented, with group games and country-and-western dancing. Regional activities include hiking, fishing, rafting, four-wheeling, and exploring numerous historic sites in the area.

**Location:** On the Lake Fork of the Gunnison River; map B2, grid e0.

**Campsites, facilities:** There are 20 full-hookup sites for tents or RVs of any length. Drinking water, picnic tables, fire grills, and bathrooms with hot showers are provided. Cabins and a public phone are available. Leashed pets are permitted.

**Elevation:** 9,000 feet.

**Reservations, fees:** Reservations are accepted. Sites are $18 a night.

**Open:** June to October.

**Directions:** From Lake City, drive 2.5 miles south on Hwy. 149 to the campground.

**Contact:** Woodlake Park, P.O. Box 400, Lake City, CO 81235; tel. (970) 944-2283 or (800) 201-2694.

## 87 Highlander RV Park    8

The Highlander is one of the newer camps in Lake City, featuring spacious sites overlooking the Lake Fork of the Gunnison River. The camp is packed with trees, including fragrant pine and spruce and lush aspens that warm to sunny shades of gold in the fall. Just a couple of miles south is beautiful Lake San Cristobal, the state's second largest natural body of water.

**Location:** South of Lake City; map B2, grid e0.

**Campsites, facilities:** There are 25 sites for tents or RVs of any length, most with full hookups. Drinking water, picnic tables, fire grills, and bathrooms with hot showers are provided. Laundry facilities, a waste disposal station, a small store, and a public phone are available. Some facilities are wheelchair accessible. Leashed pets are permitted.

**Elevation:** 9,000 feet.

**Reservations, fees:** Reservations are accepted. Sites are $18 a night.

**Open:** May to November.

**Directions:** From Lake City, drive two miles south on Hwy. 149, turn right on County Rd. 30 (Lake San Cristobal Rd.), and continue one mile to the campground.

**Contact:** Highlander RV Park, P.O. Box 880, Lako City, CO 81235; tol. (070) 044 2878; e-mail: hilander@gunnison.com.

## 88 Lakeview Resort     9

Lakeview Resort is directly across the road from the shore of stunning Lake San Cristobal, a clear, pure mountain lake settled in a tree-lined basin and surrounded by magnificent peaks. The resort encompasses a marina, lodge, and campground and offers full services and amenities including boat rentals, fishing gear, and guided jeep and horseback tours. The camp is small and intimate, with a row of small but well-kept sites. Most of the sites are tucked in among the trees, with gorgeous lake views.

**Location:** On Lake San Cristobal; map B2, grid e0.

**Campsites, facilities:** There are 12 full-hookup sites for RVs of any length. No tents are permitted. Drinking water, picnic tables, fire grills, and bathrooms with hot showers are provided. A restaurant, cabins, horse and jeep rentals, public phone, and full-service marina with boat ramps, docks, and rentals are available. Leashed pets are permitted.

**Elevation:** 9,000 feet.

**Reservations, fees:** Reservations are accepted. Sites are $20 a night.

**Open:** May to October.

**Directions:** From Lake City, drive two miles south on Hwy. 149, turn right on County Rd. 30 (Lake San Cristobal Rd.), and continue 1.5 miles. When you come to a bridge, turn east and proceed one-half mile to the campground.

**Contact:** Lakeview Resort, P.O. Box 1000, Lake City, CO 81235; tel. (970) 944-2401 or (800) 456-0170.

## 89 Williams Creek     8

Spruce, fir, and aspen trees shade this modest camp, located near the banks of the Lake Fork of the Gunnison River. Fishing is possible about a quarter mile down the road in the river and farther north at Lake San Cristobal. Just down and across the road is a trailhead for the Camp Trail. For a pleasing side trip, head south to the historic mining town of Carson (four-wheel-drive required).

**Location:** On the Lake Fork of the Gunnison River in Gunnison National Forest; map B2, grid e0.

**Campsites, facilities:** There are 23 sites for tents or RVs up to 20 feet long. Drinking water, picnic tables, fire grills, and vault toilets are provided. Leashed pets are permitted.

**Elevation:** 9,200 feet.

**Reservations, fees:** Reservations are not accepted. Sites are $10 a night.

**Open:** June to September.

**Directions:** From Lake City, drive two miles south on Hwy. 149, turn right on County Rd. 30 (Lake San Cristobal Rd.), and continue seven miles south.

**Contact:** Gunnison National Forest, Gunnison Ranger District, 216 N. Colorado St., Gunnison, CO 81230; tel. (970) 641-0471.

## 90 Mill Creek     9

I felt as if I were in an enchanted forest when I drove through this camp. The trees are so thickly clustered that one might feel alone even if the campground was full. The sites are well-spaced and private, overlooking Mill Creek, with splendid mountain views to the south. This is one of the best camps in the area for the price.

**Location:** Near Lake San Cristobal; map B2, grid e0.

**Campsites, facilities:** There are 22 sites for tents or RVs up to 35 feet long. Drinking water, picnic tables, fire grills, and vault toilets are provided. Leashed pets are permitted.

**Elevation:** 9,500 feet.

**Reservations, fees:** Reservations are not accepted. Sites are $7 a night.

**Open:** June to September.

**Directions:** From Lake City, drive two miles south on Hwy. 149, turn right on County Rd. 30 (Lake San Cristobal Rd.), and continue ten miles south.

**Contact:** Bureau of Land Management, 216 N. Colorado St., Gunnison, CO 81230; tel. (970) 641-0471.

## 91 Castle Lakes Campground Resort  7

Approximately one mile from the Lake Fork of the Gunnison River, this full-service resort offers roomy, flat sites separated by thickets of aspen, pine, and spruce trees. The resort features trails for hiking and horseback riding, plus jeep rentals for four-wheel-drive explorations. The Castle Lakes are two private, stocked fishing lakes (there is a fee to use them, but no license is needed). To the east are stunning views of the Continental Divide, and to the west is the vast expanse of Gunnison National Forest, featuring several 14ers including Sunshine Peak (14,001 feet), Redcloud Peak (14,034 feet), and Handies Peak (14,048 feet).

**Location:** South of Lake San Cristobal; map B2, grid e0.

**Campsites, facilities:** There are 14 tent sites and 37 sites for RVs of any length, many with full hookups. Drinking water, picnic tables, fire grills, and bathrooms with hot showers are provided. Laundry facilities, a store, jeep rentals, cabins, and public phone are available. Leashed pets are permitted.

**Elevation:** 9,200 feet.

**Reservations, fees:** Reservations are accepted. Sites are $15-20 a night.

**Open:** Mid-May to October.

**Directions:** From Lake City, drive two miles south on Hwy. 149, turn right on County Rd. 30 (Lake San Cristobal Rd.), and continue nine miles south.

**Contact:** Castle Lakes Campground Resort, P.O. Box 909, Lake City, CO 81235; tel. (970) 944-2622.

## 92 Slumgullion  8

Located east of beautiful Lake City and Lake San Cristobal, this high-altitude camp sits in a forest of spruce, fir, and aspen, and is a pleasant and less expensive alternative to the higher-profile camps around the lake. This camp's curious name comes from the seafaring slang term "slumgullion," referring to the yellow goo associated with butchered whale blubber. The connection arose when a landlubbing sailor caught sight of the nearby Slumgullion Slide, a 1,000-acre mass of saffron-colored earth resulting from the slump of ancient, unstable volcanic matter down the steep hillside. Cannibal Plateau Trailhead is a short distance down the road.

**Location:** Near Lake San Cristobal in Gunnison National Forest; map B2, grid e0.

**Campsites, facilities:** There are 21 tent sites. Drinking water, picnic tables, fire grills, and vault toilets are provided. Leashed pets are permitted.

**Elevation:** 11,200 feet.

**Reservations, fees:** Reservations are not accepted. Sites are $8 a night.

**Open:** July to September.

**Directions:** From Lake City, turn south on Hwy. 149 and drive nine miles to the campground.

**Contact:** Gunnison National Forest, Gunnison Ranger District, 216 N. Colorado St., Gunnison, CO 81230; tel. (970) 641-0471.

## 93 Deer Lakes      8

Surrounded by wildflower-strewn meadows, this camp is set high on a hillside in a dense grove of conifers. Deer Lakes are a small cluster of man-made ponds, each just big enough to get a decent cast from shoreline. Prospects for rainbow and cutthroat trout are good. Portions of the camp are wheelchair accessible, including a barrier-free fishing platform at one of the lakes. The Cañon Infierno Trail leaves from camp and heads north through the La Garita Wilderness and into the Powderhorn Wilderness. Note: Beware of wandering bovines. When we stayed here, we were blocked at the campground entrance road for nearly 20 minutes by a herd of good-natured but slow-moving cows.

**Location:** Near Mill Creek in Gunnison National Forest; map B2, grid e1.

**Campsites, facilities:** There are 12 sites for tents or RVs up to 30 feet long. Drinking water, picnic tables, fire grills, and vault toilets are provided. Some facilities are wheelchair accessible. Leashed pets are permitted.

**Elevation:** 10,400 feet.

**Reservations, fees:** Reservations are not accepted. Sites are $10 a night.

**Open:** July to September.

**Directions:** From Lake City, turn south on Hwy. 149 and drive 8.5 miles. Turn left on Forest Service Rd. 788 and continue three miles northeast. Turn left on Forest Service Rd. 788-IE and proceed one-half mile to the campground.

**Contact:** Gunnison National Forest, Gunnison Ranger District, 216 N. Colorado St., Gunnison, CO 81230; tel. (970) 641-0471.

## 94 Hidden Valley    7

Tiny and secluded, this wooded camp on the banks of Cebolla Creek is squeezed onto a narrow stretch of road between the north and south halves of the La Garita Wilderness. A trailhead is available to the east, at the end of the road. Fishing is possible in Cebolla Creek but, as one U.S. Forest Service Ranger put it, "hardly worth mentioning."

**Location:** On Cebolla Creek in Gunnison National Forest; map B2, grid e1.

**Campsites, facilities:** There are three tent sites. Drinking water, picnic tables, fire grills, and a vault toilet are provided. Leashed pets are permitted.

**Elevation:** 9,700 feet.

**Reservations, fees:** Reservations are not accepted. Sites are $8 a night.

**Open:** June to September.

**Directions:** From Lake City, turn south on Hwy. 149 and drive 8.5 miles. Then turn left on Forest Service Rd. 788 and drive seven miles northeast to the camp.

**Contact:** Gunnison National Forest, Gunnison Ranger District, 216 N. Colorado St., Gunnison, CO 81230; tel. (970) 641-0471.

## 95 Spruce   7

Down the hill a bit from the Hidden Valley camp is this slightly larger option, set in mixed conifer forest near the La Garita Wilderness. See the trip notes for Hidden Valley and Cebolla camps for regional information.

**Location:** On Cebolla Creek in Gunnison National Forest; map B2, grid e1.

**Campsites, facilities:** There are nine tent sites. Drinking water, picnic tables, fire grills, and vault toilets are provided. Leashed pets are permitted.

**Elevation:** 9,300 feet.

**Reservations, fees:** Reservations are not accepted. Sites are $8 a night.

**Open:** June to September.

**Directions:** From Lake City, turn south on Hwy. 149 and drive 8.5 miles. Turn left on Forest Service Rd. 788 and continue seven miles northeast to the campground.

**Contact:** Gunnison National Forest, Gunnison Ranger District, 216 N. Colorado St., Gunnison, CO 81230; tel. (970) 641-0471.

## 96 Cebolla     7

Looking for solitude, my new husband and I searched out this camp on our honeymoon. After gingerly picking our way down the somewhat rutted dirt road, we were waved down by a truckload of frantic-looking people. Fearing that something awful had happened, we quickly stopped to offer help. Turns out they weren't in trouble—just excited. They had spotted a moose, standing calmly on a hillside watching them drive by. We hopped back in the car and drove as quietly as we could, hoping to catch a glimpse, but alas, the big guy had lumbered off into the reeds. We continued along to the campground, but were dismayed to find that three of the five sites were already occupied. So much for privacy. The camp was lovely, however, with sites right next to lovely little Cebolla Creek. Lots of mosquitoes, though. The site is just a mile west of the Mineral Creek Trailhead, a major access point for the La Garita Wilderness. The trail follows Mineral Creek for several miles, eventually connecting with the Colorado Trail.

**Location:** On Cebolla Creek in Gunnison National Forest; map B2, grid e1.

**Campsites, facilities:** There are five tent sites. Drinking water, picnic tables, fire grills, and a vault toilet are provided. Leashed pets are permitted.

**Elevation:** 9,200 feet.

**Reservations, fees:** Reservations are not accepted. Sites are $8 a night.

**Open:** June to September.

**Directions:** From Lake City, turn south on Hwy. 149 and drive 8.5 miles, turn left on Forest Service Rd. 788, and continue seven miles northeast to the campground.

**Contact:** Gunnison National Forest, Gunnison Ranger District, 216 N. Colorado St., Gunnison, CO 81230; tel. (970) 641-0471.

## 97 Stone Cellar     7

It's rare to find a free camp that offers water and other basic amenities, and this one's a prize. Although it's been neglected for several years, the camp's state of disrepair is redeemed by the peaceful, natural environment surrounding it. Saguache Creek runs through camp, providing fishing access, and the sites are open and breezy, sprinkled with a few conifers and in full view of the Continental Divide. Since the camp is rather off the beaten track, you're likely to have complete privacy. Hiking trails into the La Garita Wilderness are nearby: Go west down Forest Service Rd. 744 and you'll come to a major trailhead.

**Location:** Near the La Garita Wilderness in Rio Grande National Forest; map B2, grid e3.

**Campsites, facilities:** There are three sites for tents or RVs up to 40 feet long. Drinking water, picnic tables, fire grills, and a vault toilet are provided. Leashed pets are permitted.

**Elevation:** 9,500 feet.

**Reservations, fees:** Reservations are not accepted. There is no fee, but donations are requested.

**Open:** May to October.

**Directions:** From Saguache, drive approximately 34 miles west on Hwy. 114, turn left on Forest Service Rd. 804, and drive five miles south. At County Rd. NN14, turn left and go one mile east. Turn right on Forest Service Rd. 787 and continue 15 miles south to the campground.

**Contact:** Rio Grande National Forest, Saguache Ranger District, P.O. Box 67, Saguache, CO 81149; tel. (719) 655-2553.

## 98 Poso      7

You're way out in the boonies here, but that can work to your advantage. While others are fighting for sites at more popular developed campgrounds, you'll be enjoying absolute peace and quiet in a thick, cool forest. In fact, you just may find yourself alone, with all the fish in the South Fork of Carnero Creek to yourself. And bring along your mountain bike—nearby U.S. Forest Service roads make good trails.

**Location:** On the South Fork of Carnero Creek in Rio Grande National Forest; map B2, grid e4.

**Campsites, facilities:** There are 11 sites for tents or RVs up to 20 feet long. Drinking water, picnic tables, fire grills, and vault toilets are provided. Leashed pets are permitted.

**Elevation:** 9,100 feet.

**Reservations, fees:** Reservations are not accepted. Sites are $5 a night.

**Open:** May to October.

**Directions:** From Saguache, drive 15 miles west on Hwy. 114, turn left on Forest Service Rd. 41G, and drive 18 miles south. Turn right on Forest Service Rd. 675 and continue two miles to the campground.

**Contact:** Rio Grande National Forest, Saguache Ranger District, P.O. Box 67, Saguache, CO 81149; tel. (719) 655-2553.

## 99 Storm King    7

This camp gets its name from Storm King Mountain, which looms above it at nearly 11,000 feet. The sites are near the banks of the Middle Fork of Carnero Creek, with fair fishing for rainbow and brook trout, and are set in a dispersed forest of pine, spruce, and fir.

**Location:** On the Middle Fork of Carnero Creek in Rio Grande National Forest; map B2, grid e5.

**Campsites, facilities:** There are 11 sites for tents or RVs up to 20 feet long. Drinking water, picnic tables, fire grills, and vault toilets are provided. There is no trash service; you must pack out all refuse. Leashed pets are permitted.

**Elevation:** 9,400 feet.

**Reservations, fees:** Reservations are not accepted. Sites are $5 a night.

**Open:** May to October.

**Directions:** From Saguache, drive 15 miles west on Hwy. 114, turn left on Forest Service Rd. 41G, and drive 14 miles south to the campground.

**Contact:** Rio Grande National Forest, Saguache Ranger District, P.O. Box 67, Saguache, CO 81149; tel. (719) 655-2553.

## 100 Saguache Creek RV Park   7

Here's a tip: Before you arrive, practice your pronunciation. It's "sa-watch," not "sa-gwa-chee" as many an unfortunate tourist has uttered. The locals have no compunction about laughing in your face if you say it wrong, and you'll end up feeling like a big ding-a-ling. That said, you may wonder how you ended up here at all. There's not much to do but gaze across the San Luis Valley to the distant mountains that encase it on all sides—but that's not such a bad way to spend a day. The sites are adjacent to a small motel, set on acres of grass along U.S. 285. No trees, but great views.

**Location:** South of Saguache; map B2, grid e6.

**Campsites, facilities:** There are seven full-hookup sites for tents or RVs of any length, and a separate area for tents. Drinking water, picnic tables, fire grills, and bathrooms with hot showers are provided. Laundry facilities and motel rooms are available. Leashed pets are permitted.

**Elevation:** 7,800 feet.

**Reservations, fees:** Reservations are accepted. Sites are $12-19 a night.

**Open:** April to November.

**Directions:** From Saguache, drive one mile south on U.S. 285.

**Contact:** Saguache Creek RV Park, 21495 S. U.S. 285, Saguache, CO 81149; tel. (719) 655-2264.

## 101 North Crestone Creek     7

Set on North Crestone Creek at the base of the Sangre de Cristo Mountains, this popular camp is adjacent to a major trailhead that leads up to North Crestone Lake and beyond, eventually connecting with a web of trails in the Sangre de Cristo Wilderness. Sites are scattered among pine, spruce, and fir trees and offer easy fishing access. To the south are several 14ers (peaks over 14,000 feet), including Crestone Needle, one of the most technically difficult peaks in the state.

**Location:** Northeast of Crestone in Rio Grande National Forest; map B2, grid e9.

**Campsites, facilities:** There are 14 sites for tents or RVs up to 22 feet long. Drinking water, picnic tables, fire grills, and vault toilets are provided. Leashed pets are permitted.

**Elevation:** 8,800 feet.

**Reservations, fees:** Reservations are not accepted. Sites are $7 a night.

**Open:** May to October.

**Directions:** From Crestone, drive two miles north on Forest Service Rd. 949.

**Contact:** Rio Grande National Forest, Saguache Ranger District, P.O. Box 67, Saguache, CO 81149; tel. (719) 655-2553.

## 102 Crooked Creek  6

Used more as an overflow area than a designated campground, the Crooked Creek site is a good alternative for low-budget campers who don't mind roughing it. This is strictly a do-it-yourself option set directly adjacent to the road, with no water, tables, or even fire rings. Crooked Creek runs next to camp, with fishing access nearby.

**Location:** Southwest of Creede in Rio Grande National Forest; map B2, grid f0.

**Campsites, facilities:** There are three primitive tent sites. No facilities are provided on site, but a vault toilet is available across the road. Leashed pets are permitted.

**Elevation:** 9,200 feet.

**Reservations, fees:** Reservations are not accepted. There is no fee.

**Open:** May to September.

**Directions:** From Creede, drive 20 miles west on Hwy. 149, turn left on Forest Service Rd. 520 (Rio Grande Reservoir Rd.), and continue 1.8 miles west.

**Contact:** Rio Grande National Forest, Divide Ranger District, Creede Office, P.O. Box 270, Creede, CO 81130; tel. (719) 658-2556.

## 103 Road Canyon      7

These primitive sites are situated near the western shore of Road Canyon Reservoir. The area is grassy and treeless, with easy access to fishing for rainbow and brook trout by shore or boat. The road to Rio Grande Reservoir runs close to the sites, and traffic can be bothersome at times. Trails routed into the Weminuche Wilderness are available a few miles to the west.

**Location:** On Road Canyon Reservoir in Rio Grande National Forest; map B2, grid f0.

**Campsites, facilities:** There are six sites for tents or RVs up to 16 feet long. Picnic tables, fire grills, and a vault toilet are provided, but there is no drinking water or trash service. A boat ramp is nearby. Leashed pets are permitted.

**Elevation:** 9,300 feet.

**Reservations, fees:** Reservations are not accepted. There is no fee.

**Open:** May to September.

**Directions:** From Creede, drive 20 miles west on Hwy. 149, turn left on Forest Service Rd. 520 (Rio Grande Reservoir Rd.), and continue six miles west.

**Contact:** Rio Grande National Forest, Divide Ranger District, Creede Office, P.O. Box 270, Creede, CO 81130; tel. (719) 658-2556.

## 104 River Hill      7

Located near the confluence of the Rio Grande and Little Squaw Creek, this camp is in prime fishing territory, with access available within walking distance. The campground has many trees and offers basic facilities with a few extras, such as sinks for washing dishes and lights in the vault toilets (such things can make a big difference when you've been out in the woods for awhile). Boating and fishing are possible two miles away at Rio Grande Reservoir, and wilderness trails start down the road at the Thirtymile camp.

**Location:** On the Rio Grande in Rio Grande National Forest; map B2, grid f0.

**Campsites, facilities:** There are 20 sites for tents or RVs up to 30 feet long. Drinking water, picnic tables, fire grills, and vault toilets are provided. Leashed pets are permitted.

**Elevation:** 9,300 feet.

**Reservations, fees:** Reservations are accepted; phone (877) 444-6777. There's an $8.65 reservation fee. You may also reserve sites at website: www.reserveusa.com. Sites are $11 a night.

**Open:** May to September.

**Directions:** From Creede, drive 20 miles west on Hwy. 149, turn left on Forest Service Rd. 520 (Rio Grande Reservoir Rd.), and continue 9.5 miles west.

**Contact:** Rio Grande National Forest, Divide Ranger District, Creede Office, P.O. Box 270, Creede, CO 81130; tel. (719) 658-2556.

## 105 Thirtymile     8

Because it doubles as a major trailhead into the Weminuche Wilderness, this camp gets extremely heavy use all summer long. It's in a forest of spruce, fir, and aspen with access to the Rio Grande and Squaw Creek, both of which offer good fishing for rainbow and brook trout. Two trails are available near the camp's west loop: Weminuche Trail 818, a six-mile hike that winds south, paralleling Weminuche Creek until it reaches the top of the Continental Divide at 10,600 feet; and the Squaw Creek Trail, which follows Squaw Creek for 10 miles and also ends up at the Continental Divide (but at a higher elevation—11,200 feet). Both trails offer spectacular scenery and relatively easy grades. Rio Grande Reservoir is a short distance to the west, with fishing and boating.

**Location:** On the Rio Grande in Rio Grande National Forest; map B2, grid f0.

**Campsites, facilities:** There are 35 sites for tents or RVs up to 30 feet long. Drinking water, picnic tables, fire grills, and vault toilets are provided. Leashed pets are permitted.

**Elevation:** 9,300 feet.

**Reservations, fees:** Reservations are accepted; phone (877) 444-6777. There's an $8.65 reservation fee. You may also reserve sites at website: www.reserveusa.com. Sites are $11 a night.

**Open:** May to September.

**Directions:** From Creede, drive 20 miles west on Hwy. 149, turn left on Forest Service Rd. 520 (Rio Grande Reservoir Rd.), and continue 11 miles west.

**Contact:** Rio Grande National Forest, Divide Ranger District, Creede Office, P.O. Box 270, Creede, CO 81130; tel. (719) 658-2556.

## 106 Lost Trail     7

Like Thirtymile to the east, Lost Trail is most often used as a base camp for hikers and backpackers. Sites are small, with trees scattered throughout the camp. Across the road is the Ute Creek Trail, which runs south along Ute Creek into the Weminuche Wilderness, eventually hooking up with several other remote wilderness trails. (Note: You have to cross through private property and go over a toll bridge to access this trail.) A more scenic option is the Lost Trail Creek Trail, which heads north into the adjacent national forest, connecting with the West Lost Trail Creek Trail (a designated National Scenic Trail) and the Heart Lake Trail. If you prefer fishing to hiking, you've got three choices: Ute Creek, Lost Creek, and nearby Rio Grande Reservoir.

**Location:** On Lost Trail Creek in Rio Grande National Forest; map B2, grid f0.

**Campsites, facilities:** There are seven sites for tents or RVs up to 16 feet long. Drinking water, picnic tables, fire grills, and vault toilets are provided, but there is no trash service. Leashed pets are permitted.

**Elevation:** 9,500 feet.

**Reservations, fees:** Reservations are not accepted. There is no fee.

**Open:** May to September.

**Directions:** From Creede, drive 20 miles west on Hwy. 149, turn left on Forest Service Rd. 520 (Rio Grande Reservoir Rd.), and continue 18 miles west.

**Contact:** Rio Grande National Forest, Divide Ranger District, Creede Office, P.O. Box 270, Creede, CO 81130; tel. (719) 658-2556.

## 107 Rito Hondo     7

The campground at Rito Hondo Reservoir is nothing special, consisting of simple, primitive sites with no facilities except a vault toilet. There are no trees, only open, grassy areas on a high plateau where the winds can kick up with amazing force. The primary attraction is fishing for rainbow, brown, and cutthroat trout. Shoreline access is good, and boaters can launch nonmotorized craft at a dirt boat ramp on the south end of the reservoir.

**Location:** On Rito Hondo Reservoir in Rio Grande National Forest; map B2, grid f0.

**Campsites, facilities:** There are 35 sites for tents or RVs of any length. A vault toilet is provided, but there are no tables, fire rings, drinking water, or trash service. A primitive boat ramp is available. Leashed pets are permitted.

**Elevation:** 10,200 feet.

**Reservations, fees:** Reservations are not accepted. There is no fee.

**Open:** May to September.

**Directions:** From Creede, drive 27.5 miles west on Hwy. 149, turn left on Forest Service Rd. 513, and continue 3.5 miles northwest to the campground.

**Contact:** Rio Grande National Forest, Divide Ranger District, Creede Office, P.O. Box 270, Creede, CO 81130; tel. (719) 658-2556.

## 108 Silver Thread     6

This camp is open and breezy, with lots of grass but few trees. It's surrounded by Hwy. 149 on three sides, and with no trees to screen traffic noise, it can sound like you're camping on an interstate during the busy summer months. South Clear Creek, which runs near the sites, provides fishing access, and a hiking trail starts at camp and climbs 1,000 feet up to beautiful South Clear Creek Falls.

**Location:** Near South Clear Creek in Rio Grande National Forest; map B2, grid f1.

**Campsites, facilities:** There are 11 sites for tents or RVs up to 30 feet long. Drinking water, picnic tables, fire grills, and a vault toilet are provided. Leashed pets are permitted.

**Elevation:** 9,700 feet.

**Reservations, fees:** Reservations are not accepted. Sites are $11 a night.

**Open:** May to September.

**Directions:** From Creede, drive 23.5 miles west on Hwy. 149.

**Contact:** Rio Grande National Forest, Divide Ranger District, Creede Office, P.O. Box 270, Creede, CO 81130; tel. (719) 658-2556.

## **109** North Clear Creek    8

Hidden from the road by a thick forest of aspen, fir, and spruce, the sites at this camp are cozy and private. Some are open, others are shaded, and all have easy access to fishing in North Clear Creek. This area offers a spectacular display of fall leaves in late September.

**Location:** On South Clear Creek in Rio Grande National Forest; map B2, grid f1.

**Campsites, facilities:** There are 25 sites for tents or RVs up to 30 feet long. Drinking water, picnic tables, fire grills, and vault toilets are provided. Leashed pets are permitted.

**Elevation:** 9,800 feet.

**Reservations, fees:** Reservations are not accepted. Sites are $10 a night.

**Open:** Memorial Day to Labor Day.

**Directions:** From Creede, drive 22.5 miles west on Hwy. 149, turn right on Forest Service Rd. 510, and continue 2.1 miles north to the campground.

**Contact:** Rio Grande National Forest, Divide Ranger District, Creede Office, P.O. Box 270, Creede, CO 81130; tel. (719) 658-2556.

## **110** Bristol Head     8

Situated in an open, grassy meadow ringed by aspen, spruce, and fir trees, this camp offers basic amenities and magnificent scenery. From camp you get a clear view of Bristol Head Mountain, and a pretty quarter-mile trail will lead you up to an overlook featuring views of South Clear Creek Falls and the cliffs surrounding North and South Clear Creek Canyons. South Clear Creek runs adjacent to camp, with good fishing access.

**Location:** On South Clear Creek in Rio Grande National Forest; map B2, grid f1.

**Campsites, facilities:** There are 16 sites for tents or RVs up to 30 feet long. Drinking water, picnic tables, fire grills, and vault toilets are provided. Leashed pets are permitted.

**Elevation:** 9,800 feet.

**Reservations, fees:** Reservations are not accepted. Sites are $10 a night.

**Open:** Memorial Day to Labor Day.

**Directions:** From Creede, drive 22.5 miles west on Hwy. 149, turn right on Forest Service Rd. 510, and continue one-quarter mile north to the campground.

**Contact:** Rio Grande National Forest, Divide Ranger District, Creede Office, P.O. Box 270, Creede, CO 81130; tel. (719) 658-2556.

## **111** Rio Grande    7

These simple, pretty sites are near a grove of shade trees along the banks of the Rio Grande, adjacent to a large fishing-access point. The site is also used as a put-in for boats, so the camp is an excellent choice for rafters, kayakers, and inner-tubers. Since the sites are well off the main road, campers are sheltered from traffic and road noise.

**Location:** On the Rio Grande in Rio Grande National Forest; map B2, grid f1.

**Campsites, facilities:** There are four primitive tent sites. Drinking water, picnic tables, and a vault toilet are provided. Leashed pets are permitted.

**Elevation:** 8,900 feet.

**Reservations, fees:** Reservations are not accepted. There is no fee.

**Open:** May to September.

**Directions:** From Creede, drive 8.5 miles west on Hwy. 149, turn left on Forest Service Rd. 529 (look for the Rio Grande Fisherman's Area sign), and drive one mile south to the campground. Note: The access road is steep and narrow; trailers and RVs are not recommended.

**Contact:** Rio Grande National Forest, Divide Ranger District, Creede Office, P.O. Box 270, Creede, CO 81130; tel. (719) 658-2556.

##  Ivy Creek    7

Of the four sites at this campground, the developed walk-in site is the most desirable, with a table and fire ring in a private, remote location. You may have to wrestle for it, though—since the camp is adjacent to a major wilderness trailhead, it's often overrun with backpackers looking for a base camp. The camp is surrounded by open grassland and lots of shade trees. Recreation options include fishing on Ivy Creek and hiking on the Ivy Creek Trail, which leads 10 miles south into the Weminuche Wilderness to Goose Lake.

**Location:** Near the Weminuche Wilderness in Rio Grande National Forest; map B2, grid f1.

**Campsites, facilities:** There are three primitive tent sites and one developed walk-in site. A vault toilet is provided, but there is no drinking water or trash service. The walk-in site has a picnic table and a fire ring; the primitive sites are simply clearings with room for a car. Leashed pets are permitted.

**Elevation:** 9,200 feet.

**Reservations, fees:** Reservations are not accepted. There is no fee.

**Open:** May to September.

**Directions:** From Creede, drive six miles west on Hwy. 149, turn left on Forest Service Rd. 523 (Middle Creek Rd.), and travel four miles. At Forest Service Rd. 528 (Lime Creek Rd.), turn left and go three miles (bearing left at the Y). Turn right on Forest Service Rd. 526 (Red Mountain Creek Rd.) and continue three miles to the campground.

**Contact:** Rio Grande National Forest, Divide Ranger District, Creede Office, P.O. Box 270, Creede, CO 81130; tel. (719) 658-2556.

##  Marshall Park     6

Well known as both a fishing access point and a rafting put-in, this camp is usually filled to capacity throughout the summer. It's very near Hwy. 149, with a few trees strewn between the sites. If you're looking for more privacy, try one of several U.S. Forest Service camps to the east, on Forest Service Rd. 520 (see the listings for Rd. Canyon and River Hill, numbers 99 and 100).

**Location:** On the Rio Grande in Rio Grande National Forest; map B2, grid f1.

**Campsites, facilities:** There are 16 sites for tents or RVs up to 30 feet long. Drinking water, picnic tables, fire grills, and vault toilets are provided. Leashed pets are permitted.

**Elevation:** 8,800 feet.

**Reservations, fees:** Reservations are accepted; phone (877) 444-6777. There's an $8.65 reservation fee. You may also reserve sites at website: www.reserveusa.com. Sites are $11 a night.

**Open:** May to September.

**Directions:** From Creede, drive six miles west on Hwy. 149.

**Contact:** Rio Grande National Forest, Divide Ranger District, Creede Office, P.O. Box 270, Creede, CO 81130; tel. (719) 658-2556.

## 114 Mining Camp RV Resort  8

Just outside the limits of historic Creede, this 125-acre park offers sunny sites near the Rio Grande with fantastic views of the San Juan Mountains. The camp boasts one-half mile of river frontage and excellent fishing access, and if the fish are not biting there, you can try one of two private stocked trout ponds. Other options include hiking, cruising the ponds in paddleboats, and panning for gold. If you can afford to splurge, spend a night in one of the rustically romantic log cabins next to the riverbank.

**Location:** On the Rio Grande; map B2, grid f1.

**Campsites, facilities:** There are 82 full-hookup sites for RVs of any length, and a separate area for tents. Drinking water, picnic tables, fire grills, and bathrooms with hot showers are provided. Laundry facilities, paddleboat rentals, cabins, a sports field, and public phone are available. Leashed pets are permitted.

**Elevation:** 8,900 feet.

**Reservations, fees:** Reservations are accepted. Sites are $14-19 a night.

**Open:** June to mid-September.

**Directions:** From the western edge of Creede, drive one mile west on Hwy. 149, turn right at the entrance sign, and continue west on a gravel road to the campground.

**Contact:** Mining Camp RV Resort, P.O. Box 249, Creede, CO 81130; tel. (719) 658-2814.

## 115 Blue Creek Lodge  8

This pleasant camp is across the highway from the Rio Grande, with views of rolling hills and sharp rock outcrops rising up from the rushing river. The sites are private and roomy, encircled by pine, cottonwood, and aspen trees with fishing access nearby. Adjacent to camp is a lodge with rooms and a home-style restaurant, plus a gift shop and a beauty shop. To the northeast is the Wheeler Geologic Area (accessible only by a long hike or bike ride), a natural playground featuring unique rock formations and dramatic canyons.

**Location:** On the Rio Grande west of South Fork; map B2, grid f2.

**Campsites, facilities:** There are two tent sites and 35 full-hookup sites for RVs of any length. Drinking water, picnic tables, fire grills, and vault toilets are provided.

Laundry facilities, a waste disposal station, restaurant, store, cabins, and public phone are available. Leashed pets are permitted.

**Elevation:** 8,700 feet.

**Reservations, fees:** Reservations are accepted. Sites are $18 a night. There is an extra charge for electricity.

**Open:** Year-round.

**Directions:** From Creede, drive 10 miles east on Hwy. 149 to the campground.

**Contact:** Blue Creek Lodge, HC 33, South Fork, CO 81154; tel. (719) 658-2479 or (800) 326-6408.

## **116** Palisade     7

This riverside site is popular with rafters and anglers as well as campers. Smoothly sloping riverbanks provide a perfect launching point for rafts and tubes, and good fishing access is within walking distance. Some sites are open and sunny, some shaded by aspen, spruce, or cottonwood trees. Highway noise can pose problems in peak travel months.

**Location:** On the Rio Grande in Rio Grande National Forest; map B2, grid f2.

**Campsites, facilities:** There are 12 sites for tents or RVs up to 30 feet long. Drinking water, picnic tables, fire grills, and vault toilets are provided. Leashed pets are permitted.

**Elevation:** 8,300 feet.

**Reservations, fees:** Reservations are not accepted. Sites are $11 a night.

**Open:** May to September.

**Directions:** From Creede, drive 12 miles east on Hwy. 149.

**Contact:** Rio Grande National Forest, Divide Ranger District, Creede Office, P.O. Box 270, Creede, CO 81130; tel. (719) 658-2556.

## **117** Grandview RV Park    6

Of all the RV parks in the South Fork area, this is my least favorite. I was greeted by a surly owner who seemed curiously reluctant to let people camp on his property, and once inside, I found filthy bathrooms and showers and a grimy laundry room. That said, it's in a pretty location, with lots of grassy sites, some shaded by tall pines or young aspens. Fishing on the Rio Grande is available within walking distance. Warning: Many sites are near the road, and highway traffic is a problem in summer, with lots of noise even late in the day.

**Location:** West of South Fork; map B2, grid f3.

**Campsites, facilities:** There are 92 full-hookup sites for tents or RVs of any length. Drinking water, picnic tables, and bathrooms with hot showers are provided. Laundry facilities, a waste disposal station, cabins, and a public phone are available. Leashed pets are permitted.

**Elevation:** 8,200 feet.

**Reservations, fees:** Reservations are not accepted. Sites are $19 a night.

**Open:** Year-round.

**Directions:** From South Fork, drive three-quarters of a mile west on Hwy. 149.

**Contact:** Grandview RV Park, P.O. Box 189, South Fork, CO 81154; tel. (719) 873-5541.

## 118 Aspenridge RV Park  6

This in-town RV park offers large sites made of dirt and patchy grass, sprinkled with trees and faced with stellar views of the La Garita Mountains. The three-acre camp is backed by Rio Grande National Forest, where there are trails for hiking and horseback riding; also nearby is the Rio Grande, with opportunities for fishing and rafting. Although the hosts prefer RV campers, they will allow tents if they have space, and for only six bucks, it's a great bargain.

**Location:** West of South Fork; map B2, grid f3.

**Campsites, facilities:** There are 60 full-hookup sites for RVs of any length. Tents are not allowed. Drinking water, picnic tables, fire grills, and bathrooms with hot showers are provided. Laundry facilities and cabins are available. Leashed pets are permitted.

**Elevation:** 8,100 feet.

**Reservations, fees:** Reservations are accepted. Sites are $17 a night.

**Open:** Year-round.

**Directions:** From South Fork, drive one-half mile west on Hwy. 149.

**Contact:** Aspenridge RV Park, 0710 W. Hwy. 149, South Fork, CO 81154; tel. (719) 873-5921.

## 119 Spruce Lodge  6

This resort does triple duty as an RV park, a lodge, and a rafting company. The campsites are basically slots on a large dirt lot adjacent to the main lodge, sprinkled with a few pine trees. The camp is mostly open and sunny, set about 200 yards from the river, but there is no fishing access. Rafting trips kick off here daily, with do-it-yourself options available.

**Location:** On the Rio Grande; map B2, grid f3.

**Campsites, facilities:** There are 12 full-hookup sites for RVs of any length and a separate area for tents. Drinking water, picnic tables, fire grills, and bathrooms with hot showers are provided. A hot tub, miniature golf, motel rooms, cabins, and a public phone are available. Leashed pets are permitted.

**Elevation:** 8,400 feet.

**Reservations, fees:** Reservations are accepted. Sites are $12-14 a night.

**Open:** May to October.

**Directions:** From South Fork, drive one-half mile east on U.S. 160.

**Contact:** Spruce Lodge, P.O. Box 156, South Fork, CO 81154; tel. (719) 873-5605 or (800) 228-5605.

## 120 Riversedge RV Resort  7

This park is actually an aspiring subdivision; you can buy your own site for year-round or seasonal use. Overnighters, however, are welcome, and it's not a bad place to spend a night. The sites are grassy and landscaped, set either near the resort's private pond or near the river, a Gold Medal stretch that gets heavy fishing pressure. The pond is open for fishing, along with nonmotorized boating. Shops, restaurants, and services in the town of South Fork are readily accessible.

**Location:** On the Rio Grande; map B2, grid f3.

**Campsites, facilities:** There are 65 sites for RVs of any length, most with full hookups. No tents are permitted. Drinking water, picnic tables, fire grills, and bathrooms with hot showers are provided. Laundry facilities and a public phone are available. Leashed pets are permitted.

**Elevation:** 8,200 feet.

**Reservations, fees:** Reservations are accepted. Sites are $18 a night.

**Open:** Year-round.

**Directions:** From South Fork, drive one mile east on U.S. 160.

**Contact:** Riversedge RV Resort, P.O. Box 728, South Fork, CO 81154; tel. (719) 873-5993.

## 121 Ute Bluff Lodge  6

Located across the highway from the Rio Grande, Ute Bluff offers grassy spaces next to a lodge. Most sites are open, but those on the "bluff side"—where the sites are backed up to a hillside—are sprinkled with trees and provide better protection from the wind. One drawback: The bathroom and shower facilities are near the office, well apart from the sites, so you may face a bit of a hike to wash up.

**Location:** On the Rio Grande; map B2, grid f3.

**Campsites, facilities:** There are 45 full-hookup sites for RVs of any length. No tents are permitted. Drinking water, picnic tables, fire grills, and bathrooms with hot showers are provided. Laundry facilities, a waste disposal station, a hot tub, motel rooms, cabins, and a public phone are available. Leashed pets are permitted.

**Elevation:** 8,200 feet.

**Reservations, fees:** Reservations are accepted. Sites are $17.50 a night.

**Open:** May to October.

**Directions:** From South Fork, drive 2.5 miles east on U.S. 160.

**Contact:** Ute Bluff Lodge, P.O. Box 160, South Fork, CO 81154; tel. (719) 873-5595.

## 122 South Fork Campground and RV Resort    7

This camp offers prime riverside access to the Rio Grande, with cozy sites shaded by aspen and pine trees and spectacular views of the La Garita Mountains. Although they cost a little more, the riverside sites are the best choices, not only for their ambience but because the sound of rushing water deflects much of the traffic noise from the highway. The area is particularly beautiful in the fall, when the aspens morph from green to deep yellow and pave the roads with their crisp, round leaves.

**Location:** On the Rio Grande; map B2, grid f3.

**Campsites, facilities:** There are 22 tent sites and 30 sites for RVs of any length, many with full hookups. Drinking water, picnic tables, fire grills, and bathrooms with hot showers are provided. Laundry facilities, a waste disposal station, a small store, cabins, and a public phone are available. Leashed pets are permitted.

**Elevation:** 8,100 feet.

**Reservations, fees:** Reservations are accepted. Sites are $18-21 a night.

**Open:** Year-round.

**Directions:** From South Fork, drive four miles east on U.S. 160.

**Contact:** South Fork Campground and RV Resort, 26359 W. U.S. 160, South Fork, CO 81154; tel. (719) 873-5500 or (800) 237-7322.

**123** Cathedral     8

Here is one of the best bargains in the state—a beautiful camp with basic conveniences (although you have to pack out your own trash), and it's free. A large grove of aspens surrounds the sites, set along Embargo Creek with beautiful views of Cathedral Rock. The camp is at its most spectacular in late September, when the leaves change from green to yellow and orange. Adjacent to camp is a trailhead that leads north along Cathedral Creek, skirting Cathedral Rock; if you continue to the end of the access road, you'll find another that follows Embargo Creek, with several excellent fishing spots along the way.

**Location:** On Embargo Creek in Rio Grande National Forest; map B2, grid f4.

**Campsites, facilities:** There are 33 sites for tents or RVs up to 35 feet long. Drinking water, picnic tables, fire grills, and vault toilets are provided. There is no trash service; you must pack out all refuse. Leashed pets are permitted.

**Elevation:** 9,400 feet.

**Reservations, fees:** Reservations are not accepted. There is no fee.

**Open:** May to October.

**Directions:** From Del Norte, drive 8.75 miles west on U.S. 160, turn right on the Embargo Creek Forest Access Rd. 12, and continue 12 miles north to the campground.

**Contact:** Rio Grande National Forest, Divide Ranger District, Del Norte Office, 13308 W. U.S. 160, Del Norte, CO 81132; tel. (719) 657-3321.

**124** Penitente Canyon     8

There are zillions of gorgeous, scenic campgrounds to the west of Penitente Canyon; all around Pagosa Springs are lush, green, Eden-like places to camp. Penitente, on the other hand, is dry, dusty, and plain as can be. Why would one camp here, you ask? A simple answer: rock climbing. The climbing here is famed among enthusiasts, who flock here in droves to stand in line for the chance to risk their lives on sheer rock faces. If you're not a climber, there are hiking trails, too, and if you're really into taking it easy, you can have great fun watching those climbers sweat it out 500 feet above you.

**Location:** Near La Garita; map B2, grid f5

**Campsites, facilities:** There are 10 tent sites. Vault toilets and fire rings are provided, but there is no drinking water. Leashed pets are permitted.

**Elevation:** 7.800 feet.

**Reservations, fees:** Reservations are not accepted. There is no fee.

**Open:** Year-round.

**Directions:** From U.S. 285 north of Monte Vista, turn west on Rd. G and drive four miles to La Garita. Turn south on Rd. 38 and continue about three miles to the camp. If you're coming from the south, start at Del Norte on U.S. 160. Head northeast on Hwy. 112 for about three miles, turn left on Rd. 38, and proceed about five miles to the campground.

**Contact:** Bureau of Land Management, 46525 Hwy. 114, P.O. Box 67, Saguache, CO 81149; tel. (719) 655-2547.

 CAU

## 125 San Luis Lakes State Park

      7

Huddled in the shadow of the better-known Great Sand Dunes National Monument, San Luis Lakes State Park is an oft-overlooked recreational hub. While the sand dunes, which are visible to the east, are certainly a dramatic sight, San Luis Lakes offers a larger variety of activities, including water sports, wildlife observation, hiking, and hunting. The park is overseen by both the State Park system and the Colorado Division of Wildlife, which manages the northern portion of San Luis Lake (and the smaller Head Lake) and provides opportunities to observe flora and fauna in a riparian habitat. There is a designated swimming beach on the south side of the lake; from there, a hiking trail leads east and north into the wildlife area, where keen-eyed observers might see sandhill cranes, whooping cranes, and raptors among the multitude of wildlife (the park's four miles of hiking trails offer further opportunities). All boating is allowed on San Luis Lake, including waterskiing, sailing, and windsurfing, with strong, steady winds providing excellent conditions on summer afternoons. The campsites, clustered back from the west shore, are open and mostly treeless, some set in sandy dunes, with excellent views of the Sangre de Cristo Mountains.

**Location:** Near Great Sand Dunes National Monument; map B2, grid f8.

**Campsites, facilities:** There are 51 sites for tents or RVs of any length. Electric hookups, drinking water, picnic tables, fire grills, and bathrooms with hot showers are provided. Laundry facilities, a waste disposal station, and a boat ramp are available. Some facilities are wheelchair accessible. Leashed pets are permitted.

**Elevation:** 7,500 feet.

**Reservations, fees:** Reservations are accepted. Phone (303) 470-1144 or (800) 678-CAMP (800-678-2267) outside the Denver Metro area; there's a $7 reservation fee. Sites are $10-14 a night, and there's a $4 entrance fee.

**Open:** Year-round.  ~~ · Prices ·

**Directions:** From Alamosa, turn north on Hwy. 17 and drive approximately 15 miles, through the town of Mosca, to Six Mile Lane. Turn right and continue eight miles east to the park entrance on the left.

**Contact:** San Luis Lakes State Park, P.O. Box 175, Mosca, CO 81146; tel. (719) 378-2020.

## 126 Great Sand Dunes National Monument     8

The campground is pleasant enough—modest dirt and concrete sites well separated by scrubby pines and high-desert bushes—but the dominant attraction is, of course, the mounds of ancient sand dunes. Trails lead from the campground to the base of the dunes, where you cross a riverbed and then scramble your way up. The 700-foot-high, rolling, ever-changing banks of sand are starkly romantic, jutting smoothly against clear blue skies. Delicate cornices and steep, angled slopes beckon hikers —it's quite impossible to resist the temptation to slip off your shoes and grind the silky, grainy sand beneath your toes, or roll, slide, and tumble your way down the hills. Beware when temperatures are high, however: the sand quickly absorbs and holds the heat, making the top layers of the dunes scalding. Watch out, too, for fast-rising windstorms. The blowing, stinging sand can make you feel like you're being attacked by a swarm of angry bees.

**Location:** Northeast of Alamosa; map B2, grid f9.

**Campsites, facilities:** There are 88 sites for tents or RVs up to 35 feet long. Drinking water, picnic tables, fire grills, and flush toilets are provided. Some facilities are wheelchair accessible. Leashed pets are permitted.

**Elevation:** 8,200 feet.

**Reservations, fees:** Reservations are not accepted. Sites are $10 a night, and there's a $3 entrance fee.

**Open:** Year-round.

**Directions:** From Alamosa, turn north on Hwy. 17 and drive approximately 15 miles, through the town of Mosca, to Six Mile Lane. Turn right and continue approximately 15 miles east. Then turn north on Hwy. 150, and proceed six miles.

**Contact:** Great Sand Dunes National Monument, 11999 Hwy. 150, Mosca, CO 81146; tel. (719) 378-2312.

## 127 Great Sand Dunes Oasis    7

A more developed option than the Great Sand Dunes National Monument, this full-service camp offers every possible comfort, from hot showers to ice cream, in a sandy desert locale. The dry setting is somewhat relieved by a private (though murky-looking) fishing pond and several spindly piñon pine trees. The flat, open landscape surrounding the sites affords excellent views of the dunes.

**Location:** Near Great Sand Dunes National Monument; map B2, grid f9.

**Campsites, facilities:** There are 130 tent sites and 20 sites for RVs of any length, some with full hookups. Drinking water, picnic tables, fire grills, and bathrooms with hot showers are provided. Laundry facilities, a waste disposal station, a store, a restaurant, a sports field, cabins, and a public phone are available. Leashed pets are permitted.

**Elevation:** 8,200 feet.

**Reservations, fees:** Reservations are accepted for RV sites only. Sites are $11-17.50 a night.

**Open:** Mid-April to November.

**Directions:** From Alamosa, turn north on Hwy. 17 and drive approximately 15 miles, through the town of Mosca, to Six Mile Lane. Turn right and continue approximately 15 miles east. Turn north on Hwy. 150 and proceed two miles to the campground.

**Contact:** Great Sand Dunes Oasis, 5400 N. Hwy. 150, Mosca, CO 81146; tel. (719) 378-2222.

## 128 Bridge     7

Set in a level, open area between Piedra Rd. and the banks of Williams Creek, Bridge is an option if the other U.S. Forest Service camps close to Williams Creek Reservoir are full (as they often are). The facilities are basic but adequate, with good views of the San Juan Mountains to the north and decent fishing in Williams Creek.

**Location:** On Williams Creek in San Juan National Forest; map B2, grid g0.

**Campsites, facilities:** There are 19 sites for tents or RVs up to 50 feet long.

Drinking water, picnic tables, fire grills, and vault toilets are provided. Leashed pets are permitted.

**Elevation:** 7,800 feet.

**Reservations, fees:** Reservations are not accepted. Sites are $8 a night.

**Open:** May to October.

**Directions:** From Pagosa Springs, drive 2.5 miles west on U.S. 160, turn right on Forest Service Rd. 631 (Piedra Rd.), and continue 17 miles north to the campground.

**Contact:** San Juan National Forest, Pagosa Ranger District, P.O. Box 310, Pagosa Springs, CO 81147; tel. (970) 264-2268.

## 129 Williams Creek    8

This extremely popular camp has lovely sites near the banks of Williams Creek. Some are shaded, others are open, and creekside sites are few and coveted, snatched up quickly on summer weekends. Good fishing in Williams Creek and ample room for RVs—plus easy access to Williams Creek Reservoir—keep this camp packed throughout the summer.

**Location:** South of Williams Creek Reservoir in San Juan National Forest; map B2, grid g0.

**Campsites, facilities:** There are 67 sites for tents or RVs up to 45 feet long. Drinking water, picnic tables, fire grills, and vault toilets are provided. A waste disposal station is available across the road. Leashed pets are permitted.

**Elevation:** 8,300 feet.

**Reservations, fees:** Reservations are not accepted. Sites are $9 a night.

**Open:** May to October.

**Directions:** From Pagosa Springs, drive 2.5 miles west on U.S. 160, turn right on Forest Service Rd. 631 (Piedra Rd.), and continue 20 miles north. Turn right on Forest Service Rd. 640 and proceed one-half mile north to the campground.

**Contact:** San Juan National Forest, Pagosa Ranger District, P.O. Box 310, Pagosa Springs, CO 81147; tel. (970) 264-2268.

## 130 Teal     9

These sites are within walking distance of beautiful Williams Creek Reservoir, a 350-acre mountain paradise that offers opportunities for cartop boating and fishing for rainbow, brook, and cutthroat trout as well as kokanee salmon. The camp sits back from the shore in a wide, open grove of ponderosa pines, with plenty of grass for tents but little shade. Sites fill up quickly on summer weekends.

**Location:** On Williams Creek Reservoir in San Juan National Forest; map B2, grid g0.

**Campsites, facilities:** There are 13 tent sites and three sites suitable for RVs up to 35 feet long. Drinking water, picnic tables, fire grills, and vault toilets are provided. Leashed pets are permitted.

**Elevation:** 8,300 feet.

**Reservations, fees:** Reservations are not accepted. Sites are $9 a night.

**Open:** May to October.

**Directions:** From Pagosa Springs, drive 2.5 miles west on U.S. 160, turn right on

Forest Service Rd. 631 (Piedra Rd.), and continue 20 miles north. Turn right on Forest Service Rd. 640 and proceed 1.5 miles north to the campground.

**Contact:** San Juan National Forest, Pagosa Ranger District, P.O. Box 310, Pagosa Springs, CO 81147; tel. (970) 264-2268.

## **131** Cimarrona    8

Huddled between tall spruce and fir trees, these sites are located near the edge of Cimarrona Creek. The view south of camp is wonderful: just past here is a beautiful high mountain meadow, and beyond that, sparkling blue Williams Creek Reservoir. Since there are several trailheads nearby, the camp is often used as a base for backpackers. Across the road is the Cimarrona Trail, which leads north into the Weminuche Wilderness; farther down, at the end of the road, is the Williams Creek Trail, a scenic wilderness route often used by horse packers.

**Location:** On Cimarrona Creek in San Juan National Forest; map B2, grid g0.

**Campsites, facilities:** There are 21 sites for tents or RVs up to 35 feet long. Drinking water, picnic tables, fire grills, and vault toilets are provided. Leashed pets are permitted.

**Elevation:** 8,400 feet.

**Reservations, fees:** Reservations are not accepted. Sites are $8 a night.

**Open:** May to October.

**Directions:** From Pagosa Springs, drive 2.5 miles west on U.S. 160, turn right on Forest Service Rd. 631 (Piedra Rd.), and continue 20 miles north. Turn right on Forest Service Rd. 640 and proceed three miles north to the campground.

**Contact:** San Juan National Forest, Pagosa Ranger District, P.O. Box 310, Pagosa Springs, CO 81147; tel. (970) 264-2268.

## **132** Wolf Creek    7

Wolf Creek splits this camp in two: On the east side of the creek are four secluded, well-shaded spots (best for tents); the other side offers 22 additional sites with extra room for large RVs. With decent prospects in the creek and two stocked fishing ponds nearby, anglers will hardly have to leave camp. Those who prefer to hike should try the nearby West Fork camp.

**Location:** On Wolf Creek in San Juan National Forest; map B2, grid g2.

**Campsites, facilities:** There are 26 sites for tents or RVs up to 35 feet long. Drinking water, picnic tables, fire grills, and vault toilets are provided. Leashed pets are permitted.

**Elevation:** 8,000 feet.

**Reservations, fees:** Reservations are not accepted. Sites are $8 a night.

**Open:** May to October.

**Directions:** From Pagosa Springs, drive 14 miles east on U.S. 160, turn left on Forest Service Rd. 648 (West Fork Rd.), and continue one-half mile to the campground.

**Contact:** San Juan National Forest, Pagosa Ranger District, P.O. Box 310, Pagosa Springs, CO 81147; tel. (970) 264-2268.

## 133 West Fork     10

West Fork has remained a fairly well-kept secret, set on 10 wooded acres with big, airy sites sprinkled with large conifers and wildflowers galore. The camp is far enough from the road to feel secluded and—for those who don't mind a little work—is a magical gateway to a plethora of outdoor pleasures. Since many backpackers bypass the camp in favor of primitive spots in the wilderness, you'll almost always be able to find a space. And wait 'til you see what's within walking distance. A mile beyond the camp is the trailhead for the Rainbow Trail, a beautiful but grueling hike that leads into the Weminuche Wilderness. After about four miles you'll reach the remote, rustic Rainbow Hot Springs, a sparkling collection of natural rock pools alongside the icy West Fork of the San Juan River. (Tip: Since the trail splits in places and there are no signs to the springs, carry a U.S. Forest Service map.) Don't be surprised if you find a crowd of people waiting their turns at the pool; despite the rough hike in, more and more folks seem to flock here every year.

**Location:** On the West Fork of the San Juan River in San Juan National Forest; map B2, grid g2.

**Campsites, facilities:** There are 28 sites for tents or RVs up to 35 feet long. Drinking water, picnic tables, fire grills, and vault toilets are provided. Leashed pets are permitted.

**Elevation:** 8,000 feet.

**Reservations, fees:** Reservations are not accepted. Sites are $8 a night.

**Open:** May to October.

**Directions:** From Pagosa Springs, drive 14 miles east on U.S. 160, turn left on Forest Service Rd. 648 (West Fork Rd.), and continue 1.5 miles to the campground.

**Contact:** San Juan National Forest, Pagosa Ranger District, P.O. Box 310, Pagosa Springs, CO 81147; tel. (970) 264-2268.

## 134 Wolf Creek Valley Country Store and Campground    8

Located at the base of Wolf Creek Pass, this scenic camp offers streamside fishing in Wolf Creek and spectacular views of the Continental Divide. Mature pine and spruce trees dominate the sites, with a few large aspens sprinkled in the mix. A trail leads south of camp to Treasure Pass, passing scenic Treasure Falls on the way and ending at Treasure Mountain, where legend has it there's a fortune in lost gold buried somewhere deep within the peak.

**Location:** Near Wolf Creek Pass; map B2, grid g2.

**Campsites, facilities:** There are 24 sites for RVs of any length, most with full hookups. No tents are permitted. Drinking water, picnic tables, fire grills, and bathrooms with hot showers are provided. Laundry facilities, a store, and a public phone are available. Leashed pets are permitted.

**Elevation:** 8,000 feet.

**Reservations, fees:** Reservations are not accepted. Sites are $18-20 a night.

**Open:** May to November.

**Directions:** From Pagosa Springs, drive 15 miles east on U.S. 160.

**Contact:** Wolf Creek Valley Country Store and Campground, 13341 E. U.S. 160, Pagosa Springs, CO 81147; tel. (970) 264-4853.

## 135 Bruce Spruce Ranch     8

A large, expansive ranch surrounds this campground, located near the base of the Continental Divide adjacent to San Juan National Forest. The tent and RV sites are separated by a road, and most are large and well shaded, virtually enveloped in spruce and pine trees with gorgeous mountain views. Hiking and horseback riding trails span the property and continue into the forest for miles, some heading into the Weminuche Wilderness a few miles to the west. Anglers may cast a line in a private lake (a fee is charged, but no license is required). Fishing is also possible in small natural streams across the property.

**Location:** North of Pagosa Springs; map B2, grid g2.

**Campsites, facilities:** There are six tent sites and 32 sites for RVs of any length, most with full hookups. Drinking water, picnic tables, fire grills, and bathrooms with hot showers are provided. Laundry facilities, cabins, and a public phone are available. Leashed pets are permitted.

**Elevation:** 8,200 feet.

**Reservations, fees:** Reservations are accepted. Sites are $15-17 a night.

**Open:** Mid-May to November.

**Directions:** From Pagosa Springs, drive 16 miles northeast on U.S. 160, turn left on the entrance road, and continue one-half mile to the campground.

**Contact:** Bruce Spruce Ranch, P.O. Box 296, Pagosa Springs, CO 81147; tel. (970) 264-5374.

## 136 Big Meadows       8

One-hundred-ten-acre Big Meadows Reservoir makes an excellent base for an extended vacation, with boating, fishing, wilderness hiking, and beautiful views of the Continental Divide all within walking distance of the camp. Sites are well shaded, set in mature spruce forest near the lakeshore. Fishing is fair for rainbow and brook trout, with a small boat ramp providing maximum access and a special fishing pier for anglers in wheelchairs. A wheelchair-accessible trail leads from camp to the lake, and the Archuleta Creek Trail begins on the north side of the reservoir, wandering several miles west into the Weminuche Wilderness. Note to RV campers: If you have a large rig, try one of the camp's double sites, which can accommodate two cars or one extra-large RV or trailer.

**Location:** On Big Meadows Reservoir in Rio Grande National Forest; map B2, grid g2.

**Campsites, facilities:** There are 55 sites for tents or RVs up to 45 feet long. Drinking water, picnic tables, fire grills, and vault toilets are provided. A boat ramp is nearby. Some facilities are wheelchair accessible. Leashed pets are permitted.

**Elevation:** 9,200 feet.

**Reservations, fees:** Reservations are accepted; phone (877) 444-6777. There's an $8.65 reservation fee. You may also reserve sites at website: www.reserveusa.com. Sites are $12 a night.

**Open:** May to October.

**Directions:** From South Fork, turn west on U.S. 160 and drive 11 miles. Turn right on Forest Service Rd. 410 and continue two miles southwest to the campground.
**Contact:** Rio Grande National Forest, Divide Ranger District, Del Norte Office, 13308 W. U.S. 160, Del Norte, CO 81132; tel. (719) 657-3321.

## 137 Park Creek    7

Set on Park Creek near its confluence with the South Fork of the Rio Grande, this camp provides superb fishing access in a wooded setting. The river is lined with leafy cottonwoods and drooping willows for plenty of shade, which the campsites enjoy as well. See a U.S. Forest Service map for trails in the area.
**Location:** Near the South Fork of the Rio Grande in Rio Grande National Forest; map B2, grid g3.
**Campsites, facilities:** There are 16 sites for tents or RVs up to 30 feet long. Drinking water, picnic tables, fire grills, and vault toilets are provided. Leashed pets are permitted.
**Elevation:** 8,500 feet.
**Reservations, fees:** Reservations are not accepted. Sites are $11 a night.
**Open:** May to October.
**Directions:** From South Fork, turn west on U.S. 160 and drive 6.5 miles to the campground.
**Contact:** Rio Grande National Forest, Divide Ranger District, Del Norte Office, 13308 W. U.S. 160, Del Norte, CO 81132; tel. (719) 657-3321.

## 138 Moon Valley Resort      7

Natural and scenic, this full-service camp bordered by Rio Grande National Forest offers grassy sites in a forest of aspen, cottonwood, and fir trees. A privately stocked pond is available for fishing, or you can cross the road and take your chances in the South Fork of the Rio Grande. Hiking trails lead from camp into the adjacent forest, following small mountain creeks to meet up with a large trail network that eventually heads west and south into the Weminuche Wilderness. Guided pack and hunting trips are also available.
**Location:** Southwest of South Fork; map B2, grid g3.
**Campsites, facilities:** There are 50 full-hookup sites for tents or RVs of any length. Drinking water, picnic tables, fire grills, and bathrooms with hot showers are provided. Laundry facilities and a public phone are available. Leashed pets are permitted.
**Elevation:** 8,400 feet.
**Reservations, fees:** Reservations are accepted. Sites are $16 a night.
**Open:** May to November.
**Directions:** From South Fork, turn west on U.S. 160 and drive six miles.
**Contact:** Moon Valley Resort, P.O. Box 265, South Fork, CO 81154; tel. (719) 873-5216.

## 139 Highway Springs   6

Because it's right next to the highway, this camp gets much of its use from travelers who happen to pass by in their search for a spot simply to spend the night. And that's really what it's best for—there isn't much in the way of recreation in the immediate area, although fishing on the South Fork of the Rio Grande is available within a moderate drive. The sites are large and partially shaded (and some are missing picnic tables).

**Location:** Near the South Fork of the Rio Grande in Rio Grande National Forest; map B2, grid g3.

**Campsites, facilities:** There are 11 sites for tents or RVs up to 35 feet long. Picnic tables, fire grills, and vault toilets are provided, but there is no drinking water. Leashed pets are permitted.

**Elevation:** 8,400 feet.

**Reservations, fees:** Reservations are not accepted. Sites are $5 a night.

**Open:** May to October.

**Directions:** From South Fork, turn west on U.S. 160 and drive four miles to the campground.

**Contact:** Rio Grande National Forest, Divide Ranger District, Del Norte Office, 13308 W. U.S. 160, Del Norte, CO 81132; tel. (719) 657-3321.

## 140 Riverbend Resort     6

Campers here are treated to views of rocky bluffs jutting steeply above the South Fork of the Rio Grande, which bubbles and froths its way past the campsites en route to Big Meadows Reservoir. Although the camp is mostly open and grassy, there are a few aspen, spruce, and pine trees scattered about, with excellent fishing access in between. The river-view sites, though more expensive, are the best in the camp. Hiking is possible in the adjacent Rio Grande National Forest.

**Location:** On the South Fork of the Rio Grande; map B2, grid g3.

**Campsites, facilities:** There are six tent sites and 58 sites for RVs of any length, most with full hookups. Drinking water, picnic tables, and bathrooms with hot showers are provided. Laundry facilities, a hot tub, cabins, and a public phone are available. Leashed pets are permitted.

**Elevation:** 8,300 feet.

**Reservations, fees:** Reservations are accepted. Sites are $16-21 a night.

**Open:** Mid-April to mid-November.

**Directions:** From South Fork, turn west on U.S. 160 and drive three miles to the campground.

**Contact:** Riverbend Resort, P.O. Box 129, South Fork, CO 81154; tel. (719) 873-5344.

## 141 Lower Beaver Creek     7

These sites are settled in a ponderosa pine forest on Beaver Creek, with good fishing access. Beaver Creek Reservoir is a couple miles south and has facilities for boating and fishing. Nearby is the Tewksberry Creek Trail, which runs several miles south into the adjacent national forest.

**Location:** North of Beaver Creek Reservoir in Rio Grande National Forest; map B2, grid g3.

**Campsites, facilities:** There are 19 sites for tents or RVs up to 35 feet long. Drinking water, picnic tables, fire grills, and vault toilets are provided. Leashed pets are permitted.

**Elevation:** 8,400 feet.

**Reservations, fees:** Reservations are not accepted. Sites are $11 a night.

**Open:** May to October.

**Directions:** From South Fork, turn west on U.S. 160 and drive one mile. Then turn left on Forest Service Rd. 360 and continue 4.5 miles southeast to the campground.

**Contact:** Rio Grande National Forest, Divide Ranger District, Del Norte Office, 13308 W. U.S. 160, Del Norte, CO 81132; tel. (719) 657-3321.

## 142 Upper Beaver Creek    7

A nearly identical alternative to Lower Beaver Creek, this camp is also on Beaver Creek, although a bit closer to Beaver Creek Reservoir (it's two miles away). Fishing access is quite good, and you get pleasing views of the Continental Divide to the west.

**Location:** North of Beaver Creek Reservoir in Rio Grande National Forest; map B2, grid g3.

**Campsites, facilities:** There are 15 sites for tents or RVs up to 35 feet long. Drinking water, picnic tables, fire grills, and vault toilets are provided. Leashed pets are permitted.

**Elevation:** 8,400 feet.

**Reservations, fees:** Reservations are not accepted. Sites are $11 a night.

**Open:** May to October.

**Directions:** From South Fork, turn west on U.S. 160 and drive one mile. Turn left on Forest Service Rd. 360 and continue five miles southeast to the campground.

**Contact:** Rio Grande National Forest, Divide Ranger District, Del Norte Office, 13308 W. U.S. 160, Del Norte, CO 81132; tel. (719) 657-3321.

## 143 Cross Creek     7

Nestled in pine forest at the confluence of Beaver Creek and Cross Creek, this camp is less than half a mile south of Beaver Creek Reservoir, making it a great base for fishing expeditions. You can fish in the creeks near camp, too, but your odds improve greatly as you near the reservoir. The Cross Creek Trail starts at the eastern edge of camp and follows the creek east for three miles, providing another recreation option. If you continue south about a quarter mile on the access road, you'll come to a trail that leads to the largest Douglas fir tree in the entire Rio Grande National Forest—over 100 feet tall and wide enough that even the largest tree-hugger couldn't wrap his arms around it.

**Location:** Near Beaver Creek Reservoir in Rio Grande National Forest; map B2, grid g3.

**Campsites, facilities:** There are 12 sites for tents or RVs up to 25 feet long. Drinking water, picnic tables, fire grills, and vault toilets are provided. Leashed pets are permitted.

**Elevation:** 8,800 feet.

**Reservations, fees:** Reservations are not accepted. Sites are $10 a night.

**Open:** May to October.

**Directions:** From South Fork, turn west on U.S. 160 and drive one mile. Turn left on Forest Service Rd. 360 and continue nine miles southeast to the campground.

**Contact:** Rio Grande National Forest, Divide Ranger District, Del Norte Office, 13308 W. U.S. 160, Del Norte, CO 81132; tel. (719) 657-3321.

## 144 Tucker Ponds  7

This small camp sits under silvery spruce trees between Pass Creek and Tucker Ponds, two dingy-looking miniature lakes that offer surprisingly good fishing for rainbow trout. To the west on the Continental Divide are Wolf Creek Pass and trails into the Weminuche Wilderness.

**Location:** On Pass Creek in Rio Grande National Forest; map B2, grid g3.

**Campsites, facilities:** There are 16 sites for tents or RVs up to 30 feet long. Drinking water, picnic tables, fire grills, and vault toilets are provided. Leashed pets are permitted.

**Elevation:** 9,600 feet.

**Reservations, fees:** Reservations are not accepted. Sites are $10 a night.

**Open:** May to October.

**Directions:** From South Fork, turn west on U.S. 160 and drive 13 miles. Turn left on Forest Service Rd. 390 (Pass Creek Rd.) and continue 2.5 miles south to the campground.

**Contact:** Rio Grande National Forest, Divide Ranger District, Del Norte Office, 13308 W. U.S. 160, Del Norte, CO 81132; tel. (719) 657-3321.

## 145 Rock Creek  7

Just inside the eastern border of Rio Grande National Forest, this spruce-lined camp is on the banks of Rock Creek, with good fishing. Although it doesn't see much use in the summer, hunters fill the place in the fall, using it as a base camp while they make forays into the adjacent national forest. The North Rock Creek Trail and the South Rock Creek Trail offer more opportunities for fishing and hiking.

**Location:** On the South Fork of Rock Creek in Rio Grande National Forest; map B2, grid g5.

**Campsites, facilities:** There are 23 sites for tents or RVs up to 30 feet long. Picnic tables, fire grills, and vault toilets are provided, but there is no drinking water or trash service. Leashed pets are permitted.

**Elevation:** 9,200 feet.

**Reservations, fees:** Reservations are not accepted. There is no fee.

**Open:** May to October.

**Directions:** From Monte Vista, drive two miles south on Hwy. 15, turn right on Rock Creek Rd., and continue 16 miles southwest (after 12 miles the road becomes Forest Service Rd. 265) to the camp.

**Contact:** Rio Grande National Forest, Divide Ranger District, Del Norte Office, 13308 W. U.S. 160, Del Norte, CO 81132; tel. (719) 657-3321.

## 146 Comstock  7

Although slightly run-down, Comstock is redeemed by its pleasant atmosphere, courtesy of large, shady spruce trees and a pretty stream that runs right through camp—and it offers fishing to boot. The Alamosa-Rock Creek Trail leaves camp and travels south until it reaches the Alamosa River; if you travel to the end of the access road, you'll come to trailheads to several backcountry trails, each leading to small lakes and streams in the national forest.

**Location:** On the South Fork of Rock Creek in Rio Grande National Forest; map B2, grid g5.

**Campsites, facilities:** There are eight sites for tents or RVs up to 30 feet long. Picnic tables, fire grills, and vault toilets are provided, but there is no drinking water or trash service. Leashed pets are permitted.

**Elevation:** 9,500 feet.

**Reservations, fees:** Reservations are not accepted. There is no fee.

**Open:** May to October.

**Directions:** From Monte Vista, drive two miles south on Hwy. 15, turn right on Rock Creek Rd., and continue 18 miles southwest (after 12 miles, the road becomes Forest Service Rd. 265) to the camp.

**Contact:** Rio Grande National Forest, Divide Ranger District, Del Norte Office, 13308 W. U.S. 160, Del Norte, CO 81132; tel. (719) 657-3321.

## 147 Alamosa KOA     7

Plunked at the flat bottom of the San Luis Valley, this camp offers grassy sites sprinkled with clusters of sagebrush and 360-degree mountain views. The sites are large, even, and wide open. Points of interest include Splashland Hot Springs in Alamosa, fishing in the Rio Grande, and the Colorado Alligator Farm, located to the north on Hwy. 17.

**Location:** East of Alamosa; map B2, grid g8.

**Campsites, facilities:** There are 50 sites for tents or RVs of any length, some with full hookups. Drinking water, picnic tables, fire grills, and bathrooms with hot showers are provided. Laundry facilities, a waste disposal station, a store, a sports field, and a public phone are available. Leashed pets are permitted.

**Elevation:** 7,500 feet.

**Reservations, fees:** Reservations are accepted; phone (800) KOA-9157. Sites are $18-23 a night.

**Open:** April to November.

**Directions:** From Alamosa, drive 3.5 miles east on U.S. 160.

**Contact:** Alamosa KOA, 6900 Juniper Lane, Alamosa, CO 81101; tel. (719) 589-9757.

## 148 Blanca RV Park    5

Located in downtown Blanca, this camp features grass-and-gravel sites and large cottonwoods surrounded by the vast, even expanse of the San Luis Valley. It's the only place in town to camp, and while it doesn't offer much in the way of ambience, it is central to some significant recreation destinations, including the Great Sand Dunes National Monument to the north and Smith Reservoir to the south, which offers prime boating and fishing.

**Location:** In Blanca; map B2, grid g9.

**Campsites, facilities:** There are 30 sites for tents or RVs of any length, most with full hookups. Drinking water, picnic tables, fire grills, and bathrooms with hot showers are provided. Laundry facilities, a waste disposal station, a store, and a public phone are available. Some facilities are wheelchair accessible. Leashed pets are permitted.

**Elevation:** 7,800 feet.

**Reservations, fees:** Reservations are accepted. Sites are $12-15 a night.

**Open:** April to November.

**Directions:** From Alamosa, drive 17 miles east on U.S. 160 to Blanca. The campground is located downtown at 521 Main Street.

**Contact:** Blanca RV Park, P.O. Box 64, Blanca, CO 81123; tel. (719) 379-3201.

## 149 Sportsman's Supply and RV Park      8

This one is missed by everyone but those in the know—like you. It's way the heck up there, far enough out of town to feel like the wilderness but close enough to make a quick trip into town feasible. You probably won't have to go though, because next to the campground is a full-service country store selling groceries and camping supplies. Towering ponderosa pines shade the sites, and there's a small stream nearby for fishing. The camp sits adjacent to San Juan National Forest, making it the perfect headquarters for a backpacking or horse pack trip into the Weminuche Wilderness. Nearby there's rafting and kayaking on the Upper Piedra River.

**Location:** North of Pagosa Springs; map B2, grid h0.

**Campsites, facilities:** There are 32 full-hookup sites for RVs of any length, and a separate area for tents. Drinking water, picnic tables, fire grills, and bathrooms with hot showers are provided. Laundry facilities, a store, and cabins are available. Leashed pets are permitted.

**Elevation:** 8,100 feet.

**Reservations, fees:** Reservations are accepted. Sites are $12-24 a night.

**Open:** Mid-May to mid-November.

**Directions:** From Pagosa Springs, drive two miles west on U.S. 160, turn right on County Rd. 631 (Piedra Rd.), and continue 18 miles north. When the road forks, bear right and turn into the campground.

**Contact:** Sportsman's Supply and RV Park, 2095 Taylor Lane, Pagosa Springs, CO 81147; tel. (970) 731-2300.

## 150 Ute   7

Ute used to be a group facility, but the demand for sites in the region became so great that the U.S. Forest Service decided to make the camp more accessible to highway travelers. Set on a south-facing hillside above the highway, the sites are nestled among ponderosa pines with plenty of space for large RVs. If you huff your way to the top of the hill, you'll be rewarded with a picture-perfect vista of the Chimney Rock Archaeological Area, featuring a towering column looming over the ruins of an ancient Native American pueblo.

**Location:** West of Pagosa Springs in San Juan National Forest; map B2, grid h0.

**Campsites, facilities:** There are 24 sites for tents or RVs of any length. Drinking water, picnic tables, fire grills, and vault toilets are provided. Leashed pets are permitted.

**Elevation:** 7,100 feet.

**Reservations, fees:** Reservations are not accepted. Sites are $8 a night.

**Open:** May to October.

**Directions:** From Pagosa Springs, drive 17 miles west on U.S. 160.

**Contact:** San Juan National Forest, Pagosa Ranger District, P.O. Box 310, Pagosa Springs, CO 81147; tel. (970) 264-2268.

## **151** Happy Camper RV Park  6

Set along U.S. 160 west of Pagosa Springs, this large camp features spacious, sunny sites within walking distance of a small creek. Fishing prospects are meager, but it's fun to head down to the creek and watch resident beavers go about their business on summer evenings. Pine and cottonwood trees line the creek banks, and a few young aspens dot the camp.

**Location:** On Stollsteimer Creek; map B2, grid i0.

**Campsites, facilities:** There are 83 full-hookup sites for RVs of any length and a separate areas for tents. Drinking water, picnic tables, fire grills, and bathrooms with hot showers are provided. Laundry facilities, a waste disposal station, and a store are available. Some facilities are wheelchair accessible. Leashed pets are permitted.

**Elevation:** 6,500 feet.

**Reservations, fees:** Reservations are accepted. Sites are $12-16 a night.

**Open:** Mid-April to December.

**Directions:** From Pagosa Springs, drive nine miles west on U.S. 160.

**Contact:** Happy Camper RV Park, 9260 W. U.S. 160, Pagosa Springs, CO 81147; tel. (970) 731-5822.

## **152** Hide-A-Way Campground  7

This 27-acre camp features well-kept gravel sites at the base of Packsaddle Mountain, with pleasing views of the Mitchell Range to the north. Although most sites are open and sunny, the camp is encircled by pine trees that provide some shade, and little Turkey Creek bubbles its way through the property. No fishing is available. Bird-watching is, however—the creek draws many species every year, including bluebirds, magpies, orioles, and an assortment of songbirds. Hiking trails are adjacent to camp.

**Location:** On Turkey Creek; map B2, grid i0.

**Campsites, facilities:** There are 55 sites for tents or RVs of any length, many with full hookups. Drinking water, picnic tables, fire grills, and bathrooms with hot showers are provided. Leashed pets are permitted.

**Elevation:** 6,800 feet.

**Reservations, fees:** Reservations are accepted. Sites are $12-17 a night.

**Open:** April to November.

**Directions:** From Pagosa Springs, drive 10 miles west on U.S. 160.

**Contact:** Hide-A-Way Campground, 8880 W. U.S. 160, Pagosa Springs, CO 81147; tel. (970) 731-5112.

## 153 Cool Pines RV Park    6

One of the newest campgrounds in Pagosa Springs, Cool Pines offers roomy, graveled sites, many situated on a gently sloping hillside. Though it's just off the highway, most of the camp is sheltered from highway noise. Grassy areas divide the sites, and most are shaded by pine trees. Dog owners will appreciate the pet-friendliness of the camp; a dog run and pet-sitting are included in the list of services. Fishing guides are available as well.

**Location:** In Pagosa Springs; map B2, grid h1.

**Campsites, facilities:** There are 22 sites for tents or RVs of any length, most with full hookups. Drinking water, picnic tables, and bathrooms with hot showers are provided. Laundry facilities, rec hall, a hot tub, and a public phone are also available. Some facilities are wheelchair accessible. Leashed pets are permitted.

**Elevation:** 7,100 feet.

**Reservations, fees:** Reservations are accepted. Sites are $14-20 a night.

**Open:** Mid-May to mid-November.

**Directions:** The park is located in the town of Pagosa Springs, at 1501 W. Hwy. 160.

**Contact:** Cool Pines RV Park, 1501 W. Hwy. 160, Pagosa Springs, CO 81147; tel. (970) 264-9130.

## 154 San Juan Motel and RV Park       7

Although it's next to a motel in the middle of town, this camp provides a pleasing, natural ambience, offering riverside sites and lots of pine and cottonwood trees mixed with a few firs and aspens. The tent and RV spaces are separated, with a central grassy area for tenters and larger, more defined spots for RVs. A city park within walking distance has large grassy areas for picnicking, hiking trails, stocked fishing, and an ice skating rink. You're also within minutes of two luxurious hot springs resorts in town: the beautifully landscaped Springs, located at The Spring Inn, and across the street, the simpler Spa Motel.

**Location:** In Pagosa Springs; map B2, grid h1.

**Campsites, facilities:** There are 20 full-hookup sites for RVs of any length, and a separate area for tents. Drinking water, picnic tables, and bathrooms with hot showers are provided. Laundry facilities, motel rooms, and cabins are available. Some facilities are wheelchair accessible. Leashed pets are permitted.

**Elevation:** 7,100 feet.

**Reservations, fees:** Reservations are not accepted. Sites are $15-24 a night.

**Open:** Year-round.

**Directions:** The campground is located at 191 E. Pagosa St. (U.S. 160) in downtown Pagosa Springs.

**Contact:** San Juan Motel and RV Park, P.O. Box 729, Pagosa Springs, CO 81147; tel. (970) 264-2262 or (800) 765-0250.

## 155 Pagosa Riverside Campground  8

These spacious sites sit well back from the highway, either along the San Juan River or near the shore of the resort's beautiful private lake, where you can fish or cruise around on rented paddleboats. The tent sites are on soft grass, tucked in a forest of conifers, and the RV sites are sunnier, although many do have dappled shade. Trails around the lake offer opportunities to view native wildflowers and snowcapped peaks on the western side of the Continental Divide. There's also a swimming pool and a full-service grocery store.

**Location:** On the San Juan River; map B2, grid h1.

**Campsites, facilities:** There are 35 tent sites and 50 sites for RVs of any length, many with full hookups. Drinking water, picnic tables, fire grills, and bathrooms with hot showers are provided. Laundry facilities, a waste disposal station, store, swimming pool, paddleboat rentals, cabins, and a public phone are available. Leashed pets are permitted.

**Elevation:** 7,100 feet.

**Reservations, fees:** Reservations are accepted. Sites are $16-24 a night.

**Open:** Mid-April to mid-November.

**Directions:** From Pagosa Springs, drive approximately 2.5 miles east on U.S. 160.

**Contact:** Pagosa Riverside Campground, P.O. Box 268, Pagosa Springs, CO 81147; tel. (970) 264-5874; e-mail: prc-jones@juno.com.

## 156 Elk Meadows Campground    7

Overlooking the San Juan River, Elk Meadows offers private, secluded tent sites and roomy RV sites in a setting of pine and scrub brush. Hiking trails leave directly from camp and wander through San Juan National Forest, making this an excellent base for hikers.

**Location:** On the San Juan River; map B2, grid h2.

**Campsites, facilities:** There are 10 tent sites and 35 sites for RVs of any length, many with full hookups. Drinking water, picnic tables, fire grills, and bathrooms with hot showers are provided. Laundry facilities, a waste disposal station, store, public phone, and cabins are available. Leashed pets are permitted.

**Elevation:** 7,300 feet.

**Reservations, fees:** Reservations are accepted. Sites are $14-21 a night.

**Open:** May to November.

**Directions:** From Pagosa Springs, drive five miles east on U.S. 160.

**Contact:** Elk Meadows Campground, P.O. Box 238, Pagosa Springs, CO 81147; tel. (970) 264-5482.

## 157 East Fork     7

Perched high on a bluff overlooking the East Fork of the San Juan River, these cozy sites are shaded by sweet-smelling pine and lofty oak trees. A steep, narrow trail leads down to the river, where you'll find fishing access and more trails that continue upstream. A developed trailhead is located two miles beyond the campground, at Sand Creek.

**Location:** On the East Fork of the San Juan River in San Juan National Forest; map B2, grid h2.

**Campsites, facilities:** There are 26 sites for tents or RVs up to 35 feet long. Drinking water, picnic tables, fire grills, and vault toilets are provided. Leashed pets are permitted.

**Elevation:** 7,600 feet.

**Reservations, fees:** Reservations are not accepted. Sites are $8 a night.

**Open:** May to October.

**Directions:** From Pagosa Springs, drive 10 miles east on U.S. 160, turn right on Forest Service Rd. 667 (East Fork Rd.), and continue three-quarters of a mile to the campground.

**Contact:** San Juan National Forest, Pagosa Ranger District, P.O. Box 310, Pagosa Springs, CO 81147; tel. (970) 264-2268.

## 158 Stunner    8

This small, remote site is beneath pine trees in a pretty spot along the Alamosa River. To the north are views of Lookout Mountain, one of a handful of brilliant peaks infused with spectacular colors from iron oxides and various other mineral compounds. Pretty though they may be, these compounds are highly toxic, and the runoff from the mountains into the Alamosa River has rendered it unfishable (and undrinkable—bring bottled water). Fishing is available, however, to the south in Platoro Reservoir or the Conejos River. The South San Juan Wilderness lies a few miles west, with trailheads available on U.S. Forest Service roads to the south. The site of the historic mining town of Stunner is also nearby.

**Location:** On the Alamosa River in Rio Grande National Forest; map B2, grid h3.

**Campsites, facilities:** There are 10 sites for tents or RVs up to 22 feet long. Picnic tables, fire grills, and vault toilets are provided, but there is no drinking water. Leashed pets are permitted.

**Elevation:** 9,700 feet.

**Reservations, fees:** Reservations are not accepted. There is no fee.

**Open:** June to October.

**Directions:** From Monte Vista, drive 12 miles south on Hwy. 15, turn right on Forest Service Rd. 250, and continue approximately 27 miles west. Turn right on Forest Service Rd. 380 and proceed one-half mile to the campground.

**Contact:** Rio Grande National Forest, Conejos Peak Ranger District, P.O. Box 420, La Jara, CO 81140; tel. (719) 274-5193.

## 159 Mix Lake    8

Mix Lake is a tiny, wishbone-shaped lake just north of Platoro Reservoir, with heavily wooded campsites near its northern shore. The lake is stocked regularly with rainbow trout, so you're almost guaranteed to catch at least one or two—but they'll probably be tiny. Fishing prospects are much better at the reservoir, where you can launch a boat (there's a ramp on the north shore of the lake) and troll in deeper water for bigger rainbow and brown trout.

**Location:** Near Platoro Reservoir in Rio Grande National Forest; map B2, grid h4.

**Campsites, facilities:** There are 22 sites for tents or RVs up to 22 feet long. Drinking water, picnic tables, fire grills, and vault toilets are provided. Leashed pets are permitted.

**Elevation:** 10,000 feet.

**Reservations, fees:** Reservations are not accepted. Sites are $8 a night.

**Open:** June to October.

**Directions:** From Monte Vista, drive 12 miles south on Hwy. 15, turn right on Forest Service Rd. 250, and continue approximately 32 miles west. Turn right on Forest Service Rd. 247 and proceed one-half mile to the campground.

**Contact:** Rio Grande National Forest, Conejos Peak Ranger District, P.O. Box 420, La Jara, CO 81140; tel. (719) 274-5193.

## **160** Lake Fork     8

Set on the banks of the main Conejos River—the river's Lake Fork is actually west of the campground—this camp has both shady and sunny sites with good fishing access. Down the road, off Forest Service Rd. 105, you'll find a trailhead that leads north to Big Lake (note signs designating private property) and then abruptly switches west to wander into the South San Juan Wilderness.

**Location:** On the Conejos River in Rio Grande National Forest; map B2, grid h4.

**Campsites, facilities:** There are 18 sites for tents or RVs up to 22 feet long. Drinking water, picnic tables, fire grills, and vault toilets are provided. Leashed pets are permitted.

**Elevation:** 8,800 feet.

**Reservations, fees:** Reservations are accepted; phone (877) 444-6777. There's an $8.65 reservation fee. You may also reserve sites at website: www.reserveusa.com. Sites are $8 a night.

**Open:** June to September.

**Directions:** From Monte Vista, drive 12 miles south on Hwy. 15, turn right on Forest Service Rd. 250, and continue approximately 36 miles west. Turn right on Forest Service Rd. 247 and proceed one-half mile to the campground.

**Contact:** Rio Grande National Forest, Conejos Peak Ranger District, P.O. Box 420, La Jara, CO 81140; tel. (719) 274-5193.

## **161** Alamosa     7

This camp is perfect for a weekend overnighter, being an easy drive from Alamosa and convenient to several recreation options. The banks of the Alamosa River run next to camp, with excellent fishing access. About a mile west is a trail that starts at the river and runs north through the national forest to the Comstock camp. Since it's the first U.S. Forest Service camp travelers come to when heading toward the South San Juan Wilderness on Forest Service Rd. 250, this spot gets a lot of use. If it's full, try Stunner or Mix Lake to the west (campgrounds number 154 and 155).

**Location:** On the Alamosa River in Rio Grande National Forest; map B2, grid h5.

**Campsites, facilities:** There are 10 sites for tents or RVs up to 22 feet long. Picnic tables, fire grills, and vault toilets are provided, but there is no drinking water. Leashed pets are permitted.

**Elevation:** 8,700 feet.

**Reservations, fees:** Reservations are not accepted. There is no fee.

**Open:** June to October.

**Directions:** From Monte Vista, drive 12 miles south on Hwy. 15, turn right on Forest Service Rd. 250, and continue approximately 12 miles west.

**Contact:** Rio Grande National Forest, Conejos Peak Ranger District, P.O. Box 420, La Jara, CO 81140; tel. (719) 274-5193.

## 162 Chimney Rock Campground   6

Located in an attractive valley west of Pagosa Springs, this camp offers pleasant, pine-shaded sites with a picture-perfect view of Chimney Rock (in the Chimney Rock Archaeological Area). The property encloses not only the campground but a home-style cafe and—this nearly had me running out the door—a meat processing plant. If you can tolerate the smell of raw animal flesh and the grind of heavy machinery, it's a great bargain.

**Location:** Near the Chimney Rock Archaeological Area; map B2, grid i0.

**Campsites, facilities:** There are 20 tent sites and 25 full-hookup sites for RVs of any length. Drinking water, picnic tables, and bathrooms are provided. Laundry facilities, hot showers, a waste disposal station, restaurant, store, sports field, and public phone are available. Leashed pets are permitted.

**Elevation:** 7,800 feet.

**Reservations, fees:** Reservations are accepted. Sites are $5-14 a night.

**Open:** Year-round.

**Directions:** From Pagosa Springs, drive 15 miles west on U.S. 160.

**Contact:** Chimney Rock Campground, P.O. Box 93, Chimney Rock, CO 81127; tel. (970) 731-5237.

## 163 Blanco River  7

In the remote southern reaches of San Juan National Forest is this little-known and little-used camp with large, open sites beside the Blanco River. Sun exposure is strong most of the day, relieved only slightly by a bit of shade from ponderosa pines. Since this section of river is heavily stocked with trout but gets only light fishing pressure, it's an excellent choice for anglers.

**Location:** South of Pagosa Springs in San Juan National Forest; map B2, grid i2.

**Campsites, facilities:** There are six sites for tents or RVs up to 40 feet long. Drinking water, picnic tables, fire grills, and a vault toilet are provided. Leashed pets are permitted.

**Elevation:** 7,200 feet.

**Reservations, fees:** Reservations are not accepted. Sites are $8 a night.

**Open:** May to October.

**Directions:** From Pagosa Springs, drive 15 miles south on U.S. 84, turn left on Forest Service Rd. 656, and continue two miles to the campground.

**Contact:** San Juan National Forest, Pagosa Ranger District, P.O. Box 310, Pagosa Springs, CO 81147; tel. (970) 264-2268.

## 164 Chromo RV Park  5

When there's only one option in town, you've got to take what you can get, and at this camp it's not much. The sites are right on the highway and are set up for self-contained RVs only, with grass and full hookups but no external water, showers, or even bathrooms. Bordering the camp is a full-service mercantile store operated by a cantankerous fellow with a perpetual scowl. The one redeeming feature: spectacular mountain views.

**Location:** In Chromo; map B2, grid i2.

**Campsites, facilities:** There are 15 full-hookup sites for RVs of any length. No tents are permitted. No facilities are available. A store and a public phone are adjacent to the RV park. Leashed pets are permitted.

**Elevation:** 7,500 feet.

**Reservations, fees:** Reservations are accepted. Sites are $15 a night.

**Open:** June to mid-November.

**Directions:** The park is located in downtown Chromo at 23470 U.S. 84.

**Contact:** Chromo RV Park, 23470 Hwy. 84, Chromo, CO 81128; tel. (970) 264-5483.

## 165 Conejos     7

Located in an open area between the road and the eastern edge of the South San Juan Wilderness, Conejos is an excellent base for a hiking or fishing trip. You can walk to the river from your campsite to fish for large rainbow and brook trout, or head a mile north to jump on a wilderness trailhead. This camp gets slightly less use than nearby Spectacle Lake, so you're likely to find a spot.

**Location:** On the Conejos River in Rio Grande National Forest; map B2, grid i4.

**Campsites, facilities:** There are 16 sites for tents or RVs up to 22 feet long. Drinking water, picnic tables, fire grills, and vault toilets are provided. Leashed pets are permitted.

**Elevation:** 8,700 feet.

**Reservations, fees:** Reservations are not accepted. Sites are $9 a night.

**Open:** May to October.

**Directions:** From Antonito, drive 23 miles west on Hwy. 17, turn right on Forest Service Rd. 250, and continue 6.5 miles northwest to the campground.

**Contact:** Rio Grande National Forest, Conejos Peak Ranger District, P.O. Box 420, La Jara, CO 81140; tel. (719) 274-5193.

## 166 Spectacle Lake     7

Spectacle Lake is little more than a wide spot on the Conejos River, but the four-acre reservoir is well stocked with rainbow trout. It is fished quite heavily, so you may want to try a less popular spot upstream. Just south of camp is a trailhead for ATVs that runs south along the South San Juan Wilderness border for about four miles. If you want to escape the speed demons, hike the first two miles of the trail and veer west onto one of the trails into the wilderness.

**Location:** On the Conejos River in Rio Grande National Forest; map B2, grid i4.

**Campsites, facilities:** There are 24 sites for tents or RVs up to 22 feet long. Drinking water, picnic tables, fire grills, and vault toilets are provided. Leashed pets are permitted.

**Elevation:** 8,700 feet.

**Reservations, fees:** Reservations are not accepted. Sites are $9 a night.

**Open:** May to October.

**Directions:** From Antonito, drive 23 miles west on Hwy. 17, turn right on Forest Service Rd. 250, and continue six miles northwest to the campground.

**Contact:** Rio Grande National Forest, Conejos Peak Ranger District, P.O. Box 420, La Jara, CO 81140; tel. (719) 274-5193.

## **167** Elk Creek     7

Sunny sites and good fishing are the hallmarks of this popular camp near the confluence of Elk Creek and the Conejos River. The south end of Forest Service Trail 731 begins at camp and is used primarily by ATV devotees. A more serene trail starts about a mile beyond camp at the end of the access road, heading west into the South San Juan Wilderness. Tip: Behind the main campground are several "overflow" sites, which are slightly more primitive than the developed sites but cost half the price.

**Location:** Near the Conejos River in Rio Grande National Forest; map B2, grid i4.

**Campsites, facilities:** There are 34 sites for tents or RVs up to 22 feet long. Drinking water, picnic tables, fire grills, and vault toilets are provided. Leashed pets are permitted.

**Elevation:** 8,500 feet.

**Reservations, fees:** Reservations are accepted; phone (877) 444-6777. There's an $8.65 reservation fee. You may also reserve sites at website: www.reserveusa.com. Sites are $11 a night.

**Open:** May to October.

**Directions:** From Antonito, drive approximately 24 miles west on Hwy. 17 and turn right into the campground access road.

**Contact:** Rio Grande National Forest, Conejos Peak Ranger District, P.O. Box 420, La Jara, CO 81140; tel. (719) 274-5193.

## **168** Ponderosa Campground     7

This camp features large sites carved out of a densely forested, natural setting. Many are on the water's edge with prime fishing access from a level, brushy shoreline, and in midsummer this is a superb put-in for rafters. Developed amenities such as hot showers and laundry facilities seem extra luxurious in such a remote-feeling place. Nearby is the Cumbres-Toltec Scenic Railroad and picturesque Cumbres Pass.

**Location:** On the Conejos River; map B2, grid i4.

**Campsites, facilities:** There are 35 sites for tents or RVs of any length. Drinking water, picnic tables, fire grills, and bathrooms with hot showers are provided. Electric hookups, laundry facilities, a waste disposal station, public phone, and cabins are available. Leashed pets are permitted.

**Elevation:** 8,500 feet.

**Reservations, fees:** Reservations are accepted. Sites are $20 a night.

**Open:** June to October.

**Directions:** From Antonito, drive 20 miles west on Hwy. 17.

**Contact:** Ponderosa Campground, 19600 Hwy. 17, Antonito, CO 81120; tel. (719) 376-5857.

## 169 Trujillo Meadows      8

Just a few miles north of the Colorado/New Mexico border, this high-elevation camp makes a great stopover for travel-weary campers. The sites are set back from the reservoir's southern shore, not far from the boat ramp. Motorized (no-wake) boating is permitted, and fishing is good for brown and brook trout. Scenic opportunities abound: To the north are trails into the South San Juan Wilderness; to the south is a trailhead for the Continental Divide National Scenic Trail, along with Cumbres Pass and the Cumbres-Toltec Scenic Railroad.

**Location:** On Trujillo Meadows Reservoir in Rio Grande National Forest; map B2, grid i4.

**Campsites, facilities:** There are 50 sites for tents or RVs up to 22 feet long. Drinking water, picnic tables, fire grills, and vault toilets are provided. A boat ramp is nearby. Some facilities are wheelchair accessible. Leashed pets are permitted.

**Elevation:** 10,000 feet.

**Reservations, fees:** Reservations are not accepted. Sites are $9 a night.

**Open:** June to September.

**Directions:** From Antonito, drive approximately 38 miles west on Hwy. 17, turn right on Forest Service Rd. 118, and continue four miles north to the campground.

**Contact:** Rio Grande National Forest, Conejos Peak Ranger District, P.O. Box 420, La Jara, CO 81140; tel. (719) 274-5193.

## 170 Aspen Glade     8

This camp is, indeed, in a lovely grove of aspens, right along the banks of the Conejos River. Fishing is quite good in this stretch of river, but apparently the word is out, because it gets intense pressure. Since hunting is permitted in designated areas nearby, the camp receives a fair amount of use from hunters in the fall. The rangers at the nearby River Springs Ranger Station can answer questions and give advice.

**Location:** On the Conejos River in Rio Grande National Forest; map B2, grid i6.

**Campsites, facilities:** There are 34 sites for tents or RVs up to 22 feet long. Drinking water, picnic tables, fire grills, and vault toilets are provided. Leashed pets are permitted.

**Elevation:** 8,500 feet.

**Reservations, fees:** Reservations are accepted; phone (877) 444-6777. There's an $8.65 reservation fee. You may also reserve sites at website: www.reserveusa.com. Sites are $11 a night.

**Open:** May to October.

**Directions:** From Antonito, drive approximately 17 miles west on Hwy. 17.

**Contact:** Rio Grande National Forest, Conejos Peak Ranger District, P.O. Box 420, La Jara, CO 81140; tel. (719) 274-5193.

**171** Mogote      7

Of the two loops in this camp, the River Loop has the nicer (though somewhat smaller) sites; try for one of those if you have a choice. Fishing access is available nearby. The area is sprinkled with piñon pines and fragrant juniper, but most sites are open and sunny. Like Aspen Glade to the west, this camp gets heavy use from hunters, and since it's the first U.S. Forest Service camp you hit coming from Antonito, it's often full on summer weekends. Other options are the Elk Creek, Spectacle Lake, and Conejos camps to the west.

**Location:** On the Conejos River in Rio Grande National Forest; map B2, grid i6.

**Campsites, facilities:** There are 41 sites for tents or RVs up to 22 feet long, and two group sites: one can accommodate up to 50 people, the other up to 100 people. Drinking water, picnic tables, fire grills, and vault toilets are provided. Leashed pets are permitted.

**Elevation:** 8,400 feet.

**Reservations, fees:** Reservations are accepted; phone (877) 444-6777. There's an $8.65 reservation fee. You may also reserve sites at website: www.reserveusa.com. Sites are $11 a night.

**Open:** May to October.

**Directions:** From Antonito, drive approximately 14 miles west on Hwy. 17.

**Contact:** Rio Grande National Forest, Conejos Peak Ranger District, P.O. Box 420, La Jara, CO 81140; tel. (719) 274-5193.

**172** Conejos River Campground     7

Sprawled across a large, level parcel of land adjacent to Rio Grande National Forest, this camp features grassy sites surrounded by conifer-covered foothills, plus lots of extras, including a swimming pool, a hot tub, and a miniature golf course. Most sites are open and sunny, but the camp is encircled by a thick border of pines, with shade trees dotting the property. The Conejos River, a short walk away, provides good fishing, and the Cumbres-Toltec Scenic Railroad runs nearby, offering a no-sweat way to view the region's spectacular scenery.

**Location:** West of Antonito; map B2, grid i6.

**Campsites, facilities:** There are 12 tent sites and 36 sites for RVs of any length, many with full hookups. Drinking water, picnic tables, fire grills, and bathrooms with hot showers are provided. Laundry facilities, a waste disposal station, small store, swimming pool and hot tub, miniature golf, sports field, and cabins are available. Leashed pets are permitted.

**Elevation:** 8,400 feet.

**Reservations, fees:** Reservations are accepted. Sites are $17 a night.

**Open:** Mid-May to mid-November.

**Directions:** From Antonito, drive 12 miles west on Hwy. 17.

**Contact:** Conejos River Campground, 26714 Hwy. 17, Antonito, CO 81120; tel. (719) 376-5943.

### 173 Twin Rivers Cabins and RV Park  7

Adjacent to the Conejos River in the lovely Conejos Valley, this camp features large RV sites on four acres of grassy meadow and secluded tent sites under leafy cottonwood trees. The stream runs through the campground and is privately stocked with catchable-size trout. During July and August, the hosts offer free pancake breakfasts every Sunday, and the large covered pavilion houses a sink and a stove—particularly nice for tenters—and laundry facilities. For a real wild-west experience, you can also rent a tepee or a covered wagon (each sleeps four; bring your own sleeping bags or linens).

**Location:** On the Conejos River; map B2, grid i6.

**Campsites, facilities:** There are five tent sites and 38 full-hookup RV sites. Drinking water, a few picnic tables and fire rings, and bathrooms with hot showers are provided. Laundry facilities, a sports field, and a public phone are available. Leashed pets are permitted.

**Elevation:** 8,000 feet.

**Reservations, fees:** Reservations are accepted. Sites are $16 a night.

**Open:** May to mid-October.

**Directions:** From Antonito, drive five miles west on Hwy. 17.

**Contact:** Twin Rivers Campground, 34044 Hwy. 17, Antonito, CO 81120; tel. (719) 376-5710 or (888) 689-689-6787; e-mail: twnrivrs@fone.net.

### 174 Josey's Mogote Meadow  7

Just across the highway from Twin Rivers Campground, this camp has spacious, grassy sites shaded by huge cottonwood trees. The pesky buzz from traffic bound for Platoro Reservoir poses problems in the busy summer months; try for a site at the back of the property. The hosts—self-proclaimed "good, friendly people"—offer weekly potluck dinners and pancake breakfasts.

**Location:** West of Antonito; map B2, grid i6.

**Campsites, facilities:** There are 55 sites for tents or RVs of any length, most with full hookups. Drinking water, picnic tables, fire grills, and bathrooms with hot showers are provided. Laundry facilities, cabins, and a public phone are available. Leashed pets are permitted.

**Elevation:** 8,000 feet.

**Reservations, fees:** Reservations are accepted. Sites are $15 a night.

**Open:** May to October.

**Directions:** From Antonito, drive five miles west on Hwy. 17.

**Contact:** Josey's Mogote Meadow, 34127 Hwy. 17, Antonito, CO 81120; tel. (719) 376-5774.

### 175 Narrow Gauge Railroad RV Park  4

Best for large, self-contained RVs, this park offers little more than an unprotected space to park your rig, with full hookups but no outside facilities. The camp's main attraction is its proximity to the Cumbres-Toltec Scenic Railroad depot, located just down the street. The train winds through miles of scenic territory, following the Rio de Los Pinos southeast into New Mexico. Adjacent to the camp is a small inn with motel rooms; a restaurant is next door.

**Location:** In Antonito; map B2, grid i7.

**Campsites, facilities:** There are 10 full-hookup sites for RVs of any length. No tents are permitted. No facilities are provided, but hot showers are available for a fee. Motel rooms and a restaurant are within walking distance. Leashed pets are permitted.

**Elevation:** 7,900 feet.

**Reservations, fees:** Reservations are accepted. Sites are $7-12 a night.

**Open:** May to October.

**Directions:** The campground is located on the south side of Antonito at the junction of Hwy. 17 and U.S. 285.

**Contact:** Narrow Gauge Railroad RV Park, P.O. Box 636, Antonito, CO 81120; tel. (719) 376-5441 or (800) 323-9469.

GARDEN OF THE GODS

# MAP B3

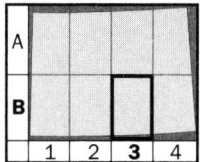

A

B

1 2 **3** 4

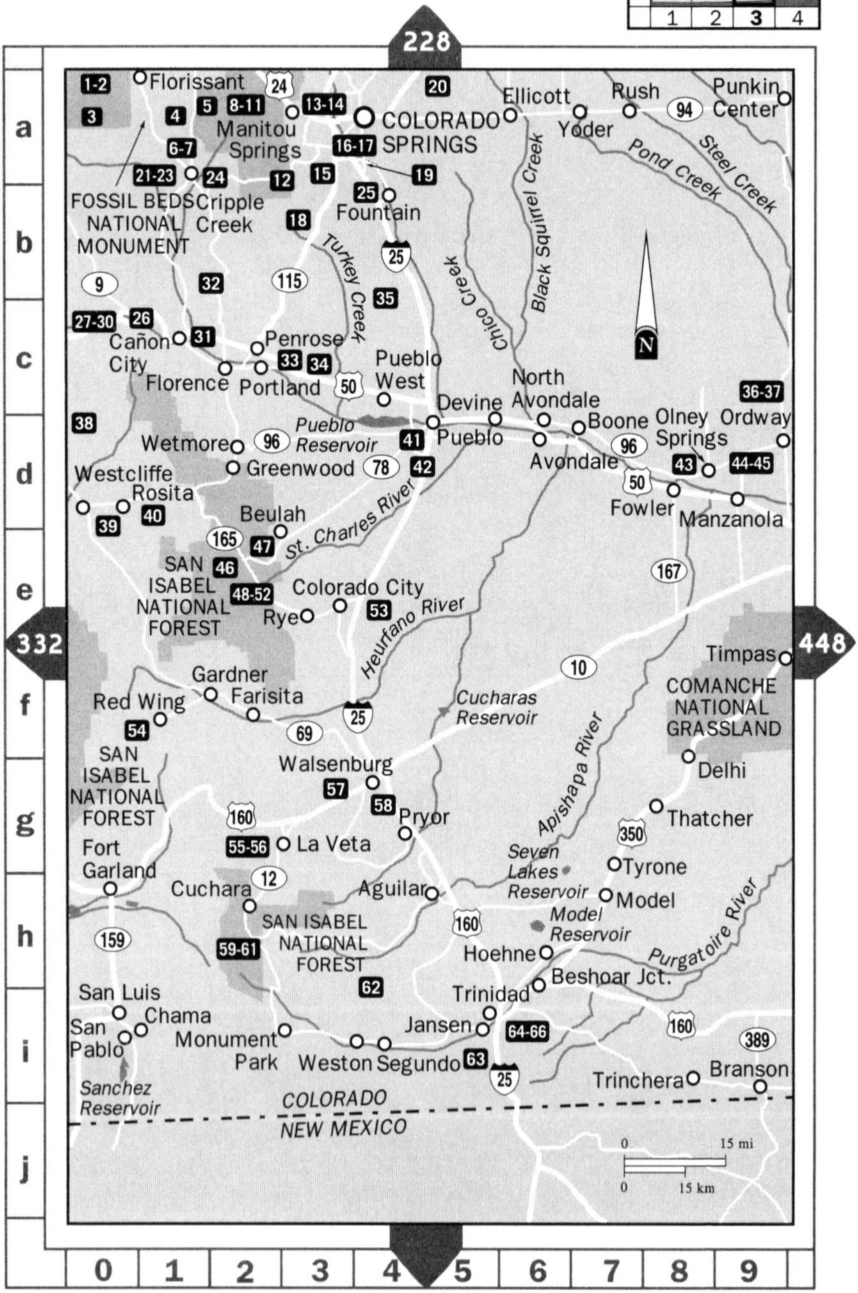

○ Florissant
1-2
3
24
4 5 8-11 13-14
6-7 Manitou
Springs
20
COLORADO
SPRINGS
Ellicott
Rush
Punkin
Center
94
Yoder
21-23 24 12
15
16-17
18
25
19
Fountain

FOSSIL BEDS
NATIONAL
MONUMENT
Cripple
Creek
32
115
25
35
9
Black Squirrel Creek
Turkey Creek
Chico Creek
Pond Creek
Steel Creek

27-30 26
Cañon
City
31
Penrose
33 34
Florence
Portland
50
Pueblo
West
North
Avondale
Boone
Olney
Springs
Ordway
36-37
38
Wetmore
96
Pueblo
Reservoir
41
42
Pueblo
Avondale
96
50
43
44-45
Westcliffe
Rosita
Greenwood
78
Fowler
Manzanola
39
40
Beulah
165 47
St. Charles River
Devine

SAN
ISABEL
NATIONAL
FOREST
46
48-52
Colorado City
Rye
53
Heurfano River
167

Red Wing
Gardner
Farisita
54
SAN
ISABEL
NATIONAL
FOREST
69
25
Cucharas
Reservoir
10
Apishapa River
Timpas
COMANCHE
NATIONAL
GRASSLAND

Walsenburg
57
58
Pryor
Delhi
160
55-56
La Veta
350
Thatcher

Fort
Garland
12
Cuchara
Aguilar
Seven
Lakes
Reservoir
Tyrone
Model
159
SAN ISABEL
NATIONAL
FOREST
59-61
62
160
Hoehne
Model
Reservoir
Beshoar Jct.
Purgatoire River

San Luis
Chama
Monument
Park
Trinidad
San
Pablo
Jansen
64-66
160
389
Weston Segundo
63
25
Trinchera
Branson
Sanchez
Reservoir
COLORADO
NEW MEXICO

N

0        15 mi
0        15 km

# CHAPTER B3

## ■ Blue Mountain    7

Set about a mile from the South Platte River, this quiet camp offers a peaceful alternative to the jam-packed sites closer to Elevenmile Canyon Reservoir. The sites are tucked under tall ponderosa pines, with a short interpretive nature trail adjacent to camp. If you head past the campground and go to the end of County Rd. 61B, you'll find a hiking trail that leads south into the surrounding national forest. There is no fishing on site, but within a short drive, access is available along the South Platte River, at Lake George, and at Elevenmile Canyon Reservoir.

**Location:** Northeast of Elevenmile Canyon Reservoir in Pike National Forest; map B3, grid a0.

**Campsites, facilities:** There are 21 sites for tents or RVs up to 35 feet long. Drinking water, picnic tables, fire grills, and vault toilets are provided. Leashed pets are permitted.

**Elevation:** 8,200 feet.

**Reservations, fees:** Reservations are not accepted. Sites are $9 a night.

**Open:** May to October.

**Directions:** From Colorado Springs, turn west on U.S. 24 and drive approximately 39 miles to Lake George. Turn south on County Rd. 96 and drive 1.5 miles. Turn left on County Rd. 61 and continue one-half mile to the campground.

**Contact:** Pike National Forest, South Park Ranger District, P.O. Box 219, Fairplay, CO 80440; tel. (719) 836-2031.

## ■ Riverside     7

This popular camp is across the highway from the South Platte River in a partially shaded clearing of young conifers. The interpretive trail that begins at the Blue Mountain camp ends here, and opportunities for fishing and hiking are available nearby.

**Location:** On the South Platte River in Pike National Forest; map B3, grid a0.

**Campsites, facilities:** There are 15 sites for tents or RVs up to 25 feet long, and four walk-in campsites. Drinking water, picnic tables, fire grills, and vault toilets are provided. Leashed pets are permitted.

**Elevation:** 8,000 feet.

**Reservations, fees:** Reservations are not accepted. Sites are $10 a night, and there's a $3 use fee.

**Open:** May to October.

**Directions:** From Colorado Springs, turn west on U.S. 24 and drive approximately 39 miles to Lake George. Turn south on County Rd. 96 and continue two miles to the campground.

**Contact:** Pike National Forest, South Park Ranger District, P.O. Box 219, Fairplay, CO 80440; tel. (719) 836-2031.

## ■ Springer Gulch   7

You'll find this camp in a tight stand of ponderosa pine trees in Elevenmile Canyon, about a quarter mile from the South Platte River. It's a quieter alternative to the crowded camps right along the banks of the river.

**Location:** Northeast of Elevenmile Canyon Reservoir in Pike National Forest; map B3, grid a0.

**Campsites, facilities:** There are 15 sites for tents or RVs up to 25 feet long. Drinking water, picnic tables, fire grills, and vault toilets are provided. Leashed pets are permitted.

**Elevation:** 8,300 feet.

**Reservations, fees:** Reservations are not accepted. Sites are $10 a night, and there's a $3 use fee.

**Open:** May to October.

**Directions:** From Colorado Springs, turn west on U.S. 24 and drive approximately 39 miles to Lake George. Turn south on County Rd. 96 and drive seven miles. Turn right on County Rd. 96E and continue one-quarter mile west to the campground.

**Contact:** Pike National Forest, South Park Ranger District, P.O. Box 219, Fairplay, CO 80440; tel. (719) 836-2031.

## ◢ Mueller State Park     10

The powers that be at Mueller State Park have achieved the rare fusion of user-friendly facilities and a pristine environment, merging beautiful, lush meadows and untouched stands of old-growth fir, aspen, pine, and spruce forest with extras like electric hookups and showers—while still preserving a wilderness feel. The park is at the western base of Pikes Peak, set on 12,000 acres of thick, hardy forest and incredibly abundant plant life, encompassing alpine meadow grasses, mosses, and wildflowers of every color—blue gentians, red paintbrush, purple columbine, yellow buttercups, white phlox. You get phenomenal mountain views from the wooded campground, and in the fall the park is one of the state's best (and least publicized) places to view the changing leaves. An astounding number of hiking trails offer various levels of difficulty; a few of the best are the Dome Rock Trail, the Rock Pond Trail, and the Outlook Ridge Trail. Fishing is available in small ponds scattered throughout the park; the ponds are well stocked but fished heavily enough that trout rarely grow beyond six inches.

**Location:** South of Divide; map B3, grid a1.

**Campsites, facilities:** There are 90 sites for tents or RVs of any length and 12 walk-in tent sites. Drinking water, picnic tables, fire grills, and bathrooms with hot showers are provided. Electric hookups, laundry facilities, and a waste disposal station are available. Some facilities are wheelchair accessible. Leashed pets are permitted.

**Elevation:** 9,500 feet.

**Reservations, fees:** Reservations are accepted. Phone (303) 470-1144 or (800) 678-CAMP (800-678-2267) outside the Denver Metro area; there's a $7 reservation fee. Sites are $10-14 a night, and there's a $4 entrance fee.

**Open:** Year-round with limited winter facilities.

**Directions:** From the junction of U.S. 24 and Hwy. 67 in Divide, turn south on Hwy. 67 and drive 3.5 miles to the park entrance.

**Contact:** Mueller State Park, P.O. Box 49, Divide, CO 80814; tel. (719) 687-2366.

# 5 The Crags    8

This out-of-the-way campground is a more private alternative to the one at nearby Mueller State Park. It's in a beautiful spot, set in a forest of ponderosa pine and blue spruce and adjacent to a trailhead for the Crags Trail, which heads east, skirting the rocky outcroppings for which it's named. Hikers can also venture south to explore the less-traveled west side of Pikes Peak. In the winter, roads in the area make excellent cross-country ski trails.

**Location:** South of Divide in Pike National Forest; map B3, grid a1.

**Campsites, facilities:** There are 17 sites for tents or RVs up to 22 feet long. Drinking water, picnic tables, fire grills, and vault toilets are provided, but there is no trash service. Leashed pets are permitted.

**Elevation:** 10,100 feet.

**Reservations, fees:** Reservations are not accepted. Sites are $9 a night.

**Open:** June to October.

**Directions:** From the junction of U.S. 24 and Hwy. 67 in Divide, turn south on Hwy. 67 and drive 4.5 miles to Forest Service Rd. 383. Turn left and continue 3.5 miles east to the campground. Note: The last few miles are steep, narrow, and rough; large RVs are not recommended.

**Contact:** Pike National Forest, Pikes Peak Ranger District, 601 S. Weber St., Colorado Springs, CO 80903; tel. (719) 636-1602.

# 6 Cripple Creek Gold Campground     8

As you wind your way up U.S. 67, the forested mountains suddenly open up to a large, grassy plain known locally as Gillette Flats, a popular starting point for horseback riders. The camp's entrance road meanders a little way through the flats before halting at the base of a wooded hillside, where well-spaced campsites are spread across a gorgeous 30-acre forest of spruce and aspen. Quiet and peaceful, the camp is far enough outside Cripple Creek to avoid the floods of gambling crowds, and sites are well off the highway. Pike National Forest, with its hundreds of miles of trails for hiking and horseback riding, is adjacent, and horse rentals are available at the campground. Nearby Cripple Creek offers limited-stakes gambling, restaurants, historic architecture, and museums.

**Location:** North of Cripple Creek; map B3, grid a1.

**Campsites, facilities:** There are 15 tent sites and 12 sites for RVs of any length. Drinking water, picnic tables, fire grills, and bathrooms with hot showers are provided. Electric hookups, laundry facilities, a waste disposal station, horse rentals, and a bunkhouse are available. Leashed pets are permitted.

**Elevation:** 10,200 feet.

**Reservations, fees:** Reservations are accepted. Sites are $12-14 a night.

**Open:** Mid-May to mid-October.

**Directions:** From Cripple Creek, drive four miles north on U.S. 67.

**Contact:** Cripple Creek Gold Campground, P.O. Box 601, Cripple Creek, CO 80813; tel. (719) 689-2342.

## ⑦ RnK Campground    5

The graveled sites at this camp a few miles outside of Cripple Creek are alarmingly close to U.S. 67. Although the camp is backed by trees, most of the sites are out in the open (the one good tent site is farther back in a grove of aspens), all with an excellent view of Pikes Peak.

**Location:** North of Cripple Creek; map B3, grid a1.

**Campsites, facilities:** There are a 14 sites for RVs of any length, and a separate area for tents. Drinking water, fire grills, and bathrooms with hot showers are provided. Electric hookups, laundry facilities, a waste disposal station, small store, and public phone are available. Some facilities are wheelchair accessible. Leashed pets are permitted.

**Elevation:** 10,000 feet.

**Reservations, fees:** Reservations are accepted. Sites are $8-16 a night.

**Open:** Year-round.

**Directions:** From Cripple Creek, drive 3.5 miles north on U.S. 67.

**Contact:** RnK Campground, P.O. Box 190, Cripple Creek, CO 80813; tel. (719) 689-3371.

## ⑧ Rocky Top Motel and Campground    6

The grassy sites at this roadside motel campground are on three separate levels. The tent sites are behind the motel; the RV sites and community facilities on the two upper levels. Most sites are sunny and open, some with young pines and aspens nearby and, alas, clear views of the adjacent highway (noise can also be bothersome at times). Your hosts can arrange bus tours of Pikes Peak and other regional attractions.

**Location:** Near Pikes Peak; map B3, grid a2.

**Campsites, facilities:** There are seven tent sites and 71 sites for tents or RVs of any length, many with full hookups. Drinking water, picnic tables, fire grills, and bathrooms with hot showers are provided. Laundry facilities, a waste disposal station, swimming pool, public phone, motel rooms, and cabins are available. Leashed pets are permitted.

**Elevation:** 8,000 feet.

**Reservations, fees:** Reservations are accepted. Sites are $10-17 a night.

**Open:** May to October.

**Directions:** From Interstate 25 in Colorado Springs, take Exit 141 and drive 13 miles west on U.S. 24.

**Contact:** Rocky Top Motel and Campground, P.O. Box 215, Green Mountain Falls, CO 80819; tel. (719) 684-9044.

## ⑨ Lone Duck Campground     7

Grassy sites shaded by leafy cottonwood trees and young aspens are one of the perks of staying at this well-landscaped camp nestled in a scenic mountain valley. Fountain Creek runs nearby, but fishing prospects are better at the privately stocked fishing pond, where campers can feed the ducks or fish from the shore. A swimming pool is next to the pond. Although Pikes Peak is just two miles away, wooded foothills block the view from here. If you want a close-up look, drive up the paved toll road; hardier souls can climb up the side.

**Location:** Near Pikes Peak; map B3, grid a2.

**Campsites, facilities:** There are 60 sites for tents or RVs of any length, many with full hookups. Drinking water, picnic tables, fire grills, and bathrooms with hot showers are provided. Laundry facilities, a waste disposal station, store, swimming pool, and public phone are available. Leashed pets are permitted.

**Elevation:** 7,500 feet.

**Reservations, fees:** Reservations are accepted. Sites are $18-24 a night.

**Open:** Mid-May to mid-September.

**Directions:** From Interstate 25 in Colorado Springs, take Exit 141 and drive 12 miles west on U.S. 24. At the first Green Mountain Falls exit, make a U-turn on U.S. 24 and backtrack about 300 yards east to the campground on your right.

**Contact:** Lone Duck Campground, P.O. Box 25, Cascade, CO 80809; tel. (719) 684-9907 or (800) 776-5925.

## 🔟 Pikes Peak RV Park     5

This city campground is on a major street in the center of Colorado Springs, convenient to most regional attractions, including Garden of the Gods, Pikes Peak, and the Cog Railway. Fountain Creek runs adjacent to camp, providing fishing access and absorption of some of the road noise. The sites are graveled, most shaded by a mix of willow, pine, elm, and cottonwood trees, with excellent mountain views (a dozen or so offer vistas of Pikes Peak). Across the street is a park with a grassy picnic area, playground, and indoor swimming pool and hot tub.

**Location:** In Manitou Springs; map B3, grid a2.

**Campsites, facilities:** There are 70 sites for tents or RVs up to 40 feet long, most with full hookups. Drinking water, picnic tables, and bathrooms with hot showers are provided. Laundry facilities and a public phone are available. Leashed pets are permitted.

**Elevation:** 6,400 feet.

**Reservations, fees:** Reservations are accepted. Sites are $15-22 a night.

**Open:** April to November.

**Directions:** From Interstate 25 in Colorado Springs, take Exit 141 and drive four miles west on U.S. 24. Turn left on Manitou Ave. and continue one-quarter mile west to the campground.

**Contact:** Pikes Peak RV Park, 320 Manitou Ave., Manitou Springs, CO 80829; tel. (719) 685-9459.

## 🔟🔟 Goldfield Campground  4

You can't miss this camp—just look for the big sign sporting a cartoonish old-time miner and his mule. Goldfield is on the outskirts of the mountain metropolis of Colorado Springs, offering quiet, graveled RV sites, some with patchy grass and a few leafy shade trees. Across the street is a city park, with a playground, sports facilities, and grassy picnic areas. If you're tired of camp food, there's a Chinese restaurant right across the street, and several local restaurants offer delivery.

**Location:** West of Colorado Springs; map B3, grid a2.

**Campsites, facilities:** There are 100 sites for RVs of any length, some with full hookups. No tents are permitted. Drinking water, picnic tables, and bathrooms with hot showers are provided. Laundry facilities, a waste disposal station, store, and public phone are available. Leashed pets are permitted.

**Elevation:** 6,500 feet.

**Reservations, fees:** Reservations are accepted. Sites are $18.50-21.50 a night.

**Open:** Year-round.

**Directions:** From Interstate 25 in Colorado Springs, take Exit 141 and drive two miles west on U.S. 24. Turn left on 26th St. and continue one block south.

**Contact:** Goldfield Campground, 411 S. 26th St., Colorado Springs, CO 80904; tel. (719) 471-0495

## 12 Wye  7

Partially wooded, partially open, Wye offers tiny, cozy tent sites and fairly easy access to a variety of recreation options, including a nearby shooting range (St. Peter's Dome), hiking trails, and fishing on Penrose-Rosemont Reservoir to the west. The camp is far enough from Colorado Springs to be quiet and secluded, and there's almost always a site available—a rarity in this area—but you're still within 40 minutes of the city.

**Location:** Southwest of Colorado Springs in Pike National Forest; map B3, grid a2.

**Campsites, facilities:** There are 21 tent sites. Picnic tables, fire grills, and vault toilets are provided, but there is no water or trash service. Leashed pets are permitted.

**Elevation:** 10,300 feet.

**Reservations, fees:** Reservations are not accepted. Sites are $9 a night.

**Open:** June to October.

**Directions:** From Colorado Springs, take Exit 138 and follow the signs west to the Broadmoor Hotel. Continue west, following the signs for the Cheyenne Mountain Zoo; when the road forks, bear right on Old Stage Rd. (the left fork will take you to the zoo) and drive seven miles southwest to Gold Camp Road. Turn right and continue five miles west. Turn right again on Forest Service Rd. 381 and continue one-half mile north to the campground.

**Contact:** Pike National Forest, Pikes Peak Ranger District, 601 S. Weber St., Colorado Springs, CO 80903; tel. (719) 636-1602.

## 13 Garden of the Gods Campground     7

As the closest campground to the popular Garden of the Gods park—a stunning natural collection of weirdly shaped red-rock formations—this place remains fully occupied throughout the camping season. Although it's within city limits, the camp is pleasant and quiet, with grassy sites shaded by elm, cottonwood, and aspen trees and hiking trails nearby. This is truly a full-service resort: the impeccable facilities include a huge pool and an indoor hot tub (adults only), and group activities from barbecues to ice cream parties keep guests busy. They'll even set up rafting trips or bus tours for your family or group. Behind the camp is Academy Riding

Stables, where you can rent horses and take tours through Garden of the Gods.

**Location:** West of Colorado Springs; map B3, grid a3.

**Campsites, facilities:** There are 50 tent sites and 280 sites for RVs of any length, most with full hookups. Drinking water, picnic tables, fire grills, and bathrooms with hot showers are provided. Laundry facilities, a waste disposal station, store, pool and hot tub, public phone, and cabins are available. Some facilities are wheelchair accessible. Leashed pets are permitted.

**Elevation:** 6,000 feet.

**Reservations, fees:** Reservations are recommended; phone (800) 248-9451. Sites are $25-30 a night.

**Open:** Mid-April to mid-October.

**Directions:** From Interstate 25 in Colorado Springs, take Exit 141 and drive 2.5 miles west on U.S. 24. Turn right on 31st St. and continue one block. Turn left on Colorado Ave. and proceed one-quarter mile to the campground.

**Contact:** Garden of the Gods Campground, 3704 W. Colorado Ave., Colorado Springs, CO 80904; tel. (719) 475-9450 or (800) 248-9451.

## 14 Fountain Creek RV Park   5

If you're looking for an in-town RV park with easy access to city sights, this camp is an excellent choice. Though pleasantly cool and shady, with tall trees and roomy sites, it's within walking distance to several shops and restaurants, and a short drive from other area attractions.

**Location:** In Colorado Springs; map B3, grid a3.

**Campsites, facilities:** There are 22 tent sites and 95 full-hookup sites for RVs of any length. Drinking water, picnic tables, and bathrooms with hot showers are provided. Laundry facilities, a waste disposal station, small store, and public phone are available. Leashed pets are permitted.

**Elevation:** 6,200 feet.

**Reservations, fees:** Reservations are accepted. Sites are $20-24 a night.

**Open:** Year-round.

**Directions:** From Interstate 25 at Colorado Springs, take Exit 141 and drive west on U.S. 24 to 31st Street. Turn right, go one block north, and turn right again onto Colorado Avenue. Continue one-half block east to the campground.

**Contact:** Fountain Creek RV Park, 3023 1/2 W. Colorado Ave., Colorado Springs, CO 80904; tel. (719) 633-2192; e-mail: info@fountaincreekrvpark.com.

## 15 Golden Eagle Ranch       8

This lovely camp is set on 1,000 acres of forested land, with a pleasing mix of ponderosa pine, fir, aspen, elm, and cottonwood trees shading the well-spaced, grassy sites. Five miles of hiking trails crisscross the property, and fishing and canoeing are possible in five small, privately stocked lakes. The campground also features the John May Museum Center, home to the May Natural History Museum and the Museum of Space Exploration—an excellent outing for children. Also on site is an enormous rally center with a stage and a 5,000-square-foot pavilion.

**Location:** South of Colorado Springs; map B3, grid a3.

**Campsites, facilities:** There are 200 tent sites and 250 full-hookup sites for RVs of any length. Drinking water, picnic tables, fire rings, and bathrooms with hot showers are provided. Laundry facilities, a waste disposal station, store, public phone, canoe rentals, a large rally pavilion, and two museums are available. Some facilities are wheelchair accessible. Leashed pets are permitted.

**Elevation:** 6,200 feet.

**Reservations, fees:** Reservations are accepted. Sites are $17-19 a night.

**Open:** May to October.

**Directions:** From Interstate 25 south of Colorado Springs, take Exit 135 and drive two miles west on Academy Boulevard. Turn left on Hwy. 115 and continue five miles south to the campground.

**Contact:** Golden Eagle Ranch, 710 Rock Creek Canyon Rd., Colorado Springs, CO 80926; tel. (719) 576-0450 or (800) 666-3841.

## 16 Peak View Inn and RV Park    4

This city campground is adjacent to a paved biking/jogging trail and is close to many urban amenities. Sites are shaded and large, set next to a motel and picnic area with a playground. The facilities include a swimming pool and hot tub.

**Location:** In Colorado Springs; map B3, grid a4.

**Campsites, facilities:** There are eight tent sites and 135 sites for RVs of any length, most with full hookups. Drinking water, picnic tables, fire grills, and bathrooms with hot showers are provided. Laundry facilities, a waste disposal station, pool, and hot tub are available. Leashed pets are permitted.

**Elevation:** 6,200 feet.

**Reservations, fees:** Reservations are accepted; phone (800) 551-2267. Sites are $16-23 a night.

**Open:** Year-round.

**Directions:** Southbound on Interstate 25 in Colorado Springs, take Exit 148A and drive a little less than a mile south on Nevada Avenue. Northbound on Interstate 25, take Exit 146 and go east on Austin Bluffs Parkway to Nevada Avenue. Turn left and drive just over a mile to the camp on the west side of the street.

**Contact:** Peak View Inn and RV Park, 4950 Nevada Ave., Colorado Springs, CO 80918; tel. (719) 598-1545.

## 17 Campers Village   5

Located a mile from downtown Colorado Springs and a short drive from Garden of the Gods, Campers Village provides easy access to the city while retaining a natural flavor. Fountain Creek runs adjacent to camp, providing a little relief from summer heat and a buffer against road noise (but no fishing access). The sites have grassy lawns and concrete pads, with plenty of shade from pine, spruce, elm, cottonwood, and maple trees, plus views of Cheyenne Mountain. A swimming pool is available in the summer, along with volleyball and badminton courts.

**Location:** In Colorado Springs; map B3, grid a4.

**Campsites, facilities:** There are 170 sites for RVs of any length, most with full hookups. Tents are not permitted. Drinking water, picnic tables, fire grills, and bathrooms with hot showers are provided. Laundry facilities, a waste disposal station, a store, a swimming pool, and a public phone are available. Leashed pets are permitted.

**Elevation:** 6,200 feet.

**Reservations, fees:** Reservations are accepted for stays between mid-May and mid-September. Sites are $15-22 a night.

**Open:** Year-round.

**Directions:** If you're heading south on Interstate 25, take Exit 140B and drive east on Arvada Ave. to Nevada Avenue. Turn left and continue one-quarter mile north. Turn right on Las Vegas St. and go one block. Turn right on Weber St. and proceed 100 feet to the campground. Northbound on Interstate 25, take Exit 140A and drive north on Nevada Ave. to Las Vegas Street. Turn right, go one block, and turn right on Weber Street.

**Contact:** Campers Village, 1209 S. Nevada Ave., Colorado Springs, CO 80903; tel. (719) 632-9737.

## 18 Mountaindale Campground    8

Set on 45 acres and adjacent to thousands of acres of public land, Mountaindale is a hiker's paradise. The campground is in a pretty, natural setting, with graveled sites sprinkled with grass and shaded by tall Ponderosa pine trees. Although the camp is easily accessible, with paved roads all the way, you get a wilderness-like feel and plenty of peace and quiet.

**Location:** In Colorado Springs; map B3, grid b3

**Campsites, facilities:** There are 30 tent sites and 60 sites for RVs of any length, some with full hookups. Drinking water, picnic tables, fire rings, and bathrooms with hot showers are provided. Laundry facilities, a waste disposal station, small store, hot tub, cabins, and public phone are available. Leashed pets are permitted.

**Elevation:** 6,000 feet.

**Reservations, fees:** Reservations are accepted. Sites are $14-19 a night.

**Open:** Year-round.

**Directions:** From Interstate 25 at Colorado Springs, take Exit 135 and drive two miles west on Academy Boulevard. Turn right on Hwy. 115 and go approximately 14 miles south. Turn right at the campground sign and continue two miles west to the camp.

**Contact:** Mountaindale Campground, 2000 Barrett Rd., Colorado Springs, CO 80926; tel. (719) 576-0619.

## 19 Wrangler RV Ranch and Motel   7

Wrangler RV Ranch offers rows of level dirt sites adjacent to a motel, some shaded by spiky pines or young aspens. The theme is decidedly Old West, with atmospheric accessories including a covered wagon and an ancient horse corral. The best feature is the view: Pikes Peak looms majestically to the west, dominating the skyline. Area attractions include the U.S. Olympic Center, the Sky Sox Baseball Stadium, and the Black Forest.

**Location:** East of Colorado Springs; map B3, grid a4.

**Campsites, facilities:** There are 10 tent sites and 90 sites for RVs of any length, most with full hookups. Drinking water, picnic tables, fire grills, and bathrooms with hot showers are provided. Laundry facilities, motel rooms, a recreation room, and a public phone are available. Leashed pets are permitted.

**Elevation:** 6,300 feet.

**Reservations, fees:** Reservations are accepted. Sites are $16.50-26 a night.

**Open:** Year-round.

**Directions:** If you're heading south on Interstate 25, take Exit 150A and drive about 10 miles south on Academy Boulevard. Then turn east on U.S. 24 and continue 2.5 miles to the campground. Northbound on Interstate 25, take Exit 135 and drive six miles north on Academy Boulevard. Turn east on U.S. 24 and continue 2.5 miles.

**Contact:** Wrangler RV Ranch and Motel, 6225 E. U.S. 24, Colorado Springs, CO 80915; tel. (719) 591-1402.

## **20** Falcon Meadow   7

Although this camp has a few full-hookup sites, they are—according to the host— jealously guarded by long-term residents, and there's a waiting list of people itching to move in. Consequently, most sites are dry or offer only water and electric hookups, best for small RVs and pop-ups or tents. Sites are grassy, bordered by a field of native grasses and deciduous trees including maple, oak, elm, and acacia, and all have postcard-quality views of Pikes Peak.

**Location:** Northeast of Colorado Springs; map B3, grid a5.

**Campsites, facilities:** There are 30 sites for tents or RVs of any length, a few with full hookups. Drinking water, picnic tables, fire grills, and bathrooms with hot showers are provided. Laundry facilities, a waste disposal station, small store, gas station, and public phone are available. Leashed pets are permitted.

**Elevation:** 6,800 feet.

**Reservations, fees:** Reservations are accepted. Sites are $11-17 a night.

**Open:** Year-round.

**Directions:** From Interstate 25 in Colorado Springs, take Exit 141 and drive 15 miles east on U.S. 24.

**Contact:** Falcon Meadow, 11150 U.S. 24, Falcon, CO 80831; tel. (719) 495-2694.

## **21** Lost Burro Campground     8

Simple and beautiful, this 17-acre camp rests in a secluded mountain valley next to a charming bed-and-breakfast. Some sites are open and sunny, set on hard-packed dirt, while others are nestled farther up the hillside under pine and aspen trees. All feature lovely views of surrounding peaks and red-rock cliffs behind the property. Hiking trails are within walking distance, and the small stream that runs through camp may have fish in it, depending on the previous winter's snowpack. Regional attractions include the Florissant Fossil Beds and Pikes Peak.

**Location:** In Cripple Creek; map B3, grid a1.

**Campsites, facilities:** There are 30 sites for tents or RVs of any length. Drinking water, picnic tables, fire grills, and bathrooms with hot showers are provided. Electric hookups, laundry facilities, and a waste disposal station are available. Leashed pets are permitted.

**Elevation:** 8,800 feet.

**Reservations, fees:** Reservations are recommended. Sites are $16-18 a night.

**Open:** Year-round.

**Directions:** From Cripple Creek, turn north on County Rd. 1 and drive four miles to the campground.

**Contact:** Lost Burro Campground, P.O. Box 614, Cripple Creek, CO 80813; tel. (719) 689-2345.

## 22 Cripple Creek Travel Park and Hospitality House     6

Probably the largest hotel in Cripple Creek, Hospitality House is a former old-west hospital transformed into a quaint Victorian inn. The campsites are behind it in a wide-open meadow with a few pine trees sprinkled about and grassy areas for games of volleyball and croquet. Casinos, the Cripple Creek District Museum, and other attractions are accessible within a short walk. Nearby Pike National Forest provides miles of hiking and horseback riding trails.

**Location:** In Cripple Creek; map B3, grid a1.

**Campsites, facilities:** There are 20 tent sites and 36 full-hookup sites for RVs of any length. Drinking water, picnic tables, fire grills, and bathrooms with hot showers are provided. Laundry facilities, a waste disposal station, a hot tub, hotel rooms, and a public phone are available. Some facilities are wheelchair accessible. Leashed pets are permitted.

**Elevation:** 9,500 feet.

**Reservations, fees:** Reservations are accepted. Sites are $16-20 a night.

**Open:** May to mid-October.

**Directions:** From Second St. in downtown Cripple Creek, turn west on Bennett Ave. and drive one-quarter mile. Turn right on B St. and continue one-half mile to the campground.

**Contact:** Cripple Creek Travel Park and Hospitality House, P.O. Box 957, Cripple Creek, CO 80813; tel. (719) 689-2513 or (800) 500-2513.

## 23 Prospector's RV Park   6

Though small and slightly dilapidated, this in-town RV park makes an adequate base camp for people who come to explore the region. A couple of trees are scattered about the property, but most sites are open and sunny, located adjacent to a store and laundry facilities. Casinos and sights in Cripple Creek are easily accessible.

**Location:** In Cripple Creek; map B3, grid a1.

**Campsites, facilities:** There are 16 full-hookup sites for tents or RVs of any length. Drinking water, picnic tables, fire grills, and bathrooms with hot showers are provided. Laundry facilities, a waste disposal station, store, and public phone are available. Leashed pets are permitted.

**Elevation:** 9,500 feet.

**Reservations, fees:** Reservations are recommended during the summer. Sites are $10-20 a night.

**Open:** Year-round.

**Directions:** From downtown Cripple Creek, turn south on Second St. and continue two blocks to the campground entrance.

**Contact:** Prospector's RV Park, P.O. Box 1237, Cripple Creek, CO 80813; tel. (719) 689-2006.

## 24 Cripple Creek KOA     7

At 10,000 feet elevation, this camp has the unique distinction of being the highest KOA campground in the world. It features open, treeless sites on a wide lot surrounded by a ring of forest, with views of mountain peaks. It's far enough away from the gambling hubbub of Cripple Creek to remain quiet and peaceful. The night air feels a bit thin up here, and it gets chilly even in the hottest summer months, so come prepared with warm gear. The camp is at the base of the foothills adjacent to wild, open Bureau of Land Management lands where you'll find miles of hiking and mountain biking trails.

**Location:** South of Cripple Creek; map B3, grid a2.

**Campsites, facilities:** There are 75 sites for tents or RVs of any length, many with full hookups. Drinking water, picnic tables, fire grills, and bathrooms with hot showers are provided. Laundry facilities, a waste disposal station, store, hot tub, public phone, and cabins are available. Some facilities are wheelchair accessible. Leashed pets are permitted.

**Elevation:** 10,000 feet.

**Reservations, fees:** Reservations are accepted; phone (800) KOA-9125. Sites are $20-25.50 a night.

**Open:** May to mid-October.

**Directions:** From Hwy. 67 in Cripple Creek, turn south on County Rd. 81 (toward Victor) and drive one-half mile.

**Contact:** Cripple Creek KOA, P.O. Box 699, Cripple Creek, CO 80813; tel. (719) 689-3376.

## 25 Colorado Springs South KOA    5

Just a short hop off Interstate 25, this large camp is a convenient stopover for highway travelers. The sites are spacious and mostly open, with small scattered trees and planted flower beds scattered in between, plus a border of large trees to block road noise. The well-kept facilities include a large indoor pool and hot tub, a miniature golf course, and even an e-mail room for campers in need of a cyber fix from the road. Regional bus tours leave regularly from camp.

**Location:** On Fountain Creek; map B3, grid b4.

**Campsites, facilities:** There are 200 sites for tents or RVs of any length, most with full hookups. Drinking water, picnic tables, and bathrooms with hot showers are provided. Laundry facilities, a waste disposal station, cafe, miniature golf course, swimming pool and hot tub, public phone, and cabins are available. Leashed pets are permitted.

**Elevation:** 6,000 feet.

**Reservations, fees:** Reservations are accepted; phone (800) KOA-8609. Sites are $22-28 a night.

**Open:** Year-round.

**Directions:** From Interstate 25 south of Colorado Springs, take Exit 132 and drive east on Hwy. 16 to Bandley Drive. Turn right and continue a short distance to the campground.

**Contact:** Colorado Springs South KOA, 8100 S. Bandley Dr., Fountain, CO 80817; tel. (719) 382-7575.

## 26 Yogi Bear's Jellystone Park Camp Resort      6

Yogi's Jellystone is the theme park of campgrounds, a fact that becomes immediately apparent at the entrance, where campers are greeted by a 12-foot statue of Yogi Bear. You get a choice of open or shaded sites with every possible amenity, from a full-service grocery and souvenir store to an extra-large swimming pool and hot tub. Nearby are white-water rafting trips, fishing access, and the Royal Gorge Bridge. On-site highlights include holiday theme weekends (parades on the Fourth of July, trick-or-treating hayrides in October), a miniature golf course, family-oriented movies, and community games.

**Location:** West of Cañon City; map B3, grid c1.

**Campsites, facilities:** There are 40 sites for tents and 40 for RVs of any length, some with full hookups. Drinking water, picnic tables, fire grills, and bathrooms with hot showers are provided. Laundry facilities, a waste disposal station, store, swimming pool, hot tub, cabins, and public phone are available. Some facilities are wheelchair accessible. Leashed pets are permitted.

**Elevation:** 6,300 feet.

**Reservations, fees:** Reservations are accepted; phone (800) 558-2954. Sites are $22-25 a night.

**Open:** Year-round.

**Directions:** From Cañon City, drive 10 miles west on U.S. 50 to the junction of U.S. 50 and Hwy. 9.

**Contact:** Yogi Bear's Jellystone Park Camp Resort, P.O. Box 1025, Cañon City, CO 81212; tel. (719) 275-2128; e-mail: yogibear@ris.net.

## 27 Royal View Campground    7

This aptly named campground does indeed sport a spectacular view of the Royal Gorge Bridge, a span that towers 1,053 feet over the rushing Arkansas River. RV sites are about one-half mile back from the highway; most are level and open with a shade tree at each site. Tenters enjoy a separate, secluded area a bit farther back from the road. You can arrange a rafting trip on site. The campground hosts are group-oriented and offer nightly movies, big pancake breakfasts, and community barbecues—not to mention the biggest swimming pool around.

**Location:** West of Cañon City; map B3, grid c0.

**Campsites, facilities:** There are 17 tent sites, 30 full-hookup sites, and two dry sites for RVs of any length. Laundry facilities, a waste disposal station, store, miniature golf course, swimming pool, public phone, and cabins are available. Leashed pets are permitted.

**Elevation:** 6,200 feet.

**Reservations, fees:** Reservations are accepted. Sites are $19-23 a night.

**Open:** All year.

**Directions:** From Cañon City, drive nine miles west on U.S. 50 to just before the junction of U.S. 50 and Hwy. 9.

**Contact:** Royal View Campground, 43590 U.S. 50W, Cañon City, CO 81212; tel. (719) 275-1900; e-mail: royalview@ris.net.

## 28 Buffalo Bill's Royal Gorge Campground  7

This camp provides a distant glimpse of the Royal Gorge Bridge, looming more than 1,000 feet over the Arkansas River, and full, unobstructed views of the dramatic-looking Sangre de Cristos. Conveniences include a pool, on-site store and restaurant, and a choice of open or shaded sites, most padded with native grasses and protected by elm trees. Tepees and cabins are also available for rent. Nearby recreation options include rafting, horseback riding, and hiking.

**Location:** West of Cañon City; map B3, grid c0.

**Campsites, facilities:** There are 10 tent sites and 34 sites for RVs of any length, many with full hookups. Drinking water, picnic tables, fire grills, and bathrooms with hot showers are provided. Laundry facilities, a waste disposal station, store, swimming pool, sports field, public phone, and cabins are available. Leashed pets are permitted.

**Elevation:** 6,300 feet.

**Reservations, fees:** Reservations are accepted; phone (800) 787-0880. Sites are $18-21 a night.

**Open:** Mid-April to mid-October.

**Directions:** From Cañon City, drive eight miles west on U.S. 50 to County Rd. 3A (Royal Gorge Rd.) and turn left. Continue 300 yards south to the campground.

**Contact:** Buffalo Bill's Royal Gorge Campground, 30 County Rd. 3A, Cañon City, CO 81212; tel. (719) 269-3211; e-mail: buffalo@ris.net.

## 29 Royal Gorge KOA  7

This KOA has the singular advantage of being the closest campground to the Royal Gorge Bridge. Sites are open, with patchy grass and just a few tall shade trees. The camp offers all the conveniences of a developed campground and a few extras: a big swimming pool and a hot tub, miniature golf, and—the main draw—a Fun Country Amusement Park, complete with hair-raising rides and a go-cart course. There's also a Dairy Queen on site for those midday ice cream cravings. Area highlights include the bridge, the Royal Gorge Scenic Railway, and Buckskin Joe, a historic old-west town.

**Location:** Near the Royal Gorge Bridge; map B3, grid c0.

**Campsites, facilities:** There are 45 tent sites and 105 sites for RVs of any length, many with full hookups. Drinking water, picnic tables, fire grills, and bathrooms with hot showers are provided. Laundry facilities, a waste disposal station, a store, a miniature golf course, a swimming pool, a sports field, and a public phone are available. Leashed pets are permitted.

**Elevation:** 6,300 feet.

**Reservations, fees:** Reservations are accepted; phone (800) KOA-5689. Sites are $20-25.50 a night.

**Open:** Mid-April to October.

**Directions:** From Cañon City, drive eight miles west on U.S. 50 to County Rd. 3A (Royal Gorge Rd.) and turn left. Continue one-half mile south to the campground.

**Contact:** Royal Gorge KOA, P.O. Box 528, Cañon City, CO 81215; tel. (719) 275-6116.

## 30 Fort Gorge Campground and RV Park   6

Although the sites at Fort Gorge are situated too close to the highway (about 100 yards back), the camp manages to provide a pleasingly comfortable setting, with large grass-and-gravel sites sheltered by piñon pine and cedar trees. The open landscape grants unobstructed views of the rugged Sangre de Cristo Mountains, and you can see the pilings of the Royal Gorge Bridge in the distance.

**Location:** West of Cañon City; map B3, grid c0.

**Campsites, facilities:** There are 53 sites for tents or RVs of any length, some with full hookups. Drinking water, picnic tables, fire grills, and bathrooms with hot showers are provided. Laundry facilities, a waste disposal station, store, public phone, and cabins are available. Leashed pets are permitted.

**Elevation:** 6,300 feet.

**Reservations, fees:** Reservations are accepted. Sites are $15-21.50 a night.

**Open:** May to November.

**Directions:** From Cañon City, drive eight miles west on U.S. 50.

**Contact:** Fort Gorge Campground and RV Park, 45044 U.S. 50, Cañon City, CO 81212; tel. (719) 275-5111.

## 31 RV Station    5

These grassy sites roll out in long rows toward the foothills. Most are open and sunny, with a border of tall shade trees on the edge of the camp. Since RV Station is directly on U.S. 50, road noise is a problem at certain sites, but many are far enough from the road to remain fairly peaceful. Shops and restaurants are nearby. Rafting enthusiasts can arrange trips on the Arkansas River's Royal Gorge by contacting outfitters in Cañon City or near the mouth of the gorge, a short drive away.

**Location:** In Cañon City; map B3, grid c2.

**Campsites, facilities:** There are 13 tent sites and 47 sites for RVs of any length, many with full hookups. Drinking water, picnic tables, and bathrooms with hot showers are provided. A waste disposal station and a public phone are available. Leashed pets are permitted.

**Elevation:** 5,300 feet.

**Reservations, fees:** Reservations are accepted. Sites are $12-17 a night.

**Open:** Year-round.

**Directions:** The campground is on the eastern edge of Cañon City at 3120 Main St. (U.S. 50).

**Contact:** RV Station, 3120 E. Main St., Cañon City, CO 81212; tel. (719) 275-4576.

## 32 Indian Springs Campground       9

Tired of highway driving and noisy city campgrounds? This place may provide the perfect balm. Indian Springs is on a working ranch, girdled by acres and acres of short grass prairie, piñon pine, and juniper forest on deep, reddish brown soil with plenty of room for free-range hiking or horseback riding. The campsites are near a wooded area at the base of the foothills, with hard-packed dirt sites for

RVs and a prairie setting for tents. Rustic and peaceful, the ranch is a registered National Natural Landmark—the site of prehistoric fossils (including the oldest known vertebrate in the world) and a historic log cabin built in 1840. The camp's owner—a no-nonsense, earthy woman with a great sense of humor—will take you on nature hikes and explain the medicinal uses of the native plants, guide a resident hummingbird to your finger, or—for the truly brave of heart (and stomach)—let you help brand the cattle. Guided horseback riding tours are available.

**Location:** Northeast of Cañon City; map B3, grid b2.

**Campsites, facilities:** There are 30 full-hookup sites for tents or RVs of any length. Drinking water, picnic tables, fire grills, and bathrooms with hot showers are provided. A swimming pool, horse rentals, and a sports field are available. Leashed pets are permitted.

**Elevation:** 5,800 feet.

**Reservations, fees:** Reservations are accepted. Sites are $11-15 a night.

**Open:** April to October.

**Directions:** From Cañon City, drive five miles east on U.S. 50, turn left on County Rd. 67, and drive four miles north. Turn left at a signed dirt road and continue about three miles to the campground.

**Contact:** Indian Springs Campground, P.O. Box 405, Cañon City, CO 81215; tel. (719) 372-3907.

## **33** Floyd's RV Park      7

Set on 17 acres of piñon pine, juniper, elm, and Russian olive trees, this pleasant camp offers roomy sites and "big sky" views of Pikes Peak and surrounding mountains. Although the camp is on U.S. 50, the sites are secluded and far enough back from the road to remain private and peaceful. Recreation options include rafting the nearby Royal Gorge, boating and fishing in Pueblo Reservoir to the east, and local attractions in Cañon City and Pueblo.

**Location:** Near Penrose; map B3, grid c3.

**Campsites, facilities:** There are seven tent sites and 37 sites for RVs of any length, many with full hookups. Drinking water, picnic tables, fire grills, and bathrooms with hot showers are provided. Laundry facilities, a waste disposal station, and a public phone are available. Leashed pets are permitted.

**Elevation:** 5,400 feet.

**Reservations, fees:** Reservations are accepted. Sites are $12-20 a night.

**Open:** April to November.

**Directions:** From the junction of U.S. 50 and Hwy. 115 in Penrose, drive three miles east on U.S. 50.

**Contact:** Floyd's RV Park, 1438 U.S. 50, Penrose, CO 81240; tel. (719) 372-3385.

## **34** Haggard's RV Campground    6

This sprawling, flat, open campground features graveled sites next to scraggly patches of grass, with distant vistas of the rolling Wet Mountains to the west and endless plains to the east (make a point to rouse yourself early for an awe-inspiring sunrise). Though basic, the camp is extremely clean and provides easy access to

U.S. 50 and Pueblo, as well as the Royal Gorge Bridge, rafting on the Arkansas River, and Pueblo State Park.

**Location:** West of Pueblo; map B3, grid c3.

**Campsites, facilities:** There are 80 sites for RVs of any length, some with full hookups, and a separate area for tents. Drinking water, picnic tables, and bathrooms with hot showers are provided. Laundry facilities, a waste disposal station, a store, and a public phone are available. Leashed pets are permitted.

**Elevation:** 5,300 feet.

**Reservations, fees:** Reservations are accepted. Sites are $20-23 a night.

**Open:** Year-round.

**Directions:** From Interstate 25 north of Pueblo, turn west on U.S. 50 and drive 15 miles.

**Contact:** Haggard's RV Campground, 7910 U.S. 50, Pueblo, CO 81007; tel. (719) 547-2101.

## 35 Pueblo KOA    5

Set in the high desert plains north of Pueblo, this well-maintained camp makes a good stopover for Interstate 25 travelers, although it's subject to heavy seasonal traffic noise. Sites are graveled, with scattered trees, a few flowering bushes, and distant views of Pikes Peak to the north. Tepees are available for rent. Pueblo State Park to the west provides opportunities for recreation and camping in a more natural setting.

**Location:** North of Pueblo; map B3, grid c4.

**Campsites, facilities:** There are 15 tent sites and 62 sites for RVs of any length, many with full hookups. Drinking water, picnic tables, fire grills, and bathrooms with hot showers are provided. Laundry facilities, a waste disposal station, store, swimming pool, sports field, public phone, and cabins are available. Leashed pets are permitted.

**Elevation:** 4,700 feet.

**Reservations, fees:** Reservations are accepted; phone (800) KOA-7453. Sites are $17 24 a night.

**Open:** Year-round.

**Directions:** From Interstate 25 north of Pueblo, take Exit 108 and head west to the frontage road. Turn right and continue one-half mile north to the campground.

**Contact:** Pueblo KOA, 4131 Interstate 25 North, Pueblo, CO 81008; tel. (719) 542-2273.

## 36 Ordway Reservoir State Wildlife Area   6

Mediocre fishing for rainbow trout, largemouth bass, channel catfish, and bluegill is the only attraction on this flat, dry stretch of land. Access is restricted to the shoreline; no boating is permitted. Camping is spartan, with no trees or facilities save for a vault toilet. The place does have one redeeming quality: the sunrises are amazing.

**Location:** Near Ordway; map B3, grid c9.

**Campsites, facilities:** Dispersed camping is permitted throughout the property. Vault toilets are provided, but there is no drinking water. Leashed pets are permitted.

**Elevation:** 4,400 feet.

**Reservations, fees:** Reservations are not accepted. There is no fee.

**Open:** Year-round.

**Directions:** From Hwy. 96 in Ordway, turn north on Hwy. 71 and drive two miles to the reservoir on the left.

**Contact:** Colorado Division of Wildlife, 2126 N. Weber St., Colorado Springs, CO 80907; tel. (719) 227-5200.

## 37 Lake Henry State Wildlife Area     6

Camping here is a rustic, do-it-yourself experience, with no drinking water or even toilets. In exchange, however, you get free sites and access to all types of boating, including waterskiing, sailing, and windsurfing, plus decent fishing for largemouth bass, blue and channel catfish, wiper, and walleye. The surrounding land is flat and treeless, with high temperatures in summer (bring something to provide shade if you plan on staying any length of time). Note: The lake is subject to drawdowns and can be too shallow for boating at times. Call before planning your trip. Hunting for small game and waterfowl is permitted.

**Location:** Near Ordway; map B3, grid c9.

**Campsites, facilities:** Several designated campsites are scattered near the shore of the lake. A boat ramp is provided, but there are no other facilities or drinking water. Leashed pets are permitted.

**Elevation:** 4,400 feet.

**Reservations, fees:** Reservations are not accepted. There is no fee.

**Open:** Last day of waterfowl season to October 31.

**Directions:** From Hwy. 96 in Ordway, turn north on County Rd. 20 and drive one mile to the reservoir.

**Contact:** Colorado Division of Wildlife, 2126 N. Weber St., Colorado Springs, CO 80907; tel. (719) 227-5200.

## 38 De Weese Reservoir State Wildlife Area     7

Covering more than 200 surface acres, this long, narrow, green-tinged reservoir offers excellent fishing for rainbow, cutthroat, and brown trout, along with splake and smallmouth bass. Camping is best on the eastern shore, where there are several level sites with established fire rings. Vegetation is fairly sparse, mostly native grasses and some scrub brush. To the north are a few crude hiking trails routed toward the De Weese Plateau, where you might catch sight of a resident antelope, deer, or coyote. Small game hunting is permitted.

**Location:** North of Westcliffe; map B3, grid d0.

**Campsites, facilities:** Dispersed camping is permitted throughout the property. Vault toilets and a boat ramp are provided, but there is no drinking water. Leashed pets are permitted.

**Elevation:** 7,700 feet.

**Reservations, fees:** Reservations are not accepted. There is no fee.

**Open:** Year-round.

**Directions:** From Westcliffe, drive five miles northwest on Hwy. 69, turn right on

Copper Gulch Rd., and go 1.5 miles north. Turn right at the signed access road and continue west to the reservoir.

**Contact:** Colorado Division of Wildlife, 2126 N. Weber St., Colorado Springs, CO 80907; tel. (719) 227-5200.

## 39 Grape Creek RV Park      8

Grape Creek RV is laid out like a huge park, with spacious, beautifully landscaped sites surrounded by wildflowers, flowering shrubs, and acres and acres of the flat, lush, green Wet Mountain Valley. The sites feature panoramic views of snowcapped peaks in the Sangre de Cristo Range to the west and the Wet Mountains to the east, and premier trout fishing on site in Grape Creek. Area attractions include wilderness hiking, rafting on the Arkansas River, the annual Wild West Rodeo, and historic ghost towns and museums.

**Location:** Near Westcliffe; map B3, grid d0.

**Campsites, facilities:** There are 35 sites for tents or RVs of any length, many with full hookups. Drinking water, picnic tables, fire grills, and bathrooms with hot showers are provided. Laundry facilities and a waste disposal station are available. Leashed pets are permitted.

**Elevation:** 7,900 feet.

**Reservations, fees:** Reservations are accepted; call (888) 783-2267. Sites are $14-20 a night.

**Open:** May to mid-September.

**Directions:** From the junction of Hwy. 96 and Hwy. 69 in Westcliffe, drive 1.5 miles south on Hwy. 69.

**Contact:** Grape Creek RV Park, 56491 Hwy. 69, Westcliffe, CO 81252; tel. (719) 783-2588.

## 40 Cross D Bar Trout Ranch       10

This spectacular camp rests in the middle of more than 300 acres of wilderness, part of a working cattle ranch in the Wet Mountain Range. The campground is refreshingly simple, offering plain sites carpeted with native grasses and screened by ancient, towering pines and aspens. Majestic views of the Sangre de Cristo Mountains frame the horizon and remain visible throughout much of the property, which is liberally crisscrossed with hiking and mountain biking trails. There are no showers or even flush toilets, but electric hookups are available for RVs and the ranch store provides a full range of supplies, including fishing gear rentals. And trout fishing is the activity of choice, with four sparkling, spring-fed lakes to choose from and every variety of trout imaginable. You don't need a license to fish here, nor fishing experience—the ranch owners will be happy to teach you how. Although most fishing is done from the shoreline, catch-and-release fishing from belly boats is permitted on one lake. One of the few camps that caters to guests in wheelchairs, this ranch makes them a priority, with full barrier-free access throughout the resort and special programs and events for wheelchair users. Horse rentals are available at a nearby ranch.

**Location:** Near Westcliffe; map B3, grid d1.

**Campsites, facilities:** There are 15 tent sites and 18 sites for RVs of any length.

Drinking water, picnic tables, fire grills, and vault toilets are provided. Electric hookups, a waste disposal station, store, public phone, and guest rooms are available. All facilities are wheelchair accessible. Leashed pets are permitted.
**Elevation:** 9,300 feet.
**Reservations, fees:** Reservations are accepted. Sites are $8-14 a night.
**Open:** May to October.
**Directions:** From the junction of Hwy 96 and Hwy. 69 in Westcliffe, drive 12 miles east on Hwy. 96. Turn right on County Rd. 347 (Rosita Rd.) and continue two miles south to the ranch entrance.
**Contact:** Cross D Bar Trout Ranch, 2299 County Rd. 347, Westcliffe, CO 81252; tel. (719) 783-2007.

## **41** Pueblo State Park

8

When the hot summer dust begins to fly in the flat, parched valley west of Pueblo, folks flock like thirsty birds to Pueblo State Park, where gleaming Pueblo Reservoir stretches lazily from east to west, lined with droopy willows and large cottonwoods. The reservoir sports 17 miles of shoreline, with dozens of tiny fingers and coves perfect for fishing a variety of species: rainbow trout, black crappie, small and largemouth bass, sunfish, channel catfish, and perch. Besides being a base for anglers, Pueblo Reservoir is something of a mecca for water sports enthusiasts, with facilities for swimming, waterskiing, and sailing and special areas on the north shore for windsurfing. The campsites are divided between the north and south shores, all open and dotted with sage, with gorgeous views of the Sangre de Cristo and Greenhorn Mountains to the west. Several trails lead through fields of native grasses (along with prickly pear and several varieties of cactus-watch your step!), and all are suitable for hiking, biking, or horseback riding. Limited hunting is permitted; call the park for details.
**Location:** West of Pueblo; map B3, grid d4.
**Campsites, facilities:** There are 401 sites for tents or RVs of any length. The Kettle Creek and Juniper Breaks areas offer only tables, fire rings, and vault toilets; all other sites have drinking water, picnic tables, fire grills, and bathrooms with hot showers. Electric hookups, laundry facilities, and a waste disposal station are also available. A marina with a restaurant, small store, boat rentals, slips, docks, and ramps is located on the north shore. Some facilities are wheelchair accessible. Leashed pets are permitted.
**Elevation:** 4,800 feet.
**Reservations, fees:** Reservations are accepted. Phone (303) 470-1144 or (800) 678-CAMP (800-678-2267) outside the Denver Metro area; there's a $7 reservation fee. Sites are $10-14 a night, and there's a $4 entrance fee.
**Open:** Year-round.
**Directions:** From Interstate 25 in Pueblo, turn west on U.S. 50 and drive four miles. Turn south on Pueblo Boulevard and go four miles. Turn west on Hwy. 96 (Thatcher Ave.) and continue six miles to the park entrance.
**Contact:** Pueblo State Park, 640 Pueblo Reservoir Rd., Pueblo, CO 81005; tel. (719) 561-9320.

## 42 Fort's Mobile Home Park  5

Basic but adequate, this full-time mobile home park is dominated by long-term inhabitants, with overnight availability dependent upon the number of seasonal residents. The park offers little character—just dry, flat, concrete spaces—but the sites are drenched with shade from ancient elms, and the facilities are spotlessly clean. Downtown Pueblo and area attractions, including the summertime State Fair and Pueblo State Park, are within a short drive.

**Location:** South of Pueblo; map B3, grid d4.

**Campsites, facilities:** There are 35 full-hookup sites for RVs of any length. No tents are permitted. Drinking water and bathrooms with hot showers are provided. Laundry facilities, a waste disposal station, and a public phone are available. Leashed pets are permitted.

**Elevation:** 4,700 feet.

**Reservations, fees:** Reservations are accepted. Sites are $21 a night.

**Open:** Year-round.

**Directions:** From Interstate 25 south of Pueblo, take Exit 94 and drive one-quarter mile west on Hwy. 45 to Lake Avenue. Turn right and proceed one block north to the campground.

**Contact:** Fort's Mobile Home Park, 3015 Lake Ave., Pueblo, CO 81004; tel. (719) 564-2327.

## 43 Olney Springs State Wildlife Area    6

This tiny reservoir (six surface acres) is more like a pond, tinged a dull green and offering dubious fishing prospects for bluegill and channel catfish. Claim one of the few small sites with fire rings near the water or traverse the plains to find your own private spot. Undeveloped hiking trails meander throughout the property.

**Location:** Near Ordway; map B3, grid d8.

**Campsites, facilities:** Dispersed camping is permitted throughout the property. There are no other facilities or drinking water. Leashed pets are permitted.

**Elevation:** 4,400 feet.

**Reservations, fees:** Reservations are not accepted. There is no fee.

**Open:** Year-round.

**Directions:** From Ordway, drive five miles west on Hwy. 96 to Olney Springs. Turn north on County Rd. 7 and continue one mile to the reservoir.

**Contact:** Colorado Division of Wildlife, 2126 N. Weber St., Colorado Springs, CO 80907; tel. (719) 227-5200.

## 44 The Junction RV Park     4

Located next to a restaurant and a store on the dry, flat plains of Ordway, this full-facility camp offers a choice of open or shaded sites set back from the road. Wilderness this is not, but neither is it a bad choice for a layover. For a small fee you can take a dip in the swimming pool at the community center next door. Meredith Reservoir, Lake Henry, and Ordway Reservoir State Wildlife Areas are all within a five-mile radius and offer opportunities for fishing and wildlife observation.

**Location:** In Ordway; map B3, grid d9.

**Campsites, facilities:** There are 40 sites for tents or RVs of any length, some with full hookups. Drinking water, picnic tables, and bathrooms with hot showers are provided. Laundry facilities, a waste disposal station, restaurant, store, sports field, gas station, and public phone are available. Leashed pets are permitted.

**Elevation:** 4,500 feet.

**Reservations, fees:** Reservations are accepted. Sites are $10-15 a night.

**Open:** Year-round.

**Directions:** The camp is in Ordway, at the southern junction of Hwy. 96 and Hwy. 71.

**Contact:** The Junction RV Park, P.O. Box 97, Ordway, CO 81063; tel. (719) 267-3262.

## 45 Meredith Reservoir State Wildlife Area  6

Like Lake Henry to the north, Meredith Reservoir provides access to all boating and warm-water fishing—with the added amenity of toilets. The surrounding country is hot, flat, and dry, but shade shelters provide a little relief. Hunting for small game and waterfowl is permitted.

**Location:** Near Ordway; map B3, grid d9.

**Campsites, facilities:** Several designated campsites are scattered near the shore of the lake. Vault toilets, shade shelters, and a boat ramp are provided, but there is no drinking water. Leashed pets are permitted.

**Elevation:** 4,400 feet.

**Reservations, fees:** Reservations are not accepted. There is no fee.

**Open:** Last day of waterfowl season to October 31.

**Directions:** From Ordway, drive three miles east on County Rd. G and then turn right on County Rd. 21 into the parking area.

**Contact:** Colorado Division of Wildlife, 2126 N. Weber St., Colorado Springs, CO 80907; tel. (719) 227-5200.

## 46 Ophir Creek   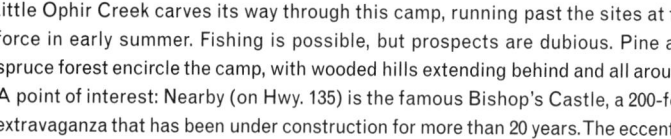 7

Little Ophir Creek carves its way through this camp, running past the sites at full force in early summer. Fishing is possible, but prospects are dubious. Pine and spruce forest encircle the camp, with wooded hills extending behind and all around. A point of interest: Nearby (on Hwy. 135) is the famous Bishop's Castle, a 200-foot extravaganza that has been under construction for more than 20 years. The eccentric ironworker from Pueblo who is building it single-handedly boasts that it's the "largest one-man project in the world." Definitely worth a look.

**Location:** North of Lake Isabel in San Isabel National Forest; map B3, grid e2.

**Campsites, facilities:** There are 31 sites for tents or RVs up to 40 feet long. Drinking water, picnic tables, fire grills, and vault toilets are provided. Leashed pets are permitted.

**Elevation:** 8,900 feet.

**Reservations, fees:** Reservations are not accepted. Sites are $9 a night.

**Open:** May to October.

**Directions:** From Pueblo, drive approximately 35 miles southwest on Hwy. 78, turn right on Hwy. 165, and drive 3.5 miles north. Turn left on Forest Service Rd. 360 and continue 100 feet to the campground entrance.

**Contact:** San Isabel National Forest, San Carlos Ranger District, 3170 E. Main St., Cañon City, CO 81212; tel. (719) 269-8500.

## 47 Davenport      7

A smaller option than nearby Ophir Creek, Davenport is set far back from the highway in a heavily forested area with a small stream running through camp. Pretty, but it's also smack in the middle of a web of motorbike trails—so if it's quiet you're after, you are better off elsewhere. Note: The trails are accessible to hikers and mountain bikers, but watch out for speeding ATVs.

**Location:** North of Lake Isabel in San Isabel National Forest; map B3, grid e2.

**Campsites, facilities:** There are 12 sites for tents or RVs up to 25 feet long. Drinking water, picnic tables, fire grills, and vault toilets are provided. Leashed pets are permitted.

**Elevation:** 8,500 feet.

**Reservations, fees:** Reservations are not accepted. Sites are $9 a night.

**Open:** May to October.

**Directions:** From Pueblo, drive approximately 35 miles southwest on Hwy. 78, turn right on Hwy. 165, and drive two miles north. Turn right on Forest Service Rd. 382 and continue two miles east to the campground entrance.

**Contact:** San Isabel National Forest, San Carlos Ranger District, 3170 E. Main St., Cañon City, CO 81212; tel. (719) 269-8500.

## 48 Southside    7

With only eight sites, Southside is the smallest and most intimate of the five camps at Lake Isabel. However, it's also the first one you come to on the access road, so it is nearly always full. The sites are spacious and wooded, not far from picnic and fishing areas on the lakeshore.

**Location:** Near Lake Isabel in San Isabel National Forest; map B3, grid e2.

**Campsites, facilities:** There are eight sites for tents or RVs up to 40 feet long. Drinking water, picnic tables, fire grills, and vault toilets are provided. Leashed pets are permitted.

**Elevation:** 8,800 feet.

**Reservations, fees:** Reservations are accepted; phone (877) 444-6777. There's an $8.65 reservation fee. You may also reserve sites at website: www.reserveusa.com. Sites are $9 a night.

**Open:** May to October.

**Directions:** From Pueblo, drive approximately 35 miles southwest on Hwy. 78, turn left on Hwy. 165, and drive four miles south. Turn right at the sign for Lake Isabel Recreation Area and continue west to the campground.

**Contact:** San Isabel National Forest, San Carlos Ranger District, 3170 E. Main St., Cañon City, CO 81212; tel. (719) 269-8500.

## 49 St. Charles    7

A basic but pleasing choice, St. Charles lies in a forest of ponderosa pine and spruce near the shore of Lake Isabel, with gorgeous mountain views nearby. Fishing is available within a short walk.

**Location:** Near Lake Isabel in San Isabel National Forest; map B3, grid e2.

**Campsites, facilities:** There are 15 sites for tents or RVs up to 35 feet long. Drinking water, picnic tables, fire grills, and vault toilets are provided. Leashed pets are permitted.

**Elevation:** 8,800 feet.

**Reservations, fees:** Reservations are accepted; phone (877) 444-6777. There's an $8.65 reservation fee. You may also reserve sites at website: www.reserveusa.com. Sites are $9 a night.

**Open:** May to October.

**Directions:** From Pueblo, drive approximately 35 miles southwest on Hwy. 78, turn left on Hwy. 165, and drive four miles south. Turn right at the sign for Lake Isabel Recreation Area and continue about a mile past Southside Campground to the campground.

**Contact:** San Isabel National Forest, San Carlos Ranger District, 3170 E. Main St., Cañon City, CO 81212; tel. (719) 269-8500.

## 50 Ponderosa Group Camp  7

Ponderosa is the largest group camp on Lake Isabel, with room for up to 150 people— plenty of space for a family reunion, company retreat, or even a wedding. The camp is quite pretty, sheltered by pine and spruce trees with a small stocked trout stream running through the middle.

**Location:** Near Lake Isabel in San Isabel National Forest; map B3, grid e2.

**Campsites, facilities:** One large site can accommodate up to 150 people and about 30 cars or small RVs. Drinking water, picnic tables, fire grills, and vault toilets are provided. Leashed pets are permitted.

**Elevation:** 8,800 feet.

**Reservations, fees:** Reservations are required; phone (877) 444-6777. There's an $8.65 reservation fee. You may also reserve sites at website: www.reserveusa.com. Fee varies depending on size of group.

**Open:** May to October.

**Directions:** From Pueblo, drive approximately 35 miles southwest on Hwy. 78, turn left on Hwy. 165, and drive four miles south. Turn right at the sign for Lake Isabel Recreation Area and continue to the turnoff for St. Charles Campground. Continue one-quarter mile past St. Charles to the campground.

**Contact:** San Isabel National Forest, San Carlos Ranger District, 3170 E. Main St., Cañon City, CO 81212; tel. (719) 269-8500.

## 51 Spruce Group Camp  7

Spruce is a more intimate option than neighboring Ponderosa Group Camp, with facilities for up to 50 people as opposed to 150. The same stocked stream that runs through Ponderosa continues through this campground, which is thickly bordered by trees. The lake is a short drive (or longer hike) away.

**Location:** Near Lake Isabel in San Isabel National Forest; map B3, grid e2.

**Campsites, facilities:** One large site can accommodate up to 50 people and about

10 cars or small RVs. Drinking water, picnic tables, fire grills, and vault toilets are provided. Leashed pets are permitted.

**Elevation:** 8,800 feet.

**Reservations, fees:** Reservations are required; phone (877) 444-6777. There's an $8.65 reservation fee. You may also reserve sites at website: www.reserveusa.com. The fee varies depending on the size of the group.

**Open:** May to October.

**Directions:** From Pueblo, drive approximately 35 miles southwest on Hwy. 78, turn left on Hwy. 165, and drive four miles south. Turn right at the sign for Lake Isabel Recreation Area and continue to the turnoff for St. Charles Campground. Continue one-quarter mile past St. Charles to the campground.

**Contact:** San Isabel National Forest, San Carlos Ranger District, 3170 E. Main St., Cañon City, CO 81212; tel. (719) 269-8500.

## 52 La Vista      8

This pretty spot is a favorite with those campers who want a little more than the basics. La Vista offers electric RV hookups and special facilities for wheelchairs, plus access to three hiking trails: the St. Charles Trail, the Snowslide Trail, and the Cisneros Trail. The first sites you pass are settled in mature pine and spruce forest; the last 12 or so are open and grassy, with pleasing mountain views. Head to Lake Isabel for fishing.

**Location:** Near Lake Isabel in San Isabel National Forest; map B3, grid e2.

**Campsites, facilities:** There are 29 sites for tents or RVs up to 50 feet long. Drinking water, picnic tables, fire grills, and vault toilets are provided. Electric hookups are available. Some facilities are wheelchair accessible. Leashed pets are permitted.

**Elevation:** 8,600 feet.

**Reservations, fees:** Reservations are accepted; phone (877) 444-6777. There's an $8.65 reservation fee. You may also reserve sites at website: www.reserveusa.com. Sites are $9-14 a night.

**Open:** May to October.

**Directions:** From Pueblo, drive approximately 35 miles southwest on Hwy. 78, turn left on Hwy. 165, and drive four miles south. Turn right at the sign for Lake Isabel Recreation Area and continue approximately one-half mile past the turnoff for St. Charles to the campground.

**Contact:** San Isabel National Forest, San Carlos Ranger District, 3170 E. Main St., Cañon City, CO 81212; tel. (719) 269-8500.

## 53 Pueblo South-Colorado City KOA    5

A bit too close to the freeway for my taste, this full-service camp is nonetheless attractive. It lies in the Greenhorn Mountain Valley in a dry, open setting with abundant piñon pine trees and teasing views of snowy mountaintops. Nearby attractions include Bishop's Castle (see the trip notes for Ophir Creek Campground), scenic Graneros Gorge, and a 27-hole championship golf course.

**Location:** Near Colorado City; map B3, grid e4.

**Campsites, facilities:** There are 17 tent sites and 55 sites for RVs of any length,

many with full hookups. Drinking water, picnic tables, fire grills, and bathrooms with hot showers are provided. Laundry facilities, a waste disposal station, store, sports field, hot tub, public phone, and cabins are available. Leashed pets are permitted.
**Elevation:** 6,000 feet.

**Reservations, fees:** Reservations are accepted; phone (800) KOA-8646. Sites are $16-23 a night.

**Open:** Year-round.

**Directions:** From Interstate 25 south of Pueblo, take Exit 74 and drive one-quarter mile east on the frontage road.

**Contact:** Pueblo South-Colorado City KOA, 9040 Interstate 25 South, Pueblo, CO 81004; tel. (719) 676-3376.

## 54 Huerfano State Wildlife Area     7

Nestled at the base of the Sangre de Cristo Mountains, this rustic wildlife area is a peaceful retreat with stunning views of high, jagged peaks to the west. The Huerfano River, which runs through the property, is valued more for its aesthetic qualities than its fishing (there are several good tent spots near the banks). Vegetation is limited, with trees sprinkled along the river and high desert wildflowers dotting the ground. Rough hiking trails lead south for several miles into the adjacent San Isabel National Forest. Limited hunting is permitted.

**Location:** Near the Sangre de Cristo Mountains; map B3, grid f0.

**Campsites, facilities:** Dispersed camping is permitted throughout the property. Vault toilets are provided, but there is no drinking water. Leashed pets are permitted.

**Elevation:** 8,200 feet.

**Reservations, fees:** Reservations are not accepted. There is no fee.

**Open:** Year-round.

**Directions:** From Gardner, drive 13 miles west on County Rd. 580 to the property.

**Contact:** Colorado Division of Wildlife, 2126 N. Weber St., Colorado Springs, CO 80907; tel. (719) 227-5200.

## 55 Circle the Wagons RV Park     6

Square dance central in the funky mountain town of La Veta is right here at this RV park, where groups come from all over the country to participate in dances and events in the camp's big clubhouse and hoof it on the shiny wooden dance floor. For those who prefer a more sedate camping experience, there are quiet, grassy sites, a little fishing pond, and restful views of the Sangre de Cristo Mountains and the Spanish Peaks.

**Location:** Near the Cuchara River; map B3, grid g2.

**Campsites, facilities:** There are 10 tent sites and 53 full-hookup sites for RVs of any length. Drinking water, picnic tables, and bathrooms with hot showers are provided. Motel rooms and a restaurant are available. Some facilities are wheelchair accessible. Leashed pets are permitted.

**Elevation:** 6,500 feet.

**Reservations, fees:** Reservations are accepted. Sites are $16-18 a night.

**Open:** Year-round.

**Directions:** From the junction of U.S. 160 and Hwy. 12 west of Walsenburg, turn south on Hwy. 12 and drive 4.75 miles to the campground, at 124 N. Main St. in La Veta.

**Contact:** Circle the Wagons RV Park, P.O. Box 122, La Veta, CO 81055; tel. (719) 742-3233.

## 56 Cuchara River Cabins and Campground

 7

Leafy maple and plum trees shelter these quiet grass-and-gravel sites nestled in a natural setting along the Cuchara River in the peaceful mountain community of La Veta. Though most sites are heavily wooded, some allow peeks at the snowcapped Sangre de Cristo Mountains and the spindly Spanish Peaks. Fishing access is available at various points along the riverside trail that leads downstream from camp. Regional attractions include fishing and hiking in the Sangre de Cristos, golfing (there's a course about a block away), and touring local historic sites.

**Location:** On the Cuchara River; map B3, grid g2.

**Campsites, facilities:** There are 14 full-hookup sites for tents or RVs of any length. Drinking water, picnic tables, fire grills, and bathrooms with hot showers are provided. Cabins and a public phone are available. Leashed pets are permitted.

**Elevation:** 7,200 feet.

**Reservations, fees:** Reservations are accepted. Sites are $14-18 a night.

**Open:** Year-round.

**Directions:** From the junction of U.S. 160 and Hwy. 12 west of Walsenburg, turn south on Hwy. 12 and drive five miles. Then turn right on Ryus St. and go one block west. Turn left on Oak St. and proceed three blocks to the campground.

**Contact:** Cuchara River Cabins and Campground, P.O. Box 397, La Veta, CO 81055; tel. (719) 742-5303.

## 57 Lathrop State Park

 8

Although Lathrop State Park covers more than 1,400 acres of high grassy plains, recreation is focused around two lakes: pretty Martin Lake, a 300-acre oasis primarily used for boating and swimming; and Horseshoe Reservoir, best known for its astounding variety of fish. Although Horseshoe is only 200 surface acres, it serves as habitat for rainbow and cutthroat trout, channel catfish, black crappie, splake, sauger, smallmouth bass, and tiger muskie, a mix that draws flocks of anglers throughout the year. The campsites encircle Martin Lake, where you'll find opportunities for water sports of all types, including waterskiing, windsurfing, and swimming (a swimming beach is available on the southwestern shore). The developed campsites are on a high bluff overlooking the northern shore, set in sparse juniper and piñon pine forest, while the primitive sites are more remote and open, set on the south shore amid yucca and cactus. The Spanish Peaks, two mountains that stand over 12,500 feet, loom in the distance to the south. A hiking trail starts near the campground and heads north for about a mile before connecting with the Hogback Ridge Trail. Limited hunting is permitted; contact the park for details.

**Location:** West of Walsenburg; map B3, grid g3.

**Campsites, facilities:** There are 17 primitive tent sites and 79 sites for tents or RVs of any length. Drinking water, picnic tables, fire grills, and bathrooms with hot showers are provided at the developed sites; water and vault toilets are provided at the primitive sites. Electric hookups, laundry facilities, a waste disposal station, and a public golf course are available. Some facilities are wheelchair accessible. Leashed pets are permitted.

**Elevation:** 6,400 feet.

**Reservations, fees:** Reservations are accepted. Phone (303) 470-1144 or (800) 678-CAMP (800-678-2267) outside the Denver Metro area; there's a $7 reservation fee. Sites are $10-14 a night, and there's a $4 entrance fee.

**Open:** Year-round.

**Directions:** From Walsenburg, drive three miles west on U.S. 160 to the park entrance.

**Contact:** Lathrop State Park, 70 County Rd. 502, Walsenburg, CO 81089; tel. (719) 738-2376.

## 58 Dakota Campground    4

The flat, dry highway stopover of Walsenburg offers little atmosphere, but it's an easy jump off Interstate 25 and provides stunning views of the Spanish Peaks and surrounding mountains. The sites at Dakota are level and paved, dotted with scraggly pine trees. There is a full-time RV mechanic on site should you run into technical problems. Nearby attractions include Lathrop State Park, the Highway of Legends, and several golf courses.

**Location:** Near Walsenburg; map B3, grid g4.

**Campsites, facilities:** There are 20 tent sites and 52 sites for RVs of any length, many with full hookups. Drinking water, picnic tables, fire grills, and bathrooms with hot showers are provided. Laundry facilities, a waste disposal station, small store, and public phone are available. Leashed pets are permitted.

**Elevation:** 6,200 feet.

**Reservations, fees:** Reservations are accepted. Sites are $15-20 a night.

**Open:** Year-round.

**Directions:** From Interstate 25 north of Walsenburg, take Exit 52 and drive three-quarters of a mile south on the Interstate 25 Business Loop.

**Contact:** Dakota Campground, P.O. Box 206, Walsenburg, CO 81089; tel. (719) 738-9912.

## 59 Bear Lake     8

Two-and-a-half-acre Bear Lake offers mediocre fishing for rainbow trout in a mountain setting near the western slope of the Culebra Range. Most sites are well shaded by fir trees, with a few sunny spots available, and spectacular mountain views await when you step out of the trees and look across the lake. The Indian Creek Trail begins at the north end of camp and heads north for several miles; you can also take the North Fork Trail south to the Blue Lake and Purgatoire campgrounds.

**Location:** Southwest of Walsenburg in San Isabel National Forest; map B3, grid h2.

**Campsites, facilities:** There are 14 sites for tents or RVs up to 40 feet long. Drinking water, picnic tables, fire grills, and vault toilets are provided. Leashed pets are permitted.

**Elevation:** 10,500 feet.

**Reservations, fees:** Reservations are not accepted. Sites are $9 a night.

**Open:** June to September.

**Directions:** From Walsenburg, drive approximately 30 miles southwest on Hwy. 12, turn right on Forest Service Rd. 422, and continue 4.5 miles west to the campground.

**Contact:** San Isabel National Forest, San Carlos Ranger District, 3170 E. Main St., Cañon City, CO 81212; tel. (719) 269-8500.

## 60 Blue Lake      8

Set at the base of the Culebra Range, with beautiful views to the west, one-acre Blue Lake qualifies better as a pond. Fishing is said to be quite good, however, with rainbow and cutthroat trout virtually boiling the lake's surface as they vie for space. The camp is surrounded by aspen and fir trees, with direct access to the North Fork Trail, which runs north and south along the North Fork of the Purgatoire River.

**Location:** Southwest of Walsenburg in San Isabel National Forest; map B3, grid h2.

**Campsites, facilities:** There are 15 sites for tents or RVs up to 40 feet long. Drinking water, picnic tables, fire grills, and vault toilets are provided. Leashed pets are permitted.

**Elevation:** 10,500 feet.

**Reservations, fees:** Reservations are not accepted. Sites are $9 a night.

**Open:** June to September.

**Directions:** From Walsenburg, drive approximately 30 miles southwest on Hwy. 12, turn right on Forest Service Rd. 422, and continue three miles west to the campground.

**Contact:** San Isabel National Forest, San Carlos Ranger District, 3170 E. Main St., Cañon City, CO 81212; tel. (719) 269-8500.

## 61 Purgatoire      7

Of the handful of basic campgrounds in the immediate area, Purgatoire is the most private and secluded, set in a lush forest of aspen and fir trees along the North Fork of the Purgatoire River. The North Fork Trail begins at camp and travels north to connect with the Blue Lake and Bear Lake campgrounds. Fishing access is decent at the campground, but better upstream along the trail.

**Location:** On the North Fork of the Purgatoire River in San Isabel National Forest; map B3, grid h2.

**Campsites, facilities:** There are 23 sites for tents or RVs up to 40 feet long. Drinking water, picnic tables, fire grills, and vault toilets are provided. Leashed pets are permitted.

**Elevation:** 9,800 feet.

**Reservations, fees:** Reservations are not accepted. Sites are $9 a night.

**Open:** June to September.

**Directions:** From Walsenburg, drive approximately 30 miles southwest on Hwy. 12, turn right on Forest Service Rd. 34, and continue three miles west to the campground.

**Contact:** San Isabel National Forest, San Carlos Ranger District, 3170 E. Main St., Cañon City, CO 81212; tel. (719) 269-8500.

## 62 Spanish Peaks State Wildlife Area     7

Camping is only allowed in one designated area here, and the public is restricted from traversing much of the property. Facilities are quite basic and the camp isn't much to look at, but it's quiet, private, and free. Although the actual Spanish Peaks are several miles to the north, you can get a decent view of them from this spot, especially West Spanish Peak (elevation 13,626 feet). A well-used hiking trail follows a small creek north through the property and provides the best vista point. For an even better view, head back on the main access road toward Hwy. 12, crossing Cordova and Cuchara Passes on the way. (Warning: The road is very rough in places and impassable when muddy.) Limited hunting is permitted.

**Location:** Northwest of Trinidad; map B3, grid h4.

**Campsites, facilities:** Several established campsites are in a large designated camping area. Drinking water and vault toilets are provided. Leashed pets are permitted.

**Elevation:** 8,100 feet.

**Reservations, fees:** Reservations are not accepted. There is no fee.

**Open:** Year-round.

**Directions:** From Aguilar, drive 18 miles southwest on Apishapa Rd., following the signs to the property. Note: The road is quite rough in spots; trailers are not recommended.

**Contact:** Colorado Division of Wildlife, 2126 N. Weber St., Colorado Springs, CO 80907; tel. (719) 227-5200.

## 63 Trinidad Lake State Park      8

As the terrain shifts from high alpine to high desert on the way south to the New Mexico border, you'll find yourself passing through scrubby foothills covered with juniper, piñon pines, and cactus. Eight hundred-acre Trinidad Lake, located just west of the city of Trinidad, looms like an oasis in the distance, sparkling blue-green and filled right up to its grassy, rocky shoreline. The state park's campground overlooks the north shore, with full facilities, even showers and electric hookups. All boating is allowed, including waterskiing, PWC riding, and sailing, but no swimming is permitted. Fishing is quite excellent for species such as rainbow and brown trout, largemouth bass, crappie, bluegill, walleye, and channel catfish. Hiking trails are a good way to view the lake, and the majority of them are open to horses and mountain bikes as well. One of the best is a mile-long interpretive trail starting at the campground; another leaves camp and leads a half mile down to the lakeshore. Limited hunting is permitted; contact the park for details.

**Location:** West of Trinidad; map B3, grid i5.

**Campsites, facilities:** There are 62 sites for tents or RVs up to 35 feet long. Drinking water, picnic tables, fire grills, and bathrooms with hot showers are provided. Electric hookups, laundry facilities, and a waste disposal station are available. A boat ramp and docks are located on the north shore of the reservoir. Some facilities are wheelchair accessible. Leashed pets are permitted.

**Elevation:** 6,300 feet.

**Reservations, fees:** Reservations are accepted. Phone (303) 470-1144 or (800) 678-CAMP (800-678-2267) outside the Denver Metro area; there's a $7 reservation fee. Sites are $10-14 a night, and there's a $4 entrance fee.

**Open:** Year-round.

**Directions:** From Trinidad, drive three miles west on Hwy. 12.

**Contact:** Trinidad Lake State Park, 32610 Hwy. 12, Trinidad, CO 81082; tel. (719) 846-6951.

## 64 Cawthon Motel and Campground   4

This quiet city campground is adjacent to a motel and a community golf course on the southern outskirts of Trinidad. Sadly, a former owner mercilessly bulldozed most of the trees in the camp, leaving just a few scattered piñon pines among the graveled sites and a small number of ponderosa pines around the office. The sites bordering the golf course are the most appealing, with lots of greenery and attractive views of the Sangre de Cristos. Restaurants and groceries are within walking distance.

**Location:** In Trinidad; map B3, grid i6.

**Campsites, facilities:** There are 42 full-hookup sites for RVs of any length. Drinking water, picnic tables, fire grills, and bathrooms with hot showers are provided. Laundry facilities, motel rooms, a golf course, and a public phone are available. Leashed pets are permitted.

**Elevation:** 6,500 feet.

**Reservations, fees:** Reservations are accepted. Sites are $16.50 a night.

**Open:** Year-round.

**Directions:** If you're southbound on Interstate 25, take Exit 13A in Trinidad and follow the signs to the Santa Fe Trail. Turn right and continue about 200 yards to the campground. Northbound on Interstate 25, take Exit 11 and drive 1.5 miles north on the frontage road (Santa Fe Trail).

**Contact:** Cawthon Motel and Campground, 1701 Santa Fe Trail, Trinidad, CO 81082; tel. (719) 846-3303.

## 65 Derrick RV Park  3

This camp is named for the enormous dinosaur of an oil derrick perched in front of the property, which is adjacent to a Budget Host motel just south of Trinidad. Close to the interstate, the concrete sites are noisy and charmless, but a smattering of piñon pine trees and panoramic (though distant) views of the Sangre de Cristo Mountains and the Spanish Peaks provide some compensation. Area attractions include art galleries, museums, and architecture in Trinidad, plus Trinidad Lake State Park and Comanche National Grassland.

**Location:** Near Trinidad; map B3, grid i6.

**Campsites, facilities:** There are 22 sites for RVs of any length, many with full hookups. No tents are permitted. Drinking water, picnic tables, fire grills, and bathrooms with hot showers are provided. Laundry facilities, a waste disposal station, a hot tub, motel rooms, and a public phone are available. Leashed pets are permitted.

**Elevation:** 6,500 feet.

**Reservations, fees:** Reservations are accepted. Sites are $17-21 a night.

**Open:** Year-round.

**Directions:** From Interstate 25 south of Trinidad, take Exit 11 and drive two blocks north on the Santa Fe Trail.

**Contact:** Derrick RV Park, 10301 Santa Fe Trail, Trinidad, CO 81082; tel. (719) 846-3307.

## 66 Summit RV Park    3

Summit RV Park is adjacent to the Budget Summit Inn just south of Trinidad. The setting is decidedly urban, with open concrete and gravel sites and a few pitiful trees virtually choked by diesel fumes from the interstate. A short hiking trail, routed up the grassy hillside behind the camp, provides a natural respite. For a small fee, you can also use the large on-site hot tub. A snack counter is available, and the hosts provide free continental breakfast in the morning.

**Location:** Near Trinidad; map B3, grid i6.

**Campsites, facilities:** There are 26 full-hookup sites for RVs of any length. No tents are permitted. Drinking water, picnic tables, fire grills, and bathrooms with hot showers are provided. Laundry facilities, a waste disposal station, restaurant, hot tub, and public phone are available. Some facilities are wheelchair accessible. Leashed pets are permitted.

**Elevation:** 6,500 feet.

**Reservations, fees:** Reservations are accepted. Sites are $17-25 a night.

**Open:** Year-round.

**Directions:** From Interstate 25 south of Trinidad, take Exit 11 and drive one-half mile south on the Santa Fe Trail.

**Contact:** Summit RV Park, 9800 Santa Fe Trail, Trinidad, CO 81082; tel. (719) 846-2251.

RIVER AND ROCK

# MAP B4

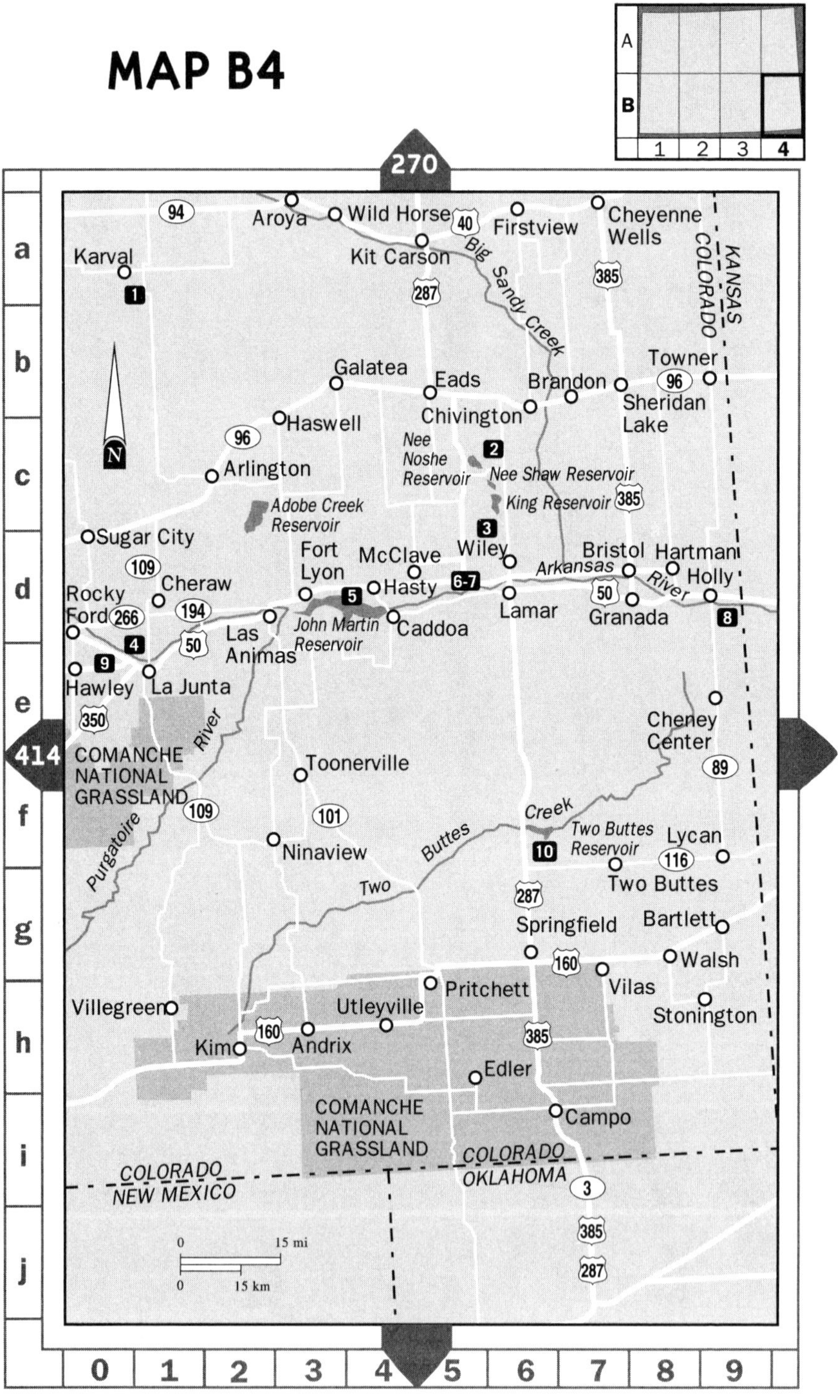

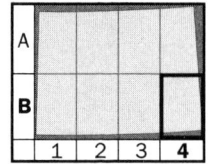
270

414

**a** Karval **1** Aroya Wild Horse **94** **40** Firstview Cheyenne Wells Kit Carson **287** **385** KANSAS COLORADO

**b** Galatea Eads Brandon Towner **96** Sheridan Lake Chivington Haswell **96**

**c** Arlington Nee Noshe Reservoir **2** Nee Shaw Reservoir King Reservoir **385**

Adobe Creek Reservoir

**d** Sugar City Fort Lyon McClave Wiley **3** Bristol Hartman Holly Cheraw **109** **194** **5** Hasty **6-7** Arkansas **50** River Granada **8** Rocky Ford **266** **50** Las Animas Caddoa John Martin Reservoir Lamar **9** Hawley La Junta

**e** **350** Cheney Center

COMANCHE NATIONAL GRASSLAND River

**f** **109** Toonerville **89**

Creek Two Buttes Reservoir Lycan

Purgatoire River Ninaview **101** **10** **116** Two Buttes

Buttes **287**

**g** Two Springfield Bartlett **160** Walsh Vilas

**h** Villegreen Utleyville Pritchett Stonington Kimo **160** Andrix **385** Edler

**i** COMANCHE NATIONAL GRASSLAND COLORADO OKLAHOMA Campo COLORADO NEW MEXICO **3**

**j** 0 15 mi **385** 0 15 km **287**

0 1 2 3 4 5 6 7 8 9

# CHAPTER B4

## 1 Karval Reservoir State Wildlife Area     6

If your desire is to escape civilization for a while, you've found the perfect retreat. This wildlife area is way out in the plains, quiet and peaceful but with little to recommend it besides fishing. Karval Reservoir is a 24-acre lake surrounded by several small ponds, each chock full of warm-water species including yellow perch, black crappie, largemouth bass, and channel catfish. nonmotorized boating is permitted. A few well-used primitive campsites have been carved out near the shoreline and are by far the preferred spots on the property. At 4,700 feet elevation, it gets blisteringly hot here in the summer, but shade shelters provide some relief. Hunting for small game and waterfowl is permitted.

**Location:** West of Kit Carson; map B4, grid a1.

**Campsites, facilities:** Dispersed camping is permitted throughout the property. A vault toilet and shade shelters are provided, but there is no drinking water. Leashed pets are permitted.

**Elevation:** 4,700 feet.

**Reservations, fees:** Reservations are not accepted. There is no fee.

**Open:** Year-round.

**Directions:** From the junction of Hwy. 94 and Hwy. 109 in Karval, drive 10 miles south on Hwy. 109 to the reservoir.

**Contact:** Colorado Division of Wildlife, 2126 N. Weber St., Colorado Springs, CO 80907; tel. (719) 227-5200.

## 2 Queens State Wildlife Area     5

Queens State Wildlife Area encompasses five reservoirs: Lower Queens, Upper Queens, Nee So Pah, Nee Gronda, and Nee Noshe. Public access is permitted at all but Nee So Pah, with warm-water fishing for species including blue and channel catfish, wiper, and walleye. Waterskiing and windsurfing are popular on Nee Noshe, but fluctuating water levels can make boating all but impossible at times; call ahead. Camping is permitted in most regions of the wildlife area—all flat and grassy—with the best spots near the reservoirs. Note that the public is not permitted at any of the lakes from November 1 until the last day of waterfowl season (January 31) except to retrieve any birds they've shot. In other words, no lakeside camping is allowed during this time, and since there are few other decent places to camp on the property, the whole place might as well be closed until February.

**Location:** South of Eads; map B4, grid c6.

**Campsites, facilities:** Dispersed camping is permitted throughout the property, except at Nee So Pah Reservoir. Boat ramps and vault toilets are provided, but there is no drinking water. Leashed pets are permitted.

**Elevation:** 3,900 feet.

**Reservations, fees:** Reservations are not accepted. There is no fee.

**Open:** Year-round with limited public access during waterfowl season.

**Directions:** To reach Upper Queens Reservoir, Lower Queens Reservoir, and Nee Gronda Reservoir, start at Eads on Hwy. 96 and drive 15 miles south on U.S.

287. Turn east on County Rd. C and continue to the property. To get to Nee Noshe Reservoir, drive 11 miles south of Eads on U.S. 287, turn east on the Kiowa County Boat Ramp access road, and continue one-half mile.

**Contact:** Colorado Division of Wildlife, 2126 N. Weber St., Colorado Springs, CO 80907; tel. (719) 227-5200.

## ▣ Thurston Reservoir State Wildlife Area

     6

Like Queens State Wildlife Area to the north, Thurston Reservoir offers fishing and waterskiing (except during waterfowl season, when boating is no-wake only) in a flat, remote setting. Camping here means risking exposure to the elements—hot sun and vicious summer thunderstorms—but in return you get expansive, open views and incredible plains sunrises. The reservoir is stocked with warm-water species including wiper, tiger muskie, and largemouth bass. Since the ragged banks make shoreline fishing challenging, your best bet is to go by boat.

**Location:** North of Lamar; map B4, grid c6.

**Campsites, facilities:** Dispersed camping is permitted throughout the property. Boat ramps and vault toilets are provided, but there is no drinking water. Leashed pets are permitted.

**Elevation:** 4,200 feet.

**Reservations, fees:** Reservations are not accepted. There is no fee.

**Open:** Year-round.

**Directions:** From U.S. 50 at Lamar, turn north on Hwy. 196 and drive nine miles. Then turn left on County Rd. TT and go one mile west. Turn right on County Rd. 7 and continue one-quarter mile to the reservoir.

**Contact:** Colorado Division of Wildlife, 2126 N. Weber St., Colorado Springs, CO 80907; tel. (719) 227-5200.

## ▤ Holbrook Reservoir State Wildlife Area

     6

One of the few state-run wildlife areas that provide a somewhat developed campground, Holbrook Reservoir nonetheless has remained a well-kept secret. You get basic amenities—water, toilets, and level campsites—plus access to all types of boating, including waterskiing, sailing, and windsurfing, as well as fishing for largemouth bass, wiper, and channel catfish. Most sites are sheltered by plenty of shade and are within walking distance of the shoreline. Small game and waterfowl hunting is permitted.

**Location:** Northwest of La Junta; map B4, grid d1.

**Campsites, facilities:** There are 30 sites for tents or RVs up to 35 feet long. Drinking water, picnic tables, and vault toilets are provided. Boat ramps are available. Leashed pets are permitted.

**Elevation:** 4,100 feet.

**Reservations, fees:** Reservations are not accepted. There is no fee.

**Open:** Year-round.

**Directions:** From Swink, drive three miles north on County Rd. 24.5, turn right on County Rd. FF, and continue one-half mile east to the reservoir.

**Contact:** Colorado Division of Wildlife, 2126 N. Weber St., Colorado Springs, CO 80907; tel. (719) 227-5200.

## 5 John Martin Reservoir State Recreation Area

     7

John Martin Reservoir State Recreation Area encompasses two lakes: huge, eel-shaped John Martin Reservoir, and the smaller Lake Hasty. The campground is east of John Martin Dam, close to Lake Hasty, and offers developed sites with modern bathrooms, showers, and electric hookups. At Lake Hasty, a designated swimming area, a wheelchair-accessible fishing pier, and shoreline access for nonmotorized craft such as canoes and rowboats are within walking distance of the campground. Cottonwoods and other deciduous trees enclose the sites and provide a welcome blanket of shade in the otherwise dry, sweltering plains environment.

John Martin Reservoir offers no developed camping, but it does have boat ramps and is large enough for all types of water sports, including waterskiing, jet skiing, and windsurfing. The shoreline is ragged and devoid of trees, a rough contrast to the lush vegetation around Lake Hasty. However, primitive camping is permitted at no charge along the north and south shorelines—a boon for budget-minded campers. There are no facilities, but if you don't mind roughing it a bit, you'll be rewarded with prime boating access and superb fishing for a variety of warm-water species. Hunting for small game and waterfowl is permitted.

**Location:** East of Las Animas; map B4, grid d4.

**Campsites, facilities:** There are 65 sites for tents or RVs of any length. Drinking water, picnic tables, fire grills, vault and flush toilets, and hot showers are provided. Electric hookups, a waste disposal station, public phone, and boat ramp are available. Some facilities are wheelchair accessible. Leashed pets are permitted.

**Elevation:** 3,900 feet.

**Reservations, fees:** Reservations are not accepted. Sites are $10-14 a night.

**Open:** Year-round.

**Directions:** From Las Animas, drive 18 miles east on U.S. 50 to Hasty. Turn south on County Rd. 24 and continue three miles to the reservoir.

**Contact:** U.S. Army Corps of Engineers, 29955 County Rd. 25.75, Hasty, CO 81044-9715; tel. (719) 336-3476.

## 6 Hud's Campground

   4

A tornado ripped through this camp in the summer of 1997, wrenching trees from their roots and blowing anything loose miles across the plains. Since then the owners have repainted and planted new trees, giving the place a fresh look. The warm, friendly hosts will cheerfully tell you their tornado story, make sure the swimming pool is clean, and give you fishing tips for nearby John Martin Reservoir State Recreation Area.

**Location:** Near John Martin Reservoir; map B4, grid d5.

**Campsites, facilities:** There are 20 full-hookup sites for RVs of any length, and a separate area for tents. Drinking water, picnic tables, fire grills, and bathrooms with hot showers are provided. Laundry facilities, a waste disposal station, store, swimming pool, sports field, and public phone are available. Leashed pets are permitted.

**Elevation:** 4,000 feet.

**Reservations, fees:** Reservations are accepted. Sites are $11-14 a night.

**Open:** Year-round.

**Directions:** From Lamar, drive 15 miles west on U.S. 50.

**Contact:** Hud's Campground, 29995 U.S. 50, McClave, CO 81057; tel. (719) 829-4344.

## 7 Lamar KOA     4

Immaculate and pleasant, this in-town camp features gravel sites and grassy lawns just a short hop from U.S. 50. A Colorado Tourist Information Center is on site, providing facts on the historic Santa Fe Trail and related points of interest. The folks there will even give you free coffee in the morning before you get back on the highway.

**Location:** On the Santa Fe Trail; map B4, grid d5.

**Campsites, facilities:** There are 50 sites for tents or RVs of any length, some with full hookups. Drinking water, picnic tables, fire grills, and bathrooms with hot showers are provided. Laundry facilities, a waste disposal station, store, swimming pool, public phone, and miniature golf are available. Some facilities are wheelchair accessible. Leashed pets are permitted.

**Elevation:** 4,000 feet.

**Reservations, fees:** Reservations are accepted; phone (800) KOA-7626. Sites are $16-22 a night.

**Open:** Year-round.

**Directions:** From Lamar, drive four miles west on U.S. 50.

**Contact:** Lamar KOA, 5385 U.S. 50, Lamar, CO 81052; tel. (719) 336-7625.

## 8 Arkansas River State Wildlife Area    5

This flat, grassy wildlife area is just west of the Kansas border along the Arkansas River. You have two options: fishing and hunting. If neither of those appeals to you, you'll be stuck sitting in the hot sun with no one around and nothing to do but watch the water go by. There are a few crudely fashioned campsites near the river that provide easy streamside access.

**Location:** Near the Kansas border; map B4, grid d9.

**Campsites, facilities:** Dispersed camping is permitted throughout the property. There are no other facilities or drinking water. Leashed pets are permitted.

**Elevation:** 4,100 feet.

**Reservations, fees:** Reservations are not accepted. There is no fee.

**Open:** Year-round.

**Directions:** From Holly, drive four miles east on U.S. 50, turn south on County Rd. 39, and drive three-quarters of a mile, crossing a canal. Turn west at a signed access road and continue one-half mile to the property.

**Contact:** Colorado Division of Wildlife, 2126 N. Weber St., Colorado Springs, CO 80907; tel. (719) 227-5200.

## 🄈 La Junta KOA 　 4

This dry, flat plains campground makes for a decent layover. The sites are level, with green lawns and a sprinkling of Russian olive and Aus trees, plus a swimming pool and a small store. All around you, for miles and miles, are level, vacant plains that go from lush green in the springtime to a dull brown by the end of summer. The draw lies not in the terrain, however, but in the region's historical flavor. This stretch of U.S. 50 is paved on what was once the Santa Fe Trail (a historic plains trade route), and towns in the region have capitalized on this wealth of history by constructing various museums and monuments. The historic trading post of Bent Fort is nearby, as is Vogel Canyon, which features ancient petroglyphs and dinosaur tracks. In La Junta is the Kashaire Indian Museum as well as the Otero Museum, where visitors can see antique displays of wagons and stagecoaches.

**Location:** On the Santa Fe Trail; map B4, grid e0.

**Campsites, facilities:** There are 20 tent sites and 30 sites for RVs of any length, many with full hookups. Drinking water, picnic tables, fire grills, and bathrooms with hot showers are provided. Laundry facilities, a waste disposal station, store, swimming pool, and public phone are available. Leashed pets are permitted.

**Elevation:** 4,000 feet.

**Reservations, fees:** Reservations are accepted; phone (800) KOA-9501. Sites are $18-22.50 a night.

**Open:** March to mid-November.

**Directions:** From La Junta, drive two miles west on U.S. 50.

**Contact:** La Junta KOA, 26680 U.S. 50, La Junta, CO 81050; tel. (719) 384-9580.

## 🄉 Two Buttes Reservoir State Wildlife Area 　 6

The terrain surrounding Two Buttes Reservoir looks much the same as that of the several other wildlife areas in this region: flat, dull, and isolated. Two Buttes hides a couple of interesting features, however. First, it's a little-known spot for rock climbing, with large outcroppings jutting knifelike from the plains floor and lovely large handholds for bouldering. Also surprising are the developed facilities, rare in these parts (especially at a no-cost site), with everything from drinking water to boat ramps to a dump station for RVs. Fishing is mediocre, with prospects for largemouth bass, channel catfish, and bluegill. Limited hunting is permitted.

**Location:** North of Springfield; map B4, grid f6.

**Campsites, facilities:** Dispersed tent or RV camping is permitted throughout the property. Drinking water, picnic tables, and vault toilets are provided. A waste disposal station, boat ramps, and boat docks are available. Leashed pets are permitted.

**Elevation:** 4,300 feet.

**Reservations, fees:** Reservations are not accepted. There is no fee.

**Open:** Year-round.

**Directions:** From U.S. 160 in Springfield, drive 18 miles north on U.S. 287, turn right on County Rd. B.5, and drive three miles east to the reservoir.

**Contact:** Colorado Division of Wildlife, 2126 N. Weber St., Colorado Springs, CO 80907; tel. (719) 227-5200.

## COLORADO'S BEST CAMPGROUNDS

Can't decide where to camp this weekend? Here are my picks for the top 10 overall campgrounds in the state, followed by the best in seven specific categories.

### Top 10 Campgrounds
- South Fork (A1, page 104)
- Rifle Falls State Park (A1, page 108)
- Colorado National Monument (A1, page 117)
- Pearl Lake State Park (A2, page 132)
- Lost Park (A2, page 216)
- YMCA Snow Mountain Ranch (A2, page 181)
- Silver Queen (A2, page 218)
- Taylor Canyon (B2, page 348)
- West Fork (B2, page 392)
- Mueller State Park (B3, page 416)

### Top 10 Camps near Hot Springs
- Indian Springs Resort (A2, page 190)
- Dry Lake (A2, page 140)
- Hot Sulphur Springs State Wildlife Area (A2, page 164)
- Radium State Wildlife Area (A2, page 175)
- 4 J + 1 + 1 RV Park (B1, page 296)
- Cement Creek (B2, page 334)
- San Juan Motel and RV Park (B2, page 401)
- Boot Leg (B2, page 351)
- West Fork (B2, page 392)
- Cottonwood Lake (B2, page 340)

### Top 10 Wheelchair-Accessible Campgrounds
- Jack's Gulch (A2, page 44)
- Thunder Ridge (A3, page 266)
- Meadow Ridge (A3, page 267)
- Cabin Canyon (B1, page 305)
- Ferris Canyon (B1, page 305)
- Ridgway State Park (B1, page 292)
- Silver Jack (B1, page 294)
- Transfer Park (B1, page 311)

- Deer Lakes (B2, page 374)
- Cross D Bar Trout Ranch (B3, page 433)

## Top 10 White-Water Rafting Camps
- Gates of Lodore (A1, page 97)
- Rock Gardens Campground and Rafting (A1, page 114)
- Bradfield (B1, page 304)
- Brown's Campground (B2, page 342)
- Shady Island Resort (B2, page 345)
- Rio Grande (B2, page 381)
- Marshall Park (B2, page 382)
- Palisade (B2, page 384)
- Lazy J Resort and Rafting (B2, page 363)
- Spruce Lodge (B2, page 385)

## Top 10 Equestrian Camps
- Marvine (A1, page 105)
- Jack's Gulch (A2, page 44)
- Shepherd's Rim (A2, page 170)
- Aspen Meadow (A3, page 242)
- Indian Creek (A3, page 256)
- Vallecito (B1, page 312)
- Lone Cone State Wildlife Area (B1, page 295)
- Soap Creek (B2, page 344)
- Sportsman's Supply and RV Park (B2, page 399)
- Cripple Creek Gold Campground (B3, page 417)

## Top 10 Fishing Camps
- Colorado River State Park: Island Acres (A1, page 120)
- Steamboat Lake State Park (A2, page 131)
- Williams Fork Reservoir (A2, page 178)
- Chapman (A2, page 208)
- Wigwam (A3, page 254)
- North Cove (A4, page 275)
- Ferris Canyon (B1, page 305)
- Mosca (B2, page 335)
- Mining Camp RV Resort (B2, page 383)
- Cross D Bar Trout Ranch (B3, page 433)

*(continues)*

## COLORADO'S BEST CAMPGROUNDS  *(continued)*

### Top 10 Bird-Watching Camps
- Swinging Bridge (A1, page 95)
- Crow Valley (A3, page 231)
- Barbour Ponds State Park (A3, page 240)
- Barr Lake RV Park (A3, page 244)
- Chatfield State Park (A3, page 250)
- Foster Grove (A4, page 274)
- Target Tree (B1, page 319)
- Navajo State Park (B1, page 328)
- San Luis Lakes State Park (B2, page 388)
- Trinidad Lake State Park (B3, page 433)

### Top 10 Camps for Hiking
- Lynx Pass (A2, page 163)
- Lost Park (A2, page 216)
- Sweetwater (A2, page 185)
- Golden Gate Canyon State Park (A3, pages 242-244)
- Transfer Park (B1, page 308)
- Pine River (B1, page 327)
- Purgatory (B1, page 310)
- Amphitheater (B1, page 297)
- Lost Lake (B2, page 333)
- Lost Trail (B2, page 379)

# INDEX

## A

A & A Mesa Verde Resort: 317
Abyss Lake Trailhead: 201
Agnes Vaille Falls: 352
Aguilar: 444
air beds/foam mattresses: 42
Alamosa: Campground 404-405; KOA 398; River 398, 403-404
Alamosa-Rock Creek Trail: 397-398
Alma State Wildlife Area: 213
Almont: 346
Alpen Rose RV Park: 322-323
Alpine: Plateau 367; Tunnel 353
Alta Lakes: 301
Alvarado/Alvarado Creek: 369-370
American Lakes: 144
Ami's Acres: 113-114
amphitheaters: 247, 250, 297
amusement park: 428
Anasazi ruins: 314-316
Angel of Shavano: 355
Animas: Overlook 320; River 303, 310, 321-322; Valley 322
Animas-Silverton Wagon Trail: 311
Antero Reservoir: 224
Anthracite Creek: 283, 333
Antonito: 407-411
Arapaho Bay: 167-168
Arapaho National Forest: 165-168, 176-181, 183-190, 195-197

archaeological sites: Chimney Rock Archaeological Area 327-328, 399, 405; Dinosaur National Monument 98-100; Florissant Fossil Beds 424; Mesa Verde National Park 316-319; petroglyphs 96, 453; Ute Mountain Tribal Park 314-315
Archuleta Creek Trail: 393
Arkansas River: 212, 340-342, 351, 355-356, 361, 363-366, 427-429, 431, 433; KOA 365; Rim Campground 340-341; South Arkansas River 354-355; State Wildlife Area 452-453
Aspen: 155-156, 198-199, 217-220
Aspen-Basalt Campground: 205
Aspen Glade: 408
Aspen Glen: 147
Aspenglen: 158
Aspen Meadow: 242-243
Aspenridge RV Park: 385
Aspen Trails Campground: 282-283
ATVs: see motorcycles/ATVs
Aurora: 249
Avalanche: 204-205

## B

Baby Doe: 210
backpacking boots: 35-36
Bailey: 202-203
Barbour Ponds State Park: 240
Barr Lake RV Park: 244
Basalt: 205-207

Basic Designs Ceramic: 57
Battlement Mesa RV Park: 111
Bayfield: 327
Bear Creek/Bear Creek Lake Park: 247-248
Bear Lake: 157, 173, 442-443
Bear River Dispersed Sites: 172
bears: general discussion 68-74; bear-proof food lockers/bags 68, 71; Lone Cone State Wildlife Area 295; West Rifle Creek State Wildlife Area 106-107; see also specific place
Beaver Creek: Reservoir 395-396; Trail 133
Beaver Lake: 293-294
Beaver Meadows Resort Ranch: 138
Bellaire Lake: 138-139
Belle of Colorado: 210-211
Bellvue: 136-137, 149
Bent Fort: 453
Berthoud Pass: 187
best campgrounds: 454-455
bicycling: see mountain biking/bicycling
Big Bend: 136-137
Big Blue: 367-368; Wilderness 294, 297, 367
Big Cimarron: 293
Big Creek: 126; Falls 133; Lakes 133-134
Big Dominguez: 285
Big J RV Park: 119
Big Lake: 404
Big Meadows/Reservoir: 393-395
Big Molas Lake: 303-304

Big South: 147
Big Thompson River: 162, 232, 235-236
Billy Creek State Wildlife Area: 288
Bishop's Castle: 436, 439
bivouac bags: 45-46
Black Canyon: 289-291; RV Park 291
Black Forest: 423
Black Hawk: 183-185, 190, 243
Blacktail Creek: 174
Blanca/Blanca RV Park: 398-399

## BIRDWATCHING

10 best birdwatching camps: 455
Barbour Ponds State Park: 240
Barr Lake RV Park: 244
Boyd Lake State Park: 236-237
Chatfield State Park: 250-251
Crook: 96
Crow Valley Recreation Area: 231
Foster Grove: 274-275
Hide-A-Way Camp-ground: 400
Indian Run State Wildlife Refuge: 99-100
Jackson Lake State Park: 238-239
Miramonte Reservoir State Wildlife Area: 294-295
Navajo Reservoir: 329
Pumphouse: 175
Rock Creek State Wildlife Area: 173-174
San Luis Lakes State Park: 388
Swinging Bridge: 95
Target Tree: 319
Viking RV Park: 112
Watson Lake: 230
Yeoman Park: 191-192

Blanco River: 405
Bliss State Wildlife Area: 136
Blodgett: 193-194
Blue Arrow Campground: 160-161
Blue Creek Lodge: 383-384
Blue Lake: 443; Trail 145
Blue Mesa Reservoir: 287, 344-345, 356-359, 367
Blue Mountain: 415; Village 100
Blue River: 178, 186
Blue Spruce RV Park: 229-230
Bogan Flats: 216
boiling water: 58-59
Bolam Pass: 300
Bonny Lake: 274-276
Boot Leg: 351
boots/shoes: 34-36
Boulder: 183; County Fairgrounds 239; Mountain Lodge 241
Box Canyon Trail: 308
Boyd Lake State Park: 236-237
Bradfield: 304-305
Brainard Lake: 168
B-R-B Crystal River Resort: 204
Breckenridge: 198
Bridge: 389-390
Brighton: 244
Bristlecone Pine Scenic Area: 213
Bristol Head: 381
Broken Arrow Campground: 362-363
Broken Rib Spring/Trail: 185
Broomfield: 244
Bross Peak: 213

Brown's Campground: 342-343
Browns Gulch: 347
Browns Park: 135-136; National Wildlife Refuge 95-96; State Wildlife Area 95
Bruce Spruce Ranch: 393
Brush Creek: 191
Brush Memorial Campground: 273-274
Buckingham: 182-183
Bucks: 171
Buena Vista: 340-343, 352; KOA 342
Buffalo: 251-252; Creek 251-252; Meadows Trail 223; Mountain Biking Area 251-252; Pass 368; Springs 224; Trail 243
Buffalo Bill's Royal Gorge Campground: 428
Burning Bear: 201-202
Burning Mountain RV Park: 113
Burnt Timber Trailhead: 311
Burro Bridge: 299
butane: 19-20
Byers Creek: 180

**C**

Cabin Canyon: 305
Cache la Poudre River: 136-138, 146-151, 230
Cache la Poudre Wilderness: 149
Cadillac Jack's: 267
Calhan: 267
Cameron Peak: 213
Camp Dick: 169-170
Campers Village: 422-423
campfires: 20-22
Campground at Woodland Park: 264

Camp Hale Memorial: 194-195
camping gear: checklist of 90-91; clothing 27-39; drinking water 54-59; first aid 48-54, 59-60; fishing gear 63-68; food/cooking gear 16-27; sleeping gear 39-42; stoves 16-20; tents 42-46; *see also specific place*
Camp Trail: 372
Cannibal Pleateau Trailhead: 373
canoeing: *see* rafting/floating/canoeing/kayaking
Cañon City: 363, 366, 427-430
Cañon Infierno Trail: 374
Canyon Creek: 353
Carbondale: 204-205, 216
Carnero Creek: 376
Carter Lake: 234-235
Carter Valley Campground: 234
Cascade: 352-353
Cascade Creek: 310, 352
casinos: Black Hawk 184; Central City 184; Cripple Creek 425-426; Towaoc 315, 328
Castle Lakes Campground Resort: 373
Castle Rock: 241; KOA 258
Cataract Creek: 176-177
Cathedral/Cathedral Rock: 387
caves/caverns: *see* spelunking
Cawthon Motel and Campground: 445
Cayton: 300

Cebolla: 375; Creek 368, 374-375
Cedar Creek RV Park: 288
Cedaredge: 283
Cement Creek: 334-335
Centennial: RV Park 287; Trail 262
Central City: 183
Central City/Black Hawk KOA: 184
Chalk: Cliffs 351; Creek 342, 350-351; Lake 352
Chambers Lake: 145-146
Chapman: 208; Reservoir 163
Chasm Lake: 159
Chasm View Nature Trail: 289
Chatfield Reservoir/State Park: 250-251
Cheesman Reservoir: 253-254
Cherry Creek: State Park 249; Valley 319
Cheyenne Mountain: 422
Chicago Creek: 188-189
Chief Hosa: 245
Chief Ouray Mine: 297
Chimney Rock: Archaeological Area 327-328, 399, 405; Campground 405
choosing a campsite: 46, 454-455
Chris Park Group: 311
Chromo RV Park: 405-406
Cimarron: 290-291
Cimarrona Creek/Trail: 391
Cimarron River: 293
Circle the Wagons RV Park: 440-441
Cisneros Trail: 439
citronella: 50-51

cleaning fish, basic steps to: 26
Clear Creek: 245
Clear Lake: 188
clothing: general discussion 27-39; checklist 90
Coachlight RV Park and Motel: 265
Coaldale: 364-365
Cobbett Lake: 122-123
Cochetopa Pass: 369
Coffee Pot Springs: 185-186
Cog Railway: 419
Coke Oven State Wildlife Area: 208-209
Cold Spring: 338
Cold Spring Mountain: 95
Cold Springs: 172-173, 183-184
Coleman Max Performance Fuel: 19-20
Collbran: 125-127
Collegiate Peaks: 340; Campground 339; Wilderness 218-220, 335-336, 339, 342
Colorado Alligator Farm: 398
Colorado Bird Observatory: 244
Colorado Campground: 261-262
Colorado National Monument: 116-117
Colorado River: 111-112, 114-115, 117, 120-121, 157, 164, 166, 175; State Park/Island Acres 120-121
Colorado Springs: 262, 419-424, 426; South KOA 426
Colorado State Forest: 144-146

Colorado Trail: 202, 209, 220-223, 252, 255, 300, 320, 339, 342, 351-352, 355, 375

Columbine: 190, 286

Comanche National Grassland: 445

Comanche Peak Wilderness: 147-148

Comstock: 397-398

Conejos: 406; Valley 410

Conejos River: 403-404, 406-410; Campground 409

Continental Divide: 131, 140-141, 157, 187, 195-196, 200, 242, 336, 350, 353, 355, 368-369, 373, 375, 379, 392-393, 396-397, 402

Continental Divide National Scenic Trail: 408

Conundrum Creek/Hot Springs: 218

cooking: checklist 90; gear 22-23; stoves/fires 16-22; tips 23-27

Cool Pines RV Park: 401

Coors Field: 248

Copper Pass: 218

Cordova Pass: 444

Corral Creek Trail: 148

Cortez: 313-315, 328

Cortez-Mesa Verde KOA: 314

costs: 24-27; see also specific place

Cotopaxi: 365

cots: 42

Cottonwood: 125; Creek 339, 364; Hot Springs 339-340; Lake 125, 339-340; RV Campground 189; RV Park 321

Cove: 344

Cow Creek: 177

Cowdrey Lake State Wildlife Area: 135

Cozy Comfort RV Park: 315

Crag Crest: 124-125

The Crags/Crags Trail: 417

Craig: 96-97, 99-100; KOA 99; Peak 191

Crawford Reservoir/State Park: 285-286

Crazy Horse Resort: 340

Creede: 378-384

Crested Butte: 283, 333-334

Crestone Needle: 377

Cripple Creek: 264, 417-418, 425; District Museum 425; Gold Campground 417; KOA 426; Travel Park and Hospitality House 425

Crook: 96, 271

Crooked Creek: 378

cross-country/downhill skiing: Aspen-Basalt Campground 205; The Crags 417; Lone Cone State Wildlife Area 295; Monarch Ski Area 354; Purgatory 310; South Meadows 262-263; Telluride 300-302; Wildhorn 261; Winter Park 181, 187

Cross Creek: 396-397

Cross D Bar Trout Ranch: 433-434

Crow Valley Recreation Area: 231

cryptosporidium: 54-56

Crystal Meadows Ranch: 283-284

Crystal River: 205, 216

Cub Lake Trail: 158

Cuchara River Cabins and Campground: 441

Culebra Pass/Range: 442-444

Cumberland Pass: 350

Cumbres Pass: 407-408

Cumbres-Toltec Scenic Railroad: 407-410

Curecanti National Recreation Area: 290-291, 344, 356-360

Cutthroat: 171

D

Dakota Campground: 442

Dakota Ridge RV Park: 246

dancing: 326, 370-371

dangers: see safety/emergencies

Davenport: 437

Davis Springs: 178

Dearhammer: 207

DeBeque Canyon: 120

Deep Lake: 110

Deer: Creek 202; Lakes 374; Mountain 158

Deerlodge Park: 98-99

DEET: 49-51

Delaney Butte Lakes State Wildlife Area: 143

Delores/West Delores River: 299-300, 308, 315; Canyon 297, 315; RV Park 308; Valley 298

Delta: 281-282, 285

Delta-Grand Mesa KOA: 282

Delux RV Park: 247-248

Democrat Peak: 213

denatured alcohol: 20

Denny Creek Trailhead: 339

Denver: 247-248; Creek 165; Denver

East/Strasburg KOA
249-250; Denver
Meadows RV Park 248-
249; Denver North
Campground 244;
Denver Northwest/
Hudson KOA 241; Mint
248; Zoo 248
Derrick RV Park: 445-446
Devil's
Head/Peak/National
Recreation Trail: 257
De Weese Reservoir
State Wildlife Area:
432-433
Dexter: 223
Diamond Campground
and RV: 263-264
diarrhea: 54-56
Difficult: 218
Dillon: 195; Pinnacles
Trail 358; Reservoir 195-
198
Dinner Station: 336
Dinosaur National
Monument: 98-100
Divide: 416
Divide Fork: 284-285
Dixon Canyon Dam: 230
Dolores/West Dolores
River: 295, 298, 304-305,
307, 309
Dorchester: 335-336
Dove Creek: 298
Dowdy Lake: 139
downhill skiing: see
cross-country/downhill
skiing
drinking water: boiling
water 58-59; filtering
systems 55-59;
giardia/cryptosporidiu
m 54-55; untreated 59;
water purification pills
59; see also specific
place

Dry Gulch: 358
Dry Lake: 140
Dumont Lake: 154
Durango: 320-323
Durango North KOA:
321-322
Dutch Hill: 131-132

E
Eads: 449-450
Eagle River: 193-194
Eagles Nest Wilderness:
186
East Beach: 276
East Brush Creek: 192
East Creek Trail: 324
East Elk Group Camp:
357-358
East Fork: 402-403
East Marvine: 106
East Portal: 290
East River: 347
Echo Basin Dude Ranch
Resort: 319
Echo Lake: 189
Echo Park: 98
Eggleston/Eggleston
Lake: 123-124
Elbert Creek: 220-221
Elevenmile Canyon
Reservoir: 343-344, 415
Eleven Mile State Park:
343-344
Elk Creek: 112, 357, 407;
Campground 156
Elkhead Mountains: 97
Elk Meadows
Campground: 402
Elk Mountains: 334
Elk River: 132-133
Elk Wallow: 208
Elliott Creek: 176
Embargo Creek: 387
emergencies: see
safety/emergencies

equestrian camps: see
horseback riding/horse
facilities
Erickson Springs: 333
Escalante State Wildlife
Area: 285
Estes Park: 158-162, 168-
169, 231-233;
Campground 161; KOA
160
ethics: 79-83
Evergreen Lake: 203

F
Fairplay: 214-215, 224
Falcon Meadow: 424
Fall Creek Trail: 192
Fall River: 158
Father Dyer: 209-210
Ferris Canyon: 305-306
fires: campfire building
20-22; dangers 19, 22
Fireside Motel: 235-236
first aid: general
discussion 47-48, 90-91;
checklist 90-91;
cryptosporidium 54-56;
drinking water 54-59;
foot care 38; giardia 54-
56; gnats 48-49;
horseflies 48-49;
hypothermia 59-60;
mosquitoes 48-51; no-
see-ums 48-51; poison
oak 52-54; repellents
49-51; sunburn 54; ticks
51-52
First Need Deluxe: 56
Fish Creek
Reservoir/Falls: 141,
152
fish/fishing: general
discussion 63-68; 10
best fishing camps 455;
cleaning fish, basic
steps to 26; fishing

gear checklist 91; *see also specific place*
Five Branches Camper Park: 325
Five Points: 366
Flatiron Reservoir: 234
Flat Rocks: 256-257
Flat Tops Wilderness: 101, 105-106, 163, 170-171
float trips: *see* rafting/floating/canoeing/kayaking
Florida: 311-312
Florissant: 261
Florissant Fossil Beds: 424
Floyd's RV Park: 430
Flying A Motel and RV Park: 281-282
Flying Saucer Park: 248
food: cleaning fish, basic steps to 26; jerky preparation 27; planning 23; stoves/cooking gear 16-23; tips 23-27
foot care: 33-39
Fort Collins: 229-231, 236; Mile High KOA 229; North KOA 229
Fort Gorge Campground and RV Park: 429
Fort Morgan: 239
Fort's Mobile Home Park: 435
Fossil Ridge: Trail 337; Wilderness 337-338, 349
fossils: Dinosaur National Monument 98-100; Florissant Fossil Beds 424
Foster Grove: 274-275
Fountain Creek: 418, 422; RV Park 421

4x4 touring: *see* off-roading
4J + 1 + 1 RV Park: 296-297
Fourmile Creek: 214
Four Seasons RV Park: 361
Fourth of July Trailhead: 182
Fraser/Fraser Experimental Forest: 180-181
Freeman: 96-98
French Creek: 185
Frisco: 195-197
Fruita Monument RV Park: 116-117
Fryingpan River: 207-208
fuels for camping stoves: 18-20
Fulford Cave: 192
Fun Country Amusement Park: 428

**G**
games: 73-87; *see also specific place*
Garden of the Gods: 419-422; Campground 420-421
Gardner: 440
Garfield: 354
The Gate: 367
Gates of Lodore: 97-98
Gateview: 356
Geneva Park/Creek: 200-201
Georgetown: 188
Georgia Pass: 199
ghost towns: 433
giardia: 54-56
Gibson Lake Trail: 200
Gillette Flats: 417
Glacier Basin/Creek: 157
Glacier Rim: 182

Glen Echo Resort: 148-149
Glenwood Hot Springs: 204
Glenwood Springs: 105, 110, 112-115
gnats: 48-49
Gold Creek: 338, 349
Golden: 242-246
Golden Clear Creek RV Park: 245
Golden Eagle Ranch: 421-422
Golden Gate Canyon: 242-243; State Park 244
Golden Terrace South RV Resort: 245-246
Goldfield Campground: 419-420
Gold Park: 194
Goose Creek: 253
Goose Lake: 382
Gore: Creek 186; Pass 174-175
Gorton's Shady Grove RV Park: 276-277
Gothic: 334
Gould: 144-145, 155
Goulding Creek Trail: 310
Graham Creek: 326
Granby: 166-168; Reservoir 122
Grand Junction: 95, 117-120, 285
Grand Lake: 156-157, 166-167
Grand Mesa: National Forest 121-126, 281-282; Scenic Byway 282
Grandview: 147-148; RV Park 384
Graneros Gorge: 439
Granite: 141
Grant: 200-202
Grape Creek RV Park: 433

Great Sand Dunes: National Monument 388-389, 398; Oasis 389
Greeley RV Park: 238
Greenhorn Mountains: 434; Valley 439
Green Mountain: 252-253; Falls 418-419; Reservoir 175-178, 186
Green Ridge: 166-167
Green River: 96-98
grizzly bears: 70-74
Grizzly Creek: 142, 220
Grizzly-Helena Trail: 141
Grizzly Lake: 220
Groundhog Reservoir State Wildlife Area: 298
group camps: East Elk Group Camp 357-358; Jack's Gulch Group Camp 151-152; Meadows Group Camp 252; Mountain Park Group Camp 150; Pickle Gulch Group Camp 184-185; Pike Communtiy Group Camp 262; Ponderosa Group Camp 438; Red Rocks Group Camp 263; Rifleman Phillips Group Camp 243-244; Spruce Group Camp 438-439; Windy Point Group Camp 197
Guanella Pass: 188-189; Scenic Byway 188
guides/outfitters: Aspen-Basalt Campground 205; Boot Leg 351; Brown's Campground 342; Cool Pines RV Park 401; Four Seasons RV Park 361; Hidden Valley Ranch 364; Indian Springs

Campground 430; Lakeview Resort 371; Moon Valley Resort 394; Pleasant Valley RV Park 362; Pollard's Ute Lodge 104; Rincon 363; Riverwood Inn and RV Park 281; Rock Gardens Campground and Rafting 114; RV Station 429; Spruce Lodge 385; Whispering Pines Campground 365; Wild Wild Rest 318
Gunnison: 345-347, 357, 360-361; KOA 360-361; National Forest 333-339, 345-350, 353-354, 367-368, 372-375; National Park 286, 289, 291; River 281-282, 289-290, 345-347, 360, 367, 370-373; Diversion Tunnel 290
Gunsight Pass: 338

**H**
Haggard's RV Campground: 430-431
Hagler Reservoir: 235
Hahns Peak Lake: 131
Halfmoon: 221
Half Moon Pass Trail: 192
Hall Valley: 200
Handcart: 200
Handies Peak: 373
The Hangin' Tree: 286-287
Hankins Pass Trail: 253
Happy Camper RV Park: 400
Happy Meadows: 260
hats: 30-31, 33
Haviland Lake: 310-311
Hayden Creek: 364-365
Haypress: 281
hazards: see safety/ emergencies

Heart Lake: 109
Heart of the Rockies Campground: 355-356
Heaton Bay: 195
Hebron: 142-143
Helena Trailhead: 133
helicopter tours: 304
Hells Hole Trail: 190
Henson Creek RV Park: 370
Hermosa: Cliffs 310; Creek Trail 309; Meadows Campground 322
Hidden Lakes: 142-243
Hidden Valley: 374; Ranch 364
Hide-A-Way Campground: 400
The Hideout Cabins and Campground: 115
Highlander RV Park: 371
Highline State Park: 115-116
Highway Springs: 394-395
hiking: 10 best hiking camps 455; boots 34-36; checklist of hiking gear 90; foot care 33-34, 38-39; socks 36-39; see also specific place; trails/trailheads
Himes Peak: 170
Hiner Springs: 105
Hinman: 132-133
Hogback Ridge Trail: 441
Holbrook Reservoir State Wildlife Area: 450-451
Holly: 452
Holy Cross: City 194; Wilderness 193, 208
Home Moraine Trailer Park: 136
Homestake Canyon/ Creek/Reservoir: 193-194

Homestake Creek: 193
Hope Pass: 222
Hornsilver: 193
horseback riding/horse facilities: general discussion 80; 10 best equestrian camps 455; Alpen Rose RV Park 322; Aspen Meadow 242-243; Aspenridge RV Park: 385; Beaver Meadows Resort Ranch 138; Big Creek Lakes 133-134; Bruce Spruce Ranch 393; Bucks 171; Buena Vista KOA 342; Buffalo Bill's Royal Gorge Campground 428; Burning Mountain RV Park 113; Carter Valley Campground 234-235; Castle Lakes Campground Resort 373; Chatfield State Park 250-251; Cherry Creek State Park 249; Colorado National Monument 117; Colorado State Forest 144-145; Cripple Creek 425; Cripple Creek Gold Campground 417; Cross D Bar Trout Ranch 433-434; East Marvine 106; Echo Basin Dude Ranch Resort 319; Estes Park KOA 160; Freeman 96-97; Garden of the Gods Campground 420-421; Glacier Basin 157; Himes Peak 170; Hornsilver 193; Horsetooth Reservoir 230; Indian Creek 256; Indian Run State Wildlife Refuge 99-100; Indian Springs Campground 429-430; Iron City 350-351; Jack's Gulch 151; Kelsey 253-254;

## HUNTING

Aspen Glade: 408
Billy Creek State Wildlife Area: 288
Coke Oven State Wildlife Area: 208-209
Crawford State Park: 285-286
De Weese Reservoir State Wildlife Area: 432-433
East Beach: 276
Eleven Mile State Park: 343
Escalante State Wildlife Area: 285
Foster Grove: 274-275
Groundhog Reservoir State Wildlife Area: 298
Holbrook Reservoir State Wildlife Area: 450-451
Hot Sulphur Springs State Wildlife Area: 164
Huerfano State Wildlife Area: 440
Jensen State Wildlife Area: 101
Joe Moore Reservoir State Wildlife Area: 316
John Martin Reservoir State Recreation Area: 451

Karval Reservoir State Wildlife Area: 449
Lake Henry State Wildlife Area: 432
Lake John State Wildlife Area: 134
Lathrop State Park: 441-442
Meredith Reservoir State Wildlife Area: 436
Middle Taylor Creek Wildlife Area: 369
Miramonte Reservoir State Wildlife Area: 294-295
Mogote: 409
Moon Valley Resort: 394
Mount Evans State Wildlife Area: 203
North Cove: 275-276
North Sterling Reservoir State Park: 272
Oak Ridge State Wildlife Area: 104
Owl Mountain State Wildlife Area: 143-144
Pearl Lake State Park: 132
Piceance State Wildlife Area: 102
Prewitt Reservoir State Wildlife Area: 273

Pueblo State Park: 434
Queens State Wildlife Area: 449-450
Radium State Wildlife Area: 175
Reverends Ridge: 242
Rock Creek State Wildlife Area: 173-174
San Luis Lakes State Park: 388
Spanish Peaks State Wildlife Area: 444
Stagecoach State Park: 152-153
Steamboat Lake State Park: 131-132
Summit Reservoir State Wildlife Area: 315-316
Thurston Reservoir State Wildlife Area: 450
Trinidad Lake State Park: 444-445
Two Buttes Reservoir State Wildlife Area: 453
Vega State Park: 125
Wagon Wheel: 275
West Rifle Creek State Wildlife Area: 106-107
see also specific place

Lakeview Resort 371-372; Lazy J Resort and Rafting 363-364; Lone Cone State Wildlife Area 295; Longs Peak 158-159; Lynx Pass 163; Marvine 105-106; Moon Valley Resort 394; Moraine Park 158; Mount Princeton RV Park 341; North Canyon 325; North Fork 101; Paonia State Park 284; Pine Point 324; Pollard's Ute Lodge 104; Ponderosa 359; Priest Gulch Campground and RV Park 309; Rabbit Valley 116; Rifle Mountain Park 108-109; Shepherd's Rim 170-171; Soap Creek 344; South Fork 104-105, 179-180; Stagecoach Campground and RV Park 103; Stagecoach State Park 152-153; Stage Stop Campground 250; Steamboat Lake State Park 131-132; Sugar Loafin' RV/ Campground 212; Sweetwater 185; Tall Texas Campground 345-346; Tiger Run Resort 198; Timber Creek Campground 157; trail ethics/manners 80; Trinidad Lake State Park 444-445; Vallecito 312-313; Weminuche Wilderness 303; Wild Wild Rest 318; Winding River Resort Village

156; YMCA Snow Mountain Ranch 181; see also specific place
horseflies: 48-49
Horseshoe: 173, 179, 214; Park 158; Reservoir 441
Horsetooth Reservoir: 230-231
hot springs: general discussion 454; 10 best camps near hot springs 454; Conundrum Hot Springs 218; Cottonwood Hot Springs 339-340; Mount Princeton Hot Springs 342, 351-352; Penny Hot Springs 204; Rainbow Hot Springs 392; Salida Hot Springs Aquatic Center 361; Splashland Hot Springs 398; Strawberry Park Hot Springs 140, 152; Yampa Hot Springs Spa and Vapor Caves 115
Hot Sulphur Springs State Wildlife Area: 164
House Creek: 306
Howard: 362
Hud's Campground: 451-452
Hudson: 241
Huerfano River/State Wildlife Area: 440
human waste: 53; see also specific place
Hunter-Fryingpan Wilderness: 208, 220-221
hypothermia: 59-60

**I**
ice skating rink: 401
Idaho Springs: 187, 189-190
Illium Valley: 300-301

Independence Pass: 221
Indian Creek: 256; Trail 442
Indian Fire Nature Trail: 286
Indian Peaks Wilderness: 169, 182-183, 229
Indian Run State Wildlife Refuge: 99-100
Indian Springs: Campground 429-430; Resort 190
Indpendence Pass: 220
information/resource guide: 89; see also specific place
insect repellents: 49-51
Insulite pads: 41
Inter Laken Historical Site: 222
Irish Canyon: 96
Iron City: 350-351
Iron Edge Trail: 192
Iron Springs: 291-292
Island Acres/Lake: 120-121
Ivy Creek/Ivy Creek Trail: 382

**J**
Jack's Gulch: 151; Group Camp 151-152
Jackson Creek: 257-258
Jackson Lake State Park: 238-239
Jackson State Wildlife Area: 238
Jefferson: 198-199, 216, 225; Creek 199; Lake 198-199
Jensen State Wildlife Area: 101
jerky preparation: 27
jet skis: see waterskiing/PWC riding

Joe Moore Reservoir State Wildlife Area: 316
Joe Wright Creek: 147
John Martin Reservoir/State Recreation Area: 451-452
John May Museum Center: 421
Johnson's Corner Campground: 237-238
Josey's Mogote Meadow: 410
Jumbo: 121; Reservoir 121, 271; State Wildlife Area 271
Junction Creek: 320
The Junction RV Park: 435-436
Junction West RV Park: 118

**K**
Karval/Karval Reservoir State Wildlife Area: 449
Kashaire Indian Museum: 453
Katadyn U.S.A. Mini Filter: 58
Kawuneeche Valley: 157
kayaking: see rafting/floating/canoeing/kayaking
Keener Lake: 172
Kelly Dahl: 183
Kelly Flat: 150
Kelsey: 253-254
Kenosha Pass: 202
kerosene: 20
kid stuff: 73-79; see also specific place
Killpecker Trailhead/Creek: 137
Kiser Creek: 123-124
Kite Lake: 213
Klines Folly: 109-110

Kremmling: 164, 174
Kroeger: 319-320

**L**
Lady Moon Trail: 139
La Garita: 387; Mountains 385-386; Wilderness 374-375
La Junta KOA: 453
Lake Charles: 192
Lake City: 367-368, 370-375
Lake Creek: 366
Lake Fork: 358-359, 404
Lake George: 259, 416
Lake Granby: 165, 167-168
Lake Hasty: 451
Lake Henry State Wildlife Area: 432, 435
Lake Irwin: 333-334
Lake Isabel: 437-438
Lake John State Wildlife Area: 134
Lake of the Rockies Resort: 265-266
Lake San Cristobal: 371-373
Lakeview: 223, 337; Resort 371-372
Lakewood: 247
Lamar: 450, 452; KOA 452
La Mesa RV Park: 313
La Plata: Canyon 319; Mountains 318-319; River 320
LaPorte: 229
La Poudre Pass Trailhead: 148
Laramie River: 145
Larkspur: 258
Lathrop State Park: 441-442
LaVeta: 440-441
La Vista: 439
layering clothing: 29-30
Lazy G Campground: 314

Lazy J Resort and Rafting: 363-364
Leadville: 209-213, 221-223; RV Corral 212-213
Leave No Trace Program: 16; see also minimum impact camping
Lemon Reservoir: 311-312
Lightner Creek Campground 320-321
Limon KOA: 258-259
Lincoln Creek: 219; Dispersed Sites 219-220
Lincoln Gulch: 219
Lincoln Peak: 213
Lindon: 274
Link McIntyre Trailhead: 135
lip balm: 33
Little Bear: 122
Little Cimarron River: 291
Little Fruita Reservoir: 281
Little Mattie: 206-207
Little Maud: 206
Little Squaw Creek: 378-379
Littleton: 251
Lizard Head Wilderness: 296, 299-300, 302
Lodgepole: 198, 337
Loma: 115-116
Lone Cone State Wildlife Area: 295
Lone Duck Campground: 418-419
Lone Rock: 254-255
Long Draw Reservoir: 147-148
Longmont: 239-240
Longs Peak: 158-159
Lon Hagler State Wildlife Area: 235
Lookout Mountain: 245, 403

loosing your way: 60-62
Los Pinos River: 324-327
Lost Burro Campground: 424-425
Lost Creek: 380; Wilderness 216, 225, 252-254, 259
Lost Lake: 145, 333; Slough 333; Trail 311
Lost Man: 220
Lostman Creek: 220
Lost Park: 216
Lost Trail Campground: 379-380
Lottis Creek: 338
Loveland: 233-238, 240; RV Village 237
Lower Beaver Creek: 395-396
Lower Piedra: 327-328
Lower Queens Reservoir: 449
Lowry: 197
LPG (liquid petroleum gas): 18
Luders Creek: 369
Lyme disease: 51-52
Lynx Pass: 163-164

**M**
McDonald Flats: 177-178
McIntyre Lake: 135
Mack Mesa Lake: 115
McPhee: 306-307; Reservoir 306-307, 315; RV Park 307
Mancos: 316-319; Reservoir 318; River 319; State Park 318
Mandall Lakes: 173
Manitou Lake: 261-262
Manitou Springs: 419
manners: 79-83
Manor RV Park: 159-160

Maroon Bells-Snowmass Wilderness: 204-205, 216-218
Maroon Creek/Trail: 217-218
Marshall Ash Village RV Park: 277
Marshall Park: 382-383
Martin Lake: 441
Marvine: 105-106
Mary's Lake Campground: 162
Mavreeso: 298-299
Maybell: 95-96
May Natural History Museum: 421
May Queen: 209
Meadow Lake: 105
Meadowlark RV Park: 274
Meadow Ridge: 267
Meadows: 153; Group Camp 252
Meeker 106
Meeker: 101-104
Meredith Reservoir State Wildlife Area: 435-436
Meridian: 202-203
Mesa Campground: 360
Mesa Oasis Campground: 314-315
Mesa Verde: 314; National Park 316-319; Point Kampark 317
Michigan Creek: 199-200; Reservoir 144
Michigan River: 155
Middle Mountain: 324
Middle Quartz: 353
Middle St. Vrain Creek: 169
Middle Taylor Creek Wildlife Area: 369
Mile High Stadium: 248
Mill Creek: 372
Miller Creek: 312

Mineral Creek: 301; Trailhead 375
minimum impact camping: campfires 22; choosing a site 46; keeping wilderness wild 78; marking trails 37; planning ahead 86; respecting others 80; sanitation 53
Mining Camp RV Resort: 383
Miramonte Reservoir State Wildlife Area: 294-295
Mirror Lake: 338-339
Mitchell Range: 400
Mix Lake: 403-404
Mizpah: 187-188
Mobile City RV Park: 118-119
Mogote: 409
Molas Lake Park: 303-304
Mollie X: 206
Molly Brown: 211
Molly Gulch: 253
Monarch: Park 354; Pass 354-355; Ski Area 354
Montrose: 286-288; RV Resort 287-288
Monumental Peak: 355
Monument Lake: 265
Moon Valley Resort: 394
Moraine Park: 158
Morefield: 316-317
Morrison: 250, 252-253; Creek 295; Divide Trail 163
Morrow Point Lake/Dam: 290
Mosca: 335, 388-389
mosquitoes: 48-51
Mosquito Pass: 209
motorcycles/ATVs: Columbine 190; Davenport 437; Elk

motorcycles/ATVs *(cont):*
Creek 407; Indian Creek
256; Island Lake 122;
Jackson Creek 257-258;
Painted Rocks 261;
Rabbit Valley 116;
Rampart Range
Motorcycle Area 256-
257; Spectacle Lake
406-407; Trail Creek 260;
Wildhorn 260-261
mountain climbing: *see*
rock/mountain climbing

Mountaindale Camp-
ground: 423
mountaineering boots: 35
Mountain Meadow
Campground: 187
Mountain Park Group
Camp: 150
Mountain Sheep Point:
297-298
Mount Bierstadt: 201
Mount Elbert: 212, 221-223;
Hydroelectric Plant 223

Mount Evans: 183, 201;
State Wildlife Area 203;
Wilderness 188-190, 202
Mount Margaret Trail: 139
Mount Massive: 221;
Wilderness 220, 222
Mount of the Holy Cross:
194
Mount Princeton: 351-352;
Hot Springs 342, 351-
352; RV Park 341-342
Mount Shavano: 355
Mount Zirkel Wilderness:
132-133, 140-142

## MOUNTAIN BIKING/BICYCLING

Barr Lake RV Park: 244
Bear Creek Lake Park: 247
Beaver Meadows Resort
Ranch: 138
Blue River: 186
Boulder Mountain Lodge:
241
Boyd Lake State Park: 236-
237
Buena Vista KOA: 342
Buffalo Mountain Biking
Area: 251-252
Buffalo Springs: 224
Byers Creek: 180
Camp Dick: 169-170
Campground at Woodland
Park: 264
Carter Valley Camp-
ground: 234-235
Centennial RV Park: 287
Chatfield State Park: 250-
251
Colorado: 261-262
Colorado National
Monument: 117
Colorado State Forest:
144-145
Cross D Bar Trout Ranch:
433-434
Davenport: 437
Delores River RV Park:
308

Diamond Campground
and RV: 263-264
Dumont Lake: 154
Estes Park KOA: 160
Five Branches Camper
Park: 325
Flying Saucer RV Park: 248
Gore Creek: 186
Groundhog Reservoir
State Wildlife Area: 298
Handcart: 200
The Hideout Cabins and
Campground: 115
Horsetooth Reservoir: 230
Indian Run State Wildlife
Refuge: 99-100
Iron City: 350-351
Iron Springs: 291-292
Island Lake: 122
Jumbo: 121
Lynx Pass: 163
Meadows Group Camp:
252
Onemile: 348
Painted Rocks: 261
Peak View Inn and RV
Park: 422
Pike Communtiy Group
Camp: 262
Pollard's Ute Lodge: 104
Poso: 376
Prospect RV Park: 246-247
Pueblo State Park: 434

Rainbow Lakes: 182
respecting others: 80
River Pines RV Park and
Cabins: 166
Rock Gardens Camp-
ground and Rafting: 114
St. Louis Creek: 181
Sawmill Creek: 97
Seedhouse: 133
Selkirk: 215
Sig Creek: 309-310
South Fork: 104-105
South Meadows: 262-263
Stagecoach Campground
and RV Park: 103
Stagecoach State Park:
152-153
Stage Stop Campground:
250
Sugar Loafin' RV/Camp-
ground: 212
Summit Lake: 140-141
Sunnyside Campground:
359-360
Tiger Run Resort: 198
Trinidad Lake State Park:
444-445
Wildhorn: 260-261
Winding River Resort Vil-
lage: 156
YMCA Snow Mountain
Ranch: 181
*see also specific place*

MSR MiniWorks: 57
MSR WaterWorks II
Ceramics: 58
Mud Springs: 117-118
Mueller State Park: 416
Mule Deer Trail: 242
museums: Cripple Creek
District Museum 425;
Denver Mint 248; John
May Museum Center
421; Kashaire Indian
Museum 453; Museum
of Space Exploration
421; Otero Museum 453;
Ute Indian Museum 287

**N**
Narrow Gauge: Railroad
RV Park 410-411; Trail
319
Narrows: 151
National Park Resort
Campground and
Cabins: 159
Native Americans:
Anasazi ruins 314-316;
Kashaire Indian
Museum 453; Mesa
Verde National Park
316-319; Navajo Indian
Reservation: 328-329;
Ute Indian Museum
287; Ute Mountain
Tribal Park 314-315; Ute
people 319, 327-328
Navajo Indian
Reservation: 328-329
Navajo Reservoir/State
Park: 328-329
Nederland: 168-170, 182-
183
Nee Gronda Reservoir:
449
Nee Noshe Reservoir:
449-450

Nee So Pah Reservoir:
449
Neota Wilderness: 148
Never Summer
Wilderness: 155
New Castle: 112-113
New Castle-Glenwood
Springs KOA: 112
noise pollution: 78
Nokhu Crags: 144
No Name Trail: 185
North Bank: 347-348
North Canyon: 325
North Clear
Creek/Canyon: 381
North Cove: 275-276
North Crestone Creek:
377
North Fork: 101
North Fork Poudre: 137-
138
North Fork Reservoir: 355
North Fork Trail: 442-443
North Park KOA: 144
North Quartz Creek: 350
North Rim: 289
North Rock Creek Trail:
397
North Sterling Reservoir
State Park: 272
North Vista Trail: 289
no-see-ums: 48-51
Nott Creek: 243

**O**
Oak Ridge State Wildlife
Area: 104
off-roading: Camp Dick
169-170; Castle Lakes
Campground Resort
373; Centennial RV
Park 287; Deep Lake
110; Dumont Lake 154;
Garfield 354; Gold Park
194; Gothic 334;
Hornsilver 193;

Horseshoe 179; Iron
City 350-351; Iron
Springs 291-292; Island
Lake 122; Jackson
Creek 257-258; Klines
Folly 109-110; Lakeview
Resort 371-372; Little
Maud 206; Middle
Quartz 353; Onemile
348; Pike Community
Group Camp 262;
Rabbit Valley 116;
Rainbow Lakes 182;
Silver Summit RV Park
304; Weir and Johnson
Reservoir 127;
Weminuche Wilderness
303; *see also*
motorcycles/ATVs;
mountain biking/
bicycling; *specific place*
O'Haver Lake: 361
Ohio City: 349
Olive Ridge: 168-169
Olney Springs Wildlife
Area: 435
Onemile: 348-349
Ophir Creek: 436-437
Ordway: 432, 435-436;
Reservoir State Wild-
life Area 431-432, 435
Osprey: 255
Otero Museum: 453
Ouray: 296-297; KOA 296
outfitters: *see*
guides/outfitters
Outlook Ridge Trail: 416
Outpost RV Park: 307-308
Ouzel: 256
Overlook Trail: 344
Owl Mountain State
Wildlife Area: 143-144

**P**
Packsaddle Mountain:
400

paddleboats: 383, 401-402
Pagosa Riverside
Campground: 401-402
Pagosa Springs: 327-328,
387, 391-393, 400-403,
405
Painted Rocks: 261
Painted Wall: 289
Palisade: 384
Panorama Point: 242
Paonia Reservoir/State
Park: 284
Parachute: 111
Paradise Travel Park: 161
Park Creek: 394
Parry Peak: 222
Parshall: 179
Pass Creek: 397
Pawnee: 168; National
Grassland 231
Peaceful Valley: 169
Peak One: 195-196
Peak View Inn and RV
Park: 422
Pearl Lake State Park:
132
Penitente Canyon: 387
Penny Hot Springs: 204
Penrose: 430
Penrose-Rosemont
Reservoir: 420
PentaPure Oasis: 56-57
petroglyphs: Irish Can-
yon 96; Vogel Canyon 453
Piceance State Wildlife
Area: 102
Pickle Gulch Group
Camp: 184-185
pickup truck campers: 46
Piedra River: 327
Pike Community Group
Camp: 262
Pike National Forest:
198-203, 213-216, 224-
225, 252-261, 263, 266-
267, 344, 415-417, 420

Pikes Peak: 265, 416-419,
423-424, 430; RV Park
419
Pine Cove: 196
Pine Point: 324
Pine River: 327
Pines: 155
Pinewood Reservoir: 233
Pitkin: 350
planning: food 23-27; tips
86
Platoro Reservoir: 403,
410
Platte River/South
Platte River: 200, 213-
214, 223, 248, 254-256,
260, 271, 344, 415-416
Pleasant Valley
Campground: 291
Pleasant Valley RV Park:
362
poison oak: 52-54
Pollard's Ute Lodge: 104
Poncha Creek: 361
Ponderosa: 359;
Campground 407-408;
Group Camp 438
Poplar Gulch: 350-351
Portal: 220
Poso: 376
Poudre Canyon: 136, 146,
149
Poudre Falls: 146
Poudre River: Canyon
229; Resort 137
Powderhorn Wilderness:
374
Prairie Point: 178
Prewitt Reservoir State
Wildlife Area: 273
Priest Gulch
Campground and RV
Park: 309
Priest Lake: 302
Primus Tri-Blend: 20
propane: 19-20

Prospector: 196
Prospector's RV Park:
425
Prospect RV Park: 246-
247
Pueblo: 430-431, 434-435,
439-440; KOA 431;
Reservoir 430, 434;
State Park 434
Pueblo South-Colorado
City KOA: 439-440
Pumphouse: 175
PUR Explorer: 57
Purgatoire/Purgatoire
River: 443
Purgatory: 310
PWC riding: see water-
skiing/PWC riding

**QR**
Quartz/Quartz Creek: 350
Queens State Wildlife
Area: 449-450
Rabbit Ears Pass: 153
Rabbit Valley: 116
Radium State Wildlife
Area: 175
rafting/floating/canoeing
/kayaking: 10 best
white-water rafting
camps 454; Animas
River 303; Arkansas
River 342, 351, 361-365,
427-429, 431, 433;
Aspen-Basalt
Campground 205;
Beaver Meadows
Resort Ranch 138; Blue
Mountain Village 100;
Burning Mountain RV
Park 113; Dolores River
304; Gates of Lodore
97-98; Gunnison River
281-282, 289, 345, 360,
367; The Hideout
Cabins and

Campground 115; Junction West RV Park 118; Lake Hasty 451; Lazy J Resort and Rafting 363-364; Los Pinos River 325; Lower Piedra 327; Pueblo Reservoir 434; Pumphouse 175; Rio Grande River 381-385; Rock Gardens Campground and Rafting 114; Spruce Lodge 385; Upper Piedra River 399

Raggeds Wilderness: 216, 283-284, 333-334

railways/train excursions: Cog Railway 419; Cumbres-Toltec Scenic Railroad 407-410; Royal Gorge Scenic Railway 428; Silverton Narrow Gauge Railroad 321

Rainbow Hot Springs: 392

Rainbow Lakes: 182

Rainbow Trail: 361, 365-366, 392

rain gear: 31-33, 85-88

Rampart Range: 254, 256-257; Motorcycle Area 256-257

Rampart Reservoir: 266-267

Rangely Camper Park: 100

Rawah: Lakes 135; Wilderness 135, 145

Red Bridge: 367

Redcliff: 193

Redcloud Peak: 373

Red Creek: 358

Red Feather Lakes: 138

Red Mountain: Motel and RV Park 303; RV Park 164

Red Rocks: Amphitheater 247, 250; Group Camp 263

Redstone: 205

Renaissance Festival: 258

resource guide: 89; see also specific place respecting others: 79-83

Reverends Ridge: 242

Richard's RV Park: 134-135

Rich Creek-Tumble Creek Trail: 223

Ridgway: 292-293; State Park 292

Rifle: 106-109, 111

Rifle Falls State Park: 107-108

Rifle Gap Reservoir/State Park: 107-108

Rifleman Phillips Group Camp: 243-244

Rifle Mountain Park: 108-109

Rimrock Campground: 103

Rim Rock Trail: 289

Rincon; 363

Rio Blanco Lake: 102; State Wildlife Area: 102-103

Rio de Los Pinos: 410

Rio Grande: 381-382; National Forest 368-369, 376-384, 387, 393-398, 403-409; Reservoir 378-380; River 382-383, 385-386, 394-395, 398

Rito Hondo/Reservoir: 380

River Bend Campground: 232-233

River Hill: 378-379

River Pines RV Park and Cabins: 166

Riversedge RV Resort: 385-386

Rivers End: 336-337

Riverside: 415; RV Park 326-327

Riverview RV Park and Campground: 233

Riverwood Inn and RV Park: 281

RnK Campground: 418

Road Canyon/Reservoir: 378

road conditions: 89

Roaring Fork River: 205, 218-219

Rock Creek: 397-398; State Wildlife Area 173-174

Rockey River Resort: 346

Rock Gardens Campground and Rafting: 114

rock/mountain climbing: Alma State Wildlife Area 213; Boulder Mountain Lodge 241; Bross Peak 213; Cameron Peak 213; Carter Lake 234-235; Castle Rock 241; Democrat Peak 213; Kite Lake 213; Lincoln Peak 213; Mount Bierstadt 201; Mount Elbert 221; Mount Evans 201; Penitente Canyon 387; Radium State Wildlife Area 175; Rifle Mountain Park 108-109; Stage Stop Campground 250; Twin Peaks 221; Two Buttes Reservoir State Wildlife Area 453

Rock Pond Trail: 416
Rocky Mountain
  Biological Laboratory:
  334
Rocky Mountain National
  Park: 148, 156-161, 168-
  169, 232-233, 236
Rocky Top Motel and
  Campground: 418
Rollers Roost: 187
Roosevelt National
  Forest: 135-139, 145-152,
  168-170, 182-183
Rosalie Trailhead: 202
Rose Park RV
  Campground: 119-120
Rosy Lane: 349
Round Mountain: 259
Routt National Forest:
  101-102, 131-134, 140-
  142, 153-155, 163-164,
  172-175
Royal Gorge: 363, 365;
  Bridge 427-429, 431;
  KOA 428; Scenic
  Railway 428
Royal View Campground:
  427
Ruby Jewel Lake Trail: 144
Ruedi Marina RV Camp:
  207
Ruedi Reservoir: 206-207,
  209
rules: 79-81
RV Ranch at Grand
  Junction: 120
RVs: general discussion
  46-47; see also specific
  place
RV Station: 429

S
safety/emergencies:
  bears 68-74; camping
  gear checklist 90-91;
  extra clothing 33; fires
19, 22; loosing your way
  60-62; see also first aid;
  specific place
Saguache: 369
Saguache Creek RV
  Park: 377
St. Charles: 437-438; Trail
  439
St. Louis Creek: 180-181
Salida: 356, 362-363
Salida Hot Springs
  Aquatic Center: 361
Sangre de Cristo:
  Mountains 362-366, 369,
  377, 388, 429, 433-434,
  440-441, 445;
  Wilderness 377
San Isabel: National
  Forest 209-212, 221-223,
  339-340, 342, 351-356,
  361, 364-366, 370, 436-
  440, 443; National Park
  341
sanitation: 53; see also
  specific place
San Juan: Motel and RV
  Park 401; Mountains
  287, 293, 296, 383, 389;
  National Forest 299-302,
  305-308, 310-314, 319-
  320, 322, 324-328, 389-
  393, 399-400, 402-403,
  405; River 392, 401-402;
  Skyway 320; Wilderness
  403-404, 406-408
San Luis: Lakes State
  Park 388; Valley 377, 398
San Miguel
  River/Mountains: 300-
  301
Santa Fe Trail: 452-453
Sapphire Point Overlook:
  196
Satanka Cove: 230
Savage Lakes: 208
Sawatch: Range 336, 350;
  Wilderness 220
Sawmill: Creek 97; Gulch
  165
Scenic Overlook Trail: 185
Scofield Pass: 334
Scottish-Irish Festival:
  159
scuba diving: Cherry
  Creek State Park 249;
  Horsetooth Reservoir
  230-231
season passes: 91
Seedhouse: 133
Seibert: 277
Selkirk: 215
Seven Lakes Trail: 133
Seven Pines Camp-
  ground and Cabins: 232
Seven Sisters Lakes: 194
Seymour Lake State
  Wildlife Park: 154-155
Shadow Mountain
  Reservoir: 166
Shady Creek RV Park: 283
Shady Island Resort: 345
Shawnee Peak: 355
Sheep Corrals: 300-301
Sheep Mountain: 291
Shelf Lake: 200
Shepherd's Rim: 170-171
Sheriff Reservoir: 163
The Shining 159
Sig Creek: 309-310
Silt: 112
Silver Bar: 217
Silver Bell: 217
Silver Dollar: 211-212;
  Lake Trail 188
Silver Jack: 294;
  Reservoir 291, 293-294
Silver Queen: 218
Silver Summit RV Park:
  304
Silver Thread: 380-381

Silverton: 302-304; Lakes Campground 303; Narrow Gauge Railroad 321

6 & 24 Trailer Park: 111

skiing: see cross-country/downhill skiing; waterskiing/PWC riding

Sky Sox Baseball Stadium: 423

Slavonia Trailhead: 133

Sleeping Elephant: 146

sleeping gear: general discussion 39-42; checklist 90

Sleeping Ute: Mountain 314, 328; RV Park and Campground 328

Sleepy Cat Ponds: 104

Slumgullion: 373

Smith Reservoir: 398

Snake River: 197

Snowblind: 353-354

Snow Hare Trail: 242

Snowshoe Hare Trail: 242-243

snow skiing: see cross-country/downhill skiing

Snowslide Trail: 439

Snowy Peaks RV And Mobile Park: 341

Soap Creek: 344-345

socks: 36-38

Somerset: 283-284

Sopris RV Park: 203-204

South Arkansas River: 354-355

South Clear Creek Canyon/Falls: 380-381

South Fork: 104-105, 179-180, 384-386, 394-396; Campground and RV Resort 386; Canyon 105

South Lottis Trail: 338, 349

South Meadows: 262-263

South Mineral: 301-302

South Park Lodge: 214-215

South Platte River: see Platte River/South Platte River

South Rim: 289

South Rock Creek Trail: 397

South San Juan Wilderness: 404, 406-408

Southside: 437

Spanish Peaks: 440-442, 444; State Wildlife Area 444

Spectacle Lake: 406-407

spelunking: Fulford Cave 192; Rifle Mountain Park 108-109

Spillway: 344

Splashland Hot Springs: 398

Sportsman's Lodge: 146-147

Sportsman's Supply and RV Park: 399

Spring Creek: 347; Reservoir 335

Springdale: 266

Springer Gulch: 415-416

Springfield: 453

Spruce: 374-375; Group Camp 438-439; Grove 121, 225; Lake RV Park 162; Lodge 385

square dancing: 326

Squaw Creek Trail: 379

Stagecoach Campground and RV Park: 103

Stagecoach State Park: 152-153

Stage Stop Campground: 250

Stanley Hotel: 159

State Fair: 435

Steamboat Lake State Park: 131-132

Steamboat Springs: 97, 140, 152-153; KOA 152

Sterling: 272-273

Stevens Creek: 356-357

Stillwater: 165-166; Reservoir 172-173

Stone Cellar: 375-376

Stoner Creek RV Park: 308-309

Storm King/Mountain: 376-377

Stove Prairie: 149

stoves: see camping stoves

Strasburg: 249-250

Stratton: 277

Strawberry Park Hot Springs: 140, 152

Stump Lake Trail: 311

Stunner: 403

Sugarbush Campground: 362

Sugarloaf: 180

Sugar Loafin' RV/Campground: 212

Summit Lake: 140-141

Summit Reservoir State Wildlife Area: 315-316

Summit RV Park: 446

sunburn: 54

Sundance RV Park: 313

sunglasses: 33

Sunnyside Campground: 359-360

Sunrise Vista: 131-132

Sunset Point: 167

Sunshine: 300

Sunshine Peak: 300, 373

Supply Basin: 109

Surface Creek: 283

Sweetwater/Trail: 185

SweetWater WalkAbout: 57

Swinging Bridge: 95

Swink: 450
Sylvan Lake State Park: 191

**T**
Tabeguache Peak: 355
Tabor, Horace: 210-211
tackle: 66

Tall Texas Campground: 345-346
Tamarack Ranch State Wildlife Area: 271
Tanglewood Trailhead: 202
Target Tree: 319

Tarryall: Creek 215, 225, 259; Reservoir State Wildlife Area 224-225
Taylor Canyon: 337, 346-347, 349; Campground 348
Taylor Park Reservoir: 336-337

## TRAILS/TRAILHEADS

Abyss Lake Trailhead: 201
Alamosa-Rock Creek Trail: 397-398
Animas-Silverton Wagon Trail: 311
Archuleta Creek Trail: 393
Beaver Creek Trail: 133
Blue Lake Trail: 145
Box Canyon Trail: 308
Broken Rib Trail: 185
Buffalo Meadows Trail: 223
Buffalo Trail: 243
Burnt Timber Trailhead: 311
Camp Trail: 372
Cannibal Pleateau Trailhead: 373
Cañon Infierno Trail: 374
Centennial Trail: 262
Chasm View Nature Trail: 289
Cimarrona Trail: 391
Cisneros Trail: 439
Colorado Trail: 202, 209, 220-223, 252, 255, 300, 320, 339, 342, 351-352, 355, 375
Continental Divide National Scenic Trail: 408
Corral Creek Trail: 148
Crag Crest Trailhead: 124
Crags Trail: 417
Cross Creek Trail: 396
Cub Lake Trail: 158
Denny Creek Trailhead: 339
Devil's Head National Recreation Trail: 257
Dillon Pinnacles Trail: 358
East Creek Trail: 324
Fall Creek Trail: 192
Fossil Ridge Trail: 337

Fourth of July Trailhead: 182
Gibson Lake Trail: 200
Goose Creek Trail: 253
Goulding Creek Trail: 310
Grizzly-Helena Trail: 141
Half Moon Pass Trail: 192
Hankins Pass Trail: 253
Helena Trailhead: 133
Hells Hole Trail: 190
Hermosa Creek Trail: 309
Hogback Ridge Trail: 441
Indian Creek Trail: 442
Indian Fire Nature Trail: 286
Iron Edge Trail: 192
Ivy Creek Trail: 382
Killpecker Trailhead: 137
Lady Moon Trail: 138-139
La Poudre Pass Trailhead: 148
Link McIntyre Trailhead: 135
Lost Lake Trail: 311
Lost Trail Creek Trail: 379-380
Maroon Trail: 218
Mineral Creek Trailhead: 375
Morrison Divide Trail: 163
Mount Margaret Trail: 139
Mule Deer Trail: 242
Narrow Gauge Trail: 319
No Name Trail: 185
North Fork Trail: 442-443
North Rock Creek Trail: 397
North Vista Trail: 289
Outlook Ridge Trail: 416
Overlook Trail: 344
Pine River Trail: 327
Rainbow Trail: 361, 365-366, 392

Rich Creek-Tumble Creek Trail: 223
Rim Rock Trail: 289
Rock Pond Trail: 416
Rosalie Trailhead: 202
Ruby Jewel Lake Trail: 144
St. Charles Trail: 439
Scenic Overlook Trail: 185
Seven Lakes Trail: 133
Silver Dollar Lake Trail: 188
Slavonia Trailhead: 133
Snow Hare Trail: 242
Snowshoe Hare Trail: 243
Snowslide Trail: 439
South Lottis Trail: 338, 349
South Rock Creek Trail: 397
Squaw Creek Trail: 379
Stump Lake Trail: 311
Sweetwater Trail: 185
Tanglewood Trailhead: 202
Tewksberry Creek Trail: 395
Texas Creek Trail: 336
Three Mile Creek Trailhead: 201
Timberline Lake Trail: 209
Timberline Trail: 336
Trail Creek: 260
Transfer Trail: 308
Turquoise Lake Trail: 210-211
Ute Creek Trail: 379
Vail Pass-10 Mile Canyon Trail: 186
West Branch Trail: 145
West Lost Trail Creek: 380
Wyoming Trailhead: 140
Yeoman Discovery Trail: 191-192

Taylor River: 335-336, 338, 346-347, 349
Teal: 390-391
Teal Lake: 141-142
Telluride: 300-302; Bluegrass Festival 300
Ten Camping Commandments for Kids: 83-85
tents: 42-46
Tewksberry Creek Trail: 395
Texas Creek: 366; Trail 336
Therm-a-Rest pads: 41-42
Thirtymile: 379
Three Forks: 107
Three Mile Creek Trailhead: 201
Three Rivers Resort: 347
Thunder Ridge: 266
Thurston Reservoir State Wildlife Area: 450
ticks: 51-52
Tiger Run Resort: 198
Tigiwon: 192-193
Timber Creek Campground: 157
Timberline Trail: 209, 336
Tincup: 339
Toll Gate Creek: 248
Tomichi Point: 289
topographical maps: 63
Towaoc: 315, 328
Town and Country Resort: 264-265
Trail Creek: 260
Trail's End Campground: 277
train rides: see railways/train excursions
Transfer: 308; Park 311; Trail 308
Trapline: 171-172
Trappers Lake: 170-171
Treasure Falls/Pass: 392
Triangle Pass: 218

Trinidad: 444-446; Lake State Park 444-445
Trujillo Meadows/ Reservoir: 408
Tucker Ponds: 397
Tunnel: 145
Turkey Creek: 400
Turquoise Lake: 209-212; Trail 210-211
Twin Eagle Trailhead: 259
Twin Lake: 126
Twin Lakes Reservoir: 222-223
Twin Peaks: 221-222
Twin Rivers Cabins and RV Park: 410
Two Buttes Reservoir State Wildlife Area: 453

U
Uncompahgre: National Forest 284-286, 288, 292-294, 296-297, 300-302; Peak 367; River 292, 296-297
United Campground of Durango: 323
Upper Beaver Creek: 396
Upper Cascade Falls: 297
Upper Piedra River: 399
Upper Queens Reservoir: 449
U.S. Olympic Center: 423
Ute: 399-400
Ute Bluff Lodge: 386
Ute Creek/Trail: 379-380
Ute Mountain Casino: 315
Ute Peak: 291
Ute people: 319, 327-328; Ute Indian Museum 287; Ute Mountain Tribal Park 314-315

V
Vail Pass-10 Mile Canyon Trail: 186
Vallecito: 312-313; Creek 312-313; Reservoir 312, 324-327; Resort 326
Vaughn Lake: 101-102
Vega Reservoir/State Park: 125-126
Venable Creek/Falls/ Peak: 370
vests/parkas: 31
Viking RV Park: 112
Vogel Canyon: 453

W
wagon rides: 231-232
Wagon Wheel: 275
Walden: 134-135, 143-144
walking shoes: 35
Walsenburg: 441-443
Walton Creek: 153-154
Ward Lake: 123
water: see drinking water
waterfalls: Agnes Vaille Falls: 352; Big Creek Falls 133; Fish Creek Falls 141, 152; Poudre Falls 146; Rifle Falls State Park 108; South Clear Creek Falls 380-381; Treasure Falls 392; Upper Cascade Falls 297; Venable Falls 370
waterproof vs. water-resistant: 32
water purification pills: 59
waterskiing/PWC riding: Big Creek Lakes 133-134; Bonny Lake 275; Boyd Lake 236-237; Chatfield Reservoir 250-251; Cherry Creek 249; Crawford Reservoir 285-286;

waterskiing/PWC riding (cont): Green Mountain Reservoir 175-176; Highline Lake 115-116; Holbrook Reservoir 450; Horsetooth Reservoir 230-231; Jackson Lake 238-239; John Martin Reservoir 451; Jumbo Lake 271; Lake Henry State Wildlife Area 432; Martin Lake 441; McPhee Reservoir 306; Meredith Reservoir 436; Miramonte Reservoir State Wildlife Area 294-295; Navajo Reservoir: 328-329; Nee Noshe Reservoir 449; North Sterling Reservoir 272; Pueblo State Park 434; Ridgway Reservoir 292; Rifle Gap Reservoir 107-108; Rio Blanco Lake 102-103; San Luis Lakes State Park 388; Stagecoach Lake 152-153; Steamboat Lake 131-132; Thurston Reservoir State Wildlife Area 450; Trinidad Lake State Park 444-445; Vallecito Reservoir 324; Vega Reservoir 125-126; see also specific place

Watson Lake State Wildlife Area: 230

Wayward Wind Campground: 239

weather: predicting the weather 85-88; rain gear 31-33; road condition information 89; tents 42-43; see also specific place

Weber's Campground: 293

Weir and Johnson Reservoir: 127

Weller: 219

Wells Fargo Stage Stop: 174

Weminuche Wilderness: 303-304, 310-312, 378-379, 382, 392-394, 397, 399

West Branch Trail: 145

West Chicago Creek: 190-191

Westcliffe: 369-370, 432-434

West Delores River: see Delores/West Delores River

West Elk Wilderness: 344

Western Inn Motel and RV Park: 215

West Fork: 392

West Lake: 139

West Lost Trail Creek: 380

West Mancos River: 308

Weston Pass: 223-224

West Rifle Creek State Wildlife Area: 106-107

Westwood Inn Campground: 240

Wet Mountains: 430, 433

Wheat Ridge: 247

wheelchair accessible campgrounds/nature trails: 454; see also specific place

Wheeler Geologic Area: 383

Whispering Pines Campground: 365-366

white gas: 18-19

White Owl Lake: 113

White River: 100-101, 103-105; National Forest 101, 105-107, 110, 113-114, 170-172, 185-186, 192-195, 205-208, 216-220

Whiteside: 201

Whitestar: 222

Wigwam: 254

Wildhorn: 260-261

Wild West Rodeo: 433

Wild Wild Rest: 318

Williams Creek: 372, 390; Reservoir 389-390

Williams Fork: Reservoir 178-179; River 179-180; Valley 179

Willow Creek: 167

Willows: 175-176

Wilson Peak: 300

Winding River Resort Village: 156

windstorms: 389

windsurfing: Blue Mesa Reservoir 357; Chatfield Reservoir 250-251; Cow Creek 177; Holbrook Reservoir 450; Horsetooth Reservoir 230-231; Jackson Lake State Park 238-239; John Martin Reservoir 451; Lake Henry State Wildlife Area 432; Martin Lake 441; Navajo Reservoir 328-329; Nee Noshe Reservoir 449; Pueblo State Park 434; San Luis Lakes State Park 388; Stagecoach Lake 152-153; Vallecito Reservoir 324; Vega State Park 125; Williams Fork Reservoir 178-179; Willows 175-176

Windy Point Group Camp: 197

Winter Park: 181, 187

Wolf Creek: 391; Pass 392, 397; Valley Country Store and Campground 392-393

Woodlake Park: 370-371

Woodland Park: 262-267

Woods Lake: 295-296

Wrangler RV Park and Motel: 423-424

Wye: 420

Wyoming Trailhead: 140

**XYZ**

Yampa: 102, 173; Hot Springs Spa and Vapor Caves 115; Reservoir 173; River 98-99, 152

Yeoman Park/Discovery Trail: 191-192

YMCA Snow Mountain Ranch: 181

Yogi Bear's Jellystone Park: Camp Resort 427;

Estes 231-232; Sterling 272-273

Youngs Creek: 282

yurts: 132

zoos/animal parks: Colorado Alligator Farm 398; Colorado Bird Observatory 244; Denver Zoo 248

## About the Author

Robyn Brewer is the author of two editions of *Colorado Camping*. She has also worked as the senior research editor on several other travel guides, including *California Camping, Pacific Northwest Camping,* and *California Fishing*. She lives and writes in the mountains of Colorado with her husband Ben and their dog Finn.

BEN BREWER

# FOGHORN ☙ OUTDOORS

Founded in 1985, Foghorn Press has quickly become one of the country's premier publishers of outdoor recreation guidebooks. Foghorn Press books are available throughout the United States in bookstores and some outdoor retailers.

| | | |
|---|---|---|
| 101 Great Hikes of the San Francisco Bay Area, 1st ed. | 1-57354-068-4 | $15.95 |
| Alaska Fishing, 2nd ed. | 0-935701-51-6 | $20.95 |
| America's Wilderness, 1st ed. | 0-935701-47-8 | $19.95 |
| Arizona and New Mexico Camping, 3rd ed. | 1-57354-044-7 | $18.95 |
| Atlanta Dog Lover's Companion, 1st ed. | 1-57354-008-0 | $17.95 |
| Baja Camping, 3rd ed. | 1-57354-069-2 | $14.95 |
| Bay Area Dog Lover's Companion, 3rd ed. | 1-57354-039-0 | $17.95 |
| Boston Dog Lover's Companion, 2nd ed. | 1-57354-074-9 | $17.95 |
| California Beaches, 2nd ed. | 1-57354-060-9 | $19.95 |
| California Camping, 11th ed. | 1-57354-053-6 | $20.95 |
| California Dog Lover's Companion, 3rd ed. | 1-57354-046-3 | $20.95 |
| California Fishing, 5th ed. | 1-57354-052-8 | $20.95 |
| California Golf, 9th ed. | 1-57354-091-9 | $24.95 |
| California Hiking, 4th ed. | 1-57354-056-0 | $20.95 |
| California Recreational Lakes and Rivers, 2nd ed. | 1-57354-065-x | $19.95 |
| California Waterfalls, 2nd ed. | 1-57354-070-6 | $17.95 |
| California Wildlife: The Complete Guide, 1st ed. | 1-57354-087-0 | $16.95 |
| Camper's Companion, 3rd ed. | 1-57354-000-5 | $15.95 |
| Colorado Camping, 2nd ed. | 1-57354-085-4 | $18.95 |
| Day-Hiking California's National Parks, 1st ed. | 1-57354-055-2 | $18.95 |
| Easy Biking in Northern California, 2nd ed. | 1-57354-061-7 | $12.95 |
| Easy Camping in Northern California, 2nd ed. | 1-57354-064-1 | $12.95 |
| Easy Camping in Southern California, 1st ed. | 1-57354-004-8 | $12.95 |
| Easy Hiking in Northern California, 2nd ed. | 1-57354-062-5 | $12.95 |
| Easy Hiking in Southern California, 1st ed. | 1-57354-006-4 | $12.95 |
| Florida Beaches, 1st ed. | 1-57354-054-4 | $19.95 |
| Florida Camping, 1st ed. | 1-57354-018-8 | $20.95 |
| Florida Dog Lover's Companion, 2nd ed. | 1-57354-042-0 | $20.95 |
| Montana, Wyoming and Idaho Camping, 1st ed. | 1-57354-086-2 | $18.95 |
| New England Camping, 2nd ed. | 1-57354-058-7 | $19.95 |
| New England Hiking, 2nd ed. | 1-57354-057-9 | $18.95 |
| Outdoor Getaway Guide: Southern CA, 1st ed. | 1-57354-011-0 | $14.95 |
| Pacific Northwest Camping, 7th ed. | 1-57354-080-3 | $19.95 |
| Pacific Northwest Hiking, 3rd ed. | 1-57354-059-5 | $20.95 |
| Seattle Dog Lover's Companion, 1st ed. | 1-57354-002-1 | $17.95 |
| Tahoe, 2nd ed. | 1-57354-024-2 | $20.95 |
| Texas Dog Lover's Companion, 1st ed. | 1-57354-045-5 | $20.95 |
| Texas Handbook, 4th ed. | 1-56691-112-5 | $18.95 |
| Tom Stienstra's Outdoor Getaway Guide: No. CA, 3rd ed. | 1-57354-038-2 | $18.95 |
| Utah and Nevada Camping, 1st ed. | 1-57354-012-9 | $18.95 |
| Utah Hiking, 1st ed. | 1-57354-043-9 | $15.95 |
| Washington Boating and Water Sports, 1st ed. | 1-57354-071-4 | $19.95 |
| Washington Fishing, 3rd ed. | 1-57354-084-6 | $18.95 |
| Washington, DC-Baltimore Dog Lover's Companion, 1st ed. | 1-57354-041-2 | $17.95 |

For more information, call 1-800-FOGHORN
email: info@travelmatters.com
or write to: Avalon Travel Publishing, Foghorn Outdoors
5855 Beaudry St., Emeryville, CA 94608

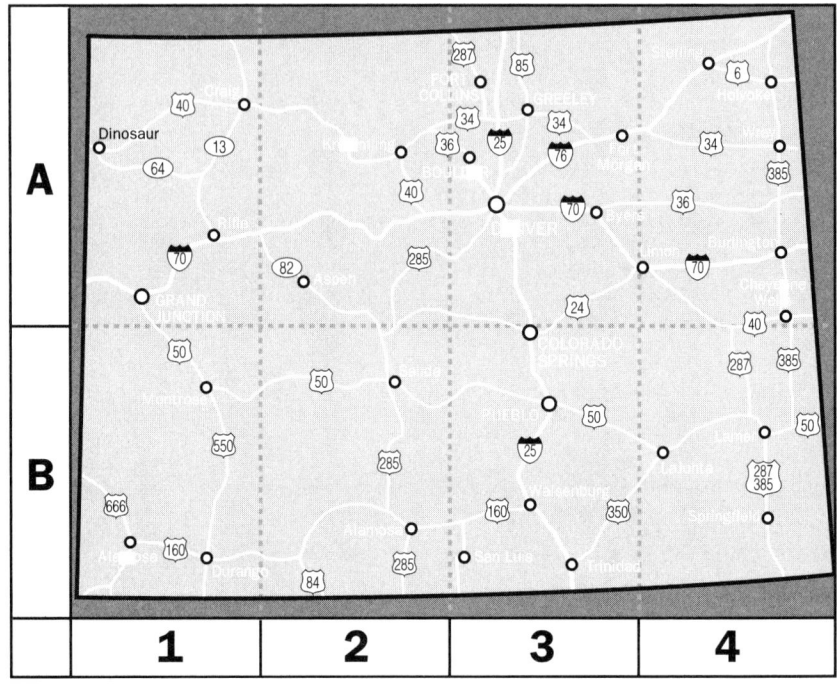

## MAPS

A1 .............................................. 94

A2 .............................................. 130

A3 .............................................. 228

A4 .............................................. 270

B1 .............................................. 280

B2 .............................................. 332

B3 .............................................. 414

B4 .............................................. 448